NUCLEAR DETERRENCE IN
SOUTHERN ASIA

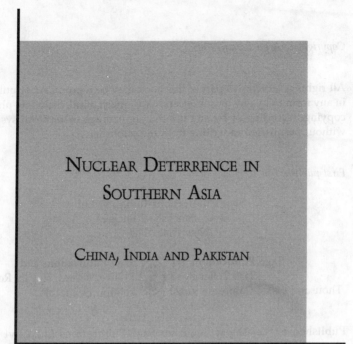

NUCLEAR DETERRENCE IN SOUTHERN ASIA

CHINA, INDIA AND PAKISTAN

Arpit Rajain

SAGE Publications
New Delhi ❖ Thousand Oaks ❖ London

Copyright © Arpit Rajain, 2005

First published in 2005 by

Sage Publications India Pvt Ltd
B-42, Panchsheel Enclave
New Delhi 110017

Sage Publications Inc
2455 Teller Road
Thousand Oaks, California 91320

Sage Publications Ltd
1 Oliver's Yard, 55 City Road
London EC1Y 1SP

Published by Tejeshwar Singh for Sage Publications India Pvt Ltd, phototypeset in 10/12 Book Antiqua by Star Compugraphics Private Limited, Delhi and printed at Chaman Enterprises, New Delhi.

Library of Congress Cataloging-in-Publication Data

Rajain, Arpit.
  Nuclear deterrence in Southern Asia: China, India and Pakistan/Arpit Rajain.
      p. cm.
  Includes bibliographical references and index.
  1. South Asia—Strategic aspects. 2. India—Military policy. 3. Pakistan—Military policy. 4. China—Military policy. 5. Nuclear weapons—India. 6. Nuclear weapons—Pakistan. 7. Nuclear weapons—China. 8. Deterrence (Strategy) I. Title.
  UA832.7.R35   355.02'17—dc22   2005   2004024866

ISBN: 0–7619–3230–5 (Hb)   81–7829–359–5 (India–Hb)
          0–7619–3284–4 (Pb)   81–7829–411–7 (India–Pb)

Sage Production Team: Shinjini Chatterjee, Neeru Handa and
                          Santosh Rawat

For
My Teachers

There lies before us, if we choose, continual progress in happiness, knowledge, and wisdom. Shall we, instead, choose death, because we cannot forget our quarrels? We appeal, as human beings, to human beings: Remember your humanity, and forget the rest. If you can do so, the way lies open to a new Paradise; if you cannot, there lies before you the risk of universal death.

—*The Einstein–Russell Manifesto*

CONTENTS

LIST OF MAPS

LIST OF FIGURES

LIST OF ABBREVIATIONS

ABM	anti-ballistic missile
AEC	Atomic Energy Commission
AMS	Academy of Military Sciences
ASLV	advanced satellite launch vehicle
BARC	Bhabha Atomic Research Centre
BJP	Bhartiya Janata Party
BMD	ballistic missile defence
BTWC	Biological and Toxin Weapons Convention
C3I	command, control, communications and intelligence
C4I	command, control, communications, computing and intelligence
C4I2	command, control, communications, computing, intelligence and information
CAEA	Chinese Atomic Energy Agency
CAEP	China Academy of Engineering Physics
CANDU	Canada Deuterium Uranium
CASC	China Aerospace Corporation
CBM	confidence-building measures
CCNS	Cabinet Committee on National Security
CD	Conference on Disarmament
CDS	Chief of Defence Staff
CDSTIC	China Defence Science and Technology Information Center
CGWIC	China Great Wall Industry Corporation
CIAE	China Institute of Atomic Energy·
CIISS	China Institute for International Strategic Studies
CMC	Central Military Commission
CMSAC	Central Military Special Artillery Corps
CNEIC	China Nuclear Energy Industry Corporation

CNS	Center for Nonproliferation Studies
CNSA	China National Space Administration
COAS	chief of army staff
COSTIND	Commission for Science and Technology and Industry for National Defence
CPC	Communist Party of China
CPMIEC	China Precision Machinery Import–Export Corporation
CSBM	confidence and security building measure
CSC	Chiefs of Staff Committee
CTBT	Comprehensive Test Ban Treaty
CWC	Chemical Weapons Convention
DF	DongFeng
DGMO	Director General of Military Operations
DPRK	Democratic People's Republic of Korea
DRDO	Defence Research and Development Organisation
ENDC	Eighteen Nation Disarmament Committee
FMCT	Fissile Material Cut-off Treaty
GAC	General Administration of Customs
GAD	General Armaments Department
GHQ	General Headquarters
GLD	General Logistic Department
GPD	General Political Department
GSD	General Staff Department
GSLV	geosynchronous satellite launch vehicle
HEU	highly enriched uranium
IAEA	International Atomic Energy Agency
IAPCM	Institute of Applied Physics and Computational Mathematics
IB	Intelligence Bureau
ICBM	intercontinental ballistic missile
IDSA	Institute of Defence Studies and Analyses
IGMDP	Integrated Guided Missile Development Programme
IPCS	Institute of Peace and Conflict Studies
IRBM	intermediate-range ballistic missile
ISI	Inter-Services Intelligence
ISRO	Indian Space Research Organisation
JCSC	Joint Chiefs of Staff Committee

JIC	Joint Intelligence Committee
JWG	Joint Working Group
KANUPP	Karachi Nuclear Power Plant
KRL	Khan Research Laboratories
LaC	line of actual control
LEAP	Lightweight Exo-atmospheric Projectile
LEU	low enriched uranium
LoC	line of control
MAD	mutually assured destruction
MEA	Ministry of External Affairs
MFA	Ministry of Foreign Affairs
MI	(Directorate of) Military Intelligence
MIRV	multiple independently targeted re-entry vehicle
MoD	Ministry of Defence
MOFTEC	Ministry of Foreign Trade and Economic Cooperation
MOST	Ministry of Science and Technology, China
MRBM	medium-range ballistic missile
MRV	multiple re-entry vehicle
MTCR	Missile Technology Control Regime
NCA	Nuclear Command Authority
NDA	National Democratic Alliance
NEA	Nuclear Energy Agency
NDU	National Defence University
NFU	no-first-use
NINT	Northwest Institute of Nuclear Technology
NMD	national missile defence
NNCA	National Nuclear Command Authority
NNSA	National Nuclear Safety Administration
NPT	Non-Proliferation Treaty
NSA	National Security Advisor
NSAB	National Security Advisory Board
NTM	National Technical Means
NTW	navy theatre wide
OIC	Organisation of the Islamic Conference
ONC	Office for the Control of Nuclear (Materials)
OSI	on-site inspection
PAEC	Pakistan Atomic Energy Commission
PINSTECH	Pakistan Institute of Nuclear Science and Technology

PLA   People's Liberation Army
PLAAF   People's Liberation Army Air Force
PLAN   People's Liberation Army Navy
PM   Prime Minister
PNE   peaceful nuclear explosion
RCA   Regional Cooperation Agreement
SAC   Second Artillery Corps
SACMPT   State Administrative Committee on Military
                Products Trade
SBMPT   State Bureau of Military Products Trade
SDI   Strategic Defence Initiative
SETC   State Economic and Trade Commission
SLBM   submarine launched ballistic missile
SNEP   Subterranean Nuclear Explosion Project
SRBM   short-range ballistic missile
SSBN   ship submersible ballistic nuclear
SUPARCO   Space and Upper Atmosphere Research
                Commission
TAPS   Tarapur Atomic Power Station
TEL   transporter-erector-launcher
TMD   theatre missile defence
TNW   tactical nuclear weapon
UAV   unmanned aerial vehicle
UPA   United Progressive Alliance
USI   United Services Institution
WMD   weapons of mass destruction
WTO   World Trade Organisation

PREFACE

The events of May 1998 pose a new challenge to Southern Asia and the strategic triangle comprising Pakistan, India and China. Conventional wisdom would have us believe that the interrelationship of strategic capabilities and policies of the three countries form a triangle of power in Southern Asia. Moreover, China dictates Indian security calculations in many ways. This has significant implications both for regional security and that of the respective countries. All three are declared nuclear weapons states. The nuclear dimension of this relationship has steadily developed since the 1960s following China's entry into the nuclear club in 1964 and the gradual nuclearisation of India and Pakistan since the early 1970s that reached its logical conclusion in May 1998.

The three states now need to appreciate the implications of this new strategic reality and stabilise their trilateral relationship, despite their past history of bilateral conflict, hostile propaganda, rhetorical diplomacy and persisting tensions. Since the Indo-Pak nuclear tests cannot be undone, the countries now need to decide upon the directions that would best serve their national and regional interests. China, India and Pakistan, with their different political systems, varying approaches to arms control regimes and variable foreign policy preferences, are now labouring with hitherto untackled issues of nuclear weaponisation and deployment, command and control, and military strategy. It, therefore, does become imperative to work on existing strands of a restraint regime and evolve new ones in this triangle. The strategic asymmetry between these three countries—India vis-à-vis China and Pakistan vis-à-vis both China and India—extends to the areas of conventional and nuclear weaponry. This is a reflection of the disparity existing in the correlation of their forces, which could persist in being an obstacle to the establishment of a plausible nuclear restraint regime or to the emplacing of credible risk reduction measures. It is not difficult to conjure up scenarios that envision the escalation of regional conflict from the subterranean level to a minor skirmish, then to a major conventional conflict, and finally to crossing the nuclear threshold. The nature of polity in the three states, ranging from a practising democracy to an authoritarian regime and a military dictatorship, is partially responsible for the difficulties in establishing nuclear restraint and risk reduction regimes in Southern Asia. The checks and balances on the political executive vary. While in India there exist strong institutional filters in decision making on nuclear issues that result in absolute civilian control over the arsenal, in Pakistan the army takes all decisions relating to the bomb; whilst in China it is believed the ultimate authority on nuclear weapons rests with the chairman of the Central Military Commission after its top leaders have reached a consensus.

Deterrence includes a mix of reassurance and accommodation, and should not focus exclusively on nuclear capabilities. It is premised on the notion that decision makers are rational individuals. The question of armed conflict, the risk of war and the issue of deterrence in Southern Asia are complicated by the fact that India has a nuclear adversarial relationship with Pakistan and China. Historically, this is an unprecedented situation where a triangular nuclear competition has been constructed, since it is geo-strategically different and more complicated than the bilateral nuclear rivalry that existed between the United States and the Soviet Union during the Cold War. Should India and Pakistan continue creeping along towards weaponisation and deployment, and China proceed with its nuclear modernisation plans, also partially resulting from the US's national missile defence programme, the three could easily enter into a triad that would be more competitive and conflictual in nature than cooperating with each other in the medium and long term.

This book seeks to investigate the nuances of the oft-repeated mantra of credible minimum deterrent, study decision making in crisis and the drivers of various processes and structures in the domestic environment that influence the existence of the bomb in these countries. It seeks to explicate the prevailing attitudes towards issues of arms control, doctrines, strategy, weaponisation and deployment. The fundamental objective here is to highlight issues and prepare decision makers and policy elites in these countries.

Towards this end, the book builds from the classical Western literature of the Cold War era and indigenous writings, particularly in India and Pakistan, on strategic issues. I have benefited from field trips and interviews and extensive reliance on open sources of information and archives. The writing of this book was substantially completed by May 2003. Needless to add that my institutional affiliations are in no way responsible for the views expressed herein.

Arpit Rajain
April 2004
New Delhi

ACKNOWLEDGEMENTS

At the very outset I consider it my duty to thank my former professors Amitabh Mattoo, Kanti Bajpai and Varun Sahni who, during the early stages of my scholarly pursuits at the School of International Studies, taught me everything I know about international relations. Shri P.R. Chari has been instrumental in sharpening my focus and a guiding force during my days at the Institute of Peace and Conflict Studies (IPCS). While I was at the ORF Institute of Security Studies, Gen V.P. Malik helped me immensely in understanding the nuances of policy at the highest levels. At the Centre for Global Studies, Dr Rajesh Basrur has been, as always, a constant source of guidance and inspiration.

I would fail in my responsibility if I do not thank the scholars, diplomats and practitioners who have taken time out to comment on the chapter drafts and made many valuable suggestions that helped me fine-tune my arguments. Professors Stephen Cohen, Kanti Bajpai, W.P.S. Sidhu and Dr Ashley Tellis took precious time out to comment on the specifics of each chapter. For commenting on the entire manuscript I am grateful to Prof Sumit Ganguly who went through each chapter diligently and helped me immensely. I remain deeply indebted to all of them.

My interactions with officials at the Ministry of External Affairs have been most useful and I have benefited in no small measure from their hospitality and in my informal interactions with them. My numerous visits to the DISA desk at the Indian Ministry of External Affairs, have exposed me to the thoughts that go into crucial foreign policy choices. I thank the many officials who have often given me generous time to explain various nuances of disarmament and proliferation issues.

Several officers of the armed forces have, over the last many months, taken time out to explain to me the forces' perspective of the Kargil conflict, the post-Parliament attack phase and the role of nuclear weapons. Gen V.P. Malik spent long hours in a very fruitful exchange of ideas, and I remain indebted to him. I thank the many officers at the army, navy and air headquarters for sharing their time and ideas.

My professional experience at IPCS, where I worked from 1997 to 2003 and where this study was completed, has been most rewarding. I remain obliged to Gen Dipankar Banerjee and Shri P.R. Chari who helped me to concentrate on the project, provided constructive policy inputs, and took valuable time out to give some very significant insights. Their vast experience and extensive writing has helped to motivate me to a great extent.

At IPCS, I sought to learn the difference between the theory and practice of the art of diplomacy. I learnt to investigate the nuances that go into decision making and why states choose to do what they do. My informal interactions with the vastly experienced group of scholars that the IPCS has gathered for its Friday seminars over the years, have been a most educating and fruitful experience. Some of finest former diplomats, academics, former chiefs of the armed forces and senior bureaucrats who are far too many to name here, have over the years enriched the discussions at the IPCS with their knowledge and expertise. Particular mention must be made of Late Air Chief Marshal (Retd) S.K. Mehra, Lt Gen (Retd) A.M. Vohra, Salman Haider, S.K. Singh, Muchkund Dubey, Dr K. Santhanam, Amb. C.V. Ranganathan, Amb. Eric Gonsalves, Amb. Arundhati Ghose, Dr C. Raja Mohan, Lt Gen (Retd) V.R. Raghvan, Rear Admiral (Retd) Raja Menon, Ram Mohan Rao, G. Parthasarthy, Air Cmde (Retd) Jasjit Singh, Air Vice Marshal (Retd) Kapil Kak, Dr Rajesh Rajagopalan, Brig Gurmeet Kanwal, Dr G. Balachandran, Cmde C. Uday Bhaskar, Lt Gen (Retd) B.S. Malik, Bharat Karnad, Dr Sanjaya Baru, Maj Gen (Retd) Ashok Mehta, Professors Mira Sinha Bhattacharjea, Madhu Bhalla, Riyaz Punjabi, Prem Shankar Jha, Dr Bhashyam Kasturi and Brig Subhash Kapila.

I have benefited in many ways from my informal discussions with Shri K. Subrahmanyam, Drs Ashis Nandy and P.K. Iyengar, who have at various stages during the writing of this book helped me focus on the role of nuclear weapons in the body politic and the various nuances of nuclear deterrence. I had the good fortune of taking guidance from the Late Giri Deshingkar who had helped me prepare a framework for Chapter 4. I have also benefited in no small measure from my long and fruitful discussions with Ambs C. Dasgupta and Hamid Ansari.

Parts of this work have been presented in various seminars around the world. My interactions at the Harvard Project, Indiana University, Chicago University, APCSS (Hawaii), Wilton Park (UK), University of St Gallen (Switzerland), Quaid-i-Azam University and Institute of Strategic Studies, Islamabad have greatly enhanced my understanding of the subject, and I have also benefited tremendously while being grilled at Annual Pugwash Conferences in Rustenburg (South Africa), Cambridge University and the University of California at San Diego. I wish to express my thanks also to the scholars and academics at various international universities and institutes whose intellectual inputs at different stages of the project have been invaluable. Among them are Professors Joseph Rotblat, David Holloway, Sumit Ganguly, Clifford Singer, John Holdren, James Clad, Stephen Walt, Pervez Hoodbhoy, Pervaiz Iqbal Cheema, David Cortwright, Steven Hoffmann, Steven Miller, David Albright, Michael Krepon, Rasul-Baksh Rais, George Rothgens, Drs Karen Hallberg, Kent Biringer, Carsten Rohr, George Perkovich, Tanvir Ahmed Khan, Jeffrey Boutwell, Dingli Shen, Peter Lavoy, Ruth Adams, Bruce G. Blair, Brian Winchester, Maj Gen (Retd) Mahmud Ali Durrani, Gen (Retd) Jahangir Karamat, Lt Gen (Retd) Talat Masood, Ejaz Haider, Najam Sethi and Sandra Ionno Butcher.

A part of the research material was collected in my repeated visits to the libraries of the University of California at San Diego, Chicago University, Cambridge University, George Washington University, Indiana University and Quaid-i-Azam University. I have benefited tremendously from the databases of Center for Nonproliferation Studies (CNS), Monterey, California. They house perhaps the world's finest database on proliferation issues. At the CNS, I would like to thank Amy Sands and Gaurav Kampani for their support. In India, the Institute of Defence Studies and Analyses (IDSA), the United Services Institution (USI), IPCS, Jawaharlal Nehru University and the Nehru Memorial Museum and Library have been extremely useful. I would also like to thank the Carnegie Endowment for International Peace for the permission to use the maps in chapters 4, 5 and 7 and the figure in chapter 4.

My colleagues at the IPCS, where majority of this study was completed, have provided the stimulating environment for carrying out my research. I wish to record my gratitude to Sonika Gupta who cheerfully held fort in my long absences from the office.

Additionally, I banked on her to fill some gaps in my arguments. Furthermore, Aisha Sultanat, Prafulla Ketkar and R. Radhakrishan have been very supportive in creating the congenial office environment for carrying out my research. I am also thankful to Mr S.L. Vermani who has helped with the administrative work involved, along with Sapna, Vijay Chauhan and Surinder Singh.

The people living around the author perhaps best appreciate such occupational hazards. My little niece, Dristi, and nephews, Dhruv, Anuj and Angad, who I hope grow up to see a different world—a world that is free from the fear of conflict and full of happiness. My parents, who were taken aback at my choice of career in policy analysis, but like all parents have always wished the best for me and remained a constant source of my inspiration. Finally, Rakhee had to suffer my long abdication from my contributions towards our house. She was kind and caring enough to put up with my inattentiveness, restlessness and long hours of working on the book. Without her love, forbearance and support, I could not have devoted so much time and effort to this book. The best parts of this endeavour are hers as much as mine. For the many shortcomings that remain, the views expressed, the methodology used and the conclusions reached in this book I am, needless to add, solely responsible.

Arpit Rajain
April 2004
New Delhi

CHAPTER I

INTRODUCTION

*History has given us the gift of time. If we use it properly and rid the species
for good of nuclear danger we will secure the greatest of time's gift:
assurance of a future.*

—Jonathan Schell

This book examines the nuances of the much chanted mantra
of minimum nuclear deterrence and limited war in the
triangular relationship of China, India and Pakistan. The
fundamental purpose is to illustrate the complex interplay between
public opinion, domestic variables and various driving forces,
sometimes from outside this region, that influence the existence
of the nuclear bomb in times of conflict and peace in the region.
From the perspective of research, one of the many objectives of this
endeavour is to probe into the concealed fundamental dynamics
that are likely to govern the relationships between nuclear armed
neighbours during any crisis. The central premise remains the
assumption that knowledge of many of these variables and driving
forces might aid a decision maker in averting a future armed conflict from escalating in this volatile region. With deterrence theory,
this research seeks to investigate the present with a hope for a secure and stable future.

The Southern Asian region[1] provides a unique strategic triangle
comprising three declared nuclear weapons states which have been
involved in limited conflict. The other uniqueness of the three states
lies in their having different political systems, varying approaches
to arms control regimes and variable foreign policy preferences,
as they now labour with hitherto untackled issues of nuclear
weaponisation and deployment, command and control, military

---

[1] By Southern Asia I mean the region encompassing South Asia and China.

strategy, and the one issue that is central to the existence of nuclear weapons—deterrence.

Thus far, the discourse on nuclear deterrence has been dominated by realist assumptions based on Western construction of the threat and the strategy to cope with it. These assumptions have underscored certain types of conflicts between states and certain types of conflict-resolving mechanisms, much of which were perhaps relevant in the Cold War paradigm of dyadic geo-strategic relationships and which remain very different from the Southern Asian setting. Thus, at the very outset, the research was left to canoe through unchartered waters, compelling it to cover much more ground, both theoretically and empirically, than originally set.

Searching for Explanations: Purpose and Propositions

Southern Asia has been faced with a new strategic reality post the May 1998 nuclear tests by India and Pakistan. The interrelationship of historical baggage, strategic capabilities and attitudes to the nuclear equation of the three states in the triangle—China, India and Pakistan—leaves a vacuum in the existing literature that this book seeks to fill. The complexity of this trilateral stand-off cannot be underestimated and historically there have been no parallels.[2]

When the research for this book began, a year after the nuclear tests, it was believed that nuclear weapons would enhance the security of both Pakistan and India, deterrence would be stable and that the region presented a 'changed strategic environment'. The highs of the Lahore Declaration, the talk of limited war, the lows of Kargil and the attack on the Indian Parliament have provided a policy analyst enough food for thought on the central premise of the raison d'être of nuclear weapons—deterrence. The passage of time and events have also helped to examine these issues with the benefit of experience of current history.

This study has two main purposes and three supplementary investigations. First and foremost, it is a conceptual investigation

[2] Historically, the only other precedent was the triangle comprising USA, USSR and China.

of the notion of deterrence. Second, it looks at the theory and practice of limited war. The three country studies that follow ascertain whether there are common features in their respective security practices which have been evaluated on approximately similar parameters, yet recognise domestic cultural variables to seek answers on stability and deterrence in this triangle. The intention is to deduce how past interactions and behaviour translate into policy choices.

The question of the risk of war and the issue of strategic stability in Southern Asia are complicated by the fact that India shares a nuclear adversarial relationship with Pakistan and China. All the three states are within 10 minutes of missile flight time from each other, share long borders, which at many places are contested, have fought wars in the past, possess nuclear weapons, have a history of hostile political rhetoric, and have not just hotly debated limited war but at some point in their recent history also fought a limited war. History informs us that this is an unprecedented situation where a triangular nuclear competition has been constructed. It is qualitatively different, has far more variables working simultaneously and remains geo-strategically more dangerous than the bilateral nuclear rivalry that existed between the United States and the Soviet Union during the Cold War. From the Indian perspective, its military calculations need to factor in a situation when it might need to simultaneously deter Pakistan and China, and cater for a conflictual rather than cooperative relationship with the two neighbours in the next decade. The likelihood of Pakistan continuing to receive support from China remains. From the Pakistani point of view, India harbours hegemonic designs and India's vast conventional forces have to be deterred. Overt nuclearisation has proved to be the great balancer. From the Chinese point of view, the US is the main concern. The three countries have different governments—a practising democracy, an authoritarian regime and a praetorian state. This in turn has implications for the maintenance of checks and balances on the political executive and the military, which have great salience for the command and control structures of these three states. This book explores nuclear stability in Southern Asia through the prism of nuclear deterrence and probes the various influences and pressures exerted on the bomb in their totality. Existing literature on nuclear issues in Southern Asia has dealt with the evolution and future of the nuclear programmes of China, India and Pakistan, or at the most with bilateral nuclear dyads.[3] This is among the few attempts to analyse the triangle comprising three declared nuclear weapons states which also have engaged in limited conflict at some time in their history.

There has been a distinct lack of historical experience in dealing with crisis in Southern Asia that risks escalation to the nuclear level. The Ussuri river clashes provide the only case, apart from Kargil, when two nuclear weapons states proceeded to armed conflict. These armed conflicts highlight the fact that they entail elements which cannot be anticipated. In Southern Asia, the added variable is domestic opinion. The Kargil crisis had all these elements of likely escalation and was a case in nuclear brinkmanship. While Kargil was still being discussed, new geopolitical realities shaped up post 9/11 with US presence in the region. The attack on the Indian Parliament further increased the chill between India and Pakistan as war clouds that had gathered took over 10 months to disperse.

In 1946, the strategic analyst Bernard Brodie famously wrote, 'Thus far the chief purpose of our military establishment has been to win wars. From now on its chief purpose must be to avert them'.[4] This sums up the basic premise of nuclear deterrence: nuclear weapons must ensure that they prevent outbreak of military

---

[3] See Abraham 1998; Ahmad 1957; Ahmad 1996a; Ahmed 1999; Ali 1999; Bajpai and Mattoo 2000; Bajpai et al. 1995; Beg 1994; Bonds 1979; Brodie 1946; Chari 1995, 1999; Chari, Cheema and Cohen 2003; Cheema 1996, 2000; Chengappa 2000; Chong-pin Lin 1988; Coats 1986; Ding 1991; Dingli Shen 1993; Durrani 2001; Elliot 1995; Ganguly 1999a, 2002; Ganguly and Greenwood 1996; Garrett and Glaser 1995/96; Amitav Ghosh 1999; Gupta 1995; Haass 1988; Hagerty 1993/94, 1998; Harrison et al. 1999; Hoffmann 1990; Hoodbhoy 1994; Hoyt 2001; Hua Di 1997; Jaspal 2001; Joeck 1997; Johnston 1996a; Kamal 1992a; Kapur 2001; Karnad 2002; Khalilzad 1985; Khan 1994; Kondapalli 1999; Krishna and Chari 2001; Lewis and Litai 1988; Lewis et al. 1991; Liu Xuecheng 1994; Lodi 1999; Manning et al. 2000; Marwah and Shulz 1975; Mattoo 1999a; Maxwell 1970; Mazari 1991, 1999a, 1999b; Milholin and White 1991; Ming Zhang 1999; Moshaver 1991; Nizamani 2001; Perkovich 1993, 1999; Pollack 1988; Pollack and Yang 1998; Pye 1988; Rahman 1998; Sattar 1994/95; Sawant 2000; Shambaugh and Yang 1997; Siddiqa-Agha 2000a; Jasjit Singh 1998; Sundarji 1993b; Swami 2000; Tellis 2001, 2002a; Ur-Rehman 1999; Weisman and Krosney 1981; Whiting 1975; Yan Xu 1993; Yang et al. 1994; Yimin Song 1986; Zou Yunhua 1999.

[4] Brodie 1946: 76.

confrontation. Since the raison d'être of the nation-state is to survive and enhance its power in a conflict-ridden international system, military security acquires special significance. While comprehending the realist response to state security, this study takes into account the societal aspect and historical influence that govern the choices a state makes towards issues of security and war. It considers Desmond Ball's definition of strategic culture: '... different countries and regions approach the key issues of war, peace and strategy from perspectives which are both quite distinctive and deeply rooted, reflecting their different geo-strategic situations, resources, history, military experience and political beliefs.'[5] These factors, he says, 'profoundly influence how a country perceives, protects, and promotes its interests and values with respect to the threat or use of force.'[6]

Perceptions and psychology play a major role in the logic, structure and stability of deterrence. Deterrence attempts to create risks strategically, militarily and psychologically to ensure that the opponent does not pursue a certain action. This is premised on the threat to use or to punitively retaliate with nuclear weapons if those actions are undertaken. For deterrence to be stable, the risk must be disproportionately higher than any conceivable gains to be acquired. Nuclear weapons were not created to deter. It was deterrence that was conceived in regard of nuclear weapons. All countries have to address issues related to nuclear doctrines—alternative response options, early warning, intelligence and alert levels. If hostilities do break out, minimum deterrence says precious little on how the war will then be shaped or when it may escalate to a different level, given the complex variables at play, especially in Southern Asia. Issues like these have to be thrashed out in peacetime, as continuing to defer discussion only increases the risk of a less than optimal decision, should a crisis occur.

Attempts to enhance a nation's security by treading the nuclear road can threaten the security perceptions of other states, thereby reducing security all around. This security dilemma is an enduring feature of an anarchic international order characterised by a pyramidal nuclear structure, and its consequences are arms races,

[5] Ball 1993: 44.
[6] Ibid.: 44.

shifting alliances and altering balances of power. Nuclear weapons are perceived as the instruments of power and as palliatives for this dilemma.

Such instruments have produced four major changes in military strategy. First, modern delivery systems ensure that there is no foolproof defence against missiles. Second, nuclear weapons and their deployment involve non-combatants, namely, the debate on counter-value or counter-force strategies. It is possible to destroy the adversary even before engaging its armed forces. Third, a nuclear war can be over within hours, leaving statesmen and leaders no time to rethink their decisions. And finally, with the concept of limited and decisive wars and quick retaliation, nuclear forces need to be on high alert. This would require conventional force structures to be geared and deployed in a certain way. The challenge of managing limited wars is huge when various forms of cognitive closures handicap the political leadership on one or both sides. This warrants a clearer understanding of the complex relationship between limited aims wars, escalation dominance, control and the breakdown of nuclear deterrence. The questions of escalation control, war termination and nuclear deterrence stability therefore gain significance.

For the success of nuclear deterrence, several conditions need to operate simultaneously, ranging from strategy and policy to an effective mind game. First, a deterrent force (be it a triad or air and land based) must be able to inflict intolerable damage on the adversary (deterrence by punishment) with the added caveat of an acceptable cost to itself, or deny the opponent (deterrence by denial) the desired objective. It could also be a combination of the two. An essential element of this policy is the safety of the nuclear arsenal. The deterring nation must ensure that its deterrent force is not destroyed in a pre-emptive strike. Second, the deterring nation must have all the necessary plans in readiness to demonstrate that it has the will and capability to deliver the 'message', either covertly or overtly. Often, this posture can lead to a dilemma: the deterring nation must also exhibit willingness to engage in the war that it is trying to deter, or prevent crossing of the threshold from deterring war to fighting war with nuclear weapons. Third, the deterring nation has to ensure the survivability of the deterrent force to absorb a first strike. The 'retaliatory force' must be protected against a 'first strike', but also inflict punitive retaliation in the 'second strike'. This can be established by technical means, but also through policy. Fourth, the deterrent message has to be conveyed with a high degree of credibility, meaning that the adversary must believe that the deterring nation *will* exercise the nuclear option. Both nations must also believe at the same time that a real probability exists that the threatening nation will indeed retaliate if required. Finally, the cost–benefit analysis: the deterring nation must communicate to the opponent the price it will have to pay for endeavouring to achieve its objective. This price has to outweigh any possible gains from attempting to achieve the objective.

One of the consequences of the break-up of the Soviet Union has been an unchecked fissile material trade and it is only a matter of time before terrorists get a nuclear weapon. They are the most likely 'proliferators', because nuclear blackmail is the ultimate expression of fanaticism and terrorism. As deterrence is based on the rational actor model, in the event of a terrorist outfit or an undeterrable leader acquiring these deadly weapons, one cannot be certain that deterrence would work in the way it was originally planned. In the absence of an established deterrent relationship, the threat may not be understood in the intended manner. Would this have unpredictable and perhaps counter-productive consequences? It is difficult to see deterrence operating against non-state actors. The threat of nuclear annihilation just cannot be used against these *fidayeen*s (suicide attackers), since a 'nuclear deterrent relationship' is not established with them. Even if they are threatened, they may call the bluff as targeting them with even a small nuclear weapon would be impossible without incurring unacceptable collateral damage and provoking global outrage. Indeed, with *fidayeen* attacks on the rise, the rationale of using nuclear weapons for deterrence is becoming increasingly problematic.

China has been a key player in Southern Asian nuclear dynamics since the early 1960s. With nuclear tests in this region, a new source of instability was brought into the security architecture of Asia. This has led to further 'triangularisation' of the region. The three nuclear weapons states of China, India and Pakistan with different political systems and approaches to arms control regimes are now continually emphasising the mantra of minimum nuclear deterrence. Their approach and the choices will have far-reaching consequences for Asian security, since possessing nuclear weapons alone does not imply having an effective deterrent force. The current strategic asymmetry between India, China and Pakistan that extends from conventional to nuclear weaponry reflects the existing disparity in their correlation of nuclear and conventional forces. Additionally, non-state actors are already at play in the region, and in such a complex situation, simple dyadic behaviour models of research are not sufficient. Given these parameters and a dynamic strategic environment, it is not difficult to conjure up scenarios that envisage the escalation of a local military engagement from the subterranean level to a minor skirmish, a major conventional conflict, and finally to crossing the nuclear threshold. The role of non-state actors in precipitating such a crisis cannot be ruled out.

Although China has an effective deterrent against India, the same cannot be said about India vis-à-vis China. Both India and Pakistan have rudimentary land- and air-based deterrent forces as they continue their slow-motion deployment and refinement of their arsenals. The open literature suggests that during the Kargil crisis, both India and Pakistan had exhibited some ambiguity regarding their intent to deploy nuclear missiles and nuclear armed aircraft. Apart from this, the Kargil crisis also came to be termed as 'limited war'. Can future wars be limited under the nuclear umbrella? Although Pakistan does not have a declared nuclear doctrine, it is widely believed that nuclear weapons are its weapons of 'first strike and last resort'; India and China, on the other hand, have a declared no-first-use (NFU) posture. Operationally, this means that both China and India are prepared to absorb a first strike, and since they do not have a launch on warning posture, they are likely to adopt a launch after attack posture. But launch after attack implies a failure of deterrence. In a crisis scenario, both Pakistan and India have to consider each other's threats as credible. The message has to be effectively communicated either covertly or overtly to each other to be perceived as credible. But will that increase the stakes of the 'nuclear flashpoint'? The gains accruing from any nuclear adventure have to outweigh the price. There could be horrendous military costs in terms of a counter-force strike or collateral damage in a counter-value strike. This needs to be well understood before any such an adventure is undertaken.

Deterrence harbours a fundamental, perhaps unsolvable, contradiction between its operational and political components. Can the conditions for stable deterrence be maintained in times of Southern Asian crises? The march of technology cannot be restricted. Nuclear scientists will almost invariably push to acquire longer-range missiles with better accuracy and miniaturised warheads. There will also be pressure to adopt strategies involving counter-force, first strike, second strike and better delivery systems. Deterrence is premised on the notion that decision makers are rational, thinking individuals. Decision making in crisis, apart from being influenced by the external strategic environment, is also the function of the psychological attitudes of decision makers and results in a range of outcomes. But is this feature similar for decision makers on either side? Do both sides to the conflict view each other's threats as credible? What role do personalities play in such a scenario? The behavioural patterns of the actors involved in decision making, the bargain initiated between adversaries, the role of deterrence, compellance or coercion, the role of allies in crisis management, the causal factors in the crisis, issues of grand strategy, competing internal power structures, bureaucratic momentum, scientific and technological imperatives, the extent to which physical and psychological attributes of decision makers influence their ability to take decisions in crisis, and power and status, all influence possible outcomes. The manner in which decision makers grapple with options before them in any crisis is therefore the outcome of a complex interplay of key variables.

The military coup in Pakistan has been a setback to prospects of formal civilian control over Pakistan's nuclear deterrence. Armed forces will anyway retain operational control over deterrence under civilian rule, but a formal civilian filter in an institutional setting can provide the necessary operational space in times of crisis for stability. China already occupies an enviable position, both in terms of attributes of power and negotiating strengths, whilst continuing to modernise its nuclear forces. US ballistic missile defence (BMD) in the region will further offset the security architecture of Asia and have far-reaching impact on China, which already has all the attributes of a great power. A qualitative and quantitative improvement of Chinese nuclear forces would lead to an increased threat perception in New Delhi. India is facing a bumpy road ahead with regard to its reform process and challenges to its secular fabric, and is faced with difficult choices regarding weaponising and deploying its forces. Pakistan has to set its house in order, reconsider its national priorities and involve the larger population in the process of political development and participation once it is able to rein in the *jihadi* forces.

Decision makers in Beijing, Islamabad and New Delhi should not lull themselves into thinking that a credible minimum deterrent posture would prevent crisis and outbreak of hostilities. Continuing to defer discussion would only increase the risk of a less than optimal response, should a crisis occur. China, Pakistan and India have to work out a restraint regime wherein nuclear weapons are used as tools of war prevention and war deterrence, rather than as weapons of fighting war. This study seeks answers to these issues that will determine the security structure and the shape of overt nuclearisation in the region.

✷ RATIONALE/STRUCTURE OF THE STUDY

This vast mandate required careful attention in meticulously presenting the security perceptions of the three states using indigenous sources, respective government statements for each country and facts, wherever needed, substantiated by American sources. An effort to address the strategic, political and military dimensions of the role of nuclear weapons, evolution of strategy and deterrence can be found in chapter 2. Three cases were carefully chosen—the Cuban missile crisis, the Ussuri river clashes and the Kargil crisis. The Cuban missile crisis was widely perceived to be the first test of the deterrent value of nuclear weapons, but fortunately not a shot was fired. The Ussuri river clashes presented a rather interesting case where two declared nuclear weapons states, Soviet Union and China, went to a limited war. There were covert threats of a 'surgical strike' by Soviet Union on the Chinese nuclear infrastructure. The Kargil crisis was another case that tested deterrence and has been termed by many as a limited war. In chapter 3, prevalent literature on the various influences on the decision maker, the rational deterrence model, notion of deterrence and limited war are discussed. Militarily, there is a fine balance between limited war and the inherent potential for escalation. To complete the 'triangularisation' of Southern Asia, three states that comprise this triangle have been evaluated on similar parameters for stability and outcomes for deterrence, with chapters on China, India and Pakistan. Finally, there are some concluding observations for a more stable Southern Asia.

The study was conducted in two parts. The first part involved the collection of materials to enable a broad understanding of the indigenous perceptions of national security. This was supported by field visits, interviews and informal discussions with many former chiefs of the armed forces, diplomats, key policy makers, senior bureaucrats and academics. One of the principal challenges has been to prioritise and encapsulate the various domestic viewpoints that influence the existence of the nuclear weapon in the security architecture of these countries. An additional challenge has been to evaluate declared governmental positions with followed practice in terms of policy. Ascertaining details of decision-making processes and their nuances proved especially difficult to uncover sometimes, and so the research had to rely on secondary sources or on interviews of key government officials and senior decision makers. Once the first drafts of these chapters were ready, they were sent out to diplomats, strategists, academics and practitioners to critique and sharpen the focus and strengthen or dilute arguments. Some of the ideas contained in this book were first aired at a number of seminars and conferences around the world and the hypothesis tested. This proved to be another rewarding task as not only were the co-panellists and participants in most occasions members of highest decision-making bodies, but in many cases former chiefs of the armed forces, ambassadors and senior diplomats. The discussions in many of these seminars often brought forward many interesting observations.

The present volume is the end result of this close to three-year project. It is sincerely hoped that this offering will stimulate more systematic efforts with additional research tools that lead to further nuanced and informed debate to discover the fuller political dimensions and strategic implications of the nuclearisation of the triangle in Southern Asia. It is my expectation that further reflection on these issues will deflect some attention away from the current fixation in the region with the nuclear and military aspects of national security, to other equally relevant non-military dimensions.

CHAPTER 2

NUCLEAR WEAPONS
AND INTERNATIONAL SYSTEM

*If we consider international agreement on total prevention of nuclear warfare as
the paramount objective...this kind of introduction of atomic weapons to the
world may easily destroy all our chances of success....[dropping an atomic bomb]
will mean a flying start toward an unlimited armaments race.*

—Franck Committee, 1945

The tests of May 1998 did two things: first, they highlighted
the declared nuclear weapons posture of India and Pakistan;
and second, they alerted the world about China's nuclear
weapons capability. All three countries comprising the strategic
triangle in Southern Asia are declared nuclear weapons states.
There are, moreover, two dyads in this triangle: the Sino-Indian
and Indo-Pak dyads. Conventional and nuclear policies in competition with each other, past history of bilateral conflict, hostile
propaganda, rhetorical diplomacy and persisting tensions inform
us of the trilateral division of power in this region. The three countries now have to decide what strategic directions would best serve
their national and regional interests. The three states, governed
by different political systems, approach to arms control and foreign
policy, now have to find answers to issues of nuclear weaponisation
and deployment, command and control and military strategy in a
dynamic strategic environment.

Cold War literature on deterrence envisages a mix of reassurance
and accommodation that focuses exclusively on nuclear capabilities. It is premised on the notion that decision makers are rational
thinking individuals. Questions of armed conflict, stability, risk
of war and deterrence in this region are compounded by the fact
that India features in both the dyads, and therefore the problem

is far more complex than the Cold War nuclear rivalry.[1] This chapter looks at the role of nuclear weapons and three crises—the Cuban missile crisis between the US and USSR, the Ussuri river clashes between USSR and China, and the Kargil War between India and Pakistan—that reflect the larger role of nuclear weapons in bilateral confrontations.

With the Soviet test in 1948 (which surprised Americans), the notion of deterrence started dominating strategic planning. Motives, interests, diplomacy and strategy were now in different compartments with the bomb available and out of the closet, and the strategic community had to figure out the most authoritative way to deliver a bomb that could hurt the vital interests of the adversary to its own maximum strategic benefit. Bernard Brodie believed that a vital first blow might not finish off the adversary and there might be enough energy in the adversary to retaliate.[2] This gradually brought the issue of targeting through strategic calculations to the forefront. It was now a choice (and in some cases a no-choice) between targeting cities and other 'vital interests'.[3] Brodie remarked that the chief task of the military would thenceforth be the prevention of war at all costs.[4]

Thus were set the parameters of the notion of deterrence: the vulnerability of world capitals, a vital first blow to the interests of a state, the helplessness of defence against intruding aircrafts and the need to build a retaliation force. The concept, of course, continued to be refined all through the Cold War years and many new elements were added with the advent of new technologies. In 1954, the then US Secretary of State, John Foster Dulles, broadly

---

[1] There was a triangle in the Cold War too: USSR, USA and China. But there are many differences between these triangles. The most prominent of the competitors, USSR and USA, had roughly similar powers. In Southern Asia, China, India and Pakistan form an asymmetric triangle.

[2] He noted that no victory is worth it if retaliation is expected. He argued for a stable balance, since 'a war in which atom bombs are not used is more likely to occur if both sides have bombs in quantity from the beginning than if neither side has it at the outset or if only one side has it' (Brodie 1946: 74).

[3] The term *vital interests* was to gain eminence in later years as its meaning expanded to include defence industries, army cantonments, nuclear installations, ammunition dumps, armoured formations and cities that were political or economic capitals.

[4] Brodie 1946: 76.

outlined the new doctrine of 'massive retaliation'. The strategic validity of mutually assured destruction (MAD) was premised on the assumption that either side protects all or most of its large population centres with anti-missile defences.[5] It is difficult to imagine whether a MAD posture would ensure long-term peace and stability, especially if one of the countries seeks to structure forces in defensive rather than offensive mode. Later refinements came in the form of 'limited war' and flexible response'.

In the initial years of the existence of nuclear weapons, theorists had to begin conceptualising from scratch. The later nuclear weapons states—China, India and Pakistan—can benefit from this literature on nuclear weapons from the Cold War period. Where can one locate the theory that best describes the nuclear posture and accompanying doctrines of China, India and Pakistan? It is unlikely that in the near future any of the states would configure their force structures towards offensive MAD. It is also unlikely that China, India or Pakistan would follow a flexible response posture, although it is clear that all states can expect an assured and punitive response, if the time comes.

The stakes were high in all the three 'crises' situations mentioned earlier. But while in the Cuban missile crisis not a shot was fired, in the Ussuri river clashes China and USSR went to armed conflict and lives were lost. In the Kargil War, there were more than a thousand causalties. In all the cases, there was the overarching presence of nuclear weapons that determined the outcome of the conflict. Often, before going to armed conflict, states pass through a phase of action–reaction and high political rhetoric, paving way for perceptions and misperceptions. This is a phase of 'crisis'—a

---

[5] The doctrine of assured destruction also attracted critics. President Nixon underlined the drawbacks of the doctrine in 1970 when he questioned, 'Should a President in the event of a nuclear attack, be left with the single option of ordering the mass destruction of enemy civilians in the face of the certainty that it would be followed by the mass slaughter of Americans? Should the concept of assured destruction be narrowly defined and should it be the only measure of our ability to deter the variety of threats we may face?' (US Congress 1974: 35). There were inherent problems with MAD. The assessment of the capability and intention of the adversary remained a function of complex variables, such as military, technological, strategic and most important, political, that had to operate in a dynamic strategic environment. In such an environment the maintenance of assured destruction capability at all times was extremely difficult.

period characterised by three key elements: a threat, the prospect of war and a sense of urgency.[6]

Cuban Missile Crisis

On 15 October 1962, American intelligence agencies discovered the first of six Soviet nuclear missiles bases under construction in Cuba. After discussing this for a week with the executive committee of the National Security Council, or the 'Ex. Comm.', President John F. Kennedy in a televised address announced this discovery to the world on 22 October 1962. He stressed that the deployment was a flagrant violation of his own warnings. He demanded withdrawal of these missiles and imposed a naval 'quarantine' on the shipment of 'offensive' weapons to Cuba. He warned Soviet Chairman Nikita Khrushchev that any missile launched from Cuban territory against any Western nation would be considered an attack by the Soviet Union on the US. Khrushchev immediately ordered construction of missile sites to be accelerated and denounced the quarantine as a violation of the Soviet Union's right to freedom of navigation. The quarantine took effect on 24 October, but Khrushchev ordered his ships not to challenge the US blockade. An immediate confrontation was thus avoided.

With the settlement of the dispute not in sight, the crisis dragged on and continued to build pressure on both sides for decisive action. While both the leaders were concerned about the outcomes of an inadvertent accidental war, neither was willing to back off, since the international and national stakes were high. A half-chance came on 26 October in the form of a long letter from Khrushchev, where he offered to withdraw in return for a US pledge not to invade Cuba and in return for the withdrawal of the 15 US Jupiter missiles from Turkey. The Ex. Comm. was against this, but President Kennedy secretly instructed his secretary of state to lay the ground-work for a contingency by which the secretary-general of the UN would propose a Cuba–Turkey missile swap.[7] On 28 October, Khrushchev offered an agreement to withdraw missiles from Cuba in return

[6] See in this context, Lebow 1981: 7–12.

[7] Blight and Welch 1989. See also Abel 1966a; Allison and Zelikow 1999; and Beggs 1971.

for a non-invasion pledge. However, Fidel Castro thought he was not consulted, felt betrayed and refused inspections to the UN inspectors. The other problem arose when Kennedy insisted that Soviets also withdraw the nuclear capable IL-28 light bombers. These bombers had been supplied to Cuba under an arrangement independent of the crisis at hand. It took Khrushchev's special envoy, Anastas Mikoyan, three weeks to persuade Castro. On 19 November, Castro relented and the quarantine was lifted on 21 November.

The Cuban missile crisis has been interpreted by some as a bold effort by Soviets to try and alter the unfavourable strategic environment in which the USSR found itself in 1962 as a result of the US intercontinental arms build-up and collapse of the 'missile gap' myth. The other postulate regarding Soviet objectives is that Soviet missiles and bombers deployed in Cuba were essentially bargaining counters which could be exchanged for a desired political or military (or both) concessions by the US. With these in the background, one can examine a public pledge by the US president not to invade Cuba, while the Soviets withdrew their missiles from Cuba in exchange of withdrawal of US missiles from Turkey.

It is doubtful that the Soviet Union merely sought to compel the US to withdraw its missiles from Turkey in exchange for the withdrawal of Soviet missiles from Cuba.[8] Khrushchev explicitly proposed a mutual missile withdrawal from Cuba and Turkey in his 27 October letter to President Kennedy. The fact that Khrushchev proposed such an exchange after the US had demanded the withdrawal of Soviet strategic weapons, does not prove that the original objective was to extract a mere promise of President Kennedy not to invade Cuba. Given geographical factors, and also the fact that the US already possessed a huge advantage on intercontinental nuclear delivery capabilities, a missile base in Cuba

---

[8] Arnold L. Horelick and Myron Rush contend, 'Since the US had only one squadron of Jupiters deployed in Turkey no more than one third the number of MRBMs [medium range ballistic missiles] with a 100 mile range known to have been shipped to Cuba would have been necessary to make such a trade seem quantitatively plausible. The costly and essentially unsalvageable fixed sites that were being prepared to receive IRBMs [intermediate-range ballistic missiles] with a 2200 mile range were altogether superfluous to any intended Cuba Turkey missile base exchange since the US had no equivalent missiles in Turkey or anywhere else for that matter' (Horelick and Rush 1966: 128).

would have been a greater military asset to the Soviet Union than the base in Turkey was to the US. Moreover, Secretary McNamara had already demanded replacing the Jupiter missiles as they had become obsolete.

The discovery of Soviet strategic missiles in Cuba provoked a US naval quarantine, a rapid build-up of tactical air force and army and a worldwide alert of the Strategic Air Command. It was clear that the crisis did reach a level where an all-out nuclear war seemed a possibility. The 26 October letter by Khrushchev to Kennedy laid the foundations for an amicable settlement.

MOTIVATIONS

Why were the missiles put in Cuba? Apparently, one of the causes that led Khrushchev, who was guided only by a small group of advisors, to take a hasty decision seems to have been to prevent the American invasion of Cuba. The invasion inevitable, especially after the US role in the Bay of Pigs and in the light of Operation Mongoose. The Bay of Pigs invasion, launched on 17–19 April 1961, was a serious attempt by the CIA to overthrow the Fidel Castro regime in Cuba. Castro's rise to power in Cuba upset a longstanding hemispheric status quo built upon a US claim to an exclusive sphere of influence in Latin America and a prohibition against the spread of communism into the region. The CIA grossly underestimated Castro's popularity, and the size, equipment and training of the invasion force proved wholly inadequate to the task at hand. The superior Cuban forces quickly defeated the invaders. Another cause was to counterbalance the massive US superiority in strategic nuclear weapons in a theatre away from Europe. A third was the desire to counterbalance the US deployment of Jupiter missiles on Soviet periphery for reasons of prestige. The following are a set of assumptions in understanding the motivations behind placing the missiles in Cuba:

1. To improve the Soviet bargaining position in a nuclear weapons balance: This was probably premised on 'bargaining from a position of strength'. Earlier, the US had been able to establish overseas bases all around the Soviet Union mainly because it was in a position of strength; now the Soviet Union wanted to do the same.

2. To deter an attack on Cuba by making a Soviet response a certainty: Technically, the missiles in Omsk had the same deterrent effect on the US as the Cuban missiles. But the Soviet Union tried to project the idea that it would take a strong position for its allies—Cuba, in this case.
3. To protect Cuba: Cuba was gradually becoming a significant element in the power projection of the Soviet Union. This move was also an extension of the socialist umbrella of USSR.
4. To improve the Soviet position in Europe, more specifically in Berlin: The main motive of the USSR in Europe was to avail an opportunity to harass West Germany.

The question that arises is, did the missiles serve their purpose?

1. The counter-bargaining strategy: It is still unclear if the Soviet Union had planned a counter-bargaining strategy, necessitating mutual concessions in the event of 'discovery'. It seems unlikely that brinkmanship could entertain the bargaining strategy even as reserve position.
2. Strengthening a bargain over Cuba: Even if recognition of Cuba and a non-aggression promise from USA was a pre-planned motive in exchange of withdrawal of missiles, the motive was only partially fulfilled as Cuba was very unhappy with the deal and took some time before it would comply.
3. Improving the Soviet bargaining position in Europe, more so in Berlin: There could have been other strategies than sending missiles to Cuba, but the Soviet Union never availed easier opportunities to harass Berlin.
4. To reassert a Soviet leadership in the socialist world: The missiles, in the first place, were not supposed to be discovered and certainly not so soon.[9] China was an emerging socialist power and presumably a Soviet victory in Cuba would have forced the Chinese to accept Soviet leadership in the socialist world.[10] With a not-so-favourable Soviet deal over Cuba, this motive too was not fulfilled.

----

[9] There is a view that if the missiles had not been discovered till Khrushchev's planned trip of the US after the November elections, their presence would have had to be disclosed privately in keeping with counter-bargaining strategy.

[10] Indeed, Soviet historian Adam Ulam even speculated that Khrushchev hoped to pressurise the Chinese into surrendering their rights to an independent nuclear capacity.

The US acted as if the offer to withdraw missiles in return of a Cuban recognition and a withdrawal of Jupiter missiles from Turkey came from the Soviet Union. Although Fidel Castro was left frustrated, Khrushchev and Kennedy settled for a tacit agreement wherein (a) the missiles would be withdrawn; (b) the withdrawal would be verified by independent reconnaissance; and (c) Jupiter missiles would be withdrawn from Turkey. Not much later, Kennedy was assassinated and Khrushchev was removed from power. Both leaders feared loss of control over events and both knew that any loss would far outweigh perceived gains. Both were willing to pay a price to extricate themselves from the predicament they had come to see as intolerably hazardous. Despite strong positions, both leaders could not afford to risk war. But there was also a view that a nuclear world war was averted by a narrow margin and deterrence was far from stable.[11]

Writers have used various theories of international relations to explain various aspects of this crisis—balance of power, military balance, the conviction that nuclear weapons would lead to stable deterrence and the psychology of decision makers under stress. In the legal sense, the crisis was never fully resolved. No treaty was ever concluded governing the settlement of the dispute, nor was the exchange of letters between Kennedy and Khrushchev formalising their terms of agreement ever made public.[12] The Cuban missile crisis also sought to improve crisis stability.[13]

Some analysts are of the view that it was not deterrence but God's grace that prevented a nuclear conflict.[14] The handling of the crisis by the two leaders came in for criticism too. Kennedy's critics lamented his unwillingness to seize the opportunity

---

[11] For instance, the title of Elie Abel's book is *The Missiles of October: Twelve Days to World War Three* (1966b).

[12] Larson 1986.

[13] In 1963 came the Hotline Agreement and the Limited Test Ban Treaty. Among the more important outcomes, was that the US and Soviet Union worked out rules of the game, limiting provocative initiatives in areas each regarded as being within its sphere of vital interest.

[14] They add that it was Kennedy and Khrushchev's personal initiatives that managed to prevent the conflict from escalating and eventually led to a solution that was satisfactory to both. They did so by avoiding irreversible steps, curtailing unwarranted bluster and refraining from giving ultimata. The Cuban missile crisis went down in history as the time the world came closest to a nuclear war.

provided by the pretext of Soviet deployment to deal decisively with Castro, even as the US enjoyed overwhelming conventional and nuclear superiority. Khrushchev's handling of the crisis has been criticised largely as a betrayal of Cuba's national interest and as yielding to US pressure. But they do have admirers who credit Kennedy for instructing Secretary of State Dean Rusk to lay the groundwork for the secretary-general of the UN in proposing the Cuba–Turkey missile swap. Khrushchev too is credited for his cautious handling of the situation. Fortunately, not a shot was fired and no lives were lost.

✣ Ussuri River Clashes

The Kargil conflict between India and Pakistan in May–July 1999 was not the first instance of conflict (where lives were lost) between two nuclear weapons states. In March 1969, China and the Soviet Union, both nuclear weapons states, with China being the smaller of the two, clashed with each other over the island of Chenpao,[15] which led to about 100 casualties (60 on the Russian side and 33 dead and 21 wounded on the Chinese side).[16]

It is imperative to situate the conflict in the context of deteriorating Sino–Soviet relations, which in 1969 had reached their lowest ebb. After defeating India in the 1962 war, China had consolidated itself politically, militarily and economically. In March 1963, China declared the Russo–Chinese border treaties of the 19th century to be 'unequal'. The Chinese premier, Mao Tse-tung, questioned the treaties between Tsarist Russia and the Ching Dynasty, since after that time Khabarovsk, Kamchatka and Vladivostok had been taken from Chinese territory and added to the Soviet Union. China did

---

[15] Chenpao is a small island about 22.5 km in length and about half a kilometre wide. The Ussuri river at this point is broad with the Soviet bank being about 400 m from the island and the Chinese bank being 100 m. The river forms the international boundary between China and the Soviet Union. At the centre of the dispute is the island itself about which the two sides do not even agree on the name (the Russians call it Damansky while it is called Chenpao by the Chinese). The island has the occasional lumberjack and fisherman, but it is generally uninhabited and covered by snow.

[16] Maxwell 1973.

not want the territories back but wanted the treaties to be negotiated again. China's repeated references to the unequal treaties
and their rapid nuclear weapon modernisation persuaded Moscow
to rethink its priorities with China, as the area that China was re-
ferring to had two major cities of the Soviet Union. Moreover, the
Trans-Siberian rail link from Leningrad to Vladivostok ran within
20 miles of the Chinese border for almost 800 miles of the route.
Any disruption in the link could block Eastern Siberia and interrupt
the primary source of oil for the Pacific fleet. With the Cultural
Revolution of the 1960s, Moscow had begun to take Chinese statements more seriously and military on the border was strengthened.
At the same time, Beijing began increasing its intimacy with
Washington. Both China and Washington had interest in containing the Soviet Union. Henry Kissinger said, 'As for the Soviets
we considered the Chinese option useful to induce restraint; but
we had to take care not to pursue it so impetuously as to provoke
a Soviet pre-emptive attack on China.'[17] After many years of
tension, China began to be termed as a long-term threat. Like its
two main adversaries, Germany and the US, China too had its
differences of opinion with the Soviet Union. What added to the
enmity was geographical proximity: a direct 2,000 mile border with
the Soviet Union and a large population base that was governed
authoritatively by a state that possessed nuclear weapons. Ideo-
logically too, there was a challenge as China followed a different
ideology within the communist movement.

The Soviet Union decided to take defensive steps against what
Kremlin saw as the 'yellow peril'. A defence treaty with Mongolia
in January 1966 resulted in huge reinforcement (100,000 men with
surface-to-surface rockets) of the already large deployment in
positions east of Lake Baikal. Besides, the Russians sought to 'take
advantage of the internal ferment caused by the Cultural Revolution and strengthen forces in the leadership that were opposed
to Mao.'[18] Another event that worsened mutual relations and
images was the Soviet Union's invasion of Czechoslovakia which
the Chinese did not support. The Chinese had supported the Soviet
Union's role in Hungary in 1956, but by 1968 many new developments had taken place. The Chinese started thinking about the

---

[17] As cited in Steele 1983: 144.
[18] Ibid.: 140.

Soviet Union's self-proclaimed right to intervene in other socialist countrsies by force if necessary.[19]

The Chinese had continued to use the Ussuri and Amur rivers for fishing and navigational purposes. The change in Soviet behaviour came following the summer of 1967 when the Soviet frontier guards started using force. Between December 1967 and February 1969, there were 16 occasions when patrols clashed on or near the island.[20] On 23 January 1969, a Chinese patrol on the island was clubbed and most of the soldiers were beaten. Following that the Chinese kept their distance. On 2 March, the Russians attacked another patrol which was substantially reinforced. Normally, the Chinese were chased off by wooden clubs but this time firepower was used. In a sustained battle in which both used small and medium weapons, many were left dead and wounded on each side.[21] The Russians retreated and made additional preparations. The Chinese too called for heavier armoury and firing began on 15 March. Accounts differ on who started the firing.[22] The Russians lost a tank, which got stuck in ice between the islands and the Chinese shore, and the rest of the battle was centred for three days on the prestige of recovering or retaining the tank. The Chinese took the tank and the island, while Russians continued to use artillery shelling and made attempts to recover and later destroy the tank. Gunfire was sporadically exchanged till 21 March, when the Chinese stopped firing.[23] The Russians, although numerically larger in number, made no more attempts take the islands. The infantry, the tanks and artillery all contributed to the battle, which lasted for about a week.

Given the technological advances and the geographical sprawl (which helps dispersal, and by implication, credibility) of both countries, it was unlikely that either China or Russia could succeed in a punishing first strike against the other. One also wonders what role the other powers like the US would have played if they had

---

[19] '...clearly implied that Moscow might feel impelled to do the same against China' (Steele 1983: 140).

[20] Maxwell 1973.

[21] According to Maxwell (ibid.), on the Russian side about 70 were killed or wounded and on the Chinese side 20 were killed and 34 wounded.

[22] Although Maxwell's account (ibid.) says the Russians began first, Steele (1983), Ambroz (1972) and Hoffman and Fleron (1980) say the Chinese fired first.

[23] This is according to Soviet accounts. See Maxwell 1973 and Robinson 1981.

been given the necessary negotiating space. The US probably did not want to play a role. It has also been proposed that at the heart of the conflict were political causes. Mao was probably trying to divert attention from the Cultural Revolution chaos—there were demonstrations against Russians—while Steele asserts, 'only if Brezhnev and his colleagues had been able to go against all their inherited assumptions and show willingness to deal with Peking as an equal could the conflict have been resolved.'[24] Besides, in the Chinese perception, 'very large Soviet forces (were) stationed along the borders and in Mongolia ... to influence the Chinese negotiating position through coercion.'[25]

The incident at least helped the two sides to come to the negotiating table. On 11 September 1969, the Russian Prime Minister Kosygin flew to Peking on his way home from the funeral of Ho Chi Minh, for a hastily arranged meeting with the Chinese Premier Chou En-lai. The two agreed on negotiations which started on 20 October and dragged on for some years. The concession that the Chinese gave was dropping their demand for Russian acknowledgement of the treaties as 'unequal', as a precondition for negotiations. These negotiations continued till China disengaged itself from them in 1979 after the Soviet Union became engaged in Afghanistan. These were subsequently restarted in 1982. Having come so close to a full-scale war, the two sides consciously left some channels of communications open until history took its own course.

Each claimed that the island was on its side. The Chinese stated that according to international law, in the case of navigable boundary rivers, the central line of the main channel should form the boundary line that determines the ownership of the islands. Chenpao and two other islands are situated on the Chinese side of the central line of the main channel of the Ussuri river and come under Chinese jurisdiction.[26] The Russians contended that according to the 1860 Peking Treaty, all land on the right side of the Ussuri belonged to Russia, while the land on the left bank was Chinese. A map appended to the treaty, they claimed, showed Damansky and many other islands on their side of the Ussuri.[27]

---

[24] Steele 1983: 143.
[25] Gelman 1980: 619.
[26] Ambroz 1972: 138.
[27] Ibid.: 138.

The Soviets attempted to raise the issue with the Americans who insisted that it was a bilateral problem. On 11 March, Ambassador Dobrynin raised the Ussuri river incident in a meeting with Henry Kissinger. Kissinger has written, 'when I tried to change the subject by suggesting that it was a Sino–Soviet problem, Dobrynin insisted passionately that China was everybody's problem.'[28] Kissinger further adds, that when he spoke to President Nixon, the latter remarked how unexpected events could have a major effect. The US saw a role for itself and some communications exchanged on general US–Soviet relations were based on 'long-term' considerations.[29]

There was repeated speculation that circumstances were just right for a Soviet pre-emptive 'surgical strike' against Chinese nuclear installations.[30] At the same time, there was perhaps no guarantee of a 100 per cent success, had a pre-emptive strike taken place.[31] Chinese nuclear installations were spread out geographically from Lop Nur (the test site) to Aksu, Urumchi and much further eastwards to Haiyen, Lanchou and Paotou. Had the Soviets decided to carry out the surgical strikes with a 75 per cent success rate, China would have retaliated with whatever nuclear weapons it had after the first strike, leading to escalation to the nuclear level.

In June 1969, when the talks opened, the Soviet premier openly admitted that they had reached a stalemate.[32] This was reflected in military affairs. The Military Affairs Commission of the Chinese Communist Party completed a report on military preparedness, 'on the basis of which some reinforcement of frontier areas may have taken place.'[33] The Soviets too had reinforced their deployments. The year 1971 saw diplomatic openings for China when it became a permanent member of the UN Security Council. An invitation to President Nixon was another example of the changing position of China in the international system. Diplomatic relations was established with 13 countries. 'All of this could be seen as a part of China's competition with the Soviet Union for ideological leadership of the under developed countries, but was also portrayed by

---

[28] Kissinger 1979: 172.
[29] Ibid.: 173.
[30] IISS 1969–71, here 1969.
[31] Ibid.
[32] IISS 1969–71, here 1970.
[33] Ibid.

China as part of the struggle against the super powers trying to divide the world.'[34]

Both the states played the brinkmanship game, fully realising that neither could win a conventional war. Militarily, the Soviets were much more powerful, and had delivery systems that could project a warhead not just to any part of China but also to any part of the world. Had Russia decided to go in for surgical strikes, much of Chinese nuclear weapons complexes would have been damaged, although perhaps a 100 per cent strike rate would not have been possible. Military build-up by both the states continued. The nuclear prowess too was enhanced. A clash that left a causalty figure of about 100 in a week suggests that had battle continued for a longer period, the figure could have been higher. Also, the border between the two states being more than 2,000 miles long, had any other sector opened, there could have been a problem of containing the conflict or even de-escalating it once it reached a different level. No external power played any role and the two sides continued their military build-up. Channels of communication were opened after the incident and talks rambled on without any result. Eventually, China agreed to come to the negotiating table, signed a one-year navigation agreement with respect to the disputed river, and gave up its insistence that the unequalness of the old treaties that had determined the Sino–Soviet border had rendered them worthless. Up to a point, the Soviet strategy seems to have worked. But in the long run, it did not. Once the crisis had been resolved, the Chinese backed away from negotiations, as they had no intention of carrying the Soviet terms to conclusion.[35]

According to international law, a boundary is not merely a line, but a line in a borderland. Boundaries are one of the most significant manifestations of territorial sovereignty.[36] It seems that with increasing claims of the Peaking Treaty being obsolete by China

---

[34] IISS 1969–71, here 1971: 55.

[35] Robinson 1981.

[36] Exceptional instances of boundaries, as in the Chenpao case, are termed 'voisinage' in international law. 'Where the borderland is of such character that, notwithstanding the boundary line running through it, the territory itself and its inhabitants are fused for all practical purposes, the two or more states concerned may tolerate (either by treaty or conduct) the existence in the borderland of administrative and other practices, for example the free movement of officials throughout the borderland ...' (Starke 1989: 189). 'In the case of a non-navigable

and the change in customary international law with a (by now) wider acceptance of the principle of *Thalweg*, the Soviet Union decided to forgo its claims on the islands: an inglorious exit no superpower would want. Or perhaps, the Soviet Union did not want to engage in a protracted conflict there.

Either way, just like the Cuban missile crisis, where shots were not fired, this conflict brought forth the point that nuclear weapons states do not necessarily deter each other and that there is always the risk of escalation arising out of many factors, including misperception, miscommunication and underestimating adversarial capabilities.

Kargil Crisis

In 1999, India and Pakistan battled over Kargil (Map 2.1) which became the second instance after the 1969 Ussuri river clashes where two overt nuclear weapons states went to war. The indisputable facts of the Kargil War were that in the summer of 1999, just a few months after the highs of the Lahore Declaration, Pakistani army regulars and irregulars occupied high positions in the mountainous Kargil sub-sector that was on the Indian side of the line of control. India was taken by surprise, as intelligence agencies failed to detect the presence of a large number of *mujahideen* intruders firmly entrenched in the heights in Kargil, overlooking the strategic highway connecting Srinagar to Leh. The Kargil region is more than 15,000 feet high and the winter temperatures are below –20ºC. These *mujahideen* forces numbering more than 3,000 men were equipped with all kinds of weapons, including shoulder fired Stinger missiles. They had rations that could last them six months and winter clothing that helped them survive the sub-zero temperatures.

river the boundary line in the absence of contrary treaty provision runs down the middle of the river ....' This is called the 'median line' and it was adopted for non-navigable rivers by the peace treaties of 1919–20. 'Where the river is navigable the boundary line as a rule runs through the middle line of the deepest navigable channel, or as it was technically called the *Thalweg*.' Only in exceptional cases, one bank of the river is the boundary, while the whole bed is under the sovereignty of the other country. 'This is an exceptional case arising under treaty or by long established peaceable occupation' (ibid.: 189).

The mission was logistically supported by Pakistan, but perhaps Pakistan had not thought out the political and strategic end clearly.[37]

Pakistan started raising the bogey of nuclear exchange—Kashmir being a nuclear flashpoint at an early stage—and the element of surprise gave the country the advantage.[38] The Prime Minister of Pakistan, Nawaz Sharif, said, 'last year's nuclear tests have given Pakistan the confidence to counter any enemy attack .... They (people) are confident for the first time in their history that in the eventuality of an armed attack they will be able to meet it on equal terms.'[39] Given the overt nuclearisation of Pakistan in May 1998, this threat was perceived to have obvious connotations in India.

India started discovering these intrusions towards the end of May 1999, by which time these intruders were well entrenched in the mountains. The Indian options were limited to either crossing the line of control to stop their supplies or continuing to bear losses as the forces tried climbing the mountain tops. If India opened up another front, there would have been tremendous domestic political pressures within Pakistan to respond with an all-out war. In an all-out war scenario, either side would have been prompted to use nuclear weapons, incurring heavy losses. Escalation to a nuclear level would not then have been ruled out. The issue of crossing the line of control was seriously debated in India.[40]

---

[37] The assumptions were probably: (*a*) The international community would intervene or stop the war at an early stage; (*b*) the coalition government in India was a mere caretaker government and would not be able to respond quickly, as it was weak; (*c*) with the pressure on the Srinagar–Leh highway and the supplies to Leh getting choked, India would respond by opening another front, whereby the onus of escalation would lie on India; (*d*) a military operation under the garb of *mujahideens* would focus the world's attention on Kashmir and the issue would be further internationalised. The nuclear status of the two countries would ring an alarm for the world at large.

[38] See Akram 1998. Also see *The Times of India* 1999a and *The News International* 1999b.

[39] *The News International* 1999a. The Pakistani Foreign Secretary, Mr Shamshad Ahmad, warned that Islamabad would use 'any weapon' in its arsenal to defend the country's territorial integrity. The Foreign Secretary told *The News/Jang* newspaper: 'We will not hesitate to use any weapon in our arsenal to defend our territorial integrity.' See *The News International* 1999a. Also see Baruah 1999a, 1999b; Dutt 1999; *The Asian Age* 1999; *The Indian Express* 1999a; *The Hindustan Times* 1999; *The News International* 1999b, 1999d; *The Times of India*, 1999a, 1999b; and Zafar 1999.

[40] See Roy Chowdhury and Singh 1999. The issue was discussed many times at the Cabinet Committee on Security as well.

It seems that India had taken a carefully considered decision at the very beginning not to cross the LoC, in spite of voices being raised in Pakistan questioning the LoC itself.[41] The argument perhaps was that the war could escalate with nuclear weapons in both countries; it would be difficult to try to contain it. There were voices in India that it was the nuclear weapons capability which prevented India from crossing the LoC. It also became clear that the bogey of Kashmir being a nuclear flashpoint was directed more at the international community and did not have credibility. Therefore, India did not cross the LoC and continued to pay a heavy personnel and material price instead.

Map × 2.1
Jammu and Kashmir (inset Kargil)

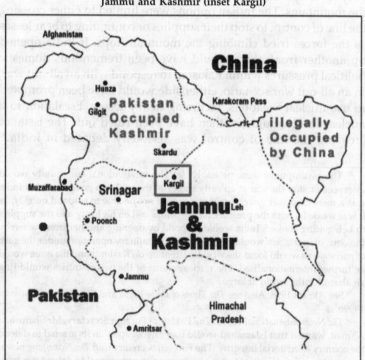

Source: www.indianembassy.org/new/Kargil/J&K_Map.html.

---

[41] This was surprising, as after the Simla Agreement in 1972, the LoC was very clearly delineated by Lt Gen P.S. Bhagat and the then Director, Military Operations, Maj Gen I.S. Gill from India, and from the Pakistani side by

Contrary to its expectations, Pakistan calculated that India's conventional advantage would be offset by mutual nuclear deterrence, and that the former could increase the activities of *mujahideens* in a calibrated manner without fear of conventional retaliation from India.[42] Despite warnings from eminent strategic thinkers over a period of time, the BJP-led NDA (National Democratic Alliance) government in India did not anticipate the emergence of such a 'stability–instability paradox'.[43] Pakistan trusted its 'strategic ally' China to provide material assistance. However, in spite of the Pakistani Foreign Minister Sartaj Aziz personally visiting Beijing, this did not happen as China distanced itself from the conflict, asking India and Pakistan to bilaterally resolve it. Pakistan had to then look towards Washington, and following the 4 July Declaration,[44] the then Prime Minister Nawaz Sharif had to make a

Lt Gen Hameed Khan and the then Director, Military Operations, Brig S.M. Abbasi. They were assisted by deputy directors of survey from India and with adequate number of trained survey personnel and survey equipment from Pakistan. The senior military commanders of the two sides were assisted by three sector commanders along the entire length of 740 km of the line of control which was divided in three segments, namely, the southern, central and the northern sectors. In turn, sector commanders were assisted by sub-sector commanders to do the groundwork on the entire line of control. For example, in the northern sector were included the four sub-sector commanders of Partapur, Kargil (including Batalik), Shingo (Kaksar) and Drass, which are the areas of current conflict. Sector and sub-sector commanders of the two countries worked in close cooperation. In the whole exercise, two sets of maps each comprising 27 maps were prepared. These marked maps were joined and 19 mosaics prepared, thus clearly delineating the entire stretch of the line of control running through 740 km, starting from Sangam and ending at Pt NJ-9842. Besides the maps, there were 19 annexures consisting of 40 pages, giving the details of every feature, landmark and coordinates of the line of control. After being signed by two senior military commanders, Lt Gen P.S. Bhagat and Lt Gen Hameed Khan, it was subsequently accepted by the two governments, and on 20 December 1972, a joint statement by the Indian and Pakistan governments was released to the media delineation in conformity with the line of control in Jammu and Kashmir. There should be absolutely no reason for any reservation in anyone's mind in India or Pakistan that there is anything vague or uncertain about the line of control in Jammu and Kashmir. See Chibber 2003. Lt Gen M.L. Chibber was Deputy Director of Military Operations after the 1971 war.

[42] Siddiqa-Agha 2001: 178–83.

[43] Krepon and Gagné 2001.

[44] Observe the language of the Clinton–Sharif 4 July 1999 Washington Declaration: 'President Clinton and Prime Minister Sharif share the view that the current fighting in the Kargil region of Kashmir is dangerous and contains the seeds of a

'personal appeal' to the intruders to withdraw. By this time, India, using its army and air force (the air force had been used in a wartime operation after 1971) had regained up to 80 per cent of the territory from the intruders. Most of the capitals around the world made strong appeals for respecting the line of control.

PAKISTAN'S STRATEGY

The strategy that Pakistan had chalked out is not difficult to understand. Calling the *mujahideen*s in Kashmir freedom fighters, Pakistan thought that the population of the Kashmir valley might end up supporting it, and India would find it extremely difficult to contain the situation. Additionally, the international opinion would oscillate between the issue of Kashmir and nuclear weapons, and Pakistan would not be blamed. Actually, Pakistani army regulars masqueraded as *mujahideen*s, although during the Kargil War Pakistan denied the presence of its army regulars. Some months later, however, the Pakistani government even gave gallantry awards to these soldiers.[45] Kashmir supported the Indian response to the intrusion like the rest of the country and did not shelter the intruders. Second, the intruders had occupied strategic heights overlooking the Srinagar–Leh highway and could prevent the movement of traffic and supplies to Leh (Map 2.2).[46] There are reports

---

wider conflict. They also agreed that it was vital for the peace of South Asia that the line of control in Kashmir be respected by both parties, in accordance with the 1972 Shimla accord. It was agreed between the President and the Prime Minister that concrete steps will be taken for the restoration of the line of control in accordance with the Shimla Agreement. The President urged an immediate cessation of the hostilities once these steps are taken' (Joint US–Pakistan statement 1999).

[45] In a function some months after the war, these war heroes were decorated. For instance, the country's highest gallantry award, the *Nishan-e-Haider*, was given to Capt Karnal Sher Khan and Havaldar Lalak Jan, both of the Northern Light Infantry. A total of 95 officers and soldiers were given battle honours—out of which 71 were posthumously awarded. 'Captain Karnal Sher Khan's valour was seen first hand by the Indian Army and an Indian Army Captain insisted that Karnal Sher Khan's memory should be treated with due respect. The Indian Captain said we are a professional army and respect another professional soldier even when he is from the enemy side. And we would feel happy if a soldier like Karnal Sher gets recognition for his bravery' (Sawant 2000). For more details on Pakistani war heroes, see PIADS 2001.

[46] There is another route to Leh from Manali in Himachal Pradesh, via the Rohtang Pass, Keylong and Sarchu.

that Pakistan had been planning such an operation and the Pakistani army could thereafter move into the Siachen region. It is also clear that Pakistan had spent money, energy and strategic planning to execute an operation of this magnitude. A passage by Altaf Gauhar, an information advisor to Field Marshal Mohammad Ayub Khan, makes this point clear: 'The occupation of the strategic hilltops in Dras (sic), Kargil and Leh has been a major objective of the Pakistan Army ... in 1987 General Zia-ul-Haq authorised the preparation of a war plan to occupy several positions in the Kargil sector.'[47] Following the political, diplomatic, and to some extent, military loss, there began a blame game in Pakistan culminating in the coup of October 1999. Many questions were raised, like 'what was this operation all about? Who was its real mastermind? When were the operations planned and what kind of forces were used to take control of the strategic heights and ridges in the Kargil–Drass region? And, most importantly, were the diplomatic fallouts, or for that matter the expected gains and losses, taken into account before embarking on this adventure?[48] There has always been a delicate balance in Pakistan between civilian and military hierarchies. These were put to test after its Kargil misadventure: both the civilian and military leaderships indulged in the blame game, covertly and publicly.[49]

If indeed nuclear weapons deter the use of nuclear weapons, does that mean that states should be more than prepared for conventional and sub-conventional conflicts? One wonders how the states would have reacted if any of the following situations had arisen—had Pakistan opened another front, or had India decided to cross the line of control. Once domestic pressures begin to accumulate, a definite result is what states look for; otherwise 'backing off' without tangible results might be conceived as a sign of weakness in a future crisis situation by the adversary. What is unclear is the connection between nuclear weapons in India and Pakistan and specific politico-military objectives in the event of outbreak of hostilities.

[47] Gauhar 1999.

[48] Abbas 1999: 65.

[49] See in this context, Jones 2002. Owen Bennett Jones was the then BBC World correspondent in Islamabad.

Map × 2.2
Kargil Battle Region

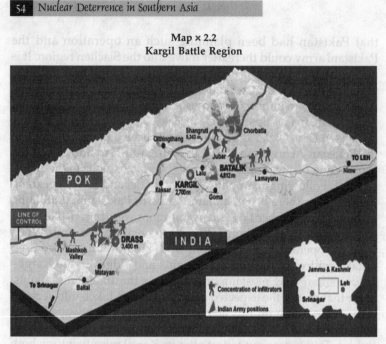

Source: Available at http://www.rediff.com/news/kargil.htm, accessed on
10 March 2003.

It became clear that Pakistan's expectation of international
mediation on Kashmir due to concern over nuclearisation in South
Asia was too optimistic. Though concerned about the situation,
the international community nevertheless wanted both countries
to exercise restraint and resolve the issue peacefully through bilateral dialogue. The Indian assessment was that Pakistan had
resorted to adventurism, having failed to secure international
mediation on Kashmir. As *The Kargil Review Committee Report* notes,
'It committed aggression in Kargil by crudely violating the LoC,
using its regular forces in civil dress along with some *mujahideen*.
It was able to re-focus international attention on Kashmir but, much
to its surprise, in a manner that was critical of its rash and unpro-
voked action in the wake of the Lahore Declaration.'[50] Once the
scale of the intrusion was known, the Indian military forces handled
the situation effectively, though with considerable restraint, since

---

[50] Kargil Review Committee 2000.

there were pressures to cross the LoC. Pakistan continued to project Kashmir as being a nuclear flashpoint. The international community did not favour alteration of the status quo through overt use of regular and irregular forces and covert nuclear blackmail. The 1990 Gulf War had strengthened the foundation of the norm against altering the status quo by use of force. Pakistan obviously overlooked this factor. International pressure mounted on Pakistan to withdraw its forces and respect the sanctity of the LoC. This underlines the message that the international community is averse to allowing nuclear blackmail to alter the long-established status quo.

The Kargil Review Committee Report notes in one place:

> what Pakistan attempted at Kargil was a typical case of salami slicing [government security deletion]. Since India did not cross the LoC and reacted strictly within its own territory, the effort to conjure up escalation of a kind that could lead to nuclear war did not succeed. Despite their best effort Pakistan was unable to link its Kargil caper with a nuclear flashpoint, though some foreign observers believe it was a near thing.[51]

After the Kargil War, the international community 'insisted with even greater vehemence than hitherto that the line of control was inviolable and that Pakistan should respect its sanctity … Pakistan had managed to enhance its image as an aggressive and unpredictable state.'[52] The belief that Pakistan was deliberately seeking to introduce a nuclear element into the Kargil conflict should be a cause for concern. The faith in the rationality of the Indo–Pak leadership in the matter of nuclear weapons therefore seems somewhat naïve, to say the least. The stakes involved in the failure of deterrence, whatever the conventional response to such a crisis, are enormous enough to occasion greater effort being made to stabilise the fragile Indo–Pak nuclear stand-off.

---

[51] Kargil Review Committee 1999: para 13.57. Although the Committee was not constituted under the Commissions of Inquiry Act, it 'was given the widest possible access to all relevant documents, including those with the highest classification and to officials of the Union and Jammu and Kashmir Governments.'
[52] Jones 2002: 104.

✠ CONCLUSION

The deterrent value of nuclear weapons during the Cold War era was premised on their ability to deter nuclear and large-scale conventional conflict. Even as assumptions have been made that they are basically unusable, there has existed a belief that they could be used as a last resort option, a position that was also argued by the P-5 in the International Court of Justice (ICJ). In spite of a growing norm against further proliferation and testing of these weapons in the post-Cold War world, the United States has stressed the deterrent value of nuclear weapons against biological or chemical weapons attack as well. A stance like this by the world's superpower has served to enhance their military value and encourage the old beliefs that nuclear weapons are just another kind of weaponry that are not to be abhorred. But the question remains, do nuclear weapons ensure a long-lasting peace in the region?

After examining three cases that involved two nuclear weapons states where direct confrontation was always in the offing, nuclear weapons have neither stabilised the region, nor have they helped in establishing lasting peace. Constant veiled threats were exchanged during all the cases examined. Even in the cases where government reactions were calm, as was the case in the Ussuri river clashes and the Kargil War, beneath the calm surface there was always the reality that both sides had the capacity to annihilate vast populations. Below the tranquil surface there were symptoms of the volatile interplay between threat and fear. What was important was the intensity of perceived threat. This was a variable independent of the military means available and led to increased pressure on the governments to use the weapon of last resort.

Once armed hostilities break out, maintaining control over events is a very complex task with uncertainty and misinformation intensifying the threat perception. This can have a catastrophic feedback loop. One thread of influence on the government's actions is domestic pressure, which is not sensitive to possible outcomes. The tension between internal and external policy is much more noticeable in democracies than in authoritarian regimes. However, depending on powerful decision-influencing sources that exist in any state, even authoritarian regimes come under pressure.

In the Ussuri river clashes, once the Chinese knew that they could match Soviet firepower, they were prepared to fight longer battles. The earlier motive of retaining the control of the island was no longer the ultimate aim. Even if the Soviets carried out a surgical strike on Chinese nuclear facilities, there was every chance of escalation as there could not have been a 100 per cent success rate of a first strike. A Chinese retaliatory strike would then have at least had the capability of knocking out a few Soviet cities. Again, in the case of the Cuban missile crisis, one does not know of the decision-making process and motivations of the Soviets.

Based on this assumption, can a similar conclusion be drawn for the Kargil War as well? It is likely that Pakistan did not calculate all possible outcomes of the high altitude adventure. The key figure in planning and executing the operation, General Musharraf, may have just informed the then Prime Minister Nawaz Sharif that he would like to increase activity along the line of control but perhaps not all details were shared.[53] After initial gains which emboldened the Pakistan backed intruders, the attention-seeking ploy turned out to be a dangerous game in brinkmanship.[54] Once Pakistan started realising that winning was out of question and no state was willing to intervene on its behalf, a face-saving formula was worked out. Internationally, Pakistan stood isolated and it was only after the 4 July 1999 Washington Agreement with US President Bill Clinton that it could find a way out of the situation. The Chinese and Western refusal to give countenance to the Pakistani operation was a big disappointment to Islamabad. A bigger disappointment was the fact that both countries being declared nuclear weapons states and democracies at the same time went to a war that had all the elements of escalation. Many Pakistanis now privately acknowledge that not just this war, but even all the earlier ones that Pakistan fought for Kashmir, never involved an assessment of all possible outcomes and it is invariably prone to change strategies midway.[55] The conclusion of the Kargil conflict did not ensure any moderation in Pakistan's behaviour; on the contrary, incidents of cross-border terrorism have only increased, as have the number

---

[53] See the chapter on the 1999 coup in Jones 2002.

[54] India lost two fighter jets and a helicopter in the first week.

[55] Personal impressions gathered in a visit to Pakistan during March–April 2000.

of *fidayeen* attacks upon Indian military and paramilitary forces, installations and administrative headquarters in Kashmir. The irrationality of this strategy arises from the reality that, 'allowing the practice of cross-border terrorism to dictate policy effectively legitimizes the behaviour, and Pakistan simply cannot afford to support a policy in Kashmir that if applied within Pakistan's borders would threaten the integrity of the state.'[56]

For years Pakistan believed that it could bleed India through Kashmir. The May 1998 tests further encouraged it as Islamabad thought that stability at the nuclear level makes sub-conventional conflict safer without the risk of escalation.[57] The Kargil conflict demonstrated that Pakistan could be a reckless adventurist and a risk-prone state that is capable of behaving astrategically and irrationally. The possession of nuclear weapons has raised the threshold for Pakistan to take risks. This was further proved by the suicide attack on the Indian Parliament on 11 December 2001. But in the post-Parliament attack phase, India decided to play tough. This time, New Delhi decided that relentless military and diplomatic pressure and war rhetoric with subtle threats of patience running out could alter the outcome of the crisis in its favour, and it could also get the Western world to build pressure on Pakistan. To be taken credibly, India had to ensure that its threat of initiating an armed conflict was taken seriously. To some extent, this strategy paid off. Indian and Western pressure resulted in General Musharraf's speech on 12 January 2002, wherein he made tall promises of Pakistan officially stopping support to terrorists. This was a change from Pakistan's stance till recently that it could manipulate the risks of a nuclear confrontation purely for political reasons, and when India upped the ante it could cry nuclear wolf, attract global attention to the Kashmir 'flashpoint' and get away with it.

The conclusion that one can draw from the three cases is that even though states want to acquire nuclear weapons to strengthen their security and to augment their forces against their adversary, this often leads to a nuclear dilemma, and the adversary too makes all efforts to acquire similar capabilities. There remain chances that

---

[56] Joeck 2000.

[57] India has sought to counter this now by seriously debating escalation control in a limited war scenario.

in any armed conflict between two adversaries, the losing state would want to use all the weapons at its disposal to ensure political, social, economic and regime survival. Often decision makers fail to calculate all possible outcomes and mid-crisis motivations change. Even against geographically small state surgical strikes, there can be no guarantee that all the nuclear assets of the adversary would be destroyed and that there would remain none to inflict a retaliatory strike, while limited wars or salami slicing tactics always have incentives for the loser to use all weapons at its disposal. Further, escalation control in any conflict operates in a dynamic strategic environment. Nuclear weapons do not prevent the outbreak of armed conflict; on the contrary, they increase the chances of skirmishes that contain seeds of escalation to the nuclear level. Moreover, nuclear weapons also encourage low intensity adventurism even if all outcomes have not been thought through, and there is no exit strategy.

CHAPTER 3

REVISITING DETERRENCE

*Escalation, while it conveys resolve, if premature or miscalculated,
risks provoking the outcome it was initiated to forestall ... military
passivity, on the other hand, is decidedly unprovocative
but may weaken or even undermine deterrence.*

—Richard Ned Lebow

C old War foes projected threats of sudden cold-blooded
attacks, whilst expressing their faith in deterrence. The idea
of deterrence is premised on the belief that rationally cal-
culating decision makers would refrain from a first strike, fearing
a massive retaliatory strike. Deterrence becomes the central theme
in military strategy once states acquire nuclear weapons. It is also
the most important issue in any armed confrontation. This chapter
investigates the nuances of deterrence in the triangular competition
between China, India and Pakistan.

After the Second World War, which ushered in the age of nuclear
strategy, two seminal works appeared—*The Absolute Weapon* by
Bernard Brodie and *There Will be No Time: The Revolution in Strategy*
by William Borden.[1] These two books broadly set the parameters
of the utility and strategic culture of nuclear weapons. Strategic
culture may be defined, in Colin Gray's words, as 'the socially constructed and transmitted assumptions, habits of mind, traditions,
and preferred methods of operation—that is, behaviour—that are
more or less specific to a particular geographically based security
community.'[2] Brodie argued that the use of nuclear weapons could
not have military objectives because of their awesome destructive
capability. Much later, the distinction between the actual use and

---

[1] Brodie 1946; Borden 1946.
[2] Gray 1999: 28.

deterrent force of nuclear weapons began to be discussed as deterrence by punishment and deterrence by denial.[3]

❖ PUNISHMENT

Deterrence by punishment fundamentally seeks to prevent aggression by threat of punishing retaliation. The 1950s American strategies of massive retaliation and assured destruction are good examples of deterrence by punishment.[4] The central objective of assured destruction was 'to deter deliberate nuclear attack upon the United States ....'[5] Massive retaliation was no different from this and was more explicit in its threat of punishment as the means to deter the Soviet Union.[6] The credibility of American massive retaliation started getting questioned once Soviet forces began growing. The fundamental concern of the American forces then became the US ability to retaliate after surviving a Soviet 'first strike'. This added the term 'second strike' to the growing nuclear literature. Credibility of the threat of a punishing retaliation, therefore, became a focal point.[7] There was a big information gap and American estimates of Soviet capability were way off the mark. This lack of information only added to the threat perception. In fact, Soviet forces were much weaker than what the US estimated.[8] Even at the beginning of this century, US policy is based on using nuclear weapons once deterrence has failed.[9]

---

[3] Barry Buzan denies that any such distinction exists. He contends that the only real difference is between deterrence and compellance. See Buzan 1987.

[4] See Dulles 1973: 62–64.

[5] See McNamara 1968: 52.

[6] Dulles 1973. Massive retaliation was not just a military strategy but was also used to deter Soviet 'aggression' in the 1970s and the 1980s.

[7] In the context of vulnerability of the American forces, see Talbott 1989.

[8] See in this context, Prados 1982.

[9] See The US Air Force 1994: para 1.2.1. If deterrence does fail, the use of nuclear weapons should have definite objectives. These objectives should: (a) forcibly change the perceptions of enemy leaders about their ability to win; (b) demonstrate to enemy leaders that if the conflict continues or escalates, certain loss outweighs any potential gain; (c) encourage negotiations; (d) preclude the enemy from achieving its objectives; (e) ensure the success of the attack by the US or its allied forces. The purpose of using nuclear weapons can range from producing a political decision at the strategic level of conflict to being used to directly support

The issue central to McNamara's strategy of assured retaliation was, what constitutes punishment? There was, for a long time, no definite answer to this question. McNamara was of the view that a level could be achieved by having the capacity to inflict damage to 20 to 25 per cent of the Soviet population along with a capability of destroying 50 per cent of the Soviet industry. The main question remained unanswered in maintaining nuclear deterrence through the threat of punishment—the amount of forces that can survive an adverse attack and are able to retaliate punitively.

⊠ DENIAL

As the term itself implies, deterrence by denial is a function of defence. But as Glenn Snyder had originally suggested, the true distinction might not be between deterrence by punishment and deterrence by denial but between deterrence and defence, as it is defence that remains the true objective of strategists.[10] The central logic of deterrence by denial is premised on the failure of deterrence. Denial strategists assume that deterrence can fail and they prepare for that eventuality. They thereby try to prevent aggression by the adversary by convincing the aggressor through defence preparations that its aggression would face certain failure. Strategically preparing for deterrence by denial is a complex task. There have to be strategic offensive forces, a command and control system[11] that can survive nuclear exchange,[12] strategic defensive forces, and

military operations in theatre warfare. All uses of nuclear weapons will have strategic implications, regardless of the targets attacked, and in all circumstances require presidential approval. Options for employing nuclear weapons may have a greater impact on conflict than operations involving only conventional weapons.

[10] See Snyder 1961.

[11] Shaun R. Gregory has given a working definition of command and control as 'an agreement of facilities, personnel, procedures and means of information acquisition, processing, dissemination and decision-making used by national command authorities and military commanders in planning, directing and controlling military operations' (Gregory 1996: 3–4).

[12] One could also include the category of accidental nuclear exchange in this, which, as Paul Bracken opines, results from the technical failure of individual components of a system or from unpredictable human error. Inadvertent war is the result of a process in which crises escape control for a variety of reasons.

a society that is prepared for nuclear war.[13] Theoretically, surviving a first strike and the capability of the force to go for retaliatory strike are difficult questions and a matter of much debate.

Typically, deterrence seeks to clarify the actions of the adversary that are to be deterred, that is, to specify the actions to which the deferrer will respond by inflicting some form of punishment on the aggressor. The other version that literature recognises is denying the adversary the actions it might want to take by an overwhelming force capability. This also implies that it may just be harder to make clear and credible deterrent threats that provide an insurance against all possible adverse actions that one wishes to prevent. Michael Howard has defined deterrence as a policy that seeks to persuade an adversary, through the threat of military retaliation, that the costs of using military force to resolve political conflict will outweigh the benefits.[14]

Deterrence theory is based on the assumption that there is a certain measure of transparency of intent and capability. In principle, the party to be deterred should be in a position to calculate the deterrer's capability and willingness to use force. Also involved in the calculation is the degree of accuracy, to determine whether or not the adversary could proceed with its desired course of action.[15] On deterrence, Bernard Brodie once rued that there was 'much dogmatism but little searching inquiry.'[16] Ever since the advent of nuclear weapons, the concept of nuclear deterrence has become central to military strategy. However, although on the face of it the concept of deterrence appears simple, it has proved extremely complicated to implement in practice. The challenge of

---

Inadvertent war 'flows from an escalation process in which each side keeps seeking an edge until the unintended eruption occurs' (Bracken 1983: 129).

[13] See in this context, Gray 1984. See also Jones and Thompson 1978.

[14] Howard 1982/83: 315.

[15] The other view on this is that there also has to be a degree of opacity and uncertainty that strengthens the process of deterrence. Most states do not reveal much beyond making a customary declaration that their command and control structure is in place. India, for instance, in announcing its Nuclear Command Authority, merely indicated that 'The Government also mentions that it has "reviewed and approved the arrangements for alternate chains of command for retaliatory nuclear strikes in all eventualities." This is a reference to a situation in which the Prime Minister may be incapacitated during a crisis' (Mohan 2003b).

[16] Brodie 1970: 168.

maintaining stable deterrence is revealed as the challenge of strategy. While this is true, neither deterrence nor strategy—to which deterrence is a highly dependent variable—can be understood to be a function of a single dominant factor. Writing in 1960, Thomas Schelling had argued, 'What is impressive is not how complicated the idea of deterrence has become, and how carefully it has been refined and developed, but how slow the process has been, how vague the concepts still are, and how inelegant the current theory of deterrence is.'[17] This was more than four decades ago. Although much has been written since then, as the world changes, new alliances are being formed to counter unforeseen enemies. Weapons of mass destruction have become linked to irrational non-state actors which make all theories of rational deterrence redundant.

The central premise of deterrence is rationality. It assumes that under certain circumstances opponents will share similar value structures. On this is premised the notion that adversaries will necessarily choose alternatives that will ensure their survival rather than destruction. Therefore, at the core of deterrence theory is a notion of rational deterrence premised on three assumptions: adequate capabilities, a clearly communicated threat and a credible willingness to carry out the threat.[18] Many theorists stress strong material cost–benefit logic to deterrence and a strong rationalism.[19] But if one assumes that decision makers in states employing nuclear weapons are rational, then self-interest naturally deters the state, as retaliation would cause overwhelming devastation to the state and society. Decision makers are not essentially dispersed along a one-dimensional yardstick that extends from complete rationality at one end to complete irrationality at the other. Thomas Schelling is of the opinion that '[r]ationality is a collection of attributes, and departures from complete rationality maybe in many different directions.'[20] Even the presence of overwhelming nuclear weapons in a state and the prospect of completely annihilating the adversary

---

[17] Schelling 1960. He goes on to say, 'on strategic matters of which deterrence is an example, those who have tried to devise policies to meet urgent problems have had little or no help from an already existing body of theory, but have had to create their own as they went along.'

[18] Kaufmann 1956a: 19.

[19] See Achen and Snidal 1989; Little 1991.

[20] Schelling 1960.

do not provide deterrence; it is rationality that stops a nation from deploying its nuclear forces. The US was perhaps facing such a dilemma during the Vietnam War, and yet it could not garner itself to use nuclear weapons on Vietnam even though it was fighting a losing battle.

The theory of nuclear deterrence assumes that before initiating armed conflict, decision makers are going to perform a cost–benefit analysis, which underlines de Mesquita's expected utility theory.[21] The literature on deterrence evolved in what Robert Jervis calls 'waves'.[22] It was only after the 1949 nuclear test by the Soviet Union and the Korean War in the 1950s that a greater interest began to be taken in the theoretical aspects of nuclear deterrence. The Korean War also led to an increase in the volume of literature on limited war. The ambiguous, costly and prolonged conflict in East Asia proved to be highly frustrating for Americans. In opposition to Gen Douglas MacArthur's thesis that in war there is no substitute for victory, the advocates of limited war argued that in the emerging nuclear era wars must be kept non-nuclear and the military objectives of war have to be kept strictly non-nuclear.[23] It was essential, in their view, to devise ground rules for preventing war from escalating, even if this meant an agonisingly bitter struggle that resulted only in stalemate.[24]

---

[21] He concedes the successful outcome of war to be a function of relative power capabilities. Here power is taken in the most comprehensive sense. In any given conflict, decision makers on both sides are likely to perceive possible outcomes from the conflict differentially. Bueno de Mesquita constructs nine hypothetical international systems with varying distributions of strong and weak states. He has included varying risk-taking orientations among decision makers. He has calculated the probability of success, the actors' risk–security levels and their expected utility of war. He concludes that no particular distribution of power has exclusive claim as a predictor of peace or war. He supports this through the empirical record of the period 1816–1965 (de Mesquita 1981, 1985).

[22] Jervis 1979: 291.

[23] The debate over nuclear deterrence gained impetus after the Eisenhower administration enunciated the doctrine of 'massive retaliation.' No longer was the US constrained to fight an indefinite number of costly and long militarily engaged wars of the type of the Korean War, without resorting to nuclear weapons. It was in this sense that deterrence was considered a self-fulfilling prophecy.The US justification of huge arsenals for massive retaliation was that these were only meant to achieve certain compromise decisions and so the sizes of arsenals were not derived from meaningful military requirements.

[24] George and Smoke 1974: 23–27.

Many theorists have concluded that it should not be assumed that nuclear weapons would make conventional forces obsolete. Barry Blechman, Stephen Kaplan, Laurence Martin, Klaus Knorr and Robert Gilpin, besides many others, have concluded that states might continue to maintain conventional forces and would use them to influence political behaviour of the adversary.[25] Authors like Bernard Brodie, Robert Osgood, Donald G. Brennan, Thomas C. Schelling, Henry Kissinger and Herman Kahn considered stable deterrence and mutual deterrence in terms that were remarkably reminiscent of theories of power. They saw the same unsustainability to the theory of deterrence as that of balance of power. This has put decision makers in a dilemma of whether deterrence is a stable security situation that is best obtained as a consequence of continued efforts of both sides in their attempts to attain military technology, or if it is a policy that requires some degree of cooperative behaviour between adversaries.

⚔ DECISION MAKING IN CRISIS: BIOPOLITICS

If the analysis is limited to the strategic equation and moral issues are kept aside, then the central premise is that all of us have a shared stake in the survival of our respective national sovereignty. Robert Jervis raises these questions: Are the psychological attitudes of decision makers and the range of outcomes in a crisis similar on either side? Do both sides to the conflict view each other's threat as credible? How are decision makers likely to respond if a situation unfavourable to their desired outcome arises? Jervis considers decision makers as burdened with 'unmotivated biases'—preconceptions, images and belief systems. He opines that the fact that people are not completely rational does not automatically vitiate the rational deterrence approach.[26]

Much literature has emanated from the West on decision making in a crisis. Perhaps the largest project undertaken towards a systematic study of international crisis behaviour was the International Crisis Behaviour Project of Michael Brecher, Jonathan Wilkenfeld

---

[25] See Blechman and Kaplan 1978; Martin 1979; Knorr 1966; and Gilpin 1981.
[26] Jervis et al. 1985: chs 1 and 2.

and Sheila Moser, who collected data on 278 international crises for a 50-year period between 1929 and 1979. It was a comparative study based on quantitative research. The main goal of this project was to bring out the dimensions of international crisis, behavioural patterns of the actors, the bargain between adversaries, the role of deterrence, the role of allies in crisis management, the causal factors in the crisis, other possible outcomes, and issues of grand strategy, power and status.[27] The more authoritarian the regime, the greater the possibility of resorting to violent crisis triggers, and lesser the numbers of individuals in decision making in crisis.[28]

The manner in which decision makers grapple with options before them in any crisis is the outcome of a complex interplay of key variables. The 'images of reality' that are viewed by decision makers are generally cognitive constructs of situations that may or may not include all possible alternatives and outcomes involved. Psychologists tend to agree that constructing these 'images of reality', as well as constructing the relationship between images and cognition—between the inputs and outputs—and converting them into a response are complex processes.[29]

Michael P. Fischer Keller and Richard K. Herrmann have suggested that it is essential to ascertain how decision makers mentally represent the situation to understand stimulus and process their choices.[30] The variables include perceptions of the enemy, the perceived power of the adversary, the behaviour and likely role of other actors, the decision makers' beliefs and preconceived notions about international systems and global responses to drastic action undertaken, and long-term implications of any of the outcomes.

---

[27] According to them, it was essential to address crisis behaviour at the micro level, from the perspective of the individual actors and their foreign policies. Therefore, foreign policy is premised on two essential conditions that owe their origins in the states' external or international politics and strategic environment: (a) a threat to core values, together with an awareness of finite time for an adequate response to the threat; and (b) a very high probability that armed hostilities are going to ensue. The authors reached the conclusion that in crisis, actors opted for smaller, rather than larger, decision-making units. The basic decision-making unit has more than 10 individuals if it is in existence for a long time (Brecher et al. 1988).

[28] Ibid.

[29] See Tetlock and Levi 1982; Sharman et al. 1989; and Gardner 1985.

[30] Keller and Herrmann 1995.

Examples of these implications are competing grand strategies and power play among various departments in the government. Decision making itself can come under various pressures, ranging from internal (public opinion, a certain outcome favoured) to external (international actors and organisations) pressures. The other important variables which are also in a position to influence outcomes in a crisis include the structure (representations, competing power structures), processing information, personalities and perceptions of key decision makers, levels of stress, domestic support, issues of coalition or party (in a multi-party democracy), and the role of the opposition.

Keller and Herrmann assert that with such a wide range of causal variables, it is difficult to precisely understand which perceptions and factors from this list will prevail over others. Martha L. Cottam, in her work on decision making, has focused on the effect of cognitive patterns of policy makers on their images of international politics.[31] Richard Ned Lebow has suggested the importance of cognitive and motivational processes as an essential foundation for analysing decision-making behaviour under crisis.[32] He contends that decision makers are likely to interpret, incorporate, get advised or discard information and maintain perceptions (of the adversary) based on their existing assumption, perceptions and predispositions (Figure 3.1).

Going a step further, Jonathan Roberts has even discussed the implications of biological factors for political decision making in crisis.[33] However, it must highlighted that research in biopolitics largely remains speculative for a lack of reliable empirical data. The study of decision-making behaviour during crisis by using the

---

[31] She criticises political scientists who do not differentiate between beliefs and cognitions or between beliefs and motivations. She warns, 'Psychology cannot be blindly applied to political analysis ... what psychology does have to offer are very general guidelines for arguments about how people make political decisions' (Cottam 1986).

[32] Lebow 1981.

[33] Like mental illness (depression, paranoia, hypomania, cerebral arteriosclerosis and schizophrenia), age factors (speech, understanding, vision, hearing, memory), fatigue, sleeplessness. See Roberts 1988: ch. 9.

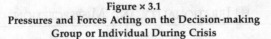

Figure × 3.1
Pressures and Forces Acting on the Decision-making
Group or Individual During Crisis

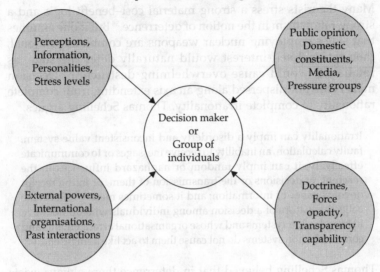

Source: Author's own illustration.

tool of political psychophysiology is considered a sub-area of bio-politics, where biological indicators are used to analyse political behaviour.

From this discussion, a broad pattern of decision making under stress and various related phenomena can be discerned. In Southern Asia, like in many other countries, there are issues, such as inter-bureaucracy competition, rationality of decision-making bodies or individuals, which are likely to have similar contours.[34] Only some variables change.

---

[34] Some theorists have stated other fundamental drawbacks. Robert Jervis maintains that a rational strategy for the employment of nuclear weapons is a contradiction in terms (Jervis 1984). Patrick Morgan has argued that 'classic criticisms of deterrence theory turn on the charge that governments simply lack the necessary rationality to make it work, that they are particularly subject to irrationality to make it work, that they are particularly subject to irrationality in times of intense crisis or actual attack' (Morgan 1983: 13).

✠ IRRATIONALITY AND MISPERCEPTION

Many theorists stress a strong material cost–benefit logic and a strong rationalism in the notion of deterrence.[35] But if one assumes that states employing nuclear weapons are completely rational, then rational self-interest would naturally deter the state, as retaliation would cause overwhelming destruction. Decision makers are not dispersed along an axis extending from complete rationality to complete irrationality. Thomas Schelling argues,

> Irrationality can imply a disorderly and inconsistent value system, faulty calculation, an inability to receive messages or to communicate effectively; it can imply random or haphazard influences in the reaching of decisions or the transmission of them, or in the receipt or conveyance of information; and it sometimes merely reflects the collective nature of a decision among individuals who do not have identical value systems and whose organisational arrangements and communication systems do not cause them to act like a single entity.[36]

Thomas Schelling believed that in deterrence there always exists an element of unpredictability,[37] and this unpredictability can reinforce deterrence. There can be many causes for the breakdown of deterrence. Purely in gaming terms, one party may take pre-emptive action and in spite of threats of use of force decide to

---

[35] Achen and Snidal 1989; and Little 1991.

[36] Schelling 1960.

[37] In his opinion 'a response that carries some risk of war can be plausible, even reasonable at a time when a final, ultimate decision to have general war would be implausible or unreasonable'. See Schelling 1966: 37. Robert Jervis comes close to Thomas Schelling's central theme of the element of unpredictability when he says, 'There is an irreducible minimum of unpredictability that operates, especially in situations which engage a state's highest values. Thus, even though there is no rational argument for a countercity response to a Soviet attack on the United States or Western Europe, the mere possibility may be an effective deterrent .... This policy makes sense when we consider threats that leave some-thing to chance; it can be rational to threaten, and carry out, a move that increases slightly the danger of an all out war, while it would be completely irrational to launch an attack. Indeed, much of deterrence rests on the fact that both sides know that events are not entirely under their control'. Jervis has admitted that deterrence theorists 'present reasonable arguments about why compellance is usually more difficult than deterrence', but he adds that 'the state trying to change

stand firm, perceiving that the other is bound to retreat, while the adversary may calculate that threats to retaliate will work and expect the attacker to back off. A constant misperception about the other, therefore, continues to build up in both states where each expects the other to back off. But beyond the dangers that remain on account of misperception and misjudgement of the potential actions of the adversary, there are a set of variables that can operate at a different level and have the potential to alter the outcome. There is always the danger of a local commander deciding to take matters in his own hands and authorising a launch. As threats are being exchanged, public opinion is built by the media and warrants a favourable outcome. All the calculations done in peacetime can suddenly go haywire. Rational deterrence is perceived to operate between national leaderships that have vital interests to guard. Local commanders or even scientists can potentially destabilise the situation. Equally dangerous is any non-state actor who takes charge of any weapon or facility and threatens to blow apart carefully manipulated deterrence. Keith Payne is of the opinion that there were several assumptions guiding the Cold War superpower relationship that contributed to stability.[38]

It has often been pointed out that the US did contemplate using nuclear weapons on many occasions, but it never used them after

---

the status quo is in a weaker bargaining position because it can drop its demand without raising the danger that the status-quo power will raise new demands. But it is hard for the latter to retreat without damaging its ability to stand firm against demands for further changes; therefore, it should be able to prevail. There is a difficulty with this argument however; one must look at what each side will gain if it prevails. Here the very advantage just ascribed to the status-quo power turns out to be a disadvantage. What the aggressor can gain is not limited to the specific issue, but includes a psychological sense of bargaining in future attempts to alter the status quo. The status-quo power, by contrast, gains only a temporary respite' (Jervis 1979: 299–300).

[38] According to him, these Cold War assumptions were (a) rational leaderships, both in the case of the US and the Soviet Union decision makers who were capable of making the cost–benefit analysis and risk–bargain analysis; (b) the ability of each side to communicate a threatened sanction effectively to an opponent that was clearly understood and regarded as decisive in developing cost–benefit calculations; (c) a level of mutual understanding and communication about the responses that actions taken by one side would elicit from the other; and (d) that threatened retaliatory action would have a level of plausibility sufficient to influence the behaviour of the adversary in a desired fashion. See Payne 1992.

the Second World War. This cannot be attributed to deterrence, because there was no deterrence operating against Vietnam, for example. Then what prevented the use of nuclear weapons? Critics may argue that it was not in the national interest to use a nuclear weapon on Vietnam, or that the Vietnamese did not have enough vital interests against which the threat could be premised. Further, the Vietnamese may well have been willing to risk everything—nothing could deter them. Richard Price and Nina Tannenwald contend, 'While a rationalist account may tell some of the nuclear story, ignoring the question about identity ... [it] leaves rational deterrence theory fundamentally unable to explain the criteria for "deterrence"—that is, what goes into leaders' calculations of "unacceptable costs"'.[39] It is for similar reasons, as Keohane argues, that rationalist regime theory has little to say about the origins and evolutions of norms and practices that cannot be conceived as simply constituting the rational calculation of national interest.[40] Even though the dilemma of using nuclear weapons may not have come about either in the Gulf War or in the recent Afghan campaign, clearly both Saddam Hussein and the Taliban were willing to risk 'unacceptable costs', knowing well that they could lose all. So the question remains, what deters them? A deterrent relationship cannot be constructed with such leaders or even a non-state actor.

Keith Payne has suggested that it is highly unlikely for leaders to be totally irrational.[41] Personality factors exist and indeed one leader might choose to seek a certain set of outcomes from a given strategic environment. This means that the preference of one leader might be different from another. But the premise still is that decision makers will choose to behave rationally. Hedley Bull points out that stability is the result of balance of terror. The dimension of stability which is deemed to be of greatest importance in the nuclear balance of terror concerns the ability to preserve peace, which is accorded a higher priority than the preservation of the component states of the system in a political sense.[42] Christopher Achen has

[39] Price and Tannenwald 1996.
[40] Keohane 1989.
[41] Payne 1992.
[42] Bull 1977: 123–24.

rejected deterrence theory as logically incoherent.[43] Ole Holsti has also sounded a warning in this context:

[I]n most times the assumption of deterrence is valid but not the notion of deterrence as it is unlikely to prove effective against a nation being attacked led by a trigger-happy paranoid individual, or by someone seeking personal or national self destruction or martyrdom ... or by those who regard the loss of most of their nation's population and resources as a reasonable cost for the achievement of foreign policy goals.[44]

The study of nuclear deterrence purely in strategic or theoretical terms without emphasis on any empirical evidence leaves the argument at the level of a half-truth. Raymond Aron has sought to fill this gap,[45] and Patrick Morgan has drawn a distinction between general deterrence and immediate deterrence.[46] Paul Huth and Bruce M. Russett, refining Morgan's definition, state that immediate deterrence is 'where at least one side is seriously considering an attack while the other is mounting a threat of retaliation in order

---

[43] Achen 1987. See also in this context, Achen and Snidal 1989. In a similar fashion, Frank Zagare has tried to compartmentalise rational and irrational decision making by distinguishing between 'procedural' and 'instrumental' rationality. According to Zagare, procedural rationality requires omniscience and does not include misperceptions, psychological and emotional deficiencies. He considers instrumental rationality as more limited and as having an order of choices that confront an actor (Zagare 1990).

[44] Holsti 1972: 8–9.

[45] He opined that 'there is no deterrent in a general or abstract sense, it is a case of knowing *who* can deter *whom, from what, in what circumstances, by what means*'. Thus, according to Aron, what deters one government in one situation might not deter another. He maintained that comparing various conflict situations and simplifying schemes would only oversimplify reality. Decision makers tend to 'over estimate the technical aspect of the diplomatic or political problems, and underestimate the importance of the psychological, moral and political data that is unique in each situation'. See Aron 1969: 69.

[46] According to him, general deterrence in an adversarial relationship means that the status quo would exist over a long period by maintaining the balance of terror. Immediate deterrence, in contrast, implies a specific situation where one side is preparing a threat of retaliation in order to prevent it, and both sides realise what is going on. See Morgan 1983: 28–43.

to prevent it'.[47] The question that still remains to be answered is whether lasting peace is the result of deterrence. In other words, does deterrence guarantee a definite time period of peace? Let us examine why deterrence fails. The strategic cause is the stability–instability relationship which is engendered by the presence of nuclear weapons. Given the risk of escalation between adversaries,[48] both sides may get involved in a proxy war. So deterrence at one level may lead to the failure of deterrence at another level. The structural cause is the 'security dilemma' and the inability of opponents to recognise each other's force posture—to be defensive or offensive. One antagonist's defensive posture may be the other's offensive posture. So, fearing a strike, one side may decide to pre-empt before being pre-empted.[49] The third cause is cognitive. Deterrence can fail because of misperception, misinterpretation and miscalculation between adversaries. Miscalculation of a first strike, absorbing a first strike or maintaining C3I for a retaliatory strike may endanger deterrence and lead to a pre-emptive strike. Another fundamental flaw in the narrative of deterrence is that it is premised on the psychology of the adversary. As Gen George Lee Butler has rightly pointed out,

> In the final analysis, it is not what you think deters, it is what your opponent thinks. And we never know what he thought. So there is an absolutely fundamental flaw in the psychology of deterrence.

[47] They made a survey of 54 cases to identify under what circumstances extended deterrence is likely to be successful. They have found deterrence to be successful in 31 (or 57 per cent) of the cases. They tested their hypothesis along three parameters: (a) relative military capabilities; (b) the role of past behaviour in signally current intentions; and (c) the nature and extent of the military, economic and other ties of mutual interest between the adversaries. See Huth and Russett 1984. Richard Ned Lebow and Janice Gross Stein have charged Huth and Russett with improperly designating attacker and defender, incorrectly identifying third parties as targets of attack or deterrence and confusing direct with extended deterrence and deterrence with compellance—discrepancies, which according to Lebow and Stein, 'reveal alarmingly low levels of cross study reliability between two teams of investigators classifying and coding precisely the same set of cases' (Lebow and Stein 1990). See also Lebow and Stein 1989. In the final analysis, one can reach the conclusion that there might be different sets of deterrence cases and each case might have its own peculiarity.

[48] Jervis 1976.

[49] Snyder 1971: 123–28.

And that is, you are not in charge of it, it is your enemy (who is in charge).[50]

It is assumed that war can be prevented if all the actors involved have nuclear weapons that can deter an attack. The possession of nuclear weapons will help ensure that the opponent will not engage in a conflict. Perceptions and psychology play the all-important role in convincing an adversary that any aggression will lead to annihilation. Stability would be 'guaranteed' since it is in neither side's interest to disturb the balance. Deterrence has in fact been an ideological, strategic and political construct born in the early phases of the Cold War, and has coexisted alongside abundant empirical evidence that it could fail. Thus, deterrence, the language of 'balance of power' and *realpolitik* leave behind the earlier notions of international relations that were based on accommodation and dialogue and enter into a world of assertiveness, which nevertheless fail to produce stability. If stability does not ensue, peace will not follow.

Triangular Deterrent Relationship

In a scenario where more than two states are engaged in trying to deter each other, the calculations are complex. All have different capabilities, weapons doctrines and intentions. This becomes important from the point of view of this study where India has to simultaneously deter China and Pakistan—two states that have different capabilities from itself. An added variable that will impact on the deterrent calculations of India is the non-state actor. It would be naïve to believe that deterring more than one state is simple, since a state may run the risk of a nuclear attack whose initiator might not be clearly identifiable. At some point, either through miscalculation or rational choice, a crisis is likely to escalate to a level where nuclear threats are exchanged. Of the many outcomes, at least one could be the breakdown of deterrence due to political causes (especially when the domestic constituents are too strong) or due to technical error that leads to the misinterpretation of a technical snag as a first strike. Or it could be simply due to the

[50] Butler 1999.

dangers inherent in the process of nuclear proliferation. Deterrence works if the aggressor is persuaded that the risks of aggression outweigh its benefits. If the costs of suffering retaliation are immense, as in the case of nuclear attack, the probability of that retaliation need not be very high to render aggression a clearly bad bargain for any plausible political gain. The challenge is to maintain stable deterrence, given a certain set of norms. In the international system, these norms have been identified and related assumptions based essentially in the context of bilateral balance of terror. These calculations become complex in the Southern Asian context as norm setting does not last long, treaties are under stress, political rhetoric is high and non-state actors play an important role.[51]

Often, the attention is limited to a superpower's choice—disarm or deter—between the basic alternatives of (a) unilateral nuclear disarmament, or (b) practising some form of deterrence that involves the threat of use of nuclear weapons against the adversary. Reciprocity can help achieve cooperation among states in the sense of refraining from an undesired action. This is the intent of the strategy of deterrence, which is the threat to punish another actor if it takes a certain negative action (such as attacking one's own state or one's allies).[52] The slogan 'peace through strength' reflects this approach. If deterrence works, its effects are almost invisible; its success is measured by attacks that did not occur and not by a phase of lasting peace. Nuclear deterrence is the threat to use nuclear weapons if another state does so. Generally, advocates of deterrence believe that conflicts are more likely to escalate into war when one party to the conflict is weak. In this view, building up military capabilities usually convinces the stronger party that a resort to military leverage would not succeed, so conflicts are less likely to escalate into violence. Deterrence in the form of a large-scale attack is viewed by the adversary leadership as capable of inflicting such damage upon its military forces or population and other economic assets, as to cripple the state completely. Deterrence assumes that an adversary's political leadership will act in the national interest, although this interest will be viewed through differing cultural perspectives and the dictates of given situations.

---

[51] For example, with a change in regime, there were voices in Pakistan that the new regime may not acknowledge the previous bilateral agreements.

[52] It is also true of limited war.

Each side in confrontation is also faced with the issue of decreasing the vulnerability of its nuclear forces against a pre-emptive first strike, while increasing its own capability, in such a scenario, to strike with its remaining forces after absorbing the first strike. The pursuit of credible and survivable second strike capability can be misperceived by the adversary as preparations for a pre-emptive strike. Often adversarial states have hostile relationships and in the absence of communication and misperception could end up making such calculations. A credible second strike capability also carries with it the inherent licence to take maximalist positions for arming the state with large forces. It further hastens the arms race. There are also incentives to strike pre-emptively. After all, inherent to NFU is absorbing a first strike and the state has to be alert against a penetrating first strike. Theoretically, states that are on NFU could have huge strategic forces that survive even after a decapitating first strike and which are able to launch a retaliatory strike. The key factor in this regard would have to be a robust command and control system. After detecting a first strike, the command and control has to function to be able to serve a retaliatory strike. Crucial to this is the function of intelligence that gathers such information. But this too has its problems. There have been cases in the Cold War when intelligence gathering agencies detected what they thought was a first strike. The problem of an accidental launch or an unauthorised launch always exists (see Figure 3.2 for stages in the escalation of conflict).

Figure × 3.2
Stages in the Escalation of Conflict

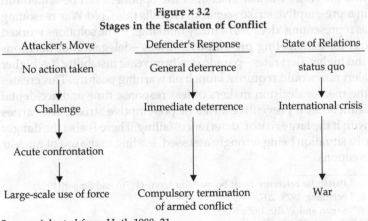

Attacker's Move	Defender's Response	State of Relations
No action taken	General deterrence	status quo
Challenge	Immediate deterrence	International crisis
Acute confrontation		
Large-scale use of force	Compulsory termination of armed conflict	War

Source: Adapted from Huth 1988: 21.

Can a state know for certain that another state will use nuclear weapons even when their use is considered irrational or there has been an accidental launch? To an extent, this can be attributed to the capability of risk taking. This could differ from state to state, and within a state, from one political leader to another. We have seen that Pakistan can attempt to take big risks to seek a change in the status quo. In the traditional debate on nuclear deterrence, this issue has received much attention.[53] The assumption that nuclear weapons promote peace was based on the single case of East–West confrontation, where culturally distinct societies provided the dividing line. Future international conflicts may or may not bear any resemblance to this situation. They may include diverse societies with incomparable norms, values and perspectives. Perceptions and analyses are influenced in a distinct way, with such diverse societies creating patterns of behaviour that may differ completely from what has been experienced so far. The risk-taking capability and threat assessment of nuclear rivals in their conduct of any crisis can differ substantially. The outcome may differ greatly; hence, the chances of escalation from a conventional to a nuclear exchange are greater.

In a potential mutual pre-emptive strike scenario, the opponents tend to completely distrust each other. Thomas Schelling called this 'the reciprocal fear of surprise attack', where there are cycles of 'he thinks, we think, he thinks, we think he'll attack; so he thinks, we shall; so he will; so we must.'[54] Kenneth Waltz does not believe that the entire nuclear arsenal of the opponent can be wiped out in a pre-emptive strike scenario. He calls this Cold War reasoning as representing 'decades of fuzzy thinking'.[55] 'The solutions worked out for anticipating pre-emptive strikes—delegation of decisions and higher alert rates—paradoxically increase instability.[56] A higher alert rate would require a launch on warning posture. This creates the risk for decision makers of less response time and accidental launch. So, a preventive strike or pre-emptive strike each carries with it the large risk of 'deterrence' failing. There is also the danger of a situation being wrongly assessed, leading to the use of nuclear weapons.

---

[53] Particular reference must be made to Jervis (1976) and Singer (1962).
[54] Schelling 1979: 207.
[55] Sagan and Waltz 1995: 67.
[56] Sauer 1998: 19.

Another dilemma is that of numbers. The question of 'how much is enough' can perhaps never be effectively answered. For the threat of retaliation to be credible, there has to be some transparency in communicating the threat. But this has to guard against being all-transparent, as the adversary may then start taking counter-measures to reduce the effectiveness of the retaliation.

Consider the possibility of deterring. The number of warheads needed to deter China with 'A' number of warheads and 'A1' number of vital interests may be different from the case than when deterrence is required against Pakistan with 'C' number of war-heads and 'C3' number of vital interests (Figure 3.3). Simply assign-ing numerical probabilities to the possible outcomes of available choices would require selecting an appropriate reference class of past situations to provide data on the respective relative fre-quencies of various outcomes. The respective outcomes will then depend on the reference class selected.

Figure × 3.3
Strategic Complexity in a Triangle: Assets and Warheads

State	Warheads	Vital Interests
China	A	A1
India	B	B2
Pakistan	C	C3

Source: Author's own illustration.

Based on the strategic planners and where they come from, planning for a strategic force in the two cases against the two adversaries can be very different (Figure 3.4).

Lasting stable deterrence is then the result of variables, none of which remain constant over a given period of time. Leaving

Figure x 3.4
Strategic Complexity in a Bilateral Relationship: Assets and Warheads

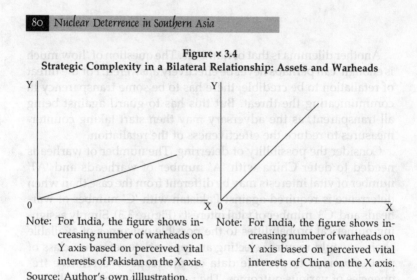

Note: For India, the figure shows increasing number of warheads on
Y axis based on perceived vital
interests of Pakistan on the X axis.

Note: For India, the figure shows increasing number of warheads on
Y axis based on perceived vital
interests of China on the X axis.

Source: Author's own illlustration.

mathematical permutations and combinations aside for reaching
definite outcomes over what constitutes stable deterrence, the past
behaviour and risk-taking capabilities of states may differ.

Threat is central to deterrence. It may have two outcomes—if a
state threatens its adversary from refraining to do something, this
threat may work under certain circumstances. If it does not have
the required influence over the adversary's behaviour, then it
may lead the adversary to respond with a counter-threat or even
actual coercion. There could also be an element of bargaining in
the process. There could be situations when threats and counter-
threats culminate into war. Jervis has commented on the lack of
knowledge on this subject in international relations: 'Two central
questions are still without answers. First, under what conditions
do threats and the use of force lead the other side to retreat and
when do they lead it to retaliation with threats and force of their
own? Second, when does a retreat or concession lead others to expect, and the state to make, other retreats?'[57] There is a considerable
body of literature that has used both theoretical analysis and some
empirical study of the use of threat especially in the context of
deterrence.[58]

When a threat is issued to an adversary, the latter has
two choices—he can either comply with the threat or defy the

[57] Jervis 1979: 292–320.
[58] Snow 1979; Weede 1983; Huth and Russett 1984; and Jervis et al. 1985.

threatener.[59] Obviously, demands will be made and a bargain initiated. The responses could vary from being specific to the strategic culture or to the individual or group taking such decisions in the state. The variation in response could also extend to the form of government, from the democratic to the totalitarian kind. An individual in a democratic form of government cannot be seen as 'backing out' under domestic compulsions, when the state itself has a culture of not 'backing off', as the weakness may then be exploited again. The Israeli government, for example, does not accede to demands from any Arab country. But states do not normally have uniform response policies—they may accede to a threat in one situation and the response may be more defiant in another situation.

This scenario is based on two powers that are more or less equal. If the scenario involves three states—with China having powerful military and economic capabilities, India being smaller than China but still powerful enough to strive for equality with China, followed by Pakistan, which is small, not powerful enough and striving for capability comparable to that of India—clearly, stable deterrence will be a big challenge (Figure 3.5).

Figure × 3.5
Strategic Complexity in a Triangle: Asymmetrical Power Structures

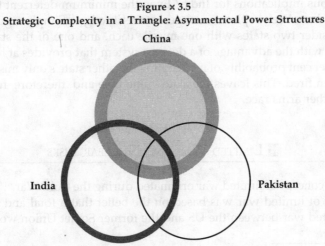

Source: Author's own illustration.

---

[59] The defiance can be varied—an immediate defiance or a promise to comply with the threatener at a later time or complying partially to the demand.

While practising nuclear deterrence, a state threatens the civilian population of the adversary if the latter's decision makers behave in an inappropriate manner. In such cases, nuclear deterrence often becomes a combination of declarative threat and risk imposition. Again, the onus of maintaining stability falls on factors like the actions of the decision makers. The outcome is a function of the decision makers acting rationally when external pressures, domestic constituency, information breakthrough about the adversary, popular perception and past behaviour of the adversary may not remain constant.

Must a state then rely on deterrence to adequately defend itself? Is defence sufficient? At least one writer has suggested this on the grounds that conventional arms alone would suffice to deter the Soviets from attack or successful nuclear blackmail.[60] If we push the argument to the stage where the focus is on defence rather than offence, so that an effective defence against intruding missiles such as a national missile defence (NMD) is thought of, the cost factor alone is so enormous that critics are up in arms against the world's lone superpower. How can lesser powers then attempt a defence like NMD? Cost and technological factors apart, what if China seeks to gear its force structure keeping in mind the US NMD, with serious implications for India? Even the minimum deterrent that may have been in place no longer retains its edge.[61] Simply argued, consider two states with one missile each, and one of the states also with the advantage of a defence system that provides at least 90 per cent probability of intercepting the other state's only missile when fired. This leaves the state vulnerable and, therefore, fuels another arms race.

✠ LIMITED WAR AND NUCLEAR RISKS

The concept of limited war originated during the Cold War.[62] The idea of limited war was based on the belief that a total and unlimited war between the US and the former Soviet Union would

---

[60] Lackey 1982. See also in the context of 'moral dilemma', Kavka 1987.

[61] This is the Chinese response to American BMD and NMD.

[62] See the following—Deitchman 1969; Osgood 1957, 1979; Halperin 1963: 107; Clark 1982; Gacek 1994; Posen 1991.

never be fought, as it would be totally disastrous for both countries in every term. The US believed that the presence of weapons of mass destruction in the hands of both the countries would result in Soviet leaders maintaining their expansionist designs, with serious implications for American security. So the idea of a short crisp war limited in operational battlespace, men, machinery used and geographical extent gained currency during the Cold War. After the Kargil War, the Indian defence minister deemed fit to juxtapose this concept in the South Asian context. In theory, maximum gain with minimum losses translated into limiting conflicts in terms of space or weaponry used or time constraints—factors that must operate simultaneously. There emerged the belief that a limited nuclear war could be fought, provided the bedrock of NATO's strategy of 'flexible response' evolved from its original conception in the 1950s.[63] The superpowers started to think beyond 'unlimited' or 'absolute' war leading to the genesis of the theory of limited war. This also seemed to reflect against the realist construction of security, on the one hand, advocating an all-out war, and the utopian attitude on the other, which desired abolition, and sought to locate the debate in the middle, premising that while wars would still occur there was a need to limit them.

Limited war is defined as:

> one in which the belligerents restrict the purposes for which they fight to concrete, well defined objectives that do not demand the utmost military effort of which the belligerents are capable and that can be accommodated in a negotiated settlement .... The battle is confined to a local geographical area and directed against selected targets—primarily those of direct military importance. It demands of the belligerents only a fractional commitment of their human and physical resources. It permits their economic, social and political patterns of existence to continue without serious disruption.[64]

A limited war means that, 'either the ends or means, or both, are limited in the conflict.'[65]

---

[63] This was considered necessary to stem the expected Warsaw Pact onslaught on West Europe during the Cold War.

[64] Osgood 1957: 1–2.

[65] Gacek 1994: 16.

The Limited War Theorists

Capt Basil Liddell-Hart was one of the first to develop an alternative to the strategy of total war. He argued that a country which is now called an enemy, might be needed as a friend in the future. He said that wars were but an unpleasant episode in relations between nations, and were usually avoidable.[66] He called this the 'indirect strategy' where the aim is the dislocation of the enemy's 'psychological and physical balance'.[67] He was of the view that atomic weapons would make total wars unthinkable.[68] What is significant to note is that Liddell-Hart's construction of the limited war doctrine was made before the advent of the nuclear age and has continued to inspire a whole range of strategic thinkers.

Bernard Brodie was one of those nuclear strategists who started writing after the advent of the nuclear age and was among those who were clearly influenced by Liddell-Hart.[69] His book, *The Absolute Weapon*, highlighted for the first time not just the destructive potential of the bomb, but also the political role that comes with its possession. His oft-quoted sentence sums up the essence of nuclear strategy: 'Thus far the chief purpose of our military establishment has been to win wars. From now on the chief purpose must be to avert them.'[70]

---

[66] Freedman 1989: 98.

[67] Liddell-Hart 1968: 25.

[68] His theory can be located in the times he was writing, in the period between the wars. One could also locate shades of risk-taking capability by an irrational decision maker in this. He brought in the rational actor factor. He was sceptical of the rational use of atomic weapons by an irrational decision maker. An element of tension was introduced in his theories with the advent of the air force that was so extensively used in the Second World War. After the world war, he became convinced that 'Total war implies that the aim, the effort and the degree of violence are unlimited ... an unlimited war waged with atomic power would be worse than nonsense; it would be mutually suicidal.' See Liddell-Hart 1946: 99–102.

[69] Brodie 1946. In fact, in a letter to Liddell-Hart in April 1957, Bernard Brodie wrote, 'you led all the rest of us in advocating the principle of limited war'. Cited in Bond 1997: 97.

[70] Brodie 1946: 76. Defining limited war, Brodie said, 'If wars were limited in ages past, the reason why they were so have little relevance for us today ... wars were kept limited by small margin of the national economic resources available for mobilisation and by the small capability for destruction that could be purchased with that narrow margin. Today, on the contrary, we speak of limited war in a sense that connotes a deliberate hobbling of a tremendous power that is already mobilised and that must in any case be maintained at a very high pitch

William Kaufmann, another nuclear strategist, edited a collection of essays which was critical of 'massive retaliation'.[71] It was Kaufmann who introduced the concept of 'nuclear threshold'. In his second book, *The McNamara Strategy*, he arrived at the conclusion that perhaps 'limited non-nuclear war' was not the best strategic–military option in the nuclear age.[72] Robert Osgood was another strategist, more in the mould of Bernard Brodie, who believed that his analyses would be theoretically sustainable even if nuclear weapons were never invented. He gave a comprehensive definition of limited war.[73] Osgood situated the 'economy of force' at the centre of his arguments when he opined that war should be a means to a certain end and not an end in itself. At the same time, he realised that 'because of the imperfection of man, force is a moral necessity.'[74] Osgood was quick to realise that limited war was not a uniform feature and that it could mean different things to different people. It could be limited in geographical terms and not in terms of the weapons used. Besides, any armed conflict could be

---

of effectiveness for the sake of only inducing the enemy to hobble himself to the like degree' (p. 311).

[71] In the opening chapter, Kaufmann emphasised the importance of 'credibility'. He questioned the US position of massive retaliation and commented that it would be 'out of character' for the US to respond in this manner, 'If the Communists should challenge our sincerity ... we would either have to put up or shut up. If we put up we would plunge into all the immeasurable horrors of atomic war. If we shut up, we would suffer a serious loss of prestige ....' Although Kaufmann conceded that this may not substitute victory, he was pragmatic enough to understand that this offered the best 'strategic space and exit' (Kaufmann 1956b: 25).

[72] Kaufmann 1964: 16–18.

[73] 'A limited war is one in which the belligerents restrict the purposes for which they fight to concrete, well defined objectives that do not demand the utmost military effort of which the belligerents are capable and that can be accommodated in negotiated settlements. Generally speaking, a limited war involves only two (or very few) major belligerents in the fighting. The battle is confined to a local geographical area and directed against selected targets—primarily those of direct military importance. It demands of the belligerents only a factional commitment of their human and physical resources, it permits their economies, social and political patterns of existence to continue without serious duplication' (Osgood 1957: 5). This definition came very close to Christopher M. Gacek's definition of limited war: 'either the ends or means, or both, are limited in the conflict' (Gacek 1994: 16).

[74] Osgood 1957: 16.

viewed as limited by one state and unlimited by another.[75] Osgood
premised the theory of limited war on the hypothesis that it 'maximizes the opportunities for the effective use of military force as a
rational instrument of national policy.'[76]

Henry Kissinger's book, *Nuclear Weapons and Foreign Policy*, immediately followed Osgood's book and was categorical in making
an appeal for espousing a limited war strategy.[77] The dilemma in
contemporary strategy that presented itself was 'how to establish
a relationship between a policy of deterrence and a strategy for
fighting war in the event of failure of deterrence.'[78] Moving to the
operational requirements of a limited war, Kissinger concluded,
'if we could develop forces capable of conducting limited war and
getting into position rapidly, we should be able to defeat the Soviet
Union or China in local engagements despite interior positions.'[79]

[75] But after the American experience in Vietnam, Osgood wrote, 'Actually there
have been two strands of the resurgence of limited war theories and doctrines
since World War II reflecting two different political perspectives in the Cold
War. One strand inspired by the concepts of Clausewitz and propounded by
Western political scientists and defense specialists has sought to make force, in
both war and deterrence, an effective instrument of containment .... The other
strand, inspired by Mao Tse-Tung and Third World nationalism and propounded
by revolutionary nationalists has sought to use guerrilla warfare to abolish
Western colonialism and hegemony and establish new nations ostensibly
dedicated to social justice' (Osgood 1979: 2).

[76] Osgood 1957: 27. According to him, during the Cold War a limited war was
considered 'more compatible with a respect for human life and an aversion to
violence ... liberal institutions and values do not thrive amid the social, economic
and political dislocations that inevitably follow in the wake of unlimited war'
(p. 27–28). Additionally, it was warranted, 'that military power should be subordinate to national policy [and] that the only legitimate purpose of military
force is to serve the nation's political objectives' (p. 13).

[77] Whereas Osgood made a semi-philosophical appeal, Kissinger made a
straightforward case for adopting a limited war strategy. Kissinger concluded
that the advent of nuclear weapons had made all traditional motivations of war
irrelevant with the awesome destructive potential of the nuclear weapon. Nuclear
weapons, he wrote, brought about a tacit non-aggression treaty: a recognition
that war is no longer a conceivable instrument of policy and that for this reason
international disputes can be settled only by means of diplomacy. Culling from
the American experience in the Korean War, Kissinger thought that American
nuclear capabilities might not be required in fighting with smaller states which
do not warrant the deployment and use of nuclear weapons. See Kissinger 1957.

[78] Ibid.: 132.

[79] He strongly felt that unnecessary destruction could be eliminated with the
strategy of limited war, as unlike an all-out war, where the targets are chosen

Klaus Knorr had contributed to Kaufmann's *Military Policy and National Security*[80] and held a belief that 'limited strategic war is a *possible* war; to fight and prepare for such a war is *possible* strategy.'[81] Both the Korean and the American experience in the Vietnam War were crucial in shaping the views of American strategists in developing the nuances of the theory of limited war. Deriving from the American experience in Vietnam and developing his argument further, Knorr concluded that the strategic role of nuclear weapons had been greatly diminished with an increasing number of states employing a level of conflict that was somewhere between traditional war and a kind of war that Knorr termed 'sub-limited'.[82]

Herman Kahn also wrote on the operational aspects of limited war and war gamed many scenarios. For instance, he thought '...*even if the United States and the Soviet Union cannot wage all-out war against each other this does not mean that the role of force will be entirely eliminated*. There will still be many disputes between the two nations—disputes which may tempt one side to use force on a small scale .... Therefore one needs limited war capabilities to meet limited provocations' (emphasis added).[83] Kahn firmly believed that a limited war capability enhances the credibility of deterrence and decreases the overall chances of a war breaking out.[84] In a 'controlled general war', Kahn conceptualised as many as 44 rungs

---

and the armed forces are geared to inflict maximum damage in the shortest possible time, a limited war may be able to restrict collateral damage being limited in objective, time and weaponry used (ibid.: 149–50, 152).

[80] Kaufmann 1956b.

[81] Knorr and Read 1962: 6.

[82] He included many other 'weapons' like propaganda, terrorism, guerrilla war, political organisation, money and key assassinations. Writing more in operational terms, he criticised the strategist's obsession with over-playing the significance of nuclear threshold in a war by invariably defining limited nuclear war as a conflict involving exclusively nuclear weapons. He believed that 'if escalation could be controlled because the interest of both antagonists to avoid large scale strategic war is overwhelming ... why should the restriction of hostilities to non-nuclear weapons be the crucial threshold?' (Knorr 1966: 97).

[83] Kahn 1961: 12.

[84] This touches on another strategic debate on capabilities versus intentions. The battle readiness of limited war capability might convey a different intention to the adversary. The lack of credibility, he opined, 'will itself make the defense seem unreliable.' In this context, he suggested that in the long run 'the west will need "safe looking" limited war forces to handle minor and moderate provocations' (ibid.: 155).

of escalation ladder where, according to him, nuclear weapons are first used at rung 15. He describes nearly 30 different stages where a limited war will remain limited until it finally reaches the stage of an all-out uncontrollable war.[85] Operationally, he advocates a counter-force strategy , since a counter-value strike carries more seeds of escalation. Elsewhere, he has written that in any war that involves the use of nuclear weapons, the first strikes would be for demonstration purposes and would essentially be counter-force. He writes, 'the first use of nuclear weapons is likely to be less for the purpose of destroying the other's military forces or handicapping its operations, than for redress, warning, bargaining, punitive, fining or deterrence purposes.'[86]

Thomas Schelling, whose book, *The Strategy of Conflict*, was essentially motivated by the development of low-yield tactical nuclear weapons, understood that limited war is premised on a tacit mutual understanding between adversaries of the limits and uncertainties that follow any potential escalation.[87] Elsewhere, he has written, 'we usually think of deterrence as having failed if a major war ever occurs. And so it has; but it could fail worse if no efforts were made to extend deterrence into war itself.'[88] He, however, does concede, 'the principal inhibition on the use of atomic weapons in limited war may disappear with their first use. It is difficult to imagine that the tacit agreement that nuclear weapons are different would be as powerfully present on the occasion of the ... limited

---

[85] Kahn 1962: 108–11.

[86] Kahn 1965: 138.

[87] He remained worried about the possible use of nuclear weapons in a limited war. He said, 'Whether limits on the use of atomic weapons other than the particular limit of no use at all, can be defined in a plausible way is made more dubious, not less so, by the increasing versatile character of atomic weapons ....' He further added, 'there seems consequently to be no "natural" break between certain limited use and others.' According to Schelling, the threat of limited war has two parts: 'one, the threat to inflict costs directly on the adversarial side in the form of causalties, loss of territory etc. and second, the threat to expose the adversaries to a heightened risk of general war.' He considered the threshold to be an important benchmark and said, 'We can ... not ... ignore the distinction and use nuclear weapons in a particular war where their use might be of advantage to us and subsequently reply on the distinction in the hope that we and the enemy might both abstain. One potential limit of war will be substantially discredited for all times' (Schelling 1979: 259–66).

[88] Schelling 1966: 191.

war after they had already been used in one.'[89] The 'tacit agreement' between adversaries was the central premise of Schelling's conception of limited war.

Ian Clark raised the essential question of whether 'any discussion of limitation in war derives from the nature of the relationship of war itself: does war entail the termination of all the rules, conventions or constraints which characterise the relations of states in peacetime?'[90] He constructed his arguments around three models of war limitation—'limitation by championship, limitation by charity, and limitation by city-swapping'.[91] Morton Halperin is another strategist who sought war limitation.[92] In the 1960s, the central premise of his thesis was how even an all-out war between the East and the West could be kept limited and controlled. A decade later he published a study, *Defence Strategies for the Seventies*,[93] in which he suggested that a counter-force strike could be a limited factor.

In practice, the Korean War is considered limited as the US restricted its objectives to restoring the status quo and did not use weapons of mass destruction against China. The Falklands War of 1982 is also considered limited, since the United Kingdom did not fight to overthrow the Argentinean government, but only to reassert its sovereignty over the Falklands.[94] Ever since the end of the Second World War, more than 40 military engagements have taken place which could be defined as limited wars.[95] Most of these

---

[89] Schelling 1979: 266.

[90] This took debate back to the philosophical level. He maintained, 'the modalities of war-limitation can best be conceived under two headings, limitation by immunity and limitation by withholding of forces-in-being. The two are interrelated, but can be distinguished in accordance with the perspective from which they are viewed.' See Clark 1982: 25.

[91] For details of these see ibid.: 38.

[92] He was of the opinion that 'the existence of thermonuclear weapons and the lack of any mechanism for guarenteeing the absence of war makes it necessary to take seriously the problem of how war, once it erupts, can be kept limited' (Halperin 1963: 2).

[93] He wrote, 'even a large scale war might be limited in terms of the targets attacked: each side might refrain from bombing each others' major cities and might concentrate instead on military targets' (Halperin 1971: 12).

[94] See Gacek 1994: 16.

[95] For the complete list the various military engagements and their objectives that could be classified into limited wars, see Deitchman 1969: 16–26.

limited wars have taken place 'among the new nations establishing their places in the scheme of post-World War II international politics.'[96]

A limited war is likely to have the following key features:

1. It is likely to be limited in topographical extent, although in terms of numbers of personnel involved, weapons used and duration of conflict it might be unlimited.
2. It is also likely to be limited in terms of its scope and objectives.
3. It may be limited from the perspective of the initiator, though this may not necessarily be the case with the defender.

Many analysts in India now believe that there is a strategic space between initiating an armed conflict and an all-out war, that is, a 'calibrated use of force' below the level of a full-scale conventional war. But any such operation always carries seeds of larger conflict, as the losing side would be predisposed to use all its weapons to avoid defeat. This could well include nuclear, biological and chemical weapons.

It can be concluded on the basis of these theories, that the objectives of limited war should be the following:

1. There has to be a very clear and concrete political objective.
2. Once the objective has been reached, the military operations must cease.
3. The limited operation should not involve the whole range of security forces and should be limited in their participation.
4. It should be limited in geographical space and its duration.
5. It should keep the social, economic and political institutions of the defending state intact.
6. As far as possible, territory seized during any such operation must be returned soon after the military operation ends.

National security is the social responsibility of the armed forces in any country. With the induction of nuclear weapons in a country's security architecture, 'total war' becomes an unthinkable proposition, although there will continue to be the view that a losing side would want to use all weapons at its disposal to win the war. Yet, if one takes the argument further, then the question arises that if

---

[96] Ibid.: 27.

bigger, larger wars are not an option, is there a strategic space for smaller 'limited' wars? There are two key drivers behind this military construct of limited war. One, as in any service, there might be a strong component of institutional interest; and second, in a changed strategic environment, where sub-conventional conflict has become the norm, moving away from the realm of strategic literature to operational battlespace, it would appear that smaller limited military engagement or limited war remains a possibility under the nuclear umbrella, howsoever escalation prone that might be. The Soviets are understood to have rejected the limited war concept at the outset, terming it as unrealistic and as a ploy used by the US to reassure its European allies.[97] Since it was in everybody's interest to avoid an all-out nuclear exchange, critics of the stalemate began calling for 'limited war'.

As the discussion in the subsequent chapters shows, all three states—China, India and Pakistan—have discussed limited war. Theoretically, the biggest problem that confronts limited war theorists is that of preventing the conflict from escalating. It is commonly accepted that even a limited war would mean a lot in terms of collateral damage. In fact, aspects like domestic politics and public opinion themselves will raise the stakes which could lead to spiralling of tensions. The horrors increase with the very first bomb that wipes out a section of forces (if it is counter-force) or wipes out large part of a major city (if it is counter-value). Once a war is initiated, both countries would want to come out of the conflict and be seen domestically and internationally as victorious. States are unlikely to leave weapons as potent as nuclear arms unutilised in a struggle for vital political interests.

The second main problem for military strategists is that of reciprocity. Even if one side in a conflict is ready and has geared up its forces for limiting war, there is no guarantee that the adversary has done the same. It may not be a wise military strategy going into war with the assumption that the adversary would play an equal part in keeping the war limited. Halperin, for instance, was of the opinion that 'limiting a central war may depend on both sides' believing that limitation is possible and that the other is likely to reciprocate restraint.'[98] The Americans, for instance, could say with

---

[97] Isby 1981: 209.
[98] Halperin 1963: 107.

any level of certainty that the Soviets were as unenamoured of limited war strategies as perhaps they themselves were.[99] Critically examining the limited war literature, Ian Clark suggested that limitations could be introduced into nuclear warfare for purposes of '(a) more effective deterrence, (b) signalling intent, (c) limiting damage in war or (d) winning a nuclear war.'[100] Even if ground rules do get negotiated it would be poor tactical sense for any army general not to break these norms if he feels his country is under threat. Another strategist, B.S. Lambeth, highlighting the Soviet disinterest in accepting artificial restrictions on war, wrote:

> [O]nce the nuclear threshold is crossed, Soviet military doctrine continues to posit—as it has throughout the past decade—that the role of nuclear weapons is simple and unambiguous attainment of military victory, a task to be achieved not by slow motion counter-force targeting, selective attacks on vital military or economic resources of the enemy, or any other limited schemes to influence his strategic behaviour, but rather through the massive application of nuclear force on all targets necessary to destroy his war waging ability and his capacity for collective strategic action.[101]

The question that presents itself is why a losing state will want to limit a conflict for some convention, when it can win the battle by not adhering to any such convention. Another unresolved dilemma is of implementing such a convention at the time of the crisis, when communication between the two leaderships would anyway be frozen. There are ways of keeping the conflict limited, but as Clark asks, 'can *either* of the parties successfully limit its own military operations and would *both* do so simultaneously?'[102]

The third main problem lies in the difficulty of gathering and interpreting the most relevant information about a conflict situation in progress and using such information to control escalation and orchestrate the conflict. Barry Posen writes that in the disarray of the 'fog of war' and analysis under the intense pressure of conflict, command, control, communications and intelligence (C4I) are

---

[99] Clark 1982: 222.
[100] Ibid.: 205.
[101] Lambeth 1977: 87–88.
[102] Clark 1982: 219.

likely to suffer, and there could occur, what he has called, 'inadvertent escalation'.[103]

❈ THE NON-STATE THREAT

In some ways, 9/11 proved to be a watershed. It changed the way the world looks at the phenomenon of terrorism, which changed from being an intra-state law and order problem to becoming an international concern. The Southern Asian region has for long encountered threats not just to the state, but also to the stability of deterrence. This has led to deeper investigation of the growing trend of suicide terrorism in the area. Popular perceptions of terrorists being undeterrable fanatics, who are willing to kill millions indiscriminately just to instil fear and chaos, belie the reality that they are cold, rational killers who employ violence to achieve specific political objectives. In suicide terrorism, the aim of the psychologically and physically war-trained terrorist is to die while destroying the 'enemy' target. It is different from the often high-risk military operations where death is not certain and the perpetrator may survive the operation. Suicide, as used in the appellation 'suicide terrorism', does not imply a psychological or pathological situation or condition. In the spectrum of political violence, from the perspective of the perpetrator, suicide terrorism is the most violent form of expression.[104] Another threat that exists is that of renegade army officers who might commandeer nuclear

---

[103] Posen 1991: 20. He says, 'analysis is difficult under the pressure of intense conventional conflict. Communications to and from the theatre of operations are likely to be uncertain and intermittent in any case.' He adds, 'critical links are quite often deliberately jammed or destroyed, as each side tries to gain a military advantage by reducing the others understanding of events and control over its forces.' He concludes that the fog of war 'increases the likelihood of inadvertent escalation because misperceptions, misunderstandings, poor communication, and unauthorised or unrestrained offensive operations could reduce the ability of civilian authorities to influence the course of the war.' He completes the argument by saying that '[i]t might also precipitate unexpected but powerful escalatory pressures due to the ever higher levels of uncertainty that would develop about the status of the other side's strategic nuclear capabilities as intense conventional conflict unfolds.'

[104] See in the context of terrorist motivations, Stern 2000a.

weapons and use them either at the adversary or even in domestic power struggles.[105]

While a section of mainstream nuclear proliferation literature maintains that these are non-strategic causal factors, Kenneth Waltz questions, 'what is hard to comprehend is why, in an internal struggle for power, any of the contenders should start using nuclear weapons. Who would they aim at? How would they use them as instruments for maintaining or gaining control?'[106] Robert Art has argued that this fear of nuclear terrorism is overstated, as even if terrorists use nuclear arms to achieve their political objectives, they can be deterred just like national governments.[107] The attack on the World Trade Center has proved, contrary to Art's analysis, that this may indeed be very difficult. The new challenge is the concept of suicide terrorism.

With a lot of fissile material available and sub-national actors willing to pay huge amounts for weapons, leading to a flourishing nuclear black market, the nuclear threat would not work on terrorists, since a 'nuclear deterrent relationship' is not established with them. Even if they are threatened, they may call off the bluff, since targeting them with even a small nuclear weapon would be impossible without incurring unacceptable collateral damage and provoking global outrage. The entire nuclear theology is based on the mind game, and with a threat from a terrorist who claims to have a nuclear device, even if its possession can be questioned, decision makers face the dilemma of considering it as a valid threat or repenting later. To be credible, deterrence must fulfil these basic conditions: (a) the opponent must have vital interests; (b) the declared nuclear threat must be credible; and (c) the opponent must be susceptible to be deterred. It is imperative that the adversary realises that the threat is authentic.

Most terrorist organisations actively study and use mind control and cult control techniques to indoctrinate members into committing horrific acts of terrorism that shock our senses. The real cause of much of today's terrorism is not what terrorists claim to be their motivation in their publicly stated agendas, rationalisations or values, but how these agendas, rationalisations or values are

[105] See Dunn 1982: 75.
[106] Waltz 1981: 10.
[107] Art 1991: 27.

implanted into the terrorists' minds by their leaders. Trends in terrorism over the past two decades indicate a definite shift from political to religious motives. Today's most fanatical terrorists are not motivated by political ideology on the far left or right, but are more likely to be extremists on the fringe of traditional religions or idiosyncratic cults with an apocalyptic mindset. Since religion acts as a legitimising force by subordinating individual responsibility to divine will, groups motivated by religious extremism experience fewer constraints on the use of violence to cause indiscriminate harm. For example, a millenarian ideology that espouses a belief in the imminence of Armageddon could justify mass casualty attacks. Many of this so-called 'new breed' of terrorists have an almost mystical fascination with nuclear, chemical and biological agents because of the ability of toxic weapons to instil a pervasive sense of dread and their similarity to biblical plagues.

Over the past decade, there has been an upsurge of interest by sub-state groups in acquiring weapons of mass destruction. The best-known instance was in March 1995, when the Japanese doomsday cult Aum Shinrikyo released sarin nerve gas in the Tokyo subway. Despite an estimated net worth of roughly $1 billion and the active recruitment of chemists and biologists from Japanese universities to create a chemical and biological weapons arsenal, Aum was unable to achieve its deadly goals. Cult scientists tried initially to produce and deliver biological agents, including anthrax and botulinum toxin, but they failed, because of technical problems, to cause genocide in nine attempted biological attacks. At the national policy level, the concepts of deterrence and foreign policy that were so useful during the Cold War do not apply in their exact sense to the threat of terrorism. When the adversary is an elusive network of enigmatic diehard operatives completely dedicated to their cause, it is nearly impossible to design a response strategy. It is, therefore, 'a "complex terrorism" that threatens modern, hi-tech societies in the world's most developed nations.'[108] Terrorists rarely have targetable assets, either financially or militarily. Efforts to freeze terrorist financial assets are hampered by the vastness and the rigid secrecy laws of the international

---

[108] Dixon 2002: 53.

banking system, and only in cases where states are supporting terrorists is it possible to find a military target.

Dr Bashiruddin Mehmood, the former chief of Pakistan Atomic Energy Commission (PAEC) and Chaudhury Abdul Majid are both under investigation for their alleged links with the Al Qaida network, as they had travelled many times to Afghanistan.[109] In a testimony before the Senate Select Committee on Intelligence in February 2002, Director of Central Intelligence, Mr George Tenet said, Osama bin Laden had declared that acquiring unconventional weapons was 'a religious duty'. 'We know that Al Qaida was working to acquire some of the most dangerous chemical agents and toxins', Mr Tenet said. 'Documents recovered from Al Qaida facilities in Afghanistan show that bin Laden was pursuing a sophisticated biological weapons research program. We also believe that bin Laden was seeking to acquire or develop a nuclear device. Al Qaida may be pursuing a radioactive dispersal device, what some call a "dirty bomb".'[110]

In the case of a terrorist outfit or an undeterrable leader acquiring these deadly weapons, one cannot be certain that an intended deterrent would work in the way intended. In the absence of an established deterrent relationship, would the threat be understood as a deterrent, the way it was perceived, and might it have some unpredictable and perhaps counter-productive consequence? It is difficult to see deterrence operating securely against proliferators. The threat of nuclear annihilation just cannot be used against terrorists. The ease with which a terrorist group can have access to fissile material and thereby construct a nuclear weapon has been discussed in detail by J. Carson Mark and his colleagues.[111]

❦

Deterrence does not emerge automatically with the possession of nuclear weapons. Nuclear deterrence accrues from the threat of a nuclear attack to prevent the opponent from using force against the vital interests of the deterrer. So, to be credible, deterrence must fulfil these basic conditions: (a) the opponent must have vital interests;

---

[109] Mufson 2001.
[110] Shankar 2002.
[111] Mark et al. 1987.

(b) the declared nuclear threat must be credible; and (c) the opponent must be susceptible to be deterred. It is imperative that the adversary realises that the threat is authentic. Threat perception is of vital importance to bring about the stabilising effect of nuclear deterrence. A potential attacker should be in a position to estimate that the probable costs of retaliation would outweigh the gains from aggression. Deterrence is a combination of capability and credibility: it succeeds if the expected costs of retaliation are added to the estimated probability that a deterrent threat will be implemented. Capability is a function of military hardware, the available delivery systems, while credibility has the following variables: perceived interests of the state, the general reputation of the state, the estimated costs of counter-retaliation and the international legitimacy of the action. The strength of these variables has to be calculated well in advance. Decision makers have to work out the cost–benefit analysis of their decision at this stage.

Although this study firmly follows the argument that nuclear weapons do not provide stability and that deterrence is a myth, it contends that following the May 1998 tests, India and Pakistan are now in a slow-motion deployment mode. Given the fact that there would be no rollback and nuclear weapons are here to stay, the only suggestions one can make are towards containing crises and steps to help maintain stability. If the risk of nuclear war can be reduced, attention has also to be paid to the ability of governments to stay in control of a crisis. Many factors determine if governments can indeed contain such a crisis. These factors are tangible or even quantifiable—such as the ability of technical intelligence, or intangible—the systematic assessment, the soundness of policies, the competence and idiosyncrasies of leaders in power and how they struggle with ignorance, knowledge, intentions, misperceptions and miscommunication. Given the peculiarities of any crisis, the manner in which these variables interact with each other normally determines the set of outcomes.

In the long and hostile history of the two dyadic relations, namely, India–Pakistan and India–China, one often comes across the term 'crisis'. Given the fact that China, India and Pakistan are nuclear weapons states (irrespective of how various international regimes define them), the escalation of any border military engagement to the nuclear level will be a quick process. The term 'crisis' may then fall short of explaining the situation.

All three states have the capability to engage in short wars or 'limited war', but by what yardstick and which regulation will such an engagement remain 'limited'? Even if one considers that 'limited war' between China and India is possible, what factors will determine that conflict does not escalate? Despite profound differences in political systems, domestic pressures will ultimately keep playing in the minds of national leaders. There is no dearth of counter-value targets in any of these countries. If indeed India does try to deter China, Pakistan will certainly want delivery systems by which it can deliver nuclear weapons to any part of India.

Crisis often develops suddenly, but if any state has a higher risk-taking capability (as Pakistan did in the Kargil War), then one can pick up strands of brinkmanship, as there are long preparations that go into it. Intelligence gathering activity normally picks up bits and pieces of information about any such large-scale preparation. Vast information and electronic networks notwithstanding, any crisis essentially has a human element, because misinformation and misperceptions impelled by fear and haste, amplified by media campaigns and elitist thinking, and miscalculation of the outcomes remain crucial to crisis.

CHAPTER 4

CHINA

The Chinese have always been a great, courageous and industrious nation;
it is only in modern time that they have fallen behind. And that was due
entirely to oppression and exploitation by foreign imperialism and
domestic reactionary governments ... ours will no longer be a nation
subject to insult and humiliation. We have stood up.

—Mao Tse-tung, 21 September 1949

Post 1949, there was a deep sense of vulnerability that pervaded Chinese thinking on security matters, which can be traced to the Chinese experience at the hands of Western nations and Japan in the 18th century. China in general, and Chinese strategic culture more specifically, was deeply affected by its experiences with almost all imperialist powers through the 19th and 20th centuries. Added to this was the feeling that China, even though it had a large territory and population, was economically and technologically very weak.[1] Chinese security thinking was dominated by its position in the global balance of power. China felt uncomfortable in the international system that was dominated by two superpowers, neither of whom it could challenge. Since the 1950s, when it was engaged in direct military confrontation with the US in the Korean War, China has continued to face American hostility in the form of diplomatic isolation, economic sanctions and military pressure. In the 1960s, the US was again engaged in Asia, this time in Vietnam.

In the new millennium, there are very few countries that will have an impact on the international system the way China would. China is fascinating, yet intriguing, and provides a challenge for policy analysts to grapple with. While thinking about China, different images come to mind—is it a superpower or is it not?

---

[1] Mao Tse-tung 1994: 175, 193.

Will it turn revisionist or will it challenge the current unipolar international system? Will economic reform and market forces help improve Chinese relations with other states? Will communism survive the winds of globalisation? What will be the future of China's relations with its neighbours and other major powers in the international system? How will China affect the Southern Asian strategic balance of which it has become an integral part? How will the US ballistic missile programme influence the strategic choices faced by China? The present discussion will limit itself to the Chinese perception of security, its strategic culture, calculations, doctrines, weapons, policies on major arms control regimes and its neighbours.

China is and always has been influenced a great deal by its past. Chinese strategists have thought differently through the ages on questions of war and peace and different variables have determined their choices. These variables locate their roots in cultural, philosophical, political and cognitive characteristics, which in turn are shaped by history. In the case of China, it is culture that shapes the outcome of many of its policies.

✠ CHINA'S STRATEGIC CULTURE

Strategic culture encompasses the threat and use of force and a country's conduct in international relations. In any state, the ideological, institutional and individual moorings of the decision-making process are often informed by its strategic culture. This concept was first conceived during the Cold War, when Jack Snyder, in a study done for the RAND Corporation, defined strategic culture as the sum total of 'ideas, conditioned emotional responses and patterns of habitual behaviour that members of national strategic community share with each other.'[2] This, however, was perceived to be a narrow definition that was limited primarily to strategic decision making, as it did not take into consideration the larger impact of strategic culture on the process of policy formulation. Ken Booth gave a broader definition of strategic culture.[3]

---

[2] Cited in Macmillan et al. 1994: 4.
[3] He defined strategic culture as 'a distinctive and lasting set of beliefs, values and habits regarding the threat and use of force which have their roots in such

China has seemingly had a consistent strategic culture through the ages. China's status as a land power, its bitter experience of foreign intervention and its traditional self-image of being at the centre of the universe, dictate that the Chinese defence establishment would focus on physical survival and national autonomy.[4]

In dynastic times, Chinese strategies of dealing with threats from 'barbarians' included:[5]

- maintaining internal stability and thereby leaving outsiders no opportunity to exploit;
- maintaining moral and cultural superiority over the barbarians so as to draw their admiration, respect and loyalty;
- engaging in skilful diplomatic manoeuvres, such as 'playing barbarians against barbarians' (*yi yi zhi yi*) and 'associating with those in the distance while attacking those in the vicinity' (*yuan jiao jin gong*); and
- giving carrots and sticks judiciously (*en wei bing shi*) so as to deter barbarians from attempting to invade China.

Some of this ancient thinking still continues, although many key variables have undergone a change due to changing security environments. Chinese analysts often measure four sub-systems of national power: (*a*) material or *hard* power (natural resources, economics, scientific and technology, and national defence); (*b*) spiritual or *soft* power (politics, foreign affairs, culture and education); (*c*) coordinated power (leadership organisation, command, management and coordination of national development); and (*d*) environmental power (natural, international and domestic). This grand strategy, which Beijing defines as 'national development strategy', can be located in Deng Xiaoping's political thought in the late 1970s and has further been reaffirmed by the post-Deng collective leadership. This strategy of development is premised on the assumption that economic power is the most essential factor in a comprehensive national power, and such an approach can

---

fundamental influences as geo-political setting, history and political culture. These beliefs, values and habits constitute a strategic culture which presents over time, and exerts some influence on the formation and execution of strategy' (Cited in Macmillan et al. 1994: 4).

[4] Shu Guang Zhang 1992: 273.

[5] Wu Xinbo 1998: 123.

lead to 'complex interdependence', thereby avoiding conflict. At the same time, Beijing also gives high priority to the development of military power as a complement to policies of reform and opening up, thereby ensuring that China's economic power will rise; for protecting important national interests; and for supporting a policy of eventually playing the role of a great power and perhaps emerging as the pre-eminent power in Asia. Nonetheless, Chinese leaders since Deng have placed military modernisation as the fourth in the priority order of the four modernisations.

In China, the state remains the key referent of security, both in domestic and international politics. Historically, the state has been thought of as a protector, rather than as the oppressor of the people. The Chinese term *guojia* (country) comprises two characters—*guo* (state) and *jia* (family). The state is regarded as a protector of both. 'This notion finds expression in such idioms as *guo po jia wang* (the country is defeated and home lost), *bao jia wei guo* (to protect our homes and defend our country), *wang guo mie zhong* (national subjugation and genocide), and *bao guo bao jiao* (to defend our country and protect our religion).'[6]

Sun Tzu's *Art of War* lays the foundation of Chinese strategic thinking. A reading of Sun Tzu would make one believe that the Chinese are anti-militaristic and rely on concepts like 'not fighting and subduing the enemy' and 'attacking' the enemy's strategic power, the worst being the attack of the enemy's cities.[7] Based on the seven Chinese military classics, Alastair Iain Johnston, who made a comprehensive study of Chinese strategic culture, concludes that these texts accept 'warfare and conflict as relatively constant features of interstate tends towards zero-sum stakes, and consequently ... violence is a highly efficacious means for dealing with conflict.'[8]

China's principal national goal is to become a strong, unified and wealthy nation that is respected as a great power in the world and as the pre-eminent power in Asia.[9] The Chinese see their country

---

[6] Ibid.

[7] There is a rich tradition of strategic thought in Chinese language.

[8] Johnston 1995: 61.

[9] Observe the language of the 2002 National Defence white paper: 'To enhance mutual trust through dialogue, to promote common security through cooperation, and to cultivate a new security concept featuring mutual trust, mutual benefit, equality and cooperation, have become the requirements of the trend of our era.

as a developing power whose nuclear forces and the permanent seat in the UN Security Council already bestow some of the attributes of a great power. They look forward, however, to achieving a status of parity in economic, political and military strength with the world's leading powers by the middle of the next century. This also governs China's grand strategy for achieving this national goal to promote rapid and sustained economic growth; raise the per capita income of its people to the global norm for advanced nations; improve the social quality of life for its people, including health and education, at par with the leading nations of the world; raise technological levels in the sciences and industry; maintain the political unity and stability of the nation; protect national sovereignty and territorial integrity; secure China's access to global resources; and promote China's role as one of the five or six major poles in a new multipolar world.

Johnston acknowledges the lack of definition of the term 'strategic culture', but says that those who use it 'explicitly or implicitly tend to mean that there are consistent and persistent historical patterns in the way particular states (or state elites) think about the use of force for political ends.'[10] He identifies the research on strategic culture as belonging to three generations.[11] According to Johnston, China's strategic culture has two characteristics: (a) a set of assumptions on questions like nature of threats to natural security, role of warfare in society, use of force in dealing with the enemy; and (b) a set of objectives that logically flow from these assumptions. The *leit-motif* in China's strategic culture, Johnston

China is always a staunch force for safeguarding world peace and promoting common development. China will unremittingly put the new security concept into practice, oppose all kinds of hegemonism and power politics, and combat terrorism in all forms and manifestations. China will strive, together with other countries in the world, to create an international environment of long-term peace, stability and security' (State Council, PRC 2002).

[10] Johnston 1995: 1.

[11] The first generation are Soviet area specialists in the early 1980s, who located the divergent behaviour of the US and Soviet Union in variations of their culture. The second generation, from the mid-1980s, recognised the possibility of a disjunction between a symbolic strategic–cultural discourse and operational doctrines, the former being used to reinforce the hegemony of strategic elites and their authority to determine the latter. The third generation has studied the role of organisational and cultural norms in strategic choice in an effort to explain choices that do not fit with dominant neorealist explanations. Johnston concedes that these generations are roughly temporal in sequence, and there is some overlap.

concludes, is the concept of absolute flexibility (*quan bian*) which suggests that the offensive application of violence is likely to be successful only if strategic conditions are ripe.[12] He further adds, 'the Chinese case suggests that strategic culture is not a trivial variable in the description or explanation of strategic behaviour.'[13]

In the 1980s, Edward Boylan too reached a similar conclusion that China had a distinctive 'cultural style' and that its strategy of use of force had roots in Sun Tzu.[14] Gerald Segal too, in his analysis of Chinese strategic behaviour, located it in historical traditions, but found that there were only a few patterns that carried the influence of ancient military thinking.[15]

Clearly, Sun Tzu's *Art of War*, out of eight military classics, had dominated China's strategic discourse through the Middle Ages. There does exist a debate where scholars have questioned the authenticity of Sun Tzu's writings—their accuracy, time in history, or even existence. Sun Tzu offered his services to King Ho Lu of Wu (514–496 BC) whose kingdom was close to the Yangtze River, and later led Wu's forces that defeated bigger states of Chu, Chi and Tsin. Sun Tzu's *Art of War* is therefore a must-read for scholars aiming to understand contemporary strategic culture not just of China but also of South-east Asia.[16] *Art of War* has influenced China's contemporary security discourse. Mao Tse-tung's two essays, 'On Protracted War' and 'Problems of Strategy in China's Revolutionary War',[17] have references to Sun Tzu's *Art of War*. Mao, of course, modified Sun Tzu's work to suit his needs and meet the requirements of the time. There is a debate about whether *The People's War* is a direct take on *Art of War*.

DECEPTION

If there is one single concept that has influenced contemporary Chinese strategic behaviour, it has been that of deception. The genesis of 'deception' can be partially located to Sun Tzu. For him,

---

[12] Ibid.
[13] Ibid.: 258.
[14] Boylan 1982: 342.
[15] Segal 1985c.
[16] Griffith 1963.
[17] These essays are part of Mao Tse-tung 1967.

'All warfare is based on deception (*bingz he guidao ye*).[18] The war doctrines in China put an excessive emphasis on deception, which is integral to China's history and geography. According to *Art of War*, 'attack where they are unprepared, go forth where they will not accept' has been a guiding principle, not just for the military, but for the citizens as well.[19] After examining the classical military texts, Johnston opined that conflict or war is the last policy option in Chinese strategic thinking. He says that under the Confucian–Mencian paradigm, it is assumed that 'when force is used, it should be applied defensively, minimally, only under unavoidable conditions, and then only in the name of the righteous restoration of a moral political order.'[20] The 'grand strategy' here seems to be defensive offence. He concludes that under the *parabellum* paradigm, given that a zero–sum context of violence is preferred, 'offensive strategies [are] followed by progressively less coercive ones, where accommodation is ranked last.'[21] This is also where the concept of absolute flexibility (*quan bian*) takes firm root. But Johnston has also said that the Confucian–Mencian paradigm is an idealised strategic discourse, whereas in reality China exhibits a *realpolitik parabellum* strategic culture. He also points out that while the Maoist–Leninist view propagates violent class struggle, the Confucian–Mencian notion of 'not fighting and subduing the enemy' can produce peace and security.[22] It is therefore argued that 'not fighting and subduing the enemy' is at the heart of the theory of deterrence 'with Chinese characteristics.'[23]

LIMITED USE OF FORCE

Another strand in Chinese strategic culture has been the shift towards minimum use of force if violence does become necessary. Offensive wars of annihilation have not been resorted to in Chinese history. This is linked to what is called 'limited war' in strategic thought.[24] China has had some degree of success in using limited

---

[18] See Sun Tzu 1910.
[19] Sawyer 1996: 43.
[20] Johnston 1995: 249.
[21] Ibid.
[22] Ibid.
[23] Ibid.: 254.
[24] This has been discussed elsewhere in the book at greater length.

force to achieve goals, in coordination with diplomatic tools to achieve clearly defined limited political aims. Grand strategic behaviour post 1949 has therefore only gone marginally further than what was planned as a non-zero–sum construction of conflict.[25]

One can locate international use of force by China from 1950–79 in these broad categories: to recover territories to which China lays claim (Sino-Indian war), to deter a perceived superpower attack (involvement in the Korean War), and to maintain regional balance of power (Sino-Vietnam border war in 1979). Most of these have been limited military engagements.

Having situated some elements of violence in Chinese historical strategic discourse, it may come as a surprise to see how most analysts of Chinese military force present a rather benign picture of China. Many writings (usually by Chinese scholars) begin by saying that the Chinese are a peaceloving people; that China has never invaded another country (with the exceptions being when it was ruled by the ethnically non-Chinese, such as the Mongol Yuan dynasty); that it has never occupied even an inch of another state's territory except to teach a lesson, and that the nation-state prefers to use political, rather than military, means to resolve disputes.[26] Gerald Segal has examined nine cases of Chinese use of force from 1949 to 1985 and concludes that there has been no set pattern. Obviously, every Chinese response was governed by 'absolute flexibility'. He says that China demonstrated strategic and tactical flexibility and a willingness to use whatever amount of force from 1949 to 1985, supplemented by wide variety of political inputs to achieve set political ends.[27] After studying China's militarised interstate dispute behaviour from 1949 to 1992, Johnston concluded that the growth in Chinese capabilities does not necessarily portend a more aggressive use of Chinese power, as long as China's territorial integrity is not challenged and it is accorded appropriate international status (involvement in international institutions, etc).[28] Johnston, however, concedes that 'the findings do suggest

---

[25] See Bobrow 1964; Godwin 1984; and Boorman 1973.
[26] See, for instance, Fang Ning 1998 and Liu Huaqing 1998.
[27] Segal 1985b.
[28] Johnston 1998.

that once in a militarised dispute China will tend to escalate to a relatively high level of force.'[29]

China has traditionally been surrounded by weak vassal states and this has supplemented what has been called 'limitation in warfare'. Against these states only a small part of China's military power was enough. But this was not sufficient against bigger states like the US and the UK and became one of the factors leading to China's colonisation. In chapter 3 of Sun Tzu's *Art of War* on 'Planning Offensive', there are details of how energy (*chi*) constitutes a basis for the kingdom's forces (*Li*) and how extended operations or battles reduce military forces.[30] For instance, in Mao's time, this principle was much in practice: China's civil war campaign at Pingjin lasted for 56 days, the Sino-Indian war 1962 lasted for 20 days, Huaihao for 65 days and the Vietnam War in 1979 for 29 days.[31] After the Cold War, China's new leaders formally pronounced limited war as a war-fighting doctrine.

Chapter 2 of *Art of War*, titled 'Waging War', has concentrated on the idea that long, protracted war may be harmful for the state. Sun Tzu suggests that short battles—'blundering swiftness'—are better than long ones.[32]

CENTRALITY OF THE ARMED FORCES

Another element of China's strategic culture is that the armed forces are considered central in the society and in national security planning. Again, the roots can be traced to the military classics. In the recent era, it was Mao Tse-tung who shouldered the responsibility for shaping the military into a prominent national institution. This process began with Western containment policies and Mao's response. Sun Tzu also played a part in shaping Mao's ideas.[33] In fact, Sun Tzu laid special emphasis on the military as another indicator of national power, a theme that continues in China's contemporary strategic culture.[34]

---

[29] Ibid.
[30] Lau 1965.
[31] The Japanese war in the late 1930s is an exception.
[32] Griffith 1963: 73.
[33] Bok 1984.
[34] Raghvan 1998.

China has, since the 1960s, placed a good deal of emphasis on developing and modernising its military. Nuclear weapons too have played an important role in shaping critical choices in China's foreign relations. China's doctrinal position on nuclear weapons and its overall military doctrines of 'defensive defence' can be located in its strategic culture. One may recall, among the Non-Proliferation Treaty (NPT)-recognised, nuclear weapons states, China is the only country that has offered an NFU. While the actual influence of the modernisation of China's forces and its enthusiastic upgradation of weapons over the region and the world remain issues of concern, ancient scholarly traditions have remained the reference point for the credibility of China's tactical and strategic positions and arguments about modern nuclear warfare.[35] If ancient Chinese military doctrines were transplanted to China's current nuclear posture, Sun Tzu would consider counter-value targeting as least desirable, counter-force only slightly better, counter-control targeting, although it does not have exact correspondence, yet a little better, with the highest form being counter-strategy.[36] The role of nuclear weapons, prominent but less than that in Western countries, confirms these principles.

PRIMACY OF MEN OVER WEAPONS AND DEFENSIVE DEFENCE

Another major theme that dominates China's contemporary strategic doctrines and can be traced to the ancient texts is the doctrine of the primacy of man. The best instance is provided by Kong Ming in *Romance of the Three Kingdoms*, where a rebel chieftain is not punished but let off seven times. The strategy involved is akin to mind over matter: 'attacking the mind is superior to attacking fortifications.'[37] Weiliao Zi, another of the ancient writers, wrote, 'A favourable weather counts less than an advantageous location, which, in turn, counts less than an army in harmony (*tianshi buru dili; buru renhe*).[38] The principle of centrality of man has evolved mainly from the Confucian–Mencian canons. The defensive

---

[35] Chong-pin Lin 1988: 6.
[36] Ibid.: 126.
[37] Ibid.: 19.
[38] Ibid.: 18.

defence thesis—'luring the enemy deep'—too can be traced to China's ancient writing mainly from the Confucian–Mencian canons. Over the last couple of decades, there has been a gradual shift in emphasis from men to materials, and while the debate in the West is still on about whether China has moved from 'defensive defence' to 'offensive defence', the Chinese contend that the doctrines have remained the same. In the late 1970s, China initiated comprehensive reorganisation (*zhengbian*), a process that is still going on. This reorganisation was based on the principle, *Suojian bujun youqi shi bubing yuan's jiaang gongjum, haijun, jige tezhing bing budai* (reduce ground forces, particularly infantry personnel, strengthen air force, navy as well as special forces—nuclear, chemical and biological weapons).[39]

Thus, China's ancient strategic military thought has been instrumental in shaping much of China's present postures and policies. Some statesmen have carried out modifications not just to suit the times, but sometimes to justify their actions. In the following discussion, an attempt will be made to explain China's securit posture and policies, both from Chinese as well as regional perceptions.

NATIONAL SECURITY PERCEPTIONS: MILITARY MODERNISATION

The roots of China's deep sense of insecurity can be located in its historical experience over the last couple of centuries, beginning with the entry of Western traders. There were little or no developments and the economy was drained by the constant pumping out of opium. Besides constructing the political infrastructure of the state, at independence China was also faced with the prospect of constructing a defence system that could stand the test of defending it against external threats.

China's defence forces of about 6 to 7 million ground troops were spread out and disorganised. Besides, internal politics played a major role in shaping the orientation of the forces. The Great Leap Forward and Cultural Revolution were full of radical elements for a long time, which reflected on the forces. Added to this, leaders like Mao Tse-tung and Deng Xiaoping believed that political power flows out of the barrel of the gun. But after 1949, the communist government was faced with the task of re-organising the military.

---

[39] Cited in Kondapalli 1999: 56.

The army was disorganised and had been used largely for internal societal purposes, and there was no navy or air force worth its name. Overall, the military in 1949 hardly had any experience in defending China, let alone in making power projections across borders.

The People's Liberation Army (PLA) has been studied by scholars, both Chinese and Western, besides other Asians.[40] The Central Military Commission (*Zhongguo Gongchandang Zhongyang Junshi Weiyuanhui*, CMC) monitors the functions, decision and the role of the PLA which is under the direct control of the CPC. The 1982 Constitution of China created another CMC. Structurally, the PLA has the following organs: various general departments (General Staff Department, General Political Department, General Logistic Department, General Armaments Department), air force (PLAAF), navy (PLAN), the Ministry of National Defence, the Second Artillery Force, military regions, military districts, military academies, colleges, etc. (under the umbrella organisation, National Defence University), and the Commission for Science and Technology and Industry for National Defence (COSTIND).

In a meeting of the CMC, Chinese Premier Deng Xiaoping said that the PLA was guilty of 'bloating, laxity, conceit, extravagance and inertia.'[41] After the shocks of the Tiananmen Square massacre, addressing a meeting of the CMC on 10–12 November 1989, Deng said the task of the armed forces was 'revolutionisation, modernisation and regularisation.'[42] One of the causes of this was the resistance put up by the PLA rank and file. The white paper released by the PRC[43] has said that the issue of demobilisation of more than 1 million personnel is a positive action towards disarmament and should be seen in terms of internal aspects rather than external ones. The PLA has traditionally played an important role in the political conditions of the PRC. The military has had representation in congress. In the fourteenth Congress in 1992, 41 out of 189 of the CPC Central Committee and 21 out of 130 alternate members belonged to the PLA. In the fifteenth Congress, 42 out of 193 members belonged to the military.

---

[40] Among others, Bonds 1979; Nelson 1977; Gittings 1967; Kondapalli 1999.
[41] Deng Xiaoping 1984: 91.
[42] Jencks 1990.
[43] State Council, PRC 1995a: 6.

The changing international environment, the end of the Cold War, the disintegration of the Soviet Union and the emerging forces of globalisation opened new windows of opportunities for China. This reflected on the PLA. As Col Xu Xiaojun of the PLA's Academy of Military Science says, 'China enjoys the best security environment since 1949. It is not facing any real military threats. There is no obvious danger of a major attack by any adversary. And the eruption of a world war or a major regional conflict which might threaten China's security, is a far away possibility.'[44]

There have been a number of reassuring moves by the PLA. Besides downsizing the PLA from 4.2 million in 1987 to 3.2 million in 1990, there were indications in the mid-1990s of another 15 per cent reduction.[45] The Shanghai Accord that was signed on 26 April 1996 between Russia, China, Kazakhstan, Tajikistan and Kyrgyzstan pledged all state members to a series of security assurances: not to attack each other, not to carry out military exercises in border regions, to give prior notification of planned military attack within border regions, and increased military consultations and exchange of military observes among parties.[46] This effort in border management or an exercise in confidence building reflected a serious effort by China in solving border problems.[47] China signed The Agreement on the Maintenance of Peace and Tranquillity along the Line of Actual Control in the India–China Border Areas, in September 1993 and again in 1996. China's other border talks included those with Vietnam, the Philippines and Malaysia;[48] with Russia, some 95 per cent of the 4,355 km long Sino-Russian border has been agreed upon. The two countries have agreed not to target each other with strategic nuclear weapons. They also have a bilateral NFU between them. This is significant as the two countries were involved in the Ussuri clashes in March 1969, when there were reports of Russian 'surgical strikes' on Chinese nuclear installations.[49] There was also speculation that there could have been a Soviet pre-emptive strike against China's nuclear installations.[50]

---

[44] Cited in Cossa 1994.
[45] *International Herald Tribune* 1996a.
[46] Yu Lei 1996.
[47] An approach that has been termed as 'solving it or shelving it'.
[48] See *International Herald Tribune* 1993, 1996b; *Financial Times* 1995a, 1995b.
[49] IISS 1969–71. See the 1969 report, p. 72.
[50] Ibid.

The Chinese nuclear installations were geographically spread out: Lop Nur (the test site) Aksu, Urumchi and much further east Haiyen Lanchou and Paotou. If the Soviets had decided to carry out the surgical strikes even with a 75 to 90 per cent success rate, China could still have retained some nuclear weapons that would then have been used for a retaliatory second strike, thereby escalating the border war to the nuclear level. Since then, there have been some encouraging steps, but there is never any guarantee of a 100 per cent success in such a pre-emptive strike.[51] On the issue of the South China Sea, China signed bilateral accords with the Philippines and Malaysia to diffuse potential disputes. On 15 May 1996, China acceded to the UN Convention on the Law of Sea.

Before focusing on proliferation concerns and China's arms control policies, it is imperative to dwell on China's perception of national security and its national security paradigms.

NATIONAL SECURITY PARADIGMS

In China's perception, national security involves a complex set of variables. It is not just the military that is of consideration, but political stability and unity as well, since historical facts state that following the opium wars, China had been reduced to the status of a semi-colony. In the subsequent period, for over 100 years, the Chinese were exploited and there was no concept of security as China was open to invaders, aggressors and economic exploiters. Given this, the Chinese speak of issues like national security and sovereignty as being influenced by history. From this perspective, the following are the security objectives of China:[52]

- To build itself into a country that is economically prosperous, politically stable and military sufficient in its own defence.[53]
- To lay particular stress on a good neighbour policy, with the purpose of establishing friendly and cooperative relations with neighbouring countries.[54]

---

[51] Ibid.
[52] Yimin Song 1986: 3.
[53] Ibid.
[54] Ibid.

- To have interdependence between security and development, striving for international economic security to strengthen international security as a whole, and thus to create a lasting and peaceful environment for China's people.[55]

The primary goal that China follows now is that of economic prosperity to raise productivity, a policy of active defence, independence and peace, and a foreign policy based on five principles.[56] The national security paradigms are discussed below.

Seeking Peace

With the thought of 'early, total nuclear strike' weighing on the minds of Chinese leaders, a recent security paradigm of 'seeking peace' has become the dominant theme. It was Mao who first saw the difference between nuclear and conventional threats and presumed that China faced an 'early total nuclear strike', thus making way for China's open-ended military modernisation in the first three decades after independence. While China constantly built up arms, the leaders repeatedly emphasised eliminating weapons of mass destruction, since they were viewed as the most drastic means to achieve the ends of peace and security. China conducted the first nuclear test at Lop Nur on 16 October 1964, and the statement released that day conveyed the shape of Chinese nuclear deterrence and policies to come.[57] The tests were to break US hegemony, and the Chinese deterrent was a part of the 'struggle to strengthen

---

[55] Ibid.

[56] These five principles are: (*a*) mutual respect for sovereignty and territorial integrity; (*b*) mutual non-aggression; (*c*) non-interference in each other's internal affairs, equality and mutual benefit; (*d*)peaceful coexistence in developing diplomatic relations; and (*e*) economic and cultural exchange with other countries. These are the same as the Panchsheel Agreement of 1954 between India and China.

[57] The highlights of the statement were: 'This is a major achievement of the Chinese people in their struggle .... The atomic bomb is a paper tiger. This famous statement by Chairman Mao Tse-tung is known to all. This was our view in the past and this is still our view at present. China is developing nuclear weapons not because it believes in their omnipotence or because it plans to use them. On the contrary, in developing nuclear weapons, China's aim is to break the nuclear monopoly of the nuclear powers and to eliminate nuclear weapons .... The Chinese Government hereby solemnly declares that China will never at any time or under any circumstances be the first to use nuclear weapons' (Government of PRC 1964).

their national defence and oppose the US imperialist policy of nuclear blackmail and nuclear threats.'[58] Although in its policy declarations and statements, China has, since 1964, maintained that it is against weapons of mass destruction, yet internally, force modernisation and a move towards winning a 'limited war under high-tech conditions' reflects a 'lean mean fighting force' that is ready for the 21st century. The force has indeed been downsized, but the laid-off soldiers have been transferred to the People's Armed Police (PAP), the strength of which has increased from 0.5 million in 1983 to 1.8 million in 1996. Thus, to seek peace regionally, the approach is to keep the borders settled, maintain a 'lean mean' force, keep the special forces (read nuclear, chemical and biological weapons) ready and updated and not engage the army in day-to-day law and order problems for which the PAP has been readied.

Limited War

Yet again, it is Sun Tzu whose dictum of a short swift war dominates and is considered better than long campaigns. 'In war, then, let your great object be victory, not lengthy campaigns.'[59] In fact, if the enemy can be defected even without fighting, it is considered supreme excellence: 'to fight and conquer in all your battles is not supreme excellence, supreme excellence consists in breaking the enemy's resistance without fighting.'[60] The chapter 2 of *Art of War*, titled 'Waging War', has constant references to the idea of a short war. Sun Tzu suggests protracted warfare can be inimical to state resources and the morale of men. A blundering speed is considered better than prolonged warfare: 'though we have heard of stupid haste in war, cleverness has never been associated with long delays.'[61] In fact, it has been clearly written that 'there is no instance of a country having benefited from prolonged warfare.'[62] The changing nature of the PLA and its transformation to a 'lean mean fighting machine' has connotations for a move towards what Sun Tzu had advised—short war. This has ably been modified to suit the present environment, and hence, special weapons and modernisation of the forces have been ordered.

---

[58] Ibid.
[59] See Sun Tzu 1910.
[60] Ibid.
[61] Ibid.
[62] Ibid.

The armed forces get the latest in weapon systems and new technologies, and coupled with new concepts in battle operations, the PLA has increased its combat effectiveness manifold. This process has been supplemented by necessary doctrinal changes.[63] This is a reflection of 'force projection' rather than occupation as the priority of the PLA, which emphasises the limited war paradigm. In the theory of conflict, an important role is played by 'such symbolic and exceptional phenomena as tradition, precedent, convention and unwritten law ....'[64] Limited war, Thomas Schelling argues, 'is not necessarily "irrational" for either party, if the alternative might have been a war that would have been less desirable for both of them.'[65] It is clear that to keep war limited there has to be norm setting. In the case of China, if tradition lays the foundations for such norms, then the adversary too should be at the same strategic wavelength to keep the conflict limited. But this may create more problems. William Kaufmann has suggested that 'any attempt to formulate rigid rules of conduct for wars whose aegis and environment we cannot foresee may create as many problems as it pretends to solve.'[66] And of course the final criticism can be that a losing state will want to use all the weapons at its disposal to continue to exist. When escalation takes place, soldiers and statesmen coming under increasing domestic pressure will then be forced to reach hasty decisions upsetting calculations that were made in peacetime. Under these circumstances, a limited war may indeed have a greater potential for escalation than a conventional conflict.[67]

Seen in this context, limited wars are not new to the literature and inherently carry the risk of escalation. It is difficult to see a concept like limited war being used to enhance stability in the region. Indeed, if force capabilities are of any indication, then China is on its way to force projection. Various strategists have been quick to point out how certain new weapon systems emphasise precision, lethality, surprise and target acquisition, thereby making space for 'limited war'.[68] Gen Qin Jiwei, Minister of Defence, addressing

---

[63] Joffe and Segal 1995.
[64] Schelling 1960.
[65] Ibid.
[66] Kaufmann 1958.
[67] See in this context, Jessup 1957; Brodie 1957; and Osgood 1957.
[68] Godwin 1992: 191–92.

the National People's Congress in 1994 said, 'in the next ten years, the international situation will be complicated and changeable. Although major war is unlikely to take place, limited local wars will be endless.'[69] In an eight-volume series prepared by the Academy of Military Science titled, 'Studies on Campaigns and Tactics in a High Tech War', 'limited high-tech' war has been described as

> a contest in science and technology: in terms of the nature of high tech limited warfare (sic) is an information contest; in terms of its manifestation a high tech limited war is a system contest; in terms of the mode of operations and the way it develops high tech limited war is highly controllable and flexible; in terms of the requirements of logistical support, high tech limited war is high on inputs and high on consumption.[70]

China has been quick to differentiate its model of limited war from Western constructs. It argues that it has still kept in mind the concept of 'people's war'. Logically, this means that China is still behind the times on weapons technologies. Second, the Chinese version of limited war pertains only to China's periphery and is not for intercontinental purposes; and finally, the Chinese believe that in a dynamic strategic environment, strategic breakthroughs will further refine this concept.

Credible Minimum Nuclear Deterrent

According to the July 1998 white paper, 'China's National Defence', the official Chinese position on nuclear deterrence and nuclear weapons is that it advocates total nuclear disarmament and complete prohibition of nuclear weapons. As a nuclear weapons state, China 'vigorously supports and participates in the international non-nuclear proliferation efforts, promotes the process of nuclear disarmament and works hard for the realisation of the final goal of the complete prohibition and thorough destruction of nuclear weapons worldwide.'[71] A couple of decades earlier, there was no indication of the formulation of a definitive nuclear strategy.

---

[69] Quoted in Shulong Chu 1994: 188.
[70] Quoted in 1998/99. See also in this context, Johnston 1995/96.
[71] State Council, PRC 1998.

It is apparent that Chinese leaders from the beginning realised that Beijing had no chance of competing against the superpowers. In the initial period in the 1960s, the Chinese strategy had major loopholes. Their thinking about nuclear war was limited to defence and survival. At that time, China had no real air defence. But since then, much thinking has gone into these issues. The PLA now understands that

> before a war breaks out, a country will, by way of military deterrence, try to make the opposite side refrain from launching an attack rashly, so as to provide a powerful backing for its own political, economic and diplomatic activities. If deterrence does not work, it will strive for a victory through actual combat, in order to remove the obstacles to its political, economic and diplomatic activities.[72]

✠ THE ROAD TO LOP NUR AND AFTER

The reasons that led China to choose the nuclear path have been fourfold: (a) its geo-strategic realities; (b) its historical experience; (c) the perceptions and beliefs of its leadership; and (d) technological, organisational and economic capabilities and limitations. The geo-strategic environment confronting the Chinese state has to a great extent contributed to its approach to WMD, and particularly to nuclear weapons. The most noteworthy and enduring features of this environment have been: (a) very long and at many places extremely porous international frontiers; and (b) international borders being shared by states with strong and well-maintained military forces, including the former Soviet Union and India, both of which have had armed conflict with China in the past.[73] Viewed from a Chinese perspective, such a security environment requires the creation of a military force large enough not just to protect the territorial sovereignty of China, but also to deter large-scale conventional and nuclear threats.

The historical experience of China since the mid-19th century has only increased its sense of insecurity and vulnerability. Western interaction with China has led to armed intervention, subjugation

---

[72] Wu Jianguo 1998: 144.
[73] Lewis 1980: 148.

and humiliation by Western powers in the past. The experience has generated various responses from the state. The statement released soon after the Lop Nur test talked of 'nuclear blackmail'. The beliefs and perceptions of the Chinese leadership have also had a major bearing on China's position, doctrines and force structure. Chinese leaders have nurtured a belief that the nuclear threat has been held out by the United States to intimidate and blackmail weaker, smaller powers and to continue its dominance of the international system.[74] The United States levelled nuclear threats against the Chinese in the early 1950s during the Korean War.

But perhaps the greatest influences on China's viewpoint towards WMD possession are fundamental technological, organisational and economic factors. The low industrial and technological base and the early reliance on Soviet weapon designs and engineering, ended up restricting the size and sophistication of China's nuclear estate. A level of indigenisation fuelled China's desire to be self-reliant, especially after the 1969 Ussuri river clashes.

China's efforts to develop nuclear weapons came in response to nuclear threats by the United States. Mao Tse-tung, with counsel from Chou En-lai, set China on its quest for nuclear weapons in January 1955.[75] The United States was the most immediate cause. The US had threatened China with nuclear weapons in the Korean War (1950–53) and was now mobilising to exert military pressure in the Taiwan Strait crisis. Chinese leaders feared that the US would threaten or actually use nuclear weapons in this crisis.[76] They also felt that the genius of the Chinese nation and the communist system would be impressed upon their citizens and the wider world by the scientific prowess displayed in the acquisition of nuclear weapons.[77] In July 1950, at the very beginning of the Korean War, President Truman ordered 10 nuclear configured B-29s to the Pacific and 'he warned China that the US would take "whatever steps are necessary" to stop Chinese intervention and that the use of nuclear weapons had been under active consideration.'[78] In 1952, President-elect Eisenhower publicly hinted that he would

[74] Lewis and Xue Litai 1988.
[75] Ibid.: 38–39.
[76] Ibid.: 37.
[77] Ibid.: 231.
[78] Nuclear Threat Initiative 2004.

authorise the use of nuclear weapons against China if the Korean War armistice talks continued to stagnate. In 1954, the leader of the US Strategic Air Command, Gen Curtis LeMay stated his support for the use of nuclear weapons if China resumed fighting in Korea. These threats prompted the Chinese to begin developing nuclear weapons in the winter of 1954–55, and the Ministry of Nuclear Industry was established in 1955. With Soviet assistance, nuclear research began at the Institute of Physics and Atomic Energy in Beijing, and a gaseous diffusion uranium enrichment plant in Lanzhou was constructed to produce weapons-grade uranium. On 15 October 1957, the USSR agreed to provide China with a sample atomic bomb and manufacturing data. However, by 1960, the rift between the Soviet Union and China had become so great that the former discontinued all assistance to China. After 1960, China was forced to continue alone.

The Beijing Nuclear Weapons Research Institute was established in 1958 and served as a transitional research facility, until it was replaced in 1962 by the Northwest Nuclear Weapons Research and Design Academy in Qinghai. The Tongxian Uranium Mining and Metallurgical Processing Institute was also established in 1958, just a few miles east of Beijing (see Map 4.1).[79] China conducted its first nuclear test at Lop Nur on 16 October 1964.[80] By the 1960s, China had begun research and design of underground nuclear testing facilities.[81]

The US was suspicious during the early 1960s that communist China would tread the nuclear path very soon. In a memorandum to Roger Hilsman, Director, Bureau of Intelligence and Research, John M. Steeves confirmed, 'it is no longer a question of whether Peking is engaged in a nuclear weapons program, but only of when a detonation may be expected.'[82] More significantly, this memorandum

---

[79] Ibid.: 90. See also Norris et al. 1994: 338, 340.

[80] In a statement after its first nuclear weapon explosion, China stated that: 'The Chinese Government pointed out long ago that the treaty on the partial halting of nuclear tests signed in Moscow in July 1963 by the United States, Britain, and the Soviet Union was a big fraud to fool the people of the world, that it was an attempt to consolidate the nuclear monopoly of the three nuclear powers and tie the hands of all peace-loving countries, and that it had increased, and not decreased, the nuclear threat of US imperialism against the people of China and of the whole world' (Government of PRC 1964).

[81] Tang Hua 1996.

[82] Steeves 1961.

sought to find out the impact of Chinese communist nuclear detonation and of the subsequent acquisition of a nuclear military capability, emphasising the impact in areas such as: (*a*) Sino-Soviet relations; (*b*) Beijing's policy towards disarmament and test ban negotiations; and (*c*) policies and attitudes of non-communist Asian countries, particularly Japan, India and free China towards the communist bloc and the West.[83] In fact, as William Burr and Jeffrey T. Richelson point out, 'The estimate that China could test a device within a few years raised alarm at the White House, and President Kennedy encouraged the CIA and other agencies to explore possibilities for preventive action against Chinese nuclear facilities.'[84] The fact that President Kennedy and his administration had considered using force against Chinese nuclear facilities has been documented by strategists.[85]

Earlier, in 1963, China had proposed a world summit to discuss nuclear disarmament. It suggested four steps towards disarmament:[86]

1. Dismantling all foreign bases and withdrawing all nuclear weapons from abroad
2. Establishing nuclear-free zones in Asia and the Pacific, Central Europe, Africa and Latin America
3. The non-export and non-import of nuclear weapons and the technical information for their production
4. A halt to all nuclear testing, including underground tests

Issues of dispersal, hardening and targets started being discussed, and the Chinese considered long-range missiles or fighter aircrafts from US or Russia as their main threats. The 1960s saw the Cuban missile crisis and in 1969 China itself was engaged in the Ussuri river clashes with the Soviet Union. Following these clashes, there was the threat of a surgical strike by the Russians which made China initiate 'war preparations'. In the midst of charges and counter-charges, a border truce was signed between the Soviet

---

[83] Ibid.
[84] Burr and Richelson 2000/2001.
[85] Chang 1988.
[86] Clemens 1993: 66.

Union and China in October 1969, but China continued to consider the Soviets as the most immediate threat. By 1971, it was clear that China wanted to become a major nuclear weapons power.

It is possible that China had deployed some DF(DongFeng) MRBMs even as early as 1969. In 1971, China rejected a Soviet proposal for the convening of a five-power conference to include the US, USSR, UK, France and China to discuss the question of nuclear disarmament. China re-emphasised its position that it would not be the first to use nuclear weapons, and urged Washington and Moscow to agree not to be the first to use them as well. Following its admission in the UN, China again rejected a Soviet proposal for a world disarmament conference placed under the twenty-sixth United Nations General Assembly. There was an indication that China would participate in the Conference of the Committee on Disarmament. While it may be apparent that China has a benign approach to the disarmament question, there has been no indication from Beijing to abandon any of its requirements of armaments or nuclear weapons and delivery warhead modernisation. Despite the overall ambiguity, there are some clear-cut attributes of China's nuclear doctrine:[87]

- China has repeatedly said that its weapons are for self-defence.
- Since 1964, China has said that it will not be the first to use nuclear weapons. China, in fact, is the only member of the NPT that has offered an NFU. It has applied NFU to Taiwan.
- China has also unconditionally said that it would not use or threaten to use nuclear weapons against non-nuclear weapons states or nuclear weapon-free zones.
- Having offered a no-first-use, China apparently follows a counter-value targeting, second strike deterrence strategy.
- China only wants to adhere to the principle of 'we must have what others have, and anyone who wants to destroy us will be subject to retaliation.'
- China provides non-nuclear weapons states with unconditional negative security assurances.

---

[87] See in this context, Pollack 1994.

Some of the other key points of Chinese nuclear diplomacy are:[88]

- China has participated in several nuclear weapon-free zone treaties in Latin America, the South Pacific, South-east Asia and Africa; these commitments prohibit China from deploying, using or threatening to use nuclear weapons in these regions.
- China has urged the United States and Russia to make deep cuts in their nuclear forces and advocates the complete destruction of nuclear weapons.

Johnston and other leading experts on this topic argue that for nearly three decades after acquiring its first nuclear weapon, China lacked a coherent nuclear doctrine.[89] In a speech in 1997 to the US Army war college, Lt Gen Li Jijun, Vice President of the PLA's Academy of Military Science, described China's nuclear strategy as:

China's nuclear strategy is purely defensive in nature. The decision to develop nuclear weapons was a choice China had to make in the face of real nuclear threats. A small arsenal is retained only for the purpose of self defence. China has unilaterally committed itself to responsibilities not yet taken by other nuclear nations including the declaration of a no-first-use policy, the commitment not to use or threaten to use nuclear weapons against non nuclear zones.... In short, China's strategy is completely defensive, focused only on deterring the possibility of nuclear blackmail being used against China by other nuclear powers.[90]

A reflection of this has been the strategic transition of the PLA from 'preparing for early, total and nuclear war to local and limited war ... to deter or fight is a medium-sized local war comparable to a PLA war zone campaign.'[91] There is a school of thought in China that advocates adopting a nuclear doctrine of limited nature seeking a capability to deter conventional, theatre and strategic nuclear war, and to control escalation in the event of a nuclear confrontation. Under this doctrine, China may need to have counter-value

---

[88] See in this context, Garrett and Glaser 1995/96; Jiang Zemin 1999; Li Daoyu 1993; Qian Qichen 1995; Sha Zukang 1995, 1997; and State Council, PRC 1995b, 2000a.

[89] Johnston 1997: 288.

[90] Li Jijun 1997: 7.

[91] Nan Li 1999: 148.

Map x 4.1
China's Nuclear Estate

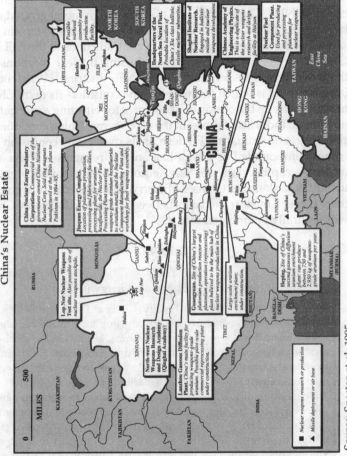

Source: Spector et al. 1995.

targets. In 1996, Johnston said, 'while the data on Chinese operational nuclear capabilities, targeting and launch doctrine are poor, it is fairly safe to say that Chinese capabilities come nowhere near the level required by the concept of limited deterrence.'[92] (See Box 4.1 for Chinese nuclear R&D at Tuoli.) For years since it first enunciated an NFU, China continued to enjoy a high moral ground and kept urging all other nuclear weapons states to take steps in the same direction. There are a couple of contradictions to the NFU, as Chinese strategists no longer regard using nuclear weapons on their own territory as a violation of the NFU doctrine.[93] What comes in sharp focus is which territories China considers its own. China has not given up the option of using force for effecting a unification of Taiwan. India also figures in these concerns. China continues to claim parts of Arunachal Pradesh as its own.[94] The confusion becomes compounded as China has not yet recognised India as a nuclear weapons state. As Yan Xeutong, a foreign policy expert in a think tank under China's Ministry of State Security argues, if there is ever a nuclear exchange between India and Pakistan, China will naturally be dragged into it.[95]

Box ✕ 4.1

Tuoli
China Institute of Atomic Energy (CIAE)

The China Institute of Atomic Energy (CIAE) at Tuoli, near Beijing, is a comprehensive research and production base in the nuclear research and development regime in China. Located in the southwest of Beijing, about 40 km from the downtown city, it is quite close to the famous Zhoukoudian site where the ancient Peking man lived about 500,000 years ago. Facilities include a laboratory-scale gaseous diffusion plant. Tuoli developed this enrichment process which was later installed at Lanzhou. Waste Management R&D includes HLW vitrification and waste form characterisation, with pilot plants to be built. Main facilities currently include large and medium-sized scientific research and production facilities:

(Box 4.1 Contd)

---

[92] Johnston 1996a.

[93] Tai Ming Cheng 1989.

[94] Until recently, China used to claim Sikkim as an independent country. This 'cartographic aggression' was set right after the Indian prime minister's visit to China in September 2003.

[95] *The China Post* 1998.

(Box 4.1 Contd)

research reactor, zero-power reactor, high- and low-energy accelerators, large and medium-sized computers and network systems, high activity cells, etc. The Department of Reactor Engineering and Technology at CIAE is the premier reactor R&D base in China. Under this are 15 research and design divisions relating to reactor physics, reactor thermal hydraulics, reactor material corrosion and protection, reactor material and radiation performance, reactor fuels and irradiated material examination, reactor fuel elements, general design of fast reactor, general design of advanced research reactor, reactor structure design, reactor loop design, reactor control and instrumentation design, sodium technology, heavy water reactor research and operation, light water reactor research and operation and miniature reactor, covering all sectors relating to reactor engineering and technology together with the necessary scientific research facilities. The Chinese Nuclear Data Center located at CIAE is a participant in the international Nuclear Energy Agency's Nuclear Science Committee and its Working Party on International Nuclear Data Evaluation Cooperation. The NEA Nuclear Science Committee has set up a Working Party on International Measurement Activities to coordinate differential nuclear data measurement activities.

Source: http://www.fas.org/nuke/guide/china/facility/tuoli.htm.

Over the last few years, there has been a shift from a posture of minimum deterrence to limited deterrence, wherein China acquires the necessary components required for a limited war fighting capability—strategically a shift from counter-value to counter-force targeting. In the words of Paul Godwin,

> Minimum deterrence, which uses a single counter-value punitive strike on cities to deter, is seen by many Chinese strategists as passive and incompatible with … a future requirement for more flexible nuclear responses. Limited deterrence incorporates nuclear war fighting, which provides China with the ability to respond to any level of nuclear attack from tactical to strategic.[96]

While Chinese strategists are still strengthening their arguments and defining the parameters of their debates that in many ways can

---

[96] Godwin 1999: 261.

only be inferential, it is the Western debate that seems to be heating up. In the words of Chinese analyst You Ji, 'To the current PLA commanders, minimum deterrence is an awkward strategy, it is too defensive, concerned mainly with how to hide .... The doctrine of minimum deterrence has total flaws but it is an unavoidable transitional guide line for deterring an all out war.'[97]

Ambiguity from the Chinese government has led to estimates and a careful use of terminology—it has been 'reported', 'it is alleged by an adversary', 'it may be possible under this scenario'— but what trajectory doctrines and their qualifying arguments will take in the future cannot be clearly predicted. This view has been reinforced by the fact that China has become more transparent in many aspects of the PLA, but ambiguity still shrouds its nuclear posture.[98]

KEY VARIABLES IN THE FUTURE

From 1964, when China first tested and articulated some of its positions on nuclear issues, till the beginning of the 21st century, the country has come a long way. Earlier, China's nuclear posture, external and internal policies were being located in the Cold War paradigm, but a host of new features of the post-Cold War period have recently been added. What then are these variables and how will they determine China's future policies?

In 1964, China justified the test in terms of threat from the Soviet Union and the US and declared that it wanted to break US hegemony. The following decades saw a systemic change—the collapse of the Soviet Union, forces of globalisation and South Asian nuclear tests. The collapse of the Soviet Union made the US the sole superpower while forces of globalisation have strengthened China's position. When India tested in May 1998, followed by Pakistan, Chinese strategic calculations were altered.

In May 1998, following its nuclear tests, India sent a letter to President Clinton[99] and clearly named China as a threat and, therefore, a motivation for testing. Following India's tests, Pakistan also

---

[97] You Ji 1999: 246.

[98] The only government source in this regard are the white papers (State Council, PRC 1995b, 2002).

[99] The Hindu 1998.

tested nuclear devices. China 'strongly condemned' India's tests and expressed its 'deep regret' over the Pakistan tests. It immediately urged both India and Pakistan to exercise utmost restraint and to abandon at once all nuclear weapons programmes in order to avoid worsening the situation and to ensure peace and stability in the region. The Chinese said, 'The South Asian region … [has] ushered in the spectre of a nuclear arms race, bringing grave consequences to world peace and security and to peace and security in the region.'[100]

China has consistently advocated the complete elimination of nuclear weapons and has argued for nuclear non-proliferation all through the 1964 Lop Nur test to the 2002 white paper. Although when China exports nuclear technology for peaceful purposes, it demands that the facility be brought under IAEA safeguards, how much of this is actually brought under the safeguards remains an unanswered question. China also wants countries of the Indian Ocean region to adopt practical measures to prevent the proliferation of nuclear weapons and other weapons of mass destruction.[101] The obvious reference here is to India and Pakistan. India has meanwhile continued to raise the issue of Chinese covert assistance to the Pakistani missile and nuclear programme. How the Sino-Pakistan relations shape up and how India reacts to that relationship will determine the level of trust that is so crucial in a trilateral relationship. How China responds to the US plans for a national missile defence will have wide-ranging strategic implications for India. From an Indian point of view the size of the deterrent may influence its relations with China. Even a minimal number will be a maximum number against Pakistan.

China articulated its nuclear policy in the white paper in July 1998, which, coming soon after the South Asian nuclear tests, was significant. China distanced itself from the tests and yet kept its original position secure: it gave some concrete proposals rather than taking any moral position on nuclear disarmament. Subsequently, in December 2002, China released another white paper on national defence.

---

[100] Government of PRC 1998.
[101] Oin Huasun 1995.

China's Arms Control and Disarmament Policy

Given that states have adjusted to the post-Cold War security architecture with the Southern Asian states going overtly nuclear, what
has been China's approach to arms control? Does China pursue
an arms control strategy? The international system too has undergone a change. When China first tested a nuclear device, there were
two blocs; by the late 1980s, one of the blocs had been dismembered
and although China kept insisting it was a bi-polar world, perhaps
it had not anticipated that it would find itself as the next great
power. Traditionally, the Chinese do not conceptualise China as a
big power that could play a role in the world. During the Cold War,
China saw arms control as one of the instruments that keeps the
weak states weak and the strong states strong. At the beginning of
the 21st century, it is China that is strong, and from an Indian point
of view, one of the five that are on top of the hegemonic pyramidal
structure (see Figure 4.1 for its arms control community).

There are several criteria, based on which one may judge a particular country's penchant for arms control. The first is the degree
of self-restraint. To judge this, one needs to situate the arms build-
up in the context of defence needs, threat perceptions, intentions
and systemic changes. Historically, China has been a weak country
and the policy that it has followed from the beginning has, even
the Americans would agree, a good degree of self-restraint—at
least as far as policy pronouncements are concerned. Second, to
evaluate the arms control policy in China: it has nuclear weapons
and a modest stockpile, and presents itself as a threat to any
country. In terms of the Indian perspective, the 1962 war was lost,
in 1964 the Lop Nur test was conducted, and continued assistance
has been made to the Pakistan nuclear weapons programme to
the extent that the US had to use sanctions on these countries.
Besides, China continues to have a huge arsenal and deliverable
systems with reports of missile bases in Tibet. Third, does China
indeed make proposals that are concrete and substantial or does
it follow policies and norms that have been set by others? Theoretically, China has forwarded proposals that if adhered to can have
an effect on nuclear disarmament. For instance, on 31 July 1963,
China proposed a world summit to discuss nuclear disarmament.[102]

---

[102] The steps that China proposed for disarmament included the dismantling
and withdrawing of foreign nuclear facilities, establishing nuclear weapon-free

But perhaps China realises that total nuclear disarmament is a difficult game. Indeed, China was the first to enunciate the policy of NFU. But there have been other models too. For instance, Japan, due to its domestic compulsions, had given a call for a UN Register for Conventional Arms Transfer and its non-nuclear policies too prove that point. The efforts by India of constantly introducing various proposals, like the Rajiv Gandhi Action Plan and various others, are also a case in point. Same is the case with efforts like the New Agenda Coalition and Middle Powers Initiative.

But as Francois Godement has argued, most approaches to arms control fall into a category 'where tough bargaining compliance with agreements, and verification are order of the day ... "Linkage" may occur in the negotiating process, as each side hunts for concessions in sometimes very different areas ... successful disarmament has been based not so much on the switch from mutual deterrence to mutual trust, but on the notion that mutual deterrence might be preserved at lower levels of armaments, irrespective of trust.'[103]

On closer scrutiny, China has sought to maintain a fine balance between, on the one hand, an idealism that is guided by high moral posturing on nuclear disarmament, and on the other hand, by a policy firmly grounded in the pragmatism of retaining and modernising the nuclear arsenal and the PLA. At the end of Cold War, there was an opportunity and a global norm towards disarmament. China has regularly sought a triad of nuclear forces, mobile deployment, multiple warheads, launch on warning, delivery vehicles of all kinds, neutron bombs, and the like. Looking at the force structure and power projection, China seems to have a disparity between policy pronouncements which look benign and forces accompanied by domestic debates that come across as belligerent.

Godement has identified three stages in China's attitude to disarmament:[104]

- The first was the stage of denial until 1964 (when Mao claimed that nuclear weapons were a 'paper tiger', while acquiring them).

---

zones, stopping the export and import of nuclear weapons and information relating to techniques of their production, and bringing to an end all forms of nuclear testing. Please see the discussion on p. 120.

[103] Godement 1997: 91.

[104] Ibid.: 97.

Figure x 4.1
China's Arms Control Community

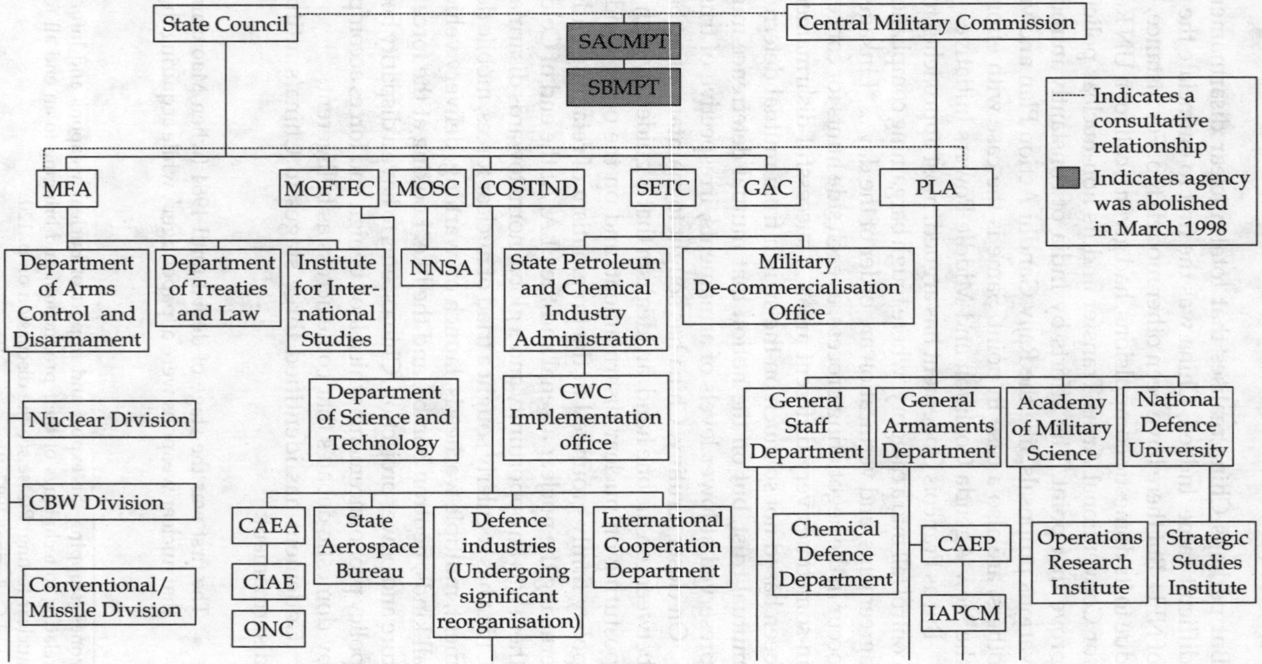

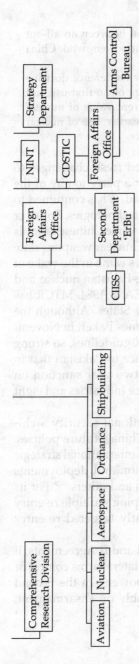

Notes: Other organisations involved in arms control and non-proliferation research are:
Beijing Institute of Nuclear Engineering; Beijing Institute of Systems Engineering; China Institute of Atomic Energy; China Institute of Contemporary International Relations; Chinese People's Association for Peace and Disarmament; Institute of American Studies Program on Arms Control; Institute for World Economics and Politics; National Defence Science Technology University; Program in Arms Control and Regional Security (Fudan University); Program in Arms Control and Disarmament (Peking University); Scientists' Group on Arms Control.

Source: © Center for Nonproliferation Studies.

- The second is the post-1964 contradiction between an all-out disarmament policy targeted at other nuclear powers, while China accepted no limitation.
- The third is the post-1979 situation. Now its defence doctrine has outgrown the initial declaratory stage of no-first-use and instead entered a phase where the deterrent value of nuclear weapons implies more gradual, but also earlier, use of nuclear arms, and is linked to conventional defence.

The post-Cold War environment has posed fresh challenges to Chinese arms control policies. China is not a party to any of the Russia–US arms control negotiations. Instead, it has continued to develop and refine its nuclear and missile technologies. For over 20 years, China refused to accede to the NPT while Chinese officials maintained that it was being a 'responsible' nuclear weapons state and not assisting any state. These assurances came in the wake of strong criticism of Chinese assistance to the Pakistan nuclear and missile programme.[105] China joined the IAEA in 1984. MTCR has been a bone of contention with the United States. Although the Chinese promised US Secretary of State, James Baker, in November 1991 that they would not violate MTCR guidelines, so strong was the evidence of Chinese M-11 assistance to Pakistan that in 1993 the State Department announced a two-year sanction on Chinese Ministries of Defence and Aerospace Industries and eight commercial companies.

Technology, market forces and international security architecture will be some of the influences on China's future policies. Nuclear weapons will be retained due to the international strategic environment. Indeed, large-scale production and deployments 'would probably alarm China's neighbours and others.'[106] For its larger missiles, China is working on developing multiple re-entry vehicles (MRVs) or multiple independently targeted re-entry vehicles (MIRVs).

Although China has praised the START I and II Agreements, it has not agreed to be a member in any multilateral arms control or arms reduction talks with other nuclear powers. In the Second Special Session of the UN General Assembly on Disarmament,

---

[105] See in this context, Sutter 1994 and Kan 1996.
[106] Sutter 1994.

China proposed 'three halts and one reduction.'[107] This had been altered in 1988 when China stated that the US and Soviet Union would have to achieve 'drastic' or 'substantial' reductions in their nuclear arsenals and not just reduce these by 50 per cent before China would be willing to enter into multilateral arms reduction negotiations. The official explanation was that the programme would have its effect on Chinese deterrence.

Given this complex interplay of key variables, what can be China's probable future posture, considering the scope, scale and sophistication of its strategic forces together with its doctrinal policies? In a study by the Council on Foreign Relations in 2000,[108] the following five options were arrived at: (*a*) small but modern,[109] (*b*) minimum deterrence restored,[110] (*c*) regional dominance, interim global irrelevance,[111] (*d*) a force *de frappe*,[112] (*e*) a parity force.[113]

---

[107] These were: 'cease all nuclear tests, stop the qualitative improvement and manufacture of any kind of nuclear weapons, and reduce by 50 per cent their existing nuclear arsenals, including all types of inter-continental, medium-range and other tactical nuclear weapons as well as their means of delivery according to a reasonable proportion and procedure to be agreed upon' (Government of PRC 1982).

[108] Manning et al. 2000.

[109] In this scenario, they suggest that China would be motivated to 'stay in the game' but not make the investments to do anything more than a modest modernisation. Therefore, China will not build more nuclear warheads or substantially increase its missile force. For the theatre force, there would be continued heavy reliance on conventionally tipped missiles (ibid.).

[110] In this scenario, China would be motivated to compete more effectively with the deployment of defence by the United States. It would increase the number of ICBMs and their effectiveness in penetrating defence with the goal of ensuring that 20 warheads get through, whatever defence is deployed by the United States.

[111] In this scenario, China would be motivated primarily by the desire to stay ahead of India and other proliferators in Asia, real or potential, and move towards more robust limited deterrence strategies at the theatre level with primary nuclear forces. At the global level, China would remain committed to minimum deterrence, but would refrain from making substantial new investments in a more robust force.

[112] In this scenario, the strategy would be guided by the principle of limited deterrence, but not extended nuclear war fighting. Broad enhancements to all aspects of the force would be pursued and fielded, including further progress in developing all legs of a triad, advanced penetration aids, an increase in the percentage of nuclear warheads in the overall force mix, and some MIRVing.

[113] In this scenario, China would be motivated to field a very robust force as part of a political strategy to signal its ascendance over Russia, its leading role in Asia, and its equal footing with America in the world scene. This scenario sees a

In the next decade or so, China would take any of the options—either only make modest investments in its nuclear force and continue a policy of minimum deterrence, or even try to fill the vacuum left by the Soviet Union, and at least in warhead count try and seek parity with the US. One of the key variables in Chinese behaviour in the next decade or so will be the US national missile defence and theatre missile defence. As of now, China seems to be investing modest amounts in its nuclear and conventional force modernisation. At the same, it might maintain minimum deterrence as the doctrinal posture.

Whatever path China may take, it should keep in mind that even a small increase in force levels or warheads will make India follow suit. This will further give Pakistan a justification for increasing its missiles and warheads. Thus, China can contribute to regional stability by keeping its force levels at a minimum, not modernising further and engaging the US and Russia in talks for warheads reduction. This would then have implications for the Indian nuclear deterrent posture.

✠ DOCTRINE, STRATEGY AND FORCE MODERNISATION

China's overarching security strategy in the 21st century is governed by its experiences during the 'century of humiliation'.[114] Beijing's political and military elites view the period between the first Opium War and the communist victory over the Kuomintang in 1949 as the time when China lost control of its own destiny to the imperial powers of Britain, Japan, France, Germany, Russia and the United States.[115] This history has passed on to China's political and military elite a strategic view that enshrines freedom from fear of domination by hostile powers as the core of national security strategy.[116] This period has also been analysed at the symptomatic level, seeking institutional and technological changes in dealing with foreigners to make China stronger.

---

substantial increase in the number of ICBMs, perhaps also an SLBM and nuclear cruise missile force, and heavy emphasis on MIRVs. Presumably, the desire for such a force may lead China to seek parity with the United States and Russia.

[114] Godwin and Schulz 1994: 7.
[115] Ibid.: 7.
[116] Ibid.: 7.

Since 1949, one can locate two major changes in the Chinese notion of security. The first was in 1949 itself, when Mao made a break with the 'feudal' past in order to establish the People's Republic of China as the dictatorship of the proletariat. Deng Xiaoping primarily affected the second change, the modernisation project, marking a departure from the Maoist legacy. The major national goal of China under Mao Tse-tung was the construction of a socialist state that worked in close conformity with a Marxist–Leninist ideology that was complemented by the practical ideology of Mao Tse-tung. The post-Mao open door policy was mainly the result of an ideological shift within the Communist Party of China (CPC). Strategies of development were renamed in terms of economic development and modernisation. There was a renewed emphasis on modernisation, as political rigidity was tempered with economic pragmatism. Politics was still very much in command and the party firmly entrenched. This reflected the resistance to alter the philosophical basis of society, while encouraging greater economic and technological development to make China stronger.

Chinese nuclear and doctrinal strategic culture was influenced a great deal by the wartime experience of the Chinese communist leadership, especially during the Chinese civil war (1927–49), as also by the war against the Japanese (1937–45). These, as Mao Tse-tung said, were successes of 'people's war' that emphasised guerrilla tactics within an overall strategy of protracted war, the importance of manpower over technology, the moral and physical attrition of the enemy over time, and the importance of controlling the strategic hinterland to surround the enemy's base in the main cities. On protracted war, Mao said,

Our strategy should be to employ our main forces to operate over extended and fluid front[s]. To achieve success, the Chinese troops must conduct their warfare with a high degree of mobility on extensive battlefields, making swift advances and withdrawals, swift concentrations and dispersals. This means large scale mobile warfare, not positional warfare depending exclusively on defence works with deep trenches, high fortresses and successive rows of defensive positions. It does not mean the abandonment of all the vital strategic points, which should be defended by positional warfare as long as profitable.[117]

---

[117] Mao Tse-tung 1994.

In nuclear doctrinal terms, this translated into (a) opposition to quick or pre-emptive military actions from a position of weakness; (b) an appreciation for 'strategic retreat' and the primacy of defence in the interest of eventual victory; (c) a subordination of a strictly military viewpoint to the political-military goals of the revolution; and (d) the ultimate superiority of man over weapons and technology.[118]

As dismissed earlier, Mao was influenced to a very great extent by Chinese classical texts on strategy, in particular, the work of Sun Tzu (*Art of War*).[119] Some of the more cited interpretations of this has been the largely defensive and non-violent nature of Chinese strategic thought: 'To win one hundred victories in one hundred battles is not the acme of skill. To subdue the enemy without fighting is the acme of skill'. Psychological warfare and deception are often considered cornerstones of traditional Chinese strategic thinking.[120] The larger context of Confucianism, the most dominant philosophy of statecraft in Chinese history, stressing abjuring violence and assuring order through moral—rather than strictly military—strength, also influences strategic thought.

In keeping with Mao's thoughts, the nature and role of the army have been changing with new objective conditions. The Chinese defence paper issued in 1998 states, 'China unswervingly pursues a national defence policy that is defensive in nature, *keeps national defence construction in a position subordinate to and in the service of the nation's economic reconstruction*, strengthens international and regional security and actively participates in the international arms control and disarmament process' (emphasis added).[121] It states that the PLA 'strengthens itself by relying on science and technology and strives to make the transition from a numerically superior type to a qualitatively superior type and from manpower intensive to technology intensive type.'[122] The tasks of the army have been identified as 'being to consolidate national defence, resist aggression, defend the motherland, *safeguard the people's peaceful labor,*

---

[118] See Hsieh 1962: chs 1–2 and Chong-pin Lin 1988.

[119] In particular, in 'Strategic Problems of China's Revolutionary War', 'On Protracted War', and 'On Guerrilla Warfare', there is a shadow of Sun on Mao's thought. See Mao Tse-tung 1967.

[120] See in this context, Johnston 1995.

[121] State Council, PRC 1998.

[122] Ibid.

participate in national construction and strive to serve the people' (emphasis added).[123]

Technology will remain a crucial element of the process of modernisation. If the PLA has to conduct war in the manner that it desires, then effective joint operations, command and control, early warning, surveillance and target acquisition that utilise advance technologies will be needed.[124] China realises that there will be no external funding for this and that it has to raise the money internally. Paul Godwin contends that 'defense industries could also benefit in that, when integrated into operational requirements, high priority weapon systems, such as tactical battlefield missiles, multiple-role combat aircraft, cruise missiles, combat, support and amphibious warfare ships, promise a steady production line.'[125]

Recent research has shown that 'military involvement is evident in all four security policy sub arenas,[126] albeit to widely varying degrees, ranging from near-total control over defence policy to limited but significant influence over foreign policy.'[127] James Mulvenon says that the military is an important actor in all phases of national security policy making, as well as including assessment, planning and implementation.[128] The overall impact of this military involvement, he says, is 'more indirect than direct: primarily the military performs a critical "shaping role" in national security policymaking with episodic attempts at intervention.'[129]

Since the Lop Nur test in 1964, when China became a declared nuclear power, it has never publicly discussed its nuclear doctrine. As Johnston put it, 'for about 30 years after China exploded its first nuclear weapon there was no coherent, publicly articulated nuclear doctrine.'[130] The only openly stated position then was that these weapons were to prevent blackmail and coercion by the other nuclear powers, principally, the US and then the Soviet Union. China's nuclear strategy has never been as explicitly stated as those

---

[123] Ibid.

[124] In this context, see Lilley and Shambaugh 1999.

[125] Godwin 1999: 61. See also Yao Yunzhu 1995.

[126] These are: national security objectives, foreign policy, intelligence, defence policy and strategic research analysis.

[127] Swaine 1996: x.

[128] Mulvenon 2001: 325.

[129] Ibid.: 325.

[130] Johnston 1996a: 552.

of some other countries. But it is believed that China has the following five objectives for its nuclear strategy: (*a*) secure superpower status; (*b*) preclude the possibility of intrusive diplomacy through nuclear coercion; (*c*) deter other nuclear regimes (such as breakaway states from the former Soviet Union); (*d*) retain a trump card for the eventuality that Japan may rescind its current pacifist policies for a military option; and (*e*) maintain political and moral ascendancy over its regional rivals (such as India). The small number of nuclear weapons in the Chinese military limits the ability to have a counter-force strategy. Consequently, the Chinese have adopted a strategy of minimum deterrence. As the October 2000 white paper on national defence says:

> From the first day it possessed nuclear weapons, China has solemnly declared its determination not to be the first to use such weapons at any time and in any circumstances, and later undertook unconditionally not to use or threaten to use nuclear weapons against non-nuclear-weapon states or nuclear-weapon-free zones.[131]

China did some moral posturing in the 2002 defence white paper: 'China holds that countries having the largest nuclear arsenals bear a special and primary responsibility toward nuclear disarmament, and that they should take the lead in drastically reducing their nuclear arsenals and destroy the reduced nuclear weapons.'[132]

Ever since the early 1990s, the main focus of Chinese military strategy has been preparing for potential military contingencies along China's south-eastern flank, specifically the Taiwan Strait. The PLA strategy has emphasised capabilities that counter regional threats, and if required, cater to a global fallout. The PLA has sought to prepare a strike capability to rapidly deploy and win a regional war under high-tech conditions around China's periphery. This has been necessitated by the need to defend against any regional adversary, maintain the credibility of territorial claims, protect national interests, maintain internal security, deter any moves by Taiwan toward *de jure* independence, and deter aggression.

---

[131] See State Council, PRC 2000a: ch. 5.
[132] State Council, PRC 2002.

On the face of it, China is downsizing its armed forces, but the manpower reduction is actually restructuring the PLA into a military force that will comprise three main components, particularly preparing for a local war under high-tech conditions: (*a*) a small number of high technology forces for flexible use in localised conflicts; (*b*) a larger number of forces that remain equipped with medium technology weapons primarily for internal security; and (*c*) a modest nuclear force that continues to maintain a viable deterrent against other nuclear powers.

This strategic shift in the PLA started taking place over a decade ago, when the focus shifted from the protracted, large-scale land warfare (Mao's 'people's war') to building capability to fight small-scale, regional conflicts along China's periphery. China's 'active defence' doctrine, christened 'people's war under modern conditions', is better portrayed as 'local wars under hi-tech conditions' with a strong component of the nuclear angle, and at its core being nuclear deterrence.

The Chinese leadership had, by the mid-1980s, come to the conclusion that the risk of a major invasion had passed, and China's People's Liberation Army was redirected towards preparations for a smaller-scale 'local war'. Unlike 'people's war', the military demands of a local war place a premium on the PLA's ability to gain the initiative at the earliest stage of the conflict, possibly through pre-emption. China's military strategy, therefore, is much more suited now to diplomatic strategies that call for 'the opportunistic or demonstrative use of force to further Chinese foreign policy interests.'[133]

This change has also been reflected in the white paper on China's national defence in 2002. It affirms,

> In response to the profound changes in the world's military field and the requirements of the national development strategy, China has formulated a military strategic guideline of active defence in the new period. This guideline is based on winning local wars under modern, especially high-tech conditions.[134]

---

[133] Burles and Shulsky 2000: vii–viii.

[134] It further said, 'In view of the various factors threatening national security, China has prepared for defensive operation under the most difficult and complex circumstances. The People's Liberation Army (PLA), in implementing the strategy of building a strong military through science and technology, has accelerated

Paul Godwin and John J. Schulz point out that China's overall deterrence strategy is designed to preclude nuclear blackmail. The idea is to create a counter-value (city-busting) deterrent of sufficient size and range to guarantee that no enemy planner could use nuclear force, or threaten to use it, without the certain knowledge of Chinese retaliation at a level sufficient to make the costs too high.[135] Recognising that their nuclear forces cannot compete with the superpowers in either numerical or technological terms (for instance accuracy), China must rely on raising the costs to a nuclear aggressor by ensuring that its own force has a survivable retaliatory capability. This deterrent strategy requires that the Chinese give the perception, real or unreal, to potential nuclear aggressors that they have the will to use nuclear force, the forces can survive a first strike, a second strike is probable, and there is a command and control apparatus in place for rapid retaliatory execution. This nuclear deterrent is advertised, but the operational employment of these nuclear forces is not. This is an important principle that deserves to be emphasised: deterrence strategies need to be advertised, whereas strategy for use (or operational strategy) under people's war requirements depends on withholding intelligence as to one's true intentions and places a high value on deception.[136]

In an effort to improve credibility and a survivable retaliatory capability of their nuclear arsenal, the Chinese emphasise mobility and pre–launch survivability.[137] The means to accomplish this goal are rooted in Chinese military art of war. Sun Tzu put forth an aphorism, well cited throughout Chinese military history: 'The essence of warfare is but the art of ambiguity.'[138] Sun Tzu also stated that 'Warfare is a matter of deception—of constantly creating false appearances, spreading disinformation, and employing trickery and deceit.'[139] To affect ambiguity in perception, routine concealment

the R&D of defense weaponry and equipment, trained high-quality military personnel of a new type, established a scientific organizational structure, developed theories for military operations with Chinese characteristics, and strengthened its capability for joint, mobile and multi-purpose operations' (State Council, PRC 2002: ch. 7).

[135] Godwin and Schulz 1993: 6.
[136] Rosita 1990.
[137] Lewis and Hua Di 1992.
[138] Chong-pin Lin 1988: 21.
[139] Sawyer 1993: 155.

is punctuated with selective and deliberate revelation.[140] China's land-based missile force is characterised by its mode of deployment: dispersal, concealment and mobility. The missiles are well concealed in man-made and natural caves amidst high mountains up to 15,000 feet above sea level, in deep gorges along the Yangtze River, and under the cover of thick tropical forestry in careful camouflage.[141] Occasionally, missiles are deliberately exposed to orbiting satellites or pictures are published in defence magazines.[142] Ambiguity is also enhanced by redundant revelation. One example is the PRC protection of its nuclear weapons testing base in Lop Nur against the reconnaissance of superpower satellites by the construction of six identical-looking bases in the area.[143] Historically, China has called upon other nuclear weapons states to give up their policy of nuclear deterrence. In June 1994, the Chinese Foreign Ministry issued a statement calling for the 'nuclear-weapon States to give up their policy of nuclear deterrence and commit themselves explicitly to the complete prohibition and total destruction of nuclear weapons.'[144]

Going by the limitations that China has imposed on itself, it is likely to follow a retaliation strategy with a delayed second strike. This implies that China will retaliate after absorbing a nuclear strike, rather than a 'launch under attack' or a 'launch on warning' posture. Some of the recent research seems to suggest that Chinese strategists are considering shifting their doctrine from *minimum* to *limited* deterrence. It is likely that China possesses a more sophisticated nuclear force structure capable of *restricting* nuclear escalation during the early stages of a conflict. This reflects a change from war-deterring capability to war-fighting capability. For this to take place in the next decade or so, Chinese nuclear forces would have to be geared up for such a role. This shift to limited deterrence would require nuclear forces that are much more advanced.

'Limited deterrence' necessitates the capability to deter conventional, theatre and strategic nuclear war, and to restrain escalation in the event of a nuclear confrontation. PLA understands that 'in

---

[140] Chong-pin Lin 1988: 69.
[141] Ibid.: 52.
[142] Ibid.: 69.
[143] Ibid.: 62.
[144] Foreign Ministry, Government of PRC 1994.

future high-tech local wars, the struggle between nuclear deterrence and counter nuclear deterrence will be even more complex.'[145]

China's development of MRV and MIRV technology, and the efforts to miniaturise its nuclear warheads, are clearly linked to US ambitions of fielding a BMD in North-east Asia. China is also developing penetration aids in addition to MRV/MIRV technology. A classified National Air Intelligence Centre report revealed that during the 1999 test of DF-31 missiles, an undetermined number of decoys decoupled from the primary warhead and 'spread out in different directions when the payload reached space.'[146] A September 1999 National Intelligence Council document concluded that 'China has had the capability to develop and deploy a multiple re-entry vehicle system for many years, including a MIRV system.'[147] China is modernising all legs of its nuclear triad: ballistic and cruise missiles, ballistic missile submarines and strategic bombers. A vast majority of China's nuclear-capable missile force remains land based. China has three ballistic missiles under development: the land-based DF-31and the DF-41 and the sea launched JL-2. The DF-31 and DF-41 are both road-mobile, solid-fuelled missiles and have launch preparation times of less than 15 minutes and 5 minutes, respectively. Much of China's nuclear delivery system modernisation has been in this area. The DF-31, DF-41 and JL-2 will also likely employ GPS for improved accuracy.[148] In addition to ballistic missiles, China is also developing land attack cruise missiles for theatre war fighting and strategic attack. China has been cooperating with Russia on the design and construction of cruise missiles.[149] It has stated that it has built two Xia-class ship submersible ballistic nuclear (SSBN) propellors, each of which can carry 12 JL-1 SLBMs. However, there are contradicting reports on their actual deployment. The 1999 National Intelligence Council report has estimated that the JL-2 is expected

---

[145] Wu Jianguo 1998: 145.

[146] Gertz 1999.

[147] National Intelligence Council 1999: 11.

[148] On 19 January 2000, Russian Deputy Prime Minister, Ilya Klebanov, announced that Russia and China were close to reaching an agreement on the bilateral use of Russia's GLONASS satellite-based global positioning system (GPS). This would enable China to be independent of the US GPS system, which is likely to be turned off by the US in the event of any crisis. See Pomfret 2000: A17.

[149] *Aviation Week and Space Technology* 1993.

to be tested within the next decade.[150] China is also in the process of developing its first indigenously produced fighter-bomber, the H-7. The H-7 was flight tested in 1988 and has the capability to deliver a 10 kT—3 MT nuclear bomb.[151]

C4I

Not much is known about China's command and control, as information continues to remain scarce. It is widely understood that the final authority to use nuclear weapons in any given situation rests with the chairman of the Central Military Commission, after the top leaders have reached a consensus. Such a decision might also require the Central Military Commission and other senior military officials to reach a consensus.

The Second Artillery Corps (SAC) is tasked with implementing the reliable and secure command and control of China's nuclear and conventional missile forces.[152] The SAC was established on 1 July 1966 under the direction of Chou En-lai as a result of a merger between the former headquarters of the Ministry of Public Security and the Central Military Special Artillery Corps (CMSAC); it maintains control over China's nuclear and conventional strategic missile forces, consisting of short-, medium-, long- and intercontinental-range ballistic missiles. One of the battalions of the CMSAC launched its first missile in October 1963.[153] The SAC as it exists now comprises approximately 90,000 personnel and six ballistic missile bases,[154] and maintains control of over 100 nuclear warheads.[155] It receives 12 to 15 per cent of the defence budget and about 20 per cent of the total procurement budget. When the PLA cut 1 million personnel in the 1980s, SAC ranks actually increased.[156]

The SAC happens to be a separate service arm, and it remains distinct from the army, navy and air force. Xishan, in the hills west of Beijing, where strategic operational orders originate, is the central

---

[150] National Intelligence Council 1999.
[151] See in this context, Norris 1996; Chong-pin Lin 1995; SIPRI 1990–2002, here 1995–2000; Godwin and Schulz 1993; Arnett 1996; Lennox 1996; Gupta 1994; and Lewis and Xue Litai 1994.
[152] This section relies on Stokes 1999.
[153] Xu Zuzhi 1999.
[154] Stokes 1999: 93.
[155] Office of the Secretary of Defense 1997.
[156] You Ji 1999.

command and control centre for all Chinese forces, including SAC. A sort of direct communication that bypasses China's military region commands and connects directly to base commands, is passed through to the SAC headquarters and its communications regiment. The base commands, in turn, communicate with their respective launch brigades.

There is very little information available on the technical aspects of Chinese nuclear C4I, as open source of information is scarce. In recent years, however, reports have surfaced that describe various new technologies and systems that have helped strengthen China's command and control system. These could be in the nature of 'leaks' or 'technology revelations'. One such 'leak' has reportedly suggested that the past level of command and control structures was not particularly advanced.[157] It further noted that the SAC 'after three years of arduous work' developed a new digital microwave communications system that allowed secure 'all-weather' communication for missile launch.[158] The Pentagon, however, continues to believe that 'China has made significant efforts to modernize and improve its command, control, communications, computers, and intelligence infrastructure.'[159] Given the primacy of nuclear weapons in the Chinese security calculus, one can safely assume that similar advances in C4I modernisation have occurred in the strategic rocket forces.

Force Modernisation

China continues a huge programme of modernisation of its nuclear forces, including improved mobility, reliability, accuracy and firepower, leaving analysts compelled to understand the Second Artillery more precisely, including its evolving doctrine, organisation and hardware, and their implications for international security.

The white paper on national defence, 2002 says, 'At the turn of the century, an important historical period, China is devoting itself to its modernization drive. China needs and cherishes dearly an environment of long-term international peace, especially a favourable peripheral environment.'[160] China is pursuing a long-term

---

[157] *People's Liberation Army Daily* 1998.
[158] Ibid.
[159] Department of Defense, US 1997a.
[160] State Council, PRC 2002: ch. 7.

military modernisation strategy that develops a power projection capability. Modernisation efforts are particularly strong towards improving the PLAN and PLAAF. Of course, the main driving force behind these modernisation efforts is the People's Liberation Army. There are many reasons for China's force modernisation. Primary among them is the desire of the PLA to address the problem of obsolete and antiquated military hardware. Among the other concerns are China's ability to cope with a variety of largely post-Cold War threats, both in and around China's periphery. Michael Swaine and Ashley Tellis view this modernisation drive as a part of its current 'calculative' strategy to sustain an expanded level of political and operational objectives.[161] According to them, these objectives include:

(*a*) securing the defence of Chinese sovereignty and national territory against threat or attacks from all manner of opponents, including highly sophisticated military forces; (*b*) acquiring the ability to counter or neutralise a range of potential short, medium and long term security threat along China's entire periphery, but especially in maritime areas; (*c*) acquiring the ability to use military power as a more potent and versatile instrument of armed diplomacy and statecraft in support of a complex set of regional and global policies; (*d*) eventually developing the power projection and extended territorial defence capabilities commensurate with the true great power status expected in the 21st century.[162]

It was during the 1970s and 1980s that China began developing lower-yield nuclear weapons and also proceeded with multimegatonne warheads. This suggests that China was also developing tactical nuclear weapons. The tests from September 1977 to October 1980 all produced yield less than 20 kT, and in 1983 the PLA published a manual that explained the different types and functions of tactical weapons.[163] The nuclear tests that were conducted in the late 1980s and the early 1990s were further geared towards modernising China's nuclear forces.

---

[161] Swaine and Tellis 2000.

[162] Ibid.: 121. See also in this regard, Shambaugh and Yang 1997.

[163] From the online database of the Center for Nonproliferation Studies, available at http://www.cns.miis.edu, accessed on 17 December 2002.

While China officially declared in 1994 that these tests were for improving safety features on existing warheads, these were also intended for the development of new, smaller warheads for China's next-generation solid-fuel ICBMs (like DF-31 and DF-41).[164] The DF-31 has a range of 8,000 km, and was first tested on 2 August 1999 and again in November 2000. The DF-31 is likely to replace the DF-4. Also under development is the Julang (JL)-2 sea-based version of the DF-31, although that may not be deployed until 2010. At this stage it is unclear whether China will have a new ballistic missile submarine for these missiles.[165] Additionally, it is possible that China might use the Russian GLONASS satellite-based global positioning system which would decrease the Chinese reliance on the US GPS system.[166] It is also likely that 'Russia could provide or China could develop, technology that would enable the missiles to deliver a Chinese nuclear warhead.'[167] A new nuclear submarine, the 09-4, may also be under development, with deployment only likely some time in the future. It has been reported that Russia is providing China with assistance in building its second generation of nuclear submarines.[168] In an effort to strengthen the air force, China's first indigenously produced fighter-bomber, the H-7, which was flight-tested in 1988 and has the capability to deliver a 10 kT–3 MT nuclear bomb, is also being developed. A modest number is being built, although production problems may delay early deployment.[169]

China's nuclear modernisation programme may be geared towards developing the capability and capacity to move from a minimum deterrence to a limited deterrence nuclear strategy. This encompasses the capability to deter conventional, theatre and strategic nuclear war and escalation control, in the event of a nuclear crisis. Theoretically, China would feel the need to have both counter-value and counter-force targeting, which would require very extensive deployment for credibility reasons. This may still be some decades away. But this process is likely to be gaining momentum

---

[164] The DF-31 and DF-41 are both expected to be road-mobile, solid-fuel missiles and have short launch preparation times.

[165] Lennox 1999; Walpole 2000.

[166] Zhang Yihong 1999.

[167] Lennox 1999: 23.

[168] Norris 1996; Godwin and Schulz 1993.

[169] Norris 1996.

with impact of the US insistence to go ahead with the BMD. The PLA is becoming more concerned with protecting institutional interests and pushing for force modernisation issues, besides having an increased mandate on the maintenance of domestic order. This would have serious strategic implications for the Indian nuclear deterrent posture. The Indian defence establishment has been observing this development for a long time. The gradual process of force modernisation is now also a feature of the Indian defence forces and the Chinese force modernisation is one of the chief drivers of this process.

✦ Foreign Policy Issues

Mark Mancall places the interpretation of Chinese foreign relations in context. According to him, China's foreign relations continue to remain an interaction 'not between different powers but between different worlds, each organised according to its own principles and perceiving the other in terms of the only reality it can know, itself.' Elsewhere he says,

> China's sense of its own civilisation did not include an aggressive mission to either civilise the rest of the world or to shoulder its burdens; the Chinese did not feel the need to bring the blessings of their technology, religious or governmental system to other peoples. When other peoples adopted and adapted elements of Chinese culture, they did so for reasons of their own and the Chinese were always welcoming to those who wished to transform themselves into members of 'civilisation'.[170]

John King Fairbank dismissed the Chinese world order as 'traditional', thereby laying the foundation of similar theorising for an entire generation of Western scholars.[171] Taking Fairbank's view further, Samuel S. Kim posits that the traditional Chinese world

---

[170] Mancall 1984.

[171] He concluded that this was not useful in interpreting contemporary Chinese foreign policy. Fairbank has argued that traditional Chinese world order can hardly be called international, since 'the participants in it did not use concepts corresponding to the Western ideas of nation, sovereignty, or equality of states each having equal sovereignty.' See Fairbank 1968: 5–9.

order has suffered a disjoint between policy pronouncement and policy performance.[172] Culture has been one of the key influences on the foreign policy choices that China makes. According to Jing Dong-Yuan, 'pre-modern Chinese history displays a blend of both the ideational, non violent and the *realpolitik*, violent approaches to external relations.'[173] As Kim opines, China lacked a dynamic and aggressive imperative to expand and impose its will upon re-calcitrant non-Chinese states.[174]

The Chinese worldview has not altered into military imperialism from dynastic rule to communist times. China explicitly recog-nises the concept of political sovereignty in the Five Principles of Peaceful Coexistence which have remained the basis of Chinese foreign policy. China has formally rejected seeking hegemony and extending its security interests beyond its borders and has not participated in creating any 'strategic balance' on the grounds that the concepts lead to interference in the internal affairs of other countries.[175] Second, contrary to Western international relations theory constructs, China does not essentially consider international cooperation as the preferred approach to world peace.[176] A reflec-tion of this is the Chinese participation in international arms con-trol and economic integration treaties. China did not endeavour for global agreement on international norms and structures to promote international interaction. In fact, the peculiarity of the Chinese approach towards foreign relations has been not to solve problems but to prevent problems from arising in the first place. 'Consequently, unique institutions and practices were developed to control what contact was deemed essential to implementing this policy.'[177] China has developed a system of conducting its foreign relations that is the institutional expression of its social ideology, with philosophical inputs from Confucius, Mencius and the Legalists.

---

[172] This phenomenon, according to him, may be explained with the help of the Chinese image of the world which is more rich in cultural symbolism than in political dynamics, more passive than active, believed to be more defensive than imperialist and more rhetorical than real (Kim 1979).

[173] Jing Dong-Yuan 1998.

[174] Kim 1979: 45.

[175] Yimin Song 1986.

[176] It is possible that with the entry of China in the World Trade Organisation, this view might have started changing.

[177] Mancall 1984: xiii.

Even in the conduct of its foreign relations, China's increasing reliance on foreign markets, maritime trade routes and energy supplies have contributed to a growing sense of strategic vulnerability, as it takes the control of events beyond China's borders. This implies that the external environment, to a great extent, will determine the degree to which China will be able to attain its key political power goals and a sphere of strategic influence.

The Sixteenth Communist Party of China (CPC) Congress, adopting the report of the Fifteenth CPC Central Committee, passed a resolution saying,

> The Congress agrees with the report on its analysis of the international situation and all the principles it puts forth for the external work, stressing the need to pursue the independent foreign policy of peace and work with all nations to safeguard the common interests of mankind, boost world multipolarization, oppose all forms of hegemonism and power politics, and advance the lofty cause of world peace and development.[178]

Various factors like values, preferences, history and culture influence the crucial foreign policy choices that Chinese policy makers make. Of course, Chinese communist leaders persist in proclaiming 'Marxist–Leninist–Maoist thought' as the ideological foundation of their state, but this is by no means fixed or static. It is continuously being reinterpreted by the CPC leadership to cater to its current needs. Lucian Pye in his analysis of Chinese pragmatism says that this is the anthropologist's notion of culture as ideology.[179] Chinese foreign policy is the praxis of ideological reinterpretation. Although written in a different context, but quite applicable to China, Michael Hunt has argued that informal ideology is a powerful variable in deciding the choices in foreign policy. He says,

> A foreign policy ideology that is carefully manufactured, neatly packaged, widely advertised, and readily available off the shelf is not necessarily more genuine or more influential. In fact the case could be made that ideologies assume formal explicit, systematic form precisely because there is resistance to them within the culture,

---

[178] Communist Party of China 2002.
[179] Pye 1988.

whereas ideology left implicit rests on a consensus and therefore exercises a greater (if more subtle) power.[180]

But then not all authors have stated ideology to be one of the pillars of Chinese foreign policy. For instance, Doak Barnett has ignored ideology completely.[181] On the other hand, there is a view that the role of ideology is decreasing in the formulation of Chinese foreign policy.

Soon after independence, the goals of Chinese foreign policy were to support the national liberation struggle in the colonial world, to oppose imperialism and to promote nuclear disarmament. This clearly laid the foundation for ideology to play a dominating role in foreign policy choices. Gradually, with changes in the international system, the non-aligned states also started playing a part, thus proving that ideology is not the only important pillar on which foreign policy can be based. As Steven Levine has perceptively noted, 'while its identity-defining dimension remained formal, ideology gradually ceased functioning as a guide to action in the foreign policy arena and was increasingly transformed into a set of abstract principles and behavioural norms used to criticise the conduct of other states.'[182] In his conclusion, he notes, 'the PRC appears to acquire what might be called a "minimum ideological framework" whose precise content varies considerably over time, but which, to the satisfaction at least of the Chinese elite, integrates the desperate strands of foreign policy.'[183]

There was a change in some of the principles that guided Chinese foreign policy. Part of the change can be located in the interaction of Nehru with Chou En-lai that led to the Panchsheel principles discussed earlier. The central premises of the Chinese foreign policy are based on principles very similar to these. Besides, during the Cold War, China realised that it should not have a close affinity with either of the superpowers. A factor affecting this decision was Moscow's initial refusal to assist China in gaining control over the Nationalist-held strongholds during the 1958 Taiwan Straits crisis, when China began shelling the off-shore Nationalist-held

---

[180] Hunt 1987: 14.
[181] See Barnett 1985.
[182] Levine 1994: 39.
[183] Ibid.: 39.

islands of Jinmen and Matzu.[184] The other factor was the Brezhnev Doctrine, wherein Moscow reserved the right to use force against 'recalcitrant socialist states.'[185]

What then is the role that China sees for itself in a world that has remained bipolar for close to four decades and is arguably unipolar and in transition now as well as increasingly interdependent and interactive? As one of the permanent five, its voice cannot be ignored in the process of conflict management, be it economic, military, social or demographic concerns. For this study, China's relations with the US, India and Pakistan will be examined.

SINO-US RELATIONS

For nearly 20 years after 1949, no American politician dared to speak openly about the relations between Washington and the People's Republic of China.[186] The Korean War, McCarthyism, a Sino-Soviet alliance, China's development of an atomic bomb, the war in Vietnam and the Cultural Revolution combined to make American leaders distrust their own countrymen as well as the Chinese.[187]

The 1968 Soviet invasion of Czechoslovakia led to the Brezhnev doctrine and the 1969 Sino-Soviet Ussuri river clashes, followed by American presence in Vietnam, which prompted a period of rapprochement in 1971–72.[188] Henry Kissinger wrote about his secret visit to China, 'When we completed drafting the communiqué announcing my secret visit to China in July 1971, Chou Enlai remarked that the announcement would shake the world. He was right.'[189]

However, US President Richard Nixon's views on China had always been more pragmatic than ideological.[190] Nixon's views regarding China, much before his becoming the president can be gathered from one of the most quoted articles that he wrote in

[184] Tow 1994.
[185] Ibid.
[186] Schulzinger 1989.
[187] cf. ibid.: 79.
[188] Besides the Nixon and Kissinger memories, see in this context, Pollack 1992.
[189] Kissinger 1979: 163.
[190] Hersh 1983.

Foreign Affairs in 1967. In that article Nixon wrote, 'Some counsel conceding to China a "sphere of influence" embracing much of the Asian mainland and extending even to the island nations beyond; others urge that we eliminate the threat by pre-emptive war.'[191]

In the aftermath of the 1965 Indo-Pak war, the United States decided to involve itself less in the South Asian region. Three factors were mainly responsible for this shift. The first was the growing détente between the US and the former Soviet Union. The second was the deep American involvement in the Vietnam War. The third factor was the result of the first two factors—the US found none of its strategic interests at stake during this period in South Asia. Whether or not China desired it, soon it came to be associated with a global power status.[192] In the early 1980s, leading Chinese think tanks and experts began suggesting a shift in China's strategic distance from the US.[193] After 1984, China started improving its relations with the US. As David Shambaugh noted, 'In the Chinese estimation, genuine superpower détente could contribute positively to a peaceful environment in East Asia which in turn was necessary for China's development during the Seventh Five-year plan period.'[194] Both domestic factors—the Tiananmen Square—and international factors—the break-up of the Soviet Union—led to sharp downslide in China's relations with the Western world. More factors contributed to security challenges for China—the break-up of the Soviet Union, the Warsaw Treaty organisation, the growing culture of Islamic fundamentalism in Central Asian republics and the Arabic world, a resurgent US after the Gulf War, and a large US military presence in Central Asia following the Afghan campaign.[195] Also at the systemic level was the process of

---

[191] He further adds, 'Clearly, neither of these courses would be acceptable to the United States or to its Asian allies …. For the short run, then this means a policy of firm restraint, of no reward, of a creative counter pressure designed to persuade Peking that its interests can be served only by accepting the basic rules of international civility. For the long run, it means pulling China back into the world community—but as a great and progressing nation, not as the epicentre of world revolution. In the long view, we can not afford to leave China forever outside the family of nations, there to nurture its fantasies, cherish its hates and threaten its neighbours' (Nixon 1967).

[192] Pollack 1980.

[193] Ross 1991.

[194] Shambaugh 1994: 204–5.

[195] See in this context, Lampton 2001.

globalisation that was fast reducing economic borders between states.

In the 1990s yet again, there were various discordant notes between the two countries. The US condemned China for violating arms limitation agreements, human rights and for engaging in unfair trade practices. Policy makers in the US Congress in the 1990s consistently focused on suspected Chinese transfer of sensitive technology to Pakistan and Iran. Since 1992, China, in view of the change in world order that led to the emergence of the US as the sole superpower, sought to alter its image. In 1992 it agreed to abide by the Missile Technology Control Regime (MTCR); in March 1992 it acceded to the NPT; in January 1993 came the signing and subsequent ratification; in October 1994 there were statements on MTCR and fissile material production; in November 1995 the white paper on arms control and disarmament was written; in May 1996 China made the statement on making only safeguarded nuclear transfers; in July 1996 came the announcement on moratorium on nuclear testing; the CTBT signing followed this in 1996 September; in October 1997 China became a member of the Zangger Committee; in August–October China released a series of export control regulations on NBC materials; and in November 2002 China released another white paper on national defence.

Meanwhile, the US policy was shifting from that of containment to engagement seeking to improve bilateral relations. As the US was trying to engage China—trying to increase interaction—it was also aware that China was not adhering to various global non-proliferation norms. In June 1997, the director of central intelligence submitted a report to Congress stating that during July–December 1996, 'China was the most significant supplier of WMD-related goods and technology to foreign countries ... there is no question that China has contributed to WMD advances' in Pakistan and Iran.[196] In early 1996, the Congress called for sanctions after there were reports of Chinese sale of 5,000 ring magnets, apparently in violation of the NPT and the US laws, including the Arms Export Control Act and the Export Import Bank Act (as amended by the Nuclear Proliferation Prevention Act of 1994). The US imposed sanction on the China National Nuclear Corporation. Sanctions continue to be a 'feel good' policy and are toothless and have no

---

[196] Kan 1998.

effect. Clandestine help to Pakistan's nuclear and missile programme continued. 'The Defence Secretary's Report' of November 1997 stated that 'China remains Pakistan's principal supplier of missile related technology and assistance.'[197] The defence secretary's report further stated that in April 1996 Iranis purchased an electro-magnetic isotope separation unit from China.[198] Citing the *International Herald Tribune*, the CRS report, further adds that '[t]he CIA reportedly found that China delivered dozens or perhaps hundreds of missile guidelines systems and computerised machine tools to Iran sometime between mid-1994 and 1995.'[199]

Core American interests of protecting the painstakingly crafted non-proliferation regime have been damaged to some extent by the Chinese. Yet, economic sense dictates American access to the Chinese market. In the 1990s, the US followed a policy of engaging China, trying to make it a member of as many international regimes from Kyoto Protocol to NPT to WTO. But the fact remains that China also participated in regimes where the costs of a unilateral defection remained high, a case in point being the CTBT. The main contemporary issues facing the two nations include Taiwan, WTO, human rights and safeguarding against piracy. The US often cites its commitments with Taiwan for an increased presence in the Asia-Pacific. But the question still remains, will the US permit use of force over the settlement of the Taiwan issue?

US plans to make a BMD or NMD have upset China and Beijing considers these plans as threatening. The main US motive behind these is defence for the whole US against a small number of ICBMs that may be launched by a 'rogue' state.[200] However, such a system would also provide some residual capability against a small accidental or unauthorised launch of strategic missiles from China or Russia.[201] The Chinese contend that with the deployment of an NMD, China will lose the very limited capacity to deter the US

---

[197] As cited in Kan 1998.

[198] Ibid.

[199] Cited in ibid.

[200] The US had officially dropped the use of the term 'rogue state', as according to a State Department spokesman, the term had outlived its use. A new coinage, 'states of concern', was used for a while in 2000 and 2001. However, George Bush used the term 'axis of evil' in his State of the Union address in early 2002.

[201] Cited in Zhu Minqnan (1999).

from inflicting a first strike on it. There are some American intentions to extend the same over Taiwan as well and, therefore, according to the Chinese this would then encroach on China's sovereignty. The Chinese Foreign Minister, Tang Jiaxuan, told a press conference in March 1999 that 'China is very much concerned about it.'[202]

It is in the interest of both Beijing and Washington to understand better what China thinks on nuclear security and regional stability. It is also in the interest of Washington to undertake policies that promote regional stability rather than exacerbate regional tensions. The US considers it in the interest of both the states to see that there is a global adherence to various arms control treaties, the CWC, NPT, BTWC and CTBT.[203] In the event of any of these treaties not being effective enough, the US may want to cooperate with China on such issues. In October 2003, Presidents Bush and Hu Jintao met to discuss 'a new, if vague, American plan to offer North Korea a five-nation commitment not to invade the country [North Korea] if it froze and then dismantled its nuclear weapons programme.'[204] The US would want to see greater transparency on nuclear issues. 'China should bring its reporting into alignment with the practices of the other *de jure* nuclear weapons states with specific information on the number and types of warheads in its arsenal and the number and general location of deployed systems.'[205] It is possible that China may seek to employ its steadily emergent military capabilities to solve local competition and establish a dominant strategic position in East Asia over the long term.

The nuclear tests by India and Pakistan highlighted the nuclear reality that China is intricately woven into the security calculations of South Asia. The US–China Joint Statement on South Asia of 27 June 1998 mentioned this categorically: 'recent nuclear tests by India and Pakistan, and the resulting increase in tension between them, are a source of deep and lasting concern to both of us.'[206]

[202] *Beijing Review* 1999: 9.

[203] This is even when the NPT is severely being tested by both Iran and North Korea.

[204] See Sanger 2003.

[205] Manning et al. 2000: 77.

[206] It further said, 'In view of the various factors threatening national security, China has prepared for defensive operation under the most difficult and complex circumstances. The People's Liberation Army (PLA), in implementing the strategy

The current US policies seek to integrate China into a variety of international regimes, attempting not to make an adversary of China and to keep the country as friendly as possible. During the Jiang–Clinton summit in Beijing in 1998, the two leaders also signed a pledge not to target strategic nuclear weapons at each other. In late July 1998, Foreign Minister Tang gave Madeleine Albright, US Secretary of State, new assurances that his government would follow through on this promise. Both sides also renewed their commitment to press India and Pakistan to stop developing nuclear armaments.[207] On its part, China would be making pragmatic calculations that will be based on the benefits and disadvantages of participation and non-participation in these regimes.

After the allied forces' successful operations in Kosovo, Afghanistan, and to some extent Iraq, Beijing has started to feel increasing difficulty in managing a potential US meddling in internal Chinese affairs and a potential conflict scenario that might involve China, particularly in the Taiwan Strait or South China Sea. Fundamental Chinese concerns involving US military intervention remain. From Beijing's perspective, the US might continue creating an international environment that might 'restrict' its efforts to develop the political, diplomatic and economic components of national power. China believes that these trends indicate that it will be difficult for Beijing to develop a special relationship with Washington that would fundamentally moderate any US intent to 'contain' China or that would encourage the United States to cooperate with China in offsetting Japan's growing power.

In its attempt to counterbalance a growing US influence in Central Asia post 9/11, China continued to insist that the Afghan campaign be carried out under the UN aegis. China did not want any dramatic shift in the existing international order, but wanted to counter an increasing US hegemony. To this effect, China 'will increasingly seek the support of Europe and Russia. Though the European Union has a long partnership with the US, their differences

---

of building a strong military through science and technology, has accelerated the R&D of defense weaponry and equipment, trained high-quality military personnel of a new type, established a scientific organizational structure, developed theories for military operations with Chinese characteristics, and strengthened its capability for joint, mobile and multi-purpose operations' (Joint US–PRC Statement 1998).

[207] Hong Kong Standard 1998.

on global issues are growing. Similarly, Russia, while seeking a partnership with the US, will want to counterbalance its growing influence.'[208]

The US may want to engage and cooperate with China to ensure that the latter does not become an adversary, but helps improve the international security environment. As Mr Bush makes good on his pledge to unfurl a missile defence umbrella over the US, Washington and Moscow would be entering an era of profound disagreement about how to maintain global security against the use of nuclear weapons, even as they continue to work to reduce their number.

SINO-PAK RELATIONS

Diplomatic relations between Islamabad and Beijing began in the 1950s, from Bandung onwards, when Chou En-lai and Mohammad Ali Bogra initiated a series of high-level contacts and visits in scientific fields. Pakistan had recognised the People's Republic of China on 4 January 1950 and the two countries established diplomatic relations a year later. The end of the 1950s also saw a downturn from the upswing *Hindi–Chini–bhai–bhai* days of Sino-Indian relations. After the 1962 Sino-Indian war, Pakistan realised that China could be an ideal friend against India. A joint communiqué, signed in February between Zulfikar Ali Bhutto and Marshal Chen Yi, urged that the Kashmir dispute should be solved according to the plebiscite that had been pledged by India.[209] Pakistan also counted on China's support during the 1965 war. It was as early as the mid-1960s that Bhutto made strong overtures requesting the Chinese to help Pakistan develop nuclear weapon capabilities that could match the Indian programme. China did not oblige then, but in 1976, following a subsequent intimation by Bhutto, the Beijing government agreed to be more forthcoming. China reportedly supplied Pakistan with blueprints for a fission weapon around or before 1983.[210] Observers attribute this to the marked warmth and upswing in Indian–Russian relations.[211] Pakistan has

---

[208] Gupta 2003a.
[209] See Baksh-Rais 1977.
[210] Department of State, US 1983.
[211] Rizvi 1971.

till date stood by China on all issues important to the latter, especially those related to the question of China's sovereignty, like
Hong Kong, Taiwan and Tibet, and other sensitive issues such as
human rights, at the UN Human Rights Commission. China often
acknowledges Pakistani support in the early 1970s, which helped
break the international isolation of Beijing.

In spite of this, Pakistan did have reasons to feel discontented
as the Chinese had a tendency to blame the British rather than India
for the Kashmir problem.[212] China was critical of the Tashkent Declaration after the 1965 war, when USSR's role as a superpower to
further its sphere of influence in South Asia was seen as a threat
to Chinese power.[213]

Chinese support for Pakistan continued well after the 1971 war,
which has been documented elsewhere in the book. China was
quiet on India's PNE of 1974. The Sikkim accession to India brought
the downslide in relations further. China refused to acknowledge
the Sikkim accession for a long time. It was only after the Indian
prime minister's visit to China in June 2003, that a 'Tibet for Sikkim'
deal ensured that Sikkim no longer remained 'an independent
country' on official Chinese websites.[214] On the Kashmir issue, it
was only after Atal Bihari Vajpayee, the Indian External Affairs
Minister, visited China in 1979 that the latter finally gave up its
persistent demand of Kashmiri self-determination.

Nuclear and Missile Assistance to Pakistan

China kept insisting that the M-11 transfer (Box 4.2) which initially
it had denied for many years was within the MTCR guidelines.
But a Congressional Research Service Report said, 'transfers of
Chinese M-11 short range ballistic missiles or related equipment
exceed MTCR guidelines, because the missile has the inherent capability to deliver a 500 kg warhead to 300 km.'[215] In fact, there was
so much evidence of Chinese assistance to the Pakistani nuclear
programme (see Box 4.2) that the US decided to impose sanctions
on some Chinese companies that engaged in exports of super-
computers, missile technology and satellites. These sanctions were
affected in June 1991 and waived in March 1993. On reports of missile

---

[212] Syed 1974: 69–71.
[213] Rizvi 1971: 192.
[214] See Baruah 2003.
[215] Kan 1998.

transfer again, in August 1993 sanctions were imposed and were waived only after a Chinese commitment to stop missile transfers to Pakistan. A joint statement by the Secretary of State, Warren Christopher and Foreign Minister, Qian Qichen on 4 October 1993 saw the lifting of the second sanctions.

Box ✖ 4.2

China–Pakistan Nuclear and Missile Cooperation

- Chinese transfer of M-11 (M-11/DF-11/CSS-7) test missile and launcher (1991).
- Direct transfers of 34 complete M-11s (1992).
- Chinese provision of M-11 components and technology (1992, 1995).
- Chinese missile technicians visited Pakistan M-11 sites (1994).
- Chinese training of Pakistani M-11 army units (1995).
- Reports of Chinese assistance with indigenous Pakistani M-11 production (1996–97).
- Continuing Chinese assistance, including a blueprint and a construction equipment missile factory in Rawalpindi for manufacture of medium-range ballistic missiles—most likely, the M-11 or a similar missile (1996–97).
- Hatf-1/1A, possibly developed with some Chinese assistance.
- Hatf-2, possibly developed with some Chinese assistance.
- Ammonium perchlorate, a chemical used in rocket fuel: alleged illegal Chinese shipment of 10 tonnes to Pakistan (1996).
- Anza surface-to-air missile: Pakistani version of that in PRC, supplied by China.
- Arms materials, special metals and electronics used in the production of Chinese-design anti-tank missiles (Pakistan's Baktar Shikhan is virtually identical to China's Red Arrow guided missile) and alleged Chinese shipment to Pakistan (1998).
- Suspicion persists regarding China's continued missile cooperation with Pakistan. It has been speculated that the Shaheen-1 IRBM, which Pakistan tested in April 1999, is actually modelled on Chinese M-9 missiles. A 1999 CIA report stated that 'Chinese and North Korean entities continued to provide assistance to Pakistan's ballistic missile program during the first half of 1998. Such assistance is critical for Islamabad's efforts to produce ballistic missiles ... China's involvement with Pakistan will continue to be monitored closely.'[216]

---

[216] CIA 2000.

The transfer of M-11 missiles had led to greater tension between the US and China as it was against core US interests of pursuing non-proliferation. From a Pakistani point of view, these relations have been good. As Pakistan's Ministry of Foreign Affairs claims,

> [O]ur ties with China constitute a cornerstone of our foreign policy and a fundamental element of our quest for regional peace and stability .... The vast spectrum of bilateral co-operation between our two countries ranges from political, economic and cultural spheres to the fields of defence and security .... The relations with China have served as a check on the hegemonistic tendencies of some other countries in the region.[217]

This broadly outlines the essence of Sino-Pak relations, which are based on mutuality of interests and cooperation in fields of defence and security to serve as a check on possibly Indian hegemonic designs. China is following the Kautilyan construction of assisting the neighbour's neighbours. This is a low cost positive sum game.

CHINA'S NUCLEAR EXPORTS AND ASSISTANCE TO PAKISTAN[218]

The Sino-Pak strategic relationship has weathered many political and diplomatic storms. Following are some of the highlights of this relationship (also refer to Box 4.2):

Nuclear Materials

- Ring magnets: These are useful in gas centrifuges that can make weapons-grade enriched uranium. Reportedly about 5,000 ring magnets were sold by China Nuclear Energy Industry Corporation (CNEIC) to A.Q. Khan's Research Lab. at Kahuta during 1994–95.
- Tritium: This is used to achieve fusion in hydrogen bombs and boost the yield of atomic bombs and was reportedly sold to Pakistan by China in 1986.

---

[217] From the website of Pakistan's Ministry of Foreign Affairs, http://www.forisb.org/Pak-majorpowers.htm.

[218] For a comprehensive coverage of this topic, see the online database of the Center for Nonproliferation Studies, Monterey Institute of International Studies, available at http://www.cns.miis.edu.

- Heavy water (D2O): D2O is required to operate certain reactors and some of it can be used in producing plutonium for nuclear weapons. Routine transfers of D2O have occurred and Chinese officials have insisted that the transfers have taken place to the safeguarded KANUPP facility only.
- Special industrial furnace: This can be used to melt plutonium or enriched uranium into the shape of a nuclear bomb core. It has reportedly been sold by China to Pakistan at the Khushab facility in 1996.
- Nuclear weapon design: Reportedly China has transferred the complete design of a 25 kT nuclear bomb—possibly a Chic-4 design—to Pakistan way back in 1983. There have also been reports of HEU being transferred around the same time.

Nuclear Infrastructure

- Kahuta lab is an unsafeguarded production facility for weapons grade fissile material. The ring magnet transfer along with re- ported presence of Chinese scientists has happened here.
- KANUPP pressurised heavy water reactor: This facility is under safeguards and China supplies D2O to this facility.
- Khushab reactor (40–100 MW [?]) is unsafeguarded and can pos- sibly produce weapons-grade plutonium. There were talks of China supplying D2O here, which got delayed.
- Chashma pressurised water reactor (300 MW) under IAEA safe- guards, fuelled by low-enriched uranium. It was sold by China to Pakistan in 1991.
- PARR-2 research reactor (27 kW) at Rawalpindi, built with Chinese help and design in 1989.

As Pakistan moves towards serial production of both intermediate-range and long-range missile systems, there will be an element of technological dependency on China and at least some more such transfers can be expected in the future. However, the fact that China has finally taken upon itself the responsibility to attempt defusing the nuclear crisis in North Korea, indicates an enhanced role that it sees for itself as a regional power, which could prove to be a restraining factor in the structure of the Sino-Pak strategic relationship.

Following the nuclear tests, China urged both India and Pakistan to exercise utmost restraint and to abandon immediately all nuclear weapons programmes in order to avoid a worsening situation and to ensure peace and stability in the region. China also firmly believes the India holds the key to peace and stability in South Asia, that it should take initiatives for peace, as it was India which initiated the nuclear process by first testing a nuclear device, thereby forcing Pakistan to conduct tests.

The Chinese nuclear and missile assistance to Pakistan has a combination of commercial strategic and foreign policy rationales. The steady supply of material and technology has helped the two countries forge a close partnership on key defence issues. Both countries had respective defence needs—in China's case, it was countering the Soviet Union, and in the case of Pakistan, the threat has been India. The economic interests in this relationship were primarily Chinese. In the early 1980s, Chinese defence industries were under tremendous pressure to tap the international arms bazaar and this resulted in locating Pakistan as a lucrative market. Beijing's assistance to Islamabad was fruitful in diplomatic terms, as it became a bargaining chip in dealing against Washington's continued assistance to Taiwan and BMD deployment in East Asia.

US objections to this were based primarily on the core US policy of non-proliferation which was being undermined. Also, the assistance to Pakistan could trigger off a missile and arms race in South Asia. The US has sought to compartmentalise non-proliferation issues on their own merits, failing to recognise and delink regional security issues from larger policy objectives. Even though India made a hue and cry of the Sino-Pak relations, perhaps the US was itself not in a position to wield the kind of authority India wanted it to. Overall, Sino-Pak relations have been mutually beneficial both in strategic and political terms and have stood the test of time. Regional stability has thus been damaged. What matters in building up an arsenal is not the intent or the morality, but the capability. China has certainly helped Pakistan to a great extent.

SINO-INDIAN RELATIONS

Given the fact that the mighty Himalayas separate the two 5000-year old civilisations, the last five decades have seen a lot of interaction and lots of tough times.

Following the signing of the Panchsheel Agreement on 29 April 1954, there were months of negotiations. For some years, there was the usual bonhomie of *Hindi–Chini–bhai–bhai*, but it came as a big surprise to India when in October–November 1962 there was a conflict between India and China. The Chinese side was far better equipped and prepared. The fact that India was taken by surprise did not absolve India of the deficiencies in its threat assessment. Within weeks of the outbreak of hostilities came the unilateral ceasefire by China. China and Pakistan had finalised their border settlements of Pakistan-occupied Kashmir (or Azad Kashmir, as Pakistan calls it) by December 1962. They reached a formal agreement in March 1963.

The agreement did carry a clause which stated that it would be renegotiated in the event of a final settlement of the Indo-Pak dispute over this area, and this led to the transfer of these areas to India. The chill in Sino-Indian relations continued for a few years. The ice was broken in August 1970 when Sardar Swaran Singh (the then Foreign Minister) made a statement in the Indian Parliament expressing the Indian government's desire to 'settle all matters ... peacefully through bilateral negotiation.'[219] Ambassadorial ties were restored in 1975 and the Indian government representatives (February 1979), prime minister (December 1988 and June 2003) and the president (May 1992 and June 2000) visited China. The Chinese too reciprocated by sending their counterparts, and China started endorsing almost all Indian positions, including bilateralism on Kashmir.

The downswing in their relations began when India tested nuclear devices in May 1998 and stated China to be one of the rationales for the test. What alienated the Chinese was the accusation against them. Most Chinese have said that it was India's right to test, but to cite the Chinese threat as justification was unnecessary and insidious. Following Vajpayee's 'famous' letter,[220]

---

[219] Singh 1972.

[220] The Indian prime minister in his letter to President Clinton had written, 'I have been deeply concerned at the deteriorating security environment, faced by India for some years past. We have an overt nuclear weapon state on our borders, a state which committed armed aggression against India in 1962. Although our relations with that country have improved in the last decade or so, an atmosphere of distrust persists mainly due to the unresolved border problem. To add to the distrust that country has materially helped another neighbour of ours to become a covert nuclear weapons state. At the hands of this bitter neighbour we have suffered three aggressions in the last 50 years' (Vajpayee 1998a).

the Chinese became the most vociferous nation among the P-5, calling for a cap and rollback of the Indian nuclear capability. The Chinese were also instrumental in getting the UN Security Council Resolution 1172 passed.[221]

Just like other nations, China too has members of the academia who hold extreme views. Consider this: 'what India is playing at present seems to be the risky game that Germany, Japan and Italy played in the 1980s and 1990s on the issue of India's nuclear test and hegemonic behaviour in South Asia ....'[222] From a Chinese point of view, it was bad enough that India should test, and it was worse that China was named as the main threat.

The Chinese believe that India continues in vain to covertly assist the Tibetan liberation struggle by sheltering the refugees who are in different cities all over India. India has given refuge not only to the Dalai Lama but also to the Karmapa. From the Chinese perspective, 'India has maintained an aggressive drive toward its northern boundary and has occupied some 90,000 square kilometres of Chinese territory since its independence from Britain. In October 1962, New Delhi continued to pursue what the Chinese called a policy of expansionism, which triggered an invasion of China.'[223] Ming Zhang adds, 'while China has assisted Pakistan's nuclear development and has provided short-range missiles to that country, a nuclear stand-off between Pakistan and India and the proliferation of nuclear weapons among Islamic countries are not necessary to China's goals.'[224]

While the nuclear tests disturbed the global non-proliferation regimes, it also drew the limelight to China's regional interests. Chinese broader foreign policy objective remains the maintenance of a strategic balance of power in Southern Asia in the post-Cold War era. Policy makers and think tanks in the US realised that China

---

[221] UN Security Council Resolution 1172 has been rejected by India as prescriptive and sovereignty violation. See response by Minister of State for External Affairs, Shri Ajit Kumar Panja, in Lok Sabha 2000f. The minister said, 'India's views on that resolution have been conveyed to our interlocutors. India's bilateral dialogue with key interlocutors is based on the premise that India is a state possessing nuclear weapons and will maintain a minimum credible nuclear deterrent in accordance with its own assessment of its national security requirements.'

[222] Zhang Wenmu 1998.

[223] Ming Zhang 1999: 15.

[224] Ibid.: 17.

did have a role in altering the South Asian security environment. As the Independent Task Force noted, 'China bears responsibility for the situation in South Asia, given its own nuclear and missile programmes.'[225] The Task Force also recommended a more constructive role for China: 'It will be difficult ... to stabilise the situation in South Asia without China's constructive participation.'[226] This gives space to an increased role to China as a security manager in South Asia. But is the US ready for China to take up such a role? As Strobe Talbott says, 'we ourselves have an ongoing strategic dialogue with China, including about critical regions, and our determination to foster peace and security in South Asia will continue very much a part of our agenda with Beijing.'[227] This changed somewhat with the visit of the Indian Prime Minister to China in June 2003. It has been necessitated by an increasingly globalised world economy and the need for both countries to promote a mature and pragmatic relationship that emphasises multilateralism on crucial regional and global issues.

Based on a changed environment, where does one locate China's relations towards India and what variables influence crucial outcomes that determine issues of stability and deterrence? One of the factors that helped shape Chinese foreign relations for a long time—ideology—no longer plays a singularly dominant role in shaping foreign policy choices now. Second, China has realised that in a world that is increasingly being influenced by forces of globalisation, the best it can do is only partially open its door, thereby staking its own claim as well. Third, on the threat perception, as Kanti Bajpai has argued, 'while the border dispute is unresolved in a formal sense, Beijing got what it wanted out of the issue. If its primary aim was to secure the route from Xinjing to Tibet, it long established the goal.' He further adds, 'India has never figured in China's threat cosmology in any serious fashion unlike the Russian expansionist, the American imperialist, and the Japanese upstart.'[228] This paints quite a benign image of China and its future role, both in the region and the international system. Fourth, if one were to

---

[225] Independent Task Force 1998:11.
[226] Ibid.: 11.
[227] Talbott 1998: 3.
[228] Bajpai 1999: 157.

situate the nuclear and missile assistance that China has provided
to Pakistan over the years in the overall strategic calculus, then
indeed China's present posture cannot be viewed as benign. As
Johnston has pointed out, 'in comparison with other major powers,
China was far more likely to use violence in a dispute over military
security questions as territory.'[229] Fifth, the Chinese view presented
by Chinese scholars cannot be dismissed. Hua Han, project leader
of the Program on Arms Control and Disarmament at Beijing University, argues there are several reasons that China is indifferent
to nuclear developments in India. 'First, even if relations soured,
conventional weapons better serve the cause of security given the
limited nature of the disagreements between China and India. In
any case, China perceives the probability of war with India to be
small. Finally, it might be inferred ... that China continues to enjoy
an advantage in nuclear capability over India, both in warheads
and in delivery systems.'[230]

What then is the Chinese image? According to Amitabh Mattoo,
'the image of the mysterious, unfathomable, inscrutable Chinese
is probably the one which strikes a chord within most sections of
public opinion.'[231] The Indian image in Beijing on the other hand
is that of a small country giving asylum to Tibetan refugees with
aspirations of big power. How seriously one takes the Chinese
threat as a legitimate threat in India and how that links to the Indian
nuclear tests is something that will take shape in the fullness of
time and depends on the time-scale one is willing to take into account. In the near future, it is unlikely that there is going to be any
outbreak of conflict leading to breakdown of nuclear deterrence.
However, in the long term, based on a number of other factors,
such as China's continued nuclear warhead and delivery system
modernisation and continued assistance to Pakistan, India's
strategic calculations are likely to be affected. In the short term, it
is possible that India would seek to solve the disputed boundary
question, although in its present form the dispute is unlikely to
escalate into a conventional war. India might also seek to counterbalance the increasing 'encirclement' by China in the short and

---

[229] Johnston 1996b.

[230] Hua Han 1998: 47. It must, however, be kept in mind that this is before the
South Asian nuclear tests. For a view on this after the nuclear tests, see Garver
1999.

[231] See Mattoo 2000: 24.

medium term.[232] Ashley Tellis, putting the long-term competitive relationship in perspective, has argued that the growth of China's economic power, its continued nuclear and conventional military modernisation, and its increasing influence in various areas of strategic relevance to South Asia, will all contribute to a serious Indo-Chinese military–strategic competition in the short to medium term. This, he says, places increased pressure on India to rejuvenate its economy and modernise its defence capability to avoid being at a disadvantage.[233]

In spite of the current Chinese view of India being that of a grand pretender, Beijing has no alternative but to treat the latter warily, even though it is by no means China's principal long-term threat. For all the dismissive condescension usually displayed in Beijing towards New Delhi, the judgement advanced by one perceptive analyst almost a decade ago still holds:

> The Sino-Indian relationship is ... an uneasy one. India still regards nuclear China as a major threat to its security. It sees China's South Asian policies as anti-Indian, divisive, opportunistic and interfering. China for its part perceives India to be an ambitious, overconfident yet militarily powerful neighbour with whom it may eventually have to have a day of reckoning.[234]

The visit of the Chinese Premier, Zhu Rongji in January 2002 was hailed as a new milestone in Sino-Indian relations. The visit was the reflection of a new mindset, a new reality.[235] On many occasions, both countries have publicly announced that they do not view each other as a security threat. The JWG on border issues also resumed regular meetings, and in November 2001 it exchanged for the first time maps on the middle sector of the line of actual control. A security dialogue has been initiated. There are other strands of a

---

[232] India could forge closer diplomatic and military ties with other countries, for instance, Vietnam.

[233] Tellis 2000a.

[234] Klintworth 1992: 96.

[235] Apart from the progress made in the economic sphere, where the two countries signed six major agreements, including the resumption of direct flights between Beijing and New Delhi, and memoranda of understanding (MOU) on tourism and cooperation in space, science and technology, some progress was also visible on the boundary dispute. China and India agreed to join efforts in combatting terrorism by setting up a joint working group (JWG).

changed Chinese perception of India that could be located in the Zhu Rongji visit. First, China demonstrated neutrality in the Kargil and the post-Parliament attack crisis. Second, a growing consensus that China and India should expand areas of mutual cooperation, particularly those in the economic sphere. The Zhu Rongji visit also provided a rare opportunity that the two countries need to build on. The two countries should seriously continue their discussions on the boundary issue. Both India and China have to realise that the line of actual control (LaC), with some minor adjustments, does offer the best chance for a settlement of their territorial issues. It is also unlikely that either side would press for a military solution as the final way to settle the boundary question. Second, while India continues to raise the issue of Sino-Pak nuclear and missile cooperation, China needs to seriously address this concern which has led to some source of instability in Southern Asia. Third, there continues to be a greater need to enhance bilateral security dialogue, and while increased contacts at the governmental level are welcome, there is need to reduce the four Ms: misunderstanding, misperception, miscalculation and mistrust. Fourth, both India and China can have a common understanding on the BMD issue and the way it is likely to impact on Southern Asia.

On the nuclear issue, there could be a sustained dialogue which could go a long way in warding off an arms race. This is particularly necessary from an Indian point of view, as it has to build a 'credible minimum deterrent' against its two immediate neighbours— Pakistan and China. Although the US, recognising India's need for a minimum credible nuclear deterrent, has moved away from UN resolution 1172, China sticks by it, at least publicly. Fifth, the PLA has also held security consultations and meetings with the Indian Ministry of Defence. There have also been anti-terrorism consultations with the Government of India. Finally, the two countries have to look ahead in their relations beyond the security prism. There are genuine concerns regarding the future shape of the international system. Both countries support the Five Principles of the Peaceful Coexistence as the basis for building a post-Cold War multipolar international order. Both oppose hegemonism and interference in domestic affairs. Zhu Rongji's visit provided the foundation on which concrete measures can be taken. The challenge lies in not losing the current momentum on issues of mutual convergence. The two countries could do well by sorting out their differences and improving their relations.[236]

Given this milieu, one can speculate on three possible trajectories of Sino-Indian relations. The first is open competition between them for regional status and global power. This would translate into continued and intensified rivalry in the political, military and economic spheres. It is possible that the scenario would be marked by a continued status quo on the territorial question or a marginal improvement thereof, by arms race and competition for regional hegemony. This is likely to occur if neither side is interested in engaging with the other on any issue. The second scenario would be of total cooperation between the two countries with India and China as complementary poles in a multipolar world. The highlights in this scenario would be marked by a resolution of all outstanding issues and reaching an understanding on regional issues, which include China's strategic relationship with Pakistan. This is likely only if both sides take the bilateral relationship to its highest level and position it above any other bilateral considerations. The third and perhaps most plausible relationship would be a combination of competition and cooperation. In the post-Cold War era, the policy of deliberate drift is not going to be adopted by either side. The areas of mutual interest will be identified and worked upon. The key to a successful relationship might well be their respective bilateral relationships with the US.[237] In a marked way, this will impact on the structure and size of the nuclear deterrent posture each country wishes to adopt in the given scenario.

BMD and China's Response

On 20 January 1999, the then US Secretary of Defense, William S. Cohen, declared that the Department of Defense had planned to allocate additional funds to NMD and BMD programmes. The rationale given was that the US faces growing ballistic missile threats from 'rogue' states (or states in the axis of evil) to the US territory, US forces deployed overseas and allies.[238] The new budget

---

[236] Tellis 2000a.

[237] See Jing Dong-Yuan and Sidhu 2002. Sidhu and Jing Dong-Yuan were among the Panellists.

[238] See *The Statesman* 2002. Also see Bumiller 2002. The State of the Union address drew sharp responses from around the world.

will request $6.6 billion to the current NMD funding levels for a total of $10.5 billion for NMD through the fiscal year 2005. The US Senate on 17 March 1999 passed the NMD Act of 1999, saying that 'it is the policy of the United States to deploy as soon as is technologically possible an effective NMD system capable of defending the territory of the United States against limited ballistic attack (whether accidental, unauthorised or deliberate).'[239]

Apart from the domestic debates within the US, which have strategic, military, domestic politics, foreign policy and theoretical variables featuring in talks on the pros and cons of having an NMD, such a policy has deep implications outside the US. Not only Russia is deeply concerned about the situation, and there are strong perspectives even within the US urging it against pushing Russia too far. Even China is deeply concerned and has been observing these debates mid-1990s onwards. As Zhu Minqnan, a Chinese analyst, sums up, 'China has taken a very sceptical and vigilant attitude on US NMD and BMD plans.'[240] The Chinese stand on missile defence is encapsulated in the white paper on China's National Defence 2002, where it says,

China is concerned about certain countries' joint research and development of theatre missile defence (BMD) systems with a view to their deployment in the Northeast Asian region. This will lead to the proliferation of advanced missile technology and be detrimental to peace and stability in the Asia-Pacific region. China resolutely opposes any country which provides Taiwan with BMD assistance or protection in any form.[241]

Within the US, analysts have argued whether NMD and BMD are technologically feasible, politically useful and financially tenable.[242] The US at this point in time seems determined to position an NMD and has sought to increase BMD cooperation with Taiwan and Japan. The Chinese reaction to this can be supplemented by these recent developments:

---

[239] *Associated Press* 1999.
[240] Zhu Minqnan 1999: 21.
[241] State Council, PRC 2002: ch. 7.
[242] See for instance, IFPA 2000 and CDI 2000.

1. The US–Japan Defence Cooperation Agreement of September 1997.
2. The US plans for extending a BMD to East Asia including Taiwan.
3. The allegations by US congressional reports of Chinese in nuclear labs engaged in transferring nuclear secrets to China and the consequent Cox Committee Report.
4. A US veto of the $450 million transfer satellite technologies package to the Singapore-based consortium on the basis that a PLA owned company was involved with China threatening to cooperate on missile technology with other Third World countries.
5. During the Taiwan president's New York visit in winter 1995–96, China conducted an unprecedented missile test across the Taiwan Straits.[243]

China's main objections to the proposed national missile defence are premised on these factors:

- An NMD would seriously undermine the credibility, effectiveness and posture of a Chinese strategic nuclear deterrent.
- An NMD would undermine Chinese capability of second strike as doctrinally China is on a no-first-use posture.
- If Russia does not agree to the proposed US amendments to the treaty, then since the US has already threatened to walk out of the agreement, what will be the future of US–Russian strategic arms reductions?

In the mid-1980s, when US President Ronald Reagan had initiated the Strategic Defense Initiative (SDI), popularly called the star wars, Chinese experts had opposed the SDI on the grounds that it would accelerate an arms race between the USSR and the US.[244] The Chinese concluded that there were three options for it to respond to SDI: (*a*) expansion of offensive forces; (*b*) development of countermeasures, such as shielding and spinning of ballistic missiles to penetrate missile defences; and (*c*) deployment of anti-satellite weapons to destroy US space-based missile defence systems.[245]

---

[243] In the middle of this crisis, some Chinese officials told former US Assistant Secretary of Defense, Chas Freeman, that China could act militarily against Taiwan without the fear of a US response because US leaders cared more about Los Angeles than they did about Taiwan. See Tyler 1996.

[244] Glaser and Garret 1986.

[245] Ibid.: 33.

Just as there are many scholars in the US who believe that the present NMD has technological roots in SDI, there are people who believe that the present Chinese response is remarkably similar to and consistent in its opposition to the SDI in the 1980s. The Chinese believe that the threat to US from rogue states (or states of concern) is vastly exaggerated and that this is another ploy to take Japanese assistance in missile research to contain China. Indeed, within the US, there are scholars who argue that as long as any state has the four long characteristics—territory, government, sovereignty and population—it can be deterred and there are various means to do so.[246]

China's Opposition to BMD in Taiwan

The fundamental rationale for China's opposition to the US provision of BMD for Taiwan is that would further assist Taiwanese separatists who may declare independence. China, of course, considers Taiwan as an inalienable part of China. As China's ambassador, Sha Zukang, said at the Carnegie Conference, 'TMD in Taiwan will give the pro-independence forces in Taiwan a sense of security, which may incite them to reckless moves. This can only lead to instability across the Taiwan Strait or even in the entire Northeast Asian region.'[247] Another reason Amb. Sha Zukang cited was that the transfer of BMD technology will lead to increased US–Taiwan military cooperation. Taiwan may then receive a large number of early warning systems, ground support and other advanced weapon systems which 'will lead to a de facto parliamentary relationship between the US and Taiwan.'[248] A third Chinese apprehension relates to missile proliferation. As Amb. Sha Zukang noted, 'transferring BMD systems to other countries or regions, or jointly developing them with other countries, will inevitably result in the proliferation missile technology. Missile and anti-missile technologies are related. Many of the technologies used in anti-missile systems are easily applicable in offensive missiles.'[249] China has also said that while the US opposes Chinese arms and nuclear materials transfer to Iran, Syria and Pakistan, it is pursuing the same policy with Taiwan and Japan. 'China's argument that missile and antimissile technologies are intimately related has led to

---

[246] Tellis 2001b.

[247] Sha Zukang 1999: 2.

[248] Ibid.: 3.

[249] Ibid.: 3.

accusations that the United States is hypocritical in proposing to sell BMD technology to Taiwan and Japan while denouncing Chinese missile technology sales to Iran and Pakistan.'[250]

Taiwan currently has Patriot Air Defence Systems that have limited anti-ballistic missile capability. On 10 February 1999, *The Financial Times* reported (based on US government sources) that China had planned increase the number of missiles in its southern regions from 30 to 50 over the next several years.[251] 'According to leaked DIA reports China was constructing two missile bases on the coast of mainland China near Taiwan in late 1999. The bases at Yongan and Xianyou, are located 220 miles and 135 miles from Taiwan, respectively.'[252] The US has linked Taiwan's need for BMD to China's missile developments. The Chinese consider their missile developments as irrelevant, as the US should not be providing BMD or any such assistance to Taiwan, the latter being China's internal affair.

China's Opposition to BMD in Japan

For years, Japanese response to collective defence rights has been governed by Article 9 of their constitution that prevents Japan from participating in a multinational global projection programme (at the same time, a bilateral agreement with the US has been possible). The Japanese Constitution has also debarred it from using space for military purposes and the legal requirements of Japan specify dual use technology can be exported only to the US.[253]

In February 1998, Japan and the US reached an agreement to conduct joint research on lightweight exo-atmospheric projectile (LEAP) technology.[254] By August 1999, the US and Japan signed an agreement for a five-year programme that focuses on the development of an advanced missile sensor, advanced kinetic warhead second stage propulsion and a lightweight nose cone design for the navy's theatre wide missile block 2 missile system (NTW). This project is scheduled for deployment in 2011 within an estimated cost of $500 million out of which Japan is expected to pay more than half.[255]

---

[250] Center for Nonproliferation Studies 2000.
[251] Fidler and Walker 1999.
[252] Ibid.
[253] Pall 1993.
[254] *Nihon Keijai Shimbun* 1999.
[255] Wall 1999.

The Chinese are opposed to BMD for Japan mainly due to these reasons: First, a Japan–US cooperation on BMD will also assist in developing NMDs, since the two are closely related. Second, as of now, the US protection of Japan restrains Japanese military ambitions; a BMD cooperation will bring Japanese military on more equal grounding. Also, 'China points to the 1997 revisions of the US–Japan defence guidelines which allow Japan to assist the US military in conflicts around Japan as evidence of this trend.'[256] Another contention is that a BMD equipped Japan may alter military strategy from defensive defence to offensive defence. Finally, China believes that if BMD in Japan is aimed at preventing North Korea from a surprise attack, thought should also be given to a possible Korean response. North Korea is already an international pariah and no amount of weaponry will help lessen the tension; only a constant process of dialogue may help. The profound Chinese mistrust of Japan, which can be traced historically to the Manchurian annexation of 1931, is at the heart of Chinese response to BMDs for Japan.

Thus, the Chinese response to BMD and NMD can be located in politico-military factors, which shape the broad contours of the Chinese nuclear deterrent posture. There are political factors, because even within the US there is a school of thought that believes as far as the threat comes from a state, it can be deterred,[257] so an NMD or BMD is not needed. The Chinese, therefore, believe that it is aimed primarily to contain them; moreover, it has become an issue in US domestic politics. Military factors are involved, because while the US has all the military weapons needed to ward off a threat, a BMD or NMD will only undermine a Chinese second strike capability, thereby making China vulnerable to US nuclear blackmail. As the white paper on national defence said, 'no state should develop or deploy outer space weapons or missile defence systems, which harm strategic security and stability.'[258] But it is likely that by 2020 China will, going by the present force modernisation drive, possess several hundred short- and medium-range ballistic missiles that will be in a position to deliver nuclear or conventional warheads to most targets in Japan with a high level of

---

[256] Center for Nonproliferation Studies 2000.

[257] Based on traditional notions of deterrence.

[258] State Council, PRC 1998.

accuracy. By 2020 it is unlikely, however, that Japan by itself or via the US would be in a position to deploy an effective missile defence system.[259]

✠ CTBT, NPT AND FMCT

CTBT

Although in 1986 China stated that it would participate in the work of an *ad hoc* group on a CTBT, in 1990 the government abstained from a UN resolution calling for the conclusion of a CTBT. At that time it was seeking a move towards universal nuclear disarmament and a no-first-use pledge from other nuclear powers. China signed the CTBT on 24 September 1996 (the second country to do so after the United States), but has not yet ratified it.[260] After its last test in July 1996, China has maintained a unilateral moratorium on testing. As Johnston has said, China's joining of the CTBT is its 'first instance where it sacrificed potential military capabilities for the sake of formal multilateral arms control',[261] although China stated its intention to revisit the issue at a review conference 10 years after the CTBT had entered into force.

---

[259] See Swaine and Tellis 2000.

[260] The signature statement carried this voice of concern from the Chinese government—'the Chinese Government solemnly makes the following appeals: (*a*) Major nuclear weapon states should abandon their policy of nuclear deterrence. States with huge nuclear arsenals should continue to drastically reduce their nuclear stockpiles. (*b*) All countries that have deployed nuclear weapons on foreign soil should withdraw all of them to their own land. All nuclear weapon states should undertake not to be the first to use nuclear weapons at any time and under any circumstances, commit themselves unconditionally to the non-use or threat of use of nuclear weapons against non-nuclear weapon states or nuclear weapon-free zones, and conclude, at an early date, international legal instruments to this effect. (*c*) All nuclear weapon states should pledge their support to proposals for the establishment of nuclear weapon-free zones, respect their status as such and undertake corresponding obligations. (*d*) No country should develop or deploy space weapon systems or missile defense systems undermining strategic security or stability. (*e*) An international convention on the complete prohibition and thorough destruction of nuclear weapons should be concluded through negotiations' (Government of PRC 1996).

[261] Johnston 1996a.

It was only in 1993 that China dropped these linkages and started supporting the creation of an *ad hoc* committee in the Conference on Disarmament for the negotiation of a CTBT. During negotiations, China's statements reflected two main concerns. First, China consistently pushed for an exemption allowing peaceful nuclear explosions under the final treaty. It was not until June 1996 that China dropped this demand.[262] Second, China objected to the use of national technical means, such as satellite reconnaissance for CTBT verification. This was premised on two main concerns: (*a*) Russian and US dominance in satellites; and (*b*) the potential misuse of these satellites. Additionally, Chinese negotiator Amb. Sha Zukang also sounded apprehensive about the use of on-site inspections for treaty verification. He said, 'China will never allow legitimizing espionage, as it infringes upon national sovereignty, in the CTBT or other future international arms control and disarmament treaties.'[263] The US and China both continued to defer for a while before they finally agreed to allow on-site inspections as a part of the CTBT.

China accepted the final CTBT text even though there remained some dissatisfaction. Following the adoption of the treaty, Sha Zukang pointed out that the CTBT text representing the results of the Conference on Disarmament (CD) negotiations over the preceding two and a half years 'basically embodies' the actual conditions of the negotiations and 'is balanced as a whole'.[264]

However, from the Chinese perspective several concerns remained. First, the CTBT final text did not contain a commitment by the nuclear weapons states not to be the first to use nuclear weapons as well as not to use or threaten to use nuclear weapons against non-nuclear weapons countries and nuclear-free zones. China held that the preamble of the treaty should reflect, as much as possible, the common desire of the international community and should

---

[262] 'Although we still need to be convinced by the various counter-arguments, we also recognize the fact that the CTBT negotiations have reached their final stage, and in order to facilitate the conclusion of the treaty within the time-frame as planned, the Chinese delegation is now ready to go along with a temporary ban on PNEs; China can agree to a treaty provision that the possibility of permitting the conduct of PNEs shall be considered by the review conference of the States' parties.' See Sha Zukang 1996a.

[263] Sha Zukang 1996b.

[264] Ibid.

point out that the international community would continue to work to realise those objectives after committing to the CTBT.[265] Second, on the issue of triggering on-site inspections, the CTBT puts the international monitoring system at par with national technical means, failing to make the necessary distinction between the positions of the two. That is to say, it fails to make a distinction between the data and information acquired for verification from the international monitoring system and the first three from NTM.[266] Third, stipulations in the CTBT treaty text regarding the procedures for examination and approval of an on-site inspection (OSI) are not entirely rational. Because of its politically confrontational and highly sensitive nature, the Chinese believe that OSI, as a last and exceptional resort for verification of the treaty, is the CTBT's most substantial obligation.[267]

Since the signing of the CTBT in 1996, China has repeatedly endorsed the treaty in public statements. At the October 1997 US–China summit, the two countries issued a joint statement noting, 'the United States and China agree to work to bring the Comprehensive Test Ban Treaty into force at the earliest possible date.'[268] Another important endorsement of the treaty came from the Chinese President, Jiang Zemin, in a speech at the CD in Geneva in March 1999, where he reiterated China's support for the CTBT and pledged ratification. He said,

Efforts should be made for early entry into force of the CTBT according to the CTBT provisions. The recent nuclear tests have made the early entry into force of the treaty a more pressing task. As one of the first countries to have signed the treaty, China will continue to work for the early entry into force of the treaty. The Chinese Government will soon officially submit the treaty to the National People's Congress for ratification.[269]

China has also completed its 'domestic legal procedure for the entry into force of the Additional Protocol to its Safeguards Agreement

---

[265] Zou Yunhua 1998.
[266] Ibid.
[267] Ibid.
[268] Joint US–PRC Statement 1997.
[269] Jiang Zemin 1999.

with the International Atomic Energy Agency, thus becoming the first among the five nuclear-weapon states that has done so.'[270]

In recent years, China has been affected by the US rejection of the CTBT. Presently, the Chinese government has submitted the treaty to the National People's Congress for examination. 'The NPC will go through the necessary procedures for the ratification of the treaty according to the relevant legal requirements.'[271] Although China officially maintains that 'there is no change at all in China's stand on this treaty',[272] it is unlikely that unless the US modifies its stance on the CTBT, any state, let alone China, will take any interest in the treaty.

NPT

When the NPT was opened for signature on 1 July 1968, the United States, United Kingdom, Soviet Union and 59 other countries signed it. China and France did not sign the treaty at that point in time.[273] The treaty came into force with US ratification in March 1970. Initially, China deplored the treaty as a conspiracy concocted by the USSR and the US to maintain their nuclear monopoly. China continued to maintain that it was in favour of complete abolition of nuclear weapons and it did not encourage nuclear proliferation. This view remained consistent from the time China tested nuclear devices in 1964. However, the Chinese position as well as behaviour towards nuclear proliferation started undergoing a change during the 1980s. China began in a rather discreet way to aid and assist Iran and Pakistan in building a nuclear estate. Although at international fora China continued to maintain that the NPT was imbalanced and discriminatory, it indicated that in principle it accepted the norm of nuclear proliferation. In 1984, China also became a member of the IAEA and agreed to place all of its nuclear-related exports under international safeguards. China attended the fourth review conference of the NPT and criticised the treaty

---

[270] Sha Zukang 2002.

[271] Foreign Ministry of PRC 2003.

[272] Joseph 1999. The news report quotes Sha Zukang.

[273] France states that it 'would behave in the future in this field exactly as the States adhering to the Treaty', while China signed the NPT in 1992.

for not banning the deployment of nuclear weapons outside national territories and for not including concrete provisions for general nuclear disarmament. In 1991, France joined the NPT and China also indicated its willingness to join the NPT, though it maintained it consistent stance about the discriminatory nature of the treaty. China acceded to the treaty in 1992 as a nuclear weapons state.[274]

The non-proliferation community has continued to raise concerns over China's compliance with its obligations under the NPT. Of specific reference has been China's role in assisting Iran and Pakistan. In Pakistan's case, the US intelligence community believed that China's nuclear assistance to Pakistan has helped it to follow the plutonium or the HEU route to its nuclear weapons. With Iran, the concern came more from the non-proliferation community in the US.

China has maintained an extensive and a rather controversial nuclear trade relationship with Iran. This has led to the US raising the issue several times with China, as Iran happens to be a part of the 'axis of evil'. This relationship goes back to 1980s, when China started training Irani nuclear technicians under a nuclear cooperation agreement, which helped in constructing Iran's primary research facility located in Isfahan. Iran was also provided subcritical or zero-yield nuclear reactors under the IAEA safeguards. When the US raised this issue with the Chinese, reports of these agreements were declared 'groundless' and 'preposterous'.

---

[274] This is what China had to say in its statement of accession: 'China maintains that the prevention of proliferation of nuclear weapons is not an end in itself, but a measure and step in the process towards the complete prohibition and thorough destruction of nuclear weapons. Non-proliferation of nuclear weapons and nuclear disarmament should be mutually complementary. Only when substantive progress is made in the field of nuclear disarmament can the proliferation of nuclear weapons be checked most effectively and the authority of the nuclear non-proliferation regime truly enhanced. At the same time, an effective nuclear non-proliferation regime is conducive to the goal of total elimination of nuclear weapons.' It further called upon all nuclear powers to issue unconditional no-first-use pledges, to issue negative and positive security assurances to the non-nuclear weapons states, to support the development of nuclear weapon-free zones, to withdraw all nuclear weapons deployed outside national territories, and to halt the arms race in outer space (Center for Nonproliferation Studies 1992).

The CNS website lists a total of eight agreements, two of which stand out.[275] In 1991, China and Iran announced China's agreement to supply Iran's first 20 MW research nuclear reactors.[276] The US concern on the nature of research led to this deal being scrapped as they were suspicious of Iran following a secret nuclear weapons programme, and Iran's heavy reliance on Chinese technology in this regard. In September 1992, Iran and China signed another nuclear agreement where China announced its intent to supply two 300 MW pressurised water reactors to Iran which had to be completed in 10 years time.[277] The US continued to maintain pressure on China, as it believed that Chinese assistance could help Iran build nuclear weapons. This in spite of the fact that Iran is a member of the NPT and it has put most of its nuclear facilities under the IAEA inspections, as other countries continue to insist that Iran sign the additional protocol.[278] Among the many 'failures' that Iran has been docked for is the failure to declare the import of 3,960 lbs of uranium from China in 1991.[279] The US continues to put pressure on China and other potential suppliers to halt nuclear cooperation programmes with Iran. In October 1997, at a press briefing, the US National Security Advisor, Sandy Berger said, 'We have received assurances from the Chinese that they will not engage in any new nuclear cooperation with Iran and that the existing cooperation—there are two projects in particular—will end. That is the assurance we have received.'[280] China, however, continues

---

[275] The agreement on 6 July 1993 included a protocol covering cooperation in several areas, including the construction of a nuclear power reactor to be constructed by China. Iran stated that the reactor would be used for peaceful purposes and would be under full IAEA safeguards. The other agreement on 19 September 1992 included a treaty on 'nuclear energy cooperation'. The agreement was intended to allow Iran to acquire two 300 MW power reactors from China. It reportedly also included cooperation in the exploration for and extraction of uranium ore. It called for the application of IAEA safeguards (Nuclear News 1993; Matveyev 1995).

[276] Hibbs 1992. However, under pressure from the US, China later cancelled the deal.

[277] Kan 1992, 1996, 1998.

[278] The IAEA has docked Iran for non-compliance as fears mount that Iran is on course to develop nuclear weapons capability within two years. See Coughlin 2003.

[279] See Srivastava and Rajain 2003. Also see Du Preez and Scheinmen 2003.

[280] Albright and Berger 1997.

to strengthen its ties with Iran. This is partially a function of China's rising energy needs, and expansion of Sino-Iranian relations is a natural and key component of Chinese strategy in extending its influence to the Central Asian region.[281] Chinese role in proliferation of nuclear materials in spite of it being a member of the NPT continues to have serious implications for the non-proliferation regime.

The main thrust of US foreign policy in the post-Cold War decades has been the proliferation of WMD, which impinges on US strategic interests in many parts of the world. The US has undertaken many measures, including strengthening the international nuclear non-proliferation regime and threatening/applying sanctions to punish/deter proliferation behaviour.

While differences with the US on nuclear non-proliferation remain and these concerns have been reinforced by the presence of the North Korean bomb, the Chinese continue to emphasise the importance of promoting peaceful use of nuclear energy. On the issue of North Korea, China has come across as a country genuinely interested in preserving peace in the region as its sustained involvement in the tripartite talks with North Korea and the US suggest. China understands that any destabilisation of the region could lead to a potentially increased US involvement in the region.[282] China favours legitimate demands of developing counties meeting their energy needs and developing peaceful use of nuclear energy and technology transfers for economic development under the pretext of preventing nuclear proliferation.

Speaking at the Conference on Disarmament in 1999, Chinese President Jiang Zemin said, 'The NPT is both the basis of the international nuclear non-proliferation regime and the prerequisite for progress in the nuclear disarmament process. The NPT must be observed in full and in good faith. Otherwise, international efforts for nuclear disarmament and non-proliferation would be seriously harmed. Those countries which have not yet joined the NPT should do so at the earliest possible date so as to make the treaty truly universal.'[283]

---

[281] See in this context, Gupta 2002c.

[282] For a perceptive look in the Chinese involvement in the crisis, see Gupta 2003b.

[283] Jiang Zemin 1999.

China also reiterated its position on the NPT in the recently released defence white paper, where it said,

> China has always been opposed to the proliferation of WMD and their means of delivery. It supports the international community's active efforts of non-proliferation, and has made its own contributions in this area. China maintains that the efforts of non-proliferation should not be confined to non-proliferation itself and should also include the identification and resolution of its root causes. Establishing a fair and rational new international order and realizing the universal improvement of international relations are the fundamental way to eliminate the threat of WMD.[284]

FMCT

The Fissile Material Cut-off Treaty (FMCT), though not negotiated so far, is about an agreement that might prohibit the production of fissile material for nuclear explosives and the production of such material outside of international safeguards. The proposed FMCT might extend verification measures to fissile material production facilities that are presently not under the international monitoring regime. Such a ban, it is expected, would place a quantitative constraint on the amount of fissile material available for use in nuclear weapons. In December 1993, the UN General Assembly passed a resolution calling for negotiation of a 'non-discriminatory, multilateral and internationally and effectively verifiable treaty banning the production of fissile material for nuclear weapons or other nuclear explosive devices.'[285] In March 1995, the CD by consensus agreed to establish an *ad hoc* committee based on the mandate given by the 1993 UN General Assembly Resolution to negotiate a cut-off treaty. Despite various calls and widespread international support for the FMCT, negotiations are still at the preliminary stage in the CD.

---

[284] See State Council, PRC 2002: ch. 7.
[285] See United Nations 1993.

China has long held the position that its nuclear weapons are solely for self-defence. It has therefore practised restraint in its nuclear weapons, as it has

> unconditionally undertaken not to be the first to use nuclear weapons. Also, without any condition, it has committed itself not to use or threaten to use nuclear weapons against non-nuclear weapon states or nuclear weapon-free zones. China has never evaded its responsibilities and obligations for nuclear disarmament and has been advocating the complete prohibition and thorough destruction of nuclear weapons.[286]

China did not support the 1993 General Assembly Resolution calling for negotiation of an FMCT. This position was altered slightly when China called the FMCT 'an important step toward nuclear disarmament'. On 4 October 1994, US Secretary of State Christopher and Chinese Foreign Minister Qian issued a joint statement promoting the 'earliest possible achievement' of an FMCT.[287] During the October 1997 US–China summit, both countries made a joint statement that they would 'agree to pursue at the UN Conference on Disarmament the early start of the formal negotiations on the Treaty on the Prohibition of the Production of Fissile Materials Use in Nuclear Weapons and Other Nuclear Explosive Devices.'[288]

China believes that the FMCT has to be conducive to the prevention of nuclear weapons proliferation and the promotion of nuclear disarmament.[289] To that end, China considers FMCT a means. China maintains that CD should answer to the requests by the United Nations General Assembly and follow the common wish and aspirations of the international community by conducting negotiations on Prevention of an Arms Race in Outer Space and nuclear disarmament, and in this context, also negotiate the FMCT.[290] Even at other fora, China has maintained that negotiations on the proposed FMCT should begin.[291]

---

[286] State Council, PRC 2000a.
[287] See Joint US–PRC Statement 1994a.
[288] See Joint US–PRC Statement 1997.
[289] Sha Zukang 2000.
[290] Hu Xiaodi 2000.
[291] See in this context, Government of PRC 2000; Shen Guofang 1999; Sha Zukang 1998.

In January 1999, Sha Zukang stated China's position on the FMCT in the Carnegie International Nonproliferation Conference in Washington, DC.[292] A few days later, the Chinese held a two-day bilateral negotiation with the US State Department concerning the US and Chinese positions on the FMCT. During the meetings, the Chinese reportedly voiced their existing concerns about the scope and the verification provisions of the treaty. Both sides also agreed that negotiations must move forward within the Geneva-based CD. A month later, the Chinese ambassador said to the CD,

China maintains that a treaty banning the production of fissile material for nuclear weapons or other nuclear explosive devices will be conducive to the prevention of nuclear proliferation and promotion of nuclear disarmament. In 2002, the UN General Assembly unanimously adopted the resolution on FMCT. The Chinese delegation supports the re-establishment of an Ad-Hoc Committee to negotiate, on the basis of the mandate contained in the 'Shannon Report', a non-discriminatory, multilateral and internationally and effectively verifiable treaty banning the production of fissile material for nuclear weapons or other nuclear explosive devices, as requested by the UNGA Resolution 48/75L.[293]

In May 1999 Prep Com of the NPT, China made three suggestions:[294]

- Establish an *ad hoc* committee on the prevention of an arms race in outer space and conduct negotiations.
- Establish an *ad hoc* committee on nuclear disarmament and conduct negotiations.
- Establish an FMCT *ad hoc* committee on the basis of the Shannon Report[295] and the mandate contained therein and conduct negotiations.

---

[292] He said: 'Negotiation should start as soon as possible. All states should make the necessary efforts and demonstrate the necessary political will to conclude a good treaty at an early date, which guarantees the adherence of all states capable of producing nuclear materials' (Sha Zukang 1999).

[293] Li Changhe 1999: 2.

[294] Preparatory Committee 1999.

[295] Amb. Gerald E. Shannon of Canada was asked by the CD in 1994 to seek the views of members of the conference on the most appropriate arrangement to negotiate a non-discriminatory, multilateral and internationally effective and verifiable treaty banning the production of fissile material for nuclear weapons or other nuclear explosive devices.

China continues to believe that 'all countries should strictly comply with existing nuclear disarmament and non-proliferation treaty obligations, and negotiate and conclude new treaties, including a fissile material cut-off treaty (FMCT).'[296]

❧❦❧

China is an important state in the international system with all the potentials of a great power: large territory, big population, large military with nuclear weapons and vast amount of resources. Having examined various factors and influences that determine and seek to explain China's strategic behaviour at present, what is the future course of action that China might take? Any change in China's behaviour or its power attributes can alter the international system and seriously impact on the regional security environment. Often, historians point out that expanding power has been the norm throughout history primarily due to the following reasons. First, a rise in power invariably leads to increased interest in international commitments and interests. Second, rising power brings about a rise in ambitions. Finally, when rising powers gain relative power they are more likely to try to advance their standing in the international system.[297] India's relationship with China to develop a more effective engagement policy would require a more nuanced understanding of the medium- and long-term evolution of China's calculative strategy and China's cooperative and assertive behaviour over time. It is imperative on India's part to understand and predict when such an engagement might fail.

How will key variables shape China's strategic behaviour in the near and distant future?

DETERMINANTS OF CHINA'S BEHAVIOUR

China's primary national goal is to become a strong, unified and wealthy nation that is respected as a great power in the world with a pre-eminent role as a major power in Asia. China terms this as comprehensive national power. The nuclear forces and the seat on the UN Security Council already bestow some of the

---

[296] Sha Zukang 2002.
[297] See Gilpin 1981. See also Kennedy 1987.

attributes of a great power on China. The Chinese look forward to achieving a status of parity in economic, political and military strength with the world's leading powers by the middle of this century.

China's grand strategy for achieving this national goal comprises raising the per capita income of its people to the global norm for advanced nations; promoting rapid and sustained economic growth; maintaining the political unity and stability of the nation; improving the social quality of life of the people (including health and education that are on a par with the leading nations of the world); raising technological levels; protecting national sovereignty and territorial integrity; securing access to global resources and markets; and promoting its role as one of the five or six major poles in a new multipolar world.

The Structure of its Economic Capabilities

A marginal increase in GDP may contribute to a marked improvement in the quality of life, which in turn may permit China to engage itself more vigorously in the international system.[298] Another variable that can be factored in, is how fast China's economy will shift from focus on primary occupations to tertiary occupations. This will further increase the flow of capital in the market. It may be very difficult for China to sustain its target of 8 per cent growth, and even if it can do a 5–6 per cent there may be a marked change in the GDP. This could then generate additional resources required for modernisation of the PLA. Even though China maintains a steady growth rate, it still remains behind many Western countries in terms of per capita GDP.[299]

Besides the economy, the nature of China's military capabilities, the modernisation of its forces and its ability to alter regional relationships will also be crucial in the future. The Chinese defence industry has also proved to be inadequate to the task of narrowing the gap between the country's aspirations and its capabilities.[300]

---

[298] Knorr termed this 'two sides to nation power', where on one side a state is concerned with what it can do to other countries, while on the other is a state's ability to limit what other countries can do to it (Knorr 1973).

[299] There are economists who maintain that Chinese growth rate may slow down in the near future.

[300] See in this context, National Defense Authorization Act 2001, where some of the following points have been raised: (a)Developments in Chinese military

This has increasingly led China to turn to foreign sources for weapons and weapons technologies. Further, it has not been successful at reverse engineering. China's forces have increasingly demanded more advanced systems:

A review of the Chinese defence industrial press as well as China's wish list the Russians reveals a concentration of attention on next generation force multipliers: C4I system cruise missile technology, laser guided bombs, satellite based sensing and guidance systems, advanced radar and jamming systems, fighter aircraft production technologies, and advanced precision guidance capabilities.[301]

RMA and other future technologies will also increasingly drive the military-industrial complex to seek more. At the same time China may have to respond to changes in the neighbourhood. If the US moves BMD in the region, China may be forced to respond. This will have serious implications for the shape of the Indian nuclear deterrent posture.

A RAND study by Michael Swaine and Ashley Tellis suggests that if the Chinese army wants to play a more dominating role, it

doctrine, focusing on (but not limited to) efforts to exploit the emerging Revolution in Military Affairs or to conduct pre-emptive strikes. (b) Efforts by China to enhance its capabilities in the area of nuclear weapons development. (c) Efforts to develop long-range air-to-air or air defence missiles designed to target special support aircraft, such as Airborne Warning and Control System aircraft, Joint Surveillance and Target Attack Radar System aircraft, or other command and control, intelligence, airborne early warning, or electronic aircraft. (d) Efforts by the People's Republic of China to develop a capability to conduct 'information warfare' at the strategic, operational and tactical levels of war. (e) Trends that would lead China towards the development of advanced intelligence, surveillance and reconnaissance capabilities, including gaining access to commercial or third-party systems with military significance. (f) Efforts by China to develop highly accurate and stealthy ballistic and cruise missiles, including sea-launched cruise missiles, particularly in numbers sufficient to conduct attacks capable of overwhelming projected defence capabilities in the Asia-Pacific region. (g) Development of command and control networks, particularly those capable of battle management of long-range precision strikes. (h) Efforts in the area of telecommunications, including common channel signalling and synchronous digital hierarchy technologies. (i) Development of capabilities for denial of sea control, including such systems as advanced sea mines, improved submarine capabilities, or land-based sea-denial systems.

[301] Gill (1998) sates this, based on his interviews with Chinese defence and technology officials.

would need significant improvement along three levels of capability. First, it would need to develop a range of military capabilities that would allow it to deny its adversaries the free use of a given battlespace. Second, they argue that 'China would move beyond merely denial capabilities to something resembling positive control thereby allowing it to operate within a given battle space without inordinate risks to its own forces'. Finally, they suggest, 'China would actually have the capability to exploit its positive control over a given battle space to bring coercive power to bear against the strategic centers of gravity valued by its adversaries.'[302] The PLA does have a large and expanding force of short- and intermediate-range cruise and ballistic missiles which can be used for political gains also.[303]

Another factor that may influence the choices China makes will be the level of communism. By this, it is implied that having opened markets to foreign goods and already in talks with the WTO for membership, a major issue is what remains of classical communism in China. As always, one school of thought says that open markets are a fair enough indicator of communism having become a thing of the past, and Hong Kong needs to be considered as the epitome of the growth of liberalism in China. The other school of thought quickly points out the Tiananmen Square massacre as an example of communist oppression. But will China make a move towards more democratisation—a move that may be detrimental to the future of the country itself? Mansfield and Snyder have argued,

> Countries do not become democracies overnight ... they go through a rocky transition period, where democratic control over foreign policy is partial, where mass politics mixes in a volatile way with authoritarian elite politics and where democratization suffers reversals. In this transitional phase of democratization, countries become more aggressive and war-prone, not less, and they do fight wars with democratic states.[304]

These findings have since been challenged by Reinhold Wolf and Erich Weede.[305]

---

[302] Swaine and Tellis 2000: 160.
[303] For PLA's present ability for power projection, see Godwin 1997.
[304] Mansfield and Snyder 1995.
[305] Wolf 1996; Weede 1996.

Yet another factor influencing the foreign policy choices of China in the struggle for resources is energy, which will be needed in large amount to fuel China's economic revolution. Only a modest increase in China's industrialisation would place a huge new strain on global suppliers. China does have enough coal, oil and natural gas and may meet the energy crunch, but over the next couple of decades the requirements are only likely to increase.[306] The next problem is the threat to environment. A few billion tonnes of coal, if burned without proper pollution control norms, may end up being an environmental threat. The most polluted place in the country may be Benxi, a Manchurian city with air like soot. It is said that many times in the 1980s, the city of Benxi completely disappeared from satellite photographs because of the haze. Another concern is that of global warming. China ranks third in emissions of greenhouse gases, behind US and Russia. But for the time being, energy security and environmental debates may take some more time before they can have an impact. As Bai Xianhong, a senior government scientist said, 'you can't say that for the sake of lowering carbon dioxide emissions, China shouldn't burn coal anymore. This is impossible.'[307] This raises regional concerns for the competition for resources, particularly energy.

Other factors involved are governance and ethnic identities. The Xinjiang–Uighur Autonomous Region in China is inhabited by Uighurs, Wei Wuers, Sarts and Kashgarliks. The area they inhabit is Xinjiang or Singkiang. Majority of Uighurs refer to this area as Eastern Turkistan. The Chinese concern is that in the process of development this ethnic group has retained its identity as in a 'salad bowl'. China has continued to mix up the ethnic pattern by infiltrating the majority Han in their society. The Chinese apprehension is that with the break-up of the Soviet Union, a 'domino effect' may affect the aspirations of this group. This is often interpreted in Western analyses as a simmer of discontent with a potential to break-up China. Strategically located between Russia and India, Xinjiang is a buffer zone between great powers. With the presence of Wahabi groups, there has been a growth in the activity of Islamic preachers. The government has sought to reduce their influence by launching a large-scale propaganda and a simultaneous

---

[306] See in the context of China's energy needs, Lague 2002.
[307] Quoted in Kristof and Wudunn 1994.

crackdown against forces of separatism. Besides, Xinjiang, which was a relatively underdeveloped area, has of late seen a fast pace, of development. The capital city, Urumqi, has had constructions of more than 80 new skyscrapers in the last 15 years. China is looking after Xinjiang with twin policies of raising living standards and lowering the levels of discontent.[308] In spite of the various efforts by the separatists, it is highly unlikely that China will relinquish the control of this province that produces one-third of China's cotton, the country's largest oil and gas reserves in the Tarim Basin and houses more than 18 million people. It borders Mongolia, many of the Central Asian republics, Pakistan, India and Russia, and is a useful springboard for projecting Chinese influence abroad. Further, any movement towards independence by the Uighurs will only embolden the separatists in Tibet and Taiwan.[309]

Xinjiang, along with Tibet, presents challenges to China in keeping together a large country that has different ethnic identities. As Mishra concludes,

> [W]hether Xinjian separatism is about religion or nationalism, whether it is a real threat or not, Beijing is taking no chances. The regime is not about to loosen its grip on the autonomous region even if that hard line pushes many Uighurs to separatism, the very outcome Beijing seeks to avoid.[310]

China's internal challenges, domestic politics and institutions will be critical inputs to the foreign policy choices that it makes.

Although there is a lack of social homogeneity, even the 94 per cent Han population vary greatly in terms of their language, belief systems, political culture and traditions.[311] A variety of cultural, economic and political conditions that exist across the Chinese provinces obscure more than they reveal. There is likely to be an inherent variability in provincial leaders' responses to these different levels of liberalisation, levels of development, social attitudes and variety of political institutions.[312] The Hainan province appears

---

[308] Harris 1993.
[309] Chien-peng Chung 2002.
[310] Mishra 2000: 348. Also see Chien-peng Chung 2002.
[311] Mosen 1985; Goodman 2003.
[312] In this context, see Minxin Pei 2002.

to be perhaps the most open part of China. There is significant foreign investment, and the area has a reputation of being China's 'wild west' where anything goes. Besides, it is a part of a special economic zone and is awarded preferential policy settings by Beijing. In Hainan province, the major proponent of social and political change was Liao Xun, who coined the term 'small government, big society' to characterise his desire to see governments withdraw from many areas of activity under state socialism, and its replacement by both a provincial government organised along new functional administrative lines, and by independent, autonomous, self-governing social groups.[313] On the other hand, one can look at Shanxi, located more inland in North China and a less open province. There is very little foreign investment which is matched by the dominating position of the state. Few small-scale initiatives, and that too in the retail sector, have increased the role of the local government, as is also the case with collective sector enterprises. The main economic strength of Shanxi is coal, but even that has not been developed very well due to lack of access to markets, which in turn depends on an increased government control. Neither has the service sector developed very much. However, '[s]ince the beginning of 1994, there has been an observable and increasing tendency for through co-operation with enterprises in other provinces seeking to invest in Shanxi.'[314] Though neither Hainan nor Shanxi can be taken up as true and complete representations of China's liberalisation, they do present some idea of relative economic development. As Gerald Segal has argued,

> The fault lines of the Chinese Empires are myriad, and history too replete with Chinas of different configurations. Today one can distinguish between China's inner and outer empires. The outer empire includes Tibet, Xingjian, Mongolia and other fringe territories, most of which have strong cases for ethnically based independence but have reaped relatively little benefit from economic decentralisation. Dialect and important cultural fault lines divide even the inner empire, which consists of areas such as Southern China, Shanghai and its hinterland and Shandong.[315]

---

[313] Liao Xun's ideas are discussed in Brodsgaard 1998.
[314] Quoted in Goodman 1997: 42.
[315] Segal 1994: 56.

And we have not touched upon the biggest 'window to the world', SAR Hong Kong. If China can manage to have an equitable distribution of foreign investment which may lead to the 'trickle-down' effect, it may help in economic development of China. Such availability of resources will naturally hasten the process of modernisation of forces.

Chinese communist leaders still believe in the two Karls—Karl Marx and Karl Von Clausewitz—in that economy is the base and politics is the superstructure, while military is the continuation of politics. The Chinese contend that the threat to the nation's survival disappeared long ago—in the 1940s with the end of the Second World War when China ended up on the winning side, and with the subsequent tide of decolonisation.[316] China does not foresee a war from any of the major powers. The end of the Cold War 'has terminated the antagonistic struggle between two systems of ideology and political economy.'[317] A more real threat that China faces is from within. As a party document said, 'keep a good government and carry out the anti corruption struggle and this is a prerequisite ... for maintaining social stability.[318] Economic development is considered most fundamental and effective as it helps improve living standards of the people, making them less rebellious and in the process increasing the international prestige of the country.[319] As Jiang Zemin also noted,

> There exists an inseparable inner link among reform, development and stability. Development is the hard core of all principles ... and is indispensable in maintaining stability and withstanding the pressures of hegemonism and power politics ... and fundamentally shaking off economic backwardness and ranking China among the world's modernised countries.[320]

It is for some of these reasons that China continues to insist to Pakistan that it should solve the Kashmir dispute with India on a

---

[316] Hua Di 1997.
[317] Ibid.: 3.
[318] *China Daily* 1995a.
[319] Hua Di 1997.
[320] *China Daily* 1995b.

bilateral basis. But these are some of the challenges that China has to address internally. How China addresses such issues will impact on its aspirations as a 'great power'.

China's primary national goal is to become a strong, modernised, unified and wealthy nation. It views its national standing in relation to the position of other 'great powers'. China considers itself a developing power whose natural resources, manpower, nuclear-capable forces, seat on the UN Security Council and growing economy give it most of the attributes of a great power. If present trends continue, Beijing believes it will achieve the status of a 'medium-sized' great power by 2050 at a minimum. Beijing clearly wants to be recognised as a full-fledged great power. It wants to achieve 'parity' in political, economic and military strength with other great powers. China also wants to become the pre-eminent Asian power by generating enough 'strength' so that no major action will be taken by any other international actor in Asia without first considering Chinese interests.

In pursuit of 'comprehensive national power', what then will be the China of 2010 or 2015? Based on the earlier analysis, some estimates can be made. Internally, there will be an overall increase in standard of living. While pursuing modernisation, the leadership has tended to relax internal controls over the population. At the same time, the PLA is marching ahead in perfect synchronisation with time and technology. Externally, China has 'solved or shelved' its border problems with its neighbours. Its disarmament diplomacy has been realistic as opposed to more idealistic Indian policies. The economy has now sustained a high rate of growth for a long time—what will then be the challenges to the international system from the rising dragon?

Optimists opine that an ever-increasing web of international interdependence will moderate the sustained growth of China's military and economic power. The pessimists point out that a growth in relative power terms may encourage Beijing to be more assertive in territorial, trade and other demands, where some other powers in the system are following a policy of appeasement. While China does calculate the relative benefits of remaining in a treaty regime, it also does a cost–benefit analysis of what other states pay in terms of remaining in the treaty. This implies, other variables being equal, that China could 'unilaterally' defect on some treaty.[321] That being so, the regional states have to cater for such an eventuality.

The sole superpower, the US, may continue to use its limited influence over China to make it conform to international norms, which over a period of time will foster changes in political, economic and military spheres that are compatible to US interests.[322]

All these variables will impact on China's nuclear deterrent posture. This, in turn, will impinge on Indian strategic calculations both in the near and far term. China is pursuing an assertive, worldwide diplomatic campaign aimed at promoting Beijing's positions on such issues as Taiwan, human rights, proliferation and trade. In recent years, China's goals have turned increasingly to the support of economic and commercial interests, as exemplified by China's participation in the Asia-Pacific Economic Cooperation forum and its efforts to join the World Trade Organisation (WTO).

On the core issues of nuclear and missile systems and force modernisation, the following can be suggested:

1. Realise the role of nuclear weapons in the post-Cold War period. Are these weapons of offence or defence—first strike or last resort? The answers to these questions will be clear in due course and will be a reflection of the grand strategy of China.
2. What strength of force is sufficient to deter? If the US has the capability to deter, then it should not thrust a BMD that may spiral a new arms race.
3. Multilaterally work out a framework for determining the end of tactical nuclear weapons. With all other members of NPT gradually decreasing their nuclear warhead count, China should be encouraged to qualitatively refine its nuclear forces.
4. At least on the declaratory policy, China is way ahead of the other NPT members—it has a no-first-use policy; it will not attack a non-nuclear state with nuclear weapons, and will not use nuclear weapons in nuclear weapon-free zones. Thus, the operational battlespace of Chinese nuclear weapons is considerably limited.
5. The other big powers should, at least declaratorily, shift the role of nuclear weapons from fighting war to deterring it.

[321] In this context, see Johnston 1996a.
[322] See in this regard, Sutter 1995b.

6. The US has already launched an 'engage China' programme. China has been made a member of various regimes. The web of regimes has now to be strengthened, so that even potential nuclear states are engaged to contain the spread of nuclear weapons. A world with few nuclear arms is in the interest of all.

7. States look up to the US and its actions. Until the process begins from the superpower, other states will not take non-proliferation initiatives seriously.

8. The US has to realise that BMD has consequences of 'trickle down effect'. Even Pakistan may be affected. Any US action will become a rationalisation for Chinese actions. India will invariably get linked to the Chinese threat, with Pakistan left to justify an increase in its missile and nuclear force because India is its main threat.

9. The force modernisation will continue regardless of what Washington may do. On issues where China disagrees and is pushed to a corner, it may offer to sell technology, thereby making the NPT irrelevant. China has sold technology and delivery systems before.

10. All the major arms control relationships are bipolar—this could be modified to include China, as the bipolar vision has obscured the emerging strategic offence/defence relationship among the US, Russia and China.

11. China may have the capability to make its missiles MIRVs. The CTBT which has been dead for a while has to be revived—but that initiative has to come from the US. Until it comes into force, even the principles of *pacta sunt suvanda* (treaties are supreme) do not apply.

12. Chinese efforts to promote credibility of its forces are often interpreted as using deception and a marked lack of transparency. This now is becoming an inseparable part of their nuclear strategy.

13. Internally, China has the ability to take care of itself. It may not break-up, and the strength of the economy will keep improving the standard of living.

14. Externally, the forces of globalisation can assist China to build up a strong nation. The capital generated from trade surplus can be used to spread economic equality internally.

15. China has to realise that there are many intended consequences of its actions—Chinese actions give legitimate strategic space to India for furthering the Chinese threat bogey.

16. Whenever political will permits, China, Pakistan and India should enter into a security dialogue. Building a credible deterrence against each other will be very difficult.

17. The American presence in Central Asia will have implications for China's military modernisation. This, coupled with the proposed national missile defence, makes the US almost impregnable and impinges on the Chinese ability to construct a credible military deterrent against growing US power. It is likely that China will increase the pace of its military modernisation.

CHAPTER 5

INDIA

Long years ago we made a tryst with destiny, and now the time comes when we shall redeem our pledge, not wholly or in full measure, but very substantially. At the stroke of the midnight hour, when the world sleeps, India will awake to life and freedom.

—Jawaharlal Nehru
Discovery of India

India conjures up images vast and varied—intermingling of civilisations, cultures, religions, ethnicities, languages, a large population, a huge market, advanced science and technology, democracy down to the grassroots and a state that is now also a nuclear power. To quote Jawaharlal Nehru, 'I feel that anything that had the power to mould hundreds of generations without a break, must have drawn its vitality from some deep well of strength, and have had the capacity to renew that vitality from age to age.'[1]

This chapter examines India's strategic culture, nuclear doctrines, weapons, policies on major arms control regimes and foreign relations to make conclusions about conflict and stability in the region and see in which direction these policies will take the country.

Indian culture has been marked by diversity from the ancient ages. History has witnessed many different groups, with divergent customs, languages and religions, gaining control over and settling down in various parts of the subcontinent. This diversity is reflected in the strategic cultures of states through the ages, forming part of the preservation of territory and people that broadly covers the term security. The determinants of security of the state have grown through the ages from mere territory, to include culture, history and population. Through the ages, India has faced many external invasions—some external rulers came for resources, while others

---

[1] Nehru 1946.

led conquests for prestige. The geo-strategic importance of India has been key to these conquests—while it beckoned invaders for its 'golden sparrow' image, there were also the resources of the Indo-Gangetic plain and the Bengal plain.

Among the ancient rulers, while Samudragupta used military force, Ashoka had a change of heart after using brute military force in the battle of Kalinga (269 BC). Thereafter, he used *dhamma* (peaceful methods) to win over enemies. Kautilya outlined various forms of foreign policy, historically the most comprehensive:

1. *Samdhi* or entering into an agreement with specific conditions, that is, concluding a treaty.
2. *Vigratha* or three kinds of war—open war, a battle in the normal sense; secret war, attacking the enemy in a variety of ways; and undeclared war.
3. *Asana* or staying quiet.
4. *Yana* or preparing for war.
5. *Samsraya* or seeking the protection, when threatened, of a stronger king or taking refuge in a fort.
6. *Dvaidhibhava* or the policy of making peace with neighbouring king in order to pursue, with his help, the policy of hostility towards another.[2]

On the growth of Indian civilisation, Jawaharlal Nehru wrote,

It seems absurd and presumptuous to talk of an impulse, or an idea of life, underlying the growth of Indian civilisation. Even the life of an individual draws sustenance from a hundred sources; much more complicated is the life of a nation or of a civilisation. There are myriad ideas that float about like flotsam and jetsam on the surface of India, and many of them are mutually antagonistic. It is easy to pick out any group of them to justify a particular thesis; equally easy to choose another group to demolish it.[3]

Therefore, varied cultural ethos, geography and histories have resulted in the absence of 'a territorial consciousness, and a strategic sense about the protection of the territory of residence.'[4]

---

[2] See Rangarajan 1987: 548.
[3] Nehru 1946: 143.
[4] Singh 1999: 16.

The India that emerged after August 1947 was a nation that had borne 200 years of British exploitation and the painful experience of partition. India as a developing nation, whose core national security interests include the preservation of sovereignty, territorial integrity and the well-being of the population, is still in the process of identifying its interests and values. This brings us to the definition of national security. Robert McNamara has provided an illustrative starting point: 'Security means development into a modernising society, security is not just military hardware, though it may include it; security is not just military force though it may involve it, security is not traditional activity though it may encompass it.'[5]

 ## STRATEGIC THOUGHT AND PRACTICE

This brings us to the questions of strategic culture and whether India has a culture of strategic thinking at all. Colin Gray has defined strategic culture as 'the socially constructed and transmitted assumptions, habits of mind, traditions, and preferred methods of operation—that is, behaviour—that are more or less specific to a particular geographically based security community.'[6] Writing on the issue of strategic thought and practice, George Tanham says that military matters in India have been marked routinely by a passive, or at best a reactive approach, that is further located in the hierarchical nature of the society, agricultural economy and the traditional civilian bureaucracy.[7] Further, Stephen Rosen has argued,

above all else, India is Hindu, and Hindus think differently from non-Hindus. This statement of course, acknowledges the presence of non-Hindus in India and has been modified to take into account the existence in India today of an elite that is relatively less traditional in its religious outlook .... But accepting that qualification, is it important that India is Hindu? If it is important, that could form one basis for arguing that there is a Hindu strategic culture.[8]

[5] McNamara 1968: 4.
[6] Gray 1999: 28.
[7] Tanham 1992.
[8] Rosen 1996: 33.

This is nowhere close to being true. Jawaharlal Nehru had written,

> Hinduism as a faith, is vague, amorphous, many sided, all things to all men. It is hardly possible to define it, or indeed to say definitely whether it is a religion or not, in the usual sense of the word. In its present form, and even in the past, it embraces many beliefs and practices, from the highest to the lowest, often opposed to or contradicting each other. Its essential spirit seems to be live and let live.[9]

He further adds, 'It is, therefore incorrect and undesirable to use "Hindu" or "Hinduism" for Indian culture, even with reference to the distant past, although the various aspects of thought, as embodied in the ancient writings, were dominant expression of that culture.'[10] However, going beyond these debates, if we simply consider the pre-Sultanate period, that is, the time before 1200 AD, we find that although there is no dearth of texts that mention actions of men, princes and kings in the past, of social systems and religious beliefs delineating right and wrong, there is an absence of these ideals in political institutions, unlike later. Ancient law-givers and their commentators have written on laws of warfare, threat or use of weapons of mass destruction, and policies to be followed against an adversary.[11] There are references to calling the elements—fire or rain—against the enemy, and instances in Indian Vedic and post-Vedic literature of righteousness of the king. There was, however, a general abhorrence against using extreme weapons and in formulating laws of warfare that had to be abided by and had the consent of the warring armies. With the invention of gunpowder, military tactics changed in the 15th century. So did techniques of assault, *durg* (fort) building, deployment of garrisons and communications. Both defensive and offensive techniques altered radically in the 18th and 19th centuries with the coming of the rifle and European strategies of warfare. On the other hand, Shri Aurobindo said, 'India's central conception is that of the Eternal, the Spirit ... [it is] her urge towards the spiritual and the external that constitute[s] the distinct value of her civilisation.'[12] Even Dr S. Radhakrishnan, a great philosopher and

---

[9] Nehru 1946: 75.
[10] Ibid.: 75.
[11] See for instance, Oppert 1967 [1880]: 32.
[12] Shri Aurobindo 1959: 2–3.

India's second president, conceded, 'India has failed to give political expression to its ideals. The importance to wealth and power though theoretically recognised was not practically realised.'[13]

Does this mean that India has no strategic culture or does India have a culture in which state power is benign? A contemporary Indian writer offers an explanation: 'The authors of the Indian state were crippled by ... often an excessive, and at times ersatz pacifism, both internal and external, [which] has twisted India's strategic culture into all kinds of absurdities.'[14] Alternatively, a civilisation 5000 years old would pass through periodic heightened activity. In some sense, India strategic culture was shaped and influenced by its history. Many influences have contributed to this: an accommodating and forgiving Hindu populace, successive Jain, Buddhist and later Vaishnav–Bhakti influences resulting in excessive piety, and much later, in the 20th century, ahimsa or non-violence. An unintended consequence of all these influences, spread over many centuries, has been a near total emasculation of the concept of state power and its proper employment as an instrument of state policy. In the service of national interest, war was shunned— a linear consequence of both Jain and Buddhist logic and a belief of non-injury.[15] However, within the overall canvas of shunning violence and finding a peaceful solution before taking up the route of armed conflict, there were militant cultures which privileged defending the land beyond all else. The Rajputs, Jats, Marathas, Dogras, the Sikh Khalsa, Gurkhas and various tribes have their names in history precisely because they took up arms for the cause of the state. This again has neither been a consistent pattern nor the dominant thinking. The Rajputs took up arms because some of them, the most prominent being Maharana Pratap, refused to enter into alliance with Akbar. The Jats of Bharatpur and parts of modern-day Haryana in North India took up arms because they could not pay the high taxes to the later Mughal rulers. The Dogras had a similar problem in Kashmir, while the Gurkhas, though fiercely loyal, could take up arms when mobilised properly. The Khalsa order came into being after nine Sikh gurus had preached peace and two of them had to pay a heavy price for not converting.

---

[13] Radhakrishnan 1974: 378.
[14] Singh 1999: 13.
[15] Ibid.

The British laid the foundations of the Indian Army (then British Army) with the Jat Regiment, Sikh Regiment, Maratha Regiment, Rajputana Regiment and Gorkha Rifles, among other martial segments.

So, while Indians in the past have written and commented on every conceivable subject on military science, the most detailed is as ancient as the *Arthashastra*. Contemporary India, which is the world's largest democracy, with the fourth largest standing army and a force that includes missiles bombers, submarines and nuclear capability, reflects this lack—it has no formal national defence policy document. If India does have a strategic culture that has not been clearly articulated, what is stopping the Parliament from doing so, as the state enters the 21st century?

One can attempt to pick up threads from what little is available of government articulated positions on the shape of India's national security interests and policy. One standard source is the Ministry of Defence (MoD) annual reports and another is the Standing Committee on Defence in the Parliament. According to the Standing Committee on Defence, 'although there has been no specifically written document called India's National Defence Policy, yet it has been articulated clearly and unambiguously through various policy statements over the years.'[16] The annual report of the Ministry of Defence (1998–99) also highlights 'national security interests'. [17]

---

[16] The report further says, 'our military capability is to be so directed to ensuring the defence of national territory over land, sea and air encompassing among others the inviolability of our land borders, island territories, offshore assets and our maritime trade routes. Government have (sic) repeatedly made it clear that it is not our objective to influence/interfere/dominate [the] region on the basis of military strength' (Standing Committee on Defence 1996a).

[17] It includes: '(a) Defence of national territory over land, sea and air, encompassing among others the inviolability of our land borders, island territories, offshore assets and our maritime trade routes; (b) To secure an internal environment whereby our Nation State is insured against any threat to its unity or progress on the basis of religion, language, ethnicity or socio-economic dissonance; (c) To enable our country to exercise a degree of influence over the nations in our immediate neighbourhood to promote harmonious relationship in tune with our national interests; (d) To be able to effectively contribute towards regional and international stability; (e) To possess an effective out-of-the-country contingency capability to prevent destabilisation of the small nations in our immediate neighbourhood that could have adverse security implications for us.' See section on

It is essential to realise that in 1947, while scientists and national leaders were aware of the potential of the atom, the strategic environment did not warrant effective decision making, although ambiguity in this area can also be attributed to the towering personalities of that time—primarily, Jawaharlal Nehru.[18] The choices India made at global fora were largely articulated by a moralistic brand of politics. It can also be argued that for a state that had just attained independence and chose to remain non-aligned in an international environment characterised by Cold War alliances, the options that presented themselves could not have altered the course of India drastically. To this effect, the use and harnessing of atomic energy was left for peaceful purposes.[19] To some extent, India's strategic and foreign policy choices can also be located in the process of political development of a state that had just rid itself of more than 200 years of colonial rule.

The official version on the absence of any written document on strategic environment is that it is the result of a conscious decision. In December 1996, the Parliament Standing Committee on Defence suggested that a national defence policy be published. The response of the Defence Ministry was that

India has a comprehensive policy on strategic and security issues based inter alia on our threat perception and the global and regional security environment. The policy is constantly under review ... the absence of such a written document should not be construed to imply ... non existence of such a policy.[20]

Does this mean that there is a disjoint between the self-image of India as a great benign power in the making and the security construct based on a declared security posture of defending the territorial integrity of the state? Perhaps yes. Gandhi wanted 'India to practise non-violence being conscious of her strength and power.'[21]

'National Security Environment' in Ministry of Defence, GOI 1985–2002, here 1998–99.

[18] 'Nuclear ambiguity' has been taken as the condition where the nuclear option is 'kept open but in a state of suspended animation.' For a good discussion on nuclear ambiguity, see Chari 1995.

[19] Ganguly 1983.

[20] Standing Committee on Defence 1996b.

[21] Gandhi 1920.

Elsewhere, he did concede, 'non-violence affords the fullest protection to one's self respect and sense of honour, but not always to possession of land or movable property, though its habitual practice does prove a better bulwark than the possession of arms to defend them.'[22] India's first Prime Minister, Jawaharlal Nehru, said,

The peace of one country cannot be assured unless there is peace elsewhere also. In this narrow and contracting world, war and peace and freedom are becoming indivisible. Therefore, it is not enough for one country to secure peace within its own borders but it is also necessary that it should endeavour, to its utmost capacity, to help in the maintenance of peace all over the world.[23]

The Nehruvian legacy, primarily based on coercion-based power politics, found itself somewhat in disharmony with the earlier and older Gandhian moral blend, that emphasised community over state and non-violence over coercion.[24] However, it is apt to note that although both Nehru and Gandhi were not pro-nuclear by any means, there was an ambivalence in their outlook about the kind of weaponry that India might require in the post-Second World War phase.[25]

Successive parliamentary standing committees may be held responsible for not providing any document on the security planning of the country. In February 2001, the government released the *Recommendations of the Group of Ministers on Reforming the National Security System*.[26] This report covered broadly four major areas of national security: intelligence, international security, border management and management of defence.[27] The Group of Ministers

---

[22] Gandhi 1936.

[23] Nehru 1988a: 24–25.

[24] Jain 1994.

[25] In the context of Nehru's ambivalence, see Kapur 1976 and Perkovich 1999.

[26] The Group of Ministers included Mr L.K. Advani (Minister of Home Affairs), Mr George Fernandes (Minister of Defence), Mr Jaswant Singh (Minister of External Affairs), Mr Yashwant Sinha (Minister of Finance). This group was constituted in April 2000 with the approval of the prime minister 'to review the national security system in its entirety and, in particular, to consider the recommendations of the Kargil Review Committee and formulate specific proposals for implementation.' Apart from the four ministers, Brajesh Mishra, the National Security Advisor, was a special invitee for the meetings of the group. See Group of Ministers, GOI 2001.

[27] Ibid.: 118.

further suggested national security management systems be re-examined periodically every five years.[28] 'This exercise', the group suggested, 'should take stock of the progress achieved in the implementation of the recommendations approved, address areas of difficulty and chart out a plan of action for the future.'[29] The group was assisted by four task forces: (a) Task Force on Intelligence Apparatus,[30] (b) Task Force on Internal Security,[31] (c) Task Force on Border Management,[32] and (d) Task Force on Management of Defence.[33] A transparency in policy not just makes it possible to analyse or modify security positions, but also to communicate likely security responses to the adversary. This helps stabilise the security environment in a given region.

The British institutionalised decision making on national security issues in governmental bureaucratic structures operating in London and New Delhi. The secretary of state in conjunction with the office of the governor-general took decisions on national security issues. The commander-in-chief along with the war member in the Viceroy's Council analysed threats and responses. The necessary domestic inputs came from the Indian Civil Service. Thus was established civilian control over the armed forces—a tradition that continued post independence. After independence, with the firming up of the parliamentary form of government, institutions like these became more powerful. Some other institutions also emerged. The Prime Minister's Office, the Planning Commission, the Scientific Advisor, the Principal Secretary, and according to the needs of the time, Department of Atomic Energy, Department of Space, and lately, the National Security Advisor and a National Security Council. Minor alterations like dropping the title of the commander-in-chief in 1955 to merge with chiefs of staff continued. The Joint Intelligence Committee (which has now become the National Security Council Secretariat) too gained in importance

---

[28] Ibid.: 119.

[29] Ibid.: 119.

[30] Chairperson G.C. Saxena, former RAW Chief and Governor of Jammu and Kashmir.

[31] Chairperson N.N. Vohra, former Home Secretary, Defence Secretary and Principal Secretary to the Prime Minister.

[32] Chairperson Dr Madhav Godbole, former Union Home Secretary.

[33] Chairperson Arun Singh, Advisor (Security) in the Ministry of External Affairs and former Minister of State for Defence.

after 1962. The other agencies on intelligence gathering, the Intelligence Bureau (IB) and Research and Analysis Wing (RAW), too began to be taken seriously. The choices of foreign policy were formulated in the Policy Planning Division of the Ministry of External Affairs with inputs from Ministry of Defence and sometimes RAW.

Whatever policies were made, they always carried the reflection of the prime minister's persona. In the initial years, the towering personality of Pandit Nehru was clearly evident in the choices of Indian foreign policy. Krishna Menon, B.N. Mullick, Lal Bahadur Shastri, Indira Gandhi, Rajiv Gandhi and Atal Behari Vajpayee have been other prime ministers who influenced the course of foreign policy. Nehru was strongly opposed to an Indian nuclear weapons programme, although he did not foreclose the possibility of the 'option' strategy.

Given the fact that India, a developing Third World country, had seen the towering personality of Mahatma Gandhi, the initial policies were firmly based on the ideals of peace and non-violence. This saw a reflection in India's foreign policy and various Indian positions and initiatives in international fora. India's unflinching faith in international organisations, particularly the UN, policies of non-alignment, Panchsheel and decolonisation, all have a reflection of these ideals. It might be easy to criticise such positions living in a different century with a vastly different international system, but when contextualised in the immediate period following independence, one may appreciate that the choices were apt for their time.

While India was talking peace and gaining moral leadership of the Third World after Suez, Korea and Bandung, it was also realistic for it to debate the uses and potential of atomic energy.[34] Externally, India continued to maintain an idealistic and moralistic position on various issues relating to war and peace, while internally Nehru's vision of using transformative science was aided by Homi J. Bhabha. Nehru realised the thin line between using science for peaceful and destructive purposes.[35] Nehru had a vision for India— that of a self-reliant, modern and peace-loving nation. He wanted

---

[34] See in this context, Abraham 1998 and Perkovich 1999.

[35] As he once said, 'This great force—atomic energy—that has suddenly come about through scientific research may be used for war or may be used for peace.

India to make use of atomic energy, as it was modern, and yet apply it only to peaceful production. He said in the Parliament, 'I should like the House to remember that the use of atomic energy for peaceful purposes is far more important for a country like India whose power resources are limited.'[36] India started taking up idealistic and moralistic positions on the question of disarmament from the very beginning.[37]

Given such moorings, the Indian nuclear disarmament policy can be located in this context. A defensive orientation of the military, with greater reliance on international institutions for inter-state dispute resolution, also made available larger resources for political and economic development. Additionally, as Verghese Koithara argues, 'in modern India the concept of security ought to be located in the interstice of human welfare and national power.'[38]

Over the years, India continued to campaign tirelessly for abolition of nuclear weapons. Various leaders in different capacities spoke about the problem of nuclear weapons in different fora. The problem was addressed from all conceivable angles of logic— philosophy, balance of power, peace, and, of course, state security. While India may not have great transparency today, there is greater talk of defence in the foreign policies followed by the country. There is also a proliferation of a body of scholars who are examining the statements by the government. With the help of archives in the UK and USA, many books on various aspects of decision making in the past and interactions with great powers have highlighted the case for a freedom of information act in India. This new body of academics is not just New Delhi-centric, but has of late spread to various parts of the country. There now exist think tanks in many

---

We cannot neglect it because it may be used for war .... We shall develop it, I hope in cooperation with the rest of the world and for peaceful purposes.' Cited in Abraham 1998: 47.

[36] To quote from a Nehru speech in the United Nations General Assembly, 'No manner of disarmament can make a weak country strong or a non-industrial country the equal of an industrial country. Nor can it make a country which is not scientifically advanced the equal of a country which is. We can, however, lessen the chances of war and the fear of war through disarmament. Ultimately, the entire question is a question of confidence and of lessening the fear of one another. Disarmament helps that purpose, although it does not equalise conditions. The dangers remain' (Nehru 1988b).

[37] Nehru 1988c: 67.

[38] Koithara 1999: 21.

cities across the country, scholars are busy analysing every state-ment and the electronic media is full of experts who are high-lighting every nuance or lack of it in foreign policy. Some view this to be an increased cacophony of voices and ill-trained scholars who do not possess the requisite research tools and are often pres-surising the government. While this may be unfortunate, this pro-liferation has helped in the larger sense of taking the debate from a handful few in Delhi to many parts of the country.

The Nuclear Programme

Indian nuclear research began in 1944 and an Indian Atomic Energy Commission was created in 1948. From 1954, steady funding started flowing into nuclear research and development under the aegis of the Department of Atomic Energy.[39] By the early 1950s, Homi J. Bhabha led a consensus among a core group in New Delhi on the right to develop nuclear energy. India's defeat in the 1962 war with China and the subsequent nuclear test by China in 1964 intensified the debate within India over the nuclear option. The Indian belief was that, while nuclear science and technology was common intel-lectual property, the end use of atomic energy was purely a state's sovereign prerogative.[40] While India continued to champion the cause of global nuclear disarmament at various international fora, it was also aware of the tremendous potential capability of the atom. The shift from idealism to realism came after the 1962 Sino-Indian war. This was perhaps Nehru's biggest failure, as 'the possibility of the Chinese launching a very carefully controlled limited operation, with very limited political objectives, appears to have been over looked altogether, both in the services and pol-itical circles, and by the prime minister.'[41] Itty Abraham and George Perkovich[42] have stated that similar arguments had been raised at that time even in the debates of the Constituent Assembly.

---

[39] Marwah 1977.

[40] See Prime Minister Jawaharlal Nehru's note of 18 April 1955 on international control of atomic energy for B.K. Nehru, member of Indian delegation to the Asian-African Conference in Bandung, opposing the creation of International Atomic Energy Agency as mooted by the US, in Kumar and Prasad 1955.

[41] Subrahmanyam 1990a.

[42] Abraham 1998; Perkovich 1999.

There are enough reports to indicate that the US was aware as far back as 1961 that India's nuclear programme had the potential to produce nuclear weapons.[43] The Trombay plutonium reprocessing plant was the essential facility required for an atomic bomb.[44] The construction of this facility went under way in April 1961. Systemic causes undermined the US focus on non-proliferation efforts at that point in time. There were even suggestions that the US should actively aid India to become a nuclear power to counter the communist threat. This is evident from a recently declassified memorandum of 13 September 1961 from George McGhee, Head, State Departments' Policy Planning Council, to the then Secretary of State, Dean Rusk.[45] Expecting that China would 'detonate a nuclear device as early as 1962', the McGhee memo suggested that 'it would be desirable if a friendly Asian power beat Communist China to the punch' and for this there was 'no likelier candidate than India.'[46] This proposal was rejected outright by Rusk, as he was not 'convinced we (the US) should depart from our stated policy that we are opposed to further extension of national nuclear weapons capability.'[47] It augments another perspective of US policy, which was to promote India's nuclear capabilities to counter communist influence in South Asia. There were also the 'possibilities of providing nuclear weapons under US Custody'[48] to some of the 'friendly' Asian countries, in case there was an attack from China or a threat of an attack. The main rationale behind such an approach was to provide low-yield tactical nuclear weapons to select friendly Asian countries, such as Japan, India, Australia, New Zealand, the Philippines, Taiwan, Pakistan, Thailand and South Korea.[49] However, the US was aware of India's capability to acquire nuclear weapons even in the 1950s.[50] According to George Perkovich, in the late 1950s, 'although the American experts recognised India's capacity to divert its nuclear programme into military applications, non proliferation was a secondary consideration to

---

[43] Cited in Foran 1992.
[44] Perkovich 1999: 52.
[45] McGhee 1961.
[46] Ibid.
[47] Quoted in Perkovich 1999: 53.
[48] Quoted in ibid.: 91.
[49] Ibid.: 91–92.
[50] Ibid.: 49.

winning nuclear industry "markets" and containing communist influence in South Asia.'[51] The space programme, the nuclear programme, and various other dual-use technologies were all assumed to be cost effective. However, when various Western states denied a number of technologies, as in the case of the second US super-computer, India put in enhanced effort into developing indigenous technologies that would presumably make the country that much stronger, because it was forced to be self-reliant. This has since become an important rallying point for nationalist groups, since India is often portrayed as defying the combined might of the West in this regard.

The ENDC (Eighteen Nation Disarmament Committee) negotiated the NPT in the late 1960s. While this was happening, India was looking for a security guarantee. Soon after taking over the reins of prime ministership, Lal Bahadur Shastri despatched Sardar Swaran Singh, his Foreign Minister, to ascertain the views of the US, USSR and UK on India's request for a nuclear guarantee. Shastri was facing increasing pressure on the domestic front, especially after the Chinese nuclear test in 1964. India failed to get a security guarantee from the major powers, especially the United States and the then Soviet Union.[52] Following this failure, India decided to militarise its nuclear programme.[53] The debate in 1964–65 centred primarily on the threat from China. After the loss in the war with China in 1962, the Chinese nuclear test was seen as a grave strategic challenge. US President Nixon's visit to China in 1971 and the US 'tilt' towards Pakistan in the 1971 war with India (the US despatched an aircraft carrier, USS Enterprise, to the Bay of Bengal) also upset Indian calculations.

Prime Minister Lal Bahadur Shastri sanctioned a Subterranean Nuclear Explosion Project (SNEP), in which, 'once the go-ahead was given, it would take three months to have an explosion.'[54] The post-Shimla phase saw India exploding a nuclear device in Pokhran on 18 May 1974, which was termed a peaceful nuclear explosion (PNE) and was a signal to the world that India had nuclear capability. Although other Western counties condemned

[51] Ibid.: 49.
[52] Noorani 1967.
[53] Chari 1995.
[54] Kapur 1976: 194.

India for the tests, the American reaction to the Pokhran tests was mild. According to a state department release, 'It was only a matter of Indian leaders making up their minds and devoting the necessary resources.'[55] Kissinger felt public castigation would not undo the event, and it would only add to US–Indian bilateral problems and reduce the influence Washington might have on India's future nuclear policy.[56] As Indo-US relations were already on a low ebb, the US decided not to highlight proliferation issues at this time. This could be observed from the fact that the United States, in the aftermath of the test, agreed to reschedule Indian debts amounting to more than $29 million, and in June 1974 decided to ship an instalment of previously approved uranium fuel to India's Tarapur reactor.[57]

Kissinger went on to testify at a hearing before the Senate Committee that the Indian test did not violate any US agreement. He said, 'We (the US) objected (to the Pokhran test by India) strongly, but since there was no violation of US agreements involved, we had no specific leverage on which to bring our objections to bear.'[58] However, the US did pressurise the Indian government not to pursue a vigorous nuclear policy.

Pakistan now faced the same dilemma that India faced in the 1960s. After a war with India in 1962, China had tested a nuclear device at Lop Nur in 1964, while after a war with Pakistan in 1971, India tested a nuclear device in 1974. This became the semi-official rationale for Pakistan to tread the nuclear path. But as proved elsewhere in this study, Pakistan had ambitions of going nuclear even before 1974. The 1970s saw Pakistan speeding up the clandestine search for nuclear materials and the unwillingness or inability of the international community to impede Pakistan's nuclear ambitions. China became Pakistan's trusted ally in furthering these ambitions, a fact which did not go unnoticed in India. The annual report of the Ministry of Defence for 1985–86 mentioned, 'China is widely believed to be involved in Pakistan's nuclear programme.'[59]

When India carried out the 15 kT PNE in 1974, Defence Minister Shri Jagjivan Ram ruled out military use and simply stated that it

---

[55] Quoted in Perkovich 1999: 183.
[56] Kux 1993.
[57] Perkovich, 1999: 184.
[58] Quoted in ibid.: 523–24.
[59] Ministry of Defence, GOI 1985–2002, here 1985–86: 2.

was a part of India's ongoing attempts to tap nuclear energy. The two scientists involved directly with the tests, Dr Raja Ramanna and Dr R. Chidambaram, maintained the same line. In October 1997, Raja Ramanna admitted that the 1974 test was that of a nuclear weapon.[60] Gradually, the nuclear programme progressed, although at a slow pace. Domestic problems at this time, mainly the 'emergency' of 1975–77 declared by Indira Gandhi, and her subsequent defeat in the national elections of 1977, led to a change of stance related to nuclear development. After the emergency, when fresh elections were called, Morarji Desai, a long-time opponent of nuclear weapons, publicly promised that India under his regime would not conduct nuclear tests.[61] With Indira Gandhi coming to power again in 1980 and with continued reports of Pakistan's clandestine nuclear programme, the Indian programme was back on track. In 1983, the funding of the DRDO (Defence Research and Development Organisation) was increased and the Integrated Guided Missile Development Programme (IGMDP) was instituted.[62] As reports of further Chinese assistance to Pakistan came in, the small pro-bomb lobby of the domestic constituency increased its pressure.[63] Dr A. P. J. Abdul Kalam, a space scientist, was moved from ISRO (Indian Space Research Organisation) and placed in charge of IGMDP.[64]

After the assassination of Mrs Gandhi in 1984, her son Rajiv Gandhi came to power with a thumping majority. He followed, what one school of thought calls, contradictory policies on the nuclear question. On the one hand, it has been argued that he continued to support the nuclear programme, while on the other hand, he presented the Rajiv Gandhi Action Plan for Disarmament to the UN. This plan called for step-by-step, time-bound elimination of all nuclear arsenals by the year 2010. It can be argued that Rajiv Gandhi's views on declaratory policy were influenced by Nehruvian policies.[65] Subrahmanyam argues that it was under Rajiv Gandhi

[60] See Sengupta 1998.
[61] Desai 1978.
[62] See Chengappa 2000.
[63] Subrahmanyam 1986b.
[64] See Chengappa 2000; also see Smith 1994.
[65] For the contradictions, see Sen Gupta 1985. Also in this context, see Subrahmanyam 1998b.

that India made the decision to acquire more missiles to form an effective deterrent.[66] It was also during Rajiv Gandhi's time that India and Pakistan reached an accord not to attack each other's nuclear installations—a CSBM (confidence and security building measure) that has ever since been honoured.[67]

The earlier discussion highlights the fact that over a period of time the Indian nuclear programme has been active, except for a brief period in the 1970s when the Congress was not in power. It further illustrates that in the coming years, both the new Congress-led UPA government and the BJP and its allies will support the nuclear programme. From India's point of view, the slow but steady pace of weaponisation and deployment will continue well into the next decade. The only factor that might slow down this process will be a change in the international security environment and progress towards nuclear disarmament. This is unlikely to happen in the near and medium term, and so India will probably continue with 'creeping' weaponisation, irrespective of alliances in the government. It is also unlikely that any pressure from the West, particularly the US, will have any impact on this process.

Nuclear Crisis

Michael Brecher and Jonathan Wilkenfeld have described an international crisis as 'a situational change characterized by an increase in the intensity of disruptive interactions between two or more adversaries with a high probability of military hostilities in peace time (and, during a war, an adverse change in the military balance).'[68] India and Pakistan underwent a couple of serious crises before going overtly nuclear. Some lessons and broad contours can be drawn from these past interactions as they provided a foundation to the overt nuclearisation that was to follow.

Brasstacks Crisis, 1986–87

Towards the closing months of 1986, a crisis associated with the so-called military exercise emerged that had a potential for escalation into a full-fledged war. This military exercise was the largest conducted by India that included 10 divisions on the Indian side,

---

[66] Ibid.

[67] This agreement was ratified as late as in 1991.

[68] Brecher and Wilkenfeld 1989: 5.

including two strike units. The exercise location chosen was Northern Rajasthan, which was perceived in Pakistan as the most likely launch area for an attack across Pakistan.[69] Failure of communication fuelled fears in Pakistan that India was striking a belligerent pose. This led to Pakistan deploying troops and moving them closer to the international border. This manoeuvre was seen as having belligerent overtures in India, as it could have disrupted communications between Jammu and Kashmir and the rest of the country, and/or even led to salami slicing in Punjab. A series of miscommunications led to misperceptions and soon the two sides were preparing for war. India undertook a massive airlift and quickly mobilised ground troops along the international border. The surcharged atmosphere also drew the attention of the Soviet Union and the United States. The US President, Ronald Reagan apparently spoke to the Indian Prime Minister, Mrs Indira Gandhi to cool down tempers, and perhaps emphasised the role of communications being maintained at all times between the highest leaderships in both countries.[70]

Soon negotiations were held between official delegations from the two sides, and they were able to work out a timetable for withdrawal of troops from the border to their peacetime locations.[71] The nuclear dimension of this crisis surfaced from a rather dramatic interview that was given by Pakistan's chief nuclear scientist and 'father' of Pakistan's nuclear bomb, Dr A.Q. Khan to an Indian journalist, Kuldip Nayyar, during the crisis, wherein a nuclear threat was purportedly conveyed to India. Nayyar was accompanied by a Pakistani journalist, Mushahid Hussain, to the residence of Dr Khan. It was during the course of this interview that Pakistan held out an overt nuclear threat when Dr Khan informed his visitors that Pakistan had succeeded in enriching uranium to weapons grade and affirmed that a nuclear device could be tested by simulation techniques and in a laboratory. Khan further added rather significantly, 'Nobody can undo Pakistan or take us for granted. We are here to stay and let it be clear that we shall use the bomb if our existence is threatened.'[72] Gen Mirza Aslam Beg, the then

---

[69] See Hoon 1999: 104.
[70] Bajpai et al. 1995: 42.
[71] Chari 1995.
[72] Nayyar 1987.

Pakistani Chief of Army Staff, confirmed this assessment in an October 1989 interview and again in 1993.[73] Although this interview was conducted on 28 January 1987, it appeared in the media only on 1 March for reasons that remain shrouded in mystery.

On 26 January, Pakistan agreed to send an official delegation to New Delhi for negotiating the withdrawal of troops from the border.[74] Dr Khan made it clear that Pakistan had succeeded in making weapons-grade uranium. Scholars in Pakistan think that he had delivered a veiled warning and thereby strengthened deterrence.[75] But the country's initial attempts at nuclear signalling failed in its purpose of stopping India from proceeding with its exercise. Perhaps the timing of the threat did not work to Pakistan's advantage. Had it been conveyed during the crisis, it could have escalated tensions between the two countries, since India would have felt compelled to respond by issuing a counter-threat to assuage domestic public opinion; thereby leading to action–reaction verbal pyrotechnics. What effect this warning would have had on the Indian government, had it been conveyed immediately after the interview, remains unsurmisable. Incidentally, serious doubts persist regarding the interview's contents, since 'much of the interview, though not its most provocative passages, was an unattributed, nearly verbatim repetition of an article Khan had written six months earlier in the Karachi English newspaper, *Dawn*.'[76] What then were the lessons one could draw with the benefit of hindsight from this episode?

- First, inherent dangers lie in large-scale military exercises, especially in the traditional Indian exercise ranges in Khetolai, Lathi and Pokhran areas in Rajasthan, close to the international border, and more so if there is a breakdown in communications between the military and political leaderships. Significantly, one of the CBMs established after this crisis was the Agreement on Advance Notice of Military Exercises, Manoeuvres and Troop Movements.[77]

---

[73] See Hussain 1989. Also see in this context, *The New York Times* 1993.

[74] Bajpai et al. 1995. Also Rikhye 1988; Hagerty 1993/94.

[75] See Shahi et al. 1999.

[76] Spector 1988: 134.

[77] The text of this agreement, signed on 6 April 1991, may be seen in Krepon and Sevak 1996.

- Second, the 'hotline' that was established between the two military operations directorates (DGMOs) was of little use to defuse the crisis: 'when the possibility of war loomed large, CBMs were distrusted or misused by one or both sides: at crucial moments, India resisted giving information that might somehow be used to its disadvantage, and both sides stopped using the DGMO hotlines after December 8.'[78] Hence, paradoxically, CBMs in the Indo-Pak context build confidence well during peacetime but are a complete failure during times of crisis. A procedure was established thereafter, whereby the 'hotline' would be used at least once a week, and the two sides would call each other on alternate weeks.

The 1990 Crisis: How Real?

From the Indian perspective, the origins of this crisis lay in the noticeable increase in Pakistan's support to cross-border terrorism in Punjab, and in the latter half of 1989, to the insurgency in Kashmir. This increase in militancy also strangely coincided with the Pakistani army not withdrawing to its peacetime locations at Zarb-e-Momin after its major military exercise in the winter of 1989. Its strike corps moved into areas that were seen by India as threatening its security. India reacted by deploying its troops in Kashmir and Punjab.[79] From Pakistan's perspective, these Indian troop movements seemed offensive and reminiscent of Brasstacks crisis.[80] Unlike the Brasstacks exercise, which started essentially as a military exercise, the 1990 event was fuelled by the outbreak of ethno-religious insurgency in Jammu and Kashmir. As the crisis precipitated, Pakistani infiltrators began crossing porous borders and joined forces with Kashmiri secessionists.[81] New Delhi accused Pakistan of waging an unconventional war with India, by arming and training Kashmiri Muslim youth. From the Indian perspective, Pakistan had developed a low-cost strategy to de-stabilise its larger and stronger neighbour without risking the near-certain prospect of defeat in a conventional military encounter. The dramatic rise in incidents of violence led

---

[78] Bajpai et al. 1995: 110.

[79] The then serving Army Chief, V.N. Sharma, has described these events in an interview to *The Economic Times*. See V.N. Sharma 1993.

[80] For an excellent analysis of the 1990 crisis from the Indian, US and Pakistani viewpoints, see Chari 2003.

[81] For Pakistan's involvement in fuelling the insurgency, see *The Hindustan Times* 2003. For an older perspective on the same issue, see Desmond 1991.

the Indian decision makers to contemplate deep strikes on terrorist training camps in Pakistan-administered Kashmir which made Pakistan put forces on alert.

The nuclear dimension entered into the crisis at this time when Pakistan placed 'its nuclear weapons arsenal on alert.'[82] It is not clear if Pakistan had planned to use nuclear weapons in the crisis, but the two states were close to a conflict.[83] As the crisis developed, US intelligence, picking up signals of a looming conflict, despatched Robert Gates, the Deputy National Security Advisor, accompanied by Richard Haass and John Kelly.[84] In New Delhi, the Gates team counselled restraint while in Islamabad, joined by Amb. Robert Oakley, they explained that in every war game scenario that the Pentagon had developed, Pakistan emerged a loser. Gates told General Beg, 'Our military has war gamed every conceivable scenario between you and the Indians and there isn't a single way you win.'[85] Robert Oakley also made it clear that in the event of war, the US would not come to the rescue of Pakistan and this was a further sobering thought.[86] It was explained to the Pakistani decision makers that in the event of outbreak of hostilities, Pakistan was likely to lose diplomatically and militarily. The Pakistani President, Ghulam Ishaq Khan, also 'assured him (Gates) that Pakistan would close the training camps for Kashmiris in Azad Kashmir.'[87] The Gates mission also explained to the Indian decision makers that if Indians carried out any strikes on the training camps, then Pakistan would be forced to respond due to domestic compulsions, and then

---

[82] Hersh 1993: 65.

[83] Other aspects of these sensational disclosures are: Some time in 'early spring' General Beg authorised technicians in Kahuta to 'put together nuclear weapons'; some time in May, as conditions in Kashmir worsened, American satellite photographs noticed 'the evacuation of thousands of workers from Kahuta'; again in May, satellite intelligence showed 'signs of a truck convoy moving from the suspected nuclear-storage site in Balochistan to a nearby Air force base'; 'eventually,' intelligence picked up 'F-16s pre-positioned and armed delivery— on full alert, with pilots in the aircraft' (Ibid.: 56–73).

[84] The US wanted a senior KGB officer to accompany them, which they thought would have greater impact on the region. But Secretary of State, James Baker was unable to convince the Soviet Foreign Minister, Eduard Sherardnadze. See Reiss 1995: ch. 5.

[85] Quoted in ibid.: 190.

[86] Quoted in ibid.: 190.

[87] Hersh 1993: 68.

de-escalation would be a difficult proposition. What role nuclear weapons played in this crisis is yet unclear. A collaborative study by an Indian, an American and a Pakistani scholar has come to the conclusion that

> the dominant American interpretation was that the crisis was made worse by the existence of nuclear weapons in India and Pakistan, and that 1990 was largely, if not entirely, *a nuclear crisis* .... On the other hand, Indians and Pakistanis seem to concur that nuclear weapons may have limited the risks of war, but did not inhibit the opportunity to pursue their conflict 'by other means' in Kashmir and elsewhere.[88]

It is widely understood that some sort of nuclear threat was conveyed by Gates, who visited Pakistan and India at this time as a special emissary of President Bush; his Indian interlocutors have expressly denied this.[89] Indeed, Indian officialdom did not believe that Pakistan possessed a deliverable nuclear weapon at that time. For instance, General Sharma was specifically asked in his interview to *The Economic Times* whether he apprehended a nuclear threat from Pakistan during this crisis. He replied:

> No, I don't think so. There is a lot of bluff and bluster from Pakistan. It is different to talk about something and totally different to do something .... In hard military terms your capacity is not judged by the bluff and bluster, but what you have in your pocket and what you can do with it.[90]

Proponents of deterrence will argue that India and Pakistan were deterred from war in 1990 by the existence of opaque nuclear weapon capabilities on both sides, and no matter what Indian and Pakistani decision makers said or did, any military clash never had the potential for escalation to the nuclear level.[91] The case for nuclear deterrence is admittedly circumstantial, since deterrence

---

[88] Chari, Cheema and Cohen 2003: 134–35.

[89] See V.N. Sharma 1993; Deshmukh 1994. Deshmukh was the then Secretary to the Indian Prime Minister.

[90] Deshmukh 1994: 62.

[91] Many Indian and Pakistani generals maintain such a position, and after the Kargil War, senior government officials too have endorsed this point of view. See in this context, Hagerty 1998.

theory, crisis stability and nuclear signalling make tracing the causality of non-events a practically impossible task. In this instance, one would have to get authoritative Indian and/or Pakistani officials to admit that they were planning to go to war, but were dissuaded from doing so by the possibility that conventional conflict might have escalated to a nuclear exchange. But this is difficult mainly for two reasons: First, such an admission would reveal that the country was actually planning to start a war, which would make it lose face internationally; second, backing down from such plans would imply national weakness. No leader would do this. A recent study has revealed that 'despite the almost daily issue of bellicose speeches from both sides, the danger of war was never regarded as realistic.'[92]

Many Indian scholars and former military personnel maintain that the story of the nuclear crisis was sensationalist, and are often dismissive of it. It is possible that there was no truth in the revelations. Why then did Seymour Hersh write it?[93] It could be that the story was planted and the US wanted to play a role. Given the level of confidence that both India and Pakistan would have on US intelligence, the story was widely accepted. This led to an increased US role in the region. The nuclear angle of the crisis was highlighted by the US. Years later, during the Kargil crisis, when the Pakistani Prime Minister, Nawaz Sharif went to meet US President, Bill Clinton, he was informed that the Pakistan Army was busy readying missiles.

The NPT Extension and After

In 1995, the NPT came up for its 25-year review and was extended indefinitely. India decided to stay outside the proceedings and did not seek even an observer status.[94] The indefinite extension of the NPT, along with continued Chinese assistance to Pakistan, perhaps became the main motivations for India to prepare for another

---

[92] Chari, Cheema and Cohen 2003: 142.

[93] Hersh wrote the story on the nuclear dimension of the crisis in *The New York Times*. See Hersh 1993.

[94] For an official view on Indian objections to the NPT, see Sood 1993. He discusses the possibility of expanding the scope of the regime to address Indian concerns. Sood was the Joint Secretary in the Disarmament and International Security Division of the Ministry of External Affairs, and later, India's Permanent Ambassador to the CD in Geneva.

test in December 1995. The other motivation was the CTBT negotiations in the CD that were nearing finalisation. US satellites picked
up increased activity at Pokhran and US Ambassador to India,
Frank Wisner, prevailed upon Narasimha Rao to resist testing.[95]
The Congress-led Narasimha Rao government was still following
the declaratory Congress position of global nuclear disarmament,
although years of work had gone into the nuclear programme. In
fact, the Congress Party, during the visit of US President Bill Clinton
in 2000, seemed unable to resolve the dilemma of maintaining its
historical position of global nuclear disarmament or accepting the
official Indian position of credible minimum nuclear deterrent.[96]
The disjoint between the work of the MEA (Ministry of External
Affairs) and the DAE (Department of Atomic Energy) may never
be fully resolved. As Bhashyam Kasturi argues, 'The divergence
of policy statements by the MEA and the actual work of the DAE
will remain until a more open form of interdepartmental cooperation is instituted in the case of the nuclear program.'[97]

By the mid-1980s and early 1990s, the domestic public opinion
was shifting from the idealistic positions of that had been nurtured
from the time of Nehru and maintained with subtle shifts till Rajiv
Gandhi's government. This is reflected in a public opinion survey
where just 8 per cent (N = 83) of those interviewed favoured the
renunciation of nuclear weapons.[98] While 581 favoured a time-
bound plan for global nuclear disarmament, 15 per cent linked
Indian renunciation of nuclear weapons to a final boundary settlement with China and the removal of Chinese nuclear weapons
from Tibet, and another 26 per cent to a verifiable renunciation of
Pakistan's nuclear option.[99] To the question of why India should
develop nuclear weapons, 57 per cent located the rationale to
threats from nuclear Pakistan, while 20 per cent felt threats from
China.[100] In an answer to the same question, an overwhelming
49 per cent felt India should develop nuclear weapons to improve

---

[95] Ganguly 1999a.

[96] See The Statesman 2000b; The Hindu 2000a; The Asian Age 2000a, 2000b; and
The Times of India 2000c.

[97] Kasturi 1999: 128.

[98] Cortright and Mattoo 1994.

[99] Ibid.: Table 7.

[100] Ibid.: Table 9.

India's bargaining power in world affairs.[101] The opposition to NPT had begun to develop, as 49 per cent supporters of official policy and 52 per cent nuclear advocates said under no circumstances should India sign the NPT.[102] Forty per cent of the respondents of this survey said information on nuclear issues is not easy to get.[103] Of nuclear advocates who had to vote for the extent of developing nuclear weapons, 34 per cent voted for the development of all components but not the actual assembling of any nuclear weapon.[104] Kashmir plays a central role in determining the decision to use nuclear weapons: 33 per cent respondents said India could use nuclear weapons if Pakistan were about to overwhelm India militarily.[105] An overwhelming 83 per cent of all respondents totally support an international agreement eliminating nuclear weapons. This gives a sense that overall the population in the mid-1990s supported an international agreement to eliminate nuclear weapons. These linkages make one point clear, that there needs to be greater international cooperation on disarmament that might reduce the tendency of elites to accept nuclear weapons development as a policy option. Another inference that can be drawn is the influence of regional security issues and their overall impact on Indian decision making. Another significant finding was, nuclear issues were ranked seventh, with communalism, poverty, economic stability, terrorism, Kashmir and GATT being ranked higher in importance than the nuclear issue.

What then motivated the government to prepare for a test in 1995? Three factors were crucial. The indefinite extension of the NPT, the passage of the Brown Amendment, leading to renewal of up to $368 million in US military assistance to Pakistan, and the impending CTBT negotiations that were gathering steam in the Conference on Disarmament in Geneva which would lead to the closing of the option of further tests. Although India had been one of the chief supporters of the treaty, when the final document came up for negotiation, it raised objections finding no link to universal nuclear disarmament at the moral plane, while at the realistic plane it was able to buy itself some time to retain its nuclear option.

---

[101] Ibid.
[102] Ibid.: Table 8.
[103] Ibid.: Table 3.
[104] Ibid.: Table 13.
[105] Ibid.: Table 14.

EXPLAINING INDIA'S NUCLEAR BEHAVIOUR

Over the last five decades, there has been continuity in India's development of a civilian nuclear programme, although this process has been rather haphazard, has had inconsistent support and has been at times incongruent with policy pronouncements. The logical conclusion of any civilian nuclear programme can be a simultaneous military programme, if need be. The nuclear programme had received government funding all through the 1980s. In December 1995, the Congress government tried to test a nuclear device, but was pressurised by the US not to do so.

India's motivations to test were a combination of international and domestic factors. First, to discuss the international factors, India has constantly argued—and continues to do so—for total disarmament, but has never been taken seriously. Various international treaties, such as the CTBT, were closing India's options. Second, China, with whom India went to war in 1962 and has a longstanding border dispute (albeit a dormant one), has had a track record of proliferation of not merely small arms, but also sensitive nuclear and missile technology to Pakistan.[106] China as a nuclear weapons power was probably the first motivation for India. Third, India thought of possessing the nuclear weapons as a ticket to a seat in the Security Council (ironically, at this moment the P-5 are also the five nuclear weapons states). Finally, since the dilution of ties between New Delhi and Moscow, there were genuine security concerns that New Delhi had to address. The South Asian security environment had deteriorated to a very great extent.

In terms of national factors, the official explanations for the May 1998 nuclear tests were threats from China and Pakistan.[107] This is at best an unconvincing justification. The motivations to test were a combination of factors. Domestic politics was a key force behind the tests. The Vajpayee-led coalition government (of the twelfth Lok Sabha) was shaky—it was constantly receiving threats from one of the coalition partners, the AIADMK led by Jayalalitha, to pull down the government. The government needed to accommodate the unreasonable demands of its other alliance partners

---

[106] Mahmood 1999.
[107] Vajpayee 1998a.

as well, which made governance almost impossible. Second, on 6 April 1998, Pakistan tested the Ghauri, and if reports are to be believed, a decision to test a nuclear weapon in India was taken two days later. Third, the Bharatiya Janata Party (BJP), which had clearly mentioned induction of the nuclear option in its manifesto, had the groundwork done to conduct the tests. Fourth, the dismemberment of the USSR—India's chief military partner—had made India rethink its policy options. Fifth, the scientific–bureaucratic establishment, which is always active in any country, was pushing for the tests. With the BJP coming to power, the pressure became stronger. Even when the BJP government came to power for 13 days in its first term, there were reports that it may have ordered the scientists to test. Sixth, the domestic constituency, which had gathered momentum post NPT's indefinite extension, would also have been pleased. As Brahma Chellaney says, 'India's main strategic gain from the tests was that the detonations—and the subsequent "provocative" Indian statements—successfully enticed Islamabad to come out of its nuclear closet.'[108] As Stephen Cohen explains it,

India's strategic environment grew both more complex and dangerous after 1990 with the renewal of the threat of war with Pakistan, Islamabad's nuclearisation, strong evidence of Chinese support for Pakistan (despite the apparent improvement of India–Chinese relations), and the rise of serious domestic insurrections in Punjab, the Northeast, and Kashmir; while objectively India's security position was manageable, the sense of insecurity grew in New Delhi.[109]

A related school of thought says that though sanctions were imminent after the tests, India could endure these and Pakistan could not. The military establishment in Pakistan was fully aware that it 'lacks the economic and technological means for a full scale weaponisation and deployment. Both would require additional expenditures—for example, for the establishment of an adequate command, control and communications infrastructure—which the country's strained economy could not possibly sustain.'[110]

---

[108] Chellaney 1999b: 147.
[109] Cohen 1998.
[110] Ahmed 1999.

The rise of BJP to power in New Delhi led to the culmination of the various pressures on the government to conduct nuclear tests.[111] Carrying a huge *swadeshi* baggage, the BJP was heir to years of work on the nuclear programme—all it had to do was provide the green signal. When the BJP made this clear in its election manifesto, most Western analysts called it a bluff. When the tests happened, there were loud noises of it being a Hindu bomb, and sands of the Shakti tests were to be distributed. A year later, the diplomatic response to Kargil proved that harsh decisions have to be supported by well-oiled diplomatic machinery.

✸ Doctrinal Issues

Perhaps no other country has laboured so much on the nuclear question as India has, yet doctrinal aspects seem to find much less resonance in debates on India's nuclear future. The military dimensions of the Indian nuclear programme only marginally figured in the debates. After a couple of decades of being under the towering personalities and ideals of Gandhi and Nehru, the country was ill-equipped to handle technical and operational aspects of nuclear weapons. Terms such as war, deterrence, compellance and hardened silos had to be imported from the West but needed an Indian flavour.

In an attempt to locate the role that nuclear weapons might play in the overall security calculus in India, it is imperative to view nuclear doctrine as a set of beliefs that identifies the role of nuclear weapons and the purpose for which these weapons have been acquired by India. Attempts were made in the early 1980s to develop a nuclear doctrine. Leading the strategists was K. Subrahmanyam, who is widely considered to be the 'father of Indian strategic thought'.[112] Former Chief of Army Staff, Gen K. Sundarji, was among the very few Indian Army officers who gave a serious thought to the issue of nuclear weapons.[113] He organised a quasi-official study of

---

[111] In this context, see Cherian 1998; Partha S. Ghosh 1999; and Graham 1990.

[112] See in this context, Subrahmanyam 1998a, 1998b.

[113] Gen K. Sundarji had spent considerable time writing an unpublished monograph, 'Strategy in the Age of Nuclear Deterrence and Its Application to Developing Countries' (1984). He later authored a novel, *Blind Men of Hindoostan, Indo-Pak Nuclear War* (1993b). See also Sundarji 1981b, 1990; On the triangle, see Sundarji 1994a, 1994b.

nuclear doctrine in 1981. In this study, civilian and military personnel of the government (including serving officers) were asked to comment on a scenario involving three states, A, B and C, thinly disguised as India, Pakistan and China. Many contributors favoured a limited nuclear programme.[114] Sundarji himself was of the opinion that nuclear deterrence 'will add to stability and peace and that the only salvation is for both countries to follow policies of cooperation and not confrontation … a mutual minimum nuclear deterrence will act as a stabilising factor … the chances of conventional war between the two will be less likely than before.'[115]

The most frequently cited argument in the strategic community in India about a role for nuclear weapons is that nuclear weapons are purely political instruments.[116] Air Cmde Jasjit Singh, building on this argument, says that over a period of time it has become obvious that a 'nuclear war cannot be won and therefore must never be fought.'[117] Elaborating further, Singh says, 'nuclear weapons [are] more an instrument of politics … than military instrument of war fighting.'[118] Taking this argument further, K. Subrahmanyam says that 'India does not subscribe to the outmoded war-fighting doctrine and the Indian nuclear weapons are meant solely for deterrence.'[119] This is a reiteration of what the Chinese have termed 'nuclear blackmail'. Speaking at an earlier occasion, K. Subrahmanyam had said, 'the main purpose of a third world arsenal is deterrence against blackmail.'[120] As another leading strategic commentator, C. Raja Mohan, has also observed,

India has taken too long to come to terms with the nuclear revolution and its impact on world military affairs … Nuclear weapons are

---

[114] Sundarji 1981b. Arun Singh and Brig Vijai K. Nair were among the many members of this project. Arun Singh later became the Minister of State for Defence in the late 1980s and almost a decade later an Officer on Special Duty in the Ministry of External Affairs.

[115] Sundarji 1995: 59.

[116] Former President, K.R. Narayanan, addressing the nation on the occasion of the golden jubilee of India's independence said, 'nuclear weapons are useful only when they are not used. They can only be a deterrent in the hands of the nation' (Narayanan 1998).

[117] Jasjit Singh 1998: 11.

[118] Ibid.: 11.

[119] Subrahmanyam 1998c.

[120] Subrahmanyam 1993a.

certainly important. And India's decision to acquire them was long overdue. But in the flush of becoming an atomic power, India could easily overstate the significance of nuclear weapons. They can only serve a limited purpose for India—of preventing the use or threat of use of nuclear weapons by its adversaries against it. There is little else that nuclear weapons can do.[121]

Over the last couple of decades, ambiguity and recessed deterrence remained the hallmark of the Indian nuclear posture. In its present avatar, India's nuclear doctrine can be located in the BJP's election manifesto, in a run-up to the March 1998 general elections.[122] This manifesto promised that if the BJP was elected, it would establish a National Security Council that would 'undertake India's first-ever Strategic Defence Review to study and analyze the security environment and make appropriate recommendations .... Re-evaluate the country's nuclear policy and exercise the option to induct nuclear weapons.'[123] This ambition was reiterated in its National Agenda for Governance.[124] When the BJP government was elected for the second time in March 1998, a three-man task force was appointed to advise on the constitution of the council. The basic problems were related to the structure of the council, the position of the national security advisor, and whether the council should have a statutory or an advisory body. The National Security Council (NSC) was to be headed by the prime minister, which included the ministers for defence, home, external affairs and finance, but also the deputy chairman of the Planning Commission (Jaswant Singh at that time). A three-tier structure was evolved under it.[125] One of the divisions was the National Security Advisory Board

---

[121] Mohan 1999c.

[122] This election brought the BJP government to power for 13 days.

[123] Full text of the BJP manifesto is available at http://bjp.org/manifes/chap8.htm, accessed on 16 July 2000.

[124] Text of National Agenda for Governance can be found at http://bjp.org/nagenda.htm, accessed on 16 July 2000.

[125] This included a Strategic Policy Group with serving civil and military officials and a 22-member National Security Advisory Board consisting of former civil and military officials, academics, scientists and journalists 'with expertise in Foreign Affairs, External Security, Defence, Strategic Analysis, Economics, Science and Technology, Internal Security and Armed Forces.' Information on the composition, structure and objectives of the National Security Council can be obtained from http://www.ipcs.org/new/nsc.htm, accessed on 25 November 1998.

(NSAB).[126] Five sub-groups of the NSAB were constituted to deal with issues relating to nuclear, internal, external, technological and economic security. The nuclear sub-group drafted a nuclear doctrine. The National Security Advisor, Brajesh Mishra and Convenor of the National Security Advisory Board, K. Subrahmanyam presided over its release (in August 1999), giving it an official character.[127] The true status of this doctrine was authoritatively declared by Foreign Minister, Jaswant Singh some three months later. The Minister in an interview given to a national daily replied, 'The National Security Advisory Board is a group of non-official strategic experts and analysts. It was tasked by the National Security Council to prepare a number of papers, including one on a possible "Indian Nuclear Doctrine"'.[128] This it prepared and submitted to the national security advisor, also releasing it publicly for a larger debate. Subsequently, in January 2003, the Government of India clarified this further when it adopted the draft doctrine as an official policy document and added another caveat, thereby increasing the operational battlespace of nuclear weapons. The draft doctrine stated, 'In the event of a major attack against India or Indian forces anywhere, by biological or chemical weapons, India will retain the option of retaliating with nuclear weapons.'[129]

The mere possession of the nuclear bomb does not constitute minimum deterrence, and the possession of a minimum deterrent should essentially be used to negotiate a better strategic balance. A stable strategic balance is required not only for India but also for the Southern Asian region, as it serves India's national interest better. It requires conveying to the world in general, and China and Pakistan in particular, that for India nuclear weapons are purely political instruments. Important and central to this role will be situating nuclear weapons in the Indian security architecture. A credible combination of arms control negotiations, a restrained articulation of the Indian interest and willingness to integrate with a global economy would do more for India than minimum deterrence. To this end, in the initial couple of years after May 1998, it was required for India to show the world its intent in being a responsible nuclear weapons state.

---

[126] The other was the National Security Council Secretariat.
[127] See *The Hindu* 1999c.
[128] See Mohan 1999d.
[129] Mohan 2003b.

On doctrinal issues, India announced a unilateral moratorium on testing, although there were demands from some quarters that India should have conducted more tests. India has also announced an unconditional no-first-use posture and brought out a draft report of the nuclear doctrine.[130] On the face of it, one could argue that the doctrine is a mere fleshing out of Vajpayee's statement in Parliament on 15 December 1998, where he spelt out the principal elements of minimum nuclear deterrence: no-first-use, no use against non-nuclear powers, and commitment to the elimination of nuclear weapons. But the draft report transcends the prime minister's statement and does some moral posturing. It makes clear that nuclear deterrence can range from a mere declaratory posture with covert demonstration of capabilities—a form of existential deterrence—to deterrence based on a near total certainty—an elaborate nuclear arsenal based on the 'triadic' nature of the deterrent: air, mobile land-based and sea assets with command and control systems, leaving no doubt about the certainty of retaliatory strike.[131] It has announced the country's intention to maintain a credible minimum nuclear deterrent. This raises the important issue of 'nuclear sufficiency', which requires an explanation about how many weapons would be required to achieve this state of deterrence. According to the draft report, deterrence requires that India maintains:[132]

- sufficient, survivable and operationally prepared nuclear forces;
- a robust command and control system;
- effective intelligence and early warning capabilities;
- comprehensive planning and training for operations in line with the strategy; and
- the will to employ nuclear forces and weapons.

There were four main elements of the nuclear doctrine, some inherent contradictions and tensions.

- **No-First-Use:** India's position on no-first-use has been explicitly dealt with in paras 1.5, 2.3, 2.4 and 8.2 of the nuclear doctrine.

---

[130] NSAB 1999.

[131] See *The Times of India* 1999c, 1999d, 1999e; *The Indian Express* 1999b; Mattoo 1999b; Sheth 1999; *The Pioneer* 1999; Rajagopalan 1999.

[132] NSAB 1999: para 2.6.

It suggests measures being taken, like de-mating of warheads and delivery systems. This would assure others that a first strike is not possible. However, this position becomes ambiguous on read-ing paras 2.5 and 3.2., especially the latter, wherein the doctrine 'envisages assured capability to shift from peacetime deployment to fully employable forces in the shortest possible time ....' Operationally, this could translate into higher rate of alert level, but it is common knowledge that India maintains de-alert, de-mated status of its nuclear arsenal. This further strengthens the NFU posture, as it is not just a political statement but also an operational commitment.[133]

- **Minimum Nuclear Deterrent:** In attempting to increase the credibility and effectiveness of the deterrent, the doctrine refrains from limiting itself to 'minimum nuclear deterrence'. How the stated maximum credibility can be achieved without becoming a maximum deterrent is left unclear.
- **Command and Control:** Whilst a greater focus on command and control structures would have been desirable, the doctrine's men-tion of 'an integrated operational plan, or a series of sequential plans' adds to the ambiguity.
- **Survivability:** Tactical nuclear weapons form an integral part of flexible response in nuclear war fighting. This has been left unmentioned, which points to an 'open option.' Left unexplained also are the types of command and control arrangements with re-spect to different forces.

In an interview with *The Hindu* on 29 November 1999, the then Indian Foreign Minister, Jaswant Singh discussed India's position on arms control issues and addressed international concerns about its nuclear doctrine being generated from the draft doctrine. Most notably, Singh downplayed the significance of the draft report, stressing that it is not an official policy document and that the talk of an Indian nuclear triad is 'premature.'[134]

---

[133] Draft Nuclear Doctrine 1999. See the point highlighted by Dr Amitabh Mattoo, one of the panelists. Dr Mattoo later became a member of the third and fourth National Security Advisory Board.

[134] Mohan 1999d. He further said, India would maintain a credible, but mini-mum nuclear deterrent; India would continue its declared moratorium on under-ground nuclear testing, but would pursue computer simulation and sub-critical tests, if necessary; an extended-range Agni missile would be developed and flight-

India has made it clear that 'the fundamental purpose of Indian nuclear weapons is to deter the use and threat of use of nuclear weapons by any State or entity against India and its forces' (Clause 2.4). There is, however, a growing global apprehension about terrorists gaining access to fissile materials.[135] How could such an 'entity' be deterred without threatening or attacking the country where it is located? The doctrine remains silent on this problem. India will not be the first to initiate a nuclear strike, but will respond with punitive retaliation if deterrence fails.[136] This implies that India should adopt a 'launch on attack', not a 'launch on warning', nuclear posture.

The draft report of the NSAB has stated that India shall 'pursue a doctrine of credible minimum nuclear deterrence' (para 2.3). In this policy of 'retaliation only' (para 2.3) the survivability of India's arsenal is critical.[137] Mr Vajpayee assured the public that the Indian nuclear capability would be defensive in nature.[138] India has also declared that it 'will not resort to the use or threat of use of nuclear weapons against States which do not possess nuclear weapons, or are not aligned with nuclear weapon powers.'[139] This further reduces operational battlespace of India's nuclear forces.

The draft report is not clear on the size and shape of the minimum nuclear deterrent and conforms to traditional nuclear deterrence found in the Western narrative. In fact, in reply to a question in the Rajya Sabha, the Indian external affairs minister stated,

> India's minimum deterrent can not be elaborated in terms of a fixed quantification; it is a policy approach dictated and determined in the context of our security environment. Government has also conveyed that matters relating to defence postures are sovereign functions and, therefore, not subjects to negotiations.[140]

tested in a non-provocative and transparent manner; in pursuance of its no-first-use declaration, India would not use nuclear weapons against non-nuclear states; a deployment posture would be adopted that ensures the survivability of assets; India would not engage in any arms race; and that India's commitment to global nuclear disarmament remains undiluted.

[135] See, for example, *The Indian Express* 2001.

[136] NSAB 1999.

[137] Ibid.

[138] See Mr Vajpayee's statement in Vajpayee 1998c. This has further been refined by the draft report.

[139] NSAB 1999: para 2.5.

[140] Rajya Sabha 1999.

The real tension in the draft is between minimum deterrence and maximum credibility. India may also need to specify the size of its deterrent, a demand that the United States has often been raising.[141] Answering a question in the Indian Parliament, the minister of state for external affairs also made it clear that

> India and the US are engaged in an ongoing dialogue on security, non-proliferation and disarmament issues. This dialogue is predicted on India maintaining a minimum credible nuclear deterrent. India's minimum deterrent is not a fixed quantification, it is a policy approach dictated and determined in the context of our security environment.[142]

What is not clear is whether the Indian government is talking in terms of quantity or quality of the proposed Indian deterrent. This becomes complicated because China figures in India's security calculus, despite Beijing's declared no-first-use policy. The draft report is also not clear on whether the naval deterrent would be submarine or ship based. Another flaw in the draft report is that there is no mention of the costs involved or the time-frame that would be needed for implementing the many concepts that have been mentioned. For instance, the report mentions that: 'The Indian defence forces shall be in a position to execute operations in an NBC environment with minimal degradation; and Space based and other assets shall be created to provide early warning, communications, damage/detonation assessment.'[143]

Deterrence cannot be quantified. If India tries to build a minimal deterrent against China it exceeds the maximum limit against Pakistan. Some estimates in India suggest that minimum deterrence is based on targeting five Pakistani cities and 20 Chinese cities.[144] Nuclearisation in the Indian context will be an expensive process and will involve the following:

- Developing a reasonable number of weapon cores and mating them with credible delivery means.

---

[141] *The Hindu* 1999b.

[142] Lok Sabha 2000e.

[143] NSAB 1999: para 5.6.

[144] Point made by a participant in IPCS 1998. See also in this context, Karnad 2002.

- Developing a command and control arrangement.[145]
- Developing an effective communications network that can survive a first strike.[146]
- Keeping these weapon cores and delivery means dispersed to ensure survivability against adversary first strike.
- Organising forces to handle and use nuclear weapons and ensure their training for delivery as part of the national security doctrine.
- Structuring conventional forces to deal with the altered security environment.
- Ensuring an effective and instantaneous communication system linking various key institutions.

All these requirements are based on the assumption of establishing a 'credible minimum nuclear deterrent'. Added to this is the cost factor, which the draft nuclear doctrine does not consider. The scenario envisaged in the draft doctrine is many years and millions of dollars away. If the aim is to built a 'credible minimum nuclear deterrent' and if the minimum is what the draft doctrine states, then the government of the day will have to think many times over before launching such an expensive programme which will include not only economic costs—appreciating that the possession of nuclear weapons will not prevent proxy wars, drug trafficking and proliferation of small arms—nor prevent inimical neighbours from abetting various insurgencies. The rhetorical statements made by people in power after the nuclear tests in May 1998 serve no purpose. The need is for India to eschew such incendiary rhetoric and develop a non-aggressive force posture that could assure international anxieties regarding the future of nuclear South Asia.[147]

At the time of the release of the draft report, there was no mention of who would control the nuclear button, except that there was common understanding that the Cabinet Committee on Security (CCS) with the prime minister as the head would have the final

---

[145] India has drafted a Rs 3.75 billion dollar five-year plan for creating a nuclear command, control, communications and intelligence infrastructure. See *The Hindustan Times* 2000a. Details of the Nuclear Command Authority were fleshed out in January 2003.

[146] Ibid.

[147] One such initiative calls for force reduction along the China border. In the foreseeable future, there seems to be no likelihood of a large-scale conflict with China.

say on such matters. Regarding the command and control structures, the draft report does mention that after nuclear weapons are inducted into the armed forces it would be the elected head of the country, that is, the prime minister, who would have the authority to release them for use. This was fleshed out in January 2003, when the government announced the Nuclear Command Authority (NCA) and made a two-tier system of command.

Through the last decade, India followed what came to be termed as existential deterrence. The draft suggests that deterrence will be based on certainty. On one hand, the doctrine declares pursuing the path of minimum nuclear deterrence; on the other hand, it has emphasised that the retaliatory capability has to be high after clearly defining the pillars on which this would be based—survivability, safety, effectiveness, security and a targeting policy. There are also recommendations on C4I2 (command, control, communications, computing, intelligence and information).

Supporting Infrastructure

Delivery systems, fissile stocks and nuclear weapons alone do not make the Indian nuclear arsenal credible as a projected nuclear deterrent; a minimal infrastructure is needed to 'stitch up' all this together. There has been a demand, not just domestically but also internationally, for India to set up a nuclear command and control authority.[148]

On 5 January 2003, India declared a set of political principles and administrative arrangements to manage its nuclear arsenal. This reflects another step in the evolution of India's gradual, yet firm process of nuclearisation. It is also a step towards the deployment of what Ashley Tellis has called India's nuclear 'force-in-being'.[149] This institutionalises the final decision to use nuclear weapons, exhibits an absolute political control over decision making and incorporates effective interface between civilian and military leaders in the final decision on nuclear weapons. The announcement was made after the India's highest decision-making body on matters of national security, the Cabinet Committee on Security,

---

[148] See Nair 1992; Menon 2000a; Kanwal 2001, 2003; Kak 1998; and Bajpai 1999.

[149] Tellis has used this term in his monumental work, *India's Emerging Nuclear Posture* (2002a).

met to review progress in implementing India's nuclear doctrine, the state of readiness of its strategic forces and the procedures for their command and control. This demand has been raised many a time. The Group of Ministers in their report, *Reforming the National Security System*, had suggested in February 2001,

> Given India's nuclear status, there is a pressing need to establish a Strategic Forces Command, to manage all strategic forces. While the operational control of the strategic forces should unambiguously vest in the highest political authority, the CDS [Chief of Defence Staff] should, as stated earlier, exercise administrative control over these forces and also be the channel of communication between the government and the Strategic Forces Commander.[150]

This report further went on to suggest that 'the highest importance must be attached to the creation of appropriate structures for the management and control of our nuclear weapons and strategic forces. The CDS should exercise administrative, as distinct from operational military control, over these strategic forces.'[151]

The establishment of the NCA reflects the maximum restraint in the final decision to use nuclear weapons, exhibits an absolute political control over decision making. It incorporates an effective interface between civilian and military leaders regarding the final decision on nuclear weapons. The NCA comprises the Political Council (presumably the prime minister, the deputy prime minister, the external affairs minister, the home minister, the finance minister, the national security advisor, the three service chiefs and the cabinet secretary) and the Executive Council (presumably comprising the chiefs of defence services, chairman, the convener of the National Security Advisory Board, the cabinet secretary, heads of intelligence agencies and secretaries of ministries represented in the CCS). The government stated that the NCA, chaired by the prime minister, 'is the sole body which can authorize the use of nuclear weapons.'[152] The Executive Council, chaired by the national security advisor to the prime minister, 'provides inputs for decision making by the NCA and executes the directives given to it by the

---

[150] Group of Ministers, GOI 2001.

[151] Ibid.

[152] Mohan 2003b.

Political Council.'[153] The CCS also approved the appointment of a 'Commander-in-Chief, Strategic Forces Command,' who would be responsible for the administration of the nuclear forces.[154] The National Security Council Secretariat aids the National Security Advisory Board. Air Chief Marshal T.M. Asthana has been made the first Head of the Strategic Forces Command. These administrative arrangements form the crucial link between the civilian and military leadership on nuclear decisions and their execution. The CCS accepted certain recommendations of the draft nuclear doctrine.[155]

Since India has a declared NFU posture, theoretically it is expected that India will absorb a first strike, which is likely to hit the command structure, perhaps a few counter-force and counter-value targets. India has made it clear that credible alternative lines of command at the political and military levels have been fully worked out.[156] If there is a nuclear attack that targets the nation's leadership, 'the alternative nuclear command authority will be in a position to take charge' and ensure massive retaliation against the adversary.[157] The NDA government said that 'there could be more than one alternative command structure' to make certain that an Indian nuclear riposte would inevitably follow an atomic attack on the nation.[158] This also means that 'it is unnecessary to delegate powers in a manner which is required if one's nuclear strategy embraced procedures for launch-on-warning or launch-on-attack or to delegate them specifically to military commanders in the field.'[159] The Indian NFU policy and consequent punitive retaliation strategy require delicate balancing between the imperatives of ensuring the survivability of the retaliatory forces by means

---

[153] Ibid.

[154] Ibid.

[155] These were: commitment to no-first-use (which has now been qualified by the assertion that the 'option of nuclear weapon use will be retained' if India or the Indian armed forces are attacked by chemical or biological weapons); acceptance of the need for building and maintaining a credible minimum deterrent; non-use of nuclear weapons against non-nuclear weapons states; moratorium on further nuclear tests; and agreement to join the negotiations on the Fissile Material Cut-off Treaty.

[156] Mohan 2003b.

[157] Doctrinally, the term used is punitive retaliation.

[158] Ibid.

[159] *The Hindu* 2003a.

of deception, camouflage, mobility and redundancy in strike capabilities. As the father of Indian strategic thought K. Subrahmanyam says, 'The alternative chain of command and arrangements to continue the vital institutions of the republic without interruption in case of a decapitation attack and the capability for punitive retaliation should be impressed on the adversary and should be credible to our own people.'[160] But nagging questions remain: There are no indications as to what shape this would take or as to its interfaces with the three defence forces. A Strategic Forces Command has been established under a separate commander-in-chief. The defence services have already worked the Tri-service Command in the Andaman and Nicobar islands. Where would the Strategic Forces Command fit in? Would it be under the prime minister, the NSA or the Chiefs of Staff Committee? Will the Strategic Forces Command have its own forces, or will its strategic regiments and squadrons remain under their respective service headquarters as they are now? Will it build, train and sustain its own corpus of leadership and human resources? In other words, will it be a special entity, as it ought to be, or will it need to hang on the apron strings of the three services?'[161] Additionally, it is also not clear,

if an adversary were to launch an attack on its nuclear forces using conventional means, would New Delhi regard this as a first use, thus giving India the right to retaliate with its second-strike nuclear capability? In which case, would it not be a violation of the no-first-use posture? Or would India confine itself to a conventional response and try to take out the nuclear assets of the adversary even at the risk that such retaliation might lead to a nuclear escalation?[162]

A few questions continue to warrant attention:[163]

1. The CCS announcement is silent on the composition and the manner in which the alternative command structure envisaged would function, should a first strike 'decapitate' the first line of leadership. Will greater transparency in identifying the chain of political and military succession in this contingency enhance or detract from the credibility of the deterrent?

---

[160] Subrahmanyam 2003.
[161] Raghvan 2003.
[162] Sidhu 2003.
[163] Chari 2003a. See, also in this context, Chari and Rajain 2003.

2. A pivotal role has been assigned to the national security advisor (NSA) in these arrangements. He will head the Executive Council, but will also be the conduit between the political and military adjuncts of the NCA. The present incumbent is also the principal secretary to the prime minister who has to handle many domestic and international crises. Is it wise to invest so much authority and responsibility in one single individual?

3. How the Strategic Forces Command would function within the NCA hierarchy is not clear. Will the Executive Council, which will have the chiefs of staff in its fold, exercise direct operational control over the Strategic Forces Command or exercise control through the Chiefs of Command Committee?[164]

4. The issue of who will control the strategic forces in peacetime has been left vague. It is widely believed that the Indian nuclear arsenal has not been not deployed. The Atomic Energy Commission is believed to have the nuclear cores; the nuclear assemblies are believed to be with the Defence Research and Development Organisation (DRDO), while the delivery systems are with the services. How these three assets are going to work together in a crisis scenario without giving the message of preparing for a pre-emptive strike, is unclear.

Although the debate may continue on the state of readiness of nuclear weapons deployment for sake of absolute credibility of deterrence, as a small step towards the future, the fundamental structure of the nuclear command has been put in place. Its rough edges can be subjected to refinement and revision depending on strategic need and to some extent political will.

India has always believed that global disarmament is in the interest of all nations. The doctrine has enunciated, 'global, verifiable and non-discriminatory nuclear disarmament is a national security objective. India shall continue its efforts to achieve the goal of a nuclear weapon-free world at an early date.'[165] After the tests, India gave a call for negotiating a gradual and progressive elimination of all nuclear weapons within a time-bound framework.[166] At the first committee of the United Nations General Assembly,

---

[164] The Group of Ministers, GOI (2001) had recommended the creation of the Chief of Defence Staff to 'administer the Strategic Forces.'

[165] NSAB 1999.

[166] At the NAM Summit meet in Durban in September 1998.

India proposed global nuclear de-alerting.[167] This initiative was intended to urge countries to retreat from the nuclear hair-trigger postures adopted during the Cold War. Mr Vajpayee said that if such initiatives were accepted in a multilateral forum like the United Nations, they would reflect the Indian position too.[168]

It remains to be seen what value such initiatives hold, coming from a state that has gatecrashed into the nuclear regime. Indian diplomacy will continually have to project idealism at multilateral fora and realism in the region with same delicate balance. At the United Nations or any other multilateral forum, India needs to spell out clearly what it means by minimum deterrence and whether it is tactical, thermonuclear, de-mated, or inducted and deployed. This would also reflect the kind of nuclear weapons state that India wants to be—whether it wants to be a nuclear weapons state with rudimentary weapons or whether it wants to have a sophisticated thermonuclear deterrent.

What one sees is a slow motion nuclear arms race evolving in South Asia. India detonated nuclear devices, followed by Pakistan in May 1998. Next came the missile tests. A draft nuclear doctrine has been spelt out and a command structure put in place. Gradually the armed forces are getting the arsenal. A slow motion induction and deployment process is on. There are provisions in the doctrine about building a credible nuclear deterrent and for having a credible and survivable arsenal, apart from the land- air- and sea-based delivery systems. While on the realistic plane, these processes are on, on the idealistic plane, India has to continue mak-ing parallel diplomatic efforts towards global disarmament and continue to engage in various arms control negotiations, depending on the regional strategic environment and the dynamics of multi-lateral arms control environment.

❋ Military Issues

In terms of military issues, it becomes imperative to understand what India possesses and what it is likely to have over the next

---

[167] Pawar 1998. India tabled the resolution 'Reducing Nuclear Danger', and this was passed. For a fine commentary on this, see Chari 1999b.

[168] Vajpayee 1998c.

couple of decades in terms of fissile stocks (see Map 5.1). Additionally, what are the delivery systems that are available to India and what are in the pipeline?

A RAND analysis by Gregory Jones has suggested that India, at the most, 'could currently produce ... only 19 kg of HEU per year.' Jones also believes that India might have produced 'kilogram quantitative of U-233 by irradiating thorium in its power reactors.'[169] In 1998, David Albright estimated that

> India has about 370 kilograms of weapons-grade plutonium, or the equivalent of about 74 nuclear weapons. India relies principally on the Dhruva reactor for weapons-grade plutonium at a rate of about 20 kilograms per year. This amount corresponds to roughly four nuclear weapons per year. At this rate in 2005 India is estimated to have enough weapons-grade plutonium for over 100 nuclear weapons. India could produce significant weapons-grade plutonium by using its CANDU [Canada Deuterium Uranium] power reactors, although it may not have sufficient facilities to separate significant quantities of plutonium from the irradiated CANDU fuel.[170]

Meanwhile, R. Ramachandran has argued that the fissile material inventory available for weapon production from India's two research reactors, CANDU and Dhruva, could not exceed 280 kg of PU^{239} in 1998.[171] It is his assumption that 8 kgs are required per critical mass and this is sufficient for 35 nuclear weapons.[172] This issue gains significance, as it directly relates to the size of the arsenal. In 1994, K. Subrahmanyam estimated that 60 nuclear warheads would be sufficient.[173] Subrahmanyam, however, had to revise his estimate and concede that perhaps 150 odd nuclear warheads might be essential to build a credible nuclear deterrent.[174] Brig Vijai K. Nair has suggested that a force strength of 132 warheads/weapons would be suitable,[175] while Rear Admiral Raja Menon believes that 200 nuclear warheads/weapons would meet

---

[169] Jones 2000: 9.
[170] Albright 1999.
[171] Ramachandran 1999.
[172] Ibid.
[173] Subrahmanyam 1994.
[174] Subrahmanyam 1999.
[175] Nair 1992.

the requirement of 'credible minimum deterrent'.[176] From the viewpoint of building the 'credible minimum deterrent', it is essential to know what India is capable of. The need arises due to the debatable notion that a state's nuclear arsenal affects the durability and quality of deterrence it can attain.[177] Developing the argument of quality further, Bharat Karnad is of the opinion, and this reflects the maximalist position, that a thermonuclear deterrent is essential.[178] But on the quantity he does concede,

> depending on what figures one assigns to how much of the deterrent survives the enemy first strike and how much of the retaliatory strike will get through, braving the mid course hazards, like warhead and missile malfunction, boost phase and terminal phase interception by ballistic missile defences and coast phase interdiction by satellite based killer technologies under development, there is simply no way to alight on any right figure for the size of one's national nuclear force.[179]

This debate ultimately raises the question central to the calculations of numbers. If India is determined to go down the nuclear path and having reiterated that it would not strike first, it needs to have retaliatory capability. The draft report of the National Security Advisory Board on the Indian nuclear doctrine has outlined that 'these (nuclear) forces will be based on a triad of aircraft, mobile land-based missiles and sea-based assets. Survivability of the forces will be enhanced by a combination of multiple redundant systems, mobility, dispersion and deception.'[180] Let us assess the current capabilities of the Indian armed forces.

LAND

The land-based deterrent and its ability to safely deliver payloads deep into adversary territory have made the development of the Indian missile system the mainstay of credible minimum deterrence: Prithvi (tested in 1988) and the Agni (tested in 1989) are

---

[176] Menon 2000a.
[177] Hagerty 1998.
[178] Karnad 2002.
[179] Ibid.: 620.
[180] NSAB 1999: para 2.3.

Map × 5.1
India's Nuclear Estate

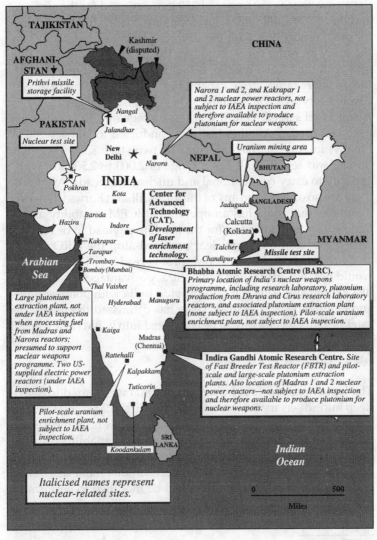

Source: Spector et al. 1995.

nuclear-capable missiles. The liquid-fuel, single-stage Prithvi comes in three versions: SS-150 with 150 km range (designed for the army), the SS-250 (range of 250 km, designed for the air force), and the SS-350 (still under development). Prithvi has been cleared for serial production, with the air force placing an order for 25 and the army an order for 50 missiles. The problem, as Ashley Tellis sees with the Prithvi missile, is that it does not add muscle to the Indian short-range strike capabilities. India has Pakistan already covered very well with aircraft.[181] The Agni I has a range of 1,400 km. A solid-fuel staged Agni II that has a range of 2,500 km has also been test fired.[182] Another test was conducted in January 2003.[183] Finally, in August 2004, an Agni III two-stage solid propellant missile was test fired. It has a range of 2,000 to 2,500 km with a capacity to carry conventional and nuclear warheads. As of now, there are no orders from any of the forces. Bharat Karnad, however, maintains that India has an operational ICBM capability and all that he says is required is 'for the satellite payload to be replaced with a megaton thermonuclear warhead atop the ISRO rockets, and a redoubtable Indian ICBM force is ready.'[184] This, he thinks, would not just offer range and accuracy advantages over missiles like Prithvi and Agni but also provide India with political power and clout. However, Ashley Tellis has dismissed the theory that satellite launch vehicles can be converted into ICBMs at a whim.[185]

AIR

The Jaguar was the first Indian aircraft that was geared to deliver deep into adversary territory. Later, the Mirage 2000 and the MiGs were acquired. The most recent acquisition has been the Russian Su-30. While the earlier aircrafts have the capability to cover Pakistan, only the Su-30 has the range to cover China and that too on a one-way mission. The critical decision that India will have to make is, which of these aircrafts will be modified to perform the role of carrying a nuclear warhead. It is unlikely that the MiGs

---

[181] Tellis 2002a.
[182] See *The Hindu* 2001.
[183] *The Hindu* 2003b.
[184] Karnad 1999: 139.
[185] See Tellis 2002a.

will have this role, given their popular perception of being 'flying coffins'.[186] Ashley Tellis believes that in the short term, only a few aircrafts will be configured for the role of building deterrence against Pakistan. But over a longer period of time, China will also figure in these calculations.[187] The Su-30s can be configured to carry nuclear warheads. They would also need mid-air refuelling if a long distance is to be covered, which is possible only after India buys the IL-78 flight tankers. The then Defence Minister, George Fernandes of the NDA cleared the purchase of these.[188] A question that still needs consideration in operational terms is, how many aircrafts can be airborne in a crisis scenario after a first strike and are to able to deliver a retaliatory strike.[189]

NAVY

As far as the navy goes, it does not have a nuclear-tipped submarine. There are voices that India should acquire one soon,[190] and the main argument given is that of the credibility and survivability of the arsenal. The Indian navy chief at a press conference said, 'any country that espouses a no-first-use policy (as India does) must have an assured second strike capability. All such countries have a triad of weapons, one of them at sea.'[191] It is significant that the Standing

[186] Answering a question in the Parliament on frequent MiG crashes, George Fernandes said, '110 numbers of MiG-21 jets had been crashed since 1992–93. Of these, 44 were due to technical defects, 43 due to human error and 13 due to bird hits' (The Pioneer 2002b).

[187] With the C-in-C of the Strategic Forces Command being Air Marshal T.M. Asthana, it is more likely that a greater emphasis will be laid on getting these 'precious' strategic assets ready. This would involve withholding them from conventional operations, isolating them from the rest of the forces, and securing them in special sanctuaries. See Tellis 2002a.

[188] See The Statesman 2000c. Mr George Fernandes 'assured the Indian Air Force that there will be no shortage of funds for the long-awaited acquisition of necessary equipment, including the advanced jet trainer, the airborne warning and control system and air to air refuelling aircraft as well as addition warfare and modern command and control system.'

[189] In such a scenario, the flight path seriously affects the range of the aircraft. A low-low-low flight path might endanger the aircraft to ground air defences while a high-high-low flight path or a dog path only reduces the flying radii.

[190] Bhaskar 2000.

[191] See The Hindustan Times 2002.

Committee on Defence of the twelfth Lok Sabha had advised the government 'to review and accelerate its nuclear policy for fabricating or for acquiring nuclear submarines to add to the (nation's) deterrent potential.'[192] The Sagarika, if reports are to be believed, is likely to be India's first such submarine. India has the technology that can deliver signals to a submarine from the shore. The Prithvi is also being designed for the navy and is likely to have a range of 330 km. This would then complete India's nuclear triad, although such a scenario is many years and millions of dollars away. India's first missile firing submarine, INS Sindhushastra, was commissioned at St Petersburg in July 2000.[193] The question that remains unresolved is, in spite of the credibility of the deterrent, if in a crisis situation the single submarine is located in a counter-force first strike and is sunk, what impact would it have on nuclear deterrence? Such a situation reflects an unhealthy and rather heavy concentration of nuclear arsenal in one submarine.[194]

After examining India's current force structures, one does reach a conclusion that India has the capability to deliver a warhead to Pakistan convincingly but not quite everywhere in China. But if 'credible minimum deterrence' means anything, one can expect this gap to be filled up soon. P.R. Chari thinks, and rightly so, that the Indian process of deployment would continue.[195] Gurmeet Kanwal is of the opinion that 'since India's targeting philosophy is not premised on "proportionate deterrence" or "flexible response", India does not need tactical or battlefield nuclear weapons.'[196] On the feasibility of such a triad, at least one Indian analyst, G. Balachandran, argues that 'in all available estimates of the cost ... the bulk of the

---

[192] Lok Sabha 1995–2002, here 1999.
[193] Radyuhin 2000.
[194] See Stefanick 1987.
[195] Chari 2001b.
[196] Kanwal 2001: 208. Kanwal further says that 'tactical nuclear weapons are essentially weapons of warfighting and their availability in the battlefield is likely to lower the nuclear threshold and cause a proclivity to use them during adverse military situations. Also inherent disadvantages of tactical nuclear weapons (primarily, the lower threshold of use, the need for "launch on warning" and "launch through attack" strategies of complex command and control and surveillance challenges, the increased cost of manufacture and maintenance, the problems of storage, transportation and handling in the field and the greater risk of accidental and even unauthorised use) should preclude the use of these weapons for deterrence.'

cost, nearly two-thirds of the total cost, goes towards the provision of a viable safe nuclear submarine force.'[197] Balachandran says, 'the cost of 20 additional [land-based] missiles will be far less than that of a nuclear ballistic missile submarine.'[198] On 5 January 2003, India sought to fill the void of a formal Nuclear Command Authority and Strategic Forces Command to create greater integration of the forces.

Ashley Tellis reckons that with the currently favoured posture, that of a 'force-in-being' with limited size, separated components and centralised control, two alternatives can be envisaged:

[A]t the one end, India could continue to settle for a force-in-being but one that is *not* limited in size. This posture, a robust force-in-being would continue to be defined by separated components and centralised control, but it would seek to incorporate the largest and the most capable nuclear force India could produce before it is constrained either by bilateral agreements or by multilateral treaties. At the other end, India could opt for a modest ready arsenal—that is, a force defined by highly integrated weapons ready for prompt operations as well as by a centralised but rapidly devolving command and control system, yet one that is nonetheless small at least in terms of the number and perhaps types of nuclear weapons it involves.[199]

✠ FOREIGN POLICY ISSUES

For some time after the tests, the Indian Ministry of External Affairs worked overtime to explain to the world the rationale behind choosing to test. Soon after the tests senior diplomats and ministers were sent to various parts of the world. India's relations with its neighbours and the US had their highs and lows. Prominent landmarks that influenced crucial foreign policy choices that India made included the Kargil crisis, the 11 September 2001 attack on the World Trade Center and the 13 December 2001 attack on the Indian Parliament.

---

[197] Balachandran 1999.

[198] Ibid. India has faced enormous difficulties in constructing even diesel-electric submarines. For an overview with regard to the Indian submarine construction programme, see Gorwitz 1996.

[199] Tellis 2002a: 722.

SINO-INDIAN RELATIONS

India damaged its relations with China to a great extent after the nuclear tests when in a letter to the US President, Mr Vajpayee wrote,

> We have an overt nuclear weapon state on our borders, a state which committed armed aggression against India in 1962. Although our relations with that country have improved in the last decade or so, an atmosphere of distrust persists mainly due to the unresolved border problem. To add to the distrust that country has materially helped another neighbour of ours to become a covert nuclear weapons state.[200]

After a couple of years of coolness, relations started improving between India and China. Foreign Minister Jaswant Singh's visit to Beijing in June 1999 was the first by an Indian minister in many years. Jaswant Singh's trip was preceded by the JWG meeting in Beijing in April 1999, and by some Indian political parties sending their teams to China. President K.R. Narayanan also visited China in June 2000 and there was warmth in Sino-Indian relations.[201] During the president's visit, the Indo-Chinese Joint Working Group (JWG) on the boundary question and related issues met, there were indications that Sino-Indian economic relations should be brought back on track and a general agreement was reached to have insti-tutionalised security dialogue with China.[202] However, by early 1999, it was clear that the two powers would restore the status quo ante, and at the height of the Kargil War (May–July 1999) between India and Pakistan, the JWG met and the Chinese also proposed the insti-tution of a security dialogue.[203] In January 2002, the Chinese Premier, Zhu Rongji, paid a visit to India with a primary interest in economic cooperation.[204] The Indian defence minister's visit to China in April 2003 further strengthened bilateral ties. While there has been no dilution of China's critical stance on India's nuclear weaponisation,

---

[200] See the text of Mr Vajpayee's letter in Vajpayee 1998a.

[201] Mohan 2000.

[202] *The Times of India* 2001b.

[203] Bajpai 2000.

[204] In this visit an MoU was signed on exchanging hydrological data on the Brahmaputra river's flow through India and China. The highlight of this visit was the Chinese premier's visit to Infosys Technologies Ltd. Gupta 2002a.

its stridency has abated because of non-ratification of the CTBT by the USA. After the US pushed for a NMD cover in South-east Asia, Indians also voiced concerns similar as the Chinese. Later India did a volte-face on its position and has supported the US on the NMD.[205] In November 2000, China pledged imposing strict export control measures against missile proliferation.[206] This has given hope to India that the China–Pakistan defence relationship may be weakening. Speaking of transfers to countries that are developing ballistic missiles, China says that it will exercise special scrutiny and caution. Beijing has now implicitly addressed New Delhi's authoritative belief that it was China that had all along been masterminding Pakistan's nuclear and missile programme. The stated Chinese aim is to 'prevent significant contributions' to unspecified countries. Till now, China has continually denied the issue of missile technology transfer to Pakistan and Iran. Declaring that it will impose restrictions over the export of this technology implies admitting of its earlier violations of the Missile Technology Control Regime (MTCR). There are concerns in India over the recent Chinese pledge of imposing strict export control measures against missile proliferation, as this declaration does not imply an end to the China–Pakistan military and nuclear cooperation. Pakistan may still remain dependent on China for spares.[207]

China and India had signed a treaty to maintain peace and tranquillity on their disputed borders.[208] It has put in place a series of confidence-building measures (CBMs) which have worked successfully. With China, India has worked hard to 'untie the knot' without sounding apologetic. Sino-Indian relations witnessed a further forward movement, with both countries exchanging maps for the first time on the 545 km line of actual control delineating a chunk of the boundary.[209] The ghosts of the past were buried.[210] A Chinese scholar has argued that 'there is the need to further enhance the bilateral security dialogue and develop other, more regular contacts between the two militaries to reduce the four "M"s:

[205] Rajagopalan 2001.
[206] *The Hindu* 2000b.
[207] See in this context, Gupta 2002b.
[208] See India–PRC Agreement (1993, 1996), discussed in chapter 4.
[209] *The Hindustan Times* 2001.
[210] *The Pioneer* 2002a. Also see the editorial in *The Hindu* 2002a.

misunderstanding, misperception, misgiving and miscalculation. The two sides must express their strategic intentions in clear terms.'[211] Observing the developing relationship between India and the US, the author argues that

> India should be forthright with its rationale for endorsing U.S. missile defence plans and its growing ties with the U.S. New Delhi needs to dispel misgivings in Beijing that it is playing the 'democracy' and 'market' cards to gain U.S. support for a greater role in global and regional affairs and that it is a potential junior partner in a U.S. global strategy to contain China.[212]

In 1998, the former ambassador to China and now the convenor of the NSAB, C.V. Ranganathan, described the world as having 'witnessed exponential changes in the last decade, brought about by a technological revolution in communications and by internal flows of investment, trade and services ....'[213] Ranganathan sees these changes leading

> [f]or the world at large, as well as China and India, to an incremental increase in what China calls 'comprehensives national strength'. [This] will cause restructuring in global resource allocations, investment decisions, financial inflows, technology development and may even affect the hitherto established power balance ... [up to now] geo-political compulsions have prevailed at the cost of geo-economic objectives. In recent years, China has set up diverse trans-border linkages across China's borders in all directions; the time has come to explore possibilities of such globalised linkages between India and China as well.'[214]

For all the attention India has received for its missile and nuclear tests, it has yet to achieve the sort of deterrent capabilities that other nuclear weapons states possess, namely, the ability to respond with a second strike if subjected to a nuclear attack. For India to pursue a 'realistic deterrence' against China, some strategists have argued that it will have to demonstrate its ability to target Chinese cities.[215]

---

[211] Jing-Dong Yuan 2002.
[212] Ibid.
[213] Ranganathan 1998: 113.
[214] Ibid.
[215] Kanwal 1999; Chellaney 1999c.

There is a need for the two Asian giants to cooperate bilaterally and globally, looking beyond the prism of security. Perhaps a better approach toward seeking convergent behaviour between India and China lies in tracing the issues where a Sino-Indian commonality of interests impels both states to seek similar outcomes from the deliberations of large multilateral groupings.

INDO-PAK RELATIONS

With a huge baggage of conflictual history, normalising Indo-Pak relations presents a very difficult situation for any decision maker. The countries have fought four wars: 1947, 1965, 1971 and the 1999 Kargil War. Indo-Pak relations have had their usual crests and troughs, but since the nuclear tests, there have been more troughs than crests. With both India and Pakistan having come out of the nuclear closet, each state has realised that it now possesses weapons that could annihilate entire societies. Therefore, it becomes imperative for them to figure out a framework that governs their strategic relationship. Soon after the tests, the idea of a subcontinental 'arms race' and 'nuclear flashpoint' caused anxiety in Western diplomatic circles. It would certainly be in the interest of the two countries to enter into a set of confidence- and security-building measures, provided the appropriate strategic environment presents itself. By declaring themselves as nuclear weapons states, both India and Pakistan have started talking the language of arms control, deterrence and military confidence-building measures. It is essential for these two countries to undertake nuclear risk reduction measures. Prominent landmarks include the much-touted Lahore Declaration followed by the Kargil crisis and the Parliament attack.

The report of the Group of Ministers aptly sums up the point of view of the Government of India:

Pakistan's weapons acquisitions from the West and China and its close collaboration with China and North Korea on nuclear and missile matters, will continue to be of grave concern to India. Pakistan will continue to seek further enhancement in the quality of its weapons to attempt to offset its conventional quantitative military inferiority vis-à-vis India.[216]

---

[216] Group of Ministers, GOI 2001: 10.

The report concludes,

> Pakistan believes that nuclear weapons can compensate for conventional military inferiority; its leaders have not concealed their desire to use nuclear weapons .... General Musharraf's proclaimed desire to talk to India rings hollow against the backdrop of continuing Pakistani support for militants and his unremitting obsession with Kashmir. Pakistan is following the policy of 'bleeding India through a thousand cuts'.[217]

Given this background, what can be the central premise of Indo-Pak relations? India and Pakistan have cooperated on nuclear issues in the past.[218] The nuclear facilities list has been exchanged punctually every year.[219] Since this was ratified in 1991, when as some argue[220] there existed non-weaponised deterrence, the argument can be made that both states might have suspected each other's adherence to it. This model of cooperative security would urge the countries to go further towards nuclear issues. Mr Vajpayee's much publicised bus diplomacy and the subsequent Lahore Declaration in February 1999 proved to be a major landmark in improving relations between the two neighbours.[221] One significant aspect of the Lahore Declaration were the nuclear CBMs which were intended to create a climate where further progress was possible. A relevant clause of the Lahore Declaration was that 'respective Governments ... shall take immediate steps for reducing the risk of accidental or unauthorised use of nuclear weapons and discuss concepts and doctrines with a view to elaborating measures for confidence building in the nuclear and conventional fields, aimed at prevention of conflict.'[222] Unfortunately, the Kargil War which followed the Lahore Declaration served to reverse any progress made.

---

[217] Ibid.: 10.

[218] See India–Pakistan Agreement 1988.

[219] There are those who argue that the lists are not comprehensive. The latest exchange of lists took place on 1 January 2004. See *Dawn* 2004.

[220] The more prominent among these scholars is George Perkovich. See Perkovich 1993.

[221] The Lahore Declaration was signed between the Indian and the Pakistani prime ministers following the much publicised bus trip by the Indian prime minister. The text of the Lahore Declaration can be seen in *The Hindu* 1999a.

[222] Ibid. Also see http://www.ipcs.org/documents/1999/1-jan-mar.htm, accessed on 15 July 2000.

India came through the Kargil crisis with the following gains: it expelled intruders from Indian soil, all the while maintaining the sanctity of the LoC, forged an equation with China—which decided to remain neutral, won international acclaim for choosing to respect the LoC and saw a new high in its relationship with the United States.

On 10 August 1999, while the Kargil conflict was winding up, an Indian Air Force MiG 21 shot down a Pakistani surveillance aircraft, Breguet Atlantique, killing all 16 Pakistan personnel on board, for intruding 10 km into Indian territory in the Kori Creek region in Gujarat. According to the Indian version, the MiG 21s tried to force the Atlantique to land in India, but the intruder aircraft turned in towards the MiG 21 in an attack position. The Pakistani official version, however, was that the Atlantique was unarmed and in a routine training within its territorial limits when it was shot without any warning. It was precisely to avoid such incidents that the countries had entered into the Agreement between Pakistan and India on Prevention of Air Space Violation in 1991.[223] Later, Pakistan took the case to the International Court of Justice and lost the case.

Against the backdrop of these events, an Indian Airlines flight from Kathmandu to New Delhi, IC-814, was hijacked and after a couple of halts at Amritsar (India), Lahore (Pakistan) and Dubai, the plane finally came to a halt in Kandahar for seven days. In return for the safety of the passengers, the Government of India had to release three terrorists—Masood Azhar, Mushtaq Zargar and Omar Sheikh. Soon after their release in Kandahar, the three terrorists reached Quetta in Baluchistan (Pakistan)—they did not travel in a clandestine manner, but started spitting anti-Indian and US venom in public rallies. India had long suspected a Pakistani hand in the hijacking, and the presence of the three terrorists in Pakistan after their release only confirmed India's suspicions.[224]

---

[223] Article 2 of the agreement states, 'the following restrictions are to be observed by military aircraft of both the forces: (a) Combat aircraft (to include fighter, bomber, reconnaissance, jet military trainer and armed helicopter aircraft) will not fly within 10 kms of each other's airspace including ADIZ. No aircraft of any side will enter the airspace over the territorial waters of the other country, except by prior permission' (India–Pakistan Agreement 1991).

[224] See in this context, Dixit 2002: ch. 1.

The Kargil conflict and the issue of cross-border terrorism lend credibility to the argument that nuclear weapons do not prevent armed conflict, and depending on the actors involved, in this case India and Pakistan, an irrational or unauthorised use of these weapons cannot be totally ruled out if such a conflict escalates.[225] Although there has been a guarded response from India and both sides have expressed confidence that they can keep such conflicts from escalating, the risks that emanate from a miscalculation are unacceptably high. There has been some concern over the change of guard in Pakistan with Gen Pervez Musharraf having seized power, but in his address to the nation on 17 October 1999, he took two reassuring steps.[226] He has also welcomed the offer of talks with India. India will find it difficult to talk business with a person who is widely believed to have carried out the Kargil operations. Still, it is in India's interest to talk, depending on the political environment. The violence in Kashmir intensified in July–August 2000 when terrorists killed more than 100 people in a week. Officially, India has put the cessation of hostilities in Kashmir as the precondition of talks.

The Agra Summit

On 24 May 2001, Mr Atal Behari Vajpayee took the rather bold decision of inviting the Pakistani chief executive (who had by now donned the mantle of president) to begin the process 'of engaging in productive dialogue'[227] for talks in the Indian city of Agra. This took place on 14–16 July 2001, and ended inconclusively. The three

---

[225] At the 4 July 1999 Blair House meeting of the US President Bill Clinton and Pakistan Prime Minister Nawaz Sharif, President Clinton asked Sharif if he 'knew how advanced the threat of nuclear war really was: 'Did Sharif know his military was preparing their nuclear tipped missiles? ... Did Sharif order the Pakistani nuclear missile force to prepare for action?' At this information, 'Sharif seemed taken aback' (See Riedel 2002: 7).

[226] 'I take this opportunity to announce a unilateral military de-escalation on our international borders with India and initiate the return of all our forces moved to the borders in the recent past. I hope this step would serve as a meaningful confidence building measure. And Pakistan will continue to pursue a policy of nuclear and missile restraint and sensitivity to global non-proliferation and disarmament objectives.' For the full text of the address, see Musharraf 1999b.

[227] The text of the letter can be seen in Vajpayee 2001.

points that came in the way of signing a joint declaration (an Agra Declaration was on the cards) were Pakistan's insistence on describing the Kashmir issue as a 'dispute', although India had at one point agreed to make it the 'first point' in the eight points to be included in the declaration that was being drafted on the second day of the summit talks, on 16 July. That flexibility shown by India came to a nought, for Pakistan in the end insisted on adding a clause to say that the entire declaration should be 'subject to' and 'dependent on' movement on the Jammu and Kashmir issue (on the ground, in terms of finding a solution). 'India was not going to accept that', it was said, for India was against holding the entire bilateral relationship hostage to the Kashmir question. The second issue on which no headway could be made was that of cross-border terrorism. 'Pakistan President, General Pervez Musharraf, did not want anything at all on this issue, he insisted it was a freedom struggle in Kashmir, and this was not acceptable to us.'[228] Finally, it was candidly admitted that the live telecast of General Musharraf's breakfast meeting with 35 editors on the morning of 16 July after the talks were under way, and even as the delicate and complex negotiations had started, was completely unacceptable. As already stated by the External Affairs Minister, Mr Jaswant Singh, it was to have been an off-the-record exchange of views which the government had felicitated. The controversy involving the Hurriyat leaders earlier was bad, but the telecast of the breakfast meeting was what finally vitiated the atmosphere completely.

The morning after the exhausting summit with the leadership of Pakistan ended inconclusively, India signalled its determination to stay on course and seek peace and reconciliation with Pakistan. Seeking to dispel the widespread perception of the failure of the Agra summit, Mr Jaswant Singh said the two nations had covered considerable ground in Agra in finding a framework to deal with their bilateral differences. Similar sentiments were expressed by Abdul Sattar in Pakistan. Fundamental differences over Kashmir and cross-border terrorism turned out to be too strong to let both countries reach a broad accommodation of each other's core political concerns. As a result, the attempts to craft an 'Agra Declaration' that would have helped India and Pakistan embark on 'the high road to peace and prosperity' collapsed. The absence of a

---

[228] Vyas 2001.

codified declaration at the inconclusive end of their meeting at Agra may indeed have much to do with the qualitative asymmetry of a different kind, that could be traced to the conflicting expectations the two sides had of the summit. Both sides at the end of the two days of hard bargaining agreed on the belief that 'the existing goodwill on both side' would at some stage lead to 'mutually desired results' in the future. Islamabad and New Delhi were unwilling to call the talks a failure, choosing instead to term the deliberations at Agra 'inconclusive' in serving as the 'foundation' for future parleys.

The Attack on the Parliament and the Rise of Compellance Strategy
The report of the Group of Ministers concluded that

> notwithstanding the deterrence provided by India's nuclear tests, the possibility of a conventional war between two nuclear power states cannot be ruled out. This was amply demonstrated by the Kargil War of 1999. The battlefield of the future, however, will be vastly different from [that of] the past—it would be non-linear in nature, with real-time surveillance, integrated Command, Control, Communications, Computer, Intelligence and Information (C4I2) assets, target acquisition, and highly lethal precision weapon systems.'[229]

The daring attack on the Parliament of India on 13 December 2001 led to the downward spiral of Indo-Pak relations. Immediately after the attack, the Government of India blamed Pakistan-based militant groups for the attack and placed a set of demands on Pakistan.[230] In the months that followed, India had to decide whether to go to war or exhaust all other options first. The military standoff was independent India's largest mobilisation that lasted more than 10 months. As the crisis between India and Pakistan de-escalated, questions were being asked regarding whether it was coercive diplomacy at its best or nuclear brinkmanship at its worst.[231] India threatened to take military action but never initiated it as it was testing the limits of coercive diplomacy—threatening to go to war but not actually doing so. The US shuttle diplomacy managed

---

[229] Group of Ministers GOI 2001.
[230] Mohan 2001b.
[231] See Rajain 2002a.

to obtain an assurance from Pakistani President, Gen Pervez Musharraf that the infiltration into India by Muslim radicals had been ended permanently. That seemed sufficient for India to de-escalate.

What were India's other options? There were primarily three options before India in handling the 13 December attacks and the subsequent attacks in Jammu: diplomatic, economic and military. India's immediate response was on the diplomatic front, when in December the government snapped road, rail and air links and asked Pakistan to recall its High Commissioner Ashraf Jahangir Qazi, while appealing to the Western world to step up the pressure on Pakistan. Additionally, visa restrictions, consulate facilities and reduction of the Pakistani high commission staff followed. As India grew impatient with the Western coalition against terrorism and on the domestic front, the NDA, faced with a growing 'adequate response' sentiment, considered a 'go at it alone' approach. Among the very few diplomatic successes between the two countries was the 1960 Indus Water Treaty, and India had been scrupulous in keeping the terms of the treaty. If India had chosen to abrogate the treaty, the impact of the denial of the water would have been felt in Pakistan, both economically and socially. But this could have proved to be politically disastrous for India, as this would have left the door open for Pakistan to walk out of the 1972 Simla Agreement that emphasised the Indian mantra of bilateralism.[232]

If India wanted to hurt Pakistan economically, there was the need to halt the illegal parallel trade that runs across the border into Pakistan and the impact of that would have been immediate and widespread. But that would also have had an impact on some of Indian states that share the international border with Pakistan. India also toyed with the idea of withdrawing the most favoured nation status of Pakistan.[233] But this was at best a blunt weapon, as there is very little official trade between the two countries. Perhaps last in the line of options was the military option, and going by the large military mobilisation, it seemed clear that India was going to press the advantage. This, however, required very clear political objectives. High on the scale of the escalation ladder of the military options was the use of air power on terrorist training camps, which

---

[232] Text of the Simla Agreement may be seen in Krepon and Sevak 1996.
[233] The argument here is that Pakistan has anyway not given India this status.

at best would have been few tents, with trainee terrorists probably dispersed deep inside Pakistan. The second option was the use of Indian special forces and air-dropping paracommandos close to where these camps are. Most of these camps, like Oghi village, Ojheri camp, Para Chinar, Saidgali and Sargodha, had quickly shut down operations. A third option was 'hot pursuit'. India, however, had to be clear on politico-military objectives—would India retain administrative control of the territories that the Indian army ran over in its hot pursuit? In an answer to this question, Gen V.P. Malik, the Chief of the Army Staff during the Kargil War said, 'Yes! There is space for such an armed action. But the politico military objective must be very clear.'[234] Was India en-visaging 'salami slicing' of Pakistan occupied Kashmir? India had to consider whether it was willing to occupy and retain territory, or whether closing down training camps would be its only object-ive. Obviously, these camps could be quickly established else-where. A fourth option could have been an all-out war involving regular armies. In response to these questions, General Malik said, 'the important point is what is our politico-military objective and what would be the final outcome of such an action.'[235]

Even if the final political objectives had been thought through, each of the three options carried the risk of escalation to a nuclear level. If indeed India had decided to cross the line of control or the international border, and Pakistan had decided to issue an implicit or even explicit warning that it was feeling 'threatened' enough for it to contemplate the use of the nuclear option (better used early enough to deter)—what then would have been India's options?[236] Would India have stopped the air strikes, recalled its troops and called off the operation? Or would it have gone ahead and con-tinued to hope that Pakistan would not make good on its nuclear threats? An element of strategic uncertainty remains here. It is pre-cisely this kind of uncertainty that could breed misperceptions which might lead to miscalculations. It seems both India and Pakistan are still learning the nuances of the nuclear deterrence game. Hence, there remains a likelihood of miscalculation in

---

[234] Malik 2002.

[235] Ibid.

[236] In any such crisis situation, the role of increasing pro-war public sentiment cannot be underestimated.

correctly reading and interpreting each other's 'red lines', especially in a crisis situation. This calls for adopting more reliable methods of signalling their intent and developing sustainable channels of communication. Additionally, if one were to see the trajectory of Indian response to a future similar situation, it seems fairly clear that India will not cross the LoC, a norm that it seems to have set, and Pakistan may continue to test the Indian threshold on this.

As the crisis wound down, there were a spate of statements from both sides about nuclear weapons and their role in managing the crisis.[237] Artillery exchanges continued as did war rhetoric. Constant nuclear sabre rattling by Pakistan drew the attention of the Western world, particularly the direct intervention of the United States. One positive outcome of the stand-off was the 12 January 2002 speech by President Musharraf, wherein he pledged the cessation of overt support to terrorism. He later promised to 'permanently' end cross-border terrorism.[238] This verbal commitment should translate into closure of training camps and the accompanying infrastructure associated with infiltration, and this could be monitored credibly by the United States, India, or both. The use of monitoring technology would go a long way towards restoring trust. Once this issue is settled, there are chances of an increased stability in the region. This would mean a loss for Pakistan in terms of trying to find 'strategic depth'.[239] It is also possible that Pakistan will not stop cross-border terrorism and only increase or decrease it according to the pressure applied on the country. India has to be prepared for such an eventuality.

Diplomatic success could mean gains for both countries. First, war is never a positive sum game or to the advantage of either. Second, any outbreak of large-scale armed hostilities always carries the seeds of escalation. Third, Pakistan's Kashmir policy, just like

---

[237] See *The Hindu* 2002c, 2002d. Also see *Dawn* 2002.

[238] *The Times of India* 2002. For the text of Musharraf's speech, see Musharraf 2002. The Pakistan Foreign Office initially issued a notice that no such promise had been made, but under pressure from the US, it later conceded the truth. See *The News International* 2002. There were concerns not just in India but also in the United States that Pakistan was not complying. See *International Herald Tribune* 2002.

[239] Pakistan's search for 'strategic depth' has often made it follow dangerous and destabilising policies both in Afghanistan and Kashmir. Both these policies have backfired and have shown to the world that Pakistan is a formentor of terrorism in the region.

its Afghan policy, has failed the country. Fourth, a war would be detrimental to US interests in the region as it would destabilise the entire region.

For the fear of escalation, perhaps no country wanted an armed conflict, as the situation could easily spiral, owing to factors that might be beyond the control of either. In the meantime, each side seems determined to convince the other that it is not blustering, maintaining the threat of actual war. Howsoever 'victorious' either side may feel from the stand-off, one thing is clear: one unresolved Kashmir issue always carries the risk of another such crisis. While Indians continue to point out that the United States has the authority and the leverage to coerce Pakistan into making substantial internal policy changes, questions continue to be raised about the credibility of Washington's role as a peacemaker and the leader of the international coalition against terrorism. From an Indian point of view, the main concern is that the US chooses to turn a blind eye to terrorist training camps in Pakistan.[240] After the attack on the Indian Parliament, the US seems to be exerting some pressure on Pakistan to stop terrorist infiltration, but from the Indian perspective much more needs to be done. And some charge that Pakistan has now realised that it can get away with testing India's patience at a threshold higher than ever before. In such a context, issues like crisis management and escalation control acquire new significance. If armed conflict is not initiated, it is probably due to either side not wanting to escalate it to the 'point of no return', and choosing to come out of the crisis with 'something to show' from the crisis bargaining as opposed to 'backing off'.[241]

- If Pakistan decided that it would comply with any of the Indian demands—stopping cross-border terrorism and handing over India's 20 most wanted criminals who have taken refuge there, it would have immediately lost out on the domestic constituency. If Pakistan had gamed that India was unlikely to attack given (a) international pressure, and (b) India's established norm of not crossing the LoC, one outcome was certain. The stand-off would remain for a while, but international pressure would slowly ensure

---

[240] See in this context, the CIA's briefings and statements over a period of time, notably DCI 2003. The US has also been aware of bin Laden and Pakistan's support to militant activity in Kashmir. See DCI 2000, 2002.

[241] Rajain 2002a.

that India withdrew its troops in a phased manner from its battle positions to peacetime locations.

- Another outcome could have been that the stand-off would continue for a while, and Pakistan would hand over some of the people named in the 20 most-wanted list (perhaps beginning with the Punjab militants and not given away anything on the Kashmir issue), and a process of de-escalation would be initiated.
- A third outcome could have been no compliance, no bargaining, no punishment—with the US ensuring that the stand-off ends peacefully. In either case, Indian demands would only have been partially met. Pakistan realised that it could get away after testing India's patience at a threshold that is substantially higher than before. Where does this leave India? After the present stand-off, India would realise that a military build-up and making demands does not work. Since this threshold did not work, India would have to raise the threshold in the next crisis to just short of an armed conflict.

At least on one occasion Pakistan made it clear, rather overtly, that it had the right to use any weapon at its disposal in the case of an Indian attack.[242] Perhaps Pakistan calculated that India may not attack due to Pakistan's nuclear capability.[243] There were far too many factors at play to fathom even complex war gaming scenarios. While Pakistan might have viewed escalation on a vertical trajectory with move 'a' leading to 'b' and then to 'c' and so on, it was likely that it may not have been the case. What if the escalation trajectory was horizontal with move 'a' followed by 'd', or to another point higher in the escalation ladder?[244] What if the adversary chose to escalate tension through the use of non-conventional military or other means?[245] Moreover, given the external influence on South Asian deterrence, playing out a nuclear conflict scenario does not appear realistic. Besides, how can success be determined at this stage, when the deterrence calculation has not changed drastically?[246]

This is what some scholars imply when they say that the threat of war was effective in creating international pressure on Pakistan,

---

[242] *Dawn* 2002.
[243] Siddiqa-Agha 2002.
[244] Ibid.
[245] Ibid.
[246] Ibid.

but maintain that the execution of any such threat would be dangerous and could lead to a breakdown of deterrence. There is a delicate
balance between nuclear capability acting as a deterrent and it
being the cause for breakdown of deterrence. The appropriate
diplomatic response lies in adopting the stance of nuclear brinkmanship: threaten to cross the brink and hope your enemy gives
in first.[247] The risk that hostility between India and Pakistan may
escalate was affirmed by several factors that ranged from the
diplomatic to the politico-strategic. Despite this, it is widely believed that India's 'experimentation with coercive diplomacy
involved an important shift to the notion of containing Pakistan'
from the notion of engaging it.[248]

Where does this leave India? After the present stand-off, India
should realise that a military build-up, coupled with far-reaching
political demands, does not work each time. The next time around,
India must exercise better judgement about the probability of
various pay-offs, including its own ability to execute a threatened
course of action.[249] There has to be an exit strategy in place before
India decides to take a certain course of action.

C. Raja Mohan concludes that while there has been no formal
articulation of India's policy of containing Pakistan, the policy has
acquired the characteristics of containment.[250] Both India and
Pakistan have to realise that many of these impediments in their
relationship will not be resolved with the aid of the nuclear weapon.
Neither does the world today approve of altering the status quo
with use of force and tacit nuclear blackmail.

INDO-US RELATIONS

Following the nuclear tests, the US imposed sanctions on India
under the Glenn Amendment. The Glenn Amendment refers to an
amendment to the Arms Export Control Act (Section 102) which stipu-
lates that if the president determines that a non-nuclear weapons

---

[247] Rajain 2002a.

[248] Mohan 2003a: 202. In fact, Mohan suggests that the policy of containment
has emerged as India's only option in dealing with Pakistan.

[249] Rajain 2002a.

[250] He suggests that 'the objective of a containment policy towards Pakistan is
to engineer, through external pressures, an internal transformation of Pakistan
that puts an end to the sources of compulsive hostility towards India' (Mohan
2003a: 202).

state, as defined by the nuclear Non-Proliferation Treaty (NPT), detonates a nuclear explosive device, certain sanctions can be applied. The sanctions would impose broad-ranging restrictions on various types of assistance, loans and trade.[251] It was believed that following the various rounds of Strobe Talbott–Jaswant Singh dialogue, India might bargain for sanction removal in exchange of signing the CTBT. Answering a question in the Parliament on his talks with US Deputy Secretary of State, Strobe Talbott, the Minister for External Affairs, Jaswant Singh said,

In addition to security, non-proliferation and disarmament issues, the two sides discussed bilateral relations and regional developments ... the two sides also agreed to hold the first meeting of the Joint Working Group on Counter-Terrorism ... the two sides are also in the process of setting up a Joint Working Group to intensify co-operation in the fields of energy and environment sector.[252]

Answering another question in the Parliament on the bilateral relations between India and the US, Jaswant Singh said, 'The two governments have also agreed to work purposefully, towards developing a broad-based relationship and intensifying mutually beneficial co-operation in trade and investment, energy and environment, science and technology, education and culture, counter terrorism and narcotics control etc.'[253] India also raised the issue of missile proliferation in the neighbourhood in its talks with the US:

[T]he issue of missile proliferation in our neighbourhood, including co-operation between China and Pakistan, has been discussed on several occasions with the United States as a part of the ongoing dialogue between India and the United States on security, proliferation, disarmament and related issues ....[254]

---

[251] The Glenn Amendment to the Arms Export Control Act of 1994 requires the president to impose these seven sanctions: (*a*) suspend foreign aid (except for humanitarian assistance or food and other agricultural commodities); (*b*) terminate sales of any military items; (*c*) terminate other military assistance; (*d*) stop credits or guarantees to the country by US government agencies; (*e*) vote against credits or assistance by international financial institutions; (*f*) prohibit US banks from making loans to the foreign government concerned; and (*g*) prohibit exports of specific goods and technology (as specified in the Export Administration Act of 1979) with civilian and military nuclear applications.

[252] Lok Sabha 2000b.

[253] Lok Sabha 2000c.

[254] Lok Sabha 2000g.

Certain sanctions were waived in October 1999, while the rest were removed in 2002. A positive aspect of the tests has been that India and the US has engaged in a serious dialogue covering nuclear issues. The Strobe Talbott–Jaswant Singh talks have had 12 rounds.[255] The talks had been

> conducted on the basis of the comprehensive proposals that India has put forward on disarmament and non-proliferation matters, our unilateral moratorium on explosive nuclear tests, willingness to discuss converting this moratorium into a *de jure* obligation, our (India's) offer to enter into constructive negotiations on the FMCT and reaffirming our (India's) policies on stringent control on export of sensitive technologies.[256]

The US seems to believe that 'either India or Pakistan will give up this (nuclear) capability or that any conceivable external pressure (from Western countries, particularly the US) will be sufficient to convince them to alter their positions.'[257] This long dialogue also meant that for the first time India was able to place its regional security apprehensions clearly on the table. It also translated into a different and qualitatively better Indo-US relationship. For years, the nuclear issue had been a major roadblock in India–US relations. Now for once there were serious discussions on it between the two countries.

The Kargil crisis ensured a new role for the US in the subcontinent. In fact, the US was apprehensive of playing a role in the South Asian crisis initially.[258] It was only after the Clinton–Sharif meeting followed by the joint statement on 4 July 1999 that led to the change

---

[255] After 10 months of sustained dialogue with India and Pakistan following their nuclear tests, Strobe Talbott has identified these five steps which the US thinks will avoid a destabilising nuclear and missile competition in South Asia: (a) moratorium on testing; (b) agree to join talks on FMCT; (c) exercise strategic restraint; (d) follow tightened export controls on sensitive technologies; and (e) continue a productive bilateral dialogue (Talbott 1999). Mr Vajpayee said in the Parliament on 15 December 1998, that India was communicating with the US as a nuclear weapons state. See Vajpayee 1998c.

[256] *The Americas* section in the 1998 report of Ministry of External Affairs, GOI (1990–2002).

[257] Independent Task Force 1998.

[258] The government stated, 'We strongly support talks between India and Pakistan to resolve this latest dispute and believe these talks should take place

of policy.[259] The immediate reason was the recognition by President Clinton that this was a very serious situation and was in danger of wider escalation.[260] According to Jaswant Singh, the US support to India on Kargil was 'both recognition of the correctness of India's case and the folly of Pakistan's misadventure. It is recognition, too, of the altering geo-strategic contours in the region.'[261] Throughout the crisis, the US continuously said that it had not played the role of a mediator. The prominent interest that guided US diplomacy in the Kargil conflict was eliminating the risk of a nuclear face-off in South Asia. 'The US realised that both India and Pakistan did not want to escalate the conflict.'[262]

After the Kargil conflict, voices were being heard on the *quid pro quo* of the 'personal interest' of President Bill Clinton.[263] With India having broken the norm against nuclear testing, an Indian accent to CTBT would have proved to be the achievement glory of Bill Clinton's presidency. But the CTBT was shelved in the US and put in a limbo. India has stepped into the new millennium with continuity of the current warmth in the Indo-US ties. Even though there were apprehensions that the US would put pressure on

---

as soon as possible. Ending the fighting in the Kargil area can only be accomplished through direct engagement by India and Pakistan. We remain in touch with the Indian and Pakistani Governments to express our strong concern, to urge them to show restraint and to prevent the fighting from spreading ...' (Krishnaswami 1999).

[259] According to the statement, the president and the prime minister agreed that respecting the line of control in Kashmir in accordance with the Simla agreement was vital for the peace of South Asia. To this end 'concrete steps' needed to be taken for the restoration of the LoC; immediate cessation of hostilities was required; the Lahore process was the best forum for resolving all issues dividing India and Pakistan, including Kashmir; the president of the US would take US 'personal interest' in resumption of bilateral dialogues; and he would pay an early visit to South Asia. See Joint US–Pakistan Statement 1999.

[260] US Information Service 1999: 2.

[261] Mohan 1999b.

[262] Schaffer and Schaffer 1999.

[263] The semantic jugglery necessitated by the phrase 'personal interest' of Bill Clinton left space for the role that the US has played in diffusing the crisis. Prof. Stephen Cohen said, 'The US has a specific role between the two sides—facilitating. There is such thing as a facilitator without being a mediator', while Prof. Robert Wirsing says, 'This (the Kargil conflict) will be dragged out with a formal additional participant in Washington. You may not call it mediation but facilitation *is* mediation' (Cited in Mitra and Sengupta 1999).

India to settle the Kashmir issue, these proved to unfounded as the US continued to insist that the best way forward in India–Pakistan relations was through dialogue. The US role and interest in the region suddenly changed post 9/11. The worldview on terrorism altered, much to India's advantage. With an increased US presence in Afghanistan and Pakistan, the spotlight turned to Pakistan's terrorist infrastructure. This helped India to a great extent, as every attack on innocent civilians in Kashmir and elsewhere in India was highlighted to India's advantage and the pressure on Pakistan to close down terrorist training infrastructure increased. This role has continued and was most evident during the military build-up after the Parliament attack phase. The relationship with the US may never be equitable. The challenge for Indian diplomacy now lies in utilising this new opportunity to forge closer relations that usher in greater empathy regarding issues of mutual concern.

The visit of US President, Bill Clinton to India in March 2000 laid the foundation of a long-term relationship with India. His speech in the Indian Parliament transformed the Indo-US relationship. President Clinton's visit to India gave added impetus to the US effort to engage India in developing a qualitatively new and closer relationship across a broad range of global, regional and bilateral issues. It underscored the reality that although significant areas of disagreement remain—including on non-proliferation—the dialogue between these two great nations, whose overall democratic values and interests have so much in common, must move forward. Informing the Parliament of India about the US president's visit, Jaswant Singh said that India and the US 'agreed to enhance bilateral co-operation in trade and commerce ....'[264] The institutional architecture for building a substantive relationship has been put in place by a provision for regular summits, proposed frequent interaction and the Joint Statement on Cooperation in Energy and Environment.[265] There are some key elements of the United States'

---

[264] The other issues were, 'finance and investment, information technology and other knowledge-based industries, energy and environment, science and technology, and health, and to work jointly for the promotion of peace and prosperity in the world in the 21st Century .... An institutional framework for dialogue on economic and commercial issues, counter-terrorism, energy and environment, and science and technology' (Lok Sabha 2000d).

[265] In the context of the US President's South Asia visit, see Joint US–India Statement 2000a, 2000b and Jenniangs 2000.

South Asia policy: The US cannot and should not attempt to make the rescue of Pakistan the centrepiece of its policy towards South Asia. It does not see India as sympathetic to its interests,[266] but realises Indian concerns. India's nuclear tests have added another dimension to this undefined relationship. Hence, locating India in the context of US policy in Southern Asia is going to be a critical task. Another major challenge for the two countries is that of redefining current Indo-US relations to reconcile the divergent expectations of the two states from an enhanced bilateral relationship that seeks to keep the nuclear issue on the backburner.

After the Bush administration took over Capitol Hill, it not just consolidated the pillars of the foundation of bilateral relations laid by Bill Clinton, but its emphasis on *realpolitik* led to some ideological repositioning by India on contentious issues (like missile defence), which consequently endeared India to the US. This indicated to the US administration that India was unwilling to carry past baggage even when the Russians were strong opponents of the US position.

At this time, some studies urged an accommodating attitude towards Indian proliferation, while some others felt that the US–India relationship should be at the core of America's Southern Asian policy. Still others called for a more balanced approach to India and Pakistan. Perhaps the most significant aspect of these studies was what they did not advocate: none felt that the United States should play a major role in settling the Kashmir problem or providing economic or military assistance in the region.[267] For India, specifically, the Council on Foreign Relations report suggested, 'The medium-term policy challenge is to complete the transition from past estrangement through constructive engagement on to genuine partnership.'[268]

The events of 11 September 2001 led to a change in US policy towards Southern Asia. There were concerns in India about the US turning a blind eye to India's offer of assistance in its war on terrorism, post 9/11. The US chose Pakistan over India as an active

---

[266] A case in point being the Indian Parliament passing a resolution against the US-led war on Iraq.

[267] Cohen 2001. Prominent among the reports are: Carnegie Task Force 1988; The Asia Society 1994, 1995; and Independent Task Force 1997, 1998, 2003.

[268] See Independent Task Force 2003: 1.

ally in its campaign in Afghanistan, and this raised concerns in India that the US tilt towards Pakistan might end up against Indian interests in Kashmir. Additionally, the US–Pakistan defence co-operation would affect India. But there were many non-visible benefits to India of the US–Pakistan relationship. The US coopted Pakistan into the war against terrorism, and as such Pakistan had to disassociate itself from the Taliban and Al Qaida. Pakistan had to be coopted mainly because of geo-political reasons. As the Taliban fled, India was moving into Afghanistan while Pakistan was groping for answers on its Afghan policy. Musharraf removed or transferred seven of the 11 senior army commanders who opposed his cooperation with the US.[269] The established US position on the ground, 'the LoC to be respected', remained unchanged. Ever since, India has been able to highlight each and every terrorist attack, raise the pitch of the rhetoric and highlight Pakistan as a perpetrator of terrorism in Jammu and Kashmir.

Although India remains reluctant to negotiate a nuclear arms control agreement, the Government of India has begun cooperating with the United States in a wide range of activities from information technology to energy security, and from regional stability to UN peacekeeping. The tenure of former US Ambassador Robert Blackwill witnessed what he himself termed, 'transforming Indo-US Relations'. This has included, in the broadest terms, a never-before witnessed Indo-US convergence of interests across a range of issues, along with the hitherto untouched military technologies. The groundwork for a closer Indo-US security relationship was laid during Mr Vajpayee's visit to Washington in November 2001.[270] This opened the doors for increased Indo-US defence cooperation.[271] But the central issues of Indo-US strategic relations continue to remain Kashmir, non-proliferation and terrorism. Of late, however,

---

[269] Of them, Generals Aziz and Mehmood Ahmed (the ISI chief) played a very active role in fomenting terrorism in Jammu and Kashmir.

[270] Eight areas were identified as being central: Afghanistan, counter-terrorism, defence, identifying a new strategic framework, civilian nuclear systems, aerospace, intelligence and economic cooperation (Thapar 2001; Mohan 2001a).

[271] It includes expediting India's request for specific weapon systems and defence procurement priorities that include multi-mission maritime patrol aircraft, radars and components for jet trainers and high performance jet engines and joint training and exercises. (Blackwill 2002a; *The Hindu* 2002b).

a large number of variables have started playing a greater role in broadening the ambit of the bilateral relations.[272] The report of the Independent Core Group on India–US Relations has concluded, 'India–US relations need not be characterized by permanent friendship nor constrained within a strategic alliance or partnership.'[273]

Emergent bilateral relations between India and the US are a far cry from the time when the nuclear issue and sanctions had dominated their relationship soon after the nuclear tests. This also reflects a sense of accommodation.

Additionally, India can use multilateral organisations to explain its viewpoint and concerns—this was done in ASEAN and ARF, apart from the Commonwealth and NAM.[274] Globally, there seems to be a greater recognition of India's behaviour as a responsible nuclear weapons state, especially after the post-Kargil phase and the attack on the Parliament. India has also exhibited a greater sense of assertiveness in tackling some issues where traditional foreign policy principles have caught up with the present pragmatism.

✹ CTBT, NPT AND FMCT

CTBT

India was one of the original sponsors of the CTBT, but in 1996 when the treaty seemed imminent, India refused to sign. The then Indian Permanent Representative to the Conference on Disarmament, Amb. Arundhati Ghose, said India would not sign, 'not now

---

[272] These include economic interaction, armed humanitarian intervention, Islamic fundamentalism, narcotics control, energy security and the role played by the vast Indian diaspora.

[273] It further says, 'They need not have permanent interests either, but rather configure their bilateral relationship around a temporary identity of interests as, for instance, the war against terrorism. The word "strategic" is greatly overused anyway to convey a sense of long-term engagement with a hint of permanence; this is wholly redundant and misleading. India and the United States could, at different times, have converging interests; these could be advanced, but without constituting the inhibitions and entanglement of an alliance or partnership' (Independent Core Group 2003: 69).

[274] Ibid.

nor later.'[275] The CTBT preamble does not contain any commitment to disarmament and sub-critical testing is not banned. The treaty was to come into force in September 1999. According to the drafting of the treaty, 44 members have to sign and ratify it and only then can the treaty come into force. Among them are India and Pakistan. If India does not become a member of the CTBT, a Conference of the States that have signed and ratified the treaty would explore ways and means of getting the non-signatories on board.[276] There still remain many imponderables. Acceptance of the CTBT is conditioned on so many factors that its finalisation does not seem likely in the near future. In any case, with the US Senate, yielding to forces of unilateralism, has rejected the CTBT.[277] The American dumping of the treaty delivers a body blow to the credibility of multilateral negotiations in the age of American pre-eminence over world affairs. With this, the chances of sub-continental approval of the CTBT have been further reduced. India adheres to the treaty in spirit as it has announced a unilateral ban on nuclear testing.

The decision to sign the CTBT at any future time should be evaluated from the security perspective. It is imperative to ask whether more tests would be required to deploy India's credible minimum nuclear deterrent. Central to this is the question of what would constitute a credible minimum deterrent and what kind of nuclear

---

[275] The reasons for the Indian rejection were: (a) that the nuclear weapons states had failed to provide a commitment to eliminate their nuclear weapons within a specified time-frame: India felt that in the absence of such a commitment the treaty would be unequal, as it would ignore the security of some countries while providing for the security of other countries; (b) the CTBT would not contribute to non-proliferation: it bans explosive testing, but states can improve the existing designs by sub-critical testing, which does not lead to disarmament; (c) the entry into force clause, Article XIV, made Indian ratification of the treaty compulsory for its coming into force. This would be contrary to international law and would be unacceptable to India. See Ghose 1996.

[276] India also refused to participate in the discussions on the CTBT in Vienna.

[277] The Republican-controlled US Senate emphatically rejected the Comprehensive Test Ban Treaty, resisting a bipartisan effort to delay the vote, and delivered a crushing blow to President Clinton's major foreign policy goals. The margin of the vote—51 to 48—along party lines may appear narrow, but it fell far short of the two-thirds majority required to ratify a treaty that has evoked controversy both within the US and internationally. This was the first time since 1920 that a major international security pact had been rejected by the senate (Chandran 1999).

weapons state India would want to be. This remains linked to India's aspirations and to the larger issue of Indian grand strategy. Would the Indian arsenal comprise unsophisticated first-generation fission devices that are mounted on aircraft or short-range missiles, which would probably be sufficient to establish a credible minimum nuclear deterrent against Pakistan? If the nuclear arsenal has to be further refined, as Bharat Karnad argues, it has to be based on thermonuclear weapons.[278] Optimally, India's nuclear force should be equipped with thermonuclear warheads as they require lesser fissile stock. In that case, can one thermonuclear test be considered sufficient for India to have gained its optimal and credible capacity? Although Indian scientists have declared that the tests have given the required results and that no further tests would be required, many analysts still believe that signing the CTBT will forever bind India to its present technological levels.[279]

India is already a signatory to the Biological and Toxin Weapons Convention and has cooperated in its negotiations. Following the US rejection of Draft Verification Protocol in the *ad hoc* Group on Biological Weapons, India is playing a leading role in taking the issue forward.

FMCT

Although the content and structure of the proposed FMCT are yet to take shape, its 'scope' seems clear. The treaty seeks to establish a non-discriminatory, multilateral and verifiable regime banning production of fissile material for military purposes. India did demand a link between the fissile material cut-off negotiations and talks on nuclear disarmament, which was turned down. Atal Behari Vajpayee reiterated India's position on engaging in negotiations on FMCT, undertaking stringent export controls on nuclear- and missile-related technologies, apart from those relating to other weapons of mass destruction.[280] The broad contours of India's position on export controls can be gauged from the then PM's

---

[278] See Karnad 2002.
[279] Menon 2000b. Also see in this context, Rasgotra 2000; Raghvan 2000; Srinivasan 2000; and Jha 2000.
[280] Kunadi 1998.

address to the UN General Assembly [281] and his statement to the Parliament.[282]

NPT

India has, since the 1970s, sought to occupy a high moral ground concerning 'horizontal proliferation' and 'vertical proliferation' as also is the case with time-bound disarmament. This has also governed the Indian response to the NPT. An instance can be cited: according to the NPT, in return for the non-nuclear weapons states promising not to acquire nuclear weapons, the five nuclear weapons states promised in Article VI of the NPT to pursue good faith negotiations for cessation of the nuclear arms race at an early date and for nuclear disarmament. The Indian position on the NPT has been that any regime seeking to control the spread of nuclear technologies has to apply evenly to all countries. 'Horizontal' proliferation could not be given precedence over 'vertical' proliferation. India also raised the point of equality for sovereign states under international law. Nuclear weapons states were making a law that was applicable to non-nuclear weapons states and would divide the world into 'nuclear haves' and 'nuclear have nots'. '[T]he redefinition of the problem of proliferation and the elevation of national sovereignty to foundational status—allowed the Indian

---

[281] Addressing the United Nations General Assembly, the Indian Prime Minister noted: 'We have an effective system of export controls and shall make it more stringent where necessary, including by expanding control lists of equipment and technology to make them more contemporary and effective in the context of a nuclear India' (Vajpayee 1998b).

[282] 'As the House would recollect, these proposals comprise: a voluntary moratorium on underground nuclear test explosions; our willingness to move towards a *de jure* formalisation of this commitment, a decision to join negotiations on a treaty for a ban on future production of fissile material for weapons purposes; and, our determination to make more stringent the existing system of export controls over sensitive materials and technology .... We have expressed our willingness to join the FMCT negotiations in the Conference on Disarmament at Geneva. It is our understanding, as that of many other countries, who have confirmed this to us, that the objective of these negotiations is to arrive at a non-discriminatory treaty, that will end the future production of fissile material for weapons purposes, in accordance with the 1993 consensus resolution of the UN General Assembly' (Vajpayee 1998c).

state to stake out a diplomatically singular and occasionally moral high ground in the UN Conference of Disarmament ....'[283]

When the NPT was extended indefinitely in 1995, the nuclear weapons states promised the 'determined pursuit ... of systematic and progressive efforts' to achieve nuclear disarmament. For most states in the world, also reflected in their voting patterns on issues like nuclear disarmament in the UN, the efforts of the nuclear weapons states in this regard have been far from satisfactory. The NPT cannot recognise India as a nuclear weapons state.[284] While India considers this as objectionable, it is waiting for the international system to find some way of accommodating its new status as a nuclear weapons state. It is for the international system to find ways and means of accommodating India into the system. For now, the NPT seems to be a victim of its own success. India has remained outside the NPT and in the future too it may continue to do so.

So, under the circumstances, the best chance of salvaging the non-proliferation regime is to accommodate India and Pakistan in the NPT. There is no provision in the present treaty to accommodate a new nuclear weapons state, but given the threat to the regime, this seems to be the viable alternative. Such inclusion, it has been argued,

> will require all three new nuclear powers to shoulder the responsibilities of the non-proliferation regime, and it would help get over the current anomaly of three of the world's nuclear powers, living in very dangerous, and possibly unstable neighbourhoods, being outside the responsibilities and oversight of the regime.[285]

This is something that statesmen, policy researchers and academics will have to grapple with.

To rectify these definitional problems as well as to maintain the regime, three suggestions can be made: First, the NPT should be amended to include the new entrants. Provision for amendment

---

[283] Abraham 1998: 303.

[284] Article IX (3) of the NPT states, 'For the purposes of this Treaty, a nuclear-weapon State is one which has manufactured and exploded a nuclear weapon or other nuclear explosive device prior to January 1, 1967' (NPT 1968).

[285] See Rajagopalan and Rajain 2004.

to the NPT is available under Article VIII.[286] An amendment process to the NPT is likely to meet with resistance from nuclear weapons states arguing that this would seem to be rewarding the states that have threatened the regime. But in the long term the benefit would be to the regime itself wherein all the declared nuclear weapons states would be under obligation not to transfer nuclear weapons or nuclear explosive devices to other states, and not to assist in the manufacture or acquisition of such weapons and devices.[287] Second, a new nuclear weapons convention should be negotiated which would then include the new entrants to the nuclear club.[288] The third suggestion is that just as France participates in the NATO meetings 'as if' it is a member of NATO, India and Pakistan too can participate in the NPT 'as if' they are the members of the NPT.[289]

❧

India is undergoing considerable internal changes. There is, as Stephen Cohen puts it, a process of 'social churning' in which 'middle and low castes and social groups compete for power against each other and against formerly dominant high castes.'[290] The other serious issue confronting the ideological mooring of the country is a major debate over state and national identity.[291] Many questions confront the policy analyst: will India be able to sustain the high

---

[286] The article states that if one-third or more of the parties submit a proposed amendment to the depository governments, which include all the parties, then a conference of all states would consider such an amendment. The article further mentions that the amendment must be approved by the majority, including nuclear weapons states and all other states which are members of the Board of Governors of the International Atomic Energy Agency. For details, see NPT 1968: Art. VIII (1 and 2).

[287] Ibid.: Art. I.

[288] A model nuclear weapons convention that has been prepared by experts and can be used for this purpose. It is available at http://www.pgs.ca./pages/a2/ialannwc.htm, accessed on 16 April 1999.

[289] I would like to thank Mr P.R. Chari for this point.

[290] Cohen 1997. See in the context of these social transformations, Naipaul 1992.

[291] Aptly summarising this debate, Stephen Cohen says that at one end of this debate are Nehruvians (those who argue that India can achieve greatness, political stability and moral grandeur only through continuation of a predominantly secular

economic rate of growth, which will be crucial in determining the size of its arsenal? Can India aim to achieve international status without internal peace? How will nuclear weapons help India stake the claim at the 'high table'? As Vice Admiral Koithara concludes, 'only an India that is less attentive to its image and more awake to its reality can make Indians, and thereby India, secure.'[292] Nuclearisation, it seems, is one part of India's grand strategy of projecting itself as a great power in the years to come.

On the issue of nuclear weapons, India remains committed to complete elimination within a specified time-frame as in the long term this serves India's national interest.[293] India's policy towards nuclear non-proliferation and nuclear weapons can be discerned from these schools of thought:

1. The 'immoral' argument that derives from Gandhian and Nehruvian thought and explains India's persistent demand for global nuclear disarmament.
2. The 'prestige' argument, which stresses the prestige more than the security value of the bomb.[294]
3. The 'security' argument which argues for possessing nuclear weapons for their deterrence value. This school of thought developed mainly during the 1970s and 1980s.

India's nuclear policy has oscillated between these three positions, often sending confused signals to its neighbours in particular and the world in general. Even when India conducted its 'PNE' in 1974, the nuclear weapons policy was never articulated and there was a clear lack of any nuclear strategic doctrine.[295] But over the last couple of years, a significant and distinguishing feature of India's declared nuclear position has emerged: that nuclear weapons are political instruments rather than instruments of war fighting. However, to put the operational component at par with the declaratory policy, a slow process of weaponisation and deployment continues. Over the last couple of years, there seems to have been a level of clarity

state), while at the other end are the Hindu revitalists who demand conformity with Hindu norms from India's non-Hindu population. (Cohen 1997).

[292] Koithara 1999: 407.
[293] Kunadi 1998.
[294] Dixit 1996.
[295] Karp 1998.

and consistency in this position as India continues to affirm an NFU and a unilateral moratorium, and maintains a strong export control regime.

The NFU reflects the traditional Indian position of operational readiness where the dispersed components are not conducive to rapid deployment and first strike. There are good reasons to believe that India will follow its commitment to NFU, especially as it is consistent with the operational component. Another striking feature of the doctrine that is reflected at the operational level is that of 'punitive retaliation', with greater emphasis on certainty of retaliation than on speed of retaliation. This process is slowed down because of the structure of the Nuclear Command Authority where the Political Council will take time and communicate to the Executive Council the need for retaliation. Once again, from a distance this may seem to be assuring, as it does re-emphasise complete civilian control over nuclear assets and eliminates any room for miscalculation or unauthorised launch.

In the true traditions of a democracy, there is a healthy debate on the pros and cons of nuclear weapons and issues related to them in India. While tests cannot be undone, India will have to tread carefully, evaluating what suits its national interests better. In a dynamic security environment, India will have to address issues of refining the weapons, and the march of technology will certainly dictate, to a great extent, the direction of the Indian nuclear weapons programme. The Indian NFU policy and retaliation strategy do require a delicate balancing among the imperatives of ensuring the survivability of retaliatory forces by camouflage, deception, mobility and redundancy of second strike forces, and transparency, to ensure that the adversary will never use his own forces to conduct a pre-emptive strike. Much of India's decisions will be borne out of China's response to an increasing US presence in the region coupled with the BMD.[296] This will only increase the dilemma of the size of the nuclear arsenal. This would eventually have bearing on the size of Pakistan's arsenal. The mantra of 'credible minimum deterrent' is likely to affect not just India's strategic calculations, but also those of China and Pakistan. If India tries to build an arsenal that meets the minimum requirements of having a stable deterrence against China, it runs the risk of being maximum against Pakistan.

---

[296] See Rajain 2001c.

This could lead to an arms race in the subcontinent. Kargil proved that India could act as a responsible nuclear weapons state. That opportunity should not be frittered away. India should use the present engagement wave to its favour.

It is also possible that on the foreign policy front, India will continue to maintain some contours of the traditional idealism and make a pitch for global nuclear disarmament. As India spends more years as a nuclear weapons state, its nuclear doctrine will be more refined, and the process of gradual weaponisation will continue. Between the Sino-Indian and the Indo-Pak dyads, the Indo-Pak dyad continues to be more conflictual and destabilising to the region, primarily due to Pakistan's anti-status quo orientation. While Pakistan's fear of Indian capabilities and intentions may be misplaced even though understandable, all through the 1990s, India has consciously pursued a policy of looking beyond South Asia.[297] To this end, India does at times follow a policy of 'ignoring'Pakistan, the 16-month long no-talk period after the attack on the Parliament being a case in point. Such situation often makes Pakistan's security managers all the more resolute in their attempts to push their nuclear and missile programmes. In the given milieu, it is possible that competitive nuclearisation will continue at feverish pace. It can be predicted that an arms race—tit-for-tat missile tests—will be the feature of the Indo-Pak dyad. Similar assumptions cannot be made of the other dyad in the triangle, that is, the Sino-Indian one. This alone may not be the cause of breakdown of deterrence. Also, in any future crisis it is unlikely, given the force of US diplomacy in the region, that any state will seek to settle 'unfinished businesses' with the use of nuclear weapons. Mutual suspicion will continue, and unfortunately, so will the low-cost high-return Pakistani support to terrorism. Beijing's response to this weaponisation in slow motion is not going to be muted either. China will continue to closely monitor all moves made by India and if necessary take preventive measures.

---

[297] The Look East policy and a greater pro-active engagement with Europe and Central Asia are only a couple of examples.

CHAPTER 6

PAKISTAN

You may belong to any religion, caste or creed—that has nothing to do with the business of the state .... I shall always be guided by the principles of justice and fair play without any, as is put in the political language, prejudice or ill will, partiality or favouritism.

—Mohammad Ali Jinnah
Speeches of Quaid-i-Azam Mohammad Ali Jinnah as Governor General of Pakistan

At the time of the British withdrawal from South Asia in 1947, a movement largely orchestrated by the All-India Muslim League under Mohammed Ali Jinnah led to the emergence of Pakistan out of the predominantly Muslim north-western and eastern extremities of the subcontinent. The partition in 1947 can be seen to be the logical conclusion of the Muslim League's intransigent championing of a sovereign Muslim state. A separate Pakistan state was in the offing since the 1942 Cripps Mission. Mahatma Gandhi, in fact, went a step further and in his talks with Jinnah in 1944 accepted the right of self-determination.

Ever since its birth, Pakistan has been beset with internal contradictions and has been an insecure and unsure state. As Ralph Braibanti described it, no other new nation which gained independence after 1947 has experienced the variety or the intensity of traumas that Pakistan has suffered.[1] Ensuring the survival of the state has been a challenge for the policy makers. A narrow 'survivalist model of national security has dominated the political discourse of the country. India was, and continues to be, a major external cause for Pakistan's insecurity, but its demonisation at the elite and popular level was also an instrument through which

[1] Braibanti 1977.

domestic consolidation could be engineered to an extent.[2] The political elite has often explained the 'India threat' to the largely illiterate population. It is this narrow militaristic framework of national security that continues to be the central pillar in Pakistan's strategic calculations. Few other states have experienced, as the political scientist Norman D. Palmer put it, 'crises of identity; of legitimacy; of integration; of participation; of penetration; and of distribution'[3] to the degree Pakistan has. The larger dimensions of security, the precarious economic condition, the growing culture of drugs, small arms proliferation, the breakdown of law and order in Sind and Karachi, besides the challenges to governance necessitated by the tardy development of political institutions do not figure in mainstream national security discourse.

Some of this can be attributed to the contradictions that Pakistan inherited at the time of the partition:

It is forgotten that Nehru, Patel and Gandhiji in 1947 were only accepting what had become inevitable because of the long term failure of the Congress to draw in the Muslim masses into the national movement and stem the surging waves of Muslim communalism, which, especially since 1937, had been beating with increasing fury.[4]

Pakistan did not have a clear roadmap for a new state ready to play a role in the comity of nations. The biggest contradiction was the geographical challenge of administering East and West Pakistan, separated by nearly 2,000 km of Indian territory. The demand for a corridor through India was turned down. Political and social integration in Pakistan has also proved to be a difficult and expensive process. As analyst Rounaq Jahan said, 'only a small elite can afford to have inter wing contact which means that the national elite tends to be narrowly oligarchic.'[5] Another contradiction was the raison d'être of Pakistan. The country was created to be a separate homeland for Muslims, but Jinnah envisioned it as a modern liberal democratic state. Jinnah was educated in Britain and was personally not deeply religious. Speaking to Pakistan's Constituent Assembly, he said, 'You may belong to any religion, caste

---

[2] Mattoo 1999c.
[3] See Palmer 1982.
[4] Chandra et al. 1989: 500.
[5] Jahan 1973: 10.

or creed—that has nothing to do with the business of the state ....'[6]
These views of the founder of the state were soon overtaken by
the Objectives Resolution passed by the Constituent Assembly in
March 1949. As Binder says, 'The fact that the Jama'at-i-Islami
accepted the Objectives Resolution as the expression of intent of
the government to make Pakistan an Islamic state testified the fact
that it had departed from the vision of its founder, M.A. Jinnah.'[7]
Each of the four constitutions since then has contained Islamic
provisions, though there have always been powerful voices both
within Islamic circles and among liberals on the interpretation of
the Islamic content of the constitution. The early constitutional debates had been conducted in the background of the battle between
Islamic fundamentalists and liberals. The first group were led by
the *Ulema* who had been demanding an Islamic state based on
Shariah and the second were those who wanted a parliamentary
form of government on the western model.[8] Clearly, Pakistan had
a problem of identity right from the beginning. History created a
deep sense of victimisation that led to a sense of insecurity. This
sense of insecurity soon made India the bigger neighbour that could
some day attack Pakistan, and this provided the justification for
the acquisition of nuclear weapons. Finally, Pakistan was not clear
about what role it would play in the new changing international
system where more and more African and Asian nations were free-
ing themselves from colonial governments. This mindset, which
left a deep imprint on the people, perhaps strengthened the role
armed forces would play in shaping the destiny of the country.

✠ STRATEGIC CULTURE: NATIONAL SECURITY DISCOURSE

On the face of it, decision making on national security issues in
Pakistan seems a much more complex task than in India, but
actually, there being lesser number of individuals in the decision-
making loop in Pakistan, and the army taking almost all decisions
regarding issues of national security, the task is made easier. This,

---

[6] Jinnah 1948: 10.
[7] Binder 1961: 195.
[8] Bahadur 1998: 16–17.

however, means that there is less filtration of decision-making processes. In times of crisis, this could make the crucial difference. The armed forces have dominated decision making on national security issues either directly or indirectly. The dominant actor in this has been the chief of army staff (COAS). Indeed, four of Pakistan's heads of state have been army chiefs. It was not that military intervention in national security decision making and governance was the result of an absence of institutions; rather it was the result of the strength of the military, bureaucracy and judiciary, and weakness of other representative bodies, political parties and lack of mass mobilisation. The intelligence wing, ISI, has rarely sought to compete with the COAS, and wherever it did appear to wield power, it may well have had the implicit consent of the army. This is often under debate in the political circles of the country. Whenever the country is under democratic governance, the leaders have tried, unsuccessfully, to reduce the leverage of the army and democratically elected leaders, and the process itself has often paid a heavy price for it. Regular consultations with the army on key security issues were the norm, but the recent turn of events proves that the army now informs political leaders of its plans.[9] The army is a powerful institution and any change in policies on India or Kashmir requires its endorsement. It is almost impossible to engineer a change of opinion or a compromise solution for any bilateral dispute without taking the army's support.[10]

After the partition from India in 1947, many leaders had hoped that the two countries would emerge as friendly neighbours. This was not to be: within days of Pakistan's creation it became clear that some popular and elite groups would project India as the great national security threat to Pakistan. The main argument put forward by these groups was that the Indian National Congress had never provided political space to Muslims during the freedom struggle and had not reconciled to the partition. Consequently,

---

[9] It is believed in India that Gen Pervez Musharraf did inform Nawaz Sharif about the Kargil operations. But while the army had thought their plan through tactically, it had not done so strategically and politically.

[10] The army did not take kindly to Nawaz Sharif's 4 July 1999 Washington Agreement, since the Kargil operations were being sold to the Pakistani population as a military victory bartered away by Sharif. A withdrawal, following the agreement, led to verbal conflicts between Nawaz Sharif and the army.

India would use fair or foul means to dismember Pakistan or unite it again with India. There were two factors that structured this feeling. First, the issue of Kashmir. The Pakistani logic was that since Kashmir is essentially Muslim populated, it should have been a part of Pakistan. Second, the partition riots and the 1948 Indo-Pak war left deep scars on the minds of thousands of people. An estimated 500,000 people were killed on both sides; history continued to be violently written with the subsequent 1965 and 1971 wars. Within Pakistan these are explained as wars that had been inflicted on Pakistan. In fact, the 1971 war left the deepest scar, as it led to the creation of Bangladesh from erstwhile East Pakistan.

India continues to be central to Pakistani security calculations. Weapons acquisitions through the Cold War years from the US are explained as necessary for security against a possible Indian attack. This narrow militaristic framework of security continues to operate in Pakistan. There have been phases when it was not so prominent, but it has always existed. Former Prime Minister, Nawaz Sharif, laid much emphasis on economic stability, and with the Gujral doctrine followed by Vajpayee's bus trip to Lahore, things seemed to be changing. But not for long. It was argued that the nuclear tests conducted by both countries would tone down their antagonism, and both countries would become responsible nuclear powers. Pakistan has tended to link its nuclear policies and posture with that of India. And the bomb is viewed as the great balancer against India's vast and superior conventional forces. The foregoing establishes the strong public opinion in favour of the bomb.

PAKISTAN'S NUCLEAR POLICIES AND POSTURE

Four sets of arguments are normally advanced by threshold states for exercising their nuclear option: political prestige, military security, economic gains and domestic compulsions. Pakistan's security calculations involve India's capabilities and intentions. India, being geographically large and having more than 15,000 km of frontiers and 6,000 km of coastline, has large conventional forces. But this comes across as belligerence to a small neighbour that is grappling with internal issues of identity and socio-economic and political development. India's intentions are explained to the people as unfriendly and anti Muslim. This mindset has existed since independence.[11]

Given this mindset it was natural for Pakistan to look for security to outside alliances and agreements. But, unlike the rationale for the Indian nuclear tests that were a combination of external threats with internal domestic compulsions, Pakistan's programme was, is and perhaps will always remain entirely Indo-centric. A close scrutiny of Pakistan's nuclear programme reveals that it has been reactive to India's capabilities. There has been a marginal contribution of other factors, such as prestige and domestic considerations. But primarily, Pakistan's nuclear programme has been to strengthen its forces to be used as a diplomatic bargaining chip and to reduce its dependence on military alliances. It is generally believed that the 1974 PNE by India made Pakistan rush into a nuclear weapons programme. But a close scrutiny reveals that Pakistan was thinking on these lines much before 1974. Clearly, Jinnah was the only national leader who could have initiated a domestic debate on nuclear issues, as he was educated in the West and knew how technology was playing a decisive role in conflicts. But he was far too preoccupied with trying to lay the foundation for a governmental infrastructure in a newly born Pakistan.

The nuclear programme of Pakistan began with the establishment of the High Tension and Nuclear Research Laboratory in 1954, the main objective of which remained providing research facilities to students.[12] Pakistan, for the first time in October 1954, announced its plan to establish an atomic research body, and in January 1955 appointed the Atomic Energy Committee under

---

[11] Consider this 'complaint against India' submitted to the UN Security Council on 15 January 1948 in response to India's complaint regarding Pakistan's stance on Kashmir—'(iii) that the security, freedom, well being, religion, culture and language of the Muslims in India are in serious danger; (iv) that Junagadh, Manavadar, and some other states of Kathiawar, which have lawfully acceded to Pakistan and form a part of Pakistani territory have been forcibly and unlawfully occupied by the armed forces of the Indian Union and extensive damage has been caused to the life and property of the Muslim inhabitants of these states by the armed forces, officials and non-Muslim nationals of the Indian Union ... (ix) that India now threatens Pakistan with direct military attack; (x) that the object of the various acts of aggression by India against Pakistan is the de-struction of the State of Pakistan' (Government of Pakistan 1948).

[12] Burki 1960: 116.

Dr Nazir Ahmad, which recommended the appointment of an atomic energy commission.[13] In 1956, the Pakistan Atomic Energy Commission (PAEC) was established.[14] The real thrust in Pakistan's nuclear programme came with Dr I.H. Usmani becoming the chairman of PAEC in 1960. Though many identify Zulfikar Ali Bhutto as the principal architect of Pakistan's nuclear programme,[15] it was Usmani who set the direction of Pakistan's nuclear programme.[16] In August 1955, the US and Pakistan signed an agreement for co-operation concerning civil uses of atomic energy.[17]

After the 1958 coup of Gen Ayub Khan, more interest grew in nuclear energy. The Pakistan Institute of Nuclear Science and Technology (PINSTECH) was established in the early 1960s at Nelore (near Islamabad) at a cost of 41.3 million Pakistani rupees,[18] and the US agreed to supply enriched uranium and plutonium for a research reactor at PINSTECH,[19] which became operational in December 1965.[20] The Karachi Nuclear Power Plant (KANUPP) was established in 1968 with assistance from Canada. The proposal

---

[13] Ahmad 1957.

[14] The main objectives of the commission were: (a) to develop peaceful uses of atomic energy; (b) to establish an atomic energy and nuclear research institute; (c) to install research and power reactors; (d) to negotiate with international atomic energy bodies; and (e) to select and train personnel (ibid.: 14).

[15] According to P.B. Sinha and R.R. Subramanian, 'Zulfikar Ali Bhutto's entry into Gen Ayub Khan's cabinet at the end of 1958 provided the essential impetus to the country's atomic energy programme which had been lacking so far' (see Sinha and Subramanian 1980).

[16] According to Ashok Kapur, 'there is no evidence of Z.A. Bhutto's commitment to develop the military use of nuclear energy in Pakistan during 1955–66. His interest in the nuclear subject and his profile as the advocate of nuclear Pakistan, blossomed after he left the government of President Ayub Khan in 1966. His claim that he was always interested in the nuclearisation of Pakistan's foreign and military policies cannot be independently verified' (Kapur 1987: 54).

[17] According to Article I of the agreement, the US and Pakistan decided to exchange information in the following fields: (a) design, construction and operation of research reactors and their use as research, development and engineering tools and in medical therapy; (b) health and safety problems related to the operation and use of research reactors; and (c) the use of radioactive isotopes in physical and biological research, medical therapy, agriculture and industry (R.K. Jain 1983: 110).

[18] Kaushik and Mehrotra 1980.

[19] Sinha and Subramanian 1980: 33.

[20] Ibid.: 33.

to purchase a nuclear reactor from Canada began in 1962 and an agreement was reached in 1965.[21] This reactor was formally inaugurated in November 1972 at a cost of 480 million Pakistani rupees.[22] The nuclear programme of Pakistan, which had a moderate commencement during the 1950s, was firmly established during the 1960s. However, the main focus was on peaceful uses of nuclear energy rather than for military purposes.

Dr Usmani wanted to explore these uses of nuclear energy. At the same time, there was a small yet influential lobby that favoured developing a nuclear capability which had the potential of acquiring an eventual nuclear weapon option.[23] This group had Z.A Bhutto in the fore, who for the first time in 1965, echoed stated that Pakistan would acquire nuclear weapons capability. 'If India developed an atomic bomb, we too will develop one *"even if we have to eat grass or leaves or to remain hungry"* because there is no conventional alternative to the atomic bomb' (emphasis added).[24] Put in perspective, this statement, which was endorsed by large sections of the society, particularly the press, was a guarded response to the Indian Prime Minister, Lal Bahadur Shastri's statement in the Lok Sabha in November 1964 that he favoured developing nuclear explosives for peaceful purposes. The Indian statement in turn was a response to the Chinese nuclear test of October 1964. In April 1965, Bhabha set up a small group for a project called the Subterranean Nuclear Explosion Project (SNEP). Bhutto was aware of these developments and in a book published in 1969 predicted that India would follow the Chinese test. Seen in this context, the statement 'even if we have to eat grass' reflects a response to an emotionally charged domestic debate ready to take on India's nuclear programme. One of the earliest systematic discussions on the nuclear question can be seen in Z.A. Bhutto's 1969 book, *The Myth of Independence*, where he starts by locating the nature of threats to Pakistan, followed by reasons behind such threats. It is as a remedy to these threats that the nuclear narrative is introduced.[25]

---

[21]Pande 1991.
[22] Kaushik and Mehrotra 1980: 69.
[23] Khalilzad 1985.
[24] Bhutto 1970: 21.
[25] See Bhutto 1969.

Pakistan rates the nuclear question higher than any other issue.[26] In a survey undertaken by the Joan B. Kroc Institute for International Peace Studies in 1996, 83 per cent of the respondents were for the nuclear weapons, as against 6 per cent for yielding to IMF/World Bank pressure for economic restructuring.[27] In response to the question of whether Pakistan could renounce nuclear weapons under any circumstances, 71 per cent of the respondents said it may be possible only after a final settlement of the Kashmir dispute.[28] This indicates how the two issues of nuclear weapons and a solution to the Kashmir dispute are linked to each other. Another 100 per cent respondents linked Pakistan's development of nuclear weapons to direct threats from India,[29] 96 per cent of the respondents said Pakistan should build an arsenal, capable of striking only India.[30] To a question of when Pakistan could use nuclear weapons, 98 per cent said, if India were about to attack Pakistan across the international border, while 77 per cent said, nuclear weapons should be used if India were to intervene militarily across Kashmir's line of control.[31]

Over the years, Jama'at-i-Islami has been at the forefront of the bomb crusaders in Pakistan. In 1994, Khurshid Ahmed, a leading ideologue of the Jama'at, claimed that 'even a single person on the streets of Pakistan would not say that we should abdicate our nuclear option.'[32] Haider Nizamani thinks that Khurshid Ahmed's views manifest tensions that can be 'expected in a narrative that invokes such diverse strands as pan-Islamism, territoriality, denial of domestic heterogeneity, and principles of modern realist theory of international relations to validate a particular version of discourse about Pakistan's security needs.'[33] Some of this reflected in writings on nuclear issues in the mid-1990s.[34]

---

[26] See two surveys in this context: Ahmed and Cortright 1996 and Nizamani 2000. The former has been used here.

[27] See Ahmed and Cortright 1996: Table 2.

[28] Ibid.: Table 7.

[29] Ibid.: Table 9.

[30] Ibid.: Table 13.

[31] Ibid.: Table 14.

[32] Ahmed 1995: 148. Khurshid Ahmed has been the director of the think tank of the Jama'at—the Institute of Policy Studies.

[33] Nizamani 2001: 107.

[34] See for instance, Khan 1995; Sattar 1995. The ICWA is a Islamabad-based think tank founded by former Foreign Minister Agha Shahi.

Soon after assuming power in December 1971, after a war that saw East Pakistan being relegated to history and the emergence of Bangladesh, Bhutto convened a meeting of Pakistani scientists and asked them to deliver the Islamic bomb.[35] Prime Minister Bhutto voiced Pakistani concerns about India's PNE in the National Assembly: 'The explosion has introduced a qualitative change in the situation between the two countries.'[36] The Indian PNE firmly brought the nuclear issue into dominant political discourse in Pakistan. There were expected protestant voices in Pakistan from the opposition, the government, intellectuals and the media. Mehrunisa Ali made an evaluation of the various options available to Pakistan,[37] while Hamid Rajput, another analyst, repeated Bhutto's statement: 'India has tested her device, it is bound to have a chain reaction, especially among her neighbours.'[38] Pakistan did not take India's word on the PNE and instead sought assurances and agreements to secure itself. 'In 1976 Pakistan signed an agreement with SGN of France to acquire a plutonium reprocessing plant to be installed at Chashma near Dera Ghazi Khan under trilateral international safeguards.'[39] In the first stage, the PINSTECH reactor building and ancillary facilities were completed and the reactor became operational on 21 December 1965. In the second stage in 1974, laboratories, workshops, a library and auditorium were opened.[40]

With the necessary infrastructure now in place, the quest to acquire nuclear weapons capability gained momentum. 'Pakistan managed to acquire a uranium hexafluoride plant from West Germany between 1977 to 1980 .... Pakistan also succeeded in operating a gas centrifuge uranium enrichment plant at Kahuta through a wide network of secret acquisitions.'[41] 'Kahuta facility is the hub of Pakistan's nuclear weapons program .... The facility may also be the site where highly enriched uranium (HEU) is formed into weapon cores.'[42] The Kahuta plant was set up with covert contributions

---

[35] Weisman and Krosney 1981.
[36] Cited in Nizamani 2001.
[37] Ali 1974.
[38] Rajput 1974.
[39] Cheema 1996: 106.
[40] PAEC 1974: 13.
[41] Cheema 1996: 106.
[42] Koch and Topping 2000.

from Britain and Canada (electrical inverters), West Germany (aluminium rods and vacuum pumps), Italy (stainless steel vessels) and Switzerland (evaporation and condensation systems).[43] David Albright estimated that Pakistan had the capacity to produce 50 kg of weapons-grade uranium per year (see Box 6.1).[44]

Box ✱ 6.1

Kahuta

Kahuta is the site of the Khan Research Laboratories (KRL), Pakistan's main nuclear weapons laboratory as well as an emerging centre for long-range missile development. The primary Pakistani fissile-material production facility is located at Kahuta, employing gas centrifuge enrichment technology to produce Highly Enriched Uranium (HEU). Dr A.Q. Khan is a German-educated metallurgist, who until 1975 was employed at the Urenco uranium enrich-ment facility in Almelo, the Netherlands.

Operating at full capacity, Kahuta has the potential to produce enough weapons-grade uranium for three to six weapons each year. But the gas centrifuge plant has been plagued by chronic delays. In 1986, it was reported that there were approximately 1,000 centrifuges operating at the facility. By the late 1980s, Pakistan began advertising its nuclear potential by publishing technical articles on centrifuge design, including a 1987 article co-authored by A.Q. Khan on balancing sophisticated ultracentrifuge rotors.

In early 1996, it was reported that the A.Q. Khan Research Laboratory received 5,000 ring magnets, which can be used in gas centrifuges, from the China National Nuclear Corporation, a state-owned facility. The US intelligence community believed the magnets were for special suspension bearings at the top of the centrifuge rotating cylinders.

The Kahuta facility has also been a participant in Pakistan's missile development programme. Pakistan operates a ballistic missile research centre at Kahuta, along with its uranium enrichment operation. KRL has successfully developed and tested IRBMs based on liquid fuel technology, and its associated sub-systems.

KRL has also undertaken many other defence projects of national importance to enable Pakistan to become self-reliant in various

(Box 6.1 Contd)

---

[43] Cited in ibid.: 109.
[44] Albright 1987.

(Box 6.1 Contd)

sophisticated weapons systems and save valuable foreign exchange. These projects include:

- Surface-to-air anti-aircraft guided missiles—Anza Mk-I and Anza Mk-II
- 'Baktar Shikan' anti-tank guided missile weapon system
- Anti-personnel mine sweeping line charges
- Anti-tank mine clearing line charge—Plofadder-195 AT
- Laser range finder
- Laser threat sensor
- Laser actuated target
- Laser aiming device
- Add-on reactive armour kit
- Anti-tank ammunition armour piercing fin stabilised discarding sabot
- Remote control mine exploder
- Digital Goniometer
- Power conditioners for weapon systems for the TOW ATGM Weapon System
- 'Anza' Training Missile System
- Switched mode power supplies for LAADS radar, skyguard radar, air defence automation system
- TOW missile modules

Ever since 1980, Pakistan has been close to crossing the threshold from nuclear capability to nuclear weapons capability. A *Washington Post* article, citing classified US intelligence reports, claimed that Pakistan had indeed started producing weapons-grade uranium.[45] When Mrs Indira Gandhi returned to power in 1980 she reassembled the team that had carried out the PNE in 1974 (this had been disbanded by Morarji Desai in 1977) which led to further speeding up of the Pakistani nuclear weapons programme. In 1982, a *Washington Post* news report, quoting intelligence sources, mentioned Indian plans to launch a pre-emptive strike on Pakistani nuclear installations, including Kahuta.[46] A threat like this compelled Pakistan to accelerate its nuclear programme. In September 1986, China and Pakistan signed a nuclear

---

[45] Woodward 1986.
[46] Benjamin 1982.

cooperation agreement.[47] Then, in March 1987, came the interview of Dr A.Q. Khan with Kuldip Nayyar, where Dr Khan admitted that Pakistan possessed nuclear weapons.[48] Another acknowledgement of Pakistan's ability to produce nuclear bombs came from General Zia himself when he told the *Time* magazine, 'Pakistan has the capability of building the bomb.'[49] Although both India and Pakistan continued to proceed with their respective nuclear programmes, in Pakistani perception its own nuclear development in 1980s 'generated an element of restraint and therefore turned out to be a positive contribution to non proliferation and peace rather than being a dangerous development.'[50] A declassified report of the US Department of State dated 23 June 1983 says,

> there is unambiguous evidence that Pakistan is actively pursuing a nuclear weapons development program. Pakistan's near-term goal evidently is to explode a nuclear device if Zia decides its appropriate for diplomatic and domestic political gains .... The Government of Pakistan is pursuing both the reprocessing of uranium enrichment routes to obtain fissile material for their program. They are building a facility near PINSTECH capable of extracting small quantities of plutonium from KANUPP power reactor fuel. In addition they are continuing to seek assistance from supplier countries to complete the larger reprocessing facility located at Chasma .... To produce sufficient quantities of plutonium for a test device for weapons Zia probably would have to abrogate or violate Pakistan's nuclear safeguards with Canada and the International Atomic Energy Agency. Pakistan is attempting to produce highly enriched uranium, which could support a test on weapons program without involving any safeguards agreements.[51]

After Ms Benazir Bhutto came to power in 1988 following General Zia's death in a plane crash, there was some moderation in Pakistan's position on nuclear weapons. During her visit to the

---

[47] This agreement sought to place all material and equipment being transferred from China to Pakistan under IAEA safeguards. This was done after the US postponed the ratification of the Sino-US nuclear cooperation agreement in 1985, leaving China to legitimise its nuclear cooperation with Pakistan.

[48] Nayyar 1987.

[49] *Time* 1987: 42–44.

[50] Cheema 1996: 106.

[51] Department of State, US 1983.

US in 1989, she reiterated that Pakistan neither had, nor intended to develop, a nuclear device. It is widely believed that she might not have had complete knowledge of the activities of the Nuclear Weapons Programme Co-ordinating Committee (chaired by President Ghulam Ishaq Khan). 'In 1989 Pakistan was reported to have conducted wind tunnel tests of the casing of a nuclear bomb designed to fit under the wing of an F16.'[52] In 1989, the Bush administration certified that Pakistan did not possess a nuclear device but in 1990 President Bush refused to certify this to Congress as required under the Pressler Amendment. US military and economic aid to Pakistan was stopped in 1990–91. However, the nuclear programme continued undeterred. In 1983 a US State Department memorandum said that Pakistan stole the gas centrifuge designs from Urenco, a European gas centrifuge enrichment consortium. It further says that Engineering Research Laboratories had acquired and produced materials for both gas centrifuges and nuclear weapons.'[53] A.Q. Khan was identified as an important agent in the transfer. A 1986 memo prepared for Henry Kissinger and the Foreign Intelligence Advisory Board asserted that Pakistan could produce enough HEU for 'several nuclear devices per year.'[54] David Albright assesses that Kahuta could make enough HEU for three to six devices a year.

Pakistan's quest to acquire technology and equipment to run its nuclear programme continued. Instances of people trying to smuggle technology or equipment were reported continually (see Box 6.2).

Box ✕ 6.2

Pakistan's Quest to Acquire Nuclear Technology and Materials

- On 16 July 1984, three Pakistanis were indicted in a US court for trying to ship parts for nuclear weapons to Pakistan.
- On 31 July 1986, it was reported that the PM of Pakistan and the PM of France had decided to end the dispute over the 1976 contract to supply Pakistan with a reprocessing plant.
- On 14 July 1987, a Canadian citizen of Pakistani origin was arrested on charges of trying to export fissile material to Pakistan.

(Box 6.2 Contd)

---

[52] Ibid.
[53] Albright 1987: 30–31.
[54] Ibid.: 30–31.

(Box 6.2 Contd)

- On 17 July 1987, the US indicted two Americans and a Hong Kong businessman for illegally exporting to Pakistan sophisticated instruments and advanced computer equipment that could be used to make nuclear weapons.
- On 28 July 1987, a retired general from Pakistan was indicted in the US for a conspiracy to obtain nuclear-related material in the US.
- On 17 December 1987, a man was convicted in the US on charges of attempting to illegally export beryllium to Pakistan. Trans Nuclear (TRAN) of the FRG may have been involved in shipping weapons grade plutonium from Belgium to Libya and Pakistan.
- On 19 January 1988, the IAEA denied a report that Libya and Pakistan obtained weapons-grade plutonium from the nuclear plants in the FRG and Belgium.
- On 21 January 1988, reports claimed that materials suitable for nuclear bombs were smuggled out of Hanau plants in the FRG, Libya and Pakistan.
- On 21 March 1989, the FRG news magazine *Stern* reported that more than 70 FRG firms had helped Pakistan develop an atomic bomb and that FRG officials ignored intelligence reports about strategic exports related to the project.
- On 21 April 1989, two small FRG companies admitted to supplying nuclear weapons related materials to Pakistan.

Source: Subrahmanyam 1990b.

By the end of the 1990s, Pakistan was not only ready with the bomb, but had even sent out 'feelers' to the world in this regard. In 1990, the former Vice Chief of Staff, General Arif said in an interview to the BBC, 'Nuclear proliferation has already occurred in South Asia. The atomic weapons are there. You cannot deny their existence because you refuse to look at them.'[55] Another indication came from Shaharyar Khan, who in an interview to *The Washington Post*, stated that Pakistan had the capability to assemble at least one nuclear device.[56] This was soon followed by an official clarification given by the Minister of State for Foreign Affairs,

---

[55] Babar 1992.
[56] See Khan 1992.

Mohammad Siddique Kanju, who stated that Pakistan neither possessed a nuclear explosive device nor had any intention of making one.[57] This was perhaps done intentionally to maintain a certain ambiguity about the nuclear programme. By the early 1990s, Pakistan's diplomats began claiming nuclear capability. In February 1992, Foreign Secretary, Shaharyar Khan said in an interview in Washington that 'the capability (nuclear) is there'. He added that his country possessed 'elements which if put together would become a device.'[58] He confirmed that these included 'cores' fashioned from HEU. Soon after this, Abida Hussain, Pakistan's Ambassador to the US, addressing George Washington University, said that Pakistan 'borrowed and stole in the face of difficulty' to acquire nuclear weapons. 'Nuclear weapons are a symbol of power and we are not willing to deny ourselves a symbol of power ... I am proud to represent a Government which had decided to tell the truth ....'[59] In March 1987, General Zia told *Time* that

> you can use it (the atomic device) for military purposes also. We have never said we are incapable of this. We said we have neither the intention nor the desire .... You can virtually write today that Pakistan can build a (nuclear) bomb whenever it wishes. What is difficult about a bomb? Once you have acquired the technology, which Pakistan has, you can do whatever you like.[60]

In July 1988, he told a delegation from the Carnegie Endowment that 'the present nuclear programme of India and Pakistan has a lot of ambiguities and therefore in the eyes of each other they have reached a particular level, and that level is good enough to create an impression of deterrence.'[61] Next, in October 1989, the army chief Gen Mirza Aslam Beg stated that 'both the nuclear option and the missiles (that Pakistan is developing) act as deterrence; and these in turn contribute to the total fighting ability of the army, which acts a deterrent to the enemy.'[62]

---

[57] *The Muslim* 1992.
[58] Shaharyar Khan 1992. See also *The New York Times* 1992b.
[59] Cited in Kargil Review Committee 2000: 194.
[60] Doerner 1987: 42.
[61] Spector 1990: 100.
[62] Beg 1989.

There is evidence that suggests that Washington knew that Pakistan had acquired nuclear weapons capability. When the US was aiding Afghan *mujahideen*s against the Soviet Union through Pakistan, it was well aware of Pakistan's nuclear weapons programme, its intentions and the capability of Pakistan to produce nuclear weapons.[63] Not only was the US aware of Pakistan's aims and potential for nuclear weapons production, but was also well aware of China's cooperation with Pakistan on the issue.[64] A former US intelligence analyst, Richard Barlow, said, 'There was never any meaningful freeze on the Pakistani program from 1987 forward.'[65] As Richard Kerr, a CIA official, most authoritatively and credibly said: '[S]ince 1987 the United States had believed that Pakistan possessed either a nuclear explosive device or all the unassembled components to make one.'[66] A Pakistani source, Gen Mirza Aslam Beg, admitted that Pakistan had attained nuclear capability in 1987.[67]

1990 SPRING CRISIS : HOW REAL?

The 29 March 1993 issue of the *New Yorker* carried a sensational article by Seymour M. Hersh, titled 'On the Nuclear Edge.' Basing his article on US intelligence sources and interviews with CIA officials Robert Gates and Richard Kerr, Hersh claimed that in the spring of 1990, India and Pakistan came close to a nuclear exchange. Richard Kerr sounded the loudest alarm: 'There's no question in my mind that we were right on the edge ... the intelligence community believed that without some intervention the two parties could miscalculate and miscalculation could lead to a nuclear

---

[63] In one of its briefing papers, the US Department of State noted, 'there is unambiguous evidence that Pakistan is actively pursuing a nuclear weapons development program. Pakistan's near term goal evidently is to have a nuclear test capability, enabling it to explode a nuclear device' (Department of State, US 1983).

[64] The US Department of State paper also noted that 'China has provided assistance to Pakistan's program to develop a nuclear weapons capability. Over the past several years, China and Pakistan have maintained contacts in the nuclear field (ibid.).

[65] Quoted in Hersh 1993.

[66] Quoted in Reiss 1995: 188.

[67] Beg 1994.

exchange.'[68] The Hersh article raked up a controversy in the US, India and Pakistan, with scholars questioning Hersh's facts.

The situation was exacerbated by actions that were misinterpreted on both sides. In December 1989, separatists escalated their operations against the state of Jammu and Kashmir. Pakistan's Inter-Services Intelligence (ISI), taking advantage of the reservoir of discontent in the valley of Kashmir, redirected fundamentalist Islamic groups from Afghanistan to Kashmir. To curb cross-border terrorism, India stepped up border patrolling along the line of control. At the same time, military exercises were held in Rajasthan with greater visibility. This action sent a threat signal to Islamabad which was recovering from the after-effects of Operation Brasstacks (1986–87). This prompted Pakistan to respond by sending more armoury close to the international border. Thus, a cycle of action–reaction, domestic political posturing and a chain of miscommunication was launched, leading to misinter-pretation of events by both sides.

The situation in Kashmir started deteriorating. As the US appealed for calm, 'Indian officials discussed pre-emptive strikes against training camps in Pakistan.'[69] India and Pakistan both had weak leaders—V.P. Singh (India), Benazir Bhutto (Pakistan)—and Ambassador Oakley was concerned that the two prime ministers did not have the personal authority or control needed to rein in their respective military establishments.[70] It may have been possible that

---

[68] Quoted in Hersh 1993: 66. The following are the highlights of Hersh's case: (a) In the early spring of 1990 US intelligence showed that Pakistan had assembled nuclear bombs; (b) some US intelligence officials believed that the Kahuta plant had been evacuated. The general inference was that Pakistan was preparing for a retaliatory strike on India; (c) in May a convoy of trucks under heavy security left a storage depot in Baluchistan and drove to an air force base where F-16s were stationed. The inference was that the trucks were carrying nuclear weapons to the F-16s. The F-16s were ready to launch on command and were presumed to deliver nuclear weapons.

[69] Ambassadors Oakley and W. Clark had the following exchange during a February 1994 on-the-record round table meeting at the Henry L. Stimson Center. Oakley said, 'General Sharma was threatening to take out the training camps and saying that it was time to teach Pakistan a lesson, put these upstarts in their place once and for all.' Clark responded, 'A boot up their backside I think he called it' (Cited in Krepon and Faruqee 1997).

[70] Oakley is quoted by Hersh as saying, 'I began to scream that what's going to happen is Brasstacks all over again ... and this time they won't stop' (Hersh 1993: 64–65).

elements within the government were exerting pressure on the weak leadership for spectacular results.

In May 1990, Robert Gates with Richard Haass and John Kelly flew to South Asia to try and defuse the crisis. Gates tried to explain to the Pakistanis that continuous support to terrorism would compel Indians to target terrorist training camps in Pakistan-administered Kashmir. This would force Pakistan to respond, perhaps for domestic political reasons. Knowing that India had a conventional force advantage, Pakistan would then use nuclear weapons not as a last resort, but early on in the conflict. During the next few days, the foreign secretaries of the two states deflected the two sides away from a possible conflict.

Some Indian analysts have sought to belittle the crisis as both countries were restrained by the realisation that war would be economically unsustainable. The prevalent internal situation also effectively checked what some outsiders considered a quick drift towards war. Although Indians view the crisis with far less alarm, a study in Pakistan does corroborate the American story.[71] Pakistan firmly believes that it was deterrence that worked in the 1990 spring crisis.[72] In a recent study, it was noted that

> there seems to be a fundamental difference of opinion as to whether or not nuclear weapons were actually brandished during the crisis. The public statements by leaders on both sides were ambiguous,

---

[71] Consider this passage: '0600 hours, 27 July 1990, the F-16 of Pakistan Air Force took a dive to release the bomb under its belly, rose like a falcon and flew away at full speed. When the bomb exploded in the air, 500 meters above the ground, the aircraft was a small speck on the horizon, well beyond the shock waves that would have been created by the bomb, had its core not been replaced by a dummy. The aircraft had just completed the trial for 'nuclear aerial device' culminating 8 months [of] long exercise by PAFC and PAD to perfect the delivery of a nuclear weapon by aircraft' (Ur-Rehman 1999).

[72] The paper by Shahi et al. (1999) states that: 'The third crisis (Pakistan believes this was the third crisis, the others being in the mid-1980s when Punjab was in turmoil and the 1986–87 Brasstacks exercise) during which the spectre of a nuclear war arose was in April–May 1990. It was precipitated by reports that, unnerved by the mass uprising for freedom in occupied Kashmir, Indian GHQ had recommended air raids on training camps allegedly established in Azad Kashmir. Such aggressive action, American analysts concluded, would provoke a Pakistani response with a high probability of escalation to general war in which Pakistan, unable to defend its territory by conventional means, would be forced to use the

yet there remains the suspicion that a nuclear threshold of one sort or another was crossed, and while there is no hard evidence, the behaviour of some of the decision-makers (especially the Indian Prime Minister and the Foreign Minister) would indicate that they were persuaded (whether by Yaqub Khan, or by other actions or statements is unclear) that a war with Pakistan was quite likely, and that it might be a nuclear war.[73]

It was the first time that the two South Asian neighbours came close to a nuclear exchange. Since Pakistan believed it was deterrence that worked, it was imperative to examine the crisis in some detail. Having got the technology to make the bomb, it had to acquire a carry system to deliver the weapon. This has both doctrinal and operational implications. Pakistan considered the nuclear option as balancing Indian conventional superiority and this translated operationally into a hunt for a delivery system.

✠ PAKISTAN'S MISSILE DEVELOPMENT

Pakistan set up a Space and Upper Atmosphere Research Commission (SUPARCO) as early as 1961. By 1970, this commission had developed the capability to fabricate rocket motors from raw materials. It now has a solid fuel manufacturing plant and maintains an instrument development facility and rocket testing range. Pakistan began its surface-to-surface ballistic missile programme in the early 1980s with the development of the Hatf I and Hatf II. The Hatf I has an estimated range of 80 km with a 500 kg payload. The Hatf II has a 300 km range with payload of 500 g. Reports of possible M-9 or M-11 sales to Pakistan from China started appearing in 1987–88.[74] Following the contract for its sale to Pakistan in February 1991, China had begun delivering M-11 transporter-erector-launchers to Pakistan.[75] Even the US Defense Department

---

weapon of last resort. So grave was the concern that the United States President sent Robert Gates as his personal emissary to Pakistan and India on a successful mission of preventive diplomacy in April.'

[73] Chari et al. 2003: 135.
[74] Jacobs and McCarthy 1992.
[75] Ibid.

reported that China had delivered M-11 missiles to Pakistan, together with inert (dummy) warheads for missile handling and launch training.[76]

The Bush Sr Administration, sensing a threat to the Missile Technology Control Regime (MTCR), announced that it would impose missile-related economic sanctions on China in three areas: (a) US companies were not allowed to sell missile technology to the China Great Wall Industry Corporation (CGWIC) and the China Precision Machinery Import–Export Corporation (CPMIEC) because of their involvement in the M-11 sale.[77] In a testimony to the Congress, US Secretary of State James Baker said, 'We think sending M-11s to Pakistan would constitute grave threats to the region and could have bilateral consequences.'[78] In fact, the early 1990s saw the US making more efforts to save the MTCR than try to curb missile proliferation. The 1991 Beijing trip only resulted in getting a verbal commitment from the Chinese not to export M-9s to Syria and M-11s to Pakistan.[79] There were reports of Chinese assistance to Pakistan's missile programme again in early 1992 when China delivered the guidance units to Pakistan for the M-11 missiles.[80] Later that year, *The Los Angeles Times* reported that the Chinese shipped about 24 M-11 missiles to Pakistan. The newspaper evidence, based on US intelligence reports, claimed that the Chinese missiles were unloaded at the Karachi port. In India, it was accepted that the M-11 missiles were stored at Pakistan's Sargodha air force base. Clearing all doubts on the M-11 transfer, Gen Mirza Aslam Beg said,

As regards the M-11 missile system that Pakistan is acquiring from China, it is covered within the six nation agreement on Missile Technology Control to which China is a signatory. The missile has a range of less than 300 kilometres and is not capable of carrying a nuclear warhead.[81]

---

[76] Ibid.

[77] Kennedy Jr 1996.

[78] Center for Nonproliferation Studies 1999.

[79] China argued that the range of M-11 was less than 200 km and under the permissible limit of MTCR.

[80] *The New York Times* 1992a.

[81] Beg 1992.

Within a week, the Chinese Major General Yang Guo Ping led a five-member military delegation to Pakistan to discuss issues of mutual interest.[82] It is a different matter that on 2 December 1992 the USA lifted missile-related sanctions on China.

The then COAS, Gen Mirza Aslam Beg, announced on 5 February 1989 that Pakistan had successfully developed the Hatf-I and Hatf-II SSMs based on French sounding rocket technology, which had a range/payload of 90 km/500 kg and 300 km/500 kg, respectively. The Hatf-I and II remained unguided rockets for quite some time as suitable on-board guidance packages and the tests conducted on these repeatedly failed. By 1991, the Chinese had begun directly transferring M-11 SRBMs (300 km/800 kg) to Pakistan and 84 of these had been transferred by 1994. The 155 Composite Rocket Regiment of the Second Army Artillery Division, Attock, soon got them. There are also reports that some missiles are located at Samungli (Quetta).[83]

The MTCR continued to be the only international norm that governed such transfers and was still under negotiation.[84] China continued to claim that the MTCR did not cover the M-11 because it had a 280 km range and carried a 800 kg payload. The US argued that the payload could be reduced to give the missile a greater MTCR restricted range.[85] On 10 May 1995, the US Secretary of State, Warren Christopher and the Chinese Foreign Minister, Qian Qichen signed the Joint United States–People's Republic of China statement on Missile Proliferation in which China promised not to 'export ground-to-ground missiles featuring the primary parameters of the MTCR.'[86] However, the missiles and their components continued to be transferred, and by mid-1996, Pakistan had deployed them.[87]

The Chinese further assisted Pakistan in the construction of a factory to build MRBMs near Islamabad. The CPMIEC provided Pakistan with gyroscopes, assessor-meters, on-board computers

[82] Yang Guo Ping 1992.

[83] JIC 1993.

[84] The MTCR is not an international agreement and has no legal authority. It is a set of voluntary guidelines which seek to control the transfer of missiles that are inherently capable of carrying a 500 kg payload to at least 300 km.

[85] Wolfsthal 1993.

[86] Ibid.

[87] Gertz 1996.

and other missile-related equipment for the M-11 missile. The US believed that this factory had the capability to manufacture key missile components based on M-11 within two years.[88] The Department of Defense report of 1997 clearly stated that 'China remains Pakistan's principal supplier of missile related technology and assistance.'[89] In July 1997, Pakistan announced a test of the 800 km Hatf III. In addition, Pakistan relied heavily on Chinese assistance to modify the missiles to permit the use of conventional warheads and possibly even chemical warheads.[90] (See Map 6.1 for Pakistan's nuclear estate.)

In the Senate testimony on 11 June 1998, Dr Gordon Oehler said,

[I]n the early 1990s the Chinese began an effort to provide Pakistan with nuclear capable ballistic missile technologies and even complete missiles. In 1990, the intelligence community detected the transfer to Pakistan of a training M-11 ballistic missile and associated transporter-erector-launcher, indicating that operational missiles were not far behind ... with this information the US imposed category II sanctions against China and Pakistan in 1991 ... however in 1992, less than eight months later [and after the US had lifted the MTCR related sanctions] the Chinese delivered 34 M-11s to Pakistan ... this led to a second sanctions ... since late 1992 China has not transferred complete MTCR covered missiles to any country. Instead it has concentrated on transferring production technologies and components. Production technologies and components are also covered under the MTCR, but they are easier to hide, or can be claimed to be from non-MTCR-related systems.[91]

THE SILENT PARTNER: DPRK

On 6 April 1998, Pakistan successfully tested a new medium-range surface-to-surface Ghauri missile (with a range of 1,500 km). While the world in general and the US in particular focused attention on the Chinese nuclear and missile assistance to Pakistan, their remains an invisible partner in Pakistan's journey to developing missile capabilities—the Democratic People's Republic of Korea (DPRK).

---

[88] The US Department of Defense confirmed the construction of this facility. See Department of Defense, US 1997b.

[89] Ibid.

[90] Center for Nonproliferation Studies 1999.

[91] Ibid.

Map × 6.1
Pakistan's Nuclear Estate

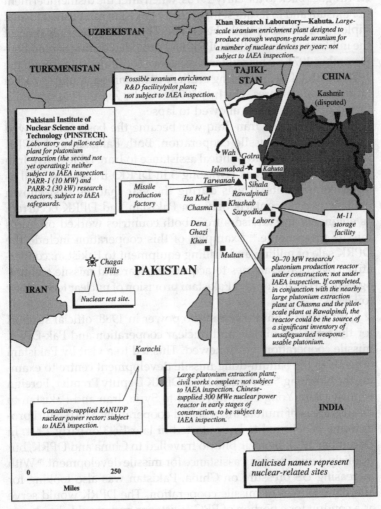

Khan Research Laboratory—Kahuta. *Large-scale uranium enrichment plant designed to produce enough weapons-grade uranium for a number of nuclear devices per year; not subject to IAEA inspection.*

Possible uranium enrichment R&D facility/pilot plant; not subject to IAEA inspection.

Pakistani Institute of Nuclear Science and Technology (PINSTECH). *Laboratory and pilot-scale plant for plutonium extraction (the second not yet operating): neither subject to IAEA inspection. PARR-1 (10 MW) and PARR-2 (30 kW) research reactors, subject to IAEA safeguards.*

Missile production factory

UZBEKISTAN

TURKMENISTAN

TAJIKI-STAN

CHINA

Kashmir (disputed)

Wah · Golra
Islamabad ★ · Kahuta
Tarwanah ▲ · Sihala
Rawalpindi
Isa Khel ■ · Khushab ▲
Chasma ■ · Sargodha
Lahore
Dera Ghazi Khan
Multan

M-11 storage facility

★ Chagai Hills

PAKISTAN

Nuclear test site.

IRAN

50–70 MW research/ plutonium production reactor under construction; not under IAEA inspection. If completed, in conjunction with the nearby large plutonium extraction plant at Chasma and the pilot-scale plant at Rawalpindi, the reactor could be the source of a significant inventory of unsafeguarded weapons-usable plutonium.

Karachi

Large plutonium extraction plant; civil works complete; not subject to IAEA inspection. Chinese-supplied 300 MWe nuclear power reactor in early stages of construction, to be subject to IAEA inspection.

INDIA

Canadian-supplied KANUPP nuclear power rector; subject to IAEA inspection.

0 ———— 250
Miles

Italicised names represent nuclear-related sites

Source: Spector et al. 1995.

The military and political relationship between Pakistan and DPRK goes back to the early 1970s, when after the dismemberment of Pakistan and in its quest for security Pakistan established formal diplomatic relations with the DPRK. This was in reciprocation of the military assistance that DPRK had provided during September–December 1971.[92] This military assistance continued all through the 1970s, with DPRK providing artillery ammunition, multiple rocket launchers and spares. The July 1977 coup by Zia-ul-Haq saw military cooperation being allowed to lapse.

In the 1980s, the Iran–Iraq war became the basis for renewed Pakistan–DPRK missile cooperation. Both Pakistan and DPRK provided military and political assistance to Iran. DPRK gave Iran 160 Scud Bs (known as Hwasong 5 in DPRK) missiles as well as other components. It was during the war that the first-known ballistic missile contacts between Pakistan and DPRK occurred, as engineers and advisors from both countries worked on Iran's missile programme.[93] Examples of this cooperation include the DPRK sale of milling and drilling equipment to Pakistan; cooperative covert programmes to acquire nuclear and missile technologies from Germany; and Pakistani provision of nuclear technology to DPRK.[94]

With Benazir Bhutto coming to power in 1988, official support for the Sino-Pak missile and nuclear cooperation and Pak-DPRK missile cooperation was renewed. This led to a visit by Pakistani officials to the Sanum-dong missile development centre to examine the No-dong.[95] In August 1992, DPRK Deputy Premier, Foreign Minister Kim Yong-Nam travelled to Syria, Iran and Pakistan to discuss areas of mutual interest and cooperation. The Ghauri programme is believed to have started in late 1993 or early 1994. In December 1994, Benazir Bhutto travelled to China and DPRK, but publicly denied seeking assistance for missile development.[96] With increasing US pressure on China, Pakistan was also looking for alternate sources of missile cooperation. The DPRK would serve as a conduit for a portion of PRC assistance and provide hardware

---

[92] Welles 1971.

[93] Bermudez Jr 1998.

[94] Milholin 1990.

[95] Bermudez Jr 1998.

[96] See Rajain 2002g.

and components from its No-dong and Taep-o-dong programmes.[97] In April 1994, a delegation of the DPRK Foreign Ministry travelled to Iran and Pakistan.[98] In November 1995, a DPRK military delegation led by Choe Kwang, Vice Chairman of the National Defence Commission, Minister of the People's Armed Forces travelled to Pakistan. This delegation had meetings with Pakistan's President, Sardar Leghari, Defence Minister, Aftab Shaban Mirani, chairman of joint chiefs of staff and various other defence personnel. Choe is believed to have visited the missile-related production facility in Faisalabad and even Jhelum (the area from where Ghauri was subsequently launched)[99] to finalise deals to provide Pakistan either with major components or a modified No-dong missile.[100]

On 25 June 1999, Indian customs officials detained a North Korean freighter allegedly bound for Malta. The ship, named Ku Wol-San, was carrying precision machine tools used in missile production. According to Indian sources, the machinery was intended for the construction of a missile production facility at Fatehjung in Pakistan.[101] The ship declared that after off-loading 13,000 metric tonnes of sugar at Kandla, India, it was scheduled to carry 177 tonnes of machinery to Malta. However, the actual cargo included:

1. Heavy duty press and lathe for flattening and milling sheets of metal.
2. Heavy plate-bending machine capable of shaping 16 mm thick sheets of metal into 700 mm diameter rocket motor casings. The bending machine can also be used to manufacture rocket nozzle cones and body structures.
3. 'Torroidal' air bottles used for guidance corrections once the warhead has separated from the missile.
4. Two sets of 'theodolides'—devices used to align a missile with its launch pad.
5. Sensitive electronic weighing machines and soldering devices.
6. Forged steel bars (1.5 mm thick) common in missile construction.
7. Water purification machinery used to produce water capable of washing missile cones.

---

[97] Ibid.

[98] KCNA (Pyongyang) 1994.

[99] *Pyongyang Korean Central Broadcasting Network* 1995; *Pyongyang Korean Central Television Network* 1995.

[100] Bermudez Jr 1998.

[101] Gupta 1999.

There is a growing concern that Pakistan may be supplying nuclear weapons technology to North Korea in exchange of missile technology.[102]

On 6 April 1998 Pakistan declared that it had tested a new ballistic missile—Ghauri. The range of the test was given as 1,100 km and it was apparently fired from a transporter-creator-launcher; it was very likely a single-stage liquid fuelled missile available only through government sources. David Wright concludes, 'the available information appears to be consistent with a missile that uses technology and a configuration similar to No-dong, but which is smaller than No-dong.'[103] It is possible that DPRK did not provide a complete missile, but instead provided major components. The technology Pakistan uses for Hatf I and Hatf II missiles is believed to be premised on solid fuel based on French sounding rockets; this may have led to indigenous technology development used in the Ghauri. DPRK is believed to be developing a two-stage missile with a range of 1,500–2,000 km that may use the No-dong as the first stage and a send engine in the second stage. Wright concludes that the information given in press reports about the Ghauri flight is compatible with the missile being liquid fuelled and using a cluster of four send engines, as does North Korea's No-dong missile. However, the missile appears to be somewhat smaller and have a shorter range that the No-dong. This confirms assertions that North Korea did not transfer a complete missile, and supports Pakistani claims that it was an indigenous design, 'albeit one that drew heavily on foreign technology, and expertise.'[104] If Pakistan uses the same technology, we may get the reported 2,000 km range Ghaznavi.[105]

There was some debate over the Ghauri test initially, regarding whether Pakistan would risk testing an unproven missile over populated areas without issuing an alert. The Indian radars that constantly monitor Pakistan air space were unable to detect the launch.[106] The US believes that a test did take place, although the

---

[102] Mohan 1999a.

[103] Wright 1998.

[104] Ibid.

[105] CDISS 1998.

[106] Of course, some commentators and 'experts' were quick to point out the weakness of the Indian surveillance system when it was argued that Indian radars may be optimised to detect aircraft.

range is still under debate. Moreover, US officials reportedly believed that the Ghauri missile is liquid fuelled and based on technology obtained from North Korea.[107] Following the test, the US imposed sanctions against a North Korean company (Changgwang Sinyonga Corporation) and Pakistan's Khan Research Laboratories.[108] Apparently, the US believed that the evidence of such a transfer was strong enough to impose sanctions.

Several days after the 6 April test, Pakistan announced that it was working on a more capable ballistic missile—the Ghaznavi with a range of 2,000 km. 'This new system will likely incorporate both technology and components from the Taepo-dong programs and the PRC.'[109]

There have been various instances over the last decade showing that the Pakistan–DPRK relationship is not limited to just one time assistance but encompasses numerous missile, nuclear and defence areas.[110] In March 1996, a DPRK cargo ship Chon Sung was detained by Taiwanese authorities for incorrectly declaring 15 tonnes (200 barrels) of ammonia per chlorate (a component used in solid rocket fuels). This was being shipped to Pakistan's SUPARCO.[111] Pakistan has in turn provided DPRK access to Western technology procured clandestinely. DPRK has been denied Western technology for long and perhaps thought fit to take Pakistan's assistance in this regard. It is likely that the DPRK's No-dong and Taep-o-dong programmes have also benefited from access to various PRC technologies that had previously been unavailable to it and Pakistan may have facilitated that process in return for DPRK's missile cooperation. In July 2001, American intelligence agencies tracked a Pakistani cargo aircraft as it landed at a North Korean airfield and took on a secret payload: ballistic missile parts made by North Korea.[112] The shipment was brazen enough, in full view of US spy satellites. But intelligence officials who described the incident say that the transport was also an embarrassment to Washington: the Pakistani

[107] Weiner 1998.
[108] Rajghatta 1998a, 1998b.
[109] Bermudez Jr. 1998.
[110] Koch 1997.
[111] KBS-1 (Pyongyang) 1996.
[112] Sanger 2002.

plane was a Lockheed-built C-130 made in the United States.[113] In November 2002, soon after North Korea declared that it had a nuclear bomb, the non-proliferation community was rife with speculation as to the origins of this bomb. Pakistan's name figured highest on the list of potential proliferators.[114] *The New York Times*, citing 'current senior American officials' said,

> The equipment, which may include gas centrifuges used to create weapons-grade uranium, appears to have been part of a barter deal beginning in the late 1990s in which North Korea supplied Pakistan with missiles it could use to counter India's nuclear arsenal [they] said. 'What you have here', said one official familiar with the intelligence, 'is a perfect meeting of interests—the North had what the Pakistanis needed, and the Pakistanis had a way for Kim Jong II to restart a nuclear program we had stopped'.[115]

---

[113] Ibid. For a perspective from Pakistan on this, see Haqqani 2002. He says, 'Pakistan's status as a key ally of the United States in the war against terrorism has not protected it from allegations of secretly supplying North Korea with uranium enrichment equipment and technical expertise in exchange for ballistic missile technology. Pakistan's military ruler, General Pervez Musharraf, described the charge as "absolutely baseless". Secretary of State Colin Powell and National Security Adviser Condoleezza Rice said they believed him, although they refused to say in absolute terms that there had never been Pakistani–North Korean cooperation. So far, no evidence has surfaced to confirm the allegations, but reports on covert weapons programs are often based on intelligence leaks. U.S. media reports have suggested that there may have been some exchange of technology under one of Pakistan's shaky civilian regimes that preceded Musharraf. Most Pakistanis are outraged over the charges that their country periodically faces, ranging from allegations of covert support of terrorists to accusations about Pakistan's nuclear and missile program.' Also see in this context, Masood Haider 2002. He reports, 'US Secretary of State, Colin Powell, said on Sunday that Pakistan has assured that no nuclear technology has been supplied to North Korea by it, nor will be in the future. He said that a 1994 US agreement with North Korea to freeze its nuclear weapons programme was effectively nullified after Pyongyang admitted violating the deal. Powell told NBC news programme "Meet the Press" that he talked to Pakistani President Pervez Musharraf on Friday and "he gave me 400 per cent assurance" that Pakistan has not supplied any nuclear know-how to North Korea. Asked about the past cooperation between the two countries, Powell said: "I cannot talk about the past; what is important is present." He added, "Musharraf knows what the consequences of their actions will be."'

[114] Sanger and Dao 2002.

[115] Ibid.

There were selected leaks from the American media as Pakistan was once again branded as 'the most dangerous place on earth', shattering 'the Bush administration's efforts to paint that country as a flawed but well-meaning member of the coalition against terror'.[116] On the other hand, North Korea's sudden admission that it has a secret uranium-based nuclear weapons programme is a fine example of Pyongyang's famous 'judo diplomacy'—sharp negotiating turns designed to extract concessions from a surprised opponent.[117]

In February 2004 media reports started appearing from all across the world, especially the Western media, about Dr A.Q. Khan's nuclear commerce. Initial investigation revealed that Dr Khan and some other scientists were involved in transferring nuclear technology from Pakistan to other states, including DPRK, Libya and Iran. In a meeting of the National Command Authority in early February 2004, it became clear that 'sensitive information regarding the nuclear technology went out of the country in which Dr Abdul Qadeer and some other scientists were involved.'[118] On 5 February 2004, coming under intense pressure, Dr A.Q. Khan confessed to the illegal trade, spoke to President General Musharraf, requested clemency during a one-hour meeting with him, appeared on national television and sought forgiveness from the nation. The Pakistani cabinet, as expected, pardoned him.[119] This, of course, left several questions unanswered and implied that he might have been forced to take the fall[120] for the more powerful military leaders, who many believe were secretly behind the technology transfers.[121] As an author has argued, 'when a dictatorship claims nuclear peddling occurred

---

[116] Hoagland 2002.

[117] Rajain 2002g.

[118] *Jang* 2004. See also in this context, Rohde 2004a, 2004b; Broad 2004; and Broad et al. 2004. The Pakistani nuclear network forced the IAEA head, Mohammed El Baradei, to warn that 'the world could be headed for destruction if it does not stop the spread of nuclear weapons technology, which has become widely accessible' (See *The Washington Post* 2004).

[119] *The Nation* 2004a.

[120] *The New York Times* 2004a.

[121] See *The Nation* 2004b; *The New York Times* 2004b. With a view to stopping future proliferation activities, the US President George Bush proposed a seven-point plan to make it far more difficult to sell nuclear equipment in the black market, declaring that the United States must 'prevent governments from developing nuclear weapons under false pretenses' (See Sanger 2004).

without its knowledge, the dangers of leakage and seizure of nuclear assets by Islamist elements becomes starkly real.'[122] Over the years, Pakistan has been quite brazen in its approach to international non-proliferation regimes. For instance, Khan Research Laboratories (KRL) have held international workshops on 'Advanced Materials' or 'Vibrations in Rapidly Rotating Machinery'.[123] The nuclear weapons programme and individuals associated with it have brought international opprobrium to Pakistan.[124]

India has monitored the North Korea–Pakistan link for a long time. In a question that was raised in the Lok Sabha on 'whether China and North Korea are providing assistance to Pakistan in building its nuclear capability', the Minister of External Affairs, Jaswant Singh answered,

> It is established that North Korea has assisted Pakistan with long range missiles, missile technology and components; Ghauri is a Pakistani version of the North Korean 'No-dong' missile capable of carrying nuclear warheads. Pakistan has also received nuclear capable M-11 solid fuel missiles from China. It also acquired technology and components related to the production of solid fuel missiles, including from China. In the nuclear field, China has provided assistance, inter alia, in setting up an unsafeguarded research reactor and plutonium reprocessing facility, provided ring magnets for Uranium enrichment, heavy water, diagnostic equipment, etc. It is assessed that external assistance to Pakistan's missiles and nuclear programme is continuing.[125]

✠ TACIT NUCLEAR DOCTRINE

The excuse that the 1974 Indian test was the reason for Pakistan deciding to follow the nuclear path is only half the truth. In fact, as long ago as 1965, Ayub Khan had turned down Zulfikar Ali Bhutto's

---

[122] Chellaney 2004.

[123] For instance, the Khan Research Laboratories (KRL), Kahuta had called for papers for the Eighth International Symposium on Advanced Materials. The objective of the symposium was 'to establish dialogue and long lasting, healthy technical cooperation among the materials, scientists and engineers of the developing and developed countries' (See KRL 2003).

[124] See in this context, Rajain 2004.

[125] Lok Sabha 2000h.

plea for a Rs (Pak) 300 million reprocessing plant on the ground that Pakistan's economy could not bear such a heavy burden.[126] According to Dr I.H. Usmani, the second Chairman of the Pakistan Atomic Energy Commission (PAEC), Pakistan did not have the necessary infrastructure at that time.[127] Interestingly, there seems to have been no connection at that time with any Indian programme or threat. The only argument that can be appreciated is that of prestige—of being the first Islamic nation to have the bomb. Pakistan knew of its technological deficiency, but realised that with the Cold War going on, getting such technology would not be difficult. In 1969, Bhutto had written,

All wars of our age have become total wars and it will have to be assumed that a war waged against Pakistan is capable of becoming a total war. It would be dangerous to plan for less and our plans should, therefore, include a nuclear deterrent.[128]

Like any other statesman, Bhutto too wanted to move with the times and the development of nuclear weapons. The timing of these statements lends credence to the argument that Pakistan entertained ambitions of becoming a nuclear state. Bhutto was not the chief decision maker in the 1960s; hence, after coming to power in December 1971, he convened a meeting of Pakistan's top scientists and asked them, 'we are going to have a bomb—can you give it to me?'[129] Of course, on 18 May 1974, India tested a device which it claimed was a Peaceful Nuclear Explosion, and this provided a rationale for Pakistan to firm up not just a nuclear weapons programme, but later on, a delivery system for a nuclear weapon.

Having established the technology, tested the device and received the means to deliver nuclear weapons, Pakistan had to enunciate a policy to use them. Pakistan has no official nuclear doctrine, but it has been evolving one with inputs from all quarters, most importantly, the army. Zulfikar Ali Bhutto had said in 1968 that Pakistan needed a nuclear deterrent. With the presence of the nuclear deterrent, the policy that began to be pursued was appropriate for the times.

---

126 Weisman and Krosney 1981.
127 Ibid.
128 Bhutto 1969: 153.
129 Cited in Weisman and Krosney 1981: 78.

One of the most significant inputs came from a serving army officer, Brig S.K. Malik, who wrote *The Quranic Concept of War*[130] in the mid-1980s. Its significance lay in the fact that General Zia, the then military ruler of Pakistan, wrote the preface to the book. In a society that has seen four coups by the army, such an input from a serving army officer becomes very important, as the army is the most powerful organisation among the political institutions in the country. To quote a paragraph from the book,

> [W]hat ever the form or type of strategy directed against the enemy, it must in order to be effective be capable of striking terror into the hearts of the enemy. A strategy that fails to attain this condition suffers from inherent drawbacks and weaknesses, and should be reviewed and modified. This rule is fully applicable to nuclear as well as conventional wars. It is equally true of the strategy of nuclear deterrence in fashion today. To be credible and effective, the strategy of deterrence must be capable of striking terror into the hearts of the enemy.[131]

Though Pakistan did not have the required delivery systems to maintain a credible deterrent and the nuclear programme was still in the process of collecting the technology and equipment, some thinking into crucial issues according to General Zia firmly linked the nuclear programme to military doctrine. Since Pakistan's nuclear option has been expressly designed to contain India, one test more than India was enough to assuage domestic alarm and political pressures.[132]

THE FINAL ARBITER: THE ARMY

At the time of independence, Pakistan was woefully short of officers, especially those that had staff and senior command experience.[133] To overcome this deficit, the government decided to retain 355 officers from the British forces, and additionally requested 129 officers

---

[130] Malik 1986.

[131] Ibid.: 60.

[132] For a perceptive analysis of public opinion surveys and views of opinion makers, see Kamal 1999.

[133] Pakistan had only one major general, two brigadiers and six colonels at the time of its independence, against the requirement of 13 generals, 40 brigadiers and 53 colonels (Khan 1963).

from England.[134] The military has also expanded its role in the economy by being active in business and industry. There are, as Rizvi says,[135] three categories of commercial interests that the military nurtures: those directly under the administrative control of the army chief,[136] those looked after by the Defence Production Division of the Ministry of Defence but headed by serving officers appointed by the army chief,[137] and the four charitable trusts that generate funds for the welfare of retired army personnel and their families.[138]

Islam has been integral to Pakistani military ideology. It has been repeatedly invoked during the wars in 1965 and 1971 to infuse a spirit of 'attack on religion' and to galvanise soldiers and civilians into action for the defence of the country. This is reflected in the calls for *Iman* (faith), *Taqwa* (piety and abstinence), *Jihad-fi-sibilillah* (holy war in the name of God) or its most recent avatar, *Jihad* (holy war).

Apart from constitutional issues, the legitimacy problem of the military is more acute than it seems. As Muthiah Allagappa says, 'it lies in the military's distaste for politics, distrust of politicians, preference for stability, order, and efficiency, lack of linkage to political and civil societies, and its unwillingness to accommodate change.'[139] He further says, 'all these attributes contribute to the military's inability to construct an acceptable political framework for the management of the state, including the acquisition and exercise of state power.'[140]

The Pakistan army, which has played a more important role in Pakistan's politics than any other institution, has always followed the 'offensive defence' doctrine. This doctrine has all the necessary

---

[134] Rizvi 2000.

[135] Ibid.: 236.

[136] These include the Frontier Works Organisation, Special Communications Organisation and the National Logistics Cell. Ibid.

[137] These include the Pakistan Ordinance factories (POF) and several defence production facilities, like the Aeronautical Complex, Kamara and several ancillary units. Ibid.

[138] These include the Fauji Foundation and the Army Welfare Trust. There were originally three agencies: the Welfare Directorate, the Post-war Reconstruction Fund and the Armed Services Boards, which were reorganised and their functions reassigned. Ibid.

[139] Alagappa 2001b: 51.

[140] Ibid.: 51.

ingredients of the Quranic concept of war. It was Gen Mirza Aslam Beg, the former Chief of Army Staff, who in 1988 (the same year that Zarb-e-Momin was created) said, 'In the past we were pursuing a defensive policy: now there is a big change since we are shifting to a policy of offensive defence.' He further added, 'should there be a war, the Pakistan army plans to take war into India launching a sizeable offensive into the Indian territory.'[141] The massive military, Zarb-e-Momin, was essentially meant to test Pakistan's new 'offensive defence' doctrine.[142] At the same time, the synchronisation of the military doctrine with the nuclear option was taking place. To cite General Beg again, 'both the nuclear option and the missile act as a deterrence and these in turn contribute to the total fighting ability of the army which then acts as a deterrent to the enemy.'[143]

In another interview, General Beg spoke at length about the establishment of a nuclear command as early the 1970s according to which the National Nuclear Command Authority (NNCA) would control the country's nuclear button. The NNCA was established in the 1970s, and is based in the army's general headquarters in Rawalpindi at the Joint Operations Centre, and the highest political functionary heads the chain of command. The decision-making body comprises the president, prime minister, the army chief and three other people.[144] It is interesting to note that Pakistan had just started entertaining thoughts of acquiring nuclear weapons in the early 1970s, and it is difficult to believe that it immediately set up a nuclear command and control structure. Further, nuclear command and control is the last thing an adversary should know about, and by revealing it, General Beg was not helping the cause. Besides, command and control is a dynamic process depending on the politico-strategic environment, as well as on the available delivery systems, that is, the way a country would react in times of crises. This story then seems to be 'planted', perhaps for an international audience. And, finally, Pakistan did establish a command and control structure some months after it had tested to assure the world that civilian command obtained over nuclear weapons.

---

[141] Beg 1989: 770.
[142] Hussain 1989.
[143] Beg 1989: 779.
[144] Rashid 1994.

At this time there was no mention of a structure, existing or a new one replacing it.

Since Pakistan's independence, there have been a number of changes in the political establishment, and the country has oscillated between democracy and dictatorship. One institution that has remained powerful at all times is the army.

The Pakistan army, which was formed in 1947, inherited a training system dependent on the British, with paucity of stores, training institutions and catering for the security needs of a country that had just been created.[145] Since Pakistan is an Islamic state, the army too was exposed to Islamic principles and practices. That the army is clearly a very powerful force in Pakistan's polity is evident from the number of coups the country has witnessed after 1947. Hasan-Askari Rizvi has sought to explain this phenomenon of the military's constant intervention in politics, and concludes that the failure of civilians 'to keep a balance between the diverse forces working in the political system' caused this problem.[146] Another argument that looks at the army's view argues that 'It had been a series of vicious circles for successive Pakistani governments. Internal instability goaded the leadership to shift emphasis upon foreign policy, which ... led to further instability.'[147] The official history of the Pakistan army which focuses on the evolution of the military tradition from Muslim rulers, claims that the officers and men of the army are descended 'from the men who fought Alexander the Great ... who established the first Muslim stronghold in India and who campaigned in the days of the great Mughal Emperors helping to conquer and stabilise nearly the whole of the subcontinent.'[148] Distortions of this nature have had an important role in shaping the perceptions of Pakistanis in general and military men in particular.[149] The army, therefore, feels that its responsibility lies in not just defending the border but also in assisting during 'crises' in

---

[145] For one of the best accounts on the Pakistan army, see Stephen P. Cohen 1989.

[146] He further adds, 'If the civilian institutions are not capable of asserting themselves on the military, the military by virtue of its qualities dominates the civil institutions. Therefore, it is the root which must be cured first' (Rizvi 1976.: 296).

[147] Ray 1975.

[148] Khan 1963: 3.

[149] Singh 1995.

the state, in general, and in governance, in particular.[150] As Professor Cohen has summed up,

> [T]he Pakistan Army like any massive bureaucracy is constrained by its own past. This heritage tells the army that intervention maybe necessary and that it must be limited in scope and time; yet the problems of diversity of Pakistani society and the slow growth of what the military would regard as a community of responsible politicians make it difficult to relinquish power. Once in power the officer corps is tempted to tinker with the political system and adjust it.[151] Often the army has sought to safeguard its corporate interests.[152]

The fourth military takeover in October 1999,[153] and the ability of the Musharraf government to manage the country's affairs without encountering any serious challenges, only reconfirms the military's strategic position in Pakistan's political system.[154] The institution of the army can be described as the most formidable and autonomous political actor in Pakistan, capable of influencing the nature and direction of political changes.[155] As Babar Sattar has written,

> [B]ecause of the preponderant role that the military has played in the history of Pakistan and its monopoly over the ultimate means of coercion, the military has arrogated to itself the right to define Pakistan's supreme national interest, gauge the civilian government's performance, and take appropriate action, which has ranged from admonition to removal of the government.[156]

---

[150] This is reflected in General Musharraf's speech on 12 October 1999 after he seized power. See Musharraf 1999a.

[151] Cohen 1989: 12.

[152] On how the Pakistani army seeks to protect its corporate interests, see Rizvi 2000.

[153] The clout of the army has been manifested in the form of direct military rule (October 1958–June 1962, March 1969–December 1971, July 1977–December 1985, and October 1999 to the present) and influence over key foreign policy and domestic issues, when out of power.

[154] See also in this context, Rashid and Gardezi 1983.

[155] Arif 2001. K.M. Arif retired as a four-star General and as Vice Chief of the Pakistani army.

[156] Sattar 2001: 386.

There are several explanations for the military's prominence in the political process. The first major interest is national security: the army continues to exercise influence in key foreign policy areas, especially the nuclear policy, relations with India, including Kashmir and Afghanistan. When in power, any civilian government is expected to keep the army well informed about major changes in foreign or nuclear policy. The military, like most civilian policy makers, would not like to improve relations with India unless it addresses the Kashmir issue. A second interest remains overseas arms and equipment procurement, which has foreign policy implications. A third interest relates to the preservation of the army's autonomy while countering any civilian interference in its internal organisation. Also related is the issue of expenditure, as the army remains opposed to unilateral cuts in defence expenditure by civilian leaders. Another associated consideration is the perks, privileges and carefully cultivated business interests that the army has developed through its four welfare foundations. And finally, the military expects civilian leaders to maintain some degree of political and economic stability, a pre-requisite to sustain its professional and corporate interests.[157] Pakistani society has developed a socio-psychological subservience to men in uniform, which is the result of a long history of indoctrination and less subtle means of cooption by successive military rulers.[158]

President, Gen Pervez Musharraf has for some time been under tremendous international pressure with increasing demands for the restoration of democracy. Just two days before the visit of the US President, Bill Clinton on 23 March 2000, Musharraf announced that he would hold local body elections later in the year throughout the country, as the first step towards the return to 'real democracy.' In May 2002, Musharraf had an overwhelming victory in the referendum to extend his mandate as president of Pakistan for a further five years. The general justified his decision thus: 'Democracy starts here at the district and local governments. From here, we will move up step by step to provincial and federal elections in due course.'[159] This promise from General Musharraf of restoring 'real democracy' was similar to what Field Marshal Ayub Khan

---

[157] See in this context, Rizvi 2000.
[158] Mustaq 2001.
[159] Musharraf 2000.

had done by holding elections in 1962. This was just another way of consolidating his power and the influence of the army.[160] Pakistani commentator Zahid Hussain believed that 'General Musharraf's local bodies plan seems clearly designed to create a new power base for the military regime.'[161] This is also what Veena Kukreja has highlighted as the all-pervasive and arbitrary role of the army and the monopolisation of power by the bureaucracy which has made civil institutions mere 'appendages of a state' that suffers from a dual crisis in mandate and legitimacy.[162]

With Pakistan possessing nuclear weapons and moving from conventional to non-weaponised and then to weaponised (?) deterrence, it seems clear that the army still retains all the security decision-making powers. The strategic conclave in Pakistan has highlighted the Indian threat case very often—that Pakistan should always make itself secure against the hegemonic designs of India and be prepared to safeguard 'national independence and territorial integrity at any cost'.[163] The main objective of possessing nuclear weapons was always clear. Mushahid Hussain, the Information Minister in the Nawaz Sharif cabinet, viewed Pakistan's nuclear programme 'as a response to India's nuclear ambition.'[164] As he said, the main objective of Pakistan was 'to seek a credible nuclear deterrent against its principal adversary, that is, India.'[165] After all, the weapons that have to be delivered and the means to deliver them are with the army; the army has always played a dominant role here. General Kidwai, head of Pakistan's Strategic Planning Division, has also stated that nuclear weapons can be used 'if the very existence of Pakistan as a state is at stake.'[166] The threshold, he says, has been lowered and now encompasses

---

[160] On the issue of local elections, see Bakhtiar 2000; also Aamer Ahmed Khan 2000.

[161] Hussain 2000.

[162] Kukreja 2002: 297. Elsewhere, she writes that 'the long years of direct rule have allowed the military to penetrate so widely into the government, the economy and society that its clout and influence no longer depend on controlling the levers of power. It is derived from its pervasive presence in all sectors of government and society' (p. 296).

[163] Shamim 1988.

[164] Hussain 1988: 233. Hussain was earlier the editor of the Islamabad-based English daily, The Muslim.

[165] Ibid.: 224.

[166] Cotta-Ramusino and Martellini 2002.

situations where (*a*) India 'conquers a large part of its [Pakistani] territory'; (*b*) 'destroys a large part either of its land or air forces'; (*c*) 'proceeds to the economic strangling of Pakistan'; (*d*) or 'creates a large scale internal subversion in Pakistan.'[167]

In an essay in the *Defence Journal* soon after the May 1998 tests, Lt Gen F.S. Lodi said, 'Pakistan's Nuclear Doctrine would ... essentially revolve around the first-strike option ... we will use nuclear weapons if attacked by India even if the attack is with conventional weapons.'[168] General Lodi endorses the views of Prof. Stephen P. Cohen when he says that Pakistan would use an 'option-enhancing policy' for a possible use of nuclear weapons.[169] It can be conjectured that the Pakistani army has identified rungs on the escalation ladder, moving from private threats, placing delivery systems on high alert status, to exploding a nuclear weapon on its own soil for demonstration purposes, to targeting military bases, and finally to targeting cities, depending on the Indian response. Shireen Mazari argues that

> the first generation of nuclear weapons that Pakistan would deploy would have large CEP (circular error probability)—that is, would not be too accurate, therefore, at least initially Pakistan would have to evolve a counter-value strategy: That is, targeting Indian economic, leadership and population centres rather than hardened military targets.[170]

Mirza Aslam Beg, in the context of deterrence, says, 'the strategy of deterrence, through flexible response is applicable, based on

---

[167] Ibid.

[168] Lodi 1999.

[169] This would entail a stage-by-stage approach in which the nuclear threat would be increased at each step to deter India from attack. The first step could be a public or private warning, the second a demonstration explosion of a small nuclear weapon on its own soil, the third step could be the use of a few nuclear weapons on its own soil against Indian attacking forces. The fourth stage would be the use of nuclear arms against critical but purely military targets in India across the border from Pakistan, probably in thinly populated areas in the desert or semi-desert, causing least collateral damage. This may prevent Indian retaliation against cities in Pakistan. Some weapon systems would be in reserve for the counter-value role. These weapons would be safe from Indian attack as some would be airborne while the ground-based ones would be mobile and can be moved around the country.

[170] Mazari 1999b.

minimum number of weapons. What comprises minimal nuclear deterrence, is a national issue, a function of the political and military judgment, related to adversary's capability.'[171] Lt Gen Asad Durrani, former head of the ISI, has stated,

> neither of us relishes the prospect of ever using them, especially when the other side could match the response …. India could consider taking out our nuclear arsenal, to deny us its use—in practice, it is an extremely risky proposition. Even on odd weapon that survived the so called 'first strike', could cause irreparable damage.[172]

Ayesha Siddiqa-Agha further argues that 'The idea is to ensure that in case of hostilities, Islamabad can manage to deliver two to three nuclear weapons to the adversary's territory. For the time being, this would be achieved with land-based missiles.'[173] On the issue of thresholds, Maria Sultan writes,

> They will be used if: India attacks Pakistan and conquers a large part of its territory (space threshold); India destroys a large part of either its land or air force (military threshold); India proceeds to the economic strangling of Pakistan (economic threshold); India pushes Pakistan into political destabilization or creates a large scale internal subversion in Pakistan (domestic destabilisation).[174]

On the other hand, Ejaz Haidar thinks that the nuclear tests placed Pakistan 'in a better position to challenge India through low intensity conflict …. This meant that India could now be denied the luxury of expanding the conflict and capitalizing on the conventional symmetries.'[175] Verbal threats from various people in power have been made on and off at various times in the past.

On the crucial issues of nuclear command and control, one of the few insights has come from Lt Gen (Retd) Sardar F.S. Lodi and

---

[171] In fact, he further argues, 'Nuclear deterrence alone cannot ensure security to Pakistan unless it is backed by an ideological propriety, aggressive diplomacy, and a viable conventional capability enjoying an optimum correlation of forces with India and adjusted correctly to the required level of operational balance' (Beg 2001).

[172] Durrani 1998. See also Durrani 2003.

[173] Siddiqa-Agha 2000a.

[174] Sultan 2002.

[175] Haidar 2002.

it is important to quote it.[176] He argues that in the case of Pakistan the following basic parameters have to be met:[177]

- The final orders to use nuclear weapons must come from the highest executive authority in the country.
- The decision must be based on a deteriorating military situation after the enemy's conventional attack is likely to break through or has already breached the main defence line.
- In case of a pre-emptive strike, it must be ensured that the enemy was preparing to launch a nuclear attack, which could cripple Pakistan's nuclear ability to strike back.

Until the paper by Agha Shahi, Zulfiqar Ali Khan and Abdul Sattar (which is considered to be Pakistan's unofficial nuclear doctrine) appeared, there was no official or unofficial communication about the doctrine of use.[178] The paper raised important questions of survivability, credibility, deterrence policy, posture and size of the strategic arsenal. It posits that a small number of weapons can deter and also that deterrence worked in the mid-1980s, 1986–87, April–May 1990, and in 1999 during the Kargil crisis. Going by this paper, if the enemy launches a general war and undertakes a piercing attack threatening to occupy large territories or communication junctions, the 'weapon of last resort' would have to be invoked. The authors argue that a massive first strike may be disastrous: 'India is too large and too well armed to be vulnerable

---

[176] Lodi 1999.

[177] Some of his other suggestions are: (*a*) 'Our standard of communication from the Chief Executive right down to the missile launch pad and the airbase concerned must be perfect and not be susceptible to interruption at all times. (*b*) Intelligence gathering agencies must be able to provide accurate, up-to-date and timely information about enemy's additional troop deployments and likely intentions. (*c*) Our final decision to employ the nuclear option must be based entirely on the security and integrity of the country, when other conventional means of defence have proved inadequate. (*d*) Our close friends and allies abroad must be kept abreast of the latest situation on the ground and eventually the urgent requirement to employ nuclear weapons. (*e*) It must be kept in mind that the nuclear option would be a weapon of last resort which may eventually produce no winners or losers and must therefore be employed with the greatest of care and caution, after discussing all the pros and cons of the situation, its impact in the region and beyond and its international ramifications' (Ibid).

[178] Shahi et al. 1999. They are influential people in Pakistan. In fact, Abdul Sattar became the Foreign Minister just days after this article was published.

to a disabling strike.' Besides, 'any such attempt would provoke retaliation with disastrous consequences.'[179] Pakistan acknowledges these to be weapons of large resort, but it sees them as a balance against India's vast conventional forces. It will, therefore, not sign a no-first-use agreement. This translates into a policy of 'weapons of last resort but first use', especially when Pakistan has fewer warheads than India. The paper bases these arguments about the size of the arsenal on the Cuban missile crisis in which the Soviet had power weapons.[180] On the size of the arsenal the paper argues, 'the size of Pakistan's arsenal and its deployment pattern have to be adjusted', and says, 'Pakistan does not need to enter into a competition with India.'[181] Quite naturally, the argument of Pakistan 'adjusting' its arsenal against India's dangerous, since it lays the foundations of an arms race which the subcontinent can ill afford. Although Pakistan considers these weapons as those of last resort, plans for their possible use are at hand. This paper also cites the NATO military doctrine of 'flexible response' as being applicable to the Pakistan–India crisis in the 1980s and 1990s. Further, it states that implicit possession of nuclear capability is a warning of actual use of nuclear weapons. Another statement makes it even clearer that 'credibility of the deterrence force does not depend on the number of nuclear bombs in the arsenal but on the survivability of the minimum number necessary for deterrence and the ability to deliver them on predetermined value targets.'[182] This statement also shows that the targeting strategy would be counter-value. The paper hints at the cost factor, stating that innovative planning should have to restructure defence forces, integrating conventional and nuclear deterrence within the limits of Pakistan's financial capacity.[183] Defining nuclear threshold, the paper says that these weapons cannot be invoked in every contingency. This leaves room for localised conflicts of the Kargil type.

---

[179] Shahi et al. 1999.

[180] Ibid. The Cuban missile crisis was a dangerous case and it has been argued that one step led to another quickly and the two states were facing each other. Besides, the Soviets and the Americans had a large number of weapons spread over different parts of the world.

[181] Ibid.

[182] Ibid.

[183] Ibid.

This argument again is dangerous, as deterrence at the nuclear level has resulted in breaking down of deterrence at the conventional level. Anyway, India has been promised 'many more Kargils'. On the key issue of C3I, the paper states that a high state of alert will become more necessary.[184] With flight time between India and Pakistan being five to seven minutes, and there being no early warning capability, accidental or unauthorised launch of even a single missile may lead to a series of escalatory steps, resulting in catastrophe. Zafar Iqbal Cheema is of the view that Pakistan's deterrence can be further augmented by its decision to assemble a small nuclear force rapidly, to diversify weapons by using designs that rely on both uranium and plutonium, to develop comprehensive missile programmes, and to take steps to miniaturise nuclear warheads.[185] Zafar Nawaz Jaspal believes that

in the present strategic scenario Pakistan possesses enough strategic weaponry ... to provide it with a minimum nuclear deterrence. The basis of this perception is that in nuclear deterrence, parity between opponents is not based on numerical equality of the number of nuclear delivery systems, or of the number of warheads or in the yield of megatons available to each opponent. Parity requires assured destruction capability.[186]

On a more defensive note, Brig S.J. Saeed Ismat has drawn the broad contours of a conceptual nuclear doctrine:[187]

(a) If nuclear deterrence fails and the aggressor seizes the initiative to launch the First Strike, we shall hit back with our Second Strike ability. (b) In case the deterrent fails by the enemy launching a meaningful conventional offensive, our forces shall resiliently defend their homeland. (c) Any time in our perception when the defences are seriously endangered and a collapse is imminent, we shall be obliged to raise the scope and nature of our response. We shall now employ tactical nuclear weapons against the invading military forces. (d) This is essentially a defensive strategy backed up by a series of controlled escalations. (e) Our response shall be directly propor-tionate to the actions of enemy provocation and threat posed to our security.

---

[184] Shahi et al. 1999.
[185] See Cheema 2000.
[186] See Jaspal 2001.
[187] Ismat 2000.

In January 1999, then Prime Minister Nawaz Sharif approved the creation of a Nuclear Regulatory Authority to minimise the chances of the export of Pakistan's nuclear expertise, while in February 2000 Pakistan set up the nuclear arms command.[188] The new organisation, dubbed the National Command Authority (NCA), was described as an institutionalised command and control mechanism consistent with Pakistan's obligations as a nuclear power by the official Associated Press of Pakistan. Following a lengthy debate in the National Security Council, Pakistan made it clear that the National Command Authority (NCA) 'will be responsible for formulation' and 'will exercise employment and development control over all strategic nuclear forces and strategic nuclear forces and strategic organisations.'[189] It comprises two committees: the Employment Control Committee, Development Control Committee as well as the Strategic Plans Division, which acts as its Secretariat. The apex Employment Control Committee is chaired by the head of the government and includes the minister for foreign affairs (deputy chairman), minister for defence, minister for interior, chairman of the Joint Chiefs of Staff Committee, services chiefs, director general of the Strategic Plans Division (secretary) and technical advisors/others as required by the chairman. The Development Control Committee is chaired by the head of the government and includes the deputy chairman, services chiefs, director general of the Strategic Plans Division and representatives of strategic organisations and the scientific community.[190]

Doubts remain about whether any civilian government would ever have access to information relating to the precise number of nuclear warheads that Pakistan has, number of delivery vehicles, operational readiness, nuclear storage sites existing fissile material stocks, future production rates, command and control chains, future plans on the architecture of the nuclear deterrent, and so forth.[191] For instance, it is entirely possible that the elected government of the late 1980s did not know about Pakistan's supposed ability to deliver nuclear weapons by aircraft soon after the onset of the Kashmir crisis.

---

[188] *The Times of India* 2000b.
[189] *The Statesman* 2000a.
[190] *Dawn* 2000.
[191] Hoodbhoy 1999a.

Thus, Pakistan's unofficial nuclear doctrine leaves room for strategic uncertainty. In some sense, ambiguity strengthens deterrence, but if a state is certain of the response an adversary should expect in case the threshold is breached then unambiguously stating it to the adversary makes more strategic sense. In this milieu what worries neighbouring states, particularly India, is that there are no civilian filters and the President, General Musharraf, controls the nuclear estate. Being premised on 'weapons of last resort and first use', some Pakistani scholars are dismissive of the unofficial nuclear doctrine—they state that it is after all just a newspaper article—while Western analysts say that Abdul Sattar, one of the authors, had become Pakistan's Foreign Minister in the Musharraf government, making it a semi-official statement. It is also entirely possible that competition between the Pakistani security establishment and the strategic enclaves might lead to building up of strategic programmes and arsenal that exceed Pakistan's near and medium-term requirements.[192]

✺ Foreign Policy Issues

Being an Islamic state, Pakistan's foreign policy has been dominated by Islamic ideals, and the state has tended to cooperate with other Muslim states. Besides the Islamic group of states, the US, which has been an ally of Pakistan for more than five decades, has maintained a close relationship with it on key foreign policy issues. Pakistan's relations with China have developed rapidly in the last couple of decades, and lastly, the country has adversarial relations with India against whom it has fought four wars.

Pakistan closely observes the Western imaging of the Islamic world. The collapse of communism influenced Samuel Huntington's 'clash of civilisation' theory, which holds that the image of a worldwide threat from Islam has filtered into the minds of policy makers in Washington. 'The US now believes in an Islamic conspiracy theory... like the red menace of the cold war era, the green peril is determining the legitimacy of western values and threatening the national security interests of US.'[193] Pakistan is very concerned that

---

[192] In this context, see Ur-Rehman 1999.
[193] Huntington 1993.

the Western media and think tanks have raised the bogey of Islamic fundamentalism.[194] It argues that Islamic movements vouch for freedom of the people and want social justice and economic well-being of their societies. Their prime interest is to preserve their cultural and economic interests, and within this framework, develop their relation with other countries based on mutual respect and recognition of each others' interests. Pakistan also recognises that Muslims lack a common goal and are pitched against each other. Such a decline is attributed to lack of tolerance for fresh ideas. Another factor has been that the masses have not been integrated into the decision-making process. Besides, in many Islamic states, the process of political development and institution building could either not take firm roots or is not complete. Many Islamic intellectuals think that Muslims have sunk into the quagmire of ignorance and Western ideas have penetrated Muslim societies, resulting in the loss of a spirit of inquiry; this has caused alienation and disintegration of fellow feeling among Muslims as against the sense of belonging to the *Ummah* which integrates Muslims.

Islam, no doubt, is a significant political player in all Muslim societies, but much depends on history and the nature of political movements, the character of the state, levels of indigenous institutionalisation, democratic experience (if any) and the degree of political institution building. Orientalists perceive two distinct, mutually contradictory schools of thought within the society in Pakistan, namely, 'Westernised modernists' and 'traditional fundamentalists'. This comes across instantly when one reads Ahmed, Bolitho, Callard, Stephens and Williams.[195] These scholars are portrayed as 'liberal' while the 'traditional fundamentalists' by implication are 'retrogressive' and 'fanatic'. South Asian scholars tend to disagree and call this compartmentalisation simplistic: as it does not 'take into account the complex and dynamic interplay of local religious, cultural and ethnic factors ... [it] cannot satisfactorily

---

[194] Samuel Huntington, Martin Kramer, Daniel Pipes, Steven Emerson, Barry Rubin and Bernard Lewis view Islam and Islamic culture as anti-modern, anti-West and anti-democracy, and by implication, a threat to Western ideas. See Lewis 1993.

[195] Ahmed 1967, 1969; Bolitho 1954; Callard 1957; Stephens 1963; and Williams 1962.

illuminate the complexity of South Asian Islam, they may end in obfuscating it.'[196]

In the case of Pakistan, one tends to forget that a vast majority of the Sunni *Ulema, Mashaikh* (mystics) and Sufis do not participate in politics. Their interpretation of Islam is based on local cultural tradition, which defines their role in the realm of soul religion, and not on issues of political power. Their understanding of Islam separates the religious sphere from the material world of political power. It is the political parties that have played a larger role in the implementation of the Shariah and transforming Pakistan into an Islamic state. Nawaz Sharif too, when he was in power before the coup, sought to impose the Shariah.[197]

General Zia-ul-Haq was really the first ruler in Pakistani history to make the Islamisation of society the state's official programme. A pendulum swing theory helps us situate a person like General Zia in the right context—he was an orthodox devout Muslim who regularly visited Saudi Arabia, abstained from alcohol, laid a great deal of emphasis on the teaching of Urdu, called the National Assembly *Majlis-e-shoora* (ideally good Muslims), termed the *Ummah* as supreme and wished to firmly draw boundaries around Islam.

General Zia's military government defined its mission as 'laying down the foundations of the Islamic system in Pakistan.' Rizvi succinctly says that he 'argued for the expansion of the role of the military in the polity by declaring time and again that the military not merely protected the geographical frontiers of the country, but was also the guardian of the "ideological frontiers".'[198] Zia worked in close cooperation with the *Ulema* and the Jama'at-i-Islami. He was able to create a network of state-sponsored institutional structures to translate the norms of the Shariah into public policies. Amongst the most significant was the establishment of a Federal Shariah Court and the revision of school textbooks to reflect an Islamic bias. 'He went on to denigrate parties, opposition parties, elections manifestos etc. as unknown in Islam ... the Islamic fundamentalists supported him in his attempts to build an alternative political system in the name of Islam.'[199] Over the centuries,

[196] Ahmed 1986: 9.
[197] See Mumtaz et al. (2002) for a broad overview on why linkages between economic strategies and outcomes have been fortuitous.
[198] Rizvi 2000: 180.
[199] Bahadur 1998: 73.

many small juridical schools, sects and doctrines also emerged among the Muslims. 'One sees a perpetual conflict among some of these sects over religious issues ... they spend more time in proving themselves on the true path of Islam and how their sects have gone astray than focussing on unifying themes of common faith.'[200] Hasan-Askari Rizvi says this 'was an attempt on the part of the military regime to cope with the legitimacy crisis which had been accentuated with the postponement of the elections and the expansion of the goals of the coup.'[201] Nawaz Sharif in April 1991 complemented this by introducing the Shariah Bill that provided a series of legislative and administrative steps to Islamise education, bureaucracy, the legal system, the mass media, the economy and the overall affairs of the state.[202]

The coming of the Zia regime in Pakistan and his Islamisation policies to gain legitimacy, the entry of Soviet troops and the subsequent Afghan *jihad* against the Soviet troops and Pakistan's involvement in the Afghanistan war—all these factors contributed to the sudden growth of the *madrassas* all through the 1980s and the 1990s. There are no official figures, but it is estimated that there are more than 15,000 *madrassas* in Pakistan. Since this figure was a mere 1,745 in 1979, the growth has been significant. These *madrassas* conform to different faiths, such as *Brelvi, Deobandi, Ahle hadith, Ahle tashi*, etc. For instance, in Punjab alone, there are around 970 *Deobandi*, 1,200 *Brelvi*, 100 *Ahle tashi* and 170 *Ahle hadith madaris*.[203] These schools also have their own political leanings. For instance, many religious scholars belong to the factions of Maulana Fazlur Rahman and Maulana Samiul Haq of the Jama'at-e-Ulama-e-Islam. This adherence to different faiths, the Shia–Sunni divide, and the divergence in political support and patronage prevent these *madrassas* from becoming a monolithic influence.

---

[200] Baksh-Rais 1999: 323.

[201] Rizvi 2000: 170–73. Rizvi further says, 'Once the elections were pushed to the background and the accountability of the ousted regime was initiated, Islamisation was employed as the raison dètre of the continuation of martial law.'

[202] Orthodox Islam is represented by the Sunni *Ulema* who are regarded as guardians of the Sunnah of the Prophet and the socio-religious institutional structures developed under the guidance of the classical jurists. See *The Oxford Encyclopaedia of the Modern Islamic World* 1995: 293.

[203] *The News International* 1999e.

One only needs to take a look at various sentences in the 12 January 2002 speech of Pakistani President, General Musharraf where he said,

> There are some negative aspects of some *madrassas* ... I know that some of these promote negative thinking and propagate hatred and violence ... we must ask what direction are we being led into by these extremists? ... [W]e must check abuse of mosques and *madrassas* and they must not be used for spreading political and sectarian pre-judices ... if any *madrassa* is found indulging in extremism, sub-version, militant activity or possessing any types of weapons, it will be closed.[204]

Coming straight from the Pakistani president, these words provide in a nutshell the ground situation in Pakistan on the *madrassa* education system. It is widely believed that *madrassas* have been breeding grounds for Islamic terrorism for a long time, while also preaching hatred, leading to an increasingly communalised society.

There is a view, particularly in India, that *madrassas* primarily have *jihadi* literature in their curriculum and their main objective is the teaching and preaching of *jihad* with a purpose of producing 'holy warriors'. This is true of some of the *madrassas*, but not all. According to the Human Rights Commission of Pakistan's report, about one-third of these schools provide military training to its students.[205] Several of these institutions also send students to fight in Kashmir and Afghanistan.[206] There are instances where students have been sent to participate in the Afghan war without the know-ledge of their parents.[207] But it is wrong to presume that all the *madrassas* advocate *jihad* and make its students *jihadis*.

These are some of the influencing variables on the choices in Pakistan's foreign policy. The kind of personality and the form of the government in power often determines the final choice of out-comes. Often fringe elements in Pakistani society seek to give Islamist colour to the nuclearisation process. The Pakistani army too has

---

[204] Musharraf 2002b.
[205] Human Rights Commission of Pakistan 1998.
[206] Ibid.
[207] There was an instance where a 13-year-old student was sent to Afghanistan and the father had to move court, which issued notices to the head of the institute, the police and the concerned ministries to bring his child back (Ibid.).

large sections that are staunch Islamic, a leftover of the time of General Zia who consider any conflict scenario with India to be a holy war. There also exists a strong *jihadi* flavour from the non-state actors who in their acts of subversion undermine the stability of the region. Needless to add, they find big support in the Pakistani army which has high stakes in the foreign policy choices that Pakistan makes, especially with regard to Kashmir, India and the nuclear option. Additionally, the army has ensured a role for itself in almost all walks of life from the public to the private sectors. So even if there is a democratically elected government in power, the army is likely to hold all reigns in the state and society even if the generals do not directly head decision making.[208] The army will continue to wield the kind of power it presently does.

PAKISTAN AND OIC

The Organisation of the Islamic Conference (OIC) brings together all the Muslim countries of the world on a single platform. There are 56 member states and four observers. Pakistan is a founder member. The OIC has extended strong and unanimous support to Pakistan on important issues. It has held three Kashmir-related summits and passed ministerial resolutions which express the Islamic world's solidarity with the Kashmiri people in their struggle for the right of self-determination. Kashmiri leaders have been invited to OIC summits and ministerial conferences and have addressed these gatherings. The OIC has also provided financial support to Kashmiris. Relations with the Islamic world are the cornerstone of Pakistan's foreign policy: the Chairman of the OIC Standing Committee on Scientific and Technological Cooperation is headquartered in Islamabad. The Islamic Chamber of Commerce and Industry also has its head offices in Pakistan. Other OIC offices located in Pakistan include the Islamic Communication Union and the Executive Committee of the Parliamentary Union of the OIC Member States in which Pakistan holds the chair. Former Foreign Minister, Mr Sharif-ud-Din Pirzada served as the Secretary General of the OIC from 1984 to 1988. Pakistan also hosted the social sessions of the OIC Foreign Ministers' Conference in 1980 and in

---

[208] On how these parameters of governance have changed, see Rizvi 2000: ch. 11.

1984. To commemorate 50 years of the independence of Pakistan, an extraordinary session of the Islamic Summit was held in Islamabad on 23 March 1997. At the behest of Pakistan, the OIC Conference of Foreign Ministers, in its session in Burkina Faso in June 1999, decided to appoint a special envoy in Kashmir. After the nuclear tests, OIC countries criticised India for initiating an arms race and linked it to the Kashmir issue. Pakistan has maintained special relations with the countries of the Middle East and has emphasised its cultural, religious, strategic, historical and economic solidarity with the region. Pakistan has supported Arab causes, starting with the de-colonisation process to Palestinian self-determination. Many Islamic states have extended economic assistance when Pakistan faced sanctions after its nuclear tests—several Arab states sent their special envoys to Pakistan as an expression of solidarity.[209]

The idea of Islamic solidarity, although hazy, has always been there since the emergence of Islam. There were several Islamic conferences in the period between the two world wars. But Pakistan's obsession with India has been so great that it became an active member of several military pacts guided by the US like CENTO and SEATO. Pakistan found itself confronting the Arab world, particularly during the Arab–Israeli Suez War in 1956. The OIC did not exist then. It was only after the burning of the Al Aqsa Mosque in Jerusalem and the Islamic Summit, called on the initiative of King Hasan of Morocco at Rabat, that the Organisation of Islamic Conference (OIC) was formed. The objective of the OIC was Islamic solidarity and consolidation.

The track record of the OIC shows that it has not been able to fulfil its objectives of Islamic solidarity and consolidation of economic, social, cultural and scientific cooperation. Within the Islamic world there are states ranging from the oil-rich Gulf countries to lawless Somalia with states like Pakistan in the middle. One of the problems confronting the OIC states is that many of them who have capital to invest have not invested in other OIC member states but have chosen to go West. Moreover, the OIC has not been able to influence its member states. A good example is the Iran–Iraq war, which could not be brought to an end by the efforts of the OIC.

---

[209] From the website of the Pakistan Ministry of Foreign Affairs, http://www.forisb.org/fpolicy.htm, accessed on 13 May 2000.

In fact, many of the Arabs states that were actively supporting Iraq deepened these divisions. Afghanistan's failure as a state, where *mujahideen* groups backed by different Arab states constantly fight among themselves, is another instance.

Despite the OIC's apparent deficiencies, Pakistan still looks to it in its relationship with India. At every OIC meet Pakistan raises the Kashmir issue and the OIC customarily passes a resolution. But the forum itself needs to reorient its goals and priorities. Independently, Pakistan has been in touch with various countries that have strong Islamic linkages. After the coup, General Musharraf went on a tour of the South-east Asian nations.[210] Iran is one country that has geo-strategic importance for the region. After the Islamic revolution in 1979, there were many changes in Iran's foreign policy. It withdrew from CENTO. The fall of the Shah regime and the emergence of Khomeini's Islamic regime helped Pakistan develop closer ties with Iran. This was happening when the Islamic world had realised the importance of the black gold—oil. General Zia's enthusiastic Islamisation programme further warmed ties between the two countries. In 1989, Iran and Pakistan signed an agreement on cooperation in defence industry and military training. With help from Iran, Pakistan has continuously raised the Kashmir issue in the OIC. Over the years, Pakistan has played the Islamic card to mobilise support of the oil-rich Arab countries to gather funds and arms for the various *mujahideen* groups. This has serious implications for issues of stability in this region as these groups have in the past proven to be a destabilising force.

Pak–US Relations

Soon after its birth, Pakistan approached the US, and the two countries have maintained close ties since then despite many ups and downs. Being insecure about India, Pakistan became a party to the US-led CENTO in its quest for security, while the US saw Pakistan as a geo-strategic ally. Gen Ayub Khan's rule (1958–69) was the high point in US–Pakistan relations. Pakistan was 'the most allied ally' then. In the initial decades of their relationship, besides military hardware, much-needed financial aid and technical help was

---

[210] The chief executive visited Malaysia and Thailand, besides stopping in Singapore.

received. Many US ambassadors like Oakley, Farland, Sidney and Sobers played important roles in shaping its domestic relations.

The US was aware that Pakistan put together an enrichment plant in 1978. Armed with the Foreign Assistance Act it decided to cut off aid to Pakistan. It was the Afghan crisis that changed their relations perceptively and the Symington Amendment, brought about in December 1981, opened the floodgates of assistance. Pakistan played the role of an ally to perfection in the long drawn-out Afghan crisis when the US pumped in arms through Pakistan to help the Afghan militants. Within days of the Soviet invasion and without even consulting Pakistan, President Jimmy Carter announced an offer of $400 million in economic and military assistance .... After President Ronald Reagan succeeded him in 1981, the US offered a new package of loans and grants amounting to $3 billion over five years.[211] It was at this time that Pakistan sought an American guarantee in the event of a Soviet or a Soviet backed Indian attack on Pakistan. 'It asked for the upgradation of the 1959 executive Agreement on Defence co-operation into a binding treaty.'[212] After the 1965 war Pakistan had expected a higher level of US assistance, which was unavailable. This weighed heavily on the minds of decision makers in Islamabad, so when American assurances were made again, their 'credibility and durability' was low.[213] On 18 April 1996, the US President approved the transfer of equipment to Pakistan that were sanctioned before 1 October 1990. 'The basic non-proliferation provision affecting Pakistan is Section 101 of the Arms Export Control Act. This provision forbids aid to countries that acquire nuclear enrichment facilities that are not under the inspection and safeguards system of the International Atomic Energy Agency (IAEA).'[214] To break this deadlock, Pakistan's foreign minister, quoting Benazir Bhutto, said that the government was considering US proposals for 'non-intrusive' means of verification since 'it was not producing enriched uranium and that it would consider "technical proposals" to that effect.'[215] The fact is, as most Pakistanis acknowledge, Pakistan no longer retains the geo-political and geo-strategic advantage as it had in the past.

[211] Sattar 1997.
[212] Ibid.: 120–21.
[213] Ibid.: 121.
[214] Ibid.: 121.
[215] Ibid.: 121.

It was used during the Afghanistan crisis and all through the 1980s, and when the Cold War ended, Pakistan also gradually became one of the many pawns at the crossroads of the post-Cold War era. Pakistan's clandestine network to acquire nuclear technology continued all through the 1980s and the US turned a blind eye to this. US-based think tanks also raised this issue a few times.[216] With the Soviet Union pulling out of Afghanistan and Pakistan no longer as important as it was previously, the US cut off arms sales to Pakistan from October 1990 because 'the President could not make a required annual certification to Congress under section 620 (E) of the Foreign Assistance Act, the so called "Pressler Amendment", that Pakistan did not possess a nuclear explosive device.'[217]

A crest in the relations between the two states was 10 rounds of dialogue involving Sartaj Aziz and Strobe Talbott. Some of the benchmarks in this dialogue were nuclear and missile restraint, CTBT, FMCT and export controls. On the issue of 'nuclear and missile restraint', Pakistan proposed a strategic regime to India with a view to maintaining nuclear deterrence at the minimum level. 'Pakistan has made it clear that any restraints will have to be mutual with India.'[218] On CTBT, Pakistan has no objection to signing the treaty, but has made the provision of lifting of sanctions and of including India as a signatory to the treaty. This is unlikely to happen in the near future. On the FMCT, although Pakistan is participating in the negotiations in the CD, 'the negotiations on the question of existing stockpiles are a special concern for Pakistan.'[219] On export controls the only official statement was that 'our assurances to the

---

[216] To quote a Carnegie Endowment report: 'In sum, on several occasions, the US has backed away from enforcing the sanctions of an aid cut off against Pakistan, permitting the waiver of the Symington Amendment in 1981 and again in 1987, waiving the Glenn Amendment by Presidential Action in 1987, declining to react to production of highly enriched uranium in 1986 and 1987, to avoid suspension of assistance even though Pakistan had acquired the wherewithal for its first nuclear device, and waiving the Solarz Amendment in early 1988, despite finding that Pakistan had attempted to smuggle material out of the US to be used in the manufacture of a nuclear explosive device (Carnegie Task Force 1988: 4).

[217] US Congress 1996.

[218] See the Pakistani government's Ministry of Foreign Affairs website at http://www.forisb.org/fpolicy.htm, accessed on 13 May 2000.

[219] Ibid.

world on the export of sensitive technologies have always been categorical.'[220]

It can be argued that Pakistan's position on some of these benchmarks exhibits consistency, like linking CTBT to India's signature; yet one comes across a paucity of debate. The CTBT relates to testing. It is up to Pakistan to decide if it needs more tests to refine its weapons, or whether the 'credible deterrent' it is trying to construct will be credible, so that the present stock of weapons can meet its security needs. Either way, until the US revives the treaty, the CTBT will continue to remain in a limbo. The FMCT is about cutting off the production of fissile material, so what Pakistan is going to negotiate for here seems clouded in confusion. Over the last couple of decades, Pakistan has imported as well as exported sensitive technologies; so the negotiating position of a country that has such a poor record on this issue seems nuclear.

While the US had welcomed the Lahore Declaration that was signed between India and Pakistan in February 1999, a devastating blow to the spirit of Lahore was dealt when Pakistan-backed *mujahideens* crossed the LoC in Kargil heights overlooking the town of Kargil and the highway connecting Srinagar to Leh. Although this operation was a good tactical move, strategically it left Pakistan diplomatically isolated with almost the whole world condemning Pakistan. The US government reacted vigorously with repeated phone calls and shuttle diplomacy. Nawaz Sharif rushed to Washington, and on 4 July signed the Washington agreement,[221] where he agreed to 'urge' the *mujahideen* to withdraw and in return the US would take 'personal interest' in the Kashmir problem. Following the *mujahideen* withdrawal there was a blame game between the army and Nawaz Sharif.

This was followed by the coup of 12 October 1999, which has not helped the international image of Pakistan. Apparently, Nawaz Sharif had an idea of things to come. A couple of months after the 1999 Washington agreement, he sent his brother Shahbaz Sharif to Washington to convey the threat of an army coup.[222] Dennis Kux

[220] Ibid.

[221] Dennis Kux, citing a participant at the talks, writes, 'Nawaz Sharif seemed like a drowning man looking for a miracle, hoping that somehow the United States would bail him out'. See Kux 2001: 353.

[222] Ibid.: 354.

writes, 'after he pressed for a US warning against a military take-over, the State Department issued such a warning.'[223] President Clinton's visit—a brief four hour stopover on 25 March 2000—did not help either, as was evident from the body language of the President who, it is reported, did not shake hands with General Musharraf. Many Pakistanis were not pleased that after more than three de-cades a US President came to Pakistan and stayed five days in India. The reaction to President Clinton's speech in Pakistan was a mixed one: some thought that his address was thoughtful and 'elderly' advice, while many others disagreed with his long list of policy prescriptions, even though a carefully worded speech made several references to Quad-i-Azam Mohammed Ali Jinnah. As Dennis Kux writes,

> although the substance of his message was blunt, he neither lectured nor scolded Musharraf .... He argued that Pakistan would benefit by lowering the temperature on Kashmir, by reining in terrorist groups, by pressing the Taliban to be more forthcoming on bin Laden and on peace talks, and by understanding non-proliferation measures.[224]

After the nuclear tests, the US imposed sanctions on Pakistan, just as it had imposed on India, and US–Pakistan relations received further a setback. There was a marginal improvement after the prime minister's meeting with President Clinton in Washington in December 1998, and the notable effect was that sanctions were eased. The remaining sanctions were lifted on 22 September 2001. Exercising the waiver authority granted by the Congress in 1999, on September 2002 President George W. Bush lifted the sanctions imposed on India and Pakistan for their 1998 nuclear tests. The president also removed other sanctions related to Pakistan's devel-opment of nuclear weapons. The decision to lift sanctions on Pakistan came in large part due to the cooperation Washington received from Islamabad after the 11 September terrorist attacks on New York and Washington. However, other sanctions imposed after the October 1999 military takeover of Pakistan's democrat-ically elected government prohibit Washington from providing

---

[223] Ibid.: 354.
[224] Ibid.: 357.

most of this assistance.[225] In addition, other sanctions imposed for the receipt of Chinese missile components do not allow certain Pakistani entities to receive US missile and space assistance.[226]

The events of 11 September 2001 brought about a major change in the US policy towards Pakistan. The US immediately looked up to Pakistan to once again provide the frontline status that it did in the 1980s. Geography dictated Pakistan's importance for the US attacks on Afghanistan. A few statements from Washington (like 'with us or against us') left Islamabad facing a Hobson's choice with no option but to support the international coalition. General Musharraf quickly went on national television and addressed his country on his choice of siding with the US. In that speech, he pulled out all the stops citing everything from international law, religious teaching and rational thought to Pakistan's strategic interests in order to persuade them that his decision to support Washington was right. Inevitably, the Indian bogey was brought into service too. Clearly, President Musharraf safeguarded the security of Pakistan, Kashmir and the nuclear programme and also managed to end his international isolation to come across as a popular leader. He also succeeded in obtaining promises of American assistance totalling almost 1 billion dollars.[227]

Commenting on the address, Ayaz Amir wrote, 'surely, a measure of self-serving calculation is involved in the decision General Musharraf has taken on behalf of the nation: a vision of gratitude

---

[225] The military coup sanctions under Section 508 of the Foreign Assistance Act of 1961 still remain in place: (a) adopted in 1988, they prohibit most forms of US economic and military assistance to any country whose elected head of government has been deposed by a military coup; (b) these were imposed in 1999 for the ousting of Pakistan's democratically elected prime minister in a military coup. See Wagner 2001.

[226] Missile sanctions also continue to remain in place under chapter 7 of the Arms Export Control Act, as required by US membership in the Missile Technology Control Regime, a voluntary regime of 33 states that seek to limit missile proliferation. These (a) bar most US missile and space cooperation for at least two years with specified entities for their sale or receipt of ballistic missiles, components, or related technology that could be used to deliver weapons of mass destruction; and (b) were imposed in 2000 on the Pakistani Ministry of Defense and the Space and Upper Atmospheric Commission for its receipt of missile components and technology transfers from China. These were also imposed in 2001 on Pakistan's National Development Complex for its receipt of missile components and technology transfers from China. Ibid.

[227] Zeb 2002.

dollars pouring in, of our debt burden easing, of India being out-smarted, and of Pakistan being treated as [an] honoured ally instead of a country down on its luck.'[228]

General Musharraf wholeheartedly supported the American war machine in humbling the Taliban regime in Afghanistan and expected Pakistan to come out on the side of victory. Rationality dictated that General Musharraf join the international coalition.[229] He allowed the US to use air force bases at Dalbandian, Jacobabad, Pesni and Penjgur. By aligning himself with the global alliance against terror, he avoided the certain diplomatic isolation that would have followed, had he tried being a fence sitter. In doing so, he took on the *jihadi* forces. But with the fall of Kabul on 13 November 2001 and the Northern Alliance entering Kabul, the worst nightmares of ISI and the Government of Pakistan turned true. Pakistan had overestimated its frontline status—it was convinced that this status would give it a virtual veto over the shape of things to come in Afghanistan. If not that, then at least its objections regarding the Northern Alliance would be respected. Nothing like this happened. In fact, it is instructive to recall that among the four reasons General Musharraf cited while justifying Pakistani support of the war, two were associated with protecting the Kashmir cause and 'nuclear assets', the irony no doubt being that the greatest strength (nukes) had turned in a moment of danger into one of its biggest weaknesses. With growing international pressure against killing innocent civilians, defining Kashmir as a freedom struggle may well lead Pakistan to lose ground there as well. Support to the US came at a lot of cost. Voices were increasingly raised against the US role and presence in the region. Pervaiz Iqbal Cheema has pointed out, 'as a consequence of Pakistan's participation in the international coalition against terrorism, it has suffered a lot ... it has experienced severe damage to its economy and creeping division within its society.'[230]

Pakistan needs to strengthen its economy, set its house in order and stop aiding terrorists, besides restoring democracy at the earliest, to have any semblance of a relationship with the US. With the

---

[228] Amir 2001.

[229] In the context of the post-9/11 impact on South Asia, see Banerjee and Kueck 2003.

[230] Cheema 2003: 49.

war against terror on, of which Pakistan is a key ally, it will continue to receive some aid from the US that just about helps the country to remain intact and reform itself.[231] In fact, the aid on which Pakistan has survived all these years seems to have backfired. Western nations are now using this very diplomatic tool to push for policy change in Pakistan. Additionally, Pakistan was never able to generate enough resources to decrease its dependence on aid. This impinges on internal resource generation that has an impact on the nuclear deterrent posture.

INDO-PAK RELATIONS

Carved out of India, in the word Pakistan 'P' stood for the Punjab, 'A' was for the Afghan Frontier or the North-West Frontier Provinces, 'K' represented Kashmir, while 'S' symbolised Sindh and 'Tan' came from Baluchistan. It is among the few states created on purely religious lines. Even within Pakistan, there were 'those who anticipated Pakistan's sudden demise; some among them had even plotted its return to mother India.'[232] Immediately after the bitter partition, Pakistani tribesmen invaded Kashmir, which had legally acceded to India. The first war between Pakistan and India over Kashmir broke out and laid the foundations of decades of rivalry. '[T]he war over Kashmir crystallised and deepened the bitterness, the suspicion, and the rivalry between the subcontinent's two most important actors.'[233] Pakistan had another war with India in 1965 and then again in 1971, which led to the dismemberment of Pakistan, a number of crises in 1984, 1986–87, 1990, 1998, the Kargil conflict in 1999 and the crisis following the attack on the Indian Parliament attack on 13 December 2001.

Indo-Pak conflicts have largely focused on Kashmir, which has remained a bone of contention between the two countries. Pakistan believes that India has not yet reconciled to its independent entity and entertains a hidden agenda to destroy Pakistan. This explains the obsession of the ruling elite with purported Indian hegemonic designs. Moreover, the powerful army 'wields considerable power and is capable of subverting any improvement in India–Pakistan

---

[231] Tellis 2000b.
[232] Ziring 1997: 96.
[233] Ibid.: 95.

relations to preserve the privileged position of the armed forces.'[234] This could be one explanation for the Kargil conflict, which occurred after the Lahore process had been initiated.

Pakistani claims to Kashmir are premised on the predominantly Muslim population of the valley. But during the partition, a greater number of Muslims decided to stay back in India rather than go to Pakistan, and second, with the loss of East Pakistan, which has a predominantly Muslim population, the argument that religion is a binding force loses credence.[235]

One of the few disputes that Pakistan and India have amicably resolved has been through the Indus Water Treaty of 1960. With mediation by the World Bank, the treaty was signed in September 1960, wherein the waters of the three Eastern rivers (Beas, Ravi and Sutlej) were allotted for use by India and the waters of the Western rivers (Indus, Jhelum and Chenab) were allotted for Pakistan.

Currently, the key foreign policy objectives of Pakistan include:

- Safeguarding vital security and geo-strategic interests, including Kashmir.
- Promoting Pakistan as a dynamic, progressive, moderate and democratic Islamic country.
- Creating a macro-political framework for the pursuit of economic and social interests abroad.
- Consolidating commercial and economic interests.[236]

Since 1988, Pakistan has been engaged in a proxy war in Kashmir and has linked this issue with the nuclear issue, thereby successfully projecting Kashmir as a nuclear flashpoint.[237] During the 1990s, Pakistan also made several bilateral proposals knowing fully well that India would not accept them. This resulted in projecting the regional hegemonic image of India. Some of these proposals included a five-power regional conference, including Pakistan, US, Russia, India and China. India rejected this. India also rejected the proposal of mutual inspections by General Zia in 1981 that was reiterated in 1984. The only successful agreement reached was on

---

[234] Rizvi 1993: 86.
[235] For the finest studies on Kashmir, see Gupta 1966; Lamb 1966.
[236] Government of Pakistan 2004.
[237] Ibid.

non-attack of each others' nuclear installations which was signed in 1988. A no-first-use agreement has been dismissed by Pakistan.[238]

The relations reached an all-time low in the aftermath of the nuclear tests in May 1998. On 28 May 1998, a day after Pakistan matched its neighbour India with five nuclear detonations, the then Pakistani Foreign Minister, Gohar Ayub Khan declared Pakistan a nuclear weapons state. Within hours of testing its nuclear devices, Pakistan's president declared a state of emergency, citing threats of 'external aggression'. Khan said Pakistan was on high alert the night prior to its nuclear testing, fearing an imminent attack by India on its nuclear installations. As a result, Pakistan scrambled its air force, contacted the ambassadors representing the five permanent members of the UN Security Council and India's ambassador to Pakistan. He said, Pakistan had 'concrete evidence' that India had armed several jet fighters with bombs that it believed were meant for its nuclear facilities. The official said that Pakistan believes the threat is reduced, not necessarily because of the testing, but because India has lost the element of surprise.[239] The Pakistani President, Rafiq Tarar also voiced a similar sentiment. It was carried by the state-run news agency (PTV). He did not identify the aggressor, but Pakistan accused India of threatening to attack its nuclear installations.[240]

According to one account, on 27 May 1998, Pakistan's director-general of military operations (DGMO) in the General Headquarters, Rawalpindi, made a series of phone calls.[241] According to Saudi intelligence, Israeli fighter jets were moving from 'Chenai' in India towards the Pakistani border.[242] Reports said the Israeli planes were tasked with destroying Pakistani nuclear capability. The DGMO said Pakistan was just seven hours away from conducting its first-ever nuclear test—and the Israelis and Indians wanted to ensure that the test would never take place.[243] Chairman, Joint Chiefs of

[238] Shahi et al. 1999.

[239] Transcript available at http://www.cnn.com/WORLD/asiapcf/9805/29/Pakistan.declaration/, acessed on 21 October 2002.

[240] Transcript available at http://www.cnn.com/WORLD/asiapcf/9805/28/Pakistan.update/, accessed on 21 October 2002.

[241] Jones 2002.

[242] If the city mentioned is Chennai (earlier Madras), any fighter jet flying from there to Pakistan would have had to refuel three times and would have taken no less than four hours to reach Pakistan.

[243] Jones 2002.

Staff, Gen Jahangir Karamat scrambled F-16 fighter planes and sent them to protect the test site in Baluchistan. Diplomats in foreign missions were informed and in New York, Pakistan's permanent representative to the UN, Ahmed Kamal informed the Secretary General Kofi Annan and the Security Council and quickly went on air via the CNN, accusing New Delhi of planning to launch an attack.[244]

The observation by Bruce Riedel, a senior US official, further substantiates this:

> After a few weeks (of the Indian 11 and 13 May tests) of agonizing, Sharif had gone forward with his own tests citing as a flimsy excuse an alleged Israel plot to destroy Pakistan's nuclear facilities in collusion with India. (I had the Israeli Chief of Staff deny categorically to the Pakistani Ambassador in Washington any such plan the night before the tests but that fact mattered little to Islamabad.)[245]

It is precisely this kind of misinformation that breeds misperception. As Owen Bennett Jones has written, 'the inability of senior decision-makers to discuss the reality of the supposed danger openly raises serious questions about Pakistan's command and control capability.'[246]

Following the nuclear tests, the Indian Prime Minister Atal Behari Vajpayee travelled by bus to Lahore, leading to the Lahore Declaration in February 1999.[247] Following Kargil, India felt betrayed. Although domestically the media portrayed a great victory for Pakistan, internationally it stood isolated, with its allies asking it to respect the LoC. Events such as the coup of 12 October 1999 further froze ties with Pakistan. Following the attack on the Indian Parliament, the 10-month stand-off had many moments during which the two countries came near armed conflict. But the larger picture is that infiltration of *jihadi* groups, such as the Laskar-e-Toiba and the Jaish-e-Muhammed into Kashmir and other parts of India, has 'created an alternative military apparatus that Islamabad funds and supplies but can't fully control.'[248] India feels

---

[244] Ibid.
[245] See Riedel 2002.
[246] Jones 2002.
[247] Text of the Lahore Declaration may be seen in *The Hindu* 1999a.
[248] Ali 2002: 301.

that until such instruments of subversion are curtailed, normal-
isation of relations would merely be cosmetic.

SINO-PAK RELATIONS

Soon after independence, Pakistan's quest for security resulted in
its close cooperation with China. 'Speaking at the UN General Assembly in October 1970, President Yahya Khan described friendly
co-operation with China as the "cornerstone" of Pakistan's policy.'[249]
Soon after the 1965 war with India it was China that provided equipment for two divisions of the army as well as MIG aircraft for its air
force. It also gave $60 million for development assistance in 1965,
a further $40 million in 1969 and $200 million for the next five-year
plan. With China, itself a low income developing country, this assistance was generous and there was emphasis on the transfer of
technology to help Pakistan achieve self-reliance.[250] After the 1970
visit of Yahya Khan to China, the Chinese reiterated their support
on Kashmir while Pakistan reciprocated by terming Taiwan as an
inalienable part of China.[251] During the 1970s and all through the
1980s, Chinese assistance to the Pakistani nuclear agenda, and in
the 1990s to the missile programme has been well documented. In
June 1998, after the South Asian nuclear tests, a Congressional
Research Service report said, 'China continues to supply missile,
nuclear and chemical technology consistent with non-proliferation
goals particularly to Pakistan and Iran.'[252] Various US organisations, including the Federation of American Scientists and the
Center for Nonproliferation Studies, have done a lot of work docu-
menting the Chinese transfer of sensitive technology to Pakistan
over the last couple of decades.[253]

In fact, the US imposed sanctions on China and Pakistan twice—
in 1990, and again in 1993.Under its non-proliferation agenda, the
US tried its best to put pressure on China 'to limit its exports of
nuclear materials, technology, and missiles, including preventing

---

[249] Sattar 1997: 97.
[250] Ibid.: 97.
[251] Ibid.
[252] US Congress 1998.
[253] See the websites of the Federation of American Scientists: http://www.
fas.org, and the Center for Nonproliferation Studies: http://www.cns.miis.edu.

such assistance to Pakistan ... China has agreed to subscribe to NPT restrictions on transfers of nuclear technology and materials, but evidence continues to accumulate that it has violated these commitments.'[254] In an effort to improve its strained relations with the US, China made concerted efforts from 1995 onwards to abide by the non-proliferation norm and has manifestly not helped Pakistan. During the Kargil crisis, the then Pakistan Foreign Minister, Sartaj Aziz came to Delhi for talks, but just before that he flew to Beijing, where he was apparently told to respect the line of control and seek a bilateral solution.

After Clinton's visit to the subcontinent there was an increase in the diplomatic isolation of Pakistan, with long-time allies such as China and Turkey not wanting to engage Pakistan in talks. This was broken only with the US Afghan campaign. Once the campaign got over, this isolation returned. One only hopes that this diplomatic isolation will give way to increased cooperation that will be beneficial to the rebuilding of Pakistan, thus making it a stable and prosperous state.

CTBT, NPT and FMCT

General and complete disarmament was a concept that was introduced in the UN in the early 1950s. Indian disarmament and arms control policies are considered reactive—they are linked to a time-bound framework for global nuclear disarmament. Pakistan's policies are no less reactive—they are invariably linked to whatever India does.

Pakistan officially

> remains firmly committed to the goal of achieving general and complete disarmament, elimination of weapons of mass destruction or the regulations of small arms, Pakistan believes that the core, principle and objective of disarmament should be to assure equal security for all states, regardless of their size and status.[255]

[254] US Congress 1996.

[255] From Pakistani Ministry of Foreign Affairs website, available at http://www.forisb.org/un3html, accessed on 17 May 2000.

In the mid-1970s, soon after the 1974 PNE, Pakistan made a proposal in the UN to keep South Asia free of nuclear weapons. India objected to this, as it saw its own security imperilled by American presence in the island of Diego Garcia in the Indian Ocean. With reports coming in of proliferation of sensitive technologies, there seemed no possibility of keeping South Asia free of nuclear weapons.[256] Pakistan argues that all these proposals have not elicited any positive response from India. These proposals seem to be only designed for bilateral purposes. The timing of these proposals is important—some of them were made in the 1970s and 1980s when Pakistan enjoyed the security patronage of the US. In the 1990s, and especially after the nuclear tests, these proposals increasingly became linked to projecting Kashmir as a nuclear flashpoint. It can of course be argued that there has been consistency in Pakistan's position, as it has always been linked to India's policies. Pakistanis believe that the Indian weapons programme is primarily directed against them and not against China. With the American government passing the Pressler Amendment to cut off military aid to Pakistan, it thought a few weapons would supplement its conventional forces to bring it at par with the larger conventional Indian force.

Domestically, the army seems to hold a veto on key security issues, defence expenditure, disarmament and arms control and Kashmir. Any change in these policies is impossible without the support of the army. It is possible that a nation that has thrived on anti-India rhetoric made proposals which it knew India would reject anyway. Another contradiction has been Pakistan's approach to arms control treaties. It acceded to the Partial Test Ban Treaty in 1963, but ratified it only in 1987, by which time the treaty had become irrelevant.

Pakistan has no real objections to being a part of the NPT per se. It has in fact participated in the NPT review meetings as an observer.

---

[256] Some of the other proposals made by Pakistan included 'a joint Pakistan–India declaration renouncing the acquisition or manufacture of nuclear weapons, mutual inspection by Pakistan and India of each other's facilities, simultaneous adherence to the NPT by both countries and acceptance of IAEA safeguards, the conclusion of bilateral or regional test ban treaty, and a proposal for a meeting to include Pakistan and India along with China, Russia and the US to discuss conventional arms control and confidence building measures as well as the promotion of nuclear restraint to prevent possible nuclear escalation in South Asia' (Ibid.).

But it has the potential to ruin the NPT regime by selling nuclear technology,[257] as it is not under any legal commitment to desist from assisting, encouraging or inducing[258] any non-nuclear weapons state to manufacture or otherwise acquire nuclear weapons. As far as the NPT is concerned, Pakistan initially voted for the resolution, commending the treaty unlike India. Now Pakistan is a *de facto* nuclear weapons state and can accede to the NPT, but only as a non-nuclear weapons state. The danger to the NPT regime may come from Pakistan exporting sensitive technologies to willing buyers in the Arab states, in case it is pushed too far by the dual pressure of sanctions and trying to match India's weaponisation programme.

The CTBT is about testing new weapon designs. It remains to be seen if Pakistan wants to retain the designs it tested in 1998 or wants to improve those designs. In mid-May 2000, there were reports that Pakistan might be planning another test. An article by Khurshid Ahmed argues that there are at least four defence needs.[259] Obviously, he believes that there is likelihood of Pakistan needing more tests in the future.

---

[257] In a full-page newspaper advertisement, the Pakistani Commerce Ministry has published an application for the export of 11 radioactive substances, including depleted uranium and tritium, and 17 types of equipment, including nuclear power reactors, nuclear research reactors and reactor control systems. See *The Hindustan Times* 2000b. Pakistan issued a denial of this advertisement two days later.

[258] Mahalingam 1999. 'Intelligence sources believe that North Korea has been bartering metals, missile components and technology and materials from Pakistan .... Ghauri is said to be a replica of North Korea's No-dong Missile, which uses liquid fuel. Shaheen is said to be based on the solid fuel technology of the Tae-po-dong missile system of North Korea ... it is understood that North Korea has been clandestinely pursuing its nuclear weapons programme and scouting for technology and materials while Pakistan has been on the lookout for metals for critical technological areas of military co-operation.'

[259] He says, 'In addition to the experiments for peaceful uses, for which we cannot forsake our right at any cost: (*a*) Weaponisation without which deterrence is just an imaginary concept; (*b*) Miniaturization through which precision can be acquired. This is essential for making the whole project cost-effective. Over and above all, the nuclear weapons can be made target-oriented and the effects of radioactivity can be minimized; (*c*) Development in the Thermo Nuclear front for its importance in a close competition; and (*d*) Harmonisation between nuclear weapons and the delivery system (Ahmed 2000).

As in most nuclear weapons states, Pakistan too has three schools of thought: the hawks or maximalists, who would like more testing, better weapons and delivery systems; the pragmatists, who want a more refined deterrent and want more testing; and the abolitionists who maintain that 'continued nuclear testing is not required to build and maintain a credible nuclear deterrent for Pakistan vis-à-vis India.'[260] There is also a small but significant group which, at most times, is dismissed as insignificant (even called American agents!), and which says, 'Pakistan must sign the CTBT because it is perfectly clear that Pakistan can never afford to test again.'[261] An argument that has been lost in the din of the coup was that before the US Senate rejected the CTBT, the US was desperate to get a signature from nuclear weapons states to sell the same to the senate. Had Pakistan signed it, it could perhaps have reaped some benefits to help its economy. However, Pakistan's position on the CTBT has also become more flexible. Like India, Pakistan has announced a moratorium after the completion of its test series. Six weeks after the tests, Pakistan officially 'de-linked' its position on the CTBT from the Indian position.[262] But the debate in the strategic community continues to link the Pakistani signing of the CTBT with the Indian signature of the treaty.[263] On 23 September 1998, Prime Minister Sharif signalled a willingness to join the CTBT:

Pakistan has consistently supported the conclusion of a CTBT for over 30 years. We voted for the Treaty when the U.N. General Assembly adopted it in 1996. We have declared a moratorium on further testing; so has India. There is no reason why the two countries cannot adhere to the CTBT. In a nuclearized South Asia, CTBT would have relevance if Pakistan and India are both parties to the Treaty. The Non-Aligned Summit has called for universal adherence to the CTBT, especially by the nuclear weapon states. This demand is consistent with the Treaty's requirement that all nuclear capable states, including India, must adhere to the CTBT before it can come into force. The Pakistani Prime Minister, Nawaz Sharif had told the

---

[260] Ali 1999: 20.

[261] Hoodbhoy 1999b: 56.

[262] 'With a proven capability to establish deterrence, Pakistan's position on the CTBT is no longer linked to our neighbours' (Akram 1998b).

[263] See for instance, Shaikh 2001.

U.N. General Assembly that Pakistan's adherence to the Treaty will take place only in conditions free from coercion or pressure.[264]

The situation has since changed with the US rejection of the treaty in the Senate. Unless the US revives the treaty, it will continue to be shelved and the world can expect to trust the moratorium on future tests from Pakistan.

On FMCT, Pakistan announced its agreement in August 1998 to commence negotiations in the Conference on Disarmament at Geneva for a non-discriminatory, multilateral and effectively verifiable treaty banning the production of fissile materials for nuclear weapons or other nuclear devices. Pakistan hopes that a Fissile Material Treaty 'should not only cut off further production of weapons grade material but also adequately address the issue of existing stockpiles of fissile materials.'[265] On the issue of export controls, Pakistan, which built its nuclear weapons programme on imports from China, has 'unilaterally and irrevocably committed not to transfer sensitive technology, material and equipment to any third country.'[266] One can estimate how tight export controls really are from a report which appeared in the press in early May 2000. According to the report, one Wahid Malik Khan claimed that he had canisters of weapons-grade uranium and plutonium for sale in Pakistan. Many people, including Osama bin Laden, will be interested to know about it.[267]

On the issue of various arms control regimes, the foregoing informs that Pakistani policies will only be reactive to Indian policies. It is fair to assume that Pakistan will stand by its moratorium on nuclear testing unless India tests another nuclear device. It is also conjectured that Pakistan might do a technology demonstration somewhere on its own soil in the event of an extreme provocation from India. One area of concern, especially in the post-9/11 and post-attack on the Indian Parliament phase, has been the physical safety of Pakistan's nuclear assets. Some of these concerns were overplayed,

---

[264] Sharif 1998.

[265] Available at the website of Pakistan's Ministry of Foreign Affairs, at http://www.forisb.org/un3.html, accessed on 17 May 2000.

[266] Ibid.

[267] The Indian Express 2000.

but even at peacetime apprehensions remain about non-state actors laying their hands on fissile stocks. Pakistan would also have to strengthen its export control laws.

❧✠❧

The future of Pakistan as a state and role of military in shaping the state and consolidating the process of nation building[268] will have significant impact on the security architecture of the region in general and on issues of deterrence in particular. With Pakistan having gone overtly nuclear, there are many unresolved dilemmas facing the state and the army. The army has to decide whether to move from its NATO type 'flexible response' strategy to, as the unofficial nuclear doctrine states, the concept of threshold, whereby the nuclear threshold might be crossed if the adversary (India) occupies a large territory or if vital communications are cut.[269] Pakistan believes that deterrence worked in the 1987 and 1990 crisis.[270] There is a belief that India and Pakistan may not fight an all-out war. 'A conventional war between India and Pakistan would probably last three to five weeks, and end in a stalemate. But should Pakistan's forces fare badly, the war might end very differently.'[271] If that happens, Pakistan may want to alter the course of events by using veiled warnings (they may continue during the conflict) and may even detonate a device. On the other hand, if Pakistan strikes first (facing a near impossible diplomatic turn around on Kashmir), Indian retaliation will be a certainty. Even if one argues that there is deterrence at the nuclear level, we have seen that deterrence at one level has in the past, during Kargil, led to breakdown of deterrence at another (conventional) level.

---

[268] As one writer has concluded, 'with neither the political nor the military elite capable of constructing a viable political framework, and the contending political parties and the military bent on ousting the incumbent government by any and all means, Pakistan has swung between civilian and military governments and ... decades of misrule by civilian and military leaders alike have deeply polarised political and civil society, creating deep cleavages over the identity of the state and system of government ...' (Alagappa 2001c: 492).

[269] Shahi et al. 1999.

[270] Ibid. Also see in this context, Hagerty 1993, 1998. For views of South Asian scholars, see Chellaney 1991 and Hussain 1991.

[271] Reiss 1995: 209.

The pressures on shaping the nuclear arsenal are only likely to increase in the years to come, partly due to the political factors of state aspirations, the anti-status quo orientation of Pakistan and the inherent sense of insecurity against India. The strategic factors of research, development and testing of new missiles, foreign acquisitions, the inter-service rivalry and the scientific–military push may, from the Islamabad point of view, continue to shape the deterrent posture. The strategic benefits that accrue from such a posture might seek to attenuate the country's acute geophysical vulnerability, but it is likely to shape substantially any outcome of a face-off with India. Islamabad has no large resource base and the economy at the present state is unable to support an open-ended arms race with India. As has been perceptively noted, this needs 'fundamental transformation in the nature of the Pakistani state which if it occurs successfully, would actually mitigate many of the corrosive forces that currently drive Islamabad's security competition with India.'[272] This was also reflected in a speech made by General Musharraf sometime back.[273]

In either case, much depends on the decision makers on both sides of the border, and if the challenge is to prevent loss of lives and outbreak of conflict, then many issues need to be resolved and many initiatives need to be taken up to ensure deterrence is not under pressure. Pakistan has been ruled by four groups alternatively—the military, the bureaucracy, the feudal lords and the industrial barons. Add to this, the 12 corps commanders and nearly 2,000 landowners who own more than half of the total cultivable land, a cadre of nearly 1,000 officers of the District Management Group and the Police Service of Pakistan and 44 industrial families. Pakistan started out as a secular welfare state and slowly degenerated into a theocratic elitist state, where it is in the interest of the ruling elite to maintain the status quo. The central premise of democracy is a sustained public participation in the process of governance. The roots of democracy lie in egalitarian political, economic and social structures, modernising entrepreneurial elite and economic policies that help build a burgeoning middle class. A judiciary that is independent of the legislative and executive organs, rule of law and checks and balances is also essential.

---

[272] Tellis 2002b.
[273] *Dawn* 2003. General Musharraf was visiting Seoul.

Pakistani political, social and economic structures and the military are still deeply feudal. Given the nature of the state and of the army, the presence of nuclear weapons without requisite filtration process in decision making is less than reassuring.

Understanding well Pakistan's failed experiments with democracy, Amb. Maleeha Lodhi reasoned, 'reform and accountability must come first before we can have a playing field for democracy. I only hope that when it does come back, people won't use it again to loot and plunder the country.'[274] After the coup, journalists and lawyers rushed to point out that though the parliament and the constitution were suspended, they had not been dissolved and the courts and the press were still being allowed to function. Over the last 55 years, Pakistan has sown the seeds of regional inequality, discontent and reaped the harvest of an alternate institutional rule of civilian elite and military bureaucracy. Having survived on constant doses of IMF loans and US aid, Pakistani economy is hollow and FDI is still negligible. Consequently, close to half the budget goes into debt financing. The Musharraf government is currently faced with options it can ill afford to exercise, and yet they are necessary to run the country: To try and restore civilian rule (the option in which he himself may be put behind bars if not sentenced to death for abusing the constitution), launch a crackdown on the corrupt elite groups that control the reins of the government in Islamabad, or under sustained US and Indian pressure try and clamp down on the *jihadi* infrastructure. It is going to be a tightrope for the general. Will he succeed in controlling the forces that helped create the Taliban and fuelled a bitter conflict in Kashmir? Will he be able to clamp down on the radical elements within the establishment that are in favour such low-intensity warfare? The world and India have to be prepared and be ready for the fact that Musharraf might remain in power for a long time.

He could be replaced by another coup, a revolution of sorts, as he tries to take radical steps towards social and economic reforms. Fundamentalism that already has strong roots would intensify, and the challenge the government and such measures would complete the Islamisation of the society. No less significant a contribution may come from the clergy that would want to keep

---

[274] Quoted in Constable 2000: 134.

the Kashmir pot boiling. As long as this continues, an anti-India sentiment will run high. A second path could be another coup by one of the 12 corps commanders, backed by the Sunni clergy (that is, if they iron out their differences). A couple of external factors may have a role in fostering this—Pakistan going the North Korea way—with increased diplomatic isolation and the world community continuing to toe the Indian line on Kashmir. On the other hand, Pakistan might be able to stabilise internally, econom-ically, socially, politically, reach some sort of a tacit understanding with India, presumably on the LoC, and thereby decrease chances of confrontation with India.

Prior to 1977, the factors that motivated young officers being trained in the military institutions were patriotism and their pride as loyal Pakistanis. General Zia, a devout *Deobandi*, changed this and introduced additional motivating factors, including their faith in Islam and their pride in being true Muslims. After 1977, those young officers who passed out started to look upon themselves as not just soldiers of the state but also of Islam. General Zia often made statements like, 'Pakistan and Islam are the names of one and the same thing and any idea or action contrary to this would mean hitting at the very roots of the ideology, solidarity, and integrity of Pakistan.'[275] General Zia faced criticism of sthis as well. Some authors maintain that 'one of the most notable features of Zia's Islamisation programme was that the contents were rich in symbolism but poor in substance.'[276] In fact, during his long tenure General Zia, who ruled longer than any other leader, never succeeded in legitimising his rule.[277] He came closest towards gaining credibility in 1985, and this was ironically the period when he talked the least about Islam.[278]

The military coup of October 1998 provided a setback to the prospects of some form of formal civilian control over Pakistan's nuclear deterrent. The armed forces would anyway have retained operational control under any civilian rule, yet a formalised civilian institutional setting would have provided more space in times of

---

[275] Quoted in Ahmad 1988: 232.

[276] Wilder 1995: 69.

[277] For a broad overview of the military's involvement in governance, see Arif 2001. Arif retired as a four-star general and served as the *de facto* Commander of the Pakistan Army under General Zia.

[278] Wilder 1995.

crisis for stability. The coup did throw some light on the sharp divisions that exist within the military establishment at the level of the corps commander. It further highlighted the institutional schism that exists between the ISI and the army. However, there is no evidence of vertical divisions or decay within the army as an institution. A bigger concern from the Indian point of view is renewed moral, diplomatic and material support by the Pakistani military to the militants fighting the Indian government in Kashmir. This policy has now become the cause of a permanent tension between New Delhi and Islamabad. 'Many more Kargils' that have been promised by Pakistan then do not seem to be far fetched.[279] This increases the chances for limited military engagements that carry the potential of escalation.

The result of this was an increasing Islamisation of the middle and lower ranks of the military and the genesis of a parallel armed force that consisted of the military-trained and equipped *madrassa* cadres, who were not under the control of the state. To strengthen religious motivation, General Zia further inducted religious teachers in large numbers into the education department. He further recognised the certificates that were issued by the *madrassas* as equivalent to university degrees for recruitment to government service. The soldiers and officers from such an Islamised system have become an army within the army that have often joined hands with the parallel force of the religious parties and have immense linkages with the various militant groups fighting in Kashmir, covertly supported by the Pakistani army and headquartered all over North Pakistan, to frustrate the attempts of any ruler who would seek to rein them in. On the issue of the future of religious groups and organisations and their impact on Pakistan's society, the threat of Pakistan getting 'Talibanised' is not as grave as it has been projected, although in the last decade it has grown.[280] These religious parties find it difficult to get any popular mandate for their programmes. So long as the objective of the *jihadi* groups is

---

[279] This issue was raised in the Indian Parliament. See Lok Sabha 2000a. The House was informed that the 'Government are aware of certain readjustments and reinforcements of Pakistani troops on the line of control and in the Sir Creek area. Movement of certain reserve formations from their permanent locations has also been reported.'

[280] In this context, also see Goodson 2000.

limited to Kashmir, they may continue to get popular support in terms of men and material; but if they try to implement any of their versions of 'Islamic' principles, they are likely to be rejected by the society. It was threats from precisely these kinds of groups that made President Musharraf walk a tightrope and issue denials about US troops undertaking 'hot pursuit' of Taliban militia into Pakistan.[281] However, these groups continue to have enormous 'nuisance value' (sometimes much more than that); because of their organisational structure and the easy availability of small arms, they pose a serious threat to the law and order situation inside Pakistan and to the region.[282]

This process is not confined merely to the armed forces, it is further spread to Pakistan's nuclear and scientific community. The younger scientists, who had their early education in the *madrassas* before they moved over to the universities or went abroad for higher education, are now a part of the nuclear establishment. Dr A.Q. Khan, the father of the Pakistani atomic bomb, though educated in Europe, had fraternised with the scientists of Saudi Arabia, Iran and Libya before 1977.

The attempts of General Musharraf or of the earlier democratically elected leaders to control the *madrassas*, disarm the *jihadis*, and pressurise the Taliban to moderate its activities have met with resistance. The Islamised army, the religious parties, militant groups and the scientific–bureaucratic community have joined hands in frustrating any attempt of the leadership to press for peace with India, reduce terrorism in Kashmir or exercise restraint over the nuclear issue.

Many scholars, especially those outside Pakistan, have on and off sounded the alarm of a total collapse of the Pakistani economy. Fortunately for India in particular, and the region in general, this has not happened until now. With the negotiations with IMF in process, it is expected that other major banks and lending institutions

---

[281] For a good discussion on this, see Weaver 2002.

[282] See in this context, Ali 2001. '*Jihadi* organizations have started visiting government schools urging the students to join their outfits for becoming "holy warriors." The new trend has been introduced by Jaish Mohammad, a *Jihadi* organization founded by Maulana Azhar Masood, who was freed from Indian jail as a result of a deal between hijackers of an Indian airliner and the New Delhi government.' See also Kumar 2001.

will start assisting Pakistan in the coming days. Additionally, the military government is expecting an increase in the foreign investment in Pakistan. Irrespective of whether this transforms Pakistan into a robust economy, it will certainly reduce the economic tensions that the government has been facing. And surely there will be no economic 'collapse'. Pakistan's economic revival depends upon generating a mass-based socio-economic atmosphere that would help regain investor confidence and make Pakistan a preferred destination for foreign direct investment and portfolio investment. Increased internally stable order is likely to make the state less insecure.

Whatever the outcome in the long term, Pakistan would need to set its house in order: have a popular elected government that lasts a full term, strengthen democratic institutions, have economic policies that strengthen the state and decrease the role of the army in influencing decisions that emanate from Islamabad, and in decision making, in general. A clearer filtration process with civilian inputs is also needed to ensure greater deliberation during the process of decision making. This impacts deterrence stability, as it seeks to eliminate unauthorised and accidental launch of nuclear weapons. As Babar Sattar has perceptively noted, 'it is the want of strong civilian institutions firmly rooted among the masses and the political leadership's doubtful commitment to democracy that makes political arena susceptible to military intervention.'[283]

Pakistan has to particularly ensure that the terrorist factories that it has created are shut down in its own long-term interest. As Jessica Stern has said, 'Pakistan's continued support of religious militant groups suggests that it does not recognize its own susceptibility to the culture of violence it has helped create. It should think again.'[284] Over a long term, the message from Pakistan is cautionary:

> while no one would be foolish enough to say that religious activism or a variant of fundamentalism will not influence Pakistan's future, the lessons of the past fifty years suggest that fundamentalist ideology will continue to elicit a limited response, its declamatory excesses more evident than its programmatic achievements.[285]

---

[283] Sattar 2001.

[284] Stern 2000b.

[285] Lawrence 1998.

Increasing dependence on Islam by regimes in power appears meaningless when the society's political, economic and social injustices are not eradicated. This raises questions concerning the long-term viability of governments that rely for their legitimacy on Islam. It is in the interest of Pakistan to send out positive signals to the world that it is a strong and responsible state with nuclear weapons, where the strength flows from democracy, strong institutions of governance, policies of social equality and justice that stand the test of time, and not from militia-breeding Kalashnikovs and heroin culture.

CHAPTER 7

CONCLUSIONS

*The most safe, sure and swift way to deal with the threat of nuclear
arms is to do away with them in every regard ... reduction and
destruction of all nuclear weapons and the means to make them should
be humanity's greatest concern.*

—Boutras Boutras Ghali
NPT Review and Extension Conference

Underlying the debate on the deterrent role of nuclear
weapons in Southern Asia is one fundamental question
—what is the role of nuclear weapons in keeping peace in
this region? Do these weapons deter war? Or do these weapons
bring about a phase of 'ugly stability'?[1] Do these weapons make
sub-conventional conflict safer? Is there strategic space for 'limited
war' under the nuclear umbrella? Is the Southern Asian triangular
situation any different from the Cold War dyad? How can nuclear
deterrence be stable in the triangle of China, India and Pakistan?

This book questions the central premise of nuclear weapons—
deterrence. The notion of deterrence and the response of any state
during a crisis situation is a function of many factors that operate
at simultaneous planes, including the military, strategic, psychological and political ones.

Any crisis has the potential of moving from localised war to
sectoral military engagement and further, every step has the potential to escalate into an all-out nuclear conflict. Past experience is
only about two relatively equal superpowers, and there exists no
instance of creating a stable deterrence in a triangle involving three
states that have different motivations, nuclear doctrines, political
systems and histories. This makes comprehending events more

---

[1] This term has been used by Tellis (1997).

problematic, with related stress and fatigues on men, machines, armies and societies all playing their part. A factor that is unique to this region is the presence of non-state actors which have in the past proven to be a big destabilising source. Prudence unambiguously dictates that avoiding any crisis by sound diplomacy that is premised on war prevention, rather than any typical general's assertion of 'we'll sort out those chaps', is needed. If states have to increase power, strength and strategic depth, then it is also in the national self-interest to maintain a robust and unprovocative defence posture. History bears testimony to the fact that if the firewood is ready, then one act can provide the spark—the murder of the Archduke in June 1914 was sufficient to initiate the First World War. States should concentrate on creating a web of crisis and escalation control and crisis management instruments that would go a long way in bringing stability and increase the response time to any aggressive action.

There has been a distinct lack of historical experience in dealing with crisis that carries a risk of escalation to the nuclear level. Given this setting, this study has sought to learn from three cases. The Cuban missile crisis became a test case much early into the Cold War between the superpowers. With stakes being so high, this crisis fortunately passed with not a shot being fired. The Ussuri river clashes have been included, as they provide the only instance apart from Kargil when two nuclear weapons states have engaged in armed conflict. These situations bring forth the truth: conflict chronically entails elements that cannot be anticipated. In Southern Asia, perhaps the added variable is domestic—politics and public opinion. Issues of nuclear weapons, war and missiles in the region are governed more by the high pitch of political rhetoric and internal politics than by technology. Finally, the Kargil crisis and the post-Parliament attack phase of troop mobilisation by India and Pakistan, which had elements of escalation and was a case in brinkmanship.[2]

Since a crisis is often just round the corner and inherently carries seeds of escalation, the study focuses on the web of structures that can be institutionalised to ensure escalation does not take place. To maintain stability in crisis, which policies and postures are useful and how can this be supplemented by technology?

---

[2] Rajain 2002a.

Quite obviously, the politico-strategic postures have to be clear. The challenge is war prevention—whatever the means. The means could range from political will to the use of scientific technology. Naturally, intelligence inputs are essential. These have to be accurate and substantiated by evidence and if need be, part of this can be conveyed to the adversary. For instance, if the intelligence has picked up any covert activity of the adversary, then the directors-general of military operations (DGMOs) could talk about it rather than remaining misinformed about it.[3] Large-scale military preparations, when observed, can also be discussed with the adversary. This kills any element of surprise attack that the adversary is planning. The West made a big noise about India's preparations for a nuclear test in 1995 and shifting of the Prithvi missile to Jalandhar (India) a few years ago. Surveillance systems and technology can be used to good affect to monitor such moves by the adversary. Constant improvement in satellite resolution sensors enables a clear picture of any such preparations. States that do not have satellites of their own can hire commercial satellites for this task. If a state has to send a message to the adversary then movement of missiles to forward bases is a militarily loud enough message and can be covertly or overtly done. After the Western nations discovered India's covert preparations to test a nuclear device in 1995, diplomatic pressure was built up against it and it was not pursued further.

Further, on the nuts and bolts of maintaining stability, the respective leaderships will have to think through the ways of deterring conflict. Possessing nuclear weapons and yet having to sustain more than 1,000 causalties (as in the Kargil War) does not help the case of those who argue for nuclear weapons. If indeed nuclear weapons are a deterrent force, does that mean that states should be more than prepared for conventional, sub-conventional limited, or even large-scale conflicts?

An intelligence source in the decision-making process during the Kargil conflict confided that India knew Pakistan had shifted seven F-16s from Sargodha to Sangauli, that is, from peacetime location to battle-ready deployment.[4] Out of these four were escorts

---

[3] There have been instances where the wrong information was conveyed. While this strengthens the case of ambiguity, it weakens that of stability.

[4] A senior Government of India intelligence service officer, in personal conversation a year after the Kargil crisis.

and three were wired for a nuclear weapons delivery. He added that Pakistan was ready for nuclear conflict, and so was India.[5] When this question was raised in the Indian Parliament, the government responded by saying that it was not aware of any such move.[6] Obviously, either the government did not want the adversary to know that it was aware about the movement of the F-16s, or it did not want to make this information public.

India had activated its three types of nuclear delivery vehicles and kept them in what is known as Readiness State 3—meaning that some nuclear bombs would be ready to be mated with the delivery vehicle at short notice. The air force was asked to keep its Mirage fighters on standby, DRDO scientists headed to where the Prithvi missiles were deployed and at least four of these were readied for a possible nuclear strike.[7] Even the Agni missile was moved to a Western Indian state and kept in a state of readiness.[8] A trajectory was worked out so that the two stages that are detached after burnout did not fall on Indian territory and hurt anyone.[9] This obviously implies that in peacetime India has a de-mated and de-alerted the status of its arsenal. Military strategy informs that if a state is losing ground in one sector of a conflict, it could open another sector and the enemy would then be forced to let off some pressure on the first sector and engage in the other sector. One wonders how India and Pakistan would have reacted if any of the following situations had arisen in Kargil—if Pakistan had opened another front, or if India had decided to cross the line of control. Once domestic pressures begin to accumulate, a definite result is what states look for.[10] What is unclear is the connection

[5] Rajain 2002b.

[6] Lok Sabha 2000i. The opposition sought to know 'whether the Government are aware that during Kargil operation Pakistan had used "wired" aircraft duly escorted by planes which was having (sic) the capacity of delivering nuclear bombs to a strategic base close to the Indian border.' Replying to this question, the Minister of Defence, George Fernandes, on the floor of the House said, 'Government have no information in this regard.'

[7] Chengappa 2000. The author says that he 'had conducted close to two hundred interviews with a range of the key people involved that included former Prime Ministers, Presidents, Ministers, Generals, Secretaries to government, diplomats, strategists and the scores of scientists both known and unknown' (Ibid.: 437).

[8] Ibid.

[9] Ibid.

[10] Rajain 2002b.

between nuclear weapons in India and Pakistan and specific politico-military objectives in the event of outbreak of hostilities. At a couple of sectors—Siachen, Poonch and Rajauri—the two countries often exchange heavy artillery fire. Firing at each other in Siachen does not require authorisation from higher authorities. The two states, more or less on an everyday basis, engage each other militarily at various other points along the line of control. This engagement, however, is limited to the Jammu and Kashmir state. This and the competing claims over Jammu and Kashmir lend credence to the arguments that any future large-scale military confrontation between India and Pakistan will be over Jammu and Kashmir.

A small window of opportunity exists with the NFU. Pakistan is unlikely to engage with India in a discussion on NFU, as this would imply permanent Pakistani strategic inferiority and vulnerability. Given India's conventional superiority, the threat of first use remains central to Pakistani calculations on the construction of its deterrent against India, while the actual use of nuclear weapons first may be vital to its defence if and when deterrence fails. Stephen Cohen suggests that the Pakistan army has conceived of a five rung escalation ladder; of these, four involve the threat of first use or actual use.[11] General Kidwai, head of Pakistan's Strategic Planning Division, has also stated that nuclear weapons could be used 'if the very existence of Pakistan as a state is at stake.'[12]

While one point of view holds that NFU is inherently a matter of faith, if the weapons are de-mated this faith can be reinforced with policy. For this there are credible monitoring technologies available for enhancing its credibility. Additionally, there has been some talk in India about a 'limited war' which could translate into

---

[11] These include: (a) private and public warnings to India not to move its forces threateningly; (b) a demonstration explosion on Pakistani territory to deter India from a conventional attack; (c) the use of a 'few' nuclear weapons on Pakistani territory against intruding Indian forces; and (d) nuclear strikes against 'critical' Indian military targets, preferably in areas with low population and without much by way of infrastructure. See Cohen 1998: 177–79.

[12] The threshold has been lowered and now encompasses the options of India (a) conquering a large part of Pakistani territory; (b) destroying a large part of its land on air forces; (c) proceeding to estrange Pakistan economically; or (d) creating a large-scale internal subversion in Pakistan (Cotta-Ramusino and Martellini 2002).

military engagement across the line of control. This, in turn, is premised on the notion that India controls escalation dominance and that any threat by Pakistan has to take into consideration India's ability to raise and control the level of escalation right up to the nuclear level. This may be very difficult, especially when it is under stress in a crisis situation and both sides look for a face-saving exit. Kanti Bajpai thinks that

the more India thinks that Pakistan is using 'first-use' threats to promote asymmetric warfare, the more it will move in the direction of limited war under nuclear conditions to indicate that Pakistan is not immune from retaliation; the more India is seen to move in the direction of limited war under nuclear conditions, the more Pakistan will emphasize first use.[13]

The coup in Pakistan gave the Indian government an excuse to stop the dialogue. When the dialogue reopened and an agendaless Agra Summit was called, it turned out to be a public relations disaster for the Indian government. The relations went down the slippery slope after the attack on the Indian Parliament. General Musharraf might not step down soon and it is possible that he will be in power for a long time. If that be so, will India not talk to Pakistan for that long a period? After the various setbacks India has experienced while doing business with the General, it is likely to tread very carefully in the future. Back channel diplomacy has been explored in the past; it can also be used in the future.[14]

The other reality that has now arisen is that China has become a part of South Asian security. Any action by China with regard to its own nuclear weapons programme or policy will necessarily result in India taking a reactive stance. This has further implications on Pakistani security calculations. If India continues the establishment of a credible minimum nuclear deterrent which has to be against all adversaries, it naturally includes China. A minimum credible deterrent against China will result in weaponisation and deployment of a deterrent force both in terms of reach and numbers. This may just be far too much for Pakistan. If an NBC news report is to

---

[13] Bajpai 2002.

[14] In 1999, R.K. Mishra from India and Niaz Naik from Pakistan were engaged in back channel diplomacy.

be taken seriously, then with able assistance from a couple of nations, Pakistan may already be ahead of India in terms of its delivery capability.[15] If this is true then India has many issues to consider. As India was decisively defeated in the 1962 war with China, the military still regards threats from China as primary and long term. China may be playing its game well by trying to contain India by assisting Pakistan—a typical Kautilyan construction of assisting an adversary's enemy (who is a friend). India and China seem to have placed the nuclear tests and the chill in bilateral ties that came about in the wake of the nuclear tests firmly behind them. India could engage China in a dialogue that includes issues such as nuclear stability, and at a later stage involve Pakistan in such a venture to bring about stability in a region widely regarded by many as the most likely place for an unauthorised accidental use of nuclear weapons. At this point in time this seems far fetched, as China is unlikely to include nuclear issues in the agenda of any dialogue with India. A humble beginning has been made with the exchange of maps on the border dispute.

Soon after the tests, the international community led by the P-5 in the Security Council and the G-8 nations met in Birmingham where it laid down some benchmarks for South Asia.[16] On the issue of export controls, the Indian government maintains 'the most stringent control on export of sensitive technologies ....'[17] India has announced a no-first-use policy, a unilateral moratorium on nuclear testing, engaged the US in a security dialogue, tabled a resolution in the first committee of the UN General Assembly for dealerting of nuclear arsenals, discussed autonomy for Kashmir, offered talks with all sections of the civil society in Kashmir and

---

[15] *The Times of India* 2000d. Many Indian strategists and policy analysts dismissed this report as fabricated.

[16] Prominent among these were: 'to conduct to further nuclear tests; sign and ratify the Comprehensive Test Ban Treaty immediately and without conditions; refrain from deploying nuclear weapons or missile systems; halt the production of fissile material for nuclear weapons; participate constructively in negotiations towards a Fissile Material Cut-Off Treaty; formalise existing policies; not to export weapons of mass destruction and missile technology or equipment; and resume a direct dialogue to address the root causes of tension between them, including Kashmir' (United Nations 1998).

[17] Lok Sabha 1998.

held the first free and fair elections there in a long time. Pakistan too has pledged not to export sensitive technologies and announced a moratorium on further tests.

China already occupies an enviable position in the international system, both in terms of attributes of power and negotiating strengths. India being firmly on the road to the reform process, depending on the issue involved either takes idealist positions (for instance, favouring a greater UN role in the Iraq crisis) or takes realist positions (for instance, not permitting any role of the UN in Kashmir); but when confronted by crucial choices, the Indian government often speaks from a position of strength. It is Pakistan that has to set its house in order to reconsider its national priorities. It is in the interest of all three states to enter into a restraint regime that works in times of crises. Decision makers in Beijing, Islamabad and New Delhi should not lull themselves into thinking that credible minimum deterrence would prevent crisis and possibly the outbreak of hostilities. All countries have to address issues related to nuclear doctrines, alternative response options, early warning, intelligence and alert levels.

Sir Michael Howard argues that deterrence includes a mix of reassurance and accommodation, and should not focus exclusively on nuclear capabilities.[18] It is common knowledge that the Indian arsenal is firmly under civilian control in de-mated and de-alerted status and will be assembled to deployable status at very short notice. K. Subrahmanyam says, that the 'Indian philosophy of deterrence is not anchored in flaunting the certainty of the destructive power of its arsenals, but in generating sufficient certainty in the minds of potential adversaries that they cannot escape retaliation if they were to resort to use of nuclear weapons.'[19]

In view of the trend of a hostile climate spread over the longer term, India and Pakistan could do well by going back to the basics of their relations: the bilateralism emphasising the Shimla Accord of 1972 and the Lahore Declaration of February 1999. They contain necessary provisions that have governed the crucial issues of international border, line of control and necessary confidence-building measures (CBMs) in nuclear and missile areas. Once a minimum

---

[18] Howard 1982/83.
[19] Subrahmanyam 1998a: 246.

level of confidence is restored, dialogue channels opened, increased communication will lead to clearer perceptions. With regard to Sino-Indian relations, two exhaustive CBMs negotiated in the 1990s provide a fine institutionalised framework for confidence and security building.[20] In the nuclear realm, there has been very little progress since China refuses to acknowledge India as a nuclear weapons state. In due course of time, this will perhaps come through, and in the aftermath of President K.R. Narayanan's visit to China in mid-June 2000 and Zhu Rongji's visit to India in 2002, relations are steadily improving. In an emerging balance of power in Asia, Japan and India remain the two countries that may pose a credible challenge to China's rise as Asia's *primus inter pares*. A process that threatens stability in Southern Asia is the Pakistan–China collusion on missile and nuclear materials. Even though both countries continue to deny this publicly, reports of Chinese assistance continue to pour in. Moreover, Chinese actions themselves at times are causes of concern to India. If the US continues to invest in theatre missile defence (TMD) in East Asia, China may be forced to respond, thereby making India rethink its strategic calculations.

❈ THE TRIANGLE: CHINA, INDIA AND PAKISTAN

Considering the fact that nuclear weapons will remain firmly entrenched in the security calculus of nation-states, and until such a time that nuclear weapons are delegitimised from the strategic fabric of nation-states, what path can China, India and Pakistan adopt that would be in their national interest without letting the guard down?

The last five decades have seen three Indo-Pak wars and one Sino-Indian conflict. If one looks at the biggest challenge that any state faces today, it is that of preventing the outbreak of a conflict. For any conflict will not just be a drain of national resources, it will further strain the relations between these states leading to a brinkmanship situation that no state would want. But such a situation is often around the corner: a chain of inadvertent events, domestic political turmoil, heightened misperceptions and weak

---

[20] See India–PRC Agreement 1993, 1996.

leaders could easily spark any crisis. The three states provide a wide range of political systems, arms control community, defence postures and nuclear doctrines. China and India have declared no-first-use policies (the only two nuclear weapons states to have done that) and it is expected that in a crisis situation these states will abide by their declared nuclear doctrines. On the other end is Pakistan which does not have an 'official' declared policy, but it is widely believed, will probably use nuclear weapons as weapons of 'last resort and first use'.

EXISTING BILATERAL AGREEMENTS

The three states could also use the framework that has been worked out under various treaties and bilateral agreements to enhance stability in the region. For instance, the Agreement on Measures to Reduce the Risk of Outbreak of Nuclear War between the US and the erstwhile USSR had the following provisions, some of which could have implications in Southern Asia, if the political will permits:

1. A pledge by each party to take measures each considers necessary to maintain and improve its organisational and technical safeguards against accidental or unauthorised use of nuclear weapons.
2. Arrangements for immediate notification should a risk of nuclear war arise from such incidents, from the detection of unidentified objects through early warning systems, or from any accidental, unauthorised, or other unexplained incident involving a possible detonation of a nuclear weapon.
3. Advance notification of any planned missile launches beyond the territory of the launching party and in the direction of the other party.

The other agreement that has broad contours for ensuring a restraint regime in South Asia is the Agreement on the Prevention of Nuclear War signed in Washington on 22 June 1973. Under this agreement, the United States and the Soviet Union agreed to reduce the danger of nuclear war and the use of nuclear weapons to practise restraint in their relations towards each other and towards all countries, and to pursue a policy of stability and peace. It was viewed as a preliminary step in preventing the outbreak of nuclear war or military conflict by adopting an attitude of international cooperation.[21]

The USA and the USSR had also negotiated The Agreement on Notifications of ICBM and SLBM Launches, signed during the 1988 Moscow Summit. India and Pakistan do not have SLBMs yet, but in due course may possess them. An agreement on the same lines, featuring short-range ballistic missiles, would reflect the continuing interest of India, China and Pakistan in reducing the risk of nuclear war as a result of misinterpretation, miscalculation or accident. The START I treaty had provisions whereby the party was under obligation to notify any flight test of an ICBM or SLBM, including those used to launch objects into the upper atmosphere or space, in addition to the requirements under the Ballistic Missile Launch Notification Agreement (under which the notifying party must provide planned launch date, launch area and re-entry impact area).

INFORMATION SHARING AND TRANSPARENCY VERSUS AMBIGUITY

Until the time that nuclear weapons are withdrawn from the security architecture of nuclear weapons states, which may be a long way off, the three states—China, India and Pakistan—can promote a stable nuclear environment by sharing information on nuclear materials. While one understands that it may be very difficult to generate political will to do so, given the pressures from the domestic constituencies, such an arrangement may work towards instilling confidence and making the region a nuclear safety zone. One particularly suspects that China may not want to be a part of any such arrangement, but once an opening has been made, data sharing can be facilitated. India and Pakistan have cooperated on nuclear issues in the past—the Bilateral Agreement on the Prohibition of Attack against Nuclear Installations and Facilities.

---

[21] This agreement broadly covers two areas: '(a) It outlines the general conduct of both countries toward each other and towards third countries regarding the avoidance of nuclear war. In this respect it is a bilateral agreement with multilateral implications; (b) the Parties agreed that in a situation in which the two countries find themselves in a nuclear confrontation or in which, either as a result of their policies towards each other or as the result of developments elsewhere in the world, there is a danger of a nuclear confrontation between them or any other country, they are committed to consult with each other in order to avoid this risk' (US–USSR Agreement 1973).

The agreement strengthens the scope of Articles 15 and 56 of the First and Second Protocols to the Geneva Convention. These articles state that

> works or installations containing dangerous forces, namely dams, dykes and nuclear electrical generating stations, shall not be made the object of attack, even where these objects are military objectives, if such attack may cause the release of dangerous forces and consequent severe losses among the civilian population.[22]

In spite of the crests and troughs of Indo-Pak relations, the lists of such installations are exchanged at the beginning of each year. A similar agreement can be negotiated with China to strengthen stability in the region. The difficulty in this may be that China is still not reconciled to the fact that India is a nuclear weapons state.

Presently, the IAEA collaborates with Sri Lanka, Pakistan, India and Bangladesh in the region on a number of projects that provide for a greater South Asian nuclear transparency. The Regional Co-operation Agreement (RCA) mentioned in the IAEA Information Circular 167 includes these four countries, among others.[23] India is one of the main countries involved in RCA. Through the RCA, the Indian Department of Atomic Energy has provided training facilities and fellowships to numerous foreign visitors. In 1999, the Bhabha Atomic Research Centre trained eight scientists, one each from Bangladesh, Myanmar, Romania, Thailand and four from Vietnam. Pakistan, which joined the RCA in September 1974, has also been active. It hosted a review meeting to analyse the regional database on marine radioactivity in 1999. The RCA provides a legitimate structure that can be used to focus on issues of mutual concern. A broad range of engagements would facilitate better understanding.

An institutionalised structure came into being in 1999, when the Indian Prime Minister, Atal Behari Vajpayee travelled by bus to Lahore and signed the Lahore Declaration with the Pakistani Prime Minister, Nawaz Sharif. A memorandum of understanding was also signed by the Indian Foreign Secretary, Mr K. Raghunath and

---

[22] India–Pakistan Agreement 1988.

[23] The others are Australia, Indonesia, Japan, Malaysia, Myanmar, Mongolia, New Zealand, the People's Republic of China, the Philippines, the Republic of Korea, Singapore, Thailand and Vietnam.

the Pakistani Foreign Secretary, Mr Shamshad Ahmad in Lahore on 21 February 1999. It had the following provisions:[24]

1. The two sides shall engage in bilateral consultations on security concepts and nuclear doctrines, with a view to developing measures for confidence building in the nuclear and conventional fields, aimed at avoidance of conflict.
2. The two sides [shall] undertake to provide each other with advance notification in respect of ballistic missile flight tests, and shall conclude a bilateral agreement in this regard.
3. The two sides are fully committed to undertaking national measures to reducing the risks of accidental or unauthorised use of nuclear weapons under their respective control. The two sides further undertake to notify each other immediately in the event of any accidental, unauthorised or unexplained incident that could create the risk of a fallout with adverse consequences for both sides, or an outbreak of a nuclear war between the two countries, as well as to adopt measures aimed at diminishing the possibility of such actions, or such incidents being misinterpreted by the other. The two sides shall identify/establish the appropriate communication mechanism for this purpose.
4. The two sides shall continue to abide by their respective unilateral moratorium on conducting further nuclear test explosions unless either side, in exercise of its national sovereignty, decides that extraordinary events have jeopardised its supreme interests. This declaration lies buried under the snows of Kargil that will take a long time to melt. The Shimla Agreement and the Lahore Declaration, emphasising bilateralism, provide a good starting point. A revival of the Lahore process can then be supplemented by the International Convention on Early Notification of a Nuclear Accident (restricted to non-weapons facilities).

Another opening that can be explored is the South Asian Seas Action Plan, of which both India and Pakistan are signatories. Annex IV of this plan includes a Regional Program of Action for the Protection of the Marine Environment of the South Asian Seas from Land-based Activities. Under this plan, the Tarapur Atomic Power Station (TAPS) in India and the Karachi Nuclear Power Plant (KANUPP)

---

[24] For the Lahore Declaration, see *The Hindu* 1999a. Also see the website of IPCS both for the text of Declaration and the MoU: http://www.ipcs.org/documents/1999/1jan–mar.htm, accessed on 21 August 2000.

in Pakistan can be made to cooperate on data that affects the environment. Both of these facilities are located on the coast, impact the coastal regions and are potential thermal, chemical and radioactive pollutant sources. One of the key features of the South Asian Seas Action Plan is to encourage collaboration among regional scientists through the establishment of coordinated regional marine pollution monitoring programmes based on inter-comparable methods for the study of the various processes occurring in the coastal areas and open ocean of the region, and the assessment of the sources and levels of pollutants and their effects on marine life and human health. This too can be strengthened. But at the heart of any Indo-Pak reconciliation is the response of both countries to the Kashmir issue. From the Pakistani side, there has to be the shutting down of the terrorist infrastructure, the support to militancy, and from the Indian side there has to be an engagement process—something that has begun in right earnest with the establishment of the N.N. Vohra Committee and the commencement of talks at the highest level. Additionally, there has to be a process of engaging the social, cultural and economic fabric of the Kashmiri society. Kashmir is the key to a stable South Asia.[25]

India and Pakistan could adopt mutual restraint in the development of nuclear weapons/missiles; provide greater transparency in their deployments; choose to negotiate confidence and security building measures (CSBMs) in the conventional and nuclear spheres; and consolidate the existing structures and instruments between them. The common/cooperative security approach ac-cepts the primacy of the state, while at the same time it does not deny the existence of tensions and instabilities between states and within states, nor does it preclude military measures being taken to assure national defence.

As this approach encourages coordinated and non-confrontational interactions between military establishments, it could extend to decisions relating to weapons acquisitions and force structuring. At the same time, this approach encourages what Jawaharlal Nehru had espoused many years ago—non-interference in each others' affairs. If external support to internal and local matters can be discouraged at the level of the state, much valuable resource can be better utilised. The cooperative and common security approach

---

[25] For two contrasting views on this, see Mattoo 2003 and Haqqani 2003.

concept also provides a new salience to the notion of national security from that based on military power to a security based on human concerns transcending state frontiers—like socio-economic development, human rights, gender equity, terrorism and environmental degradation. A general conclusion in this regard is that

> the threat of future conflict is firmly located in the developing world —where crowded peoples in poor nations are at risk from the pace of environmental change, the rapid growth in their own populations, the growing threat of infectious disease, and an array of ethnic and tribal hostilities.[26]

This reinforces the need for regional and subregional collaboration to enhance political and economic security.[27] This does not mean that the power of the state is undermined; the state remains a significant source of security as it possesses the capabilities to influence the security milieu positively or negatively, in which human security must be sought.

Additionally, some level of transparency can also instil a degree of confidence and credibility in the other state. Again, it is not the operational features or plans that need to be conveyed, but a broad understanding that the weapons are in safe hands and the command and control in civilian hands. This strengthens the credibility of deterrence rather than weakening it. The doctrinal issues, the red lines can have a degree of transparency, while the operational details can remain ambiguous to maintain credibility.

❌ LIMITED WAR UNDER NUCLEAR UMBRELLA

While territorial concerns continue to remain the fundamental factor that lead to war, it must be remembered that if armed conflict breaks out, much will depend on how disputants perceive their issue and how they negotiate over it. Richard Barringer found that one of the main distinctions between non-military and military phases of a conflict is the way issues at stake are perceived.[28]

---

[26] Kennedy et al. 1998: 21.
[27] See in this regard, IPCS 2000.
[28] Barringer 1972.

He also said that while armed conflict is under way, escalation in military tactics has two common factors: pessimism about what might happen if victory is not achieved, and a related shift in military balance.[29] The size of a dispute is probably related to the intangibility of the issue under contention.

A point of view that started emerging in the 1960s was that nuclear weapons have limited the military extent, geographical scope and strategic aim of war among states that possess such capabilities, primarily due to the awesome destructive potential of such weapons.[30] As Martin van Creveld has written, 'From Central Europe to Kashmir, and from the Middle East to Korea, nuclear weapons are making it impossible for large sovereign territorial units, or states, to fight each other in earnest without running the risk of mutual suicide.'[31] This school of thought maintains that with the emergence of nuclear weapons, total and unlimited conventional war had been relegated to the annals of history, since states would not undertake long military campaigns for economic results any more. That age of imperialism is now over. Additionally, a larger number of states simply do not have the means to conduct a total war. But does that mean that countries that have nuclear weapons may find the necessary strategic space to wage 'limited war'? This thought permeates the strategic community in India and Pakistan.

At least once in a generation, the three countries, China, India and Pakistan, have gone to war and the trend of stability–instability continues. The delicate balance of terror, particularly between India and Pakistan, therefore puts a premium upon prudent and accurate calculations of adversaries to impose disadvantageous ratio of costs to benefits upon each other, even though neither would be likely to gain an advantage if both employed their full capabilities to impose such costs.[32]

---

[29] Ibid.
[30] See chapter 2 for the theoretical aspects of limited war debates.
[31] van Creveld 1991: 194.
[32] Robert Osgood says that 'Whereas deterrence under the balance-of-power system depended largely upon estimates of relative military capabilities—which, although repeatedly miscalculated, were assumed to have fairly straightforward relationship to the will to employ them—deterrence under the balance-of-terror system depends, primarily, upon a complicated process of mutual mind-reading based upon some such highly subjective and speculative calculus as the relationship

Since May 1998, India and Pakistan have mobilised forces more than twice and there has constantly been talk of limited war. The theory of limited war entered the lexicon of the Indian strategic community when the Indian Defence Minister, George Fernandes, addressing an international conference by the country's largest think tank, the Institute of Defence Studies and Analyses (IDSA), and attended by strategists, military personnel and civil bureaucrats, propounded his thesis of limited conflicts in a nuclear environment against the backdrop of the Kargil War:

> [T]he issue was not that war had been made obsolete by nuclear weapons, and that covert war by proxy was the only option, but that conventional war remained feasible though with definite limitations if escalation across the nuclear threshold was to be avoided .... India has demonstrated in Kargil that its forces can fight and win a limited war, at a time and place chosen by the aggressor.[33]

At another seminar, this time on 'The Challenges of Limited War: Parameters and Options', the defence minister claimed that

> We had understood the dynamics of limited war especially after India declared its nuclear weapons status nearly two years ago. Nuclear weapons did not make war obsolete; they simply imposed another dimension on the way warfare could be conducted. The Kargil War, therefore, was handled within this perspective with obvious results. Pakistan, on the other hand, had convinced itself for decades, that under the nuclear umbrella it would be able to take Kashmir without India being able to punish it in return .... There was a worse error of judgement that Pakistan made after the nuclear tests in May 1998 when its elites started believing that India would be deterred in any war imposed on it, and will not fight back. There was a perception that the overt nuclear status had ensured that covert war could continue and aggression across the line of control could be carried out while India would be deterred by the nuclear factor.[34]

---

between the value of an objective at stake to the estimated effectiveness and costs of action in the light of the probability of a particular response' (Osgood 1961).

[33] Singh 2000: xvii–xviii. This statement was made in the opening address by the minister at the Second International Conference on *Asian Security in the 21st Century* organised by the Institute of Defence Studies and Analyses, New Delhi, in January 2000.

[34] Fernandes 2000.

He added further,

> while war, in our context, was kept limited in the past by choice, our interests would require that it should be kept limited in future as a matter of necessity …. We need, therefore, to ensure that conventional war, whenever imposed on us in future, is kept below the nuclear threshold. This will require close examination of our doctrine, defence strategy and force structure.[35]

At the same seminar, the then Chief of Army Staff, Gen V.P. Malik, refining this concept further, said that India would have to remain operationally prepared for the entire spectrum of war—from proxy war to an all-out war. 'The military strategy adopted for Kargil, including the line of control constraints, might not be applicable in the next war. In all limited wars the only common factor is national aim and objectives'.[36]

The question that presents itself in a dynamic strategic environment is, can India or Pakistan fight and win a limited war under the nuclear umbrella? The Indian defence minister's assertion obviously implies that India controls escalation dominance. The literature of the Cold War era informs us that in essence, there was the belief that it is possible to control patterns of conflict, and yet be able to determine outcomes even of it was not going according plans made in operations rooms. Decision makers at all times during the conflict would remain in full control of the events, in spite of the elements of surprise, use different weaponry, open other fronts and yet determine a pre-concluded set of outcomes. Herman Kahn, for instance, informs that 'This is a capacity, other things being equal, to enable the side possessing it to enjoy marked advantages in a given region of the escalation ladder.'[37] He continues, 'it depends on the net effect of the competing capabilities of the rung being occupied, the estimate by each side of what would happen if the confrontation moved to these other rungs, and the means each side has to shift the confrontation to these other rungs.'[38]

---

[35] Ibid.

[36] *The Times of India* 2000a.

[37] Kahn 1965. This appears to be premised on an 'ugly balance of terror'. The success in such a scenario depends on strategic asymmetry. Kahn's suggestion was that with nerve and skill any favourable asymmetry could be turned into bargaining advantage.

[38] Ibid.: 186, 190.

Thomas Schelling's views on this issue are slightly different. He emphasised the element of uncertainty:

> [N]ot everybody is always in his right mind. Not all the frontiers and thresholds are precisely defined, fully reliable, and known to be beyond the least temptation to test them out .... Violence, especially in war, is a confused and uncertain activity, highly unpredictable depending on decisions made by fallible human beings organized into imperfect governments depending on fallible communications and warning systems and on the untested performance of people and equipment.[39]

The inherent risk remains. As Schelling says elsewhere, 'the idea is simply that a limited war can get out of hand by degrees.'[40] When war gamed, this scenario leaves a huge element of risk. Even if the initiator of conflict[41] decides to alter the course of conflict midway[42] and moves an extra division of troops or uses air power (if none had been used so far), the other state will be tempted to thwart this. It is entirely possible that in any such event both sides would start using air power, or the defender might be tempted to use a tactical nuke on an advancing tank column. This brings us back to square one—the element of risk of escalation in a limited war cannot be ruled out.

The theory of limited war is based on the hypothesis that it 'maximizes the opportunities for the effective use of military force as a rational instrument of national policy.'[43] Limited war, Schelling argues, 'is not necessarily "irrational" for either party, if the alternative might have been a war that would have been less desirable for both of them.'[44] To keep war limited, there has to be norm setting.[45] (In the case of China, tradition lays the foundations for such norms.) The adversary too should be at the same strategic wavelength to keep the conflict limited. But this may create more problems. William Kaufmann has suggested that 'any attempt to formulate

---

[39] Schelling 1966: 93.
[40] Schelling 1979: 193.
[41] That is, the state that wants to change the status quo as it is unfavourable to it.
[42] Presumably when the course of the war is not favourable to the initiator.
[43] Osgood 1957: 27.
[44] Schelling 1960.
[45] These norms have been discussed in some detail in chapter 2.

rigid rules of conduct for wars whose aegis and environment we cannot foresee may create as many problems as it pretends to solve.'[46]

Coming back to George Fernandes' assertion of being able to control escalation dominance: does this take into account the host of variables that remain outside India's control? While controlling escalation against Pakistan might still be possible militarily, if not politically conceivable, would it be possible against China in the next 5 to 10 years?

This means that building a stable deterrent relationship with China and Pakistan is essential. While this may be easier against a smaller rival like Pakistan, building a credible deterrent against China will be difficult and controlling escalation dominance is out of question, given the present force structure. China will continue to be superior both militarily and by nuclear numbers. Even if India wants to refine its arsenal, it needs more tests; but it is restricted by the self-inflicted moratorium and limited fissile stock. It is also due to the fact that at this point in time, India does not aim to be a large nuclear weapons state; instead it seems content with modest nuclear numbers with small nuclear forces. So it is unlikely that controlling escalation during crisis would entirely be in India's hands, if left purely on nuclear numbers. Of course, now that there is much larger international attention on this region, it would be difficult for any crisis situation to reach the stage where nu-clear exchange is envisaged.[47]

Kargil demonstrated to India that Pakistan could be a reckless, adventuristic, and risk-acceptant state, capable of behaving astrategically and irrationally. As a study conducted by RAND concluded, 'For Pakistan, it (the Kargil operation) reconfirmed low intensity conflict as a legitimate tool for attaining political goals, but it probably also caused the Pakistani leadership to conclude that Kargil-like operations are not legitimate in the current international environment.'[48] Additionally, the study concluded, 'Kargil

---

[46] Kaufmann 1958.

[47] It seems clear that India has a fairly hostile border with Pakistan and it is only with Pakistan that any crisis has the potential of escalating from a limited military engagement to an all-out nuclear war. With China, the border is peaceful and it is unlikely that any crisis or issue will have the potential to escalate to a nuclear exchange.

[48] Tellis et al. 2001: ix.

stands as yet another symbol of the failure of Pakistan's grand strategy and illustrates Islamabad's inability to anticipate the international opprobrium and isolation that ensued from its actions.'[49] The possession of nuclear weapons, it seems, has elevated the threshold of Pakistan to undertake such risks. This means, stability at the nuclear level may endanger stability at the conventional and sub-conventional level.[50] In theory, it characterises the 'stability–instability' paradox. This also helps in making sub-conventional conflict safe.[51] Factors like geographical extent, weaponry used, minds of the decision makers, the pressure of external actors and time, operate simultaneously to determine the outcome of a conflict. The government of the day may not have control over many of these factors operating in the politico-strategic environment.

The assumption of the limited war concept was that wars would be localised, small and limited in geographical extent, men and machinery used. The guiding principle for nuclear weapons here was to ensure that the conflict does not become large scale, as nuclear weapons of the adversary would be a disincentive for escalating to other levels. But this argument is not strategically sustainable, as the 'use them or lose them' theory informs us that any losing side will be inclined to use all weapons at its disposal. Moreover, unless a state has fired off most of its strategic weapons, these might be lost in a pre-emptive first strike.

Even while a Kargil operation can be termed 'limited war' mainly in terms of restrictions of geographical extent, weaponry used and perhaps impact on economy, there can be no convincing answer to the predicament on either side, that nuclear capability might provide the umbrella under which such limited operations can be executed with immunity from escalation, and with a pre-determined set of rules of military engagement. A norm developed in the 1990s, and which was further strengthened by India's own position in the Kargil War, has been that the LoC is sacrosanct. It has also been found that international opinion quickly forms against states that try and alter the status quo by use of force. This has

---

[49] Ibid.: 5

[50] One can argue against stability being present at the nuclear level, given the nuclear sabre rattling in Kargil and during May 2002.

[51] See in this context, Chari 2001a. Also see in the context of stability–instability debate, Krepon 2003.

translated into reduced military options for India. P.R. Chari has argued,

> In truth, India's security has worsened after it became an overt nuclear power; however, the concerned official and non-official communities find this verity hard to accept. Hence their urging of new and risky modalities to affirm India's strategic 'superiority' over Pakistan by asserting that a limited war against Pakistan could be victoriously fought.[52]

On its part, Pakistan firmly believes that while it could engage India in a low-cost high-return game of low intensity conflict in Kashmir, it could also take some time off for a 'strategic detour' and use the overarching nuclear umbrella to pursue goals like those in Kargil. Apart from being a big domestic rallying point, altering domestic opinion and being a balancer for India's conventional superiority, the outright deterrent function of nuclear weapons for Pakistan cannot be underestimated. Apart from covert nuclear signalling, Pakistan also realised that raising the bogey of a nuclear flashpoint was a perfect way of catalysing international intervention. This assumption is unlikely to change in any future military engagement. What is also unlikely to change are the 'asymmetric strategies' that Pakistan's ISI is capable of pursuing against India.[53]

On its part, India has to realise that any future Pakistani adventurism in Kargil or any other region cannot be ruled out, given how Kashmir is played in the imagination of the Pakistani population. India realises that the large international support it received during the crisis was a function of the geo-political circumstances and will be so in the future.[54] If India has to prepare for more Kargil-type operations, then it must reinvigorate its intelligence capabilities[55] and develop robust rapid forward deployed response capabilities that remain prepared to thwart future Pakistani adventurism, and deter any Pakistani brandishing of nuclear weapons. Additionally, Indian strategists and policy makers need

---

[52] Chari 2002: 6.

[53] This could include a wide spectrum of subversive activities, ranging from economic (counterfeit currency, black marketing, money laundering, etc.), to social subversion (exploiting the fragility of Indian subaltern populations and the dissatisfied social groups).

[54] Rajain 2001a.

[55] A suggestion also made by The Kargil Review Committee (2000).

to realise that in any future Kargil-like situation, they need to get into the minds of the policy and decision makers, possibly at the general headquarters in Rawalpindi. If Pakistan is tempted to 'cry nuclear wolf' rather frequently, India is required to develop 'at least a small set of rapid-response capabilities ....'[56] Developing special forces is something that Bharat Karnad has also advocated: '[I]n a nuclearised setting, short of formal, all out conventional war ... Special Forces ... [can] wage a relentless and punishing low-intensity conflict across the border ... this has virtually no risk of escalating to conventional war, leave alone nuclear exchange.'[57]

In this milieu, it is possible that as causalties increase, domestic public opinion with the impact of media may develop against such an operation. As it has been questioned elsewhere,

> If India crosses the LoC and Pakistan decides that it is threatened and issues a warning that it would contemplate its nuclear option, what would be the Indian response? Would India recall its troops and call off the operation? Or would it go ahead and continue in the hope that Pakistan will not escalate the war to a higher or nuclear level? An element of strategic uncertainty obtains here.[58]

Ashley Tellis, in *Stability in South Asia*, had concluded that neither India nor Pakistan could attain a decisive outcome through continued conventional military conflict[59] With General Musharraf already facing a strong anti-establishment sentiment domestically, a war-like situation against India (started by India—or so would be his reasoning) may be in his best interests to serve as a domestic rallying point.[60] A way out of this conundrum for India would be to fine-tune its diplomatic moves by highlighting Pakistan's role as a perpetrator of violence in Kashmir to the world, and exert political and diplomatic pressure on Pakistan to deliver on its promises of stopping the export of terrorism. This seems to be a wiser strategy than contemplating hot pursuit, which could lead to military escalation and diplomatic isolation.[61]

---

[56] Tellis et al. 2001: 57.
[57] Karnad 2002: 497.
[58] Rajain 2002c.
[59] Tellis 1997.
[60] Rajain 2002c.
[61] Ibid.

In the post-Indian Parliament attack phase, India marched up its troops to the borders, leading to a 10-month confrontation with India testing the limits of compellance strategy. India deliberately created the recognisable risk of an armed conflict. This situation is very similar to what Thomas Schelling has termed 'brinkmanship', but he considers this 'a risk that one does not completely control',[62] because the presence of non-state action brings in complications. The crisis in the aftermath of the attack led to both sides using nuclear deterrence to seek advantageous positions, but as Lt Gen V.R. Raghvan says,

> neither side wanted deterrence to fail even as each tried to mani-
> pulate it to its advantage. Crises will therefore become the future
> test of deterrence between India and Pakistan, unless of course deter-
> rence fails both through dangerous manipulation. Attempts by India
> and Pakistan to repeatedly work up crises with nuclear under-
> pinnings will lead to a range of adverse spin-offs.[63]

In any Indo-Pak crisis, the integral role of the United States as an arbiter cannot be ignored. In the post-Parliament attack phase, there were a number of emissaries visiting South Asia, and 'the United States intervened quickly and decisively to pressure both sides toward de-escalation.'[64] But some Indian strategists, including K. Subrahmanyam, thought that war was never on the cards.[65] Some others thought that '[t]he energy and rhetoric that the news media and policymakers are devoting to conjuring doomsday scenarios would be better spent addressing the root causes of the current crisis: Pakistani support for terrorism in Kashmir and, underlying it all, the legitimate grievances of the Kashmiri people.'[66]

The reasons that the Indian government gave for the politico–military–diplomatic overdrive were to coerce Pakistan into ending

---

[62] He further argues that it is the deliberate tactic of letting the situation get somewhat out of hand, simply because its being out of hand may be intolerable to the other party and force an accommodation on his part. 'The essence of the problem seems to be a kind of controlled loss of control; putting oneself in a position where one may or may not respond, but the determining factors are not entirely subject to ones own control' (Schelling 1960).

[63] Raghvan 2002.

[64] Ignatius 2002.

[65] Subrahmanyam 2002.

[66] Ganguly 2002b.

its support for cross-border terrorism and to hand over 20 fugitives who had taken asylum in Pakistan. India initiated a bargain and threatened to use force. There was dager of the confrontation escalating after a few months of stalemate, when the army camp in Kaluchek was attacked in May 2002 and families of army soldiers were killed. Apart from not handing over the fugitives, Pakistan had also not been able to bring the terrorists under control. That raised the question of whether the country was in a position to calibrate the activities of these terrorist groups that had over the years been so faithfully nurtured by the ISI. Coming under tremendous US and Indian pressure, General Musharraf promised that Pakistan would not permit terrorists to use its territory for their activities; additionally, if these groups were found to be acting on their own, it would be a further embarrassment for Islamabad.[67]

The threat of India's use of force had to be seen as credible in Islamabad. To be taken credibly, India had to ensure that its armed forces were in their operational areas. The only danger that India faced was Pakistan's non-compliance with its demands. Failure of coercive diplomacy would have meant armed conflict with disastrous consequences and a potential for escalation. After the incident at Kaluchek, India had to control a growing public sentiment for war. The trick, as C. Raja Mohan writes,

> lay in managing this ambiguity well, taking advantage of the new openings and nudging the overall context in India's favour. This required an understanding of the limits to coercive diplomacy that by necessity involves third parties, the constraints on the third parties and the unintended consequences.[68]

As I have argued elsewhere, 'There is a delicate balance between nuclear capability acting as a deterrent and it being the cause for breakdown of deterrence. The appropriate diplomatic response lies in adopting the stance of nuclear brinkmanship: threaten to cross the brink and hope your enemy gives in first.'[69]

Meanwhile, acting on his own, Lt Gen Kapil Vij, commander of 2 Corps, moved his armoury to a tactically advantageous position

---

[67] Musharraf 2002b.
[68] Mohan 2003a: 201.
[69] Rajain 2002a.

for attack as soon as the political leadership decided to go to war. This manoeuvre was picked up by US satellites and the Government of India had to recall General Vij from his command.[70] This event, when considered alongside the shuttle diplomacy, shows that like many times in the past, the US played a very active role in defusing the crisis. It is also likely that the Western powers in general, and the US particular, were the constituency when Pakistan was raising the bogey of a nuclear flashpoint. That being so, it had the desired results.

By raising the military–diplomatic rhetoric, India too was playing to the same constituency.[71] Indian responses comprised 'nuclear signalling, conventional mobilization, border posturing, possible covert operations, political rhetoric and a diplomatic offensive.'[72] This compellance strategy paid dividends for India as well. The American media started raising the issue and called for a greater proactive approach from the Bush administration. The *New York Times* called Kashmir 'one of the most dangerous flashpoints in the world.'[73] While some American scholars, including Stephen Cohen, thought India was deliberately creating a 'sound and light show',[74] others thought that 'the risks are so cataclysmic that Washington must do more ....'[75] Perhaps, what both India and Pakistan did not take into consideration was the possibility of a process of action and reaction that could easily lead the nuclear rivals into a spiral of misperception and even misinformation, leading to catastrophe.[76]

If India's sole purpose in heading towards a potential conflict situation was to ensure that Pakistan stopped cross-border terrorism, then it was partially successful, this can be attributed to a combination of factors—from India's threat to go to war, to the US shuttle diplomacy that managed to extract a promise from General Musharraf to stop exporting terror. In doing so, India

---

[70] *The Times of India* 2001a.

[71] Additionally, an offensive posture along with political rhetoric was also aimed at drumming up domestic support for the NDA alliance.

[72] Ahmed 2002.

[73] *The New York Times* 2001.

[74] Cited in Slevin 2001.

[75] Kristof 2001. See also Gordon 2002.

[76] Raghvan 2001. General Raghvan was drawing from the experience of the Kargil War. He has been India's Director General, Military Operations.

took advantage of a global anti-terror concern post 9/11, thereby putting Pakistan in a precarious position to be either 'with or against the US in the war against terror'. But India's biggest gain was General Musharraf's tacit acknowledgement that Pakistan was exporting terror to Kashmir and that this would now stop. It is a different matter that in doing so Pakistan lost much credibility, Musharraf's popularity did a u-turn in domestic politics, and India is still debating if he is delivering on those promises. In India, this led to a school of thought which holds such a policy of combining coercive diplomacy and nuclear brinkmanship to be a viable politico–military option. Brig Subhash Kapila, for instance, thinks that the escalation was worthwhile. He locates two benefits: (*a*) the promises of General Musharraf on non-export of terrorism and (*b*) that 'Indian armed forces could train for an extended period of time in their operational areas.'[77] Somewhere in the game, India left no 'exit strategy' for itself and after Pakistan did not hand over the 20 criminals and did not stop aiding terrorists, India was left with little or no option but to keep playing to the Western pressure gallery and harping on the use of force.

With both the heads of states of India and Pakistan declaring that deterrence had worked,[78] one is left wondering if indeed it was so and whether there is a strategic space where a limited war or a calibrated use of force is possible under the nuclear umbrella. Can India and Pakistan fight and win a limited war under the nuclear umbrella?

There are no easy answers to this yet. The dynamics of military strategy and bargaining theory state that a country has to grab a piece of strategically located territory in a swift military action. The territory seized would later be useful in bargaining for altering the status quo, either territorially or in terms of state behaviour. But even as one country is making these military moves, the other country might not just be engaging itself militarily, but also initiating nuclear signalling and steadily moving towards opening

---

[77] See Kapila 2003. But Brig Kapila thinks the outcomes of the exercise would have been different if the US had not intervened. He says, 'The overall results would have been of greater effectiveness but for United States' interference. US interlocutors having got India's assurance not to declare war, passed on this information to General Musharraf. Had this not taken place Musharraf may have been forced into an exit.'

[78] See *The Hindu* 2002c, 2002d.

other fronts for comparable territorial gains. Conventional wisdom informs that in any conflict situation, visible losses often lead to restive populations being used as pawns to win the losing battle and to salvage prestige. In such a situation, it becomes impossible to ascertain when either state has crossed the 'red lines' of the opponent. That raises the question of whether *any* risk is worth the potential consequences: the political and diplomatic opprobrium of a limited aims operation turning into a large-scale military engagement and having the seeds of escalation to nuclear exchange. On the issue of undertaking a limited war, former Chief of Army Staff, Gen V.P. Malik, is of the opinion that the 'politico-military objective and what would be the final outcome of such an action' have to be clearly thought through at the very outset.[79] But he is firmly of the opinion that

> these 'grey' threshold lines can move up and down. There is no definite benchmark. There should be a reasonable justification of the decision to cross the LoC .... But the important point is what our politico-military objective is and what would be the final outcome of such an action. Political leaders need to act responsibly and not make rhetorical statements during a crisis.[80]

Hypothetically, if a vital installation in India is attacked by *fidayeens* and India moves its troops across the LoC to achieve a specific objective, like destruction of terrorist training camps without occupying territory, a nuclear threat from Pakistan could mean that India would either (a) call off the operation, pull its troops back and face adverse public opinion; or (b) continue with these operations in the hope that Pakistan does not proceed with its threatened course of action.[81] Does it also mean that even a small or medium intensity *fidayeen* attack on India's vital installations could translate

---

[79] Malik 2002.

[80] Ibid.

[81] A Pakistani view of India's options of limited war and hot pursuit informs that a 'limited war scenario could escalate quickly into nuclear exchange. It will be difficult to restrain Pakistan from the use of tactical nuclear weapons to stop naked aggression and avert danger to national security. Use of tactical nuclear weapons by either side will quickly escalate into an all out nuclear war with horrible consequences for South Asia' (Ayaz Ahmed Khan 2000). In response, V. P. Malik said, 'I do not believe that Pakistan would trigger a nuclear war and face the consequences of Indian nuclear retaliation over this counter terrorism

into a perpetual crisis situation between India and Pakistan? A politico-military environment of permanent crisis is also hardly reassuring. Neither is the solution in longstanding military build-ups.

Limited war is intrinsically escalatory. It is a politico-military strategy that involves nuclear signalling, which could easily be misperceived and the adversary might opt for pre-emptive strike. It is accompanied by conventional mobilisation along with political rhetoric and diplomatic offensive. Any crisis could lead to a minor skirmish and any brinkmanship could either lead to an all-out war or make the adversary see through the bluff. This brinkmanship is in theory termed 'game chicken'. A game chicken of sorts was being played out after the attack on the Indian Parliament. Additionally, there has to be the element of reciprocity. Halperin maintained that 'limiting a central war may depend on both sides' believing that limitation is possible and that the other is likely to reciprocate restraint.'[82] It is unlikely, given internal dynamics, that either country would be able to restrain itself from opening another front when military logic, public opinion and popular sentiment clearly warrant it.

The problem here is the risk-taking capability of political leaders, which varies from individual to individual. Pakistan has exhibited that it can take a bigger risk (by crossing the LoC in Kargil), while the same capability prevented India from crossing the LoC. Although nuclearisation of the sub-continent and terrorist activities in India have resulted in the concept of limited war, there has however been no systematic analysis as to how any limited operation across the LoC could be carried out without the risk of escalation. And, of course, the final criticism can be that a losing state will want to use all the weapons at its disposal if its survival is at stake.

---

issue. But that notwithstanding, the political objectives of any such conventional operation must be clear. We are talking of camps that are not permanent, where groups of 50–60 terrorists are being trained by the Pak ISI and ex-servicemen. Depending upon the kind of intelligence available, one would be able to eliminate some camps and terrorists. But these camps can be re-established or shifted to another location. Even if we do manage to destroy a few out of these camps, what kind of dent will that make and for how long? It would not lead to the end of cross-border terrorism. If the military is asked to strike at those camps, it will be done, but we should not expect that this act alone would solve the problem of Pak sponsored terrorism' (Malik 2002).

[82] Halperin 1963: 107.

When conflict escalates, soldiers and statesman coming under increasing domestic pressure will be forced to reach hasty decisions, upsetting calculations that were made in peacetime. There are many problems, in purely politico-military terms, in the idea of limited war between India and Pakistan. Many questions remain unanswered:

- Why would Pakistan like to keep the conflict limited, and more importantly non-nuclear, in the face of rising domestic public opinion and a militarily disadvantageous position?
- Do India and Pakistan know each other's 'red lines' as they operate in a dynamic strategic environment? Any such operation/ limited war contains the seeds of a larger conflict/escalation, particularly when the losing state would like to use all weapons at its disposal.
- In a hypothetical scenario, India launches a limited operation across the LoC or the international border (IB), and Pakistan responds with a strike on either a counter-value target (city) or uses tactical nukes on advancing Indian troops. Would India respond with a proportional nuclear strike or a full-fledged conventional attack?
- To deal with cross-border terrorism, the following military options can be exercised: (*a*) use of air power on the camps—which are at best a few mobile tents, with the trainee terrorists probably dispersed; (*b*) use of special forces against camps like Oghi village, Ojheri camp, Para Chinar, Saidgali and Sargodha that have temporarily shut down operations; (*c*) 'hot pursuit'—chasing terrorists across the LoC and the IB with the troops returning; and (*d*) 'salami slicing' of Pakistan-administered Kashmir. India has to decide whether it would occupy territory, or only close down training camps. Obviously, these camps can be quickly established elsewhere. What then would be the utility of any such operation?

If either side were to initiate a limited war, what would the political objectives of such a move be? Considering that there is a growing international acceptance of maintaining the status quo of the LoC and the IB—a norm that India sought to preserve in Kargil War—it is wishful thinking that any armed action by either side across the LoC or the IB would not invite the attention of Western countries.

On its part, can Pakistan fight and win another Kargil-like limited means operation? A growing international norm against changing international boundaries by the use of force may not prevent Pakistan from using violence as a legitimate tool in order to achieve political objectives. The danger, as General Raghvan points out, is 'not reduced by Pakistan blurring the distinction between conventional military conflict and sub conventional conflicts through the use of irregular forces.'[83] Pakistan has understood that the international fallout of its misadventure in Kargil and the covert support to *jihadi* elements in their operations against India may present a continued low–cost high–return game for itself, while introspecting not just on the misadventure but also on issues of grand strategy. Of the many articles that were written, those by Jamaluddin Naqvi[84] and Kamran Shafi[85] reflect Pakistan's sense of isolation and loss. A peep into the Pakistani establishment's thinking while planning for Kargil, reflects that it thought such a plan was applicable and would yield the required political and military results.[86]

---

[83] Raghvan 2001: 89.

[84] According to Naqvi, 'No doubt, Pakistan's initiative in Kargil was a brilliant tactical move. But being out of tune with the prevailing regional and international climate of opinion, it turned out to be self-defeating, indeed counter-productive. It was taken in a strategic vacuum and in a world environment militating against such a move .... Changing ground realities for strengthening one's argument at the bargaining table was standard practice during the Cold War period .... But the use of force is no longer a tool of diplomacy in the post-cold war world' (Naqvi 1999).

[85] According to Shafi, 'We have come a long way indeed from the time when the world listened to our entreaties on Kashmir with a certain amount of respect .... We have come a long way indeed from the time that our protector and giver of all, Amreeka Bahadur (the great America) was getting ready to mediate between India and Pakistan .... Whatever happened to us? Why do we stand at the very edge of the diplomatic precipice today?' (Shafi 1999).

[86] Brig Shaukat Qadir has written, 'The political aim underpinning the operation was "to seek a just and permanent solution to the Kashmir issue in accordance with the wishes of the people of Kashmir". However, the military aim that preceded the political aim was "to create a military threat that could be viewed as capable of leading to a military solution, so as to force India to the negotiating table from a position of weaknesses." The operational plan envisaged India amassing troops at the LoC to deal with the threat at Kargil, resulting in a vacuum in their rear areas. By July, the *Mujahideen* would step up their activities in the rear areas, threatening the Indian lines of communication at pre-designated targets, which would help isolate pockets, forcing the Indian troops to react to them. This would create an opportunity for the forces at Kargil to push forward and pose an additional threat. India would, as a consequence, be forced to the negotiating table. While it is useless to speculate on whether it could in fact have succeeded, theoretically the plan was faultless, and the initial execution, tactically

Kargil proved Pakistan's political and military objectives in blatantly pursuing a policy of irredentism. The critics of Pakistan's Kargil policy questioned why this plan of action was adopted, when Pakistan was neither in a position to sustain it to its logical conclusion, nor was able to muster at least moral and diplomatic support from the Western powers and Muslim countries.[87]

The Indian defence minister's assertion on limited war did not go unchallenged in Pakistan. General Kidwai, head of Pakistan's Strategic Planning Division, sought to fill the doctrinal gaps by lowering the Pakistani threshold to not just include territorial and economic soverignty, but also the internal subversion matrix.[88] This is in addition to the threshold already specified by Agha Shahi, Zulfiqar Ali Khan and Abdul Sattar in their seminal article.[89]

Any incursion into Pakistani territory by India would invariably be viewed as violation of its territorial sovereignty. Should such a military move take place, military logic, as Pakistani analyst Maria Sultan says, dictates that 'the obvious targets for Pakistan defence planners would be to take out strategic military targets in the Jammu and Kashmir.'[90] She questions if in such a situation it would warrant 'India to limit the war in Kashmir and not launch an offensive in other areas particularly in the south of Pakistan where India has strategic advantage.'[91] She argues that once again military logic dictates that if the ground offensive is to continue in Kashmir, there will be no easy successes for India.[92] This being a mountainous region, quick decisive victories can be ruled out. Maria Sultan thinks that India might then have to open a second front somewhere south to gain territory. This is where her argument becomes unsustainable from the Indian point of view. If India does go in

brilliant. The only flaw was that it had not catered for the "environment"' (Qadir 2002). After his retirement from the Pakistan Army, Brigadier Qadir became the Vice President of Islamabad Peace Research Institute.

[87] Haider 1999.

[88] Cotta-Ramusino and Martellini 2002.

[89] Shahi et al. 1999.

[90] Sultan 2002.

[91] She argues that '"military necessity" would dictate India to gain strategic advantages in areas other than Kashmir that would automatically lead to the expansion of the conflict zone and hence a large scale conventional war.' This line of thinking on military strategy is substantiated by many retired military generals and strategists in Pakistan.

[92] Ibid.

for a limited military action across the line of control, it will be with limited political objectives. So far this seems to be the demolition of terrorist training camps and related infrastructure. Writing on this issue, Samina Ahmed says, 'given that an exercise of the nuclear option in a limited conflict is highly unlikely, the conventional arms imbalance between the two states would work to Pakistan's disadvantage.'[93] Although even the limited military action that India might consider undertaking is ambiguous, it seems fairly unlikely that India would want to open another front in Punjab or Rajasthan to bargain territory after the war without escalation or threat of use of nuclear weapons—thereby making the whole notion of limited war rather fragile and highly unpredictable.

That brings us to George Fernandes' thesis of the likelihood of limited Indo-Pak conflict taking place in future under the umbrella of nuclear weapons. What remains unclear in the real world of warmongering politicians catering to domestic constituencies, intelligence gathering (including breakthroughs), satellites and a restive local population is, if indeed a situation does warrant a short swift limited means military operation across the border, at what stage of such a conflict would it lead to large-scale hostilities or opening of another front or the recourse to the use of nuclear weapons? Given the reality that Pakistan will continue to stoke proxy war in Jammu and Kashmir and has promised 'many more Kargils', the following modes of action present themselves to India:[94]

- First, to remain on the defensive. The next Pakistani incursion or attack could be awaited and repelled, using the same tactics used during the Kargil War. Air power could be utilised, but the sanctity of the line of control would remain inviolate; in consequence, the war would be strictly limited in space to the territories of India.
- Second, to pursue a policy of 'proportionate retaliation' by launching controlled attacks or incursions across the line of control into undefended Pakistani territory. Thus, the border war in India could be extended into Pakistan, but in a symmetrical and delimited manner to avoid escalation.

---

[93] Ahmed 1998: 361–62.
[94] Chari 2003b.

- Third, India could launch a punitive attack to degrade Pakistan's military machine. Logistics and communication centres could be selectively targeted to minimise collateral damage and inflict attrition, but without occupying territory. This option would not be risk free. Pakistan may not be deterred, but might retaliate and escalate the conflict to higher levels; this cannot be discounted.
- Fourth, to pursue either of the first two options, and simultaneously launch a diplomatic offensive to seek international support for restraining Pakistan from its military adventurism. Given its present isolation and dependence on external financial support, a judicious combination of political and financial pressure might induce Pakistan to behave responsibly within the international community. The contrary argument must be noticed. Pakistan is a desperate nation; hence, its further isolation could induce unpredictable behaviour, like North Korea. There can be no guarantees, but the old adage holds: nothing ventured, nothing gained.

Initiating a limited war without clearly identifying the political and military objectives therefore remains at best a diplomatically and strategically unviable option, and a very risky proposition at worst. Complex interplay of factors and variables even from out of the region question the power of governments alone to contain any crisis.[95] These variables and factors are tangible or even quantifiable, such as the ability of technical intelligence, or intangible, such as the systematic assessment, soundness of policies, the competence and idiosyncrasies of leaders that are in power and how they struggle with ignorance, knowledge, intentions and miscommunication. Additionally, competing grand strategies, inter-services rivalry, differences in national military capabilities, misperception of the adversarial capabilities in many areas, and poor quality of leadership quality often manifest themselves. There is also a general weakness in domestic political and organisational structures (particularly true for Pakistan), and the continual intrusion of domestic pressures on matters of high politics (very true of India). The domestic political context encourages the adoption of power politics and often leads to outbreak of wars. As John Vasquez has said, 'the driving out of accommodationist influences in the domestic

---

[95] The role of the US, in particular, can be highlighted both in the Kargil and the Parliament attack crises.

environment of both rivals is an important step toward war and a domestic prerequisite for public mobilisation.'[96] Given the peculiarities of any crisis, the manner in which these variables interact with each other normally determines a large set of outcomes. The road to deterrence stability is long, and unfortunately in Southern Asia, fraught with many crises. This gives rise to the necessity of reducing the risks that might escalate a conventional war to a nuclear level. Also required are confidence and security building measures in the nuclear realm.

This brings the argument to the issue that is central to Indo-Pak relations—Jammu and Kashmir.[97] On its part, India has made substantial political inroads towards addressing the issue. The autonomy package passed by the Jammu and Kashmir Assembly has been discussed in the Parliament, though unfortunately rejected by the central government. The Government of India should have passed the autonomy report to assuage the hurt feelings of the Kashmiri people. If and when it is implemented, one can assume that autonomy thus given may just be the maximum that the Government of India can offer under the Constitution. At least the elections that were held in late 2002 were internationally acclaimed to be 'free and fair'.[98] For its part, India too has considered every possible solution to solve the Kashmir imbroglio, from maintaining the status quo to granting greater autonomy.[99] Presently, on its part, India could work on two fronts—the political and the semi-legal: (a) India should annually review the working of all the anti-terror laws and see that the due process of law is followed against all prisoners; (b) there should be a thorough and impartial investigation of all reports of extra-judicial killing, custodial death, rape and disappearance by security and paramilitary forces and those

[96] Vasquez 1993: 223.

[97] For the crisis in Jammu and Kashmir, see Ganguly 1996, 1999b; Lamb 1992; Thomas 1991; Puri 1993; Behera 2000. For the finest historical perspectives, see Gupta 1966; Dasgupta 2002. For two reports on Kashmir (though a little dated) from different perspectives, see Bajpai et al. 1998 and Kashmir Study Group 1997.

[98] To the extent of defeating the ruling state government which is a member of the ruling coalition at the centre. Also see in this context, Blackwill 2002.

[99] This inspite of the promises to the US on stopping cross-border terrorism. But India continues to be indecisive on whether the infiltration has gone down or has remained where it is.

responsible, including military personnel, should be prosecuted; (c) the political process initiated by the October 2002 elections should be taken as the starting point to hold dialogues between representatives of ethnic, religious and political parties of Jammu, Kashmir and Ladakh. The return of Kashmiri Pandits to the valley should be facilitated and their safety and economic security ensured; and (d) local industries should be revitalised and the growth of the private sector supported. On its part, Pakistan could do well by following up firmly on commitments to prevent incursions across the line of control by militants and permanently disband all militant infrastructure in Pakistan and Kashmir. India had made many unilateral gestures of peace to the Kashmiris. Pakistan could also bring some form of representative government in Pakistan administered Kashmir. It is possible to facilitate a dialogue between Kashmiris on both sides of the LoC.

On the line of control, in the long run the only solution is accepting the *de facto* line of control as the international border.[100] P.R. Chari has argued, 'A counsel of moderation would suggest that the only practicable solution to the Kashmir problem would be acceptance of the *de facto* line of control as the international border and thereby recognize the division of Kashmir by according it *de jure* status.'[101] Though this is a minority view in India, it seems to be the only politically viable solution as borders are no longer altered by the use of force.

In such a situation, the question of the level of progress which can be achieved towards normalising bilateral relations, given the pressure from the armed forces and the domestic constituency, is better left unanswered. On its part, India has made serious mistakes in the past of rigging elections, misgovernance, lack of accountability, absence of checks and balances, and not taking into account the growing resentment in the valley of Kashmir, which made the conditions ripe for it to become a fertile ground for Pakistan's 'asymmetric strategies'. The attack on the Jammu and Kashmir Assembly on 1 October 2001, followed by the attack on the Indian

---

[100] See Chari 1995.

[101] Ibid.: 156. He further suggests, 'A resolution of the Kashmir problem does not seem possible unless these ground realities are understood and wisdom dawns on both India and Pakistan that no political solution is possible by adopting maximalist positions.'

Parliament on 13 December 2001, was a manifestation of these strategies, precipitating the Indo-Pak border confrontation crisis.

✠ LIKELY SCENARIOS OF BREAKDOWN OF DETERRENCE

This is not a comprehensive list of future wars; indeed there can be none. Based on past behaviour, risk-taking capability and the pressure of domestic constituency in these states, the following scenarios can be thought to be the likely issues over which there could be a breakdown of deterrence.

INDIA–PAKISTAN

- The most likely issue over which India and Pakistan may clash is Kashmir. It could begin as a low-key border engagement and may even involve other regions. The Pakistani motivation would be to wrest Kashmir from India, and in the course of military engagement use veiled nuclear threats to attract the attention of Western powers, particularly the US, to intervene. Pakistan may also get tired of no foreign intervention and may eventually decide to go at it alone, move forces into the chicken neck area and try to choke Indian supplies to Kashmir. India could then move armoury through Pakistani Punjab and begin air raids. Facing defeat Pakistan could call for outside intervention while threatening nuclear strikes. The US might intervene in the situation, asking both parties to withdraw to the present LoC.

This scenario is likely if the violence in Kashmir continues and the US is not able to exert further pressure on Pakistan to shut down the terror factories. A limited military engagement, often the use of small arms and artillery continues on and off along the line of control, and so the chances of limited military action on the soil of the other country exist. In the past, Pakistan has experimented with this strategy, and of late there has been talk of 'limited war' in India. In the Kargil conflict and the post-Parliament phase, India established a norm of not crossing the LoC and it is unlikely that this norm will be breached. Even if it is, the political objectives of such limited military engagement have to be very clear.

- Another scenario can be if Pakistan steps up militant activity along the line of control in any other sector that is similar to the Kargil adventure. India's patience might run out and it might launch air raids against terrorist training camps in Pakistan-administered Kashmir. Pakistan could construe this as aggression, and domestic pressures might force Pakistan to resort to the nuclear option.

This scenario assumes that India will initiate military action across the LoC. If such an action continues only against targets that are artillery shelled and does not involve soldiers or special forces crossing the LoC or air power for cross-border operation, it is possible that India could undertake such an operation without fear of escalation. The success further depends on a variety of factors. If Pakistan raises the stakes, opens another front, then domestic pressures in both countries could demand a definitive outcome.

- Having been tested at a higher threshold than ever before, that is, the attack on the Parliament, if any higher functionary in the Government of India or any government vital installation is attacked and domestic pressure builds up within India that favours an action across the line of control or international border, India might amass its troops and undertake limited action to eliminate the terrorist training infrastructure. Pakistan could then declare its sovereignty as threatened and retaliate with a nuclear attack on one of India's major cities.

Obviously such a strike in India will have to be undertaken by a fidayeen squad. There has to be credible evidence of the involvement of the non-state actor. If the Indian army crosses the LoC, Pakistan will initiate a response within its sovereign rights. After a few loud threats, it is possible that a nuclear test would also be carried out on Pakistani soil as final signal against India. It is unlikely that India would then want to escalate the conflict.

- And finally irked by India's continual snubbing of foreign intervention/mediation, Pakistan could move its forces into Kashmir. Unable to meet the challenge from the Indian forces and left with decreasing options, Pakistan might then decide to have a technology demonstration on an Indian armoury column.

Although it cannot be ruled out, it is unlikely that having lost three wars, Pakistan will still want to engage India in a conventional conflict. Conventional deterrence also works.

- Under the weight of internal contradictions, Pakistan could start facing increasing unrest and blame India for it. Reaching an extreme point, Pakistan might decide to use its 'weapon of last resort' against India, irrespective of whether or not India is to blame.

The international community is today engaged in a much greater way in helping Pakistan resolve many of these internal contradictions. The US has given a vast amount of money to reform Pakistan's education system. There is a constant inflow of aid and there is a very concerted effort to keep Pakistan from becoming a 'failed state'. A failed state with large number of non-state actors will be America's worst fear and India's biggest worry. It is unlikely that this will happen.

CHINA–INDIA

At the present levels of engagement, it is highly unlikely that India and China will ever engage each other in a nuclear war and any scenario between China and India is certainly less likely than that between India and Pakistan. However, it is likely that:

- China could try to do a 'salami slicing' of parts of India that it claims to be its own.

This is the only plausible motive for a forcible settlement of the dispute to China's advantage, howsoever remote. China is more likely to move towards a satisfactory resolution of all its border disputes with India, once it stands convinced that New Delhi poses no genuine threats to its strategic objectives.

- Irked by India's continuous raising of the issue of Chinese material assistance to Pakistan with nuclear material and technology, China might decide to 'teach India a lesson'. It could drop a nuclear bomb on Arunachal Pradesh (India's North-east state bordering China). China has border claims over this state, and its NFU does not apply to its own areas. India cannot respond with nuclear weapons because of China's superior 'third strike capability'. India's conventional forces need a lot of time to be mobilised into wartime deployment from the Western border. Arunachal could then become part of China .

The chances of such a scenario are highly unlikely. It is unlikely that China will suddenly find India's raising the issue of transfer of nuclear materials and technology irksome, since India has been doing this for a long time.

- Irked by political support to the Tibetan movement through its exiled head, the Dalai Lama, China might warn India to stop housing Tibetans. If India does not comply, a massive air raid could be carried out against India and all Tibetan camps and cultural centres could be bombarded. India cannot respond in these situations because of the fear of escalation to a different level and because it still has no credible deterrent against China.

Even this is remote. It is unlikely that China would undertake such a military operation. It will provide no strategic and political long-term gains for China. Also, India does have a deterrent relationship with China, howsoever rudimentary.

As things stand, it is likely that both the Sino-Indian and Indo-Pak dyads are likely to experience modest levels of deterrence stability in the medium and long term. But in the short term, it is likely that Pakistan would find it difficult to shut down the terror factories, and some of these non-state actors might destabilise the region. The main reason for stability in the medium and long term is that two of the bigger states in this dyad—China and India—are not revisionist states and have a pacifist approach towards solving their outstanding issues. The real unresolved issue is the territorial dispute on which substantial progress has been made (maps have been exchanged). On the other hand, Pakistan's behaviour *has been* prone to risk taking and revisionism. This has implications for deterrence stability. The use of non-state actors for political ends by Pakistan has further complicated strategic calculations and put stable deterrence under pressure. The scenarios discussed earlier involve quick advances by conventional forces and result-oriented action by special forces. While either state (India or Pakistan) could gear its military towards such an action, there is a level of conventional deterrence between India and Pakistan. That being so, in any outbreak of armed hostilities, India will have to strive for escalation dominance, which, given a dynamic strategic environment, will be extremely difficult, even if it is militarily possible.[102] The respective armed forces are not geared for rapid advances. Moreover, in both the dyads neither China nor India seek to occupy territory and retain it. Finally, neither state, even if they can find the capability for rapid advances or 'splendid strikes', will be able to support a compelling political objective for having to resort to any large military action. One caveat, however, remains. Pakistan continues to remain structurally weak, economically fragile and socially incohesive. In the past, it has resorted to risk-prone behaviour, and stability in the region continues to be a function of crucial choices by Pakistan which often seek to alter the status quo with the use of force or sub-conventional warfare. It would thus seem that there is a low level of deterrence stability, as there are several variables that severely test it.

✠ REDUCING RISKS: TOWARDS AN OVERALL STRATEGY OF PREVENTING CONFLICT

Possessing nuclear weapons does not automatically translate into stable deterrence, while the stability of the politico-military environment is not a direct function of the nuclear arms race. On the contrary, the balance of deterrence, upon which this stability essentially rests, does indeed contain an inherent component of instability, and this is exaggerated by changes in the technological and strategic environment. To alleviate this element, stability must be fundamentally achieved in all sectors of military and strategic environment, lest stability in one sector creates instability in another. In any attempt to stabilise the military–strategic environment, when deterrence is a relationship between three nuclear powers, there is always the possibility of involvement of an independent player with nuclear capability. This role in Southern Asia is completed by the presence of the United States. It has increased in the post-9/11 scenario, as history has witnessed the creation of a new imperial order with its roots in an anarchic international system. It led to the restructuring of US Cold War alliances, like that with Pakistan, and forging new ones with the Central Asian

---

[102] Even this fact is contested by many retired Indian army generals.

states. It also resulted in a massive increase of US military spending and in shaping public opinion for a specific value system designed against Islamic fundamentalism. Within the larger framework of the 'war against terror', the US military–industrial complex justified a huge increase in the military budget. Over the longer term, the US perceives China, and not Al Qaida or Islamic fundamentalism, as its primary strategic concern.[103] The US military presence in Central Asia and the military campaign in Afghanistan have serious implications for China's military modernisation, which will have a 'trickle down' effect on India and Pakistan. As has been perceptively noted,

> It demonstrated the reach of US military power across land and sea borders. Coupled with the proposed National Missile Defence, it makes the US almost invulnerable. The use of naval aircraft in the air strikes on Afghanistan is a major cause for concern to China, especially for its interests in Taiwan and South China Sea. China's bargaining power in East Asia, especially in its relations with Japan, South Korea and Taiwan, depends on its constructing a credible military deterrent against growing US power.[104]

Problems in estimating the intentions and capabilities of adversary states are not always due to the lack of information, but also attributable to the inherent difficulties of interpreting information that is available.[105] For instance, in many situations the data is inconclusive, and thus intelligence analysts and policy makers present conflicting interpretations and draw different conclusions from the same information.[106] Another unsettled debate is on the levels of transparency. It may lead analysts and policy makers, inadvertently or even deliberately, to interpret and structure selectively the information they get in order to make it consistent with their own set of pre-existing preferences, beliefs and images of the adversary.[107]

---

[103] Rajain 2002g.

[104] See Gupta 2003a.

[105] Actually, an information breakthrough during a crisis can lead to more difficult calculations in the host state. Not every scenario can be war gamed in peacetime.

[106] Betts 1978.

[107] Jervis 1976.

While India and Pakistan have started taking the first few steps on the nuclear road, China has travelled on this road since 1964. Following the May 1998 nuclear tests, there is strategic and political need for the Southern Asian states to engage in nuclear issues and stabilise their relationship, despite the baggage of hostile bilateral relationships and political rhetoric. Since the Indo-Pak nuclear tests cannot be undone, both countries need to decide what strategic options they should pursue that serve their national and regional interests. However, China, India and Pakistan have adopted different political approaches to arms control regimes and disarmament, and issues like general and complete disarmament that subsume nuclear disarmament.

India and Pakistan now have to deal with the political, strategic and military issues that are involved in nuclear weaponisation and deployment. They are in the process of establishing credible command and control arrangements over their nuclear arsenal and evolving a doctrine for the possible use of nuclear weapons (in the event of failure of deterrence) and the military strategy that guides them to such a goal. There is a marked asymmetry in the dyads that comprise this triangle—India vis-à-vis China and Pakistan vis-à-vis India—both in conventional and nuclear weaponry. This should not become an obstacle to the establishment of a plausible nuclear restraint regime or in evolving credible nuclear risk reduction measures between the three nuclear weapon powers in the region.[108] Hence, there is a distinct possibility of escalation of regional conflict from the sub-conventional level to crossing the nuclear threshold.[109] At present, India and Pakistan face an invidious choice between proceeding further to weaponising and deploying their nuclear arsenal sooner or later, or resting content with their present capabilities. This is also a function of the kind of nuclear weapons state India and Pakistan would want to become. Should India and Pakistan proceed towards weaponisation and deployment, and China continue with its nuclear modernisation plans, there are several risk-reduction measures that could be contemplated in the interest of nuclear stability of the region.[110] There were many

---

[108] See Gupta and Rajain 2003.

[109] Already Pakistan has promised more Kargils, and Indian strategists, including K. Subrahmanyam and Gen V.P. Malik, are talking in terms of 'limited war' being a possibility. This has been discussed elsewhere in this book.

[110] Gupta and Rajain 2003.

measures that were included in the ill-fated Lahore Declaration, including advance notification of missile tests, moratorium on nuclear tests, upgradation of existing communication links, undertaking measures to reduce the risk of accidental or unauthorised use of nuclear weapons, agreement to prevent incidents at sea, establishing a consultative machinery to ensure effective implementation of confidence-building measures, and bilateral consultations on security, disarmament and non-proliferation.[111] These measures need to be fleshed out. Most importantly, India and Pakistan have to discuss their exact strategic concepts pertaining to the utility of nuclear weapons.[112] Risk-reduction measures must also include exchange of information on steps to ensure safety of stockpiles, and the establishment of hotlines between their air forces and nuclear establishments.[113] Finally, risk reduction should also involve a tacit agreement to avoid inflammatory statements from people holding responsible government positions, especially in times of crisis. In this milieu, there are many more risk-reduction measures that can be suggested:

- The establishment of reliable lines of communications across borders, for both military and political leaders.
- A formal agreement not to militarily change the status quo in sensitive areas.
- An agreement to minimise dangerous military practices with a potential for escalation or accidents.
- Special reassurance measures for ballistic missiles and nuclear weapon systems, including prior notification of missile launches and transparency in the deployment and dismantling of nuclear forces.
- Reliable command and control structures with exceptional intelligence gathering capabilities.

Understanding and establishing credible deterrence can be a precarious and demanding task that is full of uncertainty, as it operates in a dynamic strategic environment. Understanding the motivation of the adversary, coupled with his military capability to respond, can pre-empt or deter the host nation to (mis)calculate

---

[111] The Lahore Declaration unfortunately lies buried in the snows of Kargil.
[112] Gupta and Rajain 2003.
[113] Ibid.

the risks and costs that are involved in any military adventure. It is possible that in order to demonstrate the resolve, firmness and credibility,[114] a state might resort to issuing repeated threats—something that both India and Pakistan often indulge in, and adopting uncompromising bargaining positions—something that India tried, perhaps unsuccessfully, in the post-Parliament attack phase.[115] Any refusal by either state in such a situation would expose the government to the risk that the other may or may not back down; hence, the one willing to accept the greater risk will prevail. In this case, both governments had a choice between accepting the demands of the other, which could have led to an automatic de-escalation of the crisis and therefore a certainty in its outcome, or accepting an uncertain outcome (back channel diplomacy, international pressure to de-escalate the crisis, which may or may not work). In turn, this would have led to a military conflict ensuing from the demands not being met.[116] Glenn Snyder has also theoretically gamed the choice of outcomes that a country might decide to accept in bargaining.[117] He contends that the main component of each country's strength in this type of situation is 'critical risk', that is, the risk of the other side standing firm, leaving the initiator of the crisis with the choice of either standing firm or accepting the demands of the other side. This, Snyder says, is the risk that a government should be willing to accept as the consequence of standing firm. There is a choice with the bargainer of comparing his critical risk with an estimated probability—the probability that the other side will also stand firm whatever the consequences. An escalation at this juncture would leave no room for a face-saving solution to the bargainer. At the end of the troop mobilisation in September–October 2002, the gain India could show from the bargain was probably a decrease in infiltration and the 12 January 2002 speech by General Musharraf. The other demands were not met, but there was no armed conflict. However, during the crisis neither side wanted to

---

[114] It can also be argued that a sense of insecurity leads a state to raise the political rhetoric.

[115] There is a view that India was able to extract some concessions from Pakistan, a case in point being the 12 January 2002 speech. But purely in bargaining terms, the demands that India had placed following the attack on the Parliament, that is, extraditing of India's 20 most wanted terrorists and the closing of terrorist training camps inside Pakistan, were met.

[116] See Rajain 2003.

[117] Snyder 1961.

be seen as 'backing off'. This resulted in gradual de-mobilisation of the troops from the international border. Figure 7.1 lists two sets of options for states engaged in a bilateral confrontation, with each option having its own consequences. Here, State A needs to make a choice between Options Y and Z. Choosing Y would mean staying firm, which could lead to confrsontation, while the Z option would mean accommodating the adversary's demands and therefore, backing off.

Figure × 7.1
Pay-offs in a Bilateral Confrontation

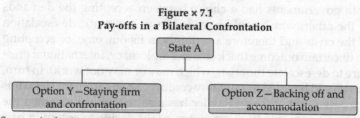

Source: Author's own illustration.

In such a situation there is also 'commitment' from either side or both sides that helps address the issue after the crisis is over. So in the post-Parliament attack phase, when Pakistan gave a commitment to clamp down on terrorist training camps, India was watchful. That commitment went a long way in addressing the core issue of terrorism (from India's point of view). Pakistan, on the other hand, suffered a setback on its core issue (Kashmir). India had to be convinced that this commitment was genuine and would yield tangible results on the ground.

The attack on the Indian Parliament has lowered the patience threshold for India but opened the window of 'risk that leaves something to chance'. The problem in such a situation is of a sudden and violent flare-up, coupled with the absence of communication. The environment that exists now has the potential of permitting incidents that are accidental and wholly unintentional—rather than the result of a deliberate provocation on the part of the state— rapidly reaching levels that neither state really wants. The outbreak of violence or another suicide attack on another Indian vital installation or an overzealous military commander might suddenly take the situation into a spiral of misperception and miscommunication. In such an environment, India has to be careful and investigate each act minutely. If the atmosphere is volatile and full of mutual suspicion, then indeed events will take their own spiral effect that any government might fisnd difficult to contain. On its part, Pakistan has to understand that the terror factory that it has supported all these years might become the initiator of any such crisis—hence, the global emphasis on closing down the terrorist training camps and supporting infrastructure.

The juxtaposition of India's nuclear doctrine of punitive retaliation with the backdrop of 'calibrated use of force' just below full conventional engagement, presents many challenges to deterrence stability. A similar grey area exists in Pakistan's nuclear doctrine. Pakistan's use of sub-conventional means to bleed India in Jammu and Kashmir on the one hand, and to immediately threaten to use 'all weapons' at any assertive response by India on the other, provide further challenges to deterrence stability. Southern Asia exhibits a test case where limited use of force under the nuclear umbrella cannot be ruled out.

One unintentional outcome of the 1998 nuclear tests has been the realisation that any bilateral confrontation in the region will receive the attention of the global community in general, and the US in particular. The presence of the US and its shuttle diplomacy often leads to another scale of coercive diplomacy that shapes the outcome in a very different way. Any state willing to undertake risks and breach established norms must take this into account— which as a matter of fact Pakistan did not, during the 1999 Kargil crisis. Sooner or later, there has to be a mutual recognition of strategic asymmetry and consequently a relative willingness on the part of Pakistan to realise that adventurist and risk-prone behaviour will no longer translate into tangible gains on the ground.

In such a crisis situation, the term 'crisis management' has serious connotations. Crisis management is primarily concerned with confronting the delicate balance of combining elements of conflictual and cooperative behaviour in an overall policy that seeks to protect national interests of a state, while avoiding armed conflict. Phil Williams, providing an excellent description of crisis management, says,

> crisis management is concerned on the one hand with procedures for controlling and regulating a crisis so that it does not get out of hand and lead to war, and on the other hand with ensuring that the

crisis is resolved on a satisfactory basis in which the vital interests of the state are secured and protected.[118]

At the heart of any calculation on coercive diplomacy is bargaining without overt nuclear signalling, something that India tried in the post-Parliament attack phase. There are many factors such as mis-perception, cognitive rigidity and effects of stress on the decision-making group that impinge on the effectiveness of crisis bargaining. A function of this are the decisions concerning the level and timing of military escalation in a crisis, invariably involving difficult questions about what trade-offs need to be made between military and political considerations. In any such situation, a defender's failure to match the military escalation of the potential attacker can encourage the latter to believe that a *fait accompli* can be achieved with the use of force, thereby deterring the attacker from actually intervening in the defence of its ally. Windows of opportunity and vulnerability perceived by the potential attacker can threaten the success of deterrence in a crisis.[119] The important implication is that the potential attacker's perception of the costs of not using force can play a critical role in the success or failure of deterrence. The emphasis in deterrence theory has been on the need for the defender to possess sufficient military strength to inflict substantial costs on the attacker in an armed conflict, and on ways to make a military response by the defender seem as credible as possible. But at the same time, it is imperative to recognise that military considerations often provide partial, if not insufficient, explanations of deterrence outcomes.[120] Paul Huth is of the opinion that for successful crisis management, the defender needs to appreciate the political costs of not pressing ahead with force, while the attacker must understand the potential damage to bargaining reputation and domestic political support.[121] The issue central to any crisis or chicken game is the establishment of the credibility of the threats, and the will to pursue the threatened course of action in the event of the bargain failing. It is argued that such a threat carries more credibility if issued publicly rather than through back channel

---

[118] Williams 1972: 30.

[119] Huth 1988.

[120] Many scholars of deterrence theory have underscored this point, including Russett 1967; Jervis et al. 1985: chs 3, 5 and 9; and George and Smoke 1974.

[121] Huth 1988.

diplomacy. Both the sides have to realise that there could be out-break of armed hostilities if the demands are not met. But this is complicated by the fact that in South Asia, the added variable of domestic politics leaves no state with a face-saving formula. A state should not head towards military action with little or no room to swerve at the last moment to prevent outbreak of hostilities. There has to be an exit strategy. Neither should it lock itself in a particular position by placing a set of demands that cannot be met. There has to be 'a last clear choice' to avoid collision. It has been noticed that Pakistan at times follows a deliberate strategy of 'the rationality of irrational', as an explicit recognition that significant benefits may accrue if India is made to believe that there are fringe elements which are not entirely rational and not completely in the control of the government. This is true for the actions of armed groups operating out of Pakistan, even though India finds it hard to believe that non-state actors can work with the kind of authority they wield, without covert or overt assistance from the Government of Pakistan.

The other deliberate strategy that Pakistan has followed in the recent past is the dramatic flouting of established conventions and norms, and leaving India guessing what the next move might be. These actions are described as initiatives that force the opponent to retaliate.[122] In such a situation, India has broadly three choices available: (*a*) India can match the escalation move by move; (*b*) India can carry on with its own course of action; or (*c*) be accommodating and concede to the game. Of these options, it is unlikely that India would ever concede to the game and be accommodating, leading to unilateral territory release. It is more likely that India would follow a combination of choices *a* and *b*. It could match the escalatory ladder to some steps in retaliation, while at the same time following a nuanced coercive diplomacy to highlight to the world Pakistan's role as a perpetrator of violence in Kashmir and other parts of the country. Either way, there is every likelihood of there remaining a 'risk that leaves something to chance'. This implies that crisis management has to be all the more robust.

A delicate task for any policy maker on either side of the border is to deter an adversary who is likely at the outset to doubt the state's commitment, while remaining sensitive to the potential threat and

---

[122] See Young 1968: ch. 14.

challenge posed by the opponent's actions. Policy makers should therefore try and devise a deterrent posture that is simultaneously credible and stable. A stable deterrent does not lead the potential attacker to be apprehensive of an offensive strike by the defender, and avoids challenging a potential attacker's bargaining reputation to an extent that leads to backing down from the threat to use force, on the one hand, and provoking the attacker and creating a spiral of escalating hostility, on the other.[123] In practice, achieving an effective and delicate balance between credibility and stability in diplomatic and military actions has been difficult for policy makers, and in Southern Asia this has been all the more difficult, given the complex interplay of forces, from public opinion, to checks and balances in the form of government, to inter-services rivalry. The equation is further complicated by the inability of any of the three states to clearly and confidently know what factors are critical in a potential attacker's calculus of loss and gain.[124]

P.R. Chari says, 'weaponisation and deployment of nuclear weapons will degrade rather than enhance its national security. Pakistan would be driven to weaponise and deploy its nuclear assets …. China would target India with its nuclear missiles.'[125] Looking internally, he adds that expanding nuclear capabilities will not

> enable India to halt the proxy war or cross-border terrorism in Kashmir … or counter the ethno-nationalism based insurgencies that bedevil Northeast India, or mitigate the growing non-military threats to the country's security. These threats are far more real and imminent than the hyped nuclear threat, which has largely been promoted by the compulsions of well-recognized groups with a vested interest.[126]

Looking externally, the argument has been made that nuclear weapons in India deterred it from crossing the line of control during the Kargil War, with Pakistani threat of using 'all weapons at disposal' perhaps being taken rather too credibly.[127]

---

[123] See Jervis 1976. Jervis presents an exceptional analysis of this problem while devising various propositions to explain when deterrent threats and actions will prevent or provoke an attack.

[124] For an elaboration of this argument, see Huth 1988: 13.

[125] Chari 2001b.

[126] Ibid.

[127] See Rajain (2002e, 2002f), for elaboration of this argument.

Therefore, the biggest confidence-building measure that can bring some stability and peace to the region is unarguably will be a peaceful resolution of the Kashmir problem. The past history of Indo-Pak wars and the festering sore of Kashmir have bedevilled the bilateral relationship between India and Pakistan. Briefly, the reasons lie in the options that India and Pakistan have exhausted on the Kashmir issue. Pakistan has attempted direct invasion (1947), inciting militancy (followed by armed attack in 1965), again direct attack (1971), and low intensity conflict starting in 1988, which continues.

✳ KEY VARIABLES
IN FUTURE INTERACTIONS IN THE TRIANGLE

Looking at the next 8 to 10 years, one can evaluate patterns of relationship based on three parameters: conflictual, cooperative, and issue-based partially cooperative, partially conflictual.

Thanks to the exigencies of geography, current history, and now economics, from an Indian perspective, while Pakistan continues to remain nettlesome, the long-term security problem continues to be China. An important element of this triangular relationship is the ability of Pakistan to draw China in its favour and this is the critical feature that will absorb Indian resources and capabilities. India also continues to be suspicious of Chinese activities in Myanmar. It is the carving of these 'spheres of influence' that will determine the nature of the Sino-Indian relationship. India feels that using this indirect means of containing and implementing a larger grand strategy is detrimental to its interests in Southern Asia. This is what many Indians see as 'strategic encirclement' of India.

As India is the weaker of the two entities in this dyadic relationship, it is not surprising to see New Delhi being far more concerned about Chinese policies, capabilities and intentions than vice versa. The same is true of the Pakistan–India relationship. Pakistan also continues to be more concerned about Indian policies, capabilities and intentions than the other way round. If India is not fixated on Beijing's policies and capabilities in the same way as Pakistan is on India, the reasons can be located in divergent histories and perceptions.

Assisted by favourable geography, adequate conventional superiority, robust nuclear forces and a helpful neighbour in Pakistan, China can afford to disregard India and Indian capabilities for some time to come. But this may not happen for long, and it is likely that in the coming decade the countries will not just be competing for the same foreign direct investment, but also for 'spheres of influence'. India's sheer size, capabilities, resources and the economy make it a strong candidate, along with Japan and Russia, in Asia. India could become a regional rival in Central Asia in the short term and in the Persian Gulf in the long term. Within South Asia, China and India are likely to continue waging what John Garver has termed a 'protracted contest' to exercise regional dominance.[128] Any containment strategy of India might therefore need to have more elements. Pakistan provides a fine low-cost high-return option for any such containment of India. Given this, the complexity of evolving Sino-Indian relations, although initially rooted in a struggle over security issues, will now have to encompass economic, ideational and institutional instruments that pertain to the recognition of spheres of influence.

In this milieu it seems Pakistan has other thoughts. Primarily because of its anti-status quo orientation in South Asia, Islamabad has sought to utilise its nuclear capabilities not simply for deterrence but also to permit the use of non-state actors to manipulate risks in order to secure certain contested political goals. Operationally, this translates into seeking to debilitate India through the mechanism of low-intensity conflict that is waged on the premise that New Delhi cannot retaliate conventionally for fear of sparking a nuclear holocaust.[129] This tool has further sought to, at least one occasion, change the status quo by force.

While it may be very difficult to predict the behaviour of China, India and Pakistan in a crisis situation, one can attempt to locate some past practices, domestic and international factors that may influence future choices that these states could make.

1. All of these states have to determine whether nuclear weapons are weapons of war or of deterrence.[130] Going by the declaratory

---

[128] Garver 2001.

[129] See in the context of how Pakistani nuclear coercion fits into its larger grand strategy, Arnett 2000.

[130] In the context of the linkage between deterrence and coercion, see Cimbala 1998.

policy—India and China are on no-first-use, while the 'un-official' Pakistan policy locates Pakistani nuclear weapon use in four scenarios—(a) when its communications are cut; (b) when there is a massive invasion; (c) economic strangulation; and (d) internal subversion.[131]

2. With the US now firmly on the road to make a ballistic missile defence, its repercussions will be felt in Beijing, which may be prompted to respond by improving its second strike capability. This will invariably lead to renewed enthusiasm in the arms race between New Delhi and Islamabad. States look up to the US for taking firm steps towards disarmament. What is happening instead is that the US pursuit of an NMD is leading to many simultaneous arms races in different parts of the world.

3. China, Pakistan and India have to work out a restraint regime wherein nuclear weapons are used as tools of war prevention and deterrence, rather than as weapons of fighting war.

4. Chinese efforts to increase credibility of its nuclear force by improving it make New Delhi suspicious. Any Indian effort to weaponise and deploy its strategic assets has an impact in Islamabad as well. This is an ongoing process and is likely to speed up with the US keen on NMD.

5. The structures of governance will have to be strengthened all over the region. China is looked upon as a state that uses an iron hand to curb all anti-state protests. If this continues, the undercurrents of discontentment are likely to affect forces of nationalism. India has been addressing such issues, but much more needs to be done than merely the increase in the number of states. The scars of Gujarat will take a long time to heal.[132] Pakistan too is a state that is facing crises not just of integration, but of economic dimensions as well. It is only when Pakistan

---

[131] This is a combination of Shahi et al. (1999) and Cotta-Ramusino and Martellini (2002). The writings of many other army officers and scholars indicate similar positions. See, for instance, articles in the *Defence Journal*, *Dawn*, *Herald*, *Newsline*, *The Nation* and *The News International*.

[132] See Varadarajan (2002) for a compelling account that is 'intended to be a permanent public archive of the tragedy that is Gujarat. Drawing upon eyewitness reports from the English, Hindi and regional media, citizens' and official fact-finding commissions, and articles by leading public figures and intellectuals, it provides a chilling account of how and why the state was allowed to burn.'

can overcome these challenges that one can hope for the process of political development to strengthen.

6. Equitable social and economic justice is the key to good governance, and this can only happen if and when the state addresses many challenges it faces on the governance front. For this, the respective states have to have political systems that facilitate such a process.

7. The notion that 'real security is connected to the enrichment of human lives' introduces the concept of humane governance, which in turn is 'dedicated to securing human development.' Over the last couple of decades, small arms proliferation, migration, environmental degradation, cross-border terrorism have threatened state sovereignty, and therefore, human development in general.

Coming to issues of 'high politics' in the armed forces, nuclear weapons, force structures, deterrence, etc., the following seem important:

1. It seems likely that China will continue to improve its nuclear weapons force, and continue making the PLA 'a lean mean fighting machine'—something that will have effect on New Delhi's options.

2. Additionally, as has been perceptively noted, India must evaluate China at what it might be 20 years hence.[133]

3. It also seems likely that New Delhi will continue on its path towards making a nuclear triad. Islamabad is going to be affected by this, and coming under immense domestic pressure it is likely to try and match up to India in this gradual arms race. This will heavily impact the economic situation of both countries, but more so that of Pakistan.

4. It may be very difficult to negotiate, but at least some movement forward can declaratorily be made. An NFU is required for all the nuclear weapons states, but being concerned with Southern Asia, a policy of NFU followed by all three states in the region will instil confidence.[134]

---

[133] See SAPRA 1996.

[134] Needless to add that Pakistan would never enter into an NFU with India. Pakistan's thinking on a nuclear policy is almost completely military–strategic (and not political).

5. There are many programmes that have been used in the context of the Cold War and can be used to bring about peace in Southern Asia. There is some talk of nuclear risk reduction centres for this region. Proposals like this could be institutionalised.[135]

6. A few institutions do exist such as the 1990 pact on non-attack of nuclear facilities between India and Pakistan—this has scrupulously been honoured in spite of the crests and troughs of Indo-Pak relations.

The CBMs that were a part of the Lahore Declaration need to be strengthened. There is a need for both India and Pakistan to arrive at a common strategic wavelength as far as weapon alert status is concerned. This could be a function of their relationship and is important to prevent escalation in any future border conflict or any larger military engagement. Any measure that aims to clearly communicate and diffuse crisis or even delay an authorised launch does merit consideration. Unilateral actions that improve command and control and cross-border monitoring will be significant steps towards regional stability.

On the central issue of deterrence stability, there is every likelihood that some form of stability will ensue, although it will be repeatedly tested. In the near future, with the Kargil War still fresh in memory, Pakistan is unlikely to undertake similar adventures, but it is likely that it will continue to seek a change in the status quo. Like China, Indian NFU is a serious policy declaration and is further reinforced at the operational levels. But if innocent lives continue to be lost in Kashmir, this phase of stability will come under increasing stress. On its part, Pakistan too does not maintain nuclear weapons at a high state of alertness. Even if Pakistan were to contemplate using nuclear weapons on Indian troops across the line of control, the stark geographic vulnerabilities of Pakistan imply that even a limited reaction by India will ensure the total destruction of functional state and society in Pakistan.

On the other hand, the Sino-Indian dyad seems to present a higher level of deterrence stability. There are currently no issues

---

[135] Even if it is a Western construct, there is no harm in exploring something that can strengthen stability in this region. Gen V.R. Raghvan (Delhi Policy Group, New Delhi) and Dr Rajesh Rajagopalan (Jawaharlal Nehru University, New Delhi) have suggested this for some time.

that warrant excessive use of force escalating up to a nuclear exchange. Both states continue to maintain forces at dispersed and low states of alertness and are doctrinally committed to using nuclear weapons as political instruments.

COUNTRY TRENDS AND OUTCOMES

Based on various internal and external factors, the possible trends for the next 10–15 years of each country are given here.

India

As far as the nature of India's nuclear capability and the doctrine of its use are concerned, India has made it clear that it would define its own requirements after an assessment of the security environment. It has formally announced an NFU policy and non-use against non-nuclear weapons states. Mr Vajpayee had informed the Parliament of the 'defensive nature of [India's] nuclear capability.'[136] He has also clarified that an NFU policy with a minimum nuclear deterrent implies 'deployment of assets in a manner that ensures survivability and capacity of an adequate response.'[137] India has defined its national security objective thus:

> [A] secure deterrent against the use or the threat of use of weapons ... including accurate and refined delivery systems, will not be circumscribed in range and payload by any outside pressure or influence but will be determined by the country's threat perception at any point of time.[138]

With the current state of the forces and delivery options, India has at best a credible deterrent against Pakistan, but to develop the same against China will take a lot of time, and it will come at a price.[139] India also sees 'no reason why the international community should shy away from a similar measure to tackle nuclear weapons ....'[140]

---

136 Vajpayee 1998c.
137 Ibid.
138 Ministry of Defence 1985–2002, here 1998–99: 2.
139 In this context, see Bajpai 1999.
140 Lahiri 1999.

Earlier Indian forays into the question of nuclear disarmament were more idealistic than realistic. 'The current disharmony, therefore, between India and the rest of the globe is that India has moved from being totally moralistic to being a little more realistic, while the rest of the world has arrived at all its nuclear conclusions entirely realistically.'[141]

It is true that the BJP election manifesto for the Twelfth Lok Sabha (Lower House of the Indian Parliament) elections had clearly mentioned that it would 're-evaluate the country's nuclear policy and exercise the option to induct nuclear weapons; and expedite the development of the Agni series of ballistic missiles with a view to increasing their range and accuracy.'[142] The fact remains that election manifestos are not taken seriously in India. The proposals that India now makes at various international institutions, be it on global 'de-alerting' at the United Nations in 1998,[143] or on NFU at the ARF meet in 1999,[144] are now looked upon by the international community as being contradictory.

In spite of this erosion of credibility, India should strive for a nuclear weapons-free world in the long term. In the short term, India is realising that arms control is a viable option. The government must continue to campaign for the global elimination of nuclear weapons in a time-bound framework as it has done for the past five-and-a-half decades, but at the same time recognise that this can at best be 'normative'. It is not an achievable policy objective in the short term.[145] India needs to find a *modus vivendi* with the global nuclear order and participate in the many arms control agreements that seek partial solutions to the nuclear problem.

---

[141] Singh 1998.

[142] The relevant chapter of the BJP's election manifesto for the Twelfth Lok Sabha elections may be seen at http://bjp.org/manifes/chap8.htm, accessed on 25 May 1998. Further, the National Agenda for Governance issued by the BJP-led coalition for the twelfth Lok Sabha stated that 'we will re-evaluate the nuclear policy and exercise the option to induct nuclear weapons.' This is available at http://bjp.org/nagenda.htm, accessed on 25 May 1998.

[143] See Pawar 1998.

[144] At the 1999 ARF meet, India argued that unambiguous no-first-use commitments, expressed in an international agreement and reflected in military doctrines and force postures, would begin the process of delegitimisation of nuclear weapons, facilitate the process of nuclear disarmament and provide effective security assurances to the non-nuclear weapons states.

[145] Mohan 1998.

South Asian nuclear testing is not only a local problem. It is a problem of the international system that leads the country of Gandhi to follow a nuclear weapons path.[146] There is only one way out of the dilemma, and that is a commitment by all nuclear weapons states towards time-bound nuclear disarmament. According to a 1996 unanimous opinion of the International Court of Justice, the complete elimination of their nuclear arsenals is now the legal obligation of the nuclear weapons states under international law.[147] If India's nuclear tests lead to sufficient pressure on the nuclear weapons states to reverse their course and become serious about ending the nuclear weapons era, we may still be able to enter the 21st century with a treaty in place to accomplish this goal. If nuclear weapons states hold firm to their present positions, however, India may be only the first of many states to become a new member in the nuclear weapons club.

A nuclear weaponised India is in a unique position in the world community to serve the cause of disarmament. Today, India is the only nuclear weapons state calling for a nuclear weapons convention which will use the global and verifiable instruments put together by the international community to tackle the other weapons of mass destruction—namely, biological and chemical weapons—to completely abolish nuclear weapons.

At the present juncture, India is undergoing a number of domestic changes, the outcome of which will shape the destiny of the country. First of all, an economic revolution began in the early 1990s. Certain sectors of the economy which are doing increasingly well, such as information technology, telecom and insurance, have given an economic boost to other sectors also. Second, there is a social revolution, which means that the regional middle classes and the low castes have been increasingly asserting themselves over the last couple of decades. Besides getting official patronage, which is symbolised by increasing reservations, political parties too are cashing in on the agenda of social transformation. Third, a federal restructuring is under way in the country, whereby development agendas are being increasingly decentralised and devolved, coalition governments ensure greater participation of regional groups at the central level and new states are being carved out to

---

[146] Krieger 1999.
[147] *International Legal Materials* 1996.

suit all ends. Three new states came into being in India in 2000. Fourth, the past decade has witnessed cultural reorientation along moral and religious lines initiated by right-wing parties. The India that will emerge from these revolutions will have all the attributes of a great power and may exert power not just in the region but also in the world. Finally, the attention that India has received after becoming a declared nuclear weapons state has added to its international prestige. As Richard Falk admits, the West realises that India is 'pursuing a security logic based on the same sort of power politics that have guided the approach of the exiting nuclear weapons states.'[148]

Pakistan

This was the fourth time in the five-and-a-half decade history of politics in Pakistan that an army chief has decided to move in to depose a democratically elected incumbent government. And surprisingly, the initiative has turned out to be popular each time. This reflects the fragility of political development and mobilisation of democracy in Pakistan. Another difficult question that remains unanswered in Pakistan's internal polity is the sectarian strife between Shias and Sunnis in Punjab, and between Sindhis and Mohajirs in Sind. Additionally, one of the biggest challenges has been the large number of militant organisations that have mushroomed in Pakistan.[149] The nexus of drug money, politics and the culture of Kalashnikovs also threatens to create a thriving underworld which might dictate both domestic and international policies.[150] A CIA report noted that

> heroin is becoming the lifeblood of Pakistan's economy and political system. Those who control the production and international transport of heroin are using their resources to purchase protection, to

---

[148] Falk 2000.

[149] The danger from these organisations is summarised thus: militant organisations currently involved in Kashmir may have come together for the time being in anticipation of some major military gains in Indian occupied territory, but once it is obvious that there are no military solutions in Kashmir, they can easily turn upon each other. One should not forget that their sectarian loyalties take precedence over all other allegiances. If that happens, it will only be a matter of time before major cities in Pakistan turn into battlegrounds quite like the ones in Srinagar and Kabul (Khan 1999: 69).

[150] Hussain and Hussain 1993.

gain access to the highest political circles in the country, and to acquire a substantial share in the banks and industries being sold to private investors ... military intelligence used heroin profits to help finance the war in Afghanistan and has developed similar funding arrangements with Sikh militants in India and Kashmiri insurgents in India controlled Kashmir ... Pakistani experts on narcotics believe narcotics money now fuels the political system, supporting party organisations and election campaigns.[151]

Fortunately, for the world in general, and India in particular, the 12 January 2002 speech by General Musharraf promised to end Pakistan's terror factory.

On the issue of the future structure of Pakistan's nuclear weapons, Maleeha Lodhi, two-time Pakistani ambassador to the US (1994–97 and 1999–2002) and present High Commissioner to the UK.

emphasised that the two nuclear capable powers should not take the region over the next threshold of deploying nuclear weapons as that would create a hair-trigger environment in the region. Both countries should instead commit not to deploying (sic) ballistic missiles, and agree to a moratorium on further testing.[152]

Another issue of concern is that the armed forces in Pakistan have undermined the growth of political institutions, thereby stalling the process of political development, and have become the decision-making centre. There are authorities within the armed forces as well, the most prominent of these being the ISI. Unsurprisingly, they are pursuing an independent foreign policy agenda. Many in India are willing to believe that the Kargil operation in May 1999 was the handiwork of Gen Pervez Musharraf and the ISI, where the prime minister may not even have been informed of the impending intrusion. Many in Pakistan's academia and military circles privately concede that Pakistan's Kashmir policy has been wrong and that they cannot win Kashmir with the low intensity war in the post-9/11 phase. In the same breath, however, they stress that Pakistan cannot be seen to give up on the issue.[153]

---

[151] *The Friday Times* 1993.

[152] Lodhi 2004.

[153] Impressions gathered during interactions with a wide variety of scholars, military strategists, journalists and academics in a field trip to Pakistan in March–April 2001.

They are now prisoners of their success in manufacturing public consent to a particular solution to Kashmir.[154]

Even if Pakistan is not paranoid about home-grown terrorism, narcotics, proliferation of small arms, money laundering, drug trafficking, and foreign money inflow, its politicians are already posing threats to its security and exacting a high price from the nation. While Pakistan is still grappling with some of the older threats facing it, it is yet to comprehend threats from issues such as energy, water and food security, and cyber war threats that are just visible over the horizon. Politicians, the army and bureaucrats who benefit from covert money inflows may have vested interests in not having an integrated professional structure to monitor threats to national security in a comprehensive sense and initiate timely counter-action. There is a near total absence of accountability that has permeated various levels of the society, the government and the military. The military justifies increasing defence expenditure in the traditional action–reaction model with respect to India. Objectively speaking, even from a Pakistani point of view, the government can make efforts to try and reduce defence expenditure. The Kargil crisis proved that diplomacy may be a bigger tool for solving the Kashmir problem rather than any military engagement with India. A military government may have the legitimacy to do so, which a democratically elected government can never wield such authority and remain in power. It is for Pakistan to decide what amount of force is required for maintaining credibility especially when the nuclear bomb has arrived and has been justified as being a great conventional force leveller. Ayesha Siddiqa-Agha has suggested that military expenditure needs to be reduced, and funds thus created can be channelled into economic activities.[155]

---

[154] See Hoodbhoy and Mian 2000.

[155] Ayesha Siddiqa-Agha suggests (a) creating an audit act whereby the auditor-general of Pakistan would have more authority to check or control the waste of resources by the defence sector; (b) starting a phased programme of introducing performance audit of defence. It is one of the important measures to fathom the link between threat perception and military spending, arms procurement, etc.; and (c) empowering the audit department to gain access to all necessary documents, and to report its proceedings to the head of the government and state—a function that is not carried out at present (Siddiqa-Agha 2000b).

While continuing to grapple with internal political instability, Pakistan is likely to be faced with these options:

1. Accept Indian dominance, which would be a very difficult and unlikely situation for Pakistan to reconcile with. But as the forces of globalisation are strengthened and the digital revolution takes deep roots, with India continuing to grow at 6–8 per cent, Pakistan may be left far behind taking solace in nuclear weapons, Kashmir and the role of the armed forces in their society.
2. Continue to encourage terrorism not just in Kashmir but also in other parts of India, keeping the Indian army and the para-military forces engaged, while continuously acquiring missiles to provide deterrence. This is a low-cost high-return option that might pay quick dividends in the short term but in the long term is detrimental to Pakistan's interests.
3. Continue to compete with India by forging closer strategic relationships with China and North Korea. This is a possible low-cost and good-return option.
4. Use its political clout in the OIC and try to take up moral leadership in championing the cause of Muslims in various countries. This is already being done by Pakistan.
5. Attempt a short quick war against India and try to take Kashmir using direct military means under nuclear cover. Even if another Kargil-like situation takes place, Pakistan will not succeed, both because of the Indian response and the international opprobrium that it will generate.

Maintaining the autonomous capability to defend a nation's sovereignty and enhancing national interests are the principal responsibilities of governments. But nobody can dispute that money spent on arms in a developing economy must be at the expense of more pressing needs of social and infrastructural development. Yet, defence expenditure continues to go up, while developmental and infrastructural needs of the country get pushed to the background.

China

In the Western sense of the term, the Chinese government has not enunciated any 'grand strategy' in its activities and approach to international affairs; but from a Chinese perspective there is a grand strategy in place.[156] The Chinese government and its leaders

---

[156] Swaine and Tellis 2000.

have been largely preoccupied with domestic concerns, especially on the crucial issues of maintaining national unity and internal stability. One can infer from official statements by senior leaders, government planning documents, white papers and government-affiliated writings that the nearest Chinese equivalent to a grand strategy would be its 'national development strategy,' which aims to comprehensively develop potential in such a way that Beijing can achieve its long-term national goals. Chinese analysts measure four sub-systems of national power: (*a*) material or hard power (natural resources, economics, science and technology, and national defence); (*b*) spirit or soft power (politics, foreign affairs, culture, and education); (*c*) coordinated power (leadership organisation, command, management and coordination of national development); and (*d*) environmental power (international, natural and domestic). Based on this intellectual foundation, China's grand strategy aims to comprehensively develop national power, so that Beijing can achieve its long-term national goals. This strategy was first initiated by Deng Xiaoping in the late 1970s and has been reaffirmed by the post-Deng government, which is led by the Communist Party of China (CPC) General Secretary, Hu Jintao, President of the PRC.

China's primary national goal is to become a strong, modernised, unified and wealthy nation. It has all the attributes of comprehensive national power. It considers itself a developing power whose natural resources, manpower, nuclear-capable forces, seat at the UN Security Council and growing economy naturally give it most of the attributes of a great power. It wishes to see itself in relation to the position of other great powers. China also wants to become the pre-eminent Asian power by generating enough 'strength', so that no major action will be taken by any other international actor in Asia without first considering Chinese interests. Quite clearly, if present trends continue, Beijing believes it will achieve the status of a 'medium-sized' great power by 2050 at a minimum. China's military capabilities, its nuclear force modernisation and its ability to alter regional relationships will also be crucial. According to the 1998 white paper, the Chinese government holds that 'the international community should promote fair, rational, comprehensive and balanced arms control and disarmament; the purpose of disarmament should be to reinforce, not weaken or undermine, the security of all countries.'[157] This was further reiterated in the 2002 white paper: 'The Constitution of the People's Republic of China (PRC) clearly specifies the tasks of the armed forces of the PRC as being to consolidate national defense, resist aggression, defend the motherland, safeguard the people's peaceful labor, participate in national construction and strive to serve the people.'[158] Beijing has frequently made public and private statements that accuse the United States of engaging in hegemonic international behaviour. The Chinese believe that the current international situation is still complex and volatile, but in general, it is moving towards relaxation. Countries are working out their economic strategies as a task of primary importance to increase their overall national strength, so as to take up their proper places in the world in the next century. China also has enunciated a 'new security concept' that has called for basing international security on multilateral dialogue and on pledges by states to foreswear the use of military threats, coercion and military intervention in the internal affairs of other countries.

The Chinese military–industrial complex has proved to be inadequate to the task of narrowing the gap between the country's aspirations and its capabilities. One of the fundamental objectives of China's military modernisation programme is to create a force that is sufficient to defend against any regional opponent, maintain the credibility of territorial claims, protect national interests, maintain internal security, deter any moves by Taiwan towards *de jure* independence, and to deter aggression.

The current Chinese policies include force reduction efforts and selective new equipment that lay emphasis on building a more mobile, combat-ready core within the larger ground force. Currently, Beijing is downsizing its armed forces. The manpower thus removed is shifting into internal policing duties, and the PLA is being revitalised. This restructuring will contribute to the PLA becoming a military force that has three components: a modest nuclear force that maintains a viable deterrent against other nuclear powers, a small number of high-technology forces for flexible use

---

[157] State Council, PRC 1998: ch. 5.

[158] Further, 'China's state interests, social system, foreign policy and historical and cultural traditions postulate that China will inevitably adopt such a national defense policy' (State Council, PRC 2002: ch. 7).

in regional contingencies, and a larger number of forces equipped with low to medium-technology weapons for internal security. Over a decade ago, the PLA started shifting its strategic focus from the protracted, large-scale land warfare that characterised Mao Tse-tung's 'people's war' to fighting small-scale, regional conflicts along China's periphery. Thus, China's 'active defence' doctrine now focuses on conducting what is officially called 'people's war under modern conditions.' In other words, it can be described as 'local wars under high-tech conditions.' As Nathan and Ross have observed, 'Of all the large countries, China has the greatest freedom to manoeuvre, to act on grand strategy, shift alignments, and conduct a strategic foreign policy in the rational pursuit of national interest.'[159]

This has increased insecurity among other states, most prominently India. Another concern that India has and that it has continuously raised with the Chinese is the transfer of missile and nuclear materials to Pakistan. Moreover, any Chinese response to the proposed NMD, now or later, will impact India. China officially maintains a no-first-use policy; the NMD would render a second strike capability problematic. China is likely to accelerate its modernisation plans to qualitatively improve its arsenal.

A qualitative and quantitative improvement of Chinese nuclear forces would lead to an increased threat perception in New Delhi. An expansion of China's nuclear arsenal could also alter India's and Pakistan's strategic calculus. Right wing hardliners in both countries will favour qualitative and quantitative improvement in their nuclear arsenals. This could accelerate an arms race between them. A purely technical improvement in the existing nuclear arsenal of the three countries warrants further tests, while tests by any of the three states have the potential of leading to another trough in relations among them. It could also lead to the breakdown of deterrence as it has been operating in Southern Asia. After the rejection of the CTBT in the US Senate and the NPT being tested by North Korea, this may be the last thing the international arms control community would want. Once better and improved delivery systems have been tested, a natural corollary would be to miniaturise the warhead. Given the pressure of domestic constituencies, no political leader would want to appear weak on

---

[159] Nathan and Ross 1997: 14.

national security issues. While India might continue to develop delivery system indigenously, Pakistan might be compelled to rely on its 'strategic allies' China and North Korea for new missiles. While Pakistan might be content with acquiring a strategic equilibrium with India, Indian ambitions may compel it to project a regional power image, thus adding an impetus to a regional arms race. An NMD for the US, if and when it comes, has the potential to become a tool for damaging the precariously balanced arms control regimes, initiate many new arms races, including the on-going one in South Asia, and weaken the notion of deterrence as it exists today.

It may not be correct to import Western constructs—patterns of proliferation and modes of deterrence that have been used in the geo-strategic dyadic Cold War setting. An effective analysis of any region requires a delicate balancing of strategic concepts and an in-depth knowledge of cultures, politics, strategic environments and geo-political realities. This is particularly true of Southern Asia.

No society has been able to halt the 'technology trajectory'. Nuclear scientists will invariably push for acquiring longer-range missiles with better accuracy and miniaturised warheads, and encourage strategies involving counter-force, first strike, second strike and better delivery systems. There is no need for South Asian states to weaponise without affirming the Clauswitzian distinction between war and diplomacy. It is imperative, meanwhile, that Pakistan, China and India determine whether nuclear weapons are military or diplomatic weapons. South Asian nations need to reassess their priorities and understand the change in threats to their security. If indeed the region has to go down the nuclear road, then a number of transparency measures aimed at instilling confidence, increasing credibility, avoiding miscommunication that may lead to misperception and misinterpretation, are needed.

Expressing shock and disbelief at the South Asian nuclear tests, Nobel Laureate, Sir Joseph Rotblat in an article raised 'an accusing finger at the main culprits, the Nuclear Weapons States, who pursue a policy characterised by hypocrisy and double standards'. He questioned 'if the US, the mightiest country militarily, declares that it needs nuclear weapons for its security, how can one deny such security to States that have real cause to feel insecure?'[160]

---

[160] Rotblat 1998. Sir Joseph may not have been hinting at India and Pakistan, but raised a pertinent point.

REFERENCES AND SELECT BIBLIOGRAPHY

Abbas, Zafar. 1999. 'Whodunnit?' *The Herald* (Karachi), August.

Abbott, F. 1966. 'Pakistan and the Secular State', in D. Smith (ed.), *South Politics and Religion*. Princeton, NJ: Princeton University Press.

———. 1968. *Islam, Critical Essays in Social Anthropology and Pakistan*. Ithaca, NY: Cornell University Press.

Abel, Elie. 1966a. *The Missile Crisis*. Philadelphia: Lippincott.

———. 1966b. *The Missiles of October: Twelve Days to World War Three*. London: Cox and Wyman Ltd.

Abraham, Itty. 1998. *The Making of the Indian Atomic Bomb*. London: Zed Books.

Achen, Christopher H. 1987. *A Darwinian View of Deterrence*. Denver, CO: University of Denver, School of International Studies.

Achen, Christopher H. and Duncan Snidal. 1989. 'Rational Deterrence Theory and Comparative Case Studies', *World Politics*, 41 (2).

Acronym Institute. n. d. *The Various Acronym Reports*. London.

Aderson, Kym. 1997. 'On the Complexities of China's WTO Accession', *The World Economy*, 20 (6).

Ahmad, Ishtiaq (ed.). 1996a. *Nuclear Non-proliferation Issues in South Asia*. Islamabad: Pakistan Scientific and Technological Information Center Press.

———. 1996b. *The Nuclear Danger: Moving Down to Minimum Deterrence*. Islamabad: National Book Foundation of Pakistan.

Ahmad, M. 1963. *Government and Politics in Pakistan*. New York: Praeger.

———. 1985. *Pakistan at the Crossroads*. Karachi: Royal Book Company.

Ahmad, Mumtaz. 1988. 'Pakistan', in Shireen T. Hunter (ed.), *The Politics of Islamic Revivalism*. Bloomington, IN: Indiana University Press.

Ahmad, Nazir. 1957. 'The Atomic Energy Commission', *Pakistan Quarterly*, 7 (3).

Ahmed, A.S. 1986. *Pakistan Society: Islam, Ethnicity, and Leadership in South Asia*. Karachi: Oxford University Press.

Ahmed, Aziz. 1967. *Islamic Modernism in India and Pakistan. 1857–1964*. London: Oxford University Press.

———. 1969. *Studies in Islamic Culture in the Indian Environment*. London: Oxford University Press.

Ahmed, Firdaus. 2002 (accessed). 'A Smoke Screen Called Limited War', available at http://www.ipcs.org/issues/800/832-ndi-firdaus.htm, accessed on 15 October.

Ahmed, Khurshid K. 1995. 'Summation: Capping the Nation', in Tarik Jan (ed.), *Pakistan's Security and the Nuclear Option*. Islamabad: Institute of Policy Studies.

———. 2000. 'CTBT and Pakistan's Nuclear Capability', available at http://www.jamaat.org/Isharat/ish022000.html.

Ahmed, M. (ed.). 1982. *Contemporary Pakistan*. Karachi: Royal Book Company.

Ahmed, Samina. 1998. 'Pakistan', in Muthiah Alagappa (ed.), *Asian Security Practice: Material and Ideational Influences*. Stanford: Stanford University Press.

———. 1999. 'Pakistan's Nuclear Weapons Programme: Turning Points and Nuclear Choices', *International Security*, 23 (4).

Ahmed, Samina and David Cortright. 1996. *Pakistan's Nuclear Choices*, A Special Report by the Joan B. Kroc Institute for International Peace Studies and the Fourth Freedom Forum. Notre Dame, IN: Joan B Kroc Institute for International Peace Studies.

———. 2001. *South Asia at the Nuclear Crossroads*, Policy Report, March. Notre Dame, IN: A Joint Publication of Managing the Atom Project at Harvard University, the Fourth Freedom Forum, and the Joan B. Kroc Institute for International Peace Studies at the University of Notre Dame.

Akram, Munir. 1998a. Statement by Amb. Munir Akram at the Special Session of the Conference on Disarmament, 2 June.

———. 1998b. Statement by Amb. Munir Akram at the Plenary Meeting of the Conference on Disarmament, 30 July.

Alagappa, Muthiah (ed.). 1998. *Asian Security Practice: Material and Ideational Influences*. Stanford: Stanford University Press.

———. (ed.). 2001a. *Coercion and Governance: The Declining Political Role of the Military in Asia*. Stanford: Stanford University Press.

———. 2001b. 'Investigating and Explaining Change', in Muthiah Alagappa (ed.), *Coercion and Governance: The Declining Political Role of the Military in Asia*. Stanford: Stanford University Press.

———. 2001c. 'Asian Civil–Military Relations: Key Developments, Explanations, and Trajectories', in Muthiah Alagappa (ed.), *Coercion and Governance: The Declining Political Role of the Military in Asia*. Stanford: Stanford University Press.

Albright, David. 1987. 'Pakistan's Bomb-making Capacity', *The Bulletin of the Atomic Scientists*, June.

———. 1999. *Fact Sheet: India and Pakistan—Current and Potential Nuclear Arsenals*. Washington, DC: Institute for Science and International Security, 27 October.

Albright, David and Mark Hibbs. 1992. 'India's Silent Bomb', *The Bulletin of the Atomic Scientists*, 48 (7).

Albright, David and Tom Zamora. 1989. 'India Pakistan's Nuclear Weapons: All the Pieces in Place', *The Bulletin of the Atomic Scientists*, 45 (5).

Albright, Madeleine and Sandy Berger. 1997. Press Briefing by Secretary of State Madeleine Albright and National Security Advisor Sandy Berger, 29 October, The White House, Office of the Press Secretary, available at http://www.cns.miis.edu.

Ali, A. 1984. *Pakistan's Nuclear Dilemma*. Karachi: Economist Research Unit.

Ali, Akhtar. 1999. *Nuclear Politics and the Challenges of Governance*. Karachi: Royal Book Company.

Ali, Mehrunisa. 1974. 'Implications of Indian Nuclear Blast', *Dawn*, 24 June.

Ali, Rafaqat. 2001. '*Jihadi* Outfits Visiting Schools to Recruit Trainees', *Dawn*, 17 February.

Ali, T. 1988. 'Pakistan: Some Dramatic Changes', *Asian Survey*, 34 (2).

Ali, Tariq. 2002. *The Clash of Fundamentalism: Crusades, Jihads and Modernity*. London and New York: Verso.

Allison, Graham T. and Philip Zelikow. 1999. *Essence of Decision: Explaining the Cuban Missile Crisis*. New York: Addison Wesley Longman.

Alpervitz, Gar. 1996. *The Decision to Use the Atomic Bomb*. New York: Random House.

Alves, Péricles Gasparini and Kerstin Hoffman (eds). 1997. *The Transfer of Sensitive Technologies and the Future of Control Regimes*. Geneva: United Nations Publication.

Ambroz, Oton. 1972. *Realignment of World Power: The Russo-Chinese Schism and the Impact of Mao Tse-tung's Last Revolution*. New York: Robert Speller and Sons.

Amin, T. 1995. 'Pakistan in 1994: The Politics of Confrontation', *Asian Survey*, 35 (2).

Amir, Ayaz. 2001. 'A Passion for Selling Ourselves Cheaply', *Dawn*, 21 September.

An American Legacy: Building a Nuclear Weapons Free World. 1997. Washington, DC: The Henry L. Stimson Center.

Arend, Anthony Clark and Robert J. Beck. 1993. *International Law and the Use of Force*. London: Routledge.

Arif, Gen K.M. 2001. *Khaki Shadows: Pakistan 1947–1997*. Karachi: Oxford University Press.

Arkin, William M., Robert S. Norris and Joshua Handler. 1998. *Taking Stock: Worldwide Nuclear Deployments 1998*. Washington, DC: NRDC Nuclear Program.

Arms Control Today. 1997. 'The Debate over NATO Expansion: A Critique of the Clinton Administration's Responses to Key Questions', 27 (6).

Arnett, Eric (ed.). 1996. *Nuclear Weapons After the Comprehensive Test Ban: Implications for Modernization and Proliferation*. Oxford: Oxford University Press.

———. (ed.). 1998. *Nuclear Weapons and Arms Control in South Asia After the Test Ban*. Oxford: Oxford University Press for the Stockholm International Peace Research Institute.

———. 2000. 'The Future Strategic Balance in South Asia', in Herro Mustafa (ed.), *The Balance of Power in South Asia*. Abu Dhabi: Emirates Center for Strategic Studies and Research.

Aron, Raymond. 1969. 'The Evolution of Modern Strategic Thought', in *Problems of Modern Strategy: Part One, Adelphi Papers*, No. 54. London: IISS.

Art, Robert J. 1991. 'A Defensible Defense: America's Grand Strategy After the Cold War', *International Security*, 15 (4).

Art, Robert J. and Kenneth N. Waltz (eds). 1988. *The Use of Force*, 3rd edn. New York: University Press of America.

Associated Press. 1999. 'House Passes Missile Defense Bill', 18 March.

Aviation Week and Space Technology. 1993. 'Cruise Missiles Becoming Top Proliferation Threat', 1 February.

Aziz, K.K. 1967. *The Making of Pakistan: A Study in Nationalism*. London: Chatto and Windus.

Babar, Farhatullah. 1992. 'Nuclear Debate in South Asia: A "Path to Sanity"', *Regional Studies*, October–December.

Babbage, R. and G. Gordon. (eds). 1991. *India's Strategic Future: Regional, State or Global Power*. London: Macmillan.

Babu, D. Shyam. 1992. *Nuclear Non-Proliferation: Towards a Universal NPT Regime*. Delhi: Konark.

Bahadur, Kalim. 1998. *Democracy in Pakistan: Crises and Conflicts*. New Delhi: Har-Anand.

Bailey, Kathleen C. (ed.). 1994. *Weapons of Mass Destruction: Costs and Benefits*. New Delhi: Manohar.

Bajpai, Kanti. 1999. 'The Fallacy of an Indian Deterrent', in Amitabh Mattoo (ed.), *India's Nuclear Deterrent: Pokharan II and Beyond*. New Delhi: Har-Anand.

———. 2000. 'India, China and Asian Security', in Kanti Bajpai and Amitabh Mattoo (eds), *The Peacock and the Dragon: India–China Relations in the 21st Century*. New Delhi: Har-Anand.

———. 2002. 'No First Use in the India–Pakistan Context' (paper presented at Pugwash Meeting no. 279 on *No First Use of Nuclear Weapons*), 15–17 November, London.

Bajpai, Kanti P. and Amitabh Mattoo (eds). 1996. *Security India: Strategic Thought and Practice, Essays by George K. Tanham with Commentaries*. New Delhi: Manohar.

———. (eds). 2000. *The Peacock and the Dragon: India–China Relations in the 21st Century*. New Delhi: Har-Anand.

Bajpai, Kanti, Maj Gen Dipankar Banerjee and Amitabh Mattoo. 1998. *Jammu and Kashmir: An Agenda for the Future*, Report of an Independent Study Team. New Delhi: Delhi Policy Group.

Bajpai, Kanti P., P.R. Chari, P.I. Cheema, Stephen P. Cohen and Sumit Ganguly. 1995. *Brasstacks and Beyond: Misperception and Crisis in Indo-Pak Relations*. Delhi: Manohar.

Baker, Philip Noel. 1958. *The Arms Race*. London: John Calder.

Bakhtiar, Idrees. 2000. 'Localising Sovereignty?', *The Herald*, September.

Baksh-Rais, Rasul. 1977. *China and Pakistan: A Political Analysis of Mutual Relations*. Lahore: Progressive Publishers.

———. 1994. *War without Winners*. Karachi: Oxford University Press.

———. 1999. 'Assessing the Threat of Islamic Revivalism in Pakistan', in Nancy Jetley (ed.), *Regional Security in South Asia. The Ethno Sectarian Dimensions*. New Delhi: Lancer's.

Balachandran, G. 1999. 'What is the Relevance of a Triad?' *The Hindu*, 10 September.

Ball, Desmond. 1993. 'Strategic Culture in the Asia-Pacific Region', *Security Studies*, 3 (1).

Banerjee, Maj Gen Dipankar (ed.). 1999. *Security in South Asia*. New Delhi: Manas Publications.

Banerjee, Maj Gen Dipankar and Gert Kueck (eds). 2003. *South Asia and the War on Terrorism: Analysing the Implications of 11 September*. New Delhi: India Research Press.

Banerjee, Sanjoy. 1987. 'Explaining the American Tilt in the 1971 Bangladesh Crisis: A Late Dependency Approach', *International Studies Quarterly*, 31 (June).

Barnaby, Frank. 1993. *How Nuclear Weapons Spread: Nuclear-Weapon Proliferation in the 1990s*. London: Routledge.

Barnet, R.J. and Richard A. Falk (eds). 1965. *Security in Disarmament*. Princeton, NJ: Princeton University Press.

Barnett, Doak. 1985. *The Making of Foreign Policy*. Boulder, CO: Westview.

Barringer, Richard. 1972. *War: Patterns of Conflict*. Cambridge, MA: MIT Press.

Baruah, Amit. 1999a. 'Any Weapon Will be Used, Threatens Pak', *The Hindu*, 1 June.
———. 1999b. 'Nuke War Likely, says Pak Website', *The Hindu*, 29 June.
———. 2003a. 'India, Pak Exchange List of N-installations', *The Hindu*, 2 January.
Baruah, Amit. 2003b. 'Sikkim, No Longer an "Independent Country" on Official Chinese Website', 9 October.
Battle, Joyce. 2000. *India and Pakistan: On the Nuclear Threshold*. National Security Archive, Washington, DC, http://www.seas.gwu.edu/nsaarchive/ NSAEBB/ NSAEBB6/index.
Baxter, Craig (ed.). 1985. *Zia's Pakistan: Politics and Stability in a Frontline State*. Lahore: Vanguard Books Ltd.
Baxter, Craig and Charles H. Kennedy. 2000. *Pakistan 2000*. Karachi: Oxford University Press.
Beg, Gen Mirza Aslam. 1989. 'Pakistan Responding to Change', Interview by Mushahid Hussain, *Jane's Defense Weekly*, 14 October.
———. 1992. Interview in *The News International*, 6 December.
———. 1994. *Development and Security*. Rawalpindi: Foundation for Research on National Development and Security (FRIENDS).
———. 2001 (accessed). 'Deterrence, Defence and Development', available at http://www.piads.com.pk/users/piads/beg2.html, accessed on 30 August.
Beggs, Robert . 1971. *Flashpoints: The Cuban Missile Crisis*. London: Longman.
Behera, Navnita Chadha. 2000. *State Identity and Violence: Jammu, Kashmir and Ladakh*. New Delhi: Manohar.
Beijing Review. 1999. 'Foreign Minister Meets Press', 42 (12).
Bermudez Jr, Joseph S. 1998. 'DPRK–Pakistan Ghauri Missile Co-operation', http://www.fas.org/news/Pakistan/1998/05/ghauri2.htm, accessed on 12 May 2000.
Bernstein, Richard and Ross H. Munro. 1997. 'The Coming Conflict with America', *Foreign Affairs*, 76 (2).
Benet, Michael. 1992. 'The People's Republic of China and the Use of International Law in the Spratly Islands Dispute', *Stanford Journal of International Law*, 28 (Spring).
Benjamin, Milton R. 1982. 'India Said to Eye Raid on Pakistani A. Plants', *The Washington Post*, 20 December.
Bennett, John. 1962. *Nuclear Weapons and the Conflict of Conscience*. New York: Charles Scribner's Son.
Bertsch, Gary, Seema Gahlaut and Anupam Srivastava (eds). 1999. *Engaging India: US Strategic Relations with the World's Largest Democracy*. New York: Routledge.
Betts, Richard K. 1978. 'Analysis, War, and Decision: Why Intelligence Failures are Inevitable', *World Politics*, 31 (2).
Bhalla, Madhu. 1997. Review Article, 'East Beats West', *Sunday*, 14–20 September.
———. 1998. 'China's Security Perceptions', *International Studies*, 35 (2).
Bhargva, G.S. 1978. 'India's Nuclear Policy', *India Quarterly*, 34 (2).
Bhaskar, C. Uday. 2000. 'Staying on Course: Subs Have Vital Role in Deterrence', *The Times of India*, 31 August.
Bhatia, A. 1985. 'India's Space Program: Cause for Concern?', *Asian Survey*, 25 (10).
Bhatia, Shyam. 1979. *India's Nuclear Bomb*. New Delhi: Vikas Publishing House.

Bhattacharjea, Ajit. 1994. *Kashmir: The Wounded Valley*. New Delhi: UBSPD.

Bhola, P.L. 1993. *Pakistan's Nuclear Policy*. New Delhi: Sterling Publishers.

Bhutto, B. 1983. *Pakistan: The Gathering Storm*. New Delhi: Vikas.

Bhutto, Z.A. 1969. *The Myth of Independence*. London: Oxford University Press.

———. 1970. *Awakening the People: Speeches of Zulfiqar Ali Bhutto 1966–69*. Rawalpindi: Pakistan Publications.

———. 1979. *If I am Assassinated ...*, Indian repr. New Delhi: Vikas Publishing House.

Bienefeld, M. and M. Godrey (eds). 1982. *The Struggle for Development: National Strategies in an International Context*. New York: John Wiley and Sons.

Binder, Leonard. 1961. *Religion and Politics in Pakistan*. Los Angeles: University of California Press.

Binkley, Cameron. 1994. 'Pakistan's Ballistic Missile Development: The Sword of Islam?', in William C. Potter and Harlan W. Jencks (eds), *The International Missile Bazaar: The New Suppliers' Network*. Boulder, CO: Westview.

Binnendijk, Hans and Ronald N. Monteperto. 1997. 'PLA Views on Asia Pacific Security in the 21st Century', *Strategic Forum 114*, Institute for National Strategic Studies.

Bitzinger, Richard. 1982. 'Arms to Go: Chinese Arms Sales to the Third World', *International Security*, Fall.

———. 1991. *Chinese Arms Production and Sales to the Third World*, WD-5289-USDP. Santa Monica, CA: RAND.

Blackett, P.M.S. 1956. *The Military and Political Consequences of Atomic Energy*. London: Turnstile.

Blackwill, Robert. 2002a. 'The Transformation of US–India Relations: A Status Report', Address to the Delhi Policy Group, *USIS Official Text*, 26 February.

———. 2002b. 'If India, Pak don't Talk Seriously, How will this Crisis Ever Go Away?', Interview with Robert Blackwill by Jyoti Malhotra, *The Indian Express*, 19 October.

Blair, Bruce G. and Kurt Gottfried (eds) 1988. *Crisis Stability and Nuclear War*. Oxford: Oxford University Press.

Blair, Bruce G., Harold A. Feiveson and Frank N. von Hippel. 1997. 'Taking Nuclear Weapons off Hair-Trigger Alert', *Scientific American*, November.

Blair, Bruce G., John E. Pike and Stephen I. Schwartz. 1998. 'Targeting and Controlling the Bomb', in Stephen I. Schwartz (ed.), *Atomic Audit*. Washington, DC: Brookings Institution.

Blechman, Barry M. and Stephan S. Kaplan. 1978. *Force without War: US Armed Forces as a Political Instrument*. Washington, DC: Brookings Institution.

Blight, James G. and David A.Welch. 1989. *On the Brink: Americans and Soviets Re-examine the Cuban Missile Crisis*. New York: Hill and Wang.

Bobrow, Davis. 1964. 'Peking's Military Calculus', *World Politics*, 16 (2).

Bok, Georges Tan Eng. 1984. 'Strategic Doctrine', in Gerald Segal and William T. Tow (eds), *Chinese Defence Policy*. Chicago: University of Chicago Press.

Bolitho, H. 1954. *Jinnah: Creator of Pakistan*. London: John Murray.

Bond, Brian. 1997. *Liddell-Hart: A Study of His Military Thought*. London: Casell.

Bonds, Ray (ed.). 1979. *The Chinese War Machine*. London: Salamander.

Boorman, Scott A. 1973. 'Deception in Chinese Strategy', in William Whitson (ed.), *The Military and Political Power in China in the 1970s*. New York: Praeger.

Booth, Ken and Russell Trood (eds). 1999. *Strategic Cultures in the Asia-Pacific Region*. London: Macmillan.

Borden, William L. 1946. *There Will be No Time: The Revolution in Strategy*. New York: Macmillan.

Bose, Sumantra. 1999. 'Kashmir: Sources of Conflict, Dimensions of Peace', *Survival*, 41 (3).

Bottome, Edger. 1971. *The Balance of Terror*. Boston: Beacon.

Boylan, Edward S. 1982. 'The Chinese Cultural Style of Warfare', *Comparative Strategy*, 3 (4).

Bozeman, Adda B. 1960. *Politics and Culture in International History*. Princeton, NJ: Princeton University Press.

Bracken, Paul. 1983. *The Command and Control of Nuclear Forces*. New Haven, CT: Yale University Press.

———. 1999. *Fire in the East: The Rise of Asian Military Power and the Second Nuclear Age*. New Delhi: Harper Collins.

Braibanti, Ralph. 1977. 'The Research Potential of Pakistan's Development', in Lawrence Ziring, Ralph Braibanti and W. Howard Higgins (eds), *Pakistan: The Long View*. Durham: Duke University Press.

Brass, Paul R. 1994. *The Politics of India Since Independence*, 2nd edn. Cambridge: Cambridge University Press.

Brecher, Michael and Jonathan Wilkenfeld. 1989. *Crisis, Conflict and Instability*. Oxford: Pergamon.

Brecher, Michael, Jonathan Moser and Shiela Moser. 1988. 'Crisis in the Twentieth Century', in *Handbook of International Crisis*, vol. I. Oxford: Pergamon.

Brennan, Donald G. 1975. *Arms Treaties with Moscow: Unequal Terms Unevenly Applied?* New York: National Strategy Information Center.

Bretton, Henry L. 1986. *International Relations in the Nuclear Age*. New York: State University of New York Press.

Broad, William J. 2004. 'Libya's A-Bomb Blueprints Reveal New Tie to Pakistani', *The New York Times*, 9 February.

Broad, William J., David E. Sanger and Raymond Bonner. 2004. 'A Tale of Nuclear Proliferation: How Pakistani Built His Network', *The New York Times*, 12 February.

Brodie, Bernard (ed.). 1946. *The Absolute Weapon: Atomic Power and World Order*. New York: Harcourt, Brace.

———. 1957. 'More about Limited War', *World Politics*, 10 (1).

———. 1965. *Strategy in the Missile Age*. Princeton, NJ: Princeton University Press.

———. 1970. 'Technology, Politics and Strategy', in Alastair Buchan (ed.), *Problems of National Strategy*. London: Chatto and Windus.

Brodsgaard, K.E. 1998. 'State and Society in Hainan: Liao Xun's Ideas on "Little Government, Big Society"', in K.E. Brodsgaard and D. Strand (eds), *Reconstructing Twentieth Century China: State Control, Civic Society and National Identity*. Oxford: Oxford University Press.

Brown, Sheryl. J. 1992. *Resolving Third World Conflict: Challenges for a New Era*. Washington, DC: US Institute for Peace Press.

Brown, W. Norman. 1967. *The United States and India and Pakistan*, 2nd edn. New York: Oxford University Press.

Brzoska, M. and T. Ohlson. 1985. 'The Future of Arms Trade', *Bulletin of Peace Proposals*, 16 (2).

Buchan. A. (ed.). 1983. *A World of Nuclear Powers*. New York: Harper and Row.

Bull, Hedley. 1961. *The Control of the Arms Race: Disarmament and Arms Control in the Missile Age*. New York: Praeger.

———. 1977. *The Anarchical Society*. London: Macmillan.

Bumiller, Elisabeth. 2002. 'In Asia, Bush Faces a Test over His "Axis of Evil" Warning', *The New York Times*, 16 February.

Bundy, Mc George. 1998. *Danger and Survival: Choices about the Bomb in the Fifty Years*, New York: Random House.

Bunn, George and John B. Rhinelander. 1997. 'The Duma-Senate Logjam on Arms Control: What Can be Done?' *The Nonproliferation Review*, 5 (1).

Bunn, Matthew. 1998. 'Act now, Mr President', *The Bulletin of the Atomic Scientists*, March/April.

Bunn, Matthew and John P. Holdren. 1997. 'Managing Military Uranium and Plutonium in the United States and the Former Soviet Union', *Annual Review of Energy and the Environment*, 22 (Fall).

Burke, S.J. 1986. *Pakistan: A Nation in the Making*. Boulder, CO: Westview.

Burke, S.M. and Shahid Javed. 1990. *Pakistan under Bhutto 1971–1977*. New York: St Martin's Press.

Burke, S.M. and Lawrence Ziring. 1990. *Pakistan's Foreign Policy: An Historical Analysis*. Karachi: Oxford University Press.

Burki, S.J. 1960. 'High Tension and Nuclear Laboratory', *Pakistan Quarterly*, 10 (2).

Burles, Mark and Abram N. Shulsky. 2000. *Patterns in China's Use of Force: Evidence from History and Doctrinal Writings*, MR–1160–AF. Santa Monica: RAND.

Burney, I.H. 1996. *No Illusions, Some Hopes, and No Fears*. Karachi: Oxford University Press.

Burr, William and Jeffrey T. Richelson. 2000/2001. 'Whether to Strangle the Baby in the Cradle: The United States and the Chinese Nuclear Program, 1960–64', *International Security*, 25 (3).

Burroughs, John. 1997. *The (Ill) legality of Threat or Use of Nuclear Weapons: A Guide to the Historic Opinion of the International Court of Justice*. Munster: LIT.

Burrow, William E. and Windrem Roberts. 1994. *Critical Mass*. New York: Simon and Schuster.

Bush, Vannevar. 1950. *Modern Arms and Free Men*. London: Heinemann.

Butler, Gen George Lee. 1999. 'Interview', *Frontline*, 16 (12).

Buzan, Barry. 1983. *People, States and Fear: The National Security Problem in International Relations*. Brighton: Harvester.

———. 1987. *An Introduction to Strategic Studies: Military Technology and International Relations*. London: Macmillan for IISS.

Caldwell, John. 1994. 'China's Conventional Military Capabilities, 1994–2004', Washington, DC: Center for Strategic and International Studies.

Callard, K. 1957. *Pakistan: A Political Study*. London: Allen and Unwin.

Cameron, Gavin. 1999. *Nuclear Terrorism: A Threat Assessment for the 21st Century*. New York: St Martins Press.

Canberra Commission on the Elimination of Nuclear Weapons. 1996. *Report of the Canberra Commission on the Elimination of Nuclear Weapons*. Canberra: Commonwealth of Australia.

Carnegie Task Force.1988. *Nuclear Weapons and South Asian Security*, Report of the Carnegie Task Force on Non-Proliferation and South Asian Security. Washington, DC: Carnegie Endowment for International Peace.

Carnegie Task Force. 1999. 'China's Nuclear Modernization', *Carnegie Endowment for International Peace Proliferation Brief*, 2 (8).

Carter, Ashton B., John D. Steinbruner and Charles A. Zraket (eds). 1987. *Managing Nuclear Operations*. Washington, DC: Brookings Institution.

Carter, Jimmy. 1982. *Keeping Faith: Memoirs of a President*. New York: Bantam Books.

CDI. 2000. *National Missile Defense: What Does it All Mean?* Washington, DC: Center for Defense Information.

CDISS (Centre for Defense and International Security Studies). 1998. 'Pakistan to Accelerate Missile Program', *Current News*, http://www.cdiss. org/98 April2.htm, accessed on 20 April 1998.

Center for Nonproliferation Studies. 1992. 'China's Instrument of Accession to the Non-proliferation Treaty (NPT)', 11 March, http://www. cns.miis.edu, accessed on 28 April 2002.

——. 1999 (accessed). 'Chinese Missile Exports and Assistance to Pakistan— Statements and Developments', http://www.cns.miis.edu/research/India / China/mpakchr. htm, accessed on 29 November.

——. 2000 (accessed). 'China's Opposition to US Missile Defense Programs', http://www/cns.miis.edu, accessed on 6 May.

Changing Grand Strategies in South Asia. 2000. RAND Studies in Public Policy. Cambridge: Cambridge University Press.

Chai, Joseph C.H. 1992. 'Consumption and Living Standards in China', *The China Quarterly*, September.

Chan, Gerald. 1991. 'International Studies in China: Origin and Development', *Issues and Studies*, 33 (2).

——. 1998. 'Toward an International Relations Theory with Chinese Characteristics?' *Issues and Studies*, 34 (6).

Chanda, Nayan. 1995. 'Fear of the Dragon', *Far Eastern Economic Review*, 13 April.

Chandra, Bipan, K.N. Panikkar, Mridula Mukherjee and Sucheta Mahajan. 1989. *India's Struggle for Independence*. Delhi: Penguin.

Chandran, Ramesh. 1999. 'US Senate Rejects CTBT', *The Times of India*, 15 October.

Chang, Gordon. 1988. 'JFK, China, and the Bomb', *Journal of American History*, 74 (4).

Chari, P.R. 1978. 'An Indian Reaction to US Nonproliferation Policy', *International Security*, 3 (2).

——. 1990. 'Pakistan's Quest for Nuclear Technology', *Australian Outlook*, 34 (1).

——. 1991. 'Prospect for Nuclear Freeze in South Asia', *Asian Defence Journal*, December.

——. 1994. 'Pakistan's Nuclear Dilemma', *Defence Journal*, 2 (May).

——. 1995. *The Indo-Pak Nuclear Standoff: The Role of the United States*. New Delhi: Manohar.

——. 1998. 'Newer Sources of Insecurity: The Crisis of Governance in India', RCSS Policy Studies 3. Colombo: Regional Centre for Strategic Studies.

——. (ed.). 1999a. *Perspectives on National Security in South Asia: In Search of a New Paradigm*. New Delhi: Manohar.

——. 1999b (accessed). 'India's Global Nuclear Initiative', http://www.ipcs.org/ issues/articles/157-ndi-chari.htm, accessed on 12 December.

Chari, P.R. 2001a. 'Nuclear Restraint, Nuclear Risk Reduction, and the Security–Insecurity Paradox in South Asia', in Michael Krepon and Chris Gagnè (eds), *The Stability–Instability Paradox: Nuclear Weapons and Brinkmanship in South Asia*, Report no. 38. Washington, DC: The Henry L. Stimson Center.

———. 2001b (accessed). 'India's Slow-motion Nuclear Deployment', Non-proliferation Section, Carnegie Endowment for International Peace website, www.ciep.org, accessed on 17 January.

———. 2002. 'Limited War Against the Nuclear Backdrop', *Peace and Conflict*, 5 (6).

———. 2003a. 'Nuclear Command Authority: Strategic Forces Command', *Issue Brief*, 3 (February). New Delhi: Institute of Peace and Conflict Studies.

———. 2003b. 'Nuclear Stability in Southern Asia—An Indian Perspective', in P.R. Chari, Sonika Gupta and Arpit Rajain (eds), *Nuclear Stability in Southern Asia*. New Delhi: Manohar.

Chari, P.R. and Arpit Rajain. 2003. 'Nuclear Command Authority: Strategic Forces Command', *Peace and Conflict*, 6 (4).

Chari, P.R., P.I. Cheema and S.P. Cohen. 2003. *Perception, Politics and Security in South Asia: The Compound Crisis of 1990*. London and New York: Routledge Curzon.

Chari, P.R., P.I. Cheema and Iftekharuzzaman (eds). 1996. *Nuclear Non-Proliferation in India Pakistan: South Asian Perspectives*. New Delhi: Manohar, RCSS.

Chari, P.R., Sonika Gupta and Arpit Rajain (eds). 2003. *Nuclear Stability in Southern Asia*. New Delhi: Manohar.

Cheema, P.I. 1983. 'The Afghanistan Crisis and Pakistan's Security Dilemma', 23 (3).

———. 2003. 'Post 11 September Developments: A Pakistani Perspective', in Maj Gen Dipankar Banerjee and Gert Kueck (eds), *South Asia and the War on Terrorism: Analysing the Implications of 11 September*. New Delhi: India Research Press.

Cheema, Z.I. 1992. 'Nuclear Diplomacy in South Asia During the 1980s', *Regional Studies*, 1 (3).

———. 1996. 'Pakistan's Nuclear Policies: Attitudes and Posture', in P.R. Chari, P.I. Cheema and Iftekharuzzaman (eds), *Nuclear Non Proliferation in India and Pakistan*. New Delhi: Manohar.

———. 2000. 'Pakistan's Nuclear Use Doctrine and Command and Control', in Peter R. Lavoy, Scott D. Sagan and James J. Wirtz (eds), *Planning the Unthinkable. How New Powers Will Use Nuclear, Biological, and Chemical Weapons*. London: Cornell University Press.

Chellaney, Brahma. 1991. 'South Asia's Passage to Nuclear Power', *International Security*, 16 (1).

———. 1993. *Nuclear Proliferation: The US–Indian Conflict*. New Delhi: Orient Longman.

———. 1994. 'An Indian Critique of US Export Controls', *Orbis*, 38 (3).

———. (ed.). 1999a. *Securing India's Future in the New Millennium*. New Delhi: Orient Longman.

———. 1999b. 'Nuclear-deterrent Posture', in Brahma Chellaney (ed.), *Securing India's Future in the New Millennium*. New Delhi: Orient Longman.

Chellaney, Brahma. 1999c. 'India's Nuclear Planning, Force Structure, Doctrine and Arms Control Posture', *Australian Journal of International Affairs*, 53 (1).

———. 2004. 'Pakistan's Nuclear Inquiry is a Sham', *International Herald Tribune*, 11 February.

Chengappa, Raj. 2000. *Weapons of Peace*. New Delhi: Harper Collins.

Chen Qida. 1998. 'Panchseela: History, Past and Present Relevant', *Chinese Institute of Contemporary International Relations*, 5 (2).

Chen-min Chao. 1986. 'Communist China's Independent Foreign Policy: The Link with Domestic Affairs', *Issues and Studies*, 22 (10).

Cherian, John. 1998. 'The BJP and the Bomb', *Frontline*, 24 April.

Chibber, Lt Gen (Dr) M.L. 2003 (accessed). 'Line of Control in Jammu and Kashmir. A Part of Simla Agreement', available at http://meadev.nic.in/OPn/kargil/chibb-loc.htm, accessed on 27 March.

Chien, Frederick F. 1991/92. 'A View from Taipei', *Foreign Affairs*, Winter.

Chieh Hsiung, James. 1972. *Law and Policy in China's Foreign Relations: A Study of Attitudes and Practice*. New York : Columbia Press.

Chien-peng Chung. 2002. 'China's "War on Terror": September 11 and Uighur Separatism', *Foreign Affairs*, July–August.

Chin-Yu Shih. 1993a. 'Contending Theories of Human Rights with Chinese Characteristics', *Issues and Studies*, 29 (11).

———. 1993b. *China's Just World: The Morality of Chinese Foreign Policy*. Boulder, CO: Lynne Rienner.

China Daily. 1995a. 'Li Explains Plenums Development Plan', 6 October.

———. 1995b. 'Principles on Modernisation Drive', 9 October.

———. 1999. Interview with Chinese Foreign Minister Tang Jiaxuan, 3 August.

Chinese Foreign Minister. 1992. 'Address to UN General Assembly', *China Report*, 28 (4).

Chishti, F.A. 1989. *Betrayals of Another Kind: Islam, Democracy and the Army in Pakistan*. Delhi: Tricolour Books.

Chong-pin Lin. 1988. *China's Nuclear Strategy: Tradition within Evolution*. Lexington, MA: Lexington Books.

———. 1995. 'Red Fist: China's Army in Transition', *International Defense Review*, February.

Chopra, P. (ed.). 1983. *Contemporary Pakistan: New Aims and Images*. New Delhi: Vikas.

———. 1994. *India, Pakistan, and the Kashmir Tangle*. New Delhi: Indus.

Chowdhury, Rahul Roy. 1990. 'Regional Stability and Weapons Proliferation in South Asia', *Strategic Analysis*, September.

Christenson, Thomas, J. 1996. 'Chinese Realpolitik', *Foreign Affairs*, 75 (5).

Chun-Hi Hsuch. 1977. *Dimension of China's Foreign Policy Relations*. New York: Praeger.

CIA. 2000. Unclassified Report to Congress on the Acquisition of Technology Relating to Weapons of Mass Destruction and Advanced Conventional Munitions, 1 January–30 June, http://www.cia.gov/cia/reports/721_reports/jan_jun2000.htm.

Cimbala, Stephen J. 1988. *Rethinking Nuclear Strategy*. Wilmington, DE: Scholarly Resources.

Cimbala, Stephen J. 1998. *Coercive Military Strategy* . College Station: A and M University Press.

Cirincione, Joseph (ed.). 2000. *Repairing the Regime: Preventing the Spread of Weapons of Mass Destruction*. New York: Routledge.

Clark, Ian. 1982. *Limited Nuclear War: Political Theory and War Conventions*. Oxford: Martin Robertson.

Clemens Jr, Walter C. 1993. 'China', in Richard Dean Burns (ed.), *Encyclopaedia of Arms Control and Disarmament*, vol. 1. New York: Charles Scribner's Sons.

Coats, Ken (ed.). 1986. *China and the Bomb*. Atlantic Highlands, NJ: Humanities Press.

Cohen, Jerome A. (ed.). 1972. *China's Practice of International Law: Some Case Studies*. Cambridge, MA: Harvard University Press.

Cohen, Paul A. 1984. *Discovering History in China: American Historical Writing in the Recent Chinese Past*. New York: Columbia University Press.

Cohen, Stephen P. 1975. 'US Weapons and South Asia: A Policy Analysis', *Pacific Affairs*, December.

——. (ed.). 1987. *Nuclear Proliferation in South Asia: Asian and American Perspectives*. Urbana: University of Illinois.

——. 1989. *The Pakistan Army*. Berkeley, CA: University of California Press.

——. (ed.). 1991. *Nuclear Proliferation in South Asia: The Prospects for Arms Control*. New Delhi: Lancer's.

——. 1997. 'Indian Perspectives on War, Peace and International Order' (paper presented at the conference on *Conflict or Convergence: Global Perspectives on War, Peace, and International Order*, held at Harvard Academy for International and Area Studies), 13–15 November, Cambridge, MA.

——. 1998. 'Nuclear Weapons and Conflict in South Asia' (paper presented to the Harvard/MIT Transnational Security Project Seminar), 23 November, Harvard.

——. 2001. *India: Emerging Power*. Washington, DC: Brookings Institution.

College of Combat. 1981. 'Effects of Nuclear Asymmetry on Conventional Deterrence', *Combat Paper*, 1 (May). Mhow, India: College of Combat.

Collina, Tom Zamora. 1995. 'Cut-off Talks Delayed', *The Bulletin of the Atomic Scientists*, 51 (2).

Communist Party of China. 2002. Resolution of the Sixteenth National Congress of the Communist Party of China on the Report of the Fifteenth CPC Central Committee, adopted on 14 November, Beijing.

Constable, Pamela. 2000. 'Will Two and Two Equal Five?' in *On the Abyss: Pakistan after the Coup*. New Delhi: Harper Collins.

Cordesman, Anthony H. 2000. *The Asian and Chinese Military Balance*. Washington, DC: Center for Strategic and International Studies.

Cortright, David and Amitabh Mattoo. 1994. *A Study of India's Nuclear Choices: A Public Opinion Survey* (conducted by the Joan B. Kroc Institute). Notre Dame, IN: University of Notre Dame.

——. (eds). 1996. *India and the Bomb: Public Opinion and Nuclear Options*. Indiana: Notre Dame Press.

Cossa, Ralph A. 1994. 'The PRC's National Security Objectives in the Post-Cold War Era and the Role of the PLA', *Issues and Studies*, 30 (9).

Cotta-Ramusino, Paulo and Maurizio Martellini. 2002 (accessed). *Nuclear Safety, Nuclear Stability and Nuclear Strategy in Pakistan*, Report of a Field Visit to Pakistan. Centro Volta, Italy: Landau Network, available at www.mi.infn.it/~landnet, accessed on 21 December.

Cottam, Martha L. 1986. *Foreign Policy Decision-Making: The Influence of Cognition*. Boulder, CO: Westview.

Cottrell, Alvin J. and R.M. Burrell (eds). 1972. *The Indian Ocean: Its Political, Economic and Military Importance*. New York: Praeger.

Coughlin, Con. 2003. 'UN Report Describes Expansive Nuclear Facility', *The Washington Times*, 8 September.

Council for a Livable World Education Fund. 1998a. *Briefing Book on NATO Enlargement*, April.

———. 1998b. *Briefing Book on Ballistic Missile Defense*, April.

Cranmer-Byng, J.L. 1965/66. 'The Chinese Attitude Towards External Relations', *International Journal*, 21 (1).

———. 1973. 'The Chinese View of Their Place in the World: An Historical Perspective', *The China Quarterly*, 53 (January–March).

Cronin, Richard P. and Barbara Leith Le Poer. 1993. *South Asia: U.S. Interest and Policy Issues*, 12 February. Washington, DC: Congressional Research Service Report.

Daalder, Ivo H. 1993. 'Nuclear Weapons in Europe: Why Zero is Better', *Arms Control Today*, 23 (1).

Dahl, Robert. 1985. *Controlling Nuclear Weapons: Democracy versus Guardianship*. New York: Syracuse University Press.

Dalby, Simon. 1992. 'Security, Modernity, Ecology: The Dilemmas of Post-Cold War Security Discourse', *Alternatives*, 17 (1).

Dasgupta, C. 2002. *War and Diplomacy in Kashmir 1947–48*. New Delhi: Sage.

Davis, Z. 1991. *Nuclear Non-proliferation Regimes: A Comparative Analysis of Policies to Control the Spread of Nuclear, Chemical and Biological Weapons and Missiles*, 1 April. Congressional Research Service Report. Washington, DC: The Library of Congress.

Davis, Z. and Benjamin Frankel (eds). 1993. *The Proliferation Puzzle—Why Nuclear Weapons Spread and What Results*. London: Frank Cass and Co.

Dawn. 2000. 'Nuclear Command Authority Formed', 3 February.

———. 2002. 'Pakistan Has the Right to Use N. Arms: Karamat', 6 June.

———. 2003. 'Nukes, Missiles Needed to Check Indian Threat: Musharraf', 8 November.

———. 2004. 'Lists of N-facilites Exchanged', 1 January.

DCI (Director, Central Intelligence). 2000. Statement before the Senate Select Committee on Intelligence, in *The Worldwide Threat in 2000: Global Realities of Our National Security*, 2 February, available at http://www.cia.gov/cia/public_affairs/speeches/archives/2000/dci_speech_020200.html.

———. 2002.'Afghanistan Provided Bin Ladin a Relatively Safe Operating Environment to Oversee his Organization's Worldwide Terrorist Activities', written statement for the record of the Director of Central Intelligence before the Joint Inquiry Committee, 17 October, available on.http://www.cia.gov/cia/public_affairs/speeches/archives/2002/dci_testimony_10172002.html.

DCI (Director, Central Intelligence). 2003. 'Pakistan Continues to Support Groups that Resist India's Presence in Kashmir in an Effort to Bring India to the Negotiating Table', in *The World-wide Threat in 2003: Evolving Dangers in a Complex World*, Worldwide Threat Briefing, 11 February, available at http://www.cia.gov/cia/public_affairs/speeches/dci_speech_02112003.html.

De Grazia, Sebastian. 1973. *Masters of Chinese Political Thought: From the Beginning to the Han Dynasty*. New York: Viking Press.

de Mesquita, Bruce Bueno. 1981. 'Risk, Power Distributions, and the Likelihood of War', *International Studies Quarterly*, 25 (4).

———. 1985. 'The War Trap Revised: A Revised Expected Utility Model', *American Political Science Review*, 79 (March).

Deitchman, Seymour J. 1969. *Limited War and American Defense Policy*. Cambridge, MA: MIT Press.

Deng Xiaoping. 1984. *Selected Works of Deng Xiaoping (1975–82)*. Beijing: Foreign Languages Press.

Deng Yong. 1998. 'The Chinese Conception of National Interest in International Relations', *The China Quarterly*, 15 (June).

Department of Defense, US. 1962–65 and 1990–2002. *Annual Reports*. Washington, DC: Department of Defense, Federal Government of the United States.

———. 1997a. 'Selected Military Capabilities of the People's Republic of China', Report to Congress pursuant to Section 1305 of the FY97 National Defense Authorization Act, April.

———. 1997b. *Proliferation: Threat and Response*. Washington, DC: Department of Defense, Federal Government of the United States.

Department of State, US. 1973. *United States' Policy Towards South Asia*. Washington, DC: Department of State.

———. 1983. 'The Pakistani Nuclear Programme', Briefing Paper, 22 June, available at the declassified files on India and Pakistan at the National Security Archives *On the Nuclear Threshold*, National Security Archive, George Washington University, Washington, DC.

———. 1995–2002. *Annual Reports of the Secretary of State*. Washington, DC: Department of State.

Derian, James D. 1987. *On Diplomacy: A Genealogy of Western Estrangement*. Oxford: Basil Balchwell Inc.

Desai, Morarji. 1978. Statement of the Prime Minister of India on Peaceful Nuclear Explosions, Rajya Sabha, 31 July. New Delhi: Press Information Bureau.

Deshmukh, B.G. 1994. 'The Inside Story', *India Today*, 28 February.

Deshpande, G.P. 1990. 'The World and China: Four Decades of China's Foreign Policy', *China Report*, 26 (1).

Desmond, Edward. 1991. 'Pakistan's Hidden Hand', *Time*, 22 July.

Devabhaktuni, Sony (ed.). 1997. 'Regional Cooperation in South Asia: Prospects and Problems', Occasional Paper No. 32 (February), The Henry L. Stimson Center.

Dick, Wilson. 1994. 'The Asian Security Management Challenge: A Future "Trinity" of China, Japan and India', RGICS, Paper 10. New Delhi: Rajiv Gandhi Institute of Contemporary Studies.

Ding, Arthur S. 1991. 'Peking's Foreign Policy in the Changing World', *Issues and Studies*, 27 (8).

Dingli Shen. 1993. 'Towards a Nuclear Tiger: The Search for Security in South Asia', *Arms Control Today*, 23 (5).

Dittmer, Lowell and Samuel S. Kim (eds). 1993. *China's Quest for National Identity*. Ithaca: Cornell University Press.

Divine, Robert A. 1978. *Blowing on the Wind: The Nuclear Test Ban Debate 1954–60*. New York: Oxford University Press.

Dixit, Aabha. 1996. 'Status Quo: Maintaining Nuclear Ambiguity', in David Cortright and Amitabh Mattoo (eds), *India and the Bomb*. Notre Dame, IN: University of Notre Dame.

Dixit, J.N. 1998. *Across Borders, Fifty Years of India's Foreign Policy*. New Delhi: Thomson Press.

———. 2002. *India–Pakistan in War and Peace*. New Delhi: Books Today.

Dixon, Thomas Homer. 2002. 'The Rise of Complex Terrorism', *Foreign Policy*, January/February.

Doerner, William R. 1987. 'Pakistan Knocking at the Nuclear Door', *Time*, 30 March.

Donelly, Warren H. 1987. 'Pakistan and Nuclear Weapons', *Issue Brief, Congressional Research Service*, Order Code IB 86110, 11 June. Updated on 9 November.

Dougherty, James E. and Robert L. Pfaltzgraff Jr. 1981. *Contending Theories of International Relations: A Comprehensive Survey*. New York: Harper and Row.

Draft Nuclear Doctrine. 1999. Report of the seminar on *India's Draft Nuclear Doctrine*, held at IPCS on 27 August 1999, available at http://www.ipcs.org/issues/articles/255-ndi-mallika.htm.

Drake, Fred W. 1975. *China Charts the World*. London: Harvard University Press.

Duara, Prasenjit. 1995. *Rescuing History from the Nation*. London: University of Chicago Press.

Du Gong. 1992. 'On the Changing Pattern of International Relations', *China Report*, 28 (1).

Du Preez, Jean and Lawrence Scheinmen. 2003 (accessed). 'Iran Rebuked for Failing to Comply with IAEA Safeguards', *Research Story of the Week*, available at http://cns.miis.edu/pubs/week/030618.htm, accessed on 2 November.

Dulles, John Foster. 1957. 'Challenge and Response in US Policy', *Foreign Affairs*, 36 (1).

———. 1973. 'The Doctrine of Massive Retaliation', in Richard G. Head and Ervin J. Rokke (eds), *American Defense Policy*, 3rd edn. Baltimore, MD: Johns Hopkins University Press.

Dunn, Lewis A. 1982. *Controlling the Bomb*. New Haven, CT: Yale University Press.

———. 1991. *Containing Nuclear Proliferation*. London: International Institute of Strategic Studies, *Adelphi Papers*, 263 (Winter).

Durrani, Lt Gen (Retd) Asad. 1998. 'Whither with the Nukes' (paper presented at the conference on *Peace and Security in South Asia After the Indo-Pakistan Nuclear Tests*), 3–5 December, Islamabad.

———. 2003. 'Doctrinal Doublespeak' (paper presented at Pugwash Meeting no. 280 *Avoiding an India-Pakistan Nuclear Confrontation*), 11–12 March, Lahore, Pakistan.

Durrani, Mahmud Ali. 2001. *India and Pakistan: The Cost of Conflict and the Benefits of Peace*. Karachi: Oxford University Press.

Dutt, Vijay. 1999. 'Pak does not Rule Out Use of N-arms', *The Hindustan Times*, 25 June.

Edmonds, Robin. 1983. *Soviet Foreign Policy: The Brezhnev Years*. Oxford: Oxford University Press.

Eikenberry, Karl W. 1995. 'Explaining and Influencing Chinese Arms Transfers', McNair Paper 36. Washington, DC: Institute for National Strategic Studies, National Defense University.

Eisenhower, Dwight D. 1965. *The White House Years, Waging Peace 1956–61*. Garden City, NY: Doubleday.

Elegant, R.S. 1964. *The Centre of the World: Communism and the Mind of China*. New York: Doubleday.

Elliot, John. 1995. 'India and China—Asia's New Giants: Stepping Stones to Prosperity', Paper No. 26. New Delhi: Rajiv Gandhi Institute of Contemporary Studies.

Ellis, Jason D. and Todd Perry. 1997. 'Nunn-Lugar's Unfinished Agenda', *Arms Control Today*, 27 (7).

Engineer, Asghar Ali (ed.). 1991. *Secular Crown on Fire: The Kashmir Problem*. Delhi: Ajanta.

Enthoven, Alain C. and K. Wayne Smith. 1971. *How Much is Enough? Shaping the Defense Program 1961–1969*. New York: Harper and Row.

Fairbank, John King (ed.). 1968. *The Chinese World Order: Traditional China's Foreign Relations*. Cambridge: Harvard University Press.

———. 1974a. *China Perceived: Images and Policies in Chinese–American Relations*. London: Alfred A. Knopf.

———. 1974b. *The United States and China*. Cambridge: Harvard University Press.

Fairbank, John King and Roderick MacFarquhar (eds). 1992. *The Cambridge History of China*. Cambridge: Cambridge University Press.

Falk, Richard. 1997. 'Nuclear Weapons and International Law: A Historic Opportunity', *American Journal of International Law*, 91 (1).

———. 2000. 'India's Nuclearism and the New Shape of World Order', Transnational Foundation for Peace and Future Research, Meeting Point Forum, March 2000, available at http://www.transnational.org/forum/ meet /2000/ falk-India.html.

Fallows, James. 1981. *National Defense*. New York: Random House.

Fang Ning. 1998. 'Defence Policy in the New Era', in Michael Pillsbury (ed.), *Chinese Views of Future Warfare*. New Delhi: Lancer's.

Faruqui, Ahmed. 2003. *Rethinking the National Security of Pakistan: The Price of Strategic Myopia*. Hampshire: Ashgate.

Feaver, Peter D. 1992/93. 'Command and Control in Emerging Nuclear Nations', *International Security*, 17 (3).

Federal Government (US). 1997. 'Plan for Designing Nuclear Weapons and Simulating Nuclear Explosions Under the Comprehensive Test Ban Treaty', Natural Resources Defense Council, August.

Feinberg, Richard E. 1983. *The Intemperate Zone: The Third World Challenge to U.S. Foreign Policy*. New York: Norton.

Feldman, H. 1972. *From Crisis to Crisis: Pakistan, 1962–1969*. London: Oxford University Press.

Felix, Chang. 1996. 'Beijing's Reach in the South China Sea', *Strategic Digest*, 26 (9).

Fernandes, George. 2000. Inaugural Address by Defence Minister George Fernandes at the National Seminar on *The Challenges of Limited War: Parameters and Options*, 5 January, organised by the IDSA, New Delhi, available at http://www.idsa-india.org/defmin5-2000.html.

Ferrell, Robert H. 1994. *Harry S. Truman—A Life*. Columbia, MO: University of Missouri Press.

Fetter, S. 1988. *Towards a Comprehensive Test Ban*. Cambridge, MA: Ballinger.

Fidler, Stephen and Tony Walker. 1999. 'China Builds Up Taiwan Missiles', *Financial Times* (internet edition), 10 February.

Financial Times. 1995a. 'Philippines Agrees Bilateral Spratly's Deal with China', 11 August.

———. 1995b. 'China–Malaysia Spratly Accord', 27 October.

Fingar, Thomas (ed.). 1980. *China's Quest for Independence: Policy Evolution in the 1970s*. Boulder, CO: Westview.

Fischer, David. 1992. *Stopping the Spread of Nuclear Weapons: The Past and Prospects*. London: Routledge.

Fisher, C.S. 1991. 'Build Confidence Not Weapons', *The Bulletin of the Atomic Scientists*, June.

Fitzgerald, C.P. 1964. *The Chinese View of Their Place in the World*. London: Oxford University Press.

———.1966. 'The Chinese Foreign Policy', in Ruth Adams (ed.), *Contemporary China*. New York: Pantheon.

Foreign Ministry of PRC. 2003. Foreign Ministry Spokesperson's Press Conference, Permanent Mission of the People's Republic of China to the UN, 9 April, available at http://un.fmprc.gov.cn/eng/55691.html.

Frankel, Benjamin (ed.). 1991. *Opaque Nuclear Proliferation*. London: Frank Cass.

Frankel, Francine R. 1986. 'Play the India Card', *Foreign Policy*, 62 (Spring).

Freedman, Lawrence. 1987. 'On the Tigers Back: The Concept of Escalation', in Roman Kolkowicz (ed.), *The Logic of Nuclear Terror*. Boston: Allen and Unwin.

———. 1989. *The Evolution of Nuclear Strategy*. London: Macmillan.

Friedman, Edward. 1996. 'Why China Matters', *Journal of International Affairs*, 49 (2).

Foran, Virginia. 1992. *US Nuclear Non Proliferation Policy, 1945–1991*. Alexandria: Chadwyck-Healey.

Fruchtwanger, E.J. and Peter Nailor (ed.). 1981. *The Soviet Union and the Third World*. London: Macmillan Press.

Fuerwerker, Albert. 1972. 'Chinese History and the Foreign Relations of Contemporary China', *The Annals of the American Academy of Political and Social Science*, July.

Gabriel, Jurg M. 1995. *Worldviews and Theories of International Theory*. Delhi: Macmillan.

Gacek, Christopher M. 1994. *The Logic of Force: The Dilemma of Limited War in American Foreign Policy*. New York: Columbia University Press.

Gandhi, M.K. 1920. 'The Doctrine of the Sword', *Young India*, 11 August.

———. 1936. 'God of Love, Not Wars', *Harijan*, 5 September.

———. 1946. 'Atom Bomb and Ahimsa', *Harijan*, 7 July.

Gandhi, Rajiv. 1988. *A World Free of Nuclear Weapons: An Action Plan*. Address to Third Special Session on Disarmament, UN General Assembly, 9 June. New Delhi: Rajiv Gandhi Foundation.

Ganguly, Sumit. 1983. 'Why India Joined the Nuclear Club', *The Bulletin of the Atomic Scientists*, 39 (4).

Ganguly, Sumit. 1985. *The Crisis in Kashmir: Portents of War, Hopes of Peace.* Cambridge: Cambridge University Press.

Ganguly, Sumit. 1996. 'Political Mobilization and Institutional Decay: Explaining the Crisis in Kashmir', *International Security,* 21 (2).

———. 1999a. 'India's Pathway to Pokhran II', *International Security,* 23 (4).

———. 1999b. *The Crisis in Kashmir: Portents of War, Hopes of Peace.* Cambridge: Cambridge University Press.

———. 2002a. *Conflict Unending: India–Pakistan Tensions since 1947.* New Delhi: Oxford University Press.

———. 2002b. '"Nuclear Cloud" is Full of Hot Air', *The Indian Express,* 12 June.

Ganguly, Sumit and Ted Greenwood (eds). 1996. *Mending Fences: Confidence and Security Building Measures in South Asia.* Boulder, CO: Westview.

Gardner, Howard. 1985. *The Mind's New Science: A History of Cognitive Revolution.* New York: Basic Books.

Garrett, Banning N. and Bonnie S. Glaser. 1995/96. 'Chinese Perspectives on Nuclear Arms Control', *International Security,* 20 (3).

Garver, John W. 1999. 'Nuclear Weapons and the China–India Relationship' (paper presented at conference on *South Asian Nuclear Dilemma*), 18–19 February, Weatherhead Centre for International Affairs, Harvard University.

———. 2001. *Protracted Contest: Sino-Indian Rivalry in the 20th Century.* New Delhi: Oxford University Press.

Garwin, Richard. 1993. 'Nuclear Weapons for the United Nations', in Joseph Rotblat, Jack Steinberger and B. Udgaonkar (eds), *A Nuclear Weapon-free World: Desirable, Feasible?* Boulder, CO: Westview.

Gates, David. 1991. *Non-offensive Defence: An Alternative Strategy for NATO?* London: St Martin's Press.

Gauhar, Altaf. 1999. 'Four Wars, One Assumption', *The Nation,* 5 September.

Gelman, Harry. 1980. 'Outlook for Sino-Soviet Relations', in Eric P. Hoffman and Fredric J. Fleron Jr (eds), *The Conduct of Soviet Foreign Policy.* New York: Aldine.

George, Alexander L. and Richard Smoke. 1974. *Deterrence in American Foreign Policy: Theory and Practice.* New York: Columbia University Press.

Gerhart, Lt Gen John K. 1961. 'Long-range Threat of Communist China', Memorandum from Lt Gen. John K. Gerhart, Deputy Chief of Staff, Plans and Programs, US Air Force, to Air Force Chief of Staff Thomas White, 8 February.

Gertz, Bill. 1996. 'Pakistan Deploys Chinese Missiles', *The Washington Times,* 12 June.

———. 1999. 'China Develops Warhead Decoys to Defeat US Defenses', *The Washington Times,* 16 September.

Ghali, Boutras Boutras. 1995. Speech of Boutras Boutras Ghali, United Nations Secretary General, during the 1995 NPT Review and Extension Conference, 17 April, New York.

Ghose, Arundhati. 1996. Statement by Amb. Arundhati Ghose at the United Nations General Assembly, 10 September.

Ghosh, Amitav. 1999. *Countdown.* New Delhi: Ravi Dayal.

Ghosh, Partha S. 1999. *BJP and the Evolution of Hindu Nationalism.* New Delhi: Manohar.

Gill, Bates. 1993. *The Challenge of Chinese Arms Proliferation: U.S. Policy for the 1990s.* Carlisle Barracks, PA: Strategic Studies Institute, U.S. Army War College.

Gill, Bates. 1998. 'Chinese Military Modernisation and Arms Proliferation in the Asia-Pacific', in Jonathan D. Pollack and Richard H. Yang (eds), *In China's Shadow: Regional Perspectives on Chinese Foreign Policy and Military Developments.* Washington, DC: RAND.

Gilpin, Robert. 1981. *War and Change in World Politics.* Cambridge: Cambridge University Press.

——. 1987. *The Political Economy of International Relations.* Princeton, NJ: Princeton University Press.

Ginsburg, Norton. 1968. 'On the Chinese Perception of a World Order', in Tang Tsou (ed.) *China in Crisis*, 2 vols. Chicago: University of Chicago.

Gittings, John. 1967. *The Role of Chinese Army.* London: Oxford University Press.

——. 1989. *China Changes Face: The Road from Revolution 1949–1989.* New York: Oxford University Press.

Gjelstad, John and Olav Njolstad (eds). 1996. *Nuclear Rivalry and International Order.* London: Sage.

Glaser, Bonnie S. 1993. 'China's Security Perceptions: Interests and Ambitions', *Asian Survey*, 33 (3).

Glaser, Bonnie S. and Banning N. Garret. 1986. 'Chinese Perspectives on the Strategic Defence Initiative', *Problems of Communism*, March–April.

Godement, Francois. 1997. 'Does China Have an Arms Control Policy', in David S.G. Goodman and Gerald Segal (eds), *China Rising*. London and New York: Routledge.

Godwin, Paul. 1984. 'Soldiers and Statesmen in Conflict: Chinese Defence and Foreign Policies in the 1980s', in Samuel S. Kim (ed.), *China and the World: Chinese Foreign Policy in the Post-Mao Era.* Boulder, CO: Westview.

——. 1992. 'Chinese Military Strategy Revised: Local and Limited War', *The Annals of the American Academy of Political Science*, January.

——. 1997. 'From Continent to Periphery: PLA Doctrine, Strategic And Capabilities Towards 2000', in David Shambaugh and Richard H. Yang (eds), *China's Military in Transition.* Oxford: Clarendon Press.

——. 1999. 'The PLA Faces the Twenty-First Century', in James R. Lilley and David Shambaugh (eds), *China's Military Faces the Future.* New York: American Enterprise Institute for Public Policy Research.

Godwin, Paul and John J. Schulz. 1993. 'Arming the Dragon for the 21st Century: China's Defense Modernization Program', *Arms Control Today*, 23 (December).

——. 1994. 'China and Arms Control: Transition in East Asia', *Arms Control Today*, 24 (9).

Goodman, David (ed.). 1989. *China's Regional Development.* London: Routledge.

——. 1994. *China Deconstructs: Politics, Trade and Regionalism.* London: Routledge.

——. 1997. 'How Open is Chinese Society?' in David S.G. Goodman and Gerald Segal (eds), *China Rising: Nationalism and Interdependence.* London and New York: Routledge.

——. 2003. 'Qinghai and the Emergence of the West: Nationalists, Communal Interaction and National Integration', (paper presented at conference on *Opening Up the West: China's Regional Development Policy*), 8–10 May, Hamburg.

Goodman, David and Gerald Segal (eds). 1997. *China Rising: Nationalism, and Interdependence*. London: Routledge.

Goodson, Larry. 2000. 'Foreign Policy Gone Awry: The Kalashnikovisation and Talibanisation of Pakistan', in Craig Baxter and Charles H. Kennedy (eds), *Pakistan 2000*. Karachi: Oxford University Press.

Gordon, Michael R. 2002. 'As Threat Eases, US Still Sees Peril in India–Pakistan Buildup', *The New York Times*, 20 January.

Gordon, Sandy (ed.). 1992. *India's Strategic Future*. New York: St Martin's Press.

———. 1994. 'Capping South Asia's Nuclear Weapons Programs: A Window of Opportunity?' *Asian Survey*, 34 (7).

Gorwitz, Mark. 1996. 'The Indian Strategic Nuclear Submarine Project: An Open Literature Analysis', December, available at http://www.fas.org/nuke/guide/india/sub/ssn/index.html.

Government of Pakistan. 1948. Complaint submitted to the UN Security Council on 15 January, UN Document No. S/646.

———. 2004. 'Foreign Policy Objectives', in *Pakistan Foreign Relations 2003–04*. Islamabad: Ministry of Foreign Affairs.

Government of PRC. 1964. 'Break the Nuclear Monopoly: Eliminate Nuclear Weapons', Statement of the Government of the People's Republic of China, 16 October, available at http://www.cns.miis.edu.

———. 1982. 'China's Proposal on Essential Measures for an Immediate Halt to the Arms Race and for Disarmament', submitted at the Second Special Session of the UN General Assembly on Disarmament, 21 June.

———. 1994. Statement of the Spokesman of the Foreign Ministry of the People's Republic of China, 10 June, available at http://www.cns.miis.edu, accessed on 27 August 2002.

———. 1996. Statement upon Signature of the Comprehensive Test Ban Treaty (CTBT), 24 September, available at http://www.cns.miis.edu.

———. 1998. Text of the Chinese Statement in Response to the Indian Tests, available at http://www.ipcs.org/documents/1998/06-Jun.htm.

———. 2000. Working Paper Submitted by China, Main Committee I at the 2000 NPT Review Conference, 1 May, New York.

Graham, Bruce. 1990. *Hindu Nationalism and Indian Politics: The Origins and Development of the Bhartiya Jana Sangha*. Cambridge: Cambridge University Press.

Gray, Colin S. 1977. 'Across the Nuclear Divide: Strategic Studies, Past and Present', *International Security*, 2 (1).

———. 1984. 'War-fighting for Deterrence', *The Journal of Strategic Studies*, 7 (1).

———. 1999. *Modern Strategy*. Oxford: Oxford University Press.

Gray, Jack (ed.). 1969. *Modern Chinese Search for a Political Form*. New York: Oxford University Press.

Gregory, Shaun R. 1996. *Nuclear Command and Control in NATO*. London: Macmillan.

Griffith, Samuel B. 1963. *Sun Zi: The Art of War*. London: Oxford University Press.

Group of Ministers, GOI. 2001. *Recommendations of the Group of Ministers on Reforming the National Security System*. New Delhi: Government of India.

Gupta, Shekhar. 1995. 'Nuclear Weapons in the Subcontinent', *A Stimson Center Occasional Paper*, 21 (May).

Gupta, Sisir. 1966. *Kashmir: A Study in India–Pakistan Relations*. Bombay: Asia Publishing.

——. 1999. 'India Detains Ship Carrying Tools for Missile Production', *The Hindustan Times*, 4 July.

Gupta, Sonika. 2002a (accessed). 'Sino-Indian Ties: New Orientation', available at http://www.ipcs.org/ipcs/newarticles/685-cr-sonika.html, accessed on 3 March.

——. 2002b (accessed). 'Missile Technology Export Control Declaration by China: Reasons for Restraint', available at http://www./ipcs.org/issues/articles/441-cr-sonika.html, accessed on 21 September.

——. 2002c. 'China's Strategic Concerns', *The Hindu*, 26 June.

——. 2003a (accessed). 'China After September 11', available on the IPCS website at http://www.ipcs.org, accessed on 17 January.

——. 2003b (accessed).'The Six Nation Talks: A Balance Sheet', available at http://www.ipcs.org, accessed on 22 October.

Gupta, Sonika and Arpit Rajain. 2003. 'Introduction', in P.R.Chari, Sonika Gupta and Arpit Rajain (eds), *Nuclear Stability in Southern Asia*. New Delhi: Manohar.

Gupta, Vipin. 1994. 'The Status of Chinese Nuclear Weapons Testing', *Jane's Intelligence Review*, January.

Gurtov, Melvin. 1971. *China and South East Asia—The Politics of Survival*. Lexington: Heath Lexington Press.

Gurtov, Melvin and Byong-Moo Hwang. 1980. *China Under Threat*. New York: Johns Hopkins University Press.

——. 1998. *China's Security: The New Roles of the Military*. Boulder, CO: Lynne Rienner.

Haass, Richard. 1988. 'South Asia: Too Late to Remove the Bomb', *Orbis*, 32 (1).

Haendel, Dan. 1977. *The Process of Priority Formation: U.S. Foreign Policy in the Indo-Pakistan War of 1971*. Boulder, CO: Westview.

Hagerty, Devin T. 1993. 'The Power of Suggestion: Opaque Proliferation, Existential Deterrence, and the South Asian Nuclear Arms Competition', *Security Studies*, 2 (3/4).

——. 1993/94. 'Nuclear Deterrence in South Asia: The 1990 Indo-Pakistani Crisis', *International Security*, 20 (3).

——. 1998. *The Consequences of Nuclear Proliferation: Lessons from South Asia*. Cambridge, MA: MIT Press.

Haidar, Ejaz. 2002. 'Stable Deterrence and Flawed Pakistani Nuclear Strategy', *The Friday Times Week*, 2 February.

Haider, Iqbal. 1999. 'Questions Not Answered', *The News International*, 20 July.

Haider, Masood. 2002. 'N-material Not Supplied to N. Korea, Powell Assured', *Dawn*, 21 October.

Hall, Brian. 1998. 'Overkill is Not Dead', *The New York Times Magazine*, 15 March.

Halperin, A.M. (ed.). 1965. *Policies Toward China, Views from Six Continents*. New York: McGraw Hill.

Halperin, Morton H. 1963. *Limited War in the Nuclear Age*. New York: John Wiley and Sons.

——. 1971. *Defense Strategies for the Seventies*. Boston: Little Brown and Co.

——. 1987. *Nuclear Fallacy: Dispelling the Myth of Nuclear Strategy*. Cambridge, MA: Ballinger.

Hamilton, Edward K. (ed.). 1989. *America's Global Interests: A New Agenda*. New York: Norton.

Haqqani, Hussain. 2002. 'The Pakistan–North Korea Connection', *International Herald Tribune*, 26 October.

Haqqani, Hussain. 2003. 'Pakistan's Endgame in Kashmir', in Sumit Ganguly (ed.), *The Kashmir Question: Retrospect and Prospect*. London: Frank Cass.

Hardin, Russell, John J. Mearsheimer, Gerald Dworkin and Robert E. Goodin (eds). 1985. *Nuclear Deterrence: Ethics and Strategy*. Chicago and London: University of Chicago Press.

Harris, Lilliam Craig. 1993. 'Xinjiang, Central Asia and the Implications for China's Policy in the Islamic World', *China Quarterly*, 133 (March).

Harrison, Selig S. 1960. *India: The Most Dangerous Decades*. Princeton, NJ: Princeton University Press.

———. 1986. 'Fanning Flames in South Asia', *Foreign Policy*, 60 (Spring).

Harrison, Selig S.and Kemp Geoffrey (eds). 1993. *India and America after the Cold War*. Washington, DC: Carnegie Endowment for International Peace.

Harrison, Selig S., Paul H. Kreisberg and Dennis Kux (eds). 1999. *India and Pakistan: The First Fifty Years*. Cambridge: Cambridge University Press.

Hart, David. 1983. *Nuclear Power in India: A Comparative Analysis*. London: Allen and Unwin.

Harvard Nuclear Study Group. 1983. *Living with Nuclear Weapons*. Cambridge, MA: Harvard University Press.

Hayes, L.D. 1984. *Politics in Pakistan: The Struggle for Legitimacy*. Boulder, CO: Westview.

Hersh, Seymour. 1983. *The Price of Power: Kissinger in the Nixon White House*. New York: Summit Books.

———. 1993. 'On the Nuclear Edge', *The New Yorker*, 29 March.

Herz, John. 1950. 'Idealist Internationalism and the Security Dilemma', *World Politics*, 2.

Hewitt, Vernon. 1995. *Reclaiming the Past: The Search for Political and Cultural Unity in Contemporary Kashmir*. London: Portland Books.

Hibbs, Mark. 1992. 'Sensitive Iran Reactor Deal May Hinge on MFN for China', *Nucleonics Week*, 1 October.

Hoagland, Jim. 2002. 'The Most Dangerous Place on Earth', *International Herald Tribune*, 25 October.

Hoffman Eric P. and Fredric J. Fleron Jr (eds). 1980. *The Conduct of Soviet Foreign Policy*. New York: Aldine.

Hoffmann, Steven. 1990. *India and the China Crisis*. Berkeley, CA: University of California Press.

Hollen, Christopher Van. 1980. 'Leaning on Pakistan', *Foreign Policy*, 38 (Spring).

Holsti, Ole R. 1972. *Crisis, Escalation, War*. Montreal: McGill-Queen University Press.

Hong Kong Standard (Internet edition). 1998. 'Beijing to Honor Joint Arms Pledge', 28 July.

Hoodbhoy, Pervez. 1994. *Nuclear Issues Between India and Pakistan: Myths and Realities*, Occasional Paper No. 18. Washington, DC: Henry L. Stimson Center.

———. 1999a. 'Why a Civilian Set-up Won't Work', *Dawn*, 16 October.

———. 1999b. 'Too Little and Too Late But Sign the CTBT Anyway', in *Pakistan–India Nuclear Peace Reader*. Lahore: Mashal.

Hoodbhoy, Pervez and Zia Mian. 2000 (accessed). 'Turning Pakistan Away from the Nuclear Abyss', available at http://www.mnet.fr/aiindex/hoodbmian. html, accessed on 23 May.

Hoon, P.N. 1999. *Unmasking Secrets of Turbulence: Midnight Freedom to a Nuclear Dawn*. New Delhi: Manas Publications.

Horelick, Arnold L. and Myron Rush. 1966. *Strategic Power and Soviet Foreign Policy*. Chicago: The University of Chicago Press.

Horsman, Mathew and Andrew Marshall. 1994. *After the Nation-State: Citizens, Tribalism and the New World Disorder*. London: Harper Collins Publishers.

Hough, Jerry F. 1986. *The Struggle for the Third World: Soviet Debates and American Options*. Washington: Brookings Institution.

House of Representatives, US. 1968. *Report of the Special Study Mission to the Far East, South East Asia, India and Pakistan, 1 November–12 December 1965*. Washington, DC: US Government Printing Office.

Howard, Michael. 1982/83. 'Reassurance and Deterrence: Western Defense in the 1980's', *Foreign Affairs*, 61 (2).

Hoyt, Timothy D. 2001. 'Pakistani Nuclear Doctrine and the Dangers of Strategic Myopia', *Asian Survey*, 41 (6).

Hsieh, Alice Langley. 1962. *Communist China's Strategy in the Nuclear Era*. Englewood Cliffs, NJ: Prentice-Hall.

Hsu, Immanuel C.Y. 1995. *The Rise of Modern China*. Oxford: Oxford University Press.

Hsu, John C. 1989. *China's Foreign Trade Reforms: Impact on Growth and Stability*. Cambridge: Cambridge University Press.

Hu Xiaodi. 2000. Statement of Hu Xiaodi, Head of the Chinese Delegation, at the Plenary Meeting of the Conference on Disarmament on the Issue of the Conference on Disarmament's Work Program, 10 February.

Hua Di. 1997. 'China's Security Dilemma to the Year 2010', Working Paper, Stanford: CISAC.

Hua Han. 1998. 'Sino-Indian Relations and Nuclear Arms Control', in Eric Arnett (ed.), *Nuclear Weapons and Arms Control in South Asia After the Test Ban*. Oxford: Oxford University Press for the Stockholm International Peace Research Institute.

Huang, Philip C. 1991. 'The Paradigmatic Crisis in Chinese Studies', *Modern China*, 17 (3).

Huck, Arthur. 1972. *The Security of China: Chinese Approaches to Problems of War and Strategy*. London: Cox and Wyman Ltd.

Human Rights Commission of Pakistan. 1998. *State of Human Rights in 1997*. Lahore: Human Rights Commission of Pakistan.

Hungdah Chiu. 1996. 'Communist China's Attitude Toward International Law', *The American Journal of International Law*, 60 (1).

Hunt, Michael. 1987. *Ideology and US Foreign Policy*. New Haven, CT: Yale University Press.

Huntington, Samuel P. 1993. 'The Clash of Civilizations', *Foreign Affairs*, 72 (3).

Hussain, Akmal and Mushahid Hussain. 1993. *Pakistan: Problems of Governance*. New Delhi: Konark.

Hussain, Mushahid. 1988. *Pakistan and the Changing Regional Scenario: Reflections of a Journalist*. Lahore: Progressive Publishers.

Hussain, Mushahid. 1989. 'The Strike of a True Believer: Pakistan Tests New Doctrine', *Jane's Defense Weekly*, 2 December.

———. 1991. 'A Bomb for Security', *Newsline* (Karachi), November.

Hussain, Zahid. 2000. 'Empowering the Khakis?' *Newsline* (Karachi), September.

Huth, Paul K. 1988. *Extended Deterrence and the Prevention of War*. New Haven and London: Yale University Press.

Huth, Paul K. and B. Russett. 1984. 'What Makes Deterrence Work ? Cases from 1900 to 1980', *World Politics*, 36.

ICDSI. 1982. *Common Security: A Programme for Disarmament: The Report of the Independent Commission on Disarmament and Security Issues* (under the Chairmanship of Olof Palme). London: Pan Books.

IFPA. 2000. 'National Missile Defense: Policy Issues and Technological Capabilities', July. Washington, DC: Institute of Foreign Policy Analysis.

Ignatius, David. 2002. 'Stepping Back From the Edge', *The Washington Post*, 14 June.

IISS. 1969–71, 1990–91 and 1999–2000. *Strategic Survey*. London: Oxford University Press for IISS.

Ikle, Charles Fred. 1973. 'Can Deterrence Last Out the Century?', *Foreign Affairs*, 51 (2).

Independent Core Group. 2003. *India–US Relations: Promoting Synergy*, Report of an Independent Core Group. New Delhi: Institute of Peace and Conflict Studies.

Independent Task Force. 1997. *A New US Policy Toward India and Pakistan*, Report of the Independent Task Force. Washington, DC: Council on Foreign Relations.

———. 1998. *After the Tests: US Policy Towards India and Pakistan*, Report of the Independent Task Force. Washington, DC: Council on Foreign Relations and the Brookings Institution.

———. 2003. *New Priorities in South Asia*, Report of the Independent Task Force. Washington, DC: Council on Foreign Relations.

India–Pakistan Agreement. 1988a. Bilateral Agreement on the Prohibition of Attack against Nuclear Installations and Facilities, 31 December, Islamabad.

———. 1988b. Agreement on the Non-Attack of Nuclear Facilities between India and Pakistan (ratified in 1991).

———. 1991. Agreement between Pakistan and India on Prevention of Air Space Violation.

India–PRC Agreement. 1993. Agreement on the Maintenance of Peace and Tranquillity along the Line of Control.

———. 1996. Agreement on Confidence Building Measures in the Military Field along the Line of Actual Control in the India–China Border Areas.

Institute of Foreign Policy Analysis. 2000. *National Missile Defense: Policy Issues and Technological Capabilities*. Washington, DC: Institute of Foreign Policy Analysis.

Institute for National Strategic Studies. 1999. *Strategic Assessment 1998: Engaging Power for Peace*, National Defense University. Washington, DC: US Government Printing Press Office.

Institute of Peace and Conflict Studies (IPCS). 1998. 'Strategic and Doctrinal Implications: Post Pokharan', Fourth IPCS Seminar, 10 July, New Delhi.

International Herald Tribune. 1993. 'China and Vietnam Sign Border Pact', 20 October.

———. 1996a. 'Cuts Seen in Chinese Military', 17 January.

International Herald Tribune. 1996b. 'Beijing Hanoi Border Talks', 24 January.

———. 2002. 'Musharraf Isn't Complying' (editorial), 16 May.

International Legal Materials. 1996. 'International Court of Justice: Advisory Opinion on the Legality of the Threat or Use of Nuclear Weapons', 35 (4).

IPCS (Institute of Peace and Conflict Studies). 1998. Seminar on *Strategic and Doctrinal Implications: Post Pokharan*, Fourth IPCS Seminar, 10 July, New Delhi.

———. 2000. Report of the seminar, *Evolving a Theoretical Perspective on Human Security*, No. 394, 30 July, available at http://www.ipcs.org/issues/articles/394-ind-suba.html.

Iqbal, Mohammed. 1983. 'India's Space Programme', *Regional Studies* (Islamabad), 2 (1).

Isby, David C. 1981. *Weapons and Tactics of the Soviet Army*. London: Janes.

Ismat, Brig S.J. Saeed. 2000. 'Strategy for Total Defence: A Conceptual Nuclear Doctrine', *Defence Journal*, available at http://www.defencejournal.com/2000/mar/doctrine.htm.

Issac, Harold R. 1980. *Scratches on Our Minds: American View on China and India*. New York: Harper Torchbooks.

Jackson, William D. 1979. 'The Soviets and Strategic Arms: Towards an Evaluation of the Record', *Political Science Quarterly*, 94 (2).

Jacobs, Gordon and Tim McCarthy. 1992. 'China's Missile Sales—Few Changes for the Future', *Jane's Intelligence Review*, December.

Jagmohan. 1991. *My Frozen Turbulence in Kashmir*. New Delhi: Allied.

Jahan, Rounaq. 1973. *Pakistan: Failure in National Integration*. Dacca: Oxford University Press.

Jain, B.M. 1994. *Nuclear Politics in South Asia*. New Delhi: Rawat.

Jain, J.P. (ed.). 1974. *Nuclear India*, vols 1 and 2. New Delhi: Radiant.

Jain, R.K. (ed.). 1983. *US–South Asian Relations, 1947–1982*, vol. 2. New Delhi: Radiant Publishers.

Jaipal, Rikhi. 1986. *Nuclear Arms and the Human Race*. New Delhi: Allied.

Jalal, A. 1985. *The Sole Spokesman: Jinnah, the Muslim League and the Demand for Pakistan*. Cambridge: Cambridge University Press.

———. 1991. *The State of Martial Rule: The Origins of Pakistan's Political Economy of Defence*. Lahore: Vanguard.

Jan, Tarik (ed.). 1995. *Pakistan's Security and the Nuclear Option*. Islamabad: Institute of Policy Studies.

Jang. 2004. 'Shared Information with Iran, Libya and N-Korea, says Dr Qadeer', 3 February.

Jaspal, Zafar Nawaz. 2001. 'Reassessing Pakistan's Nuclear Strategy', available at http://www.defencejournal.com/2001/july/reassessing.htm.

Jencks, Harlan. 1990. 'Party Authority and Military Power: Communist China's Continuing Crisis', *Issues and Studies*, 26 (7).

Jennings, Peter. 2000. Interview of the President on ABC World News, 21 March, New Delhi, available at http://www.ipcs.org/documents/2000/02-mar-apr.htm.

Jervis, Robert. 1976. *Perception and Misperception in International Politics*. Princeton, NJ: Princeton University Press.

———. 1979. 'Deterrence Theory Revisited', *World Politics*, 31 (4).

———. 1982/83. 'Deterrence and Perception', *International Security*, 7 (Winter).

Jervis, Robert. 1984. *The Illogic of American Nuclear Strategy*. Ithaca, NY: Cornell University Press.

———. 1989. 'Rational Deterrence: Theory and Evidence,' *World Politics*, Vol. 41, (1989), pp. 183–207.

Jervis, Robert, Richard N. Lebow and J.G. Stein. 1985. *Psychology and Deterrence*. Baltimore, MD: Johns Hopkins University Press.

Jessup, Philip C. 1957. 'Political and Humanitarian Approaches to Limitation of Warfare', *American Journal of International Law*, 51 (4).

Jetly, Nancy (ed.). 1999. *Regional Security in South Asia: The Ethno Sectarian Dimensions*. New Delhi: Lancer's.

Jha, Prem Shankar. 2000. 'Significance of the CTBT', *The Hindu*, 10 January.

Jiang Zemin. 1999. 'Promote Disarmament Process and Safeguard World Security', Address of the President of the People's Republic of China at the Conference on Disarmament Geneva, 26 March, available online at http://www.cns.iis.edu.

JIC. 1993. *Pakistan's Ballistic Missile Capabilities*, 27 December.

Jillani, A. 1993. 'Judicial Activism and Islamization after Zia: Toward the Prohibition of Riba', in C.H. Kennedy (ed.), *Pakistan: 1992*. Boulder, CO: Westview.

Jing-DongYuan. 1998. 'Culture Matters: Chinese Approaches to Arms Control and Disarmament', *Contemporary Security Policy*, 9 (1).

———. 2000. 'Asia-Pacific Security: China's Conditional Multilaterialism and Great Power Entente', Strategic Studies Institute, January.

———. 2002. 'Sino-Indian Ties', *The Hindu*, 31 January.

Jing-Dong Yuan and W.P.S. Sidhu. 2002. Panel discussion on 'Sino-Indian Relations', 30 January, http://www.ipcs.org/issues/newarticles/692-cr-semrep.html, accessed on 17 January 2002.

Jinnah, Mohammad Ali. 1948. *Speeches of Quaid-I-Azam Mohammad Ali Jinnah as Governor General of Pakistan*. Karachi: Sind Observers Press.

Joeck, Neil. 1986. *Strategic Consequences of Nuclear Proliferation in South Asia*. London: Frank Cass.

———. 1997. 'Maintaining Nuclear Stability in South Asia', *Adelphi Paper*, No. 312. New York: Oxford University Press for IISS.

———. 2000. 'Nuclear Relations in South Asia', in Joseph Cirincione (ed.), *Repairing the Regime: Preventing the Spread of Weapons of Mass Destruction*. New York: Routledge.

Joffe, Ellis and Gerald Segal. 1995. 'The PLA Under Modern Conditions', *Survival*, 27 (4).

Johnston, Alastair Iain. 1995. *Cultural Realism: Strategic Culture and Grand Strategy in Chinese History*. Princeton, NJ: Princeton University Press.

———. 1995/96. 'China's New' Old Thinking: The Concept of Limited Deterrence', *International Security*, 20 (3).

———. 1996a. 'Prospects for Chinese Nuclear Force Modernisation: Limited Deterrence versus Multilateral Arms Control', *The China Quarterly*, 146 (June).

———. 1996b. 'Cultural Realism and Strategy in Maoist China', in Peter J. Katzenstein (ed.), *The Culture of National Security: Norms and Identity in World Politics*. New York: Columbia University Press.

———. 1997. 'Prospects for Chinese Nuclear Force Modernization: Limited Deterrence versus Multilateral Arms Control', in David Shambaugh and

Richard H. Yang (eds), *China's Military in Transition*. Oxford: Oxford University Press.

Johnston, Alastair Iain. 1998. 'China's Militarised Interstate Dispute Behaviour 1949–1992: A First Cut at the Data', *The China Quarterly*, 153 (March).

Johnson, James Turner. 1981. *Just War Tradition and Restraint of War: A Moral and Historical Inquiry*. Princeton, NJ: Princeton University Press.

Johnson, Robert H. 1963. *Chinese Communist Nuclear Detonation and Nuclear Capability: Major Conclusions and Key Issues*. State Department Policy Planning Council, Washington, 15 October.

Joint US–India Statement. 2000a. *Indo-US Vision Statement*, 21 March, available at http://www.ipcs.org/ documents/2000/02-mar-apr.htm.

———. 2000b. Joint Statement on Cooperation in Energy and Environment, Agra, 22 March, available at http://www.ipcs.org/documents/2000/02-mar-apr.htm.

Joint US–Pakistan Statement. 1999. 'Text of Joint Statement Issued After Nawaz–Clinton Meeting', (AFP) Washington, 4 July, available at http://www.ipcs.org/what'snew/ kargil.

Joint US–PRC Statement. 1994a. *Stopping Production of Fissile Materials for Nuclear Weapons*, 4 October.

———. 1994b. Joint Statement on Missile Proliferation, *USIS Fact Sheet*, 5 October.

———. 1997. Jonint Statement on 29 October, available at http://www.cns.miis.edu, accessed on 21 April 2002.

———. 1998. Joint US–PRC Statement on South Asia, available at http://www.fas.org/news/china/1998/sasia.htm, accessed on 22 May 2000.

Jones, Gregory S. 2000. 'From Testing to Deploying Nuclear Forces: The Hard Choices Facing India and Pakistan', IP-192. Santa Monica, CA: RAND.

Jones, Owen Bennett. 2002. *Pakistan: Eye of the Storm*. New Delhi: Viking.

Jones, Rodney. W. 1981. *Nuclear Proliferation: Islam, the Bomb and South Asia*. The Washington Papers, No.82. Beverly Hills, CA: Sage.

———. (ed.). 1983. *Small Nuclear Forces and American Security Policy: Potential Threats and Conflicts in the Middle East and South Asia*. Lexington, MA: Lexington Books.

Jones, Rodney W. and Nikolai N. Sokov. 1997. 'After Helsinki, the Hard Work', *The Bulletin of the Atomic Scientists*, 53 (4).

Jones, Rodney W. and Hildreth A. Steven (eds). 1986. *Emerging Powers—Defence and Security in the Third World*. New York: Praeger.

Jones, T.K. and W. Scott Thompson. 1978. 'Central War and Civil Defence', *Orbis*, 22 (3).

Joseph, Anil K. 1999. 'China Intends to Ratify CTBT: Official', *The Pioneer*, 27 November.

Joshi, Manoj. 1994. 'Dousing the Fire: Indian Missile Programme and United States' Non-proliferation Policy', *Strategic Analysis*, August.

Kadian, Rajesh. 1993. *The Kashmir Tangle: Issues and Options*. Boulder, CO: Westview.

Kahn, Herman. 1961. *On Thermonuclear War*. Princeton, NJ: Princeton University Press.

———. 1962. *Thinking about the Unthinkable*. New York: Horizon.

———. 1965. *On Escalation: Metaphors and Scenario*. New York: Praeger.

Kak, Kapil. 1998. 'Command and Control of Small Nuclear Arsenals', in Jasjit Singh (ed.), *Nuclear India*. New Delhi: Knowledge World.

Kamal, Nazir. 1992a. 'China's Arms Export Policy and Responses to Multilateral Restraints', *Contemporary Southeast Asia*, 14 (Spring).

———. 1992b. 'Nuclear and Missile Proliferation Issues: Some Approaches to Stability', *Contemporary Southeast Asia*, 13 (4).

———. 1999. 'Pakistani Perceptions and Prospects of Reducing the Nuclear Danger in South Asia', Occasional Paper No. 6, Cooperative Monitoring Center, Sandia National Laboratories, Albuquerque, NM.

Kampani, Gaurav. 2001. 'In Praise of Indifference Toward India's Bomb', *Orbis*, Spring.

Kan, Shirley. 1992. 'Chinese Missile and Nuclear Proliferation: Issues for Congress', *Congressional Research Issue Brief*, 24 August, Washington, DC.

———. 1996. 'Chinese Proliferation of Weapons of Mass Destruction: Current Policy Issues', *Congressional Research Issue Brief*, 17 October, Washington, DC.

———. 1997. 'China's Compliance with International Arms Control Agreements', *Congressional Research Service Report*, Washington, DC.

———. 1998. 'Chinese Proliferation of Weapons of Mass Destruction: Current Policy Issues', *Congressional Research Service Report* 12056, updated June 1998, available at http://www.fas.org/spp/starwars/crs 92056.htm, accessed on 3 November 1999.

Kan, Shirley and Robert Shuey. 1997. 'China: Ballistic and Cruise Missiles', *Congressional Research Service Report*, Washington, DC.

Kanwal, Gurmeet. 1999. 'China's Long March to World Power Status: Strategic Challenge for India', *Strategic Analysis*, 22 (11).

———. 2001. *Nuclear Defense: Shaping the Arsenal*. New Delhi: Knowledge World.

———. 2003. 'Command and Control of Nuclear Weapons in India', *Strategic Analysis*, 23 (10).

Kapila, Brig Subhash. 2003 (accessed). Response to IPCS e-debate no. 4 on 'India–Pakistan Troop Mobilisation', available at http://www.ipcs.org/ipcs/debatePage.jsp, accessed on 7 March.

Kaplan, Stephen S. (ed.). 1981. *Diplomacy and Power: Soviet Armed Forces as a Political Instrument*. Washington, DC: Brookings Institution.

Kaplan, Stephen S. and W.H. Lewis.1978. *Arms across the Sea*. Washington: Brookings Institution.

Kapur, Ashok. 1974. 'India and the Atom', *The Bulletin of the Atomic Scientists*, 30 (7).

———. 1976. *India's Nuclear Option: Atomic Diplomacy and Decision-Making*. New York: Praeger.

———. 1987. *Pakistan's Nuclear Development*. New York: Croom Helm.

———. 2001. *Pokhran and Beyond: India's Nuclear Behaviour*. New Delhi: Oxford University Press.

Kapur, Harish. 1987. *As China Sees the World*. London: France Pinter.

Kapur, K.D. 1993. *Nuclear Non-Proliferation Diplomacy*. New Delhi: Lancer's.

Kargil Review Committee. 1999. *The Kargil Review Committee Report* (mimeographed version). New Delhi: Government of India.

———. 2000. *From Surprise to Reckoning. The Kargil Review Committee Report*. New Delhi: Sage.

Karnad, Bharat (ed.). 1994. *Future Imperilled: India's Security in the 1990s and Beyond*. New Delhi: Viking.

——. 1999. 'A Thermonuclear Deterrent', in Amitabh Matto (ed.), *India's Nuclear Deterrent: Pokharan II and Beyond*. New Delhi: Har-Anand.

——. 2002. *Nuclear Weapons and Indian Security: The Realist Foundations of Strategy*. New Delhi: Macmillan.

Karp, Jonathan. 1998. 'India Faces the Task of Creating a Nuclear Weapons Doctrine', *Asian Wall Street Journal*, 28 May.

Kashmir Study Group. 1997. *1947–1997. The Kashmir Dispute at Fifty: Charting Paths to Peace*, Report on the visit of an Independent Study Team to India and Pakistan, sponsored by the Kashmir Study Group.

Kasturi, Bhashyam. 1999. 'India', in P.R. Chari (ed.), *Perspectives on National Security in South Asia*. New Delhi: Manohar.

Katz, Mark N. 1982. *The Third World in Soviet Military Thought*. London: Croom Helm.

Katzenstein, Peter J. (ed.). 1996. *The Culture of Nuclear Security: Norms and Identity in World Politics*. New York: Colombia University Press.

Kaufmann, William W. 1956a. 'The Requirements of Deterrence', in William W. Kaufmann (ed.), *Military Policy and National Security*. Princeton, NJ: Princeton University Press.

——. (ed.) 1956b. *Military Policy and National Security*. Princeton, NJ: Princeton University Press.

——. 1958. 'Crisis in Military Affairs', *World Politics*, 10 (4).

——. 1964. *The McNamara Strategy*. New York: Harper and Row.

Kaul, B.N. 1980. *Dulles Resurrected*. New Delhi: Pulse.

Kaul, Lt Gen B.N. 1967. *The Untold Story*. Bombay: Allied.

Kaul, T.N. 1980. *The Kissinger Years: Indo-American Relations*. New Delhi: Arnold-Heinemann.

Kaushik, B.M. and O.N. Mehrotra. 1980. *Pakistan's Nuclear Bomb*. New Delhi: Sopan Publishing.

Kavka, Gregory S. 1987. *Moral Paradoxes of Nuclear Deterrence*. Cambridge: Cambridge University Press.

KBS-1 (Pyongyang). 1996. 'Taiwan Reportedly Finds "Nuclear Material" on DPRK Ship', 10 March.

KCNA (Pyongyang). 1994. 'Foreign Ministry Group Leaves for Iran, Pakistan', 31 March.

Keller, Michael P. Fischer and Richard K. Herrmann. 1995. 'Beyond the Enemy Image and Spiral Model: Cognitive-strategic Research After the Cold War', *International Organization*, 49 (3).

Kemp, Geoffrey. 1978. 'Scarcity and Strategy', *Foreign Affairs*, 56 (2).

Kennan, George. 1982. *The Nuclear Delusion*. New York: Pantheon.

Kennedy Jr, Bingham. 1996. 'Curbing Chinese Missile Sales: From Imposing to Negotiating China's Adherence to the MTCR', *Journal of Northeast Asian Studies*, 15 (Spring).

Kennedy, Donald (with David Holloway, Erika Weinthal, Walter Falcon, Paul Ehrlich, Roz Naylor, Michael May, Steven Schneider, Stephen Fetter and Jor-San Choi). 1998. *Environmental Quality and Regional Conflict: A Report to the Carnegie Commission on Preventing Deadly Conflict*. New York: Carnegie Corporation.

Kennedy, Paul M. 1987. *The Rise and Fall of Great Powers*. New York: Random House.

Keohane, Robert O. (ed.). 1986. *Neorealism and its Critics*. New York: Columbia University Press.

———. 1989a. *International Institutions and State Power: Essays in International Relations Theory*. Boulder, CO: Westview.

———. 1989b. 'International Institutions: Two Approaches', in Robert Keohane (ed.), *International Institutions and State Power: Essays in International Relations Theory*. Boulder, CO: Westview.

Keohane, Robert O. and Joseph Nye. 1989. *Power and Interdependence: World Politics in Transition*. Boston: Little Brown.

Khakwani, Abdul Shakoor. 2003. 'Civil–Military Relations in Pakistan: The Case of the Recent Military Intervention (October 12, 1999) and its Implications for Pakistan's Security Milieu', ACDIS Occasional Paper, May, University of Illinois.

Khalilzad, Zalmay. 1985. 'Pakistan', in Joseph Goldbat (ed.), *Nuclear Proliferation: The Why and Wherefore*. London: Taylor and Francis.

Khan, Aamer Ahmed. 2000. 'Devolving Destruction', *The Herald*, September.

Khan, Akhtar Ali. 1994. 'Towards Regional Non-Proliferation in South Asia: Review and Update', *Defence Journal*, 20 (3–4).

Khan, Air Marshal (Retd) Ayaz Ahmed. 2000. 'Hot Pursuit, Air Strikes, Limited War', *Defence Journal*, available at http://www.defencejournal.com/2000/oct/pursuit.htm.

Khan, Hafiz R. 1986. 'The Kahuta Story', *Defence Journal*, August.

Khan, Mohammad Ayub. 1967. *Friends Not Masters*. London: Oxford University Press.

Khan, R.A., Rasul B. Rais and K. Waheed. 1989. *South Asia: Military Power and Regional Politics*. Islamabad: Islamabad Council of World Affairs.

Khan, S. Agha (ed.). 1986. *Nuclear War, Nuclear Proliferation and Their Consequence*. Oxford: Clarendon.

Khan, Shaharyar. 1992. 'Pakistan Official Affirms Capacity for Nuclear Device', Pakistan Foreign Secretary Shaharyar Khan's interview, *The Washington Post*, 7 February.

Khan, Zaigham. 1999. 'Unholy Dividends', *The Herald* (Karachi), August.

Khan, Air Chief Marshal Zulfiqar Ali. 1988. *Pakistan's Security: The Challenge and the Response*. Lahore: Progressive Publishers.

———. 1995. 'Pakistan's Security and Nuclear Option', *Nuclear Issues in South Asia*, Islamabad Council for World Affairs (ICWA), Special Issue (Spring).

Kilmarx, Robert A. 1962. *A History of Soviet Air Power*. New York: Frederick A. Praeger.

Kim, Samuel S. 1979. *China, the UN and World Order*. Princeton, NJ: Princeton University Press.

———. (ed.). 1984. *China and the World: Chinese Foreign Policy in the Post-Mao Era*. Boulder, CO: Westview.

———. 1992a. 'China as a Regional Power', *Current History*, 91 (September).

———. 1992b.'International Organizations in Chinese Foreign Policy', *Annals of the American Association of Political and Social Science*, January.

Kissinger, Henry. 1957. *Nuclear Weapons and Foreign Policy*. New York: Harper and Row.

———. 1979. *White House Years*, Indian repr. New Delhi: Vikas.

———. 1998. 'No Room for Nostalgia', *Newsweek*, 160 (26).

Klare, M. 1984. *American Arms Supermarket*. Austin, TX: University of Texas Press.

Klare, Michael T. 1988. 'US Policy on Arms Transfers to the Third World', in Thomas Ohlson (ed.), *Arms Transfer Limitations and Third World Security*. New York: Oxford University Press.

Klintworth, Gary. 1992. 'Chinese Perspectives on India as a Great Power', in Ross Babbage and Sandy Gordon (eds), *India's Strategic Future*. New York: St Martin's Press.

Knorr, Klaus. 1966. *On the Uses of Military Power in the Nuclear Age*. Princeton, NJ: Princeton University Press.

———. 1973. *Power and Wealth*. New York: Basic.

Knorr, Klaus and Thornton Read (eds). 1962. *Limited Strategic War*. London: Pall Mall.

Koch, Andrew. 1997.'Pakistan Persists with Nuclear Procurement', *Jane's Intelligence Review*, 9 (3).

Koch, Andrew and Jennifer Topping. 2000 (accessed). 'Pakistan's Nuclear Related Facilities,' available at http://cns.miis.edu/pubs/reports/pdfs/9707paki.pdf.

Koithara, Verghese. 1999. *Society, State and Security: The Indian Experience*. New Delhi: Sage.

Kondapalli, Srikanth. 1999. *China's Military: The PLA in Transition*. New Delhi: Knowledge World.

Korbel, J. 1966. *Danger in Kashmir*. Princeton, NJ: Princeton University Press.

Korbonski, Andrzej and Francis Fukuyama. 1982. *The Soviet Union in the Third World: The Last Three Decades*. London: Cornell University Press.

Kreisberg, Paul. 1989. 'The United States, South Asia and American Interests', *Journal of International Affairs*, 43 (Summer/Fall).

Krepon, Michael. 1984. *Strategic Stalemate: Nuclear Weapons and Arms Control in American Politics*. New York: St Martin's Press.

———. (ed.). 1997. 'Chinese Perspectives on Confidence-building Measures', *Report of The Henry L. Stimson Center*, No. 23 (May), Washington, DC.

———. 2003. *The Stability–Instability Paradox: Misperception, and Escalation Control in South Asia*. Washington, DC: Henry L. Stimson Center.

Krepon, Michael and Mishi Faruqee (eds). 1997. 'Conflict Prevention and Confidence-Building Measures in South Asia: The 1990 Crisis', Occasional Paper No. 17, April. Washington, DC: The Henry L. Stimson Center.

Krepon, Michael and Chris Gagné (eds). 2001. *The Stability–Instability Paradox: Nuclear Weapons and Brinkmanship in South Asia*. Washington, DC: Henry L. Shimson Center.

———. (eds). 2003. *Nuclear Risk Reduction in South Asia*. New Delhi: Vision Books for Henry L. Stimson Center.

Krepon, Michael and Amit Sevak. 1996. *Crisis Prevention, Confidence Building, and Reconciliation in South Asia*. New Delhi: Manohar.

Krepon, Michael, Jenny S. Drezin and Michael Newbill (eds). 1999. *Declaratory Diplomacy: Rhetorical Initiatives and Confidence Building*, Report of the Henry L. Stimson Center, 27 (May), New York.

Krieger, David. 1999 (accessed). 'India's Nuclear Testing is a Wake Up Call to the World', available at http://www.meadev.gov.in/govt/krieger.htm accessed on 7 August.

Krishna, Maj Gen (Retd) Ashok and P. R. Chari (eds). 2001. *Kargil: The Tables Turned*. New Delhi: Manohar.

Krishnaswami, Sridhar. 1999. 'US Extends Support to Indo-Pak Talks', *The Hindu*, 6 June.

Kristof, Nicholas D. 2001. 'This is Not a Test', *The New York Times*, 28 December.

Kristof, Nicholas D. and Wudunn, Sheryl. 1994. *China Wakes: The Struggle for the Soul of Rising Power*. London: Nicholas Brealey.

KRL (Khan Research Laboratories). 2003. Call for Papers for the Eighth International Symposium on Advanced Materials, available at http://www.krl.com. pk/isam2003/INDEX1.HTM.

Kubalkova, V. and A. Cruickshank 1980. *Marxism-Leninism and Theory of International Relations.* London: Routledge and Kegan Paul.

Kueh, Y.Y. 1992. 'Foreign Investment and Economic Change in China', *The China Quarterly*, September.

Kukreja, Veena. 2002. *Contemporary Pakistan: Political Processes, Conflicts and Crises*. New Delhi: Sage.

Kumar, Ravinder and H.Y. Sharada Prasad (eds). 1955. *Selected Works of Jawaharlal Nehru* (second series), vol. 28 (1 February–31 May), a project of the Jawaharlal Nehru Memorial Fund. New Delhi: Oxford University Press.

Kumar, Satish. 1981. *CIA and the Third World: A Study in Crypto Diplomacy*. New Delhi: Vikas.

Kumar, Saurabh and P.K.Iyengar. 1995. 'Atoms for Peace: Retrieving a Lost Ideal', RGICS Paper No. 25. New Delhi: Rajiv Gandhi Institute for Contemporary Studies.

Kumar, Sumita. 2001. 'Pakistani *Jihadi* Apparatus: Goals and Methods', *Strategic Analysis*, 24 (12).

Kunadi, Savitri. 1998. Statement by Amb. Savitri Kunadi, Permanent Representative of India, at the plenary meeting of the Conference on Disarmament, 2 June.

Kurian, Nimmi. 2001. *Emerging China and India's Policy Options*. New Delhi: Lancer's.

Kux, Dennis. 1993. *Estranged Democracies: India and the U.S.* New Delhi: Sage.

———. 2001. *The United States and Pakistan 1947–2000: Disenchanted Allies*. Karachi: Oxford University Press.

Lackey, Douglas. 1982. 'Missiles and Morals: A Utilitarian Look at Nuclear Deterrence', *Philosophy and Public Affairs*, 2 (Summer).

Lague, David. 2002. 'The Quest for Energy to Grow', *Far Eastern Economic Review*, 14 November.

Lahiri, Dilip. 1999. Statement by Mr Dilip Lahiri, Permanent Mission of India, United Nations, at the United Nations Disarmament Commission, 13 April, New York, available at http://www.meadev.gov.in/govt/stm-undc.htm.

Lamb, Alastair. 1966. *The Kashmir Problem*. New York: Praeger.

———. 1973a. *The McMahon Line: A Study in the Relations between India, China and Tibet*, vols I and II. Canberra: Australian National University Press.

Lamb, Alastair. 1973b. *The Sino-Indian Border in Ladakh*. Canberra: Australian National University Press.

———. 1992. *Kashmir: A Disputed Legacy, 1846–1990*. Karachi: Oxford University Press.

Lambeth, B.S. 1977. 'Selective Nuclear Operations and Soviet Strategy', in J.J. Holst and U. Nerlich (eds), *Beyond Nuclear Deterrence*. New York: Crane, Russak and Co.

Lampton, David M. 2001. 'Cycles, Process, Constraints and Opportunities in US–China Relations' (paper presented at the conference on *Post-APEC China–US Relations*), 3–4 September, Shanghai, China.

Larson, David L. (ed.). 1986. *The 'Cuban Crisis' of 1962: Selected Documents, Chronology and Bibliography*, 2nd edn. Lanham, MD: University Press of America.

Lasswell, Harold and Abraham Kaplan. 1976. *Power and Society*. New Haven, CT and London: Yale University Press.

Latham, Robert. 1996. 'Getting Out from Under: Rethinking Security Beyond Liberalism and the Levels of Analysis Problem', *Millennium: Journal of International Studies*, 25 (1).

Lau, D.C. 1965. 'Some Notes on Sun Tzu', *Bulletin of the School of Oriental and African Studies*, 28 (2).

Lawrence, Bruce B. 1998. *Shattering the Myth: Islam Beyond Violence*. Princeton, NJ: Princeton University Press.

Lebow, Richard Ned. 1981. *Between Peace and War: The Nature of International Crisis*. Baltimore, MD: John Hopkins Press.

Lebow, Richard Ned and Janice Gross Stein. 1989. 'Rational Deterrence Theory: I Think Therefore I Deter', *World Politics*, 41 (January).

———. 1990. 'Deterrence: The Elusive Dependent Variable', *World Politics*, 42 (April).

Lee, Teng-Hui. 1999. 'Understanding Taiwan', *Foreign Affairs*, 78 (6).

Lefever, Ernest W. 1979. *Nuclear Arms in the Third World: U.S. Policy Dilemma*. Washington, DC: Brookings Institution.

Lennox, Duncan. 1996. 'Briefing: Ballistic Missiles', *Jane's Defense Weekly*, 17 April.

———. 1999. 'A Consistent Policy', *Jane's Defense Weekly*, 11 August.

Leonard, James F. and M. Adam Scheinman. 1993. 'Denuclearizing South Asia: Global Approach to a Regional Problem', *Arms Control Today* (June).

Leventhal, P. and Y. Alexander (eds). 1987. *Preventing Nuclear Terrorism*. Lexington: Lexington Books.

Levine, Steven I. 1994. 'Perception and Ideology in Chinese Foreign Policy', in Thomas W. Robinson and David Sambaugh (eds), *Chinese Foreign Policy: Theory and Practice*. Oxford: Clarendon Press.

Lewis, Bernard. 1993. 'Islam and Liberal Democracy', *The Atlantic*, February.

Lewis, George and Theodore Postol. 1997. 'Portrait of a Bad Idea', *The Bulletin of the Atomic Scientists*, July/August 1997.

Lewis, George and He Yingbo. 1998. 'U.S. Missile Defense Activities and the Future of the ABM Treaty', *Physics and Society*, 27 (1).

Lewis, John W. 1980. 'China's Military Doctrines and Force Posture', in Thomas Fingar (ed.), *China's Quest for Independence: Policy Evolution in the 1970s*. Boulder, CO: Westview.

Lewis, W. John and Hua Di. 1992. 'China's Ballistic Missile Programs: Technologies, Strategies, Goals', *International Security*, 17 (2).

Lewis, John W. and Xue Litai. 1988. *China Builds the Bomb*. Stanford, CA: Stanford University Press.

———. 1994. *China's Strategic Seapower: The Politics of Force Modernization in the Nuclear Age*. Stanford: Stanford University Press.

Lewis, John W., Hua Di and Xue Litai. 1991. 'Beijing's Defense Establishment: Solving the Arms-Export Enigma', *International Security*, 15 (4).

Li Changhe. 1999. Statement by Li Changhe, Ambassador for Disarmament Affairs of China, at the Plenary Meeting of the Conference on Disarmament, 11 February, Geneva.

Li Daoyu. 1993. 'Foreign Policy and Arms Control: The View From China', *Arms Control Today*, December.

Li Jijun, Lt Gen. 1997. Address at the US Army War College by Li Jijun, Vice President of the Academy of Military Science, The Chinese People's Liberation Army, Letort Paper No. 1, 29 August, available at http://www.cns.miis.edu, accessed on 25 May 2000.

Liddell-Hart, B.H. 1946. *The Revolution in Warfare*. London: Faber and Faber.

———. 1968. *Strategy: The Indirect Approach*. London: Faber and Faber.

Lieberthal, Kenneth G. and David M. Lampton (eds). 1992. *Bureaucracy, Politics and Decision Making Post-Mao China*. Berkeley, CA: University of California Press.

Lilley, James R. and David Shambaugh (eds). 1999. *China's Military Faces the Future*. New York: American Enterprise Institute for Public Policy Research.

Lindbeck, J.M.H. 1971. *Understanding China*. London: Praeger.

Lisbeth, Gronlund and David Wright. 1997. 'Missile Defense: The Sequel', *Technology Review*, May/June .

———. 1998. 'ABM: Just Kicking the Can', *The Bulletin of the Atomic Scientists*, 54 (1).

Liska, George. 1973. *States in Evolution: Changing Societies and Traditional Systems in World Politics*. Baltimore, MD: Johns Hopkins University Press.

Little, Daniel (ed.). 1991. 'Rational Choice Theory', in Daniel Little (ed.), *Varieties of Social Explanation*. Boulder, CO: Westview.

Litwak, Robert S. 1984. *Detente and the Nixon Doctrine, American Foreign Policy and the Pursuit of Stability, 1969–76*. Cambridge: Cambridge University Press.

Litwak, Robert S. and Samuel F. Wells (eds). 1988. *Super Power Competition and the Security of Third World*. Massachusetts: Ballinger.

Liu Huaqing. 1998. 'Defence Modernisation in Historical Perspective', in Michael Pillsbury (ed.), *Chinese Views of Future Warfare*. New Delhi: Lancer's.

Liu Xuecheng. 1994. *The Sino-Indian Border Dispute and Sino-Indian Relations*. Washington, DC: University Press of America.

Lodal, Jan. 2001. *The Price of Dominance*. New York: Council on Foreign Relations Press.

Lodi, Lt Gen (Retd) Sardar F.S. 1999. 'Pakistan's Nuclear Doctrine', available at http://www.defencejournal.com/apr99/pak-nuclear-doctrine.htm, accessed on 27 July 2001.

Lodhi, Maleeha. 2004. Statement at the High Commissioners' Forum at the International Institute for Strategic Studies, 20 January, London, available at http://www.iiss.org/showpage.php?pageID=77.

Lohalekar, Devidas B. 1991. *U.S. Arms to Pakistan: A Study in Alliance Relationship*. New Delhi: Ashish Publishing.

Lok Sabha [Lower House]. 1995–2002. *Standing Committee on Defence* (1995–2002), Tenth–Thirteenth Lok Sabha, New Delhi: Lok Sabha Secretariat.

———. 1998. *Evolution of India's Nuclear Policy*, paper laid on the Table of the House, 27 May, available at http://www.ipcs.org/documents/ statements/ may98.htm.

Lok Sabha [Lower House]. 2000a. 'Opening of New Kargil Like Fronts by Pakistan', starred question no. 9, answered on 24 February.

———. 2000b. 'Talks with US Deputy Secretary of State', unstarred question no. 1079, answered on 1 March.

———. 2000c. 'Bilateral Relations between India and US', unstarred question no. 1057, answered on 1 March.

———. 2000d. 'Clinton Visit', starred question no. 363, answered on 19 April.

———. 2000e. 'India's Stand on Nuclear Doctrine', unstarred question no. 4987, answered on 26 April.

———. 2000f. Response by Minister of State for External Affairs, Shri Ajit Kumar Panja, 'Discussion on India's Nuclear Doctrine', unstarred question no. 5862, answered on 3 May.

———. 2000g. 'Supply of Missiles to Pakistan', unstarred question no. 6929, answered on 10 May.

———. 2000h. 'Pakistan's Nuclear Capability', starred question no. 49, answered on 26 July.

———. 2000i. 'Use of Wired Aircraft by Pakistan During Kargil Conflict', unstarred question no. 1795, answered on 3 August.

Low, D.A. 1991. *The Political Inheritance of Pakistan*. New York: St Martin's Press.

Ma Jiali. 1994. 'Panchsheela: Fundamental Principle for Contemporary International Relations', *Chinese Institute of Contemporary International Relations*, 4 (6).

Mabbet, Ian. 1985. *Modern China: The Mirage of Modernity*. London: Croom Helm.

Macdonald, Huge. 1981.'The Place of Strategy and the Idea of Security', *Millennium Journal of International Studies*, 10 (3).

Macfarquhar, Roaderick (ed.). 1993. *The Politics of China 1949–1989*. Cambridge: Cambridge University.

Macmillan, Alan, Ken Booth and Russell Trood. 1999. 'Strategic Culture' in Ken Booth and Russell Trood (ed.), *Strategic Cultures in the Asia-Pacific Region*. London: Macmillan.

Mahalingam, Sudha. 1999. 'Sensitive Cargo', *Frontline*, 30 July.

Mahapatra, Chintamani. 1998. *Indo-US Relations: Into the 21st Century*. New Delhi: Knowledge World.

Mahmood, Afzal. 1999. 'Ties with China in Perspective', *Dawn*, 3 October.

Majumdar, Anindya (ed.). 2000. *Nuclear India into the New Millennium*. New Delhi: Lancer's.

Malik, Brig S.K. 1986. *The Quranic Concept of War*, Indian repr. Delhi: Himalayan Books.

Malik, Gen V.P. 2002. Interview with Gen V.P. Malik, former Chief of Army Staff, conducted with Sonika Gupta, 28 July, Chandigarh.

Maluka, Z.K. 1995. *The Myth of Constitutionalism*. London: Oxford University Press.

Mancall, Mark. 1963. 'The Persistence of Tradition in Chinese Foreign Policy', *Annals of the American Academy of Political and Social Science*, September.
——. 1984. *China at the Center: 300 Years of Foreign Policy*. New York: The Era Press.
Manhelin, J.B. 1994. *Strategic Public Diplomacy and American Foreign Policy*. London: Oxford University Press.
Manning, Robert A., Ronald Monaperto and Brad Roberts. 2000. *China, Nuclear Weapons and Arms Control*. New York: Council on Foreign Relations.
Mansfield, Edward D. and Jack Snyder. 1995. 'Democratisation and the Danger of War', *International Security*, 20 (1).
Mao Tse-tung. 1967. *Selected Works of Mao Tse-tung*, vol. II. Beijing: Foreign Languages Press.
——. 1994. *Mao Tse-tung Weijiao Wenxuan* (Selected Diplomatic Works of Mao Tse-tung). Beijing: Central Document Press and World Knowledge Press.
March, Andrew. 1974. *The Idea of China: Myth and Theory in Geographic Thought*. New York: Praeger.
Mark, J. Carson, Theodore Taylor, Eugene Eyster, William Maraman and Jacob Wechsler. 1987. 'Can Terrorists Build Nuclear Weapons?' in P. Leventhal and Y. Alexander (eds), *Preventing Nuclear Terrorism*. Lexington, MA: Lexington Books.
Martin, Laurence. 1979. *Strategic Thought in the Nuclear Age*. Baltimore, MD: Johns Hopkins University Press.
Marwah, Onkar. 1977. 'India's Nuclear and Space Programs: Intent and Policy', *International Security*, 2 (2).
Marwah, Onkar and Ann Shulz (eds). 1975. *Nuclear Proliferation in the Near-Nuclear Countries*. Cambridge, MA: Ballinger.
Masataka, Banno. 1964. *China and the West, 1858–1869: The Origins of the Tsungli Yamen*. Cambridge: Harvard University Press.
Masters, Dexter and Katherine Way (eds). 1941. *One World or None*. New York: McGraw-Hill.
Mattoo, Amitabh. 1994. 'Sanctions, Incentives and Nuclear Proliferation: The Case of India', *Journal of Peace Studies* (July/August).
——. (ed.). 1999a. *India's Nuclear Deterrent: Pokharan II and Beyond*. New Delhi: Har-Anand.
——. 1999b. 'India's Nuclear Doctrine in Search of Strategic Autonomy', *The Times of India*, 19 August.
——. 1999c. 'Pakistan', in P.R. Chari (ed.), *Perspectives on National Security in South Asia: In Search of a New Paradigm*. New Delhi: Manohar.
——. 2000. 'Imagining China', in Kanti Bajpai and Amitabh Mattoo (ed.), *The Peacock and the Dragon: India China Relations in the 21st Century*. New Delhi: Har-Anand.
——. 2003. 'India's "Potential" Endgame in Kashmir', in Sumit Ganguly (ed.), *The Kashmir Question: Retrospect and Prospect*. London: Frank Cass.
Matveyev, Konstantin. 1995. 'Russia, PRC, Links to Iranian Nuclear Program Assessed', *Al-Majallah* (London), 17 December.
Maxwell, Neville. 1970. *India's China War*. Bombay: Jaico.
——. 1973. 'The Chinese Account of the 1969 Fighting at Chenpao', *The China Quarterly*, 56 (October–December).

Mazari, Shireen M. 1991. 'The Nuclear Issue: Options for Pakistan', *Strategic Perspectives*, 1 (1).

———. 1999a. 'India's Nuclear Doctrine in Perspective and Pakistan's Options', *Defence Journal*, October.

———. 1999b. 'Formulating a Rational Strategic Doctrine', paper available on the website of the Pakistan Institute for Air Defence Studies, http://www.piads.com.pk/users/piads/mazari3.html, accessed on 30 August 2001.

McGhee, George. 1961. Declassified memorandum from George McGhee, Head, State Departments' Policy Planning Council, to Secretary of State, Dean, Rusk, 'Anticipatory Action Pending Chinese Communist Demonstration of a Nuclear Capability', September, FOIA files: India, National Security Archive, Washington, DC, available at http:www.gwu.edu/~nsarchiv/nsa/DOCUMENT/950428.htm.

McGrath, Allen. 1997. *The Destruction of Pakistan's Democracy*. Karachi: Oxford University Press.

McNamara, Robert S. 1968. *The Essence of Security: Reflections in Office*. London: Hodder and Stoughton.

———. 1996. '1968: The Essence of Security', in Lt Gen V. R. Raghvan (ed.), *India's Need for Strategic Balance: Security in the Post Cold War World*. New Delhi: Delhi Policy Group.

Mearsheimer, John. 1983. *Conventional Deterrence*. Ithaca, NY: Cornell University Press.

Meisner, Maurice. 1977. *Mao's China*. New York: The Free Press.

Mellor, John D. (ed.). 1979. *India: Rising Middle Power*. Boulder, CO: Westview.

Mendelsohn, Jack. 1997. 'The U.S.-Russian Strategic Arms Control Agenda', *Arms Control Today*, 27(8).

Menon, Raja. 2000a. *A Nuclear Strategy for India*. New Delhi: Sage.

———. 2000b. 'Not in National Interest', *The Hindustan Times* , 5 January.

Michael, Franz. 1972. 'Is China Expansionist: A Design for Aggression', *Problems of Communism*, January–April.

Milholin, Gary. 1986. 'Dateline New Delhi: India's Nuclear Cover-up', *Foreign Policy*, Fall.

———. 1990. 'Asia's Nuclear Nightmare: The German Connection', *The Washington Post*, 10 June.

Milholin, Gary and Gerard White. 1991. 'Bombs from Beijing: A Report on China's Nuclear and Missile Exports', Wisconson Project on Nuclear Arms Control, May, Washington, DC.

Ming Zhang. 1999. *China's Changing Nuclear Posture: Reactions to the South Asian Nuclear Test*. Washington, DC: Brookings Institution.

Ministry of Defence, GOI. 1985–2002. *Ministry of Defence Annual Reports*. New Delhi: Government of India.

Ministry of External Affairs, GOI. 1962. The *Report of the Officials of the Governments of India and the People's Republic of China on the Boundary Question*. New Delhi: Government of India.

———. 1988a. *Disarmament: India's Initiatives*. New Delhi: External Publicity Division, Government of India.

———. 1988b. *India and Disarmament: An Anthology*. New Delhi: Government of India.

Ministry of External Affairs, GOI. 1990–2002. *Annual Reports*. New Delhi: Government of India.

———. 1998. 'PM's Statement in Parliament on 15 December 1998 on Bilateral Talks with the United States', available at www.meaindia.nic.in.

Ministry of External Affairs, PRC. 1999a. 'Explanation of the Parade's Advanced Weapons', *Brief*, 2 October. Beijing: Government of China.

———. 1999b. 'The Big Parade Shows China's High-tech Military Power', *Brief*, 3 October. Beijing: Government of China.

———. 1999c. 'Summary of Chinese Foreign Minister's Comments on International Situation and PRC Foreign Policy', *Brief*, 15 December. Beijing: Government of China.

Minxin Pei. 2002. 'China's Governance Crisis', *Foreign Affairs*, 81 (5).

Mirchandani, G.G. 1968. *India's Nuclear Dilemma*. New Delhi: Popular.

Mishra, Manoj. 2000. 'China's Xinjiang Conundrum', in Kanti Bajpai and Amitabh Mattoo (eds), *The Peacock and the Dragon: India–China Relations in the 21st Century*. New Delhi: Har-Anand.

Mitra, A. and Ramananda Sengupta. 1999. 'Us, Them and the US', in *Outlook*, 19 July.

Modelski, George. 1972. *Principles of World Politics*. London: The Free Press.

Modelski, George and William Thompson. 1989. 'Long Cycles and Global War', in Manus I. Midlarsky (ed.), *Handbook of War Studies*. Boston: Unwin Hyman.

Moeller, Bjorn. 1992. *Common Security and Non-offensive Defense: A Neorealist Perspective*. Boulder, CO: Lyne Rienner.

Mogy, R.B. and Pruitt, D.G. 1974. 'The Effect of a Threatener's Enforcement Costs on Threat Credibility and Compliance', *Journal of Personality and Social Psychology*, 29.

Mohan, C. Raja. 1987. 'US–Pakistan Strategic Consensus and India', *Strategic Analysis*, 11 (12).

———. 1993. 'India's Nuclear Policy at the Crossroads', in Kathleen C. Bailey (ed.), *The Director's Series on Proliferation*. Livermore, CA: Lawrence Livermore National Laboratory.

———. 1998. 'Nuclear Defiance and Reconciliation: Post Pokhran II' (paper presented at the seminar on *The National Way Ahead*), 19–20 September, New Delhi.

———. 1999a. 'Pak Nuclear Exports to N. Korea?' *The Hindu*, 11 July.

———. 1999b. 'A Chance to Shed Preoccupations of the Past: Jaswant', *The Hindu*, 24 July.

———. 1999c. 'Beyond the Nuclear Obsession', *The Hindu*, 25 November.

———. 1999d. 'India Not to Engage in an N-arms Race: Jaswant', *The Hindu*, 29 November.

———. 2000. 'President Commends Idea of Road, Rail Links with China', *The Hindu*, 3 June.

———. 2001a. 'Haass Promises to Further Relax Sanctions', *The Hindu*, 5 December.

———. 2001b. 'Diplomacy Precedes Military Response', *The Hindu*, 15 December.

———. 2003a. *Crossing the Rubicon: The Shaping of India's New Foreign Policy*. New Delhi: Viking.

———. 2003b. 'Nuclear Command Authority Comes into Being', *The Hindu*, 5 January.

Mohanty, Monoranjan (ed.). 1992. *Chinese Revolution*. Delhi: Ajanta.

Moonis, Ahmar. 1993. 'Conflict Management and Confidence Building: Relevance of Cooperation in Non-military Area' (paper presented at *Conference on Confidence and Security-Building Measures in South Asia*). New Delhi and Islamabad, 24–30 May.

Morgan, Patrick. 1983. *Deterrence: A Conceptual Analysis*, 2nd edn. Beverly Hills, CA: Sage.

Morgenthau, Hans J. 1978. *Politics Among Nations: The Struggle for Power and Peace*, 5th rev. edn. New York: Knopf.

Mosen, Leo J. 1985. *The Chinese Mosaic: The Peoples and Provinces of China*. Boulder, CO: Westview.

Moshaver, Ziba. 1991. *Nuclear Weapons Proliferation in the Indian Subcontinent*. New York: St Martin's Press.

Mudumbai, Srinivas. 1980. *United States Foreign Policy Towards India, 1947–54*. New Delhi: Manohar.

Mueller, John. 1989. *Retreat from Doomsday: The Obsolence of Major War*. New York: Basic.

Mufson, Steven. 2001. 'US Nightmare: Broken Arrow from Pak N-arsenal', *Los Angeles Times–Washington Post*, 6 November.

Mukerjee, Dilip. 1987. 'U.S. Weaponry for India', *Asian Survey*, 27 (June).

Mullins, Robert E. 1995. 'The Dynamics of Chinese Missile Proliferation', *Pacific Review*, 8 (1).

Mulvenon, James. 2001. 'China: Conditional Compliance', in Muthiah Alagappa (ed.), *Coercion and Governance: The Declining Political Role of the Military in Asia*. Stanford: Stanford University Press.

Mulvenon, J.C. and Richard H. Yang (eds). 1999. *The People's Liberation Army in the Information Age*. Santa Monica, CA: RAND.

Mumtaz, Soofia, Jean-Luc Racine and Imran Anwar Ali (eds). 2002. *Pakistan: The Contours of State and Society*. Karachi: Oxford University Press.

Muni, S.D. 1987. 'Indo-U.S. Relations: The Pakistan Factor', *Man and Development*, 8 (3).

Musharraf, Gen Pervez. 1999a. Address to the nation, 12 October, available at http://www.ipcs.org/documents/1999/5-oct-dec.html.

———. 1999b. Address to the nation, *Dawn*, 17 October.

———. 2000. Announcement of local body elections, *Asian Recorder*, 21 March.

———. 2002a. Presidential address, text of 12 January speech http://www.pak.gov.pk/public/President_address.htm, accessed on 17 January 2002.

———. 2002b. Presidential address, text of 27 February speech http://www.pak.gov.pk/public/Presidentaddress-27-2-2002.htm, accessed on 3 March 2002.

Mustaq, Najam. 2001. 'The Idea of Pakistan', *Outlook*, 23 July.

Myres, Ramon H. 1982. *U.S. Foreign Policy for Asia the 1980s and Beyond*. Stanford: Hoover Press.

Naidu, A.G. 1981. 'U.S. Policy Toward India: A National Interest Model', *India Quarterly*, 37 (1).

Naipaul, V.S. 1992. *India: A Million Mutinies Now*. New York: Penguin.

Nair, Vijai K. 1992. *Nuclear India*. New Delhi: Lancer's.

Nan Li. 1999. 'The PLAs, Evolving Campaign Doctrine and Strategies', in Richard Yang and James Mulvenon (eds), *The People's Liberation Army in the Information Age*. Washington, DC: RAND.

Nandy, Ashis. 1974. 'Between Two Gandhis: Psycho-political Aspects of the Nuclearization of India', *Asian Survey*, 14 (11).

Naqvi, Jamaluddin. 1999. 'Lessons to Learn from Kargil', *Dawn*, 10 August.

Narayanan, K.R. 1998. Address to the Nation by Shri K.R. Narayanan, President of India, at the closing function of the Golden Jubilee of India's Independence, 15 August, Parliament House, New Delhi.

Nathan, Andrew J. and Robert Ross (eds). 1997. *The Great Wall and the Empty Fortress: China's Search for Security*. London: W.W. Norton and Co.

National Academy of Sciences. 1997. *The Future of U.S. Nuclear Weapons Policy*. Washington, DC: National Academy Press.

National Defense Authorization Act. 2001 (accessed). *Future Military Capabilities and Strategy of the People's Republic of China*. Report to Congress Pursuant to Section 1226 or the FY98, Washington: The Library Congress.

National Intelligence Council. 1999. *Foreign Missile Developments and Ballistic Missile Threat to the United States Through 2015*, September. Washington, DC.

National Intelligence Estimate. 1962. 'Chinese Communist Advanced Weapons Capabilities', *National Intelligence Estimate 13-2-62*, 25 April.

Navias, M. 1990. 'Ballistic Missile Proliferation in the Third World', *Adelphi Papers*, 252 (Summer). London: Brassey's for IISS.

Nayar, Baldev Raj. 1975. 'Treat India Seriously', *Foreign Policy*, 18 (Spring).

———. 1976. *American Geo-Politics and India*. New Delhi: Manohar.

———. 1991. *Super Power Dominance and Military Aid to Pakistan*. New Delhi: Manohar.

Nayyar, Kuldip. 1987. 'We have the A-Bomb, Says Pakistan's Dr. Strangelove', *The Observer* (London), 1 March.

Nehru, Jawaharlal. 1946. *The Discovery of India*. Calcutta: Signet Press.

———. 1988a. 'Indivisibility of Peace', Speech delivered in the Canadian Parliament, Ottawa, 24 October 1949, in *India and Disarmament: An Anthology*. New Delhi: Ministry of External Affairs, GOI.

———. 1988b. 'Control of Nuclear Energy', Statement at the Lok Sabha 10 May 1954, in *India and Disarmament: An Anthology*. New Delhi: Ministry of External Affairs, GOI.

———. 1988c. 'Towards a World Community', Speech at the United National General Assembly, New York, 20 December 1956, in *India and Disarmament: An Anthology*. New Delhi: Ministry of External Affairs, GOI.

Nelson, Harvey W. 1977. *The Chinese Military System: An Organisational Study of the Chinese Peoples Liberation Army*. Boulder, CO: Westview.

Newaz, Shamsa. 1985. *India's Nuclear Weapons Programme*. Lahore: Progressive Publishers.

Newman, James. 1962. *The Rule of Folly*. London: George Allen and Unwin.

Nitze, Paul. 1956. 'Strategy and Policy', *Foreign Affairs*, 24 (January).

Nihon Keijai Shimbun. 1999. 'Japan to Join US on Anti-missile Research', 14 February.

Nixon, Richard. 1967. 'Asia After Vietnam', *Foreign Affairs*, 46 (October).

———. 1978. *The Memoirs of Richard Nixon*. New York: Grosset and Dunlap.

Nizamani, Haider. 2000. 'Whose Bomb is it Anyway? Public Opinion and Perceptions about Nuclear Weapons and Policy in the Post-Explosions Phase in Pakistan', a public opinion survey conducted between June–August, http://sarn.ssrc.org/publications/nizamani.pdf, accessed on 12 December 2002.

Nizamani, Haider. 2001. *The Roots of Rhetoric: Politics of Nuclear Weapons in India and Pakistan*. New Delhi: India Research Press.

Nolan, Janne (ed.). 1994. *Global Engagement: Cooperation and Security in the 21st Century*. Washington, DC: Brookings Institution.

Noorani, A.G. 1967. 'India's Quest for a Nuclear Guarantee', *Asian Survey*, 7 (7).

———. 1981. 'Indo-US Nuclear Relations', *Asian Survey*, 21 (4).

NPT (Non-Proliferation Treaty). 1968. Text of the treaty is available at http://www.basicint.org/NPT/text.htm.

NSAB. (National Security Advisory Board) 1999 (accessed). *Draft Report of National Security Advisory Board on Indian Nuclear Doctrine*, available at www.meadev.gov.in/govt/indnucld.htm, accessed on 18 August.

Norris, Robert S. 1996. 'Nuclear Arsenals of the United States, Russia, Great Britain, France and China: A Status Report' (paper presented at the 5th ISODARCO Beijing Seminar on Arms Control), November, Chengdu, China.

Norris, Robert S., Andrew S. Burrows and Richard W. Fieldhouse. 1994. *Nuclear Weapons Databook*, vol. V: *British, French, and Chinese Nuclear Weapons*. Boulder, CO: Westview.

Nuclear News. 1993. 'Iran Ratified Nuclear Agreements With Russia and China', May.

Nuclear Threat Initiative. 2004 (accessed). 'China's Nuclear Weapon Development, Modernisation and Testing', available at http://www.nti.org/db/china/wnwmdat.htm, accessed on 24 February.

Nye, Joseph S. 1984. 'NPT: The Logic of Inequality', *Foreign Policy*, Summer.

———. 1997/98. 'China's Re-emergence and the Future of the Asia-Pacific', *Survival*, 39 (4).

Office of the Secretary of Defense. 1997. *Proliferation: Threat and Response*, Washington, DC: Department of Defense, USA.

Oin Huasun. 1995. Speech of Oin Huasun, China's Ambassador and Permanent Representative to the United Nations, at the Indian Ocean Special Council, 28 June.

Okesenberg, Michael. 1986. 'China's Confident Nationalism', *Foreign Affairs*, 65 (3).

Ollapally, Deepa and Raja Ramanna. 1995. 'US-India Tensions', *Foreign Affairs*, 74 (1).

Oppert, Gustav. 1967 [1880]. *Weapons, Army Organisation and Political Maxims of Ancient Hindus with Special Reference to Gunpowder and Firearms*. Ahmedabad: The New Order Book Co.

Orgsanski, A.F.J. 1958. *World Politics*. New York: Alfred A. Knopf.

Osgood, Robert E. 1957. *Limited War: The Challenge to American Strategy*. Chicago: University of Chicago Press.

———. 1961. 'Stabilising the Military Environment', *The American Political Science Review*, 55 (1).

———. 1973. *Retreat from Empire? The First Nixon Administration*. Baltimore, MD: Johns Hopkins University Press.

———. 1979. *Limited War Revisited*. Boulder, CO: Westview.

Oye, Kenneth A., Donald S. Rothchild and Robert J. Lieber. 1979. *Eagle Strangled: U.S. Foreign Polices in a Complex World*. New York: Longman.

PAEC. 1974. *Annual Report 1973–74*. Islamabad: Pakistan Atomic Energy Commission.

Pahwa, Lt Gen PVSM (Retd) Prem. 1999. 'Organisation and Concept of Strategic Rocket Forces', National Security Paper, National Security Series—1988. New Delhi: United Service Institution of India.

Palit, Maj Gen D.K. and P.K.S. Namboodiri. 1979. *Pakistan's Islamic Bomb*. New Delhi: Vikas Publishing.

Pall, Barbara O. 1993. 'Japan Resists Joint Missile Defense', *Defense News*, 13 December.

Palmer, Norman D. 1966. *South Asia and United States Policy*. Boston: Houghton Mifflin.

———. 1977. 'Pakistan: The Long Search for Foreign Policy', in Lawrence Ziring, R. Braibanti and W.H. Wriggins (eds), *Pakistan: The Long View*. Durham, NC: Duke University Press.

———. 1982. 'Changing Patterns of Politics in Pakistan', in Manzooruddin Ahmed (ed.), *Contemporary Pakistan*. Karachi: Royal Book Company.

———. 1984. *The U.S. and India: Dimensions of Influence*. New York: Praeger.

Palmer, Norman D. and Howard C. Perkins. 1997. *International Relations: The World Community in Transition*. New Delhi: AITBS Publishers.

Pande, Savita. 1991. *Pakistan's Nuclear Policy*. Delhi: B.R. Publishing.

Patchen, Martin. 1988. *Resolving Disputes Between Nations: Coercion or Conciliation?* Durham: Duke University Press.

Pawar, Sharad. 1998. Statement at the General Debate of the First Committee of the UN General Assembly, *Reducing Nuclear Danger*, UN Resolution 53/77 H, introduced by India, adopted on 3 December, available at www.meaindia.nic.in.

Payne, Keith B. 1992. 'Deterrence and US Strategic Force Requirements After the Cold War', *Comparative Strategy*, July–September.

———. 1996. *Deterrence in the Second Nuclear Age*. Lexington, KY: University of Kentucky Press.

Peck, Jim and John K. Fairbank. 1970. 'An Exchange', *Bulletin of Concerned Asian Scholar*, 2 (3).

People's Liberation Army Daily (Jiefangjun Bao). 1998. 'Missile Launch "all-weather" Communications Secured', 5 January, http://www.cns.miis.edu, accessed on 21 November 2002.

Perkovich, George. 1993. 'A Nuclear Third Way in South Asia', *Foreign Policy*, 91 (Summer).

———. 1999. *India's Nuclear Bomb: The Impact on Global Proliferation*. Los Angeles, CA: University of California Press.

PIADS. 2001 (accessed). 'Heroes of Kargil', Pakistan Institute for Air Defence Studies, available at http://www.piads.com.pk/users/piads/kargilheroes.html, accessed on 30 July.

Pillsbury, Michael. 1998. *Chinese Views of Future Warfare*. New Delhi: Lancer's.

Pollack, Jonathan D. 1979. 'The Logic of Chinese Military Strategy', *The Bulletin of the Atomic Scientists*, 34 (January).

———.1980. *China's Potential as a World Power*. Santa Monica, CA: RAND.

———. 1988. *The Course of Chinese Nuclear Development*. Santa Monica, CA: RAND.

Pollack, Jonathan D. 1992. 'The Opening to America, 1968–1982', in John K. Fairbank and Roderick MacFarquhar (eds), *The Cambridge History of China*. Cambridge: Cambridge University Press.

———. 1994. 'The Future of China's Nuclear Weapons Policy', in Johnston Hopkins and Weixing Hu (eds), *Strategic Views From the Second Tier: The Nuclear Weapons Policies of France, Britain and China*. La Jolla, CA: University of California, Institute of Global Conflict and Cooperation.

Pollack, Jonathan D. and Richard H. Yang (eds). 1998. *In China's Shadow: Regional Perspectives on Chinese Foreign Policy and Military Development*. Washington, DC: RAND.

Pomfret, John. 2000. 'Russians Help China Modernize its Arsenal', *Washington Post*, 10 February.

Posen, Barry R. 1991. *Inadvertent Escalation: Conventional Wars and Nuclear Risks*. London and Ithaca, NY: Cornell University Press.

Poulose, T.T. (ed.). 1978. *Perspectives of India's Nuclear Policy*. New Delhi: Young Asia Publications.

———. 1982. *Nuclear Proliferation and the Third World*. New Delhi: ABC Publishing.

Power, Thomas S. 1964. *Design for Survival*. New York: Coward McCann.

Prados, John. 1982. *The Soviet Estimates: US Intelligence Estimate and Russian Military Strength*. New York: The Dial Press.

Preparatory Committee. 1999. Proposals for Inclusion in the Report of the Third Session of the Preparatory Committee for the 2000 Review Conference of the Parties the meeting on the Non-Proliferation of Nuclear Weapons, Fissile Material Cut-off Treaty, 10–21 May 1999, New York.

Press Information Bureau. 2000. *Indo-US Vision Statement*. New Delhi: Government of India.

Price, Richard and Nina Tannenwald. 1996. 'Norms and Deterrence: The Nuclear and Chemical Weapons Taboos', in Peter J. Katzenstein (ed.), *The Culture of Nuclear Security: Norms and Identity in World Politics*. New York: Colombia University Press.

Pruitt, Dean G. 1965. 'Definition of the Situations as a Determinant of International Action', in Herbert Kelman (ed.), *International Behaviour: A Social Psychological Analysis*. New York: Holt, Rinhart and Winston.

Puri, Balraj. 1993. *Kashmir: Towards Insurgency*. New Delhi: Orient Longman.

Pye, Lucian. 1980. 'China, Erratic State, Frustrated Society', *Foreign Affairs*, Fall.

———. 1985. *Asian Power and Politics: The Cultural Dimensions of Authority*. Cambridge: Harvard University Press.

———. 1988. *The Mandarin and the Cadre: China's Political Cultures*. Ann Arbor, MI: Center for Chinese Studies University of Michigan.

Pyongyang Korean Central Broadcasting Network. 1995. 'Choe-Kwang Led Delegation Arrives in Pakistan', 20 November.

Pyongyang Korean Central Television Network. 1995. 'Military Delegation Leaves for Pakistan', 19 November.

Qadir, Brig Shaukat. 2002. 'An Analysis of the Kargil Conflict', *RUSI Journal*, April.

Qian Qichen. 1995. Statement at the 1995 Review and Extension Conference of the Parties to the Treaty on the Non-Proliferation of Nuclear Weapons, 18 April.

Quester, George H. 1986. *The Future of Nuclear Deterrence*. Lexington, MA: Lexington Books.

Radhakrishnan, S. 1974. *The Supreme Spiritual Ideal*. Delhi: Oxford University Press.

Radyuhin, Vladimir. 2000. 'INS Sindhushastra Commissioned', *The Hindu*, 20 July.

Raghvan, Lt Gen (Retd) V.R. 1996. *India's Need for Strategic Balance: Security in the Post Cold War World*. New Delhi: Delhi Policy Group.

———. 1998. 'Arthashastra and Sun Zi's Binfa', in Tan Chung (ed.), *Across the Himalayan Gap: An Indian Quest for Understanding China*. New Delhi: Gyan.

———. 2000. 'Nuclear Realpolitik', *The Hindu*, 18 January.

———. 2001. 'Limited War and Nuclear Escalation in South Asia', *The Nonproliferation Review*, 8 (3).

———. 2002. 'Manipulating Nuclear Deterrence', *The Hindu*, 3 July.

———. 2003. 'Nuclear Building Blocks', *The Hindu*, 7 January.

Rahman, A. 1982. *Pakistan and America: Dependency Relations*. New Delhi: Young Asia.

Rahman, S.M. 1998. 'Dual Deterrence: Pakistan's Strategic Bonus', available at http://www.defencejournal.com/july98/dualdeterrence1.htm.

Rajagopalan, Rajesh. 1999. 'A Welcome Debate', *The Hindu*, 28 August.

Rajagopalan, Rajesh and Arpit Rajain. 2004. 'Pakistan and Proliferation: Implications and Options for Indian Policy', *ORF Policy Brief*, February, available at http://www.orfonline.org/reports/py040219.pdf.

Rajagopalan, S. 2001. 'NMD: US Euphoric over India's Support', *The Hindustan Times*, 8 May.

Rajain, Arpit. 2001a. 'India's Political and Diplomatic Response to the Kargil Crisis', in Maj Gen Ashok Krishna and P.R. Chari, *Kargil: The Tables Turned*. New Delhi: Manohar.

———. 2001b (accessed). 'Arms Control: A Dead End?' available at http://www.ipcs.org/ issues/ndi-index.html, accessed on 15 January.

———. 2001c (accessed). 'The US National Missile Defence and South Asia', available at http://www.ipcs.org/ issues/ndi-index.html, accessed on 15 January.

———. 2002a (accessed). 'Coercive Diplomacy or Nuclear Brinkmanship?' available at http://www.ipcs.org/issues/700/796-ndi-arpit.html, accessed on 15 July.

———. 2002b (accessed). 'The 1999 Indo-Pak Nuclear Crisis', available at http://www.ipcs.org/issues/700/769-ndi-arpit.html, accessed on 15 July.

———. 2002c (accessed). 'Debating Hot Pursuit', available at http://www.ipcs.org/issues/newarticles/674-ter-arpit.html, accessed on 17 July.

———. 2002d (accessed). 'The US National Missile Defence and South Asia', available at http://www.ipcs.org/issues/articles/395-ndi-arpit.html, accessed on 17 July.

———. 2002e (accessed). 'Nuclear Deterrence in Southern Asia I', available at http://www.ipcs.org/issues/newarticles/616-ndi-arpit.html, accessed on 16 August.

———. 2002f (accessed). 'Nuclear Deterrence in Southern Asia II', available at http://www.ipcs.org/issues/newarticles/615-ndi-arpit.html, accessed on 16 August.

———. 2002g. 'The North Korean Bomb', *IPCS Issue Brief*, 2 (December).

———. 2002h (accessed). 'Post September 11: Continuities and Dis-continuities', available on the IPCS website at http://www.ipcs.org/issues/800/872-usr-arpit.html, accessed on 3 October.

Rajain, Arpit. 2003 (accessed). 'Bargaining in Crisis', available on the IPCS website at http://www.ipcs.org/issues/newarticles/695-ip-arpit.html, accessed on 2 February.

———. 2004. 'Pakistan's Nuclear Blackmarketing: North Korea, Iran and Libya', *ORF Occasional Paper*, March, available at http://www.orfonline.org/ publications/OccasionalPapers/occpaper.pdf.

Rajan, M.S. 1970. *Non-Alignment: India and the Future*. Mysore: University of Mysore Press.

Rajghatta, Chidanand. 1998a. 'US Curbs on Pak Lab over Ghauri', *The Indian Express*, 5 May.

———. 1998b. 'US Imposes Sanctions on KRL, Korean Firm', *The Indian Express*, 5 May.

Rajput, A.B. 1987. *Religion, Politics, and Society*. New York: Oxford University Press.

Rajput, Hamid S. 1974. 'Indian Nuclear Tests: Threat to Peace', *Dawn*, 30 May.

Rajya Sabha [Upper House]. 1999. Unstarred question No. 1763, answered on 11 March.

Ramachandran, R. 1999. 'Pokharan II: The Scientific Dimension', in Amitabh Mattoo (ed.), *India's Nuclear Deterrent*. New Delhi: Har-Anand.

Rana, A.P. (ed.). 1994. *Four Decades of Indo-US Relations: A Commemorative Retrospective*. New Delhi: Har-Anand.

Ranganathan, C.V. 1998. 'India–China Relations: Problems and Perspectives', *World Affairs*, 2 (2).

Rangarajan, L.N. (tr.). 1987. *The Arthashastra*, by Kautilya. New Delhi: Penguin.

Rao, R.V.R. Chandrashekhara. 1987. 'India and the Nuclear Weapons Option: Eclipse of the Ethical Profile', *Swords and Ploughshares*, May.

Rasgotra, M.K. 2000. 'Misgivings on CTBT', *The Pioneer*, 6 January.

Rashid, Ahmad. 1994. 'Bare All and be Damned: Ex Army Chief Reveals Nuclear Secrets', *Far Eastern Economic Review*, 5 May.

Rashid, Jamil and Hasan Gardezi (eds). 1983. *Pakistan: The Roots of Dictatorship*. London: Zed Press.

Rathjens, George. 1977. 'The Verification of Arms Control Agreements', *Arms Control Today*, 7 (7–8).

Ray, Aswini. 1975. *Domestic Compulsions and Foreign Policy*. New Delhi: Manas.

Raza, Rafi (ed.). 1997. *Pakistan in Perspective: 1947–1997*. Karachi: Oxford University Press.

Reiss, Mitchel. 1988. *Without the Bomb: The Politics of Nuclear Proliferation*. New York: Columbia University Press.

———.1995. *Bridled Ambition: Why Countries Constrain their Nuclear Capabilities*. Baltimore, MD: John Hopkins Press.

Riedel, Bruce. 2002. *American Diplomacy and the 1999 Kargil Summit at Blair House*, Policy Paper. Philadelphia: Center for the Advanced Study of India.

Rikhye, Ravi. 1988. *The War that Never Was: The Story of India's Strategic Failures*. Delhi: Chanakya.

Rizvi, Gowher. 1993. *South Asia in a Changing International Order*. New Delhi: Sage.

Rizvi, Hasan-Askari. 1976. *The Military and Politics in Pakistan*, revised edn. Lahore: Progressive Publishers.

———. 2000. *Military, State and Society in Pakistan*. New York: St Martin's Press.

Rizvi, Mujtaba. 1971. *The Frontiers of Pakistan*. Karachi: National Publishing.

Roberts, Jonathan M. 1988. *Decision-making During International Crisis*. New York: St Martin's Press.

Robinson, Thomas W. 1981. 'The Sino-Soviet Border Conflict', in Stephen S. Kaplan (ed.), *Diplomacy and Power: Soviet Armed Forces as a Political Instrument*. Washington, DC: Brookings Institution.

Rohde, David. 2004a. 'Pakistanis Question Official Ignorance of Atom Transfers', *The New York Times*, 3 February.

———. 2004b. 'Pakistani Finger-Pointing and Denials Spread in the Furore over Nuclear Transfers Abroad', *The New York Times*, 4 February.

Rosen, Stephen P. 1996. *India and its Armies, Societies and Military Power*. Delhi: Oxford University Press.

Rosenberg, David A. 1983. 'The Origins of Overkill: Nuclear Weapons and American Strategy, 1945–1960', *International Security*, 7 (4).

Rosita, Dellios. 1990. *Modern Chinese Defence Strategy, Present Developments, Future Directions*. New York: St Martin's Press.

Ross, Robert. 1991. 'China Learns to Compromise: Change in US–China Relations, 1982–1984', *The China Quarterly*, 28 (December).

Rotblat, Joseph. 1998. 'New Dangers to World Security', *Pugwash Newsletter*, 25 (2).

Rotblat, Joseph, Jack Steinberger and B. Udgaonkar. 1993. *A Nuclear Weapon-free World*. San Francisco, CA: Westview.

Roy, Denny. 1994. 'Hegemony on the Horizon? China's Threat to East Asian Security', *International Security*, 19 (1).

Roy Chowdhury, Gen Shankar and Jasjit Singh. 1999. 'Should India Cross the Line of Control in Kargil? A Debate', *The Times of India*, 20 June.

Rubin, J.Z. and B.R. Brown. 1975. *The Social Psychology of Bargaining and Negotiation*. New York: Academic Press.

Rudolph, Lloyd I. and Susanne Hoeber Rudolph. 1999. *The Modernity of Tradition: Political Development in India*. New Delhi: Orient Longman.

Russell, Bertrand. 1966. *The Problem of China*. London: Allen and Unwin.

Russett, Bruce. 1963. 'The Calculus of Deterrence', *Journal of Conflict Resolution*, 7 (June).

———. 1967. 'Pearl Harbor: Deterrence Theory and Decision Theory', *Journal of Peace Research*, 4 (2).

Sagan, Scott D. 1996/97. 'Why do States Build Nuclear Weapons: Three Models in Search of a Bomb', *International Security*, 21 (6).

———. 2000. 'The Commitment Trap: Why the United States Should Not Use Nuclear Threats to Deter Biological and Chemical Weapons Attacks', *International Security*, 24 (4).

Sagan, Scott D. and Kenneth N. Waltz. 1995. *The Spread of Nuclear Weapons: A Debate*. New York: W.W. Norton.

Said, Edward W. 1978. *Orientalism*. London: Routledge and Kegan Paul.

Sanger, David E. 2002. 'Atomic Ties Link North Korea and Pakistan', *International Herald Tribune*, 25 November.

———. 2003. 'Bush Yields a Bit on North Korea', *International Herald Tribune*, 20 October.

———. 2004. 'Bush Proposes Strict Limits on Back Market Sale of Equipment to Make Nuclear Fuel', *The New York Times*, 12 February.

Sanger, David E. and James Dao. 2002. 'U.S. Says Pakistan Gave Technology to North Korea', *The New York Times*, 18 October.

SAPRA. 1996. 'SAPRA Backgrounder: The China Poser', *SAPRA India Monthly Bulletin*, April–May.

Sattar, Abdul. 1994/95. 'Reducing Nuclear Dangers in South Asia', *Regional Studies* (Islamabad), 8 (Winter).

———. 1995. 'Nuclear Stability in South Asia', *Nuclear Issues in South Asia*, Islamabad Council for World Affairs (ICWA), Special Issue (Spring).

———. 1997. 'Foreign Policy', in Rafi Raza (ed.), *Pakistan in Perspective: 1947–1997*. Karachi: Oxford University Press.

Sattar, Babar. 2001. 'Pakistan: Return to Praetorianism', in Muthiah Alagappa (ed.), *Coercion and Governance: The Declining Political Role of the Military in Asia*. Stanford: Stanford University Press.

Sauer, Tom. 1998. *Nuclear Arms Control: Nuclear Deterrence in the Post-Cold War Period*. New York: St Martin's Press.

Sawant, Gaurav C. 2000. *Dateline Kargil: A Correspondent's Nine-Week Account from the Battleground*. New Delhi: Macmillan.

Sawyer, Ralph D. 1993. *The Seven Military Classics of Ancient China*. New York: Westview.

———. 1996. *The Complete Art of War: Sun Zi and Sun Pin*. Boulder, CO: Westview.

Schaer, James (ed.). 1984. *Nuclear Weapons and Nuclear Risk*. New York: St Martin's Press.

Schaffer, Teresita C. and Howard B. Schaffer. 1999. 'Finding Common Interests', *The Hindu*, 10 August.

Schell, Jonathan. 1984. *The Abolition*. New York: Alfred A. Knopf.

Schelling, Thomas C. 1960. 'The Retarded Science of International Strategy', *Midwest Journal of Political Science*, 4 (2).

———. 1966. *Arms and Influence*. New Haven, CT: Yale University Press.

———. 1976. 'Who Will Have the Bomb?' *International Security*, 1 (1).

———. 1979. *The Strategy of Conflict*. Cambridge, MA: Harvard University Press.

Schulzinger, Robert D. 1989. *Henry Kissinger: Doctor of Diplomacy*. New York: Colombia University Press.

Schurman, Frederick L. 1998. *International Politics, the Western State System and the World Community*. London: McGraw-Hill.

Schurmann, Franz and Orville Schell. 1967. *Communist China: Revolutionary, Reconstruction and International Confrontation since 1949 to the Present*. New York: Vintage.

Schwartz, Stephen I. (ed.). 1998. *Atomic Audit: The Costs and Consequences of US Nuclear Weapons Since 1940*. New York: Brookings Institution.

Scott, R.T. (ed.). 1987. *The Race for Security: Arms and Arms Control in the Reagan Years*. Lexington, MA: Lexington Books.

Seaborg, Glenn T. and Benjamin Loeb. 1987. *Stemming the Tide: Arms Control in the Johnson Years*. Lexington, MA and Toronto: Lexington Books.

Seabury, P. (ed.). 1965. *Balance of Power*. San Francisco: Chandler.

Segal, Gerald. 1985a. *China and the Arms Trade*. New York: St Martin's Press.

———. 1985b. *Defending China*. Oxford: Oxford University Press.

———. 1985c. 'Defence Culture and Sino-Soviet Relations', *Journal of Strategic Studies*, 8.

Segal, Gerald. (ed.). 1990. *Chinese Politics and Foreign Policy Reform*. New York: Kegan Paul.

———. 1994. 'The Middle Kingdom? China's Changing Shape', *Foreign Affairs*, May/June.

———. 1999. 'The Myth of Chinese Power', *Newsweek*, 20 September.

———. 2000. 'Does China Matter?' *Foreign Affairs*, 79 (2).

Segal, Gerald and William Tow (eds). 1998. *Chinese Defence Policy*. Chicago: University of Illinois.

Sen Gupta, Bhabani (ed.). 1983. *Nuclear Weapons? Policy Options for India*. New Delhi: Sage.

———. 1985. 'The Nuclear Option: Ambivalent Stand', *India Today*, 31 May.

Sengupta, Adirupa. 1998. 'Scientist says Bomb was Tested in 74', *India Abroad*, 17 October.

Seshagiri, N. 1975. *The Bomb: Fall-out of India's Nuclear Explosion*. New Delhi: Vikas.

Sha Zukang. 1995. Statement at the General Debate of the First Committee of the 50th Session of the United Nations General Assembly, 17 October.

———. 1996a. Statement by Sha Zukang, Chinese Ambassador to the Conference on Disarmament, 6 June (CD/PV.737).

———. 1996b. Statement by Sha Zukang, Chinese Ambassador to the Conference on Disarmament, 1 August (CD/PV.743).

———. 1997. Statement at the First Session of the Preparatory Committee for the 2000 Review Conference of the Parties in the Treaty on the Non-Proliferation of Nuclear Weapons, 8 April, New York.

———. 1998. Statement by Sha Zukang, Head of Delegation of the People's Republic of China at the Second Session of the Preparatory Committee for the 2000 NPT Review Conference, 27 April, Geneva.

———. 1999. 'Some Thoughts on Non-proliferation', Speech at the Seventh Annual Carnegie International Non-proliferation Conference, *Repairing the Regime*, 11–12 January, Washington.

———. 2000. Statement at the 2000 Review Conference of the Parties to the Treaty on the Non-Proliferation of Nuclear Weapons, 24 April, New York.

———. 2002. 'Reinforcing Efforts to Prevent Nuclear Proliferation: China's Perspective', Speech by Ambassador Sha Zukang at the Wilton Park Conference, *Reinforcing Efforts to Prevent Nuclear Proliferation*, 17 December, Wilton Park, UK.

Shafi, Kamran. 1999. 'Friendless in Kashmir', *The News International*, 21 June.

Shahi, Agha. 1988. *Pakistan Security and Foreign Policy*. Lahore: Progressive Publishers.

Shahi, Agha, Zulfiqar Ali Khan and Abdul Sattar. 1999. 'Securing Nuclear Peace', *The News International*, 5 October.

Shaikh, M. Naim. 2001 (accessed). 'Credible Nuclear Deterrence and Doctrine for Pakistan', policy paper of the Pakistan Institute for Air Defence Studies, available at http://www.piads.com.pk/users/piads/mnshaikh1.html, accessed on 30 July.

Shambaugh, David. 1991. *Beautiful Imperialist: China Perceives America, 1972–1990*. Princeton, NJ: Princeton University Press.

———. 1992. 'The U.S. and China: A New Cold War?' *Current History*, 91 (56).

Shambaugh, David. 1994. 'Patterns of Interaction in Sino-American Relations', in Thomas W. Robinson and David Shambaugh (eds), *Chinese Foreign Policy: Theory and Practice*. Oxford: Clarendon Press.

———. 1999. 'Liberation Army and the People's Republic at 50', *The China Quarterly*, 159 (September).

Shambaugh, David and Thomas W. Robinson (eds). 1994. *Chinese Foreign Policy. Theory and Practice*. Oxford: Clarendon Press.

Shambaugh, David and Richard H. Yang (eds). 1997. *China's Military in Transition*. Oxford: Clarendon Press.

Shamim, Air Marshal (Retd) M. Anwar. 1988. 'Pakistan's Security Concerns', *Dawn*, 2 November.

Shankar, Thom. 2002. 'US Analysts Find No Sign bin Laden had Nuclear Arms', *The New York Times*, 26 February.

Shao Xixin. 1996. 'The Clinton Administration's China Policy and Sino-US Relations', *Foreign Affairs Journal*, 39 (March).

Sharif, Nawaz. 1998. Statement by Prime Minister of Pakistan Nawaz Sharif to the UN General Assembly, 23 September.

Sharma, Dhirendra. 1983. *India's Nuclear Estate*. New Delhi: Lancer's.

———. 1986. *The Indian Atom: Power and Proliferation*. New Delhi: Philosophy and Social Action.

Sharma, Shalendra (ed.). 1999. *Asia Pacific in the New Millennium: Geopolitics, Security, and Foreign Policy*. Berkeley, CA: Institute of East Asian Studies.

Sharma, Gen V.N. 1993. 'Its All Bluff and Bluster', *The Economic Times* (Bombay), 18 May.

Sharman, Steven, Charles M. Judd and Bernadette Park. 1989. 'Social Cognition', *Annual Review of Psychology*, 48.

Sheehan, Michael. 1996. *The Balance of Power: History and Theory*. London: Routledge.

Shen Guofang. 1999. Statement at the First Committee of the 54th Session of the UNGA, 13 October.

Sheth, Ninad D. 1999. 'Fragile Consensus on Draft Nuclear Weapons Doctrine', *The Hindustan Times*, 19 August.

Shri Aurobindo. 1959. *The Foundations of Indian Culture*. Pondicherry: Sri Aurobindo Ashram Trust.

Shu Guang Zhang. 1992. *Deterrence and Strategic Culture: Chinese–American Confrontations, 1949–58*. London and Ithaca, NY: Cornell University Press.

Shulong Chu. 1994. 'China and Strategy: The PRC Girds for Limited, Hi-tech War', *Orbis*, 38 (2).

Siddiqa-Agha, Ayesha. 2000a. 'Nuclear Navies', *The Bulletin of the Atomic Scientists*, 56 (5).

———. 2000b. 'Defence a Public Good? A Case Study of Pakistan's Military Expenditure, 1982–98', in P.R. Chari and Ayesha Siddiqa-Agha (eds), *Defence Expenditure in South Asia: India and Pakistan*, RCSS Policy Studies No. 12, Colombo.

Siddiqa-Agha, Ayesha. 2001. *Pakistan's Arms Procurement and Military Buildup, 1979–99*. Basingstoke and New York: Palgrave.

———. 2002. 'War-gaming in a Nuclear Environment', *The Friday Times*, 26 July–1 August.

Siddiqui, K. 1972. *Conflict, Crisis and War in Pakistan*. New York: Praeger.

Sidhu, W.P.S. 1998. 'India Sees Safety in Nuclear Triad and Second Strike Potential', *Jane's Intelligence Review*, July.

——. 2003. 'Strategic Mis-step', *The Hindu*, 13 January.

Singer, J. David. 1962. *Deterrence, Arms Control and Disarmament: Towards a Synthesis in National Security*. Columbus, OH: Ohio State University Press.

Singh, Jasjit. 1986. 'Prospects for Nuclear Proliferation', in K. Subrahmanyam (ed.), *Nuclear Myths and Realities: India's Dilemma*. New Delhi: Lancer's.

——. 1995. 'The Army in the Power Structure of Pakistan', *Strategic Analysis*, 18 (7).

——. (ed.). 1998. *Nuclear India*. New Delhi: Knowledge World.

——. 2000. *Asia's New Dawn: The Challenges to Peace and Security*. New Delhi: Knowledge World.

Singh, Jaswant. 1998. 'Against Nuclear Apartheid', *Foreign Affairs*, September–October.

——. 1999. *Defending India*. Bangalore: Macmillan.

Singh, Sardar Swaran. 1972. 'Statement by the Minister of External Affairs on India's Policy Towards China, 26 August 1970', in A. Appadorai (ed.), *Selected Documents on India's Foreign Policy and Relations, 1947–72*, vol. I. New Delhi: Oxford University Press.

Singh, Swaran. 1998/99. 'China's Doctrine of Limited Hi tech War', *Asian Strategic Review*.

Sinha, P.B. and R.R. Subramanian. 1979. *Nuclear Ambitions: The Spread of Nuclear Weapon Proliferation*. London: Taylor and Francis.

——. 1980. *Nuclear Pakistan: Atomic Threat to South Asia*. New Delhi: Vision Books.

SIPRI. 1990–2002. *Year Book on Armaments, Disarmament and International Security*. Stockholm: Oxford University Press.

Slevin, Peter. 2001. 'Pakistan Groups Called Terrorist Organizations', *The Washington Post*, 27 December.

Smith, Chris. 1994. *India's ad hoc Arsenal: Direction or Drift in Defence Policy?* Oxford: Oxford University Press.

Snow, D.M. 1979. 'Current Nuclear Deterrence Thinking: An Overview and Review', *International Studies Quarterly*, 23.

Snyder, Glenn. 1961. *Deterrence and Defence: Towards a Theory of National Security*. Princeton, NJ: Princeton University Press.

——. 1971. 'The Conditions of Stability', in Robert J. Art and Kenneth N. Waltz (eds), *The Use of Force: International Politics and Foreign Policy*. Boston: Little Brown.

Snyder, Glenn and P. Diesing. 1977. *Conflict Among Nations*. Princeton, NJ: Princeton University Press.

Sokov, Nikolai N. 1997. 'Russia's Approach to Deep Reductions of Nuclear Weapons: Opportunities and Problems', 2nd edn, Occasional Paper No. 27 (September). Washington, DC: Henry L. Stimson Center.

Sondhi, M.L. (ed.). 2000. *Nuclear Weapons and India's National Security*. New Delhi: Har-Anand.

Sood, Rakesh. 1993. 'The NPT and Beyond' (paper presented at a seminar entitled *Non-proliferation and Technology Transfer*), 3–6 October, University of Pennsylvania.

Spector, Leonard S. 1988. *The Undeclared Bomb*. Cambridge, MA: Ballinger.

Spector, Leonard S. 1990. *Nuclear Ambitions*. Washington, DC: Westview for Carnegie Endowment for International Peace.

Spector, Leonard S., Mark G. McDonough and Evan S. Medeiros. 1995. *Tracking Nuclear Proliferation: A Guide in Maps and Charts, 1995*. Washington, DC: Carnegie Endowment for International Peace.

Spence, Jonathan. D. 1990. *The Search for Modern China*. New York: W. W. Norton.

Spence, Jonathan D. and John E. Wills (eds). 1979. *From Ming to Ching*. London: Yale University Press.

Srinivasan, M.R. 2000. 'CTBT: A Phoney Consensus', *The Hindu*, 18 January.

Srivastava, Divya and Arpit Rajain. 2003. 'Nuclear Iran and the US: A Status Report', *Observer Research Foundation Issue Brief*, vol. 1, 15 September, available at http://www.orfonline.org/analysis/ir030915.htm.

Standing Committee on Defence. 1996a. 'Defence Policy, Planning and Management', *Sixth Report* (1995–96), 10th Lok Sabha, March. New Delhi: Lok Sabha Secretariat.

———. 1996b. *Second Report* (1996–97), 11th Lok Sabha, December. New Delhi: Lok Sabha Secretariat.

Starke, J.G. 1989. *Introduction to International Law*. London: Butterworths.

State Council, PRC. 1995a. *White Paper: China's National Defense*, July. Beijing: Information Office of the State Council of the People's Republic of China.

———. 1995b. *White Paper. China: Arms Control and Disarmament Information*, November. Beijing: Office of the State Council of the People's Republic of China.

———. 1998. *White Paper: China's National Defense*. Beijing: Information Office of the State Council of the People's Republic of China.

———. 2000a. *White Paper: China's National Defense*. Beijing: Information Office of the State Council of the People's Republic of China.

———. 2000b. *Chinese White Paper on Taiwan*, February. Beijing: Information Office of the State Council of the People's Republic of China.

———. 2002. *White Paper. China's National Defense*, November. Beijing: Information Office of the State Council of the People's Republic of China.

Steele, Jonathan. 1983. *World Power: Soviet Foreign Policy under Brezhnev and Andropov*. London: Michael Joseph.

Steeves, John M. 1961. Memorandum from John M. Steeves, Bureau of Far Eastern Affairs, to Roger Hilsman, Director, Bureau of Intelligence and Research, 'National Intelligence Estimate on Implications of Chinese Communist Nuclear Capability', 12 April, National Archives, Record Group 59, Records of the Department of State, Assistant Secretary for Far Eastern Affairs Subject, Personnel and Country Files, 1960–63, box 4, Communist China Jan–June 1961, at http://www.gwu.edu/~nsarchiv/NSAEBB/NSAEBB38/, accessed on 23 July 2001.

Stefanick, Tom. 1987. *Strategic Antisubmarine Warfare and Naval Strategy*. Lexington, KY: Lexington Books.

Stephens, I. 1963. *Pakistan*. London: Benn.

Stern, Jessica. 2000a. 'Terrorist Motivations and Unconventional Weapons', in Peter Lavoy, Scott Sagan and James Wirtz (eds), *Planning the Unthinkable*. Ithaca, NY: Cornell University Press.

Stern, Jessica. 2000b. 'Pakistan's Jihad Culture', *Foreign Affairs*, 69 (6).

Stoessinger, John G. 1961. *The Might of Nations: World Politics in Our Times.* New York: Random House.

Stokes, Mark A. 1999. *China's Strategic Modernization: Implications for the United States.* Carlisle Barracks: Strategic Studies Institute, US Army War College.

Subrahmanyam, K. (ed.). 1981. *Nuclear Myths and Realities: India's Dilemma.* New Delhi: ABC Publishing.

——. 1982. *India's Security Perspective.* New Delhi: ABC Publishing.

——. (ed.). 1985. *Nuclear Proliferation and International Security.* New Delhi: Institute for Defence Studies and Analyses.

——. (ed.). 1986a. *India and the Nuclear Challenge.* New Delhi: Lancer's.

——. 1986b. 'Pak Bomb in Basement', *The Times of India*, 7 November.

——. 1990a. 'Evolution of Indian Defence Policy 1947–64', in *A History of the Congress Party.* Delhi: AICC and Vikas.

——. 1990b. 'Commentator Scores US Stand on Pakistan Bomb', *The Hindu*, 2 March.

——. 1993a. 'Nuclear Policy, Arms Control and Military Cooperation' (paper presented at the Carnegie Endowment for International Peace–India International Centre conference on *India and the United States After the Cold War*), 7–9 March, New Delhi.

——. 1993b. 'An Equal Opportunity NPT', *The Bulletin of the Atomic Scientists*, June.

——. 1994. Nuclear Forces Design and Minimum Deterrence Strategy for India', in Bharat Karnad (ed.), *Future Imperilled: India's Security in the 1990s and Beyond.* New Delhi: Viking.

——. 1998a. 'India's Security Perspectives', in P.R.Chari (ed.), *India Towards Millennium.* New Delhi: Manohar.

——. 1998b. 'Indian Nuclear Policy—1964–98 (A Personal Recollection)', in Jasjit Singh (ed.), *Nuclear India.* New Delhi: Knowledge World.

——. 1998c. 'Talbott is Stuck in Pre-85 Nuclear Groove', *The Times of India*, 17 November.

——. 1999. 'A Credible Deterrent: The Logic of Nuclear Doctrine', *The Times of India*, 4 October.

——. 2002. 'War was Never on the Cards', *The Times of India*, 24 June.

——. 2003. 'Essence of Deterrence', *The Times of India*, 7 January.

Sultan, Maria. 2002. 'Deterrence and Limited War', *The News International*, 3 June.

Sun Tzu. 1910. *The Art of War*, trans. Lionel Giles, available at http://www.fas.org/man/artofwar.htm, accessed on 29 May 2000.

Sundarji, Gen K. 1981a. 'Nuclear Weapons in a Third World Context', Combat Paper No. 2, Mhow, India: College of Combat.

——. 1981b. *Effects of Nuclear Asymmetry on Conventional Deterrence*, Combat Paper No. 1. Mhow: College of Combat.

——. 1984. 'Strategy in the Age of Nuclear Deterrence and its Application to Developing Countries' (unpublished monograph), Shimla.

——. 1990. 'The Nuclear Threat', *India Today*, 30 November.

——. 1992. 'Nuclear Deterrence Doctrine for India—Part I', *Trishul*, 5 (2).

——. 1993a. 'Nuclear Deterrence: Doctrine for India—Part II', *Trishul*, 6 (1).

Sundarji, Gen K. 1993b. *Blind Men of Hindoostan: Indo-Pak Nuclear War*. New Delhi: UBS Publishers.

———. 1993c. 'The World Power Structure in Transition from Quasi Unipolar to a Quasi Multipolar States and the Options of a Middle Power in this Milieu', USI National Security Lecture, New Delhi: United Service Institution.

———. 1994a. 'Indian Nuclear Doctrine—I: Notions of Deterrence', *The Indian Express*, 26 November.

———. 1994b. 'Indian Nuclear Doctrine—II: Sino-Indo-Pak Triangle', *The Indian Express*, 26 November.

———. 1995. 'Proliferation of WMD and the Security Dimensions in South Asia: An Indian View', in William H. Lewis and Stuart E. Johnson (eds), *Weapons of Mass Destruction: New Perspectives on Counterproliferation*. Washington, DC: National Defense University Press.

———. 1996. 'Imperatives of Indian Minimum Nuclear Deterrence', *Agni*, 2 (1).

Sur, Serge (ed.). 1992. *Verification of Disarmament or Limitation of Armaments: Instruments, Negotiations, Proposals*. Geneva: United Nations Publication.

———. (ed.). 1993. *Nuclear Deterrence: Problems and Perspectives in the 1990's*. Geneva: United Nations Publication.

———. (ed.). 1994. *Disarmament and Arms Limitation Obligations: Problems of Compliance and Enforcement*. Dartmouth: Aldershot for UNIDIR.

Susheng Zhao. 1997. *Power Competition in East Asia*. Hampshire: Macmillan.

Sutter, Robert G. 1994. 'Chinese Nuclear Weapons and Arms Control Policies: Implication and Options for the United States', *Congressional Research Service Report*, 94–4225. Washington, DC.

———. 1995a. 'China's Sinister View of U.S. Policy: Origins, Implications and Options', *Congressional Research Service Report*, Washington, DC.

———. 1995b. 'China in World Affairs—US Policy Concerns', *Congressional Research Service Report*, 95–265, January, Washington, DC.

———. 1996. 'China's Rising Military Power and Influence', *Congressional Research Service Report*, Washington, DC.

———. 1998. 'China's Changing Conditions: Possible Implications for U.S. Interests', *Congressional Research Service Report*, Washington, DC.

Swaine, Michael. 1996. *The Role of Chinese Military in National Security Policymaking*. Santa Monica, CA: RAND.

Swaine, Michael and Ashley J. Tellis. 2000. *Interpreting China's Grand Strategy: Past, Present and Future*. Washington DC: RAND.

Swami, Praveen. 2000. *The Kargil War*. New Delhi: Leftworld.

Syed, Anwar H. 1974. *China and Pakistan: Diplomacy of an Entente Cordiale*. London: Oxford University Press.

Synnott, Hillary. 1999. 'The Causes and Consequences of South Asia's Nuclear Tests', *Adelphi Papers* No. 332. London: IISS.

Tahir-Kheli, S. (ed.). 1982a. *U.S. Strategic Interests in Southwest Asia*. New York: Praeger.

———. 1982b. *The United States and Pakistan: The Evolution of an Influence Relationship*. New York: Praeger.

Tai Ming Cheng. 1989. 'New Bomb Makers', *Far Eastern Economic Review*, 16 March.

Talbott, Strobe. 1989. *The Master of the Game: Paul Nitze and the Nuclear Peace*. New York: Vintage.

Talbott, Strobe. 1998. Remarks at Brookings Institution on South Asia on 12 November.

———. 1999. 'Dealing with the Bomb in South Asia', *Foreign Affairs*, March/April.

Tan Chung. 1992. 'Review Essay: Western Scholarship and Chinese History', *China Report*, 28 (4).

———. (ed.). 1998. *Across the Himalayan Gap: An Indian Quest for Understanding China*. New Delhi: Gyan.

Tang Hua. 1996. 'Background to China's Suspension of Nuclear Testing', *Beijing Review*, 2–8 December.

Tanham, George K. 1992. *Indian Strategic Thought: An Interpretative Essay*. Paper prepared for the Under Secretary of Defence for Policy.

Taylor, Gen Maxwell D. 1963. 'Chinese Nuclear Development', Memorandum by Gen Maxwell D. Taylor, Chairman, Joint Chiefs of Staff, to General LeMay, General Wheeler, Admiral McDonald, General Shoup, 18 November.

Tellis, Ashley J. 1986. 'Hawkeyes for Pakistan: Rationale and Logic of the E-2C Request', *Journal of South Asian and Middle Eastern Studies*, 10 (1).

———. 1987. 'Nuclear Arms, Moral Questions, and Religious Issues', *Armed Forces and Society*, 13 (4).

———. 1996a. 'South Asia', in Zalmay Khalilzad (ed.), *Strategic Appraisal 1996*, MR-543-AF. Santa Monica, CA: RAND.

———. 1996b. *India: Assessing Strategy and Military Capabilities in the Year 2000*, P-7978. Santa Monica, CA: RAND.

———. 1997. *Stability in South Asia*, Documented Briefing. Santa Monica, CA: RAND.

———. 2000a. *Changing Grand Strategies in South Asia*, RAND Studies in Public Policy. Cambridge: Cambridge University Press.

———. 2000b. Talk at a seminar on *Sino-US–South Asia Relations*, 6 June, Institute of Peace and Conflict Studies, New Delhi (personal notes taken at the seminar).

———. 2001. 'The Changing Political–Military Environment: South Asia', in Zalmay Khalilzad, David T. Orletsky, Jonathan D. Pollack, Kevin Pollpeter, Angel M. Rabasa, David A. Shlapak, Abram N. Shulsky and Ashley J. Tellis (eds), *The United States and Asia Toward a New US Strategy and Force Posture*, MR-1315-AF. Santa Monica, CA: RAND.

———. 2002a. *India's Emerging Nuclear Posture: Between Recessed Deterrence and Ready Arsenal*. Oxford: Oxford University Press.

———. 2002b. 'The Strategic Implications of a Nuclear India', *Orbis*, 46 (1).

Tellis, Ashley J. and Michael Swaine. 2000. *Interpreting China's Grand Strategy*. Washington, DC: RAND.

Tellis, Ashley J., C. Christine Fair and Jamison Jo Medby. 2001. *Limited Conflict under the Nuclear Umbrella: Indian and Pakistani Lessons from the Kargil Crisis*, MR 1450 USCA. Santa Monica, CA: RAND.

Tetlock, Philip and Ariel Levi. 1982. 'Attribution Bias: On the Inclusiveness of the Cognition-Motivation Debate', *Journal of Experimental Social Psychology*, 18.

Thapar, Vishal. 2001. 'Making Strategic Sense of an Indo-US Tie-up', *The Hindustan Times*, 12 November.

The Asia Society. 1994. *South Asia and the United States After the Cold War*, Study Mission Report. New York: The Asia Society.

The Asia Society. 1995. *Preventing Nuclear Proliferation in South Asia*. New York: The Asia Society.

The Asian Age. 1999. 'Pakistani has Enough Nuclear Weapons' (AP), 27 May.
———. 2000a. 'What is the Congress Line on the Nuclear Issue?' 27 April.
———. 2000b. 'Cong (I) Panel Takes Fresh Look at Nuclear Policy', 3 May.
The China Post. 1998. 'Nuclear Power PRC Mulls Nuclear Empowered India', 27 May.
The China Quarterly. 1993. 'The Chinese Communist Party and the Collapse of Soviet Communism', March.
The Friday Times (Lahore). 1993. 'CIA Report: Heroin in Pakistan: Sowing the Wind', 3 September.
The Harvard Study Group (Albert Carnesale, Paul Doty, Stenley Hoffman, Samuel P. Huntington, Joseph S. Nye Jr. and Scott Sagan). 1983. *Living with Nuclear Weapons*. New York: Bantam Books.
The Hindu. 1998. 'Text of Vajpayee's Letter to Clinton', 14 May.
———. 1999a. 'Lahore Declaration', 22 February.
———. 1999b. 'Define "Minimum Deterrent" India Told' (PTI), 15 April.
———. 1999c. 'Create Credible N-arsenal', 18 August.
———. 1999d. 'Pak also can Build a Neutron Bomb', 20 August.
———. 2000a. 'Cong. Confused over Sonia's Remark on N-policy', 27 March.
———. 2000b. 'China's Pledge of Restraint' (editorial), 25 November.
———. 2001. 'Agni-II Second Test Successful', 18 January.
———. 2002a. 'Towards a Realistic Engagement' (editorial), 17 January.
———. 2002b. 'Towards Closer Strategic Cooperation' (editorial), 21 January.
———. 2002c. 'Deterrence Theory Has Worked: Musharraf', 19 June.
———. 2002d. 'Nuclear Weapons Helped Avert War: Kalam', 20 June.
———. 2003a. 'Command and Control' (editorial), 7 January.
———. 2003b. 'Agni Missile Test Fired Successfully', 19 January.
The Hindustan Times. 1999. 'Pak May Use N-weapons, Fears Fernandes' (UNI), 30 June.
———. 2000a. 'India Drafts New N-Command, Control System' (PTI), 12 January.
———. 2000b. 'Pakistan to Export Nuclear Material', 4 August.
———. 2001. 'Sino-Indian Experts Groups to Meet and Exchange Maps', 15 January.
———. 2002. 'Navy Chief Cagey About a Sea-based Nuke Capability', 17 January.
———. 2003a. 'Command and Control' (editorial), 7 January.
———. 2003b. 'Pak Continues to Back Terrorists in J&K: CIA', 12 February.
The Indian Express. 1999a. 'Sharif Makes N-Sounds, Pak Vows to Defend Position' (ENS and Agencies), 28 May.
———. 1999b. 'Nuclear Buccaneers' (editorial), *The Indian Express*, 20 August.
———. 2000. 'Buy it Up'(editorial), 31 May.
———. 2001. 'Osama Acquired 10 Nuclear Warheads' (Quoted in *Khabrain*), 19 January.
The Muslim. 1992. 'Nuclear Programme Entirely Peaceful', 21 February.
The Nation. 2004a. 'Cabinet Recommends Pardon for Dr Abdul Qadeer Khan', 6 February.
———. 2004b. 'Many Questions Left Unanswered' (editorial), 6 February.
The New York Times. 1992a. 'China Said to Sell Parts for Missiles', 31 January.
———. 1992b. 'Pakistan Tells of its A-Bomb Capacity', 8 February.
———. 1993. 'Pakistani Quoted as Citing Nuclear Test in '87', 25 July.

The New York Times. 2001. 'South Asian Brinkmanship' (editorial), 26 December.
——. 2004a. 'Pakistani Nuclear Scientist Takes the Rap for Leaks', 4 February.
——. 2004b. 'Half a Proliferation Program' (editorial), 16 February.
The News International (Islamabad). 1999a. 'Pakistan Reserves Right to Retaliate: Foreign Office', 27 May.
——. 1999b. 'Pakistan May Use Any Weapon: Shamshad Says Pakistan Not to Sign the CTBT', 31 May.
——. 1999c. 'N-weapons Can Be Used for National Security: Zafar', 1 June.
——. 1999d. 'N-weapons May Be Used in Indo-Pak War: Agha Shahi', 7 June.
——. 1999e. 'Foreign Funding to *Deeni Madaris* Alarming: Special Branch', 19 August.
——. 2002. 'Pakistan Doing Best to End Infiltration', 25 August.
The Oxford Encyclopaedia of the Modern Islamic World. 1995. Oxford: Oxford University Press.
The Pioneer. 1999. 'Purely Deterrent' (editorial), 19 August.
——. 2002a. 'China Poses No Threat Now', 22 January.
——. 2002b. 'Fernandes Faces Opposition Ire over MiG', 28 November.
The Statesman. 2000a. 'Musharraf to Head Pak Nuclear Command', 4 February.
——. 2000b. 'Confusion in Congress over Stand on N-issue', 28 March.
——. 2000c. 'No Shortage of Funds for IAF: Fernandes', 26 April.
——. 2002. 'Dangerous Jingoism! Bush's State of the Union' (editorial), 2 February.
The Times of India. 1999a. 'Islamabad May Not Shy Away from N-option', 25 June.
——. 1999b. 'Pak again Threatens to Use N-weapons', 1 July.
——. 1999c. 'India's Nuclear Doctrine: In Search of Strategic Autonomy', 19 August.
——. 1999d. 'Virtue of Restraint' (editorial), 20 August.
——. 1999e. 'Let's Talk Nuclear' (editorial), 26 August.
——. 2000a. 'Limited War Can Erupt Anytime: Malik', 6 January.
——. 2000b. 'Pakistan Sets Up N-arms Command' (DPA), 4 February.
——. 2000c. 'Panel to Firm Up Cong Line on N-deterrent', 2 May.
——. 2000d. 'India Speculates over NBC N-report', 9 June.
——. 2001a. 'Lt-Gen Vij Moved Forces "Too Close" to the Border', 22 January.
——. 2001b. 'India, China Security Dialogue Next Month', 23 January.
——. 2002. 'Armitage Wanted to Ensure Musharraf's Commitment: US' (PTI), 18 June.
The US Air Force. 1994. 'Nuclear Operations', *The Air Force Doctrine*, Document 23, Secretary of The Air Force, 26 August, available at http://www.fas.org/spp/military/docops/usaf/afdd23.htm, accessed on 3 March 2001.
The Washington Post. 2004. 'World May be Headed for Nuclear Destruction, El Baradei Says', 12 February.
The White House. 2002. *The National Security Strategy of the United States of America.* Washington, DC: The White House.
Theatre Missile Defences in the Asia-Pacific Region. 2000. Working Group Report, Report No. 34 (June). Washington: Henry L. Stimson Center.
Thomas, Raju G.C. 1983. 'Prospects for Indo-U.S. Security Ties', *Orbis*, 27 (Summer).
——. (ed.). 1991. *Perspectives on Kashmir: The Roots of Conflict in South Asia.* Boulder, CO: Westview.

Thomas, Raju G.C. 1993. 'South Asian Security in the 1990s', *Adelphi Papers* No. 278. London: Brassey's for IISS.

Time. 1987. 'Knocking at the Nuclear Door', 30 March 1987.

Tow, William T. 1994. 'China and the International Strategic System', in W. Robinson and David Sambaugh (eds), *Chinese Foreign Policy: Theory and Practice*. Oxford: Ciarendon Press.

Townsend, James. 1992. 'Chinese Nationalism', *The Australian Journal of Chinese Affairs*, 27 (January).

Truman, Harry S. 1955. *Memoirs: Years of Decision*. New York: Doubleday.

Turner, Stansfield. 1985. *Terrorism and Democracy*. Boston: Houghton Mifflin.

Tyler, Patrick E. 1996. 'As China Threatens Taiwan, US Listens', *The New York Times*, 24 January.

United Nations. 1970–80. Hearings before the Subcommittee on State Department Organization and Foreign Affairs.

———. 1971. 'The Indian Ocean: Political and Strategic Future'. Hearings before the Subcommittee on National Security Policy and Scientific Developments, 92nd Congress, First session, 20, 22, 27 and 28 July.

———. 1974a. 'Proposed Expansion of U.S. Military Facilities in the Indian Ocean'. Hearings before the Subcommittee on the Near East and South Asia, 93rd Congress, Second session, 21 February, 6, 12, 14 and 20 March 1974.

———. 1974b. 'South Asia, 1974: Political, Economic and Agricultural Challenges', Hearings Before the Subcommittee on Near East and South Asia, 93rd Congress, Second session, 19 and 24 September.

———. 1978. *Declaration Made by China on Unilateral Security Assurances*, United Nations Document, No. A/S-10/AC.1/17, 7 June.

———. 1980. *Comprehensive Study on Nuclear Weapons*, UN General Assembly Document No. A/33/392, New York.

———. 1993. UN Document A/RES/48/75, 81st plenary meeting, 16 December.

———. 1995. *The United Nations and Nuclear Non-Proliferation*, The United Nations Blue Book Series, Vol. III. New York: United Nations DPI.

———. 1998. Security Council Resolution 1172, UN Document No. S/RES/1172 adopted by the Security Council at its 3,890th meeting on 6 June.

Ur-Rehman, Shahid. 1999. *Long Road to Chagai*. Islamabad: Printwise.

US Atomic Energy Commission. 1950. *The Effects of the Atomic Bombs at Hiroshima and Nagasaki*, Report of the British Mission to Japan, 1946. Prepared for and in Cooperation with the US Atomic Energy Commission.

US Congress. 1974. Report of the Secretary of Defense to Congress on the FY 1975 budget and the FY 1975–79 Defense Program, 4 March.

———. 1996. *Pakistan Aid Cut Off: US Non Proliferation and Foreign Policy Consider-ations*, Congressional Research Service Report 90149, 6 December, available at http://www/fas.org/spp/starwars/GS/90-149.htm.

———. 1998. *Chinese Proliferation of Weapons of Mass Destruction: Current Policy Issues*, Congressional Research Service Report 92056, available at http://www:fas:org/spp/starwars/ers/ers92056.htm.

US Information Service. 1993a. 'Toward Regional Non-Proliferation in South Asia', *Official Text*, 7 May.

———. 1993b. 'South Asia Bureau Chief Gives Overview of US Policy', *Official Text*, 21 September.

US Information Service. 1993c. 'Clinton Warns of Perils Ahead Despite Cold War's End, Addresses to UN General Assembly, *Wireless File*, 28 September.
———. 1993d. 'A Spin Outline, New US Counter-Proliferation Policy', *Wireless File*, 8 December.
———. 1999. *Official Text*, 7 July.
US–USSR Agreement. 1973. Agreement on the Prevention of Nuclear War, 22 June, Washington, available at http://www.fas.org/nuke/control/prevent/intro.htm.
Usman, Ali. 1999. *Takbeer*, 10 June, cited in POT (Pakistan), 21 June 1999, p. 2143.
Vajpayee, Atal Behari. 1998a. Text of the letter to US President Bill Clinton, available at http://www.ipcs.org/documents/statements/ May 98.htm.
———. 1998b. Speech at the United Nations General Assembly on 23 September, available at http://www.ipcs.org/documents/statements/Sept-Oct.98.htm.
———. 1998c. Statement in the Parliament on 15 December, http://www.meadev.nic.in/parl15.htm, accessed on 16 April 1999.
———. 2001. Letter of Prime Minister Atal Behari Vajpayee to Pakistan CEO General Musharraf, 24 May, available at http://www.ipcs.org /documents/ 2001/03-may-jun.html#VajpayeeLetter.
van Creveld, Martin. 1991. *On Future War*. London: Brassey's.
Varadarajan, Siddharth (ed.). 2002. *Gujarat: The Making of a Tragedy*. New Delhi: Penguin.
Vasquez, John A. 1983. *The Power of Power Politics*. New Jersey: New Brunswick.
———. 1993. *The War Puzzle*. Cambridge: Cambridge University Press.
Venkatramani, M.S. 1966. 'America's Military Alliance with Pakistan: The Evolution and Course of an Uneasy Partnership', *International Studies*, 8 (3).
Verba, Sidney. 1961. 'Assumption of Rationality and Non-Rationality in Models of the International Systems', in Klaus Knorr and Sidney Verba (eds), *The International System: Theoretical Essays*. Princeton, NJ: Princeton University Press.
Vinod, M.J. 1992. 'Conflicting Strategic Interests of the United States and India: Evaluating US Arms Supply to Pakistan', *International Studies*, 29 (3).
Vyas, Neena. 2001. 'India against Holding Ties Hostage to Kashmir Question', *The Hindu*, 19 June.
Wagner, Alex. 2001. 'Bush Waives Nuclear-related Sanctions on India, Pakistan', *Arms Control Today*, October, available at http://www.armscontrol.org/act/ 2001_10/sanctionsoct01.asp.
Walker, J. Samuel. 1997. *Prompt and Utter Destruction: Truman and the Use of Atomic Bombs against Japan*. Chapel Hill, NC: University of North Carolina Press.
Wall, Robert. 1999. 'US-Japan Agree on Cooperative Missile Defense', *Aviation Week and Space Technology*, 23 August.
Walpole, Robert. 2000. 'The Ballistic Missile Threat to the United States', Statement for the Record to the Senate Subcommittee on International Security, Proliferation and Federal Services, 9 February.
Waltz, Kenneth N. 1959. *Man, the State and War: A Theoretical Analysis*. New York: Columbia University Press.
———. 1979. *Theory of International Politics*. New York: Random House.
———. 1981. 'Spread of Nuclear Weapons: More May Be Better', *Adelphi Papers* No.171. London: IISS.

Waltz, Kenneth N. 1998. 'The Origins of War in Neorealist Theory', *Journal of Interdisciplinary History*, 18 (Spring).

Wang Chong Jie. 1996. 'The World Trend Towards Multipolarity Past, Present and Future', *Foreign Affairs Journal*, 39 (March).

Wang Gung Wu. 1977. *China and the World Since 1949*. London: Macmillan.

Wang Jisi. 1997. 'Multipolarity versus Hegemonism: Chinese Views of International Politics Today. Division of Conflict or Convergence: Global Perspectives on War, Peace and International Order', *Harvard Academy for International and Area Studies*, 13–15 November, Harvard.

Wang Jisi and Zou Sicheng. 1996. 'Civilizations: Clash or Fusion?' *Beijing Review*, 39 (3).

Wang Zhongren. 1997. 'China Threat Theory Groundless', *Beijing Review*, 40 (28).

Weaver, Mary Anne. 2002. *Pakistan: In the Shadow of Jihad and Afghanistan*. London: Penguin.

Weber, Steve. 1990. 'Realism, Détente, and Nuclear Weapons', *International Organisation*, 44 (1).

Weede, Erich. 1983. 'Extended Deterrence by Superpower Alliance', *Journal of Conflict Resolution*, 27.

———. 1996. 'Correspondence', *International Security*, 20 (4).

Weinbaum, Martin and Chetan Kumar (eds). 1995. *South Asia Approaches the Millennium: Re-examining National Security*. Boulder, CO: Westview.

Weiner, Time. 1998. 'US Says North Korea Helped Develop a New Pakistani Missile', *The New York Times*, 11 April.

Weisman, Steve and Herbert Krosney. 1981. *The Islamic Bomb*. New York: Times Books.

Welles, Benjamin. 1971. 'Pakistan Said to Have Received North Korean Arms', *The New York Times*, 15 October.

Wendt, Alexander. 1995. 'Anarchy is What States Make of It', *International Security*, (Summer).

Wen-Wei Chang, David. 1990. 'Confucianism, Democracy and Communism: The Chinese Example of Search of a New Political Typology for Systemic Integration', *Issues and Studies*, 26 (11).

Whiting, Allen S. 1975. *The Chinese Calculus of Deterrence: India and Indo-China*. Ann Arbor, MI: University of Michigan Press.

———. 1994. 'Chinese Nationalism and Foreign Policy after Deng', *The China Quarterly*, 14 (2).

Whitson, William (ed.). 1973. *The Military and Political Power in China in the 1970s*. New York: Praeger.

Wielgele, Thomas C., Gordon Hilton, Kent Layne Oots and Susan K. Kieshell. 1985. *Leaders Under Stress: A Psychological Analysis of International Crisis*. Durham, NC: Luke University Press.

Wilder, Andrew. 1995. 'Islam and Political Legitimacy', in Muhammad Aslam Syed (ed.), *Islam and Democracy in Pakistan*. Islamabad: National Institute of Historical and Cultural Research.

Wilesner, B. Jerome, Philip Morison and Kosta Tipis. 1993. 'Ending Overkill', *The Bulletin of the Atomic Scientists*, March.

William, Joseph A. (ed.). 1994. *China Briefing*. Boulder, CO: Westview.

Williams, Phil. 1972. Crisis Management: Confrontation and Diplomacy in the Nuclear Age. New York: Wiley.

Williams, Rushbook L.F. 1962. *The State of Pakistan*. London: Faber and Faber.

Williams, Shelton, L. 1969. *The U.S., India and the Bomb*. Baltimore, MD: John Hopkins Press.

Wirsing, Robert G. 1985. 'The Arms Race in South Asia: Implications for the United States', *Asian Survey*, 25 (March).

———. 1989. 'The Siachen Glacier Dispute: Can Diplomacy Untangle It?' *Indian Defence Review*, July.

Wohlsteller, Albert. 1959. 'The Delicate Balance of Terror', *Foreign Affairs*, 37 (January).

Wolf, Reinhold. 1996.'Correspondence: Democratisation and the Dangers of War', *International Security*, 20 (1).

Wolfers, Arnold. 1952. '"National Security" as an Ambiguous Symbol', *Political Science Quarterly*, 67 (4).

Wolfgang, Franke. 1967. *China and the West*. Oxford: Basic Blackwell.

Wolfsthal, Jon B. 1993. 'US China Reach New Accords on MTCR, Fissile Cut-off Issues', *Arms Control Today*, December.

Wolpert, S. 1984. *Jinnah of Pakistan*. New York: Oxford University Press.

———. (ed.). 1992. *A New History of India*. New York: Oxford University Press.

———. 1993. *Zulfikar Ali Bhutto of Pakistan: His Life and Times*. New York: Oxford University Press.

Woodward, Bob. 1986. 'Pakistan Reported Near Atom Arms Production', *The Washington Post*, 4 November.

Wortzel, Larry M. (ed.). 1999. *The Chinese Armed Forces in the 21st Century*. Carlisle, PA: Strategic Studies Institute, US Army War College.

Wright, David C. 1998. 'An Analysis of the Pakistan Ghauri Missile Test of 6 April 1998', available at http://www.fas.org/news/Pakistan/1998/05/980512-ghauri.htm.

Wu Jianguo, Maj Gen. 1998. 'Nuclear Shadows on High-tech Warfare', in Michael Pillsbury (ed.), *Chinese Views of Future Warfare*. New Delhi: Lancer's.

Wu Xinbo. 1998. 'China: Security Practice of a Modernising and Ascending Power', in Muthiah Alagappa (ed.), *Asian Security Practice: Material and Ideational Influences*. Stanford: Stanford University Press.

Xiaowei Zhao. 1992. 'The Threat of a New Arms Race Dominates Asian Geo-politics', *Global Affairs*, Summer.

Xu Zuzhi. 1999. 'China's Strategic Missile Unit Now Possesses Fighting Capability Under High-tech Conditions', *Zhongguo Xinwen She*, 1 October in FBIS, Background of China's Strategic Missile Unit, FTS19991002000093.

Yager, Joseph (ed.). 1980. *Non-proliferation and US Foreign Policy*. Washington, DC: Brookings Institution.

Yahuda, Michael. 1983. *Towards the End of Isolationism: China's Foreign Policy after Mao*. London: Macmillan.

Yan Xu. 1993. *Zhong Yin Bian Jiezhi Zhan Lishi Zhenxiang* (The True History of the Sino-India Border War). Hong Kong: Tiandi Tusho.

Yang, Richard H. and James Mulvenon (eds). 1999. *The People's Liberation Army in the Information Age*. Washington, DC: RAND.

Yang, Richard H., Jason C. Hu, Peter K. H. Yu and Andrew N. D. Yang (eds). 1994. *Chinese Regionalism: The Security Dimension*. Boulder, CO: Westview.

Yang Guo Ping. 1992. 'Chinese Major General Yang Guo Ping's Visit to Pakistan', *Agence France-Presse* (Hong Kong), 6 December.

Yao Yunzhu. 1995. 'The Evolution of Military Doctrine of the Chinese PLA from 1985 to 1995', *The Korean Journal of Defense Analysis*, 7 (2).

Yimin Song. 1986. *On China's Concept of Security*. Geneva: UNIDIR.

You Ji. 1999. *The Armed Forces of China*. London: I.B. Taurus.

Young, Oran. 1968. *The Politics of Force: Bargaining During Superpower Crises*. Princeton, NJ: Princeton University Press.

Yu Lei. 1996. 'Five-way Border Pledge Signed', *China Daily*, 27 April.

Zagare, Frank C. 1990. 'Rationality and Deterrence', *World Politics*, 62 (2).

Zaheer, H. 1994. *The Separation of East Pakistan*. Karachi: Oxford University Press.

Zeb, Rizwan. 2002 (accessed). 'The Story of Successes: The Journey from 9/11 to October Election', available at http://www.ipcs.org/issues/800/890-pak-rizwan.html, accessed on 9 October.

Zhang Longxi. 1988. 'The Myth of the Other: China in the Eyes of West', *Critical Inquiry*, 15 (1).

Zhang Wenmu. 1998. 'Issue of South Asia in Major Power Politics', *Ta Kong Pao* (Chinese), 23 September.

Zhang Yihong. 1999. 'Beijing Develops New Radar-absorbing Materials', *Jane's Defense Weekly*, 24 February.

Zheng Yongman. 1999. *Discovering Chinese Nationalism*. Cambridge: Cambridge University Press.

Zhu Minqnan. 1999. 'US Plans on National Missile Defence (NMD) and Theatre Missile Defence (BMD): A Chinese Perspective', available at http://www.cns.miis.edu/db/Chinaengdocs/Zhu/1999.htm, accessed on 5 June 2000.

Ziring, Lawrence. 1978. *The Subcontinent in World Politics*. London: Praeger.

——. 1984. 'Government and Politics', in Richard F. Nyrop (ed.), *Pakistan: A Country Study*. Washington, DC: US Government Printing Office.

——. 1990. 'Pakistan in 1989: The Politics of Stalemate', *Asian Survey*, 30 (2).

——. 1991. 'Pakistan in 1990: The Fall of Benazir Bhutto', *Asian Survey*, 31 (2).

——. 1993a. 'The Second Stage in Pakistan Politics: The 1993 Elections', *Asian Survey*, 33 (12).

——. 1993b. 'Dilemma and Challenge in Nawaz Sharif's Pakistan', in C.H. Kennedy (ed.), *Pakistan: 1992*. Boulder, CO: Westview.

——. 1997. *Pakistan in the Twentieth Century: A Political History*. Karachi: Oxford University Press.

Ziring, Lawrence, Ralph Braibanti and W. Howard Wriggins (eds). 1977. *Pakistan: The Long View*. Durham: Duke University Press.

Zou Yunhua. 1998. 'China and the CTBT Negotiations', Center for International Security and Cooperation, Stanford University, December.

——. 1999. 'Chinese Perspectives on the South Asian Nuclear Tests', Center for International Security and Cooperation, Stanford University, January.

WEBSITES AND ONLINE DATABASES

Center for Non-proliferation Studies, http://www.cns.miis.edu
Council for a Liveable World, http://www.clw.org
Centre for Defence Information, http://www.cdi.org
Council on Foreign Relations, http://www.cfr.org
Federation of American Scientists, http://www.fas.org
Stockholm International Peace Research Institute, http://www.sipri.se
The Stimson Centre, http://www.stimson.org
The Brookings Institution, http://www.brook.edu
The Institute of Peace and Conflict Studies, http://www.ipcs.org
The Nuclear Age Peace Foundation, http://www.wagingpeace.org
The Indian Ministry of External Affairs, http://www.meadev.gov.in
Pakistan's Ministry of Foreign Affairs, http:// www.forisb.org

INDEX

ABOUT THE AUTHOR

Arpit Rajain is a Senior Policy Analyst at the New Delhi office of the Centre for Global Studies, Mumbai. Prior to joining the Centre, he was a Research Fellow at the ORF Institute of Security Studies, New Delhi. He has also worked at the Institute of Peace and Conflict Studies (IPCS), New Delhi, on WMD issues for six years and been part of projects with the Ministry of External Affairs and the Office of the Integrated Defence Staff, Government of India.

The author is currently involved in policy risk analysis and assessment with several multinational companies. He has previously co-edited three books, including *Nuclear Stability in Southern Asia* (2003), *Biological Weapons: Issues and Threats* (2003) and *Working Towards a Verification Protocol for Biological Weapons* (2001). He has also published more than 55 research papers on WMD issues in reputed journals, as chapters in edited volumes, as issue briefs, and as monographs, as well as more than 75 articles in newspapers/websites in India and abroad.